D0929047

A publication of
The National Vocational Guidance Association

Designing
Careers

❧ ❧ ❧ ❧ ❧ ❧ ❧ ❧

Counseling
to Enhance Education,
Work, and Leisure

Norman C. Gysbers
and Associates

Designing
Careers

❧ ❧ ❧ ❧ ❧ ❧ ❧ ❧

Jossey-Bass Publishers
San Francisco • Washington • London • 1984

DESIGNING CAREERS
Counseling to Enhance Education, Work, and Leisure
by Norman C. Gysbers and Associates

Copyright © 1984 by: Jossey-Bass Inc., Publishers
433 California Street
San Francisco, California 94104
&
Jossey-Bass Limited
28 Banner Street
London EC1Y 8QE

Library of Congress Cataloging in Publication Data
Main entry under title:

Designing careers.

(The Jossey-Bass higher education series) (The Jossey-
Bass social and behavioral science series)
Includes bibliographies and index.
1. Vocational guidance—Addresses, essays, lectures.
I. Gysbers, Norman C. II. Series. III. Series: Jossey-
Bass social and behavioral science series.
HF5381.D4533   1984   331.7′02   84-47986
ISBN 0-87589-618-9

Manufactured in the United States of America

The paper in this book meets the guidelines for
permanence and durability of the Committee on
Production Guidelines for Book Longevity of the
Council on Library Resources.

JACKET DESIGN BY WILLI BAUM

29398

FIRST EDITION

Code 8430

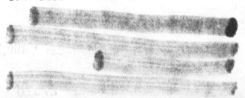

A joint publication in
The Jossey-Bass Higher Education Series
and
The Jossey-Bass
Social and Behavioral Science Series

Consulting Editors
Student Services
and
Counseling Psychology

Ursula Delworth
University of Iowa

Gary R. Hanson
University of Texas, Austin

Foreword

This volume is being published on the occasion of the seventieth anniversary of the National Vocational Guidance Association (NVGA). During each decade since the 1960s, NVGA has developed a decennial volume to help the association and the profession set goals for the future. In 1964 the landmark book, *Man in a World at Work*, edited by Henry Borow, was published. The second in the series, *Vocational Guidance and Human Development*, edited by Edwin Herr, was published in 1974. The goals of each decennial volume have been to examine the emerging context for career guidance, to summarize major developments in theory and practice during the preceding decade, and to point directions for vocational guidance in the upcoming decade. The NVGA Board of Directors views this activity as essential to the continued growth and revitalization of the profession.

The National Vocational Guidance Association, founded in 1913, is the oldest association dedicated to promoting and improving guidance programs to meet the career development needs of youth and adults. In his 1942 book, *History of Vocational Guidance*, John M. Brewer stated that the vocational guidance movement had been initiated in response to the need to "assist youth in making progress in occupational experience,

with an eye to both individual success and . . . social well-being"
(p. 2). He described four causes that had stimulated the development of the National Vocational Guidance Association in
1913: the increased use of division of labor, the growth of technology, the extension of vocational education, and the spread
of modern forms of democracy (p. 3).

These themes still have relevance today if redefined in the
light of current and future trends. The application of high technology to increase American productivity is a current national
interest and is resulting in new divisions of labor. The major
concern today is with human/machine interactions. As new
technologies such as uses of computers, robots, and lasers are
developed, new work roles are emerging that require humans to
assume high-level skills as machines assume lower-level work
functions. The extension of vocational education has expanded
to include increases in employer-sponsored training programs
and in adult education opportunities. As research has expanded
our understanding of the career development process, acceptance
of the need to develop life career planning experience for adults
throughout the life span has increased. Finally, the last several
decades have evidenced strides in improving the equalization of
opportunities for all Americans, thus furthering the spread of
democracy.

The planning and development of this volume have been
supported by several NVGA presidents, including Edwin Herr
(1979-1980), Harry Drier (1980-1981), Katherine Cole (1981-
1982), Juliet Miller (1982-1983), and Robert Smith (1983-
1984). Creative leadership in planning the volume was provided
by the Decennial Volume Committee, chaired by Henry Borow,
with members including Edwin Herr, Carl McDaniels, Anita
Mitchell, and Donald Super. NVGA is pleased to have had
Norman Gysbers serve as editor of this volume and extends its
appreciation to him for his leadership in working with authors,
establishing publishing arrangements, and monitoring the overall
quality of the volume.

On the occasion of its seventieth anniversary, the National Vocational Guidance Association presents *Designing*

Careers: Council to Enhance Education, Work, and Leisure, to provide direction and focus for career guidance and counseling during the coming decade.

August 1984   Juliet V. Miller
President
National Vocational Guidance Association
(1982–83)

Preface

In the United States and many other countries, the relationships between work and career are being rethought and reformulated. Work, instead of being seen as an important but separate part of life, is being seen as the basis for one life role—the worker role— that is closely related and linked to other life roles. Career, instead of being defined as job or occupation only, is being defined as the combinations and sequences of life roles, the settings in which life roles unfold, and the events that occur in the lives of individuals all through the life span.

What is causing this rethinking and reformulating? First, vast and far-reaching changes are taking place in the nature and structure of the social and economic systems in which people live and the industrial and occupational structures in which they work. Second, the values and beliefs individuals hold about themselves, about others, and about the world are changing. Third, more and more people are seeking meaning and coherence in their life roles.

Whatever the causes may be, the rethinking and reformulating process is changing career development theory, research, and practice. And, since these changes have been taking place at an accelerated pace since 1974, there is a need in 1984 to exam-

ine the substantial impact these changes are having. To fill this
need, the National Vocational Guidance Association (NVGA)
commissioned this book, the third in the prestigious NVGA Decennial Volume Series. It provides the profession, the public,
and policy makers with the best in contemporary thought
about work, education, and leisure and the impact they have on
human growth and development—the human career. It reflects
the state of the art, but at the same time it is forward looking—
examining and discussing future trends and issues. The book is
intended for a wide audience of professionals around the world,
including counselors in public and private agencies and institutions, training and development professionals in business and industry, higher education personnel, and adult and continuing
education specialists. It also is intended for use by would-be
professionals in guidance, counseling, personnel, and employment and training, as well as vocational education, social work,
human resource development, and sociology.

Designing Careers examines in detail the relation between
work and career from psychological, sociological, and economic
perspectives. It presents the reformulations that are emerging as
well as the implications these reformulations have for individuals, for society, and for theory, research, and practice. Illustrative, innovative career development practices, tools, and techniques for use with people of all ages and circumstances are
presented. This book is a professional source of ideas, techniques, and resources to help professionals work more effectively with individuals and their career development needs, concerns, and plans.

The contributors to the volume, all writing by invitation,
represent the best thinking in the field. They are seasoned professionals with substantial experience and expertise. The special
introduction by C. Gilbert Wrenn provides a unique, historical
perspective for the rest of the book. He contrasts the world as it
was in 1913 when NVGA was founded with the world as it is
today. The twenty-three chapters that follow are grouped into
four major parts, providing professionals with up-to-date, in-
depth review and analyses of key topics and issues.

Part One, "The World of Work Today: Personal, Social,

and Economic Perspectives," considers the meaning, nature, and structure of work in our society. The changing relationships and links among education, training, employability, and employment also are explored. Next follows a discussion of the challenges and myths of establishing and maintaining effective partnerships between education and business and industry. Throughout this part, the authors underscore the need for professionals to understand the work world and its relationship to education, training, and employability to carry out their professional responsibilities with individuals.

Part Two, "Knowledge Base of Career Development," describes what we know about career development—the career development of young people and adults and of men and women working in a variety of settings and living in differing circumstances. Discussion centers on how career development theory and practice need to connect for the purpose of improving career guidance and counseling practices. In addition, the roles and impact of family, school, peers, work experience, and the media in the occupational socialization of young people are highlighted, particularly as these factors influence the transition from school to work. Next authors describe career development from an organizational perspective, the impact that gender has on the career development of individuals, and various measures for assessing career development. The last chapter looks at what theory and research have to say about job satisfaction, worker aspirations, and work attitudes, and how these affect, and are affected by, worker behavior.

Part Three, "Facilitating Career Development: Practices and Programs," describes innovative and exemplary career development programs and practices, systematically organized and theory-based, designed to assist individuals of all ages and circumstances. Chapters present practical individual and group techniques and procedures as well as a wide variety of career guidance and counseling tools, resources, and programs available to assist individuals in their career development. Authors also describe career development programs and practices as they are taking place today in schools, postsecondary institutions, and business and industry.

Part Four, "Responding to Emerging Views of Work and Leisure," looks into the future and presents a challenging discussion of the changes that may take place in our society. Changes in the way the work force is educated, problems of work and retirement for older workers, and the relation of work and leisure are described and discussed in detail. In addition, the implications of these changes as well as the implications of the reformulation of work and career for the preparation of career development specialists are described and discussed in detail. The concluding chapter presents major trends that have emerged in the continuing evolution of career development theory and practice.

Acknowledgments

This book has a story behind it, as all books do. It is a story of many people working together. Among the people involved from the beginning were the members of the NVGA Decennial Volume Committee—Henry Borow (chair), Edwin L. Herr, Carl McDaniels, Anita Mitchell, and Donald Super. To them I express my thanks and appreciation for their vision, support, and encouragement. In addition, I acknowledge the work of the many individuals who assisted me in reviewing chapters. My thanks and appreciation go to David Adams, John Bailey, Marita S. Barkis, William C. Bingham, James E. Bottoms, Robert E. Campbell, Claire Cole, D. Stuart Conger, Harry N. Drier, Dennis J. Dunn, Russell B. Flanders, Geraldine O. Garner, Patrick Handley, Robert N. Hansen, Mary J. Heppner, P. Paul Heppner, Joseph A. Johnston, Steven M. Jung, William Knaak, Anita Sklare Lancaster, Morgan Lewis, Randy D. McAlister, Richard Miguel, Richard E. Nelson, Sandra K. Olson, Evelyn Peevy, David Roberts, Nancy Schlossberg, Robert Smith, Nita Snipes, Clemmont E. Vontress, Frank Wellman, and Helen Wood. Third, I express my thanks and appreciation to my secretary, Della Rains, for her help and support with the many details involved in putting this book together. Finally, to my wife and family, my love and my thanks.

Columbia, Missouri   Norman C. Gysbers
September 1984

Contents

Traces the changing meaning and value of work; describes how work is viewed from, and in relation to, the broader perspective of life roles and the quality of life; and discusses the implications of these changes for practice.

The Authors

Libby Benjamin is consultant to the Educational Resources Information Center, Counseling and Personnel Services (ERIC/CAPS) Clearinghouse at the University of Michigan. She was an elementary and junior high school teacher and high school and college counselor in California and Alaska schools, professor of counselor education at the University of Alaska, and admissions counselor for the University of Alaska state system before 1974, when she moved to Michigan to become associate director of ERIC/CAPS. She earned her B.Mus. degree from the University of the Pacific (1948), her M.S. degree in secondary education from San Jose State University (1963), and her Ph.D. degree in counseling psychology from Oregon State University (1973). She was vice president of the California Scholarship Federation, president of the Alaska Personnel and Guidance Association, senator to the Association for Counseling and Development, and an officer in the western region of the Association for Counselor Education and Supervision.

Benjamin was senior editor of the ERIC/CAPS publication program and has been author or coauthor of numerous monographs and journal articles on futurism, change agentry, and career development and of a three-part series on counseling adults in transition. She also coedited a nine-volume series ti-

tled *New Vistas in Counseling.* She has been project codirector
for four federally funded programs and developed several staff
training modules for a national consortium on competency-
based staff development in career guidance. She is coauthor of a
widely used career development training program, the Life Career Development System (LCDS). She has presented programs
at many local, state, and national meetings and has trained
counseling specialists in the use of the LCDS in forty states, the
Philippines, Malaysia, and Australia. Currently Benjamin is semi-
retired but continues to work actively with ERIC/CAPS as an
author, editor, program presenter, and workshop leader.

     Norman L. Berven is associate professor in the rehabilita-
tion counseling program, Department of Studies in Behavioral
Disabilities, University of Wisconsin-Madison. He previously
served as an assistant professor in rehabilitation counseling at
Seton Hall University, as a research associate at the International
Center for the Disabled in New York City, and as a rehabilitation counselor at the San Mateo County (California) Mental
Health Service. He received his B.S. degree (1967) in psychology and general science and his M.A. degree (1969) in rehabilitation counseling, both from the University of Iowa, and his
Ph.D. degree (1973) in rehabilitation counseling psychology
from the University of Wisconsin-Madison.

     Berven has focused his research on assessment practices
for individuals with disabilities, professional education and credentialing in rehabilitation counseling, and the use of simulation
in evaluating professional competence. He received special recognition for his research in 1981 and 1984 from the American
Rehabilitation Counseling Association.

     Henry Borow is professor of psychological studies in the
Division of Social and Behavioral Sciences and counseling psychologist in the Department of Educational Psychology at the
University of Minnesota. He earned his B.A., M.S., and Ph.D.
degrees in psychology at Pennsylvania State University in 1939,
1942, and 1945, respectively. Between 1942 and 1946 he
served as personnel research technician with the Engineering,

Science, and Management Training Program and as psychology instructor at Pennsylvania State. He has been on the faculty at the University of Minnesota since 1946. His leaves have included appointments with the Japanese Universities Counseling and Guidance Institutes (1951–52) and with the Horace Mann-Lincoln Institute of School Experimentation at Teachers College, Columbia University (1959–60); visiting professorships at New York University, University of Western Ontario, and Virginia Polytechnic Institute and State University; and in-residence research consultantships with the American College Testing Program and the National Center for Research in Vocational Education at Ohio State University.

Borow is author and editor of more than one hundred articles, books, and tests on counseling psychology, academic behavior, and career development, including editorship of *Man in a World at Work* (1964), NVGA's fiftieth anniversary volume, and coeditorship of the Research Frontier department of the *Journal of Counseling Psychology*. He is a past president of the National Vocational Guidance Association and the American Psychological Association's Division of Counseling Psychology and was the recipient of NVGA's Eminent Career Award.

John O. Crites is a research professor in the College of Education at Kent State University, where he also has established the Career R&D Laboratory. He has previously held appointments as professor of psychology and director of the University Counseling Service, University of Iowa, and professor of psychology, University of Maryland. He received his A.B. degree at Princeton University (1950) and his Ph.D. degree in counseling psychology at Columbia University (1957). He is a Diplomate in Counseling Psychology (American Board of Professional Psychology).

Crites has contributed chapters to each of the previous NVGA commemorative volumes. He is also author of *Vocational Psychology* (1969) and *Career Counseling: Models, Methods, and Materials* (1981) as well as the *Career Maturity Inventory* (1973, 1978). His research interests and journal articles are largely in the fields of vocational psychology and test psychology. He received the APGA Research Award for his *Psychological Monograph* (1965) on the initial development and validation of the Career Maturity Inventory, and he was recently presented the Eminent Career Award by NVGA for his "contributions to the assessment of career maturity, improvement of career counseling, and understanding of career development."

René V. **Dawis** is professor of psychology and director of the Counseling Psychology Training Program, Department of Psychology, University of Minnesota. He also is codirector of the Vocational Assessment Clinic and coprincipal investigator of the Work Adjustment Project (with L. H. Lofquist). Dawis is a native of the Philippines, where in 1951 he received his B.A. degree from the University of the Philippines. He was awarded his M.A. and Ph.D. degrees in psychology from the University of Minnesota (1955 and 1956, respectively).

Dawis has published many articles, book chapters, and monographs on work adjustment, psychological measurement, applied psychology, and vocational psychology. He is coauthor (with L. H. Lofquist) of *Adjustment to Work* (1969) and *A Psychological Theory of Work Adjustment* (1984).

Howard E. **Figler** is director of the Career Center at the University of Texas at Austin. From 1970 to 1982, he was director of the Counseling and Career Centers at Dickinson College in Carlisle, Pennsylvania. Prior to his work as a counseling psychologist, he was a research associate for the U.S. Office of Education in Washington, D.C., and had four years of personnel experience at the Prudential Insurance Company and the Port of New York Authority.

Figler earned his B.A. degree in economics from Emory University (1960), his M.B.A. degree in marketing from New York University (1961), and his Ph.D. degree in educational research and testing from Florida State University (1968), in addition to being a 1966 summer graduate fellow at the Educational Testing Service in Princeton. He was awarded the Diplomate in Counseling Psychology by the American Board of Professional Psychology in 1982.

Figler is the author of numerous books and articles in the

field of career development, including *The Complete Job Search Handbook* (1980) and *PATH: A Career Workbook for Liberal Arts Students* (1975, 1979). Other books include *The Athlete's Game Plan for College and Career* (with S. K. Figler, 1984) and *Outreach in Counseling* (with D. J. Drum, 1973). His articles have focused on the expression of personal values in career choice, the application of job search methods to diverse populations, and the need for standards in career counseling. His current professional interests are individual-centered models of career success and career strategies for liberal arts graduates.

Harold Goldstein is an economic consultant in Washington, D.C., specializing in labor economics and statistics. Up to 1972 he was assistant commissioner for Manpower and Employment Statistics in the Bureau of Labor Statistics, U.S. Department of Labor, and was responsible for the statistics on employment and unemployment and for research on manpower. He received the B.A. degree from the University of Illinois (1934) and the M.A. degree from the University of Chicago and has taught at New York University and American University in Washington, D.C.

Publications developed at the Bureau of Labor Statistics under his direction include the *Occupational Outlook Handbook* and other studies for use in guidance and in planning education. He is author of *Training and Education by Industry* (1980), "Two Hundred Years of Work in America" (a chapter in the *Employment and Training Report of the President, 1976*), *A Critical Look at the Measuring of Work* (with W. Wirtz, 1975), and studies on employment, unemployment, and the forecasting of employment trends.

Goldstein has conducted manpower studies in Japan, Korea, Israel, Jamaica, and Venezuela and has been a consultant to the World Bank, the Organization for Economic Cooperation and Development (Paris), the National Academy of Sciences, and the National Science Foundation.

Norman C. Gysbers is professor of educational and counseling psychology at the University of Missouri-Columbia. He received his B.A. degree (1954) in education from Hope College and his M.A. (1959) and Ph.D. (1963) degrees in counseling from the University of Michigan.

Gysbers was editor of the *Vocational Guidance Quarterly,* 1962–1970; president of the National Vocational Guidance Association, 1972–73; president of the American Association of Counseling and Development (formerly the American Personnel and Guidance Association), 1977–78; and vice-president of the American Vocational Association, 1979–1982. Currently, he is the editor of the *Journal of Career Development.* Since 1967 he has served as director of numerous national and state projects on career development and career counseling.

Gysbers has been a visiting professor at the University of Nevada-Reno, Virginia Polytechnic Institute and State University, and the Université libre de Bruxelles. In 1978 he received the American Vocational Association's Guidance Division Merit Award and the Missouri Guidance Association's Outstanding Service Award. In 1981 he was awarded the National Vocational Guidance Association's National Merit Award and in 1983 the American Association of Counseling and Development's Distinguished Professional Service Award. He is the author of thirty-four journal articles, ten chapters in recently published books, eight monographs, and three books.

JoAnn Harris-Bowlsbey is assistant vice-president of the American College Testing Program, heading the DISCOVER Center in Hunt Valley, Maryland. Prior to 1982, she was president of the DISCOVER Foundation and in that role was a major developer of the DISCOVER products, computer-based systems to provide career guidance to individuals of all ages. She has also served as associate and full professor at Northern Illinois University, Western Maryland College, Towson State University, and the Johns Hopkins University.

Harris-Bowlsbey received her B.A. degree in Spanish and chemistry from Wheaton College (1953), her M.A. degree in Spanish literature from the University of Wisconsin-Madison (1955), and her Ed.D. degree in counselor education from Northern Illinois University (1972).

She is author of many articles and chapters in the content

and delivery of systematic career guidance by computer and other modes. She is coauthor of two curricula—*Guided Career Exploration* (with D. E. Super, 1979) and *Take Hold of Your Future* (with R. S. Lisansky and J. D. Spivack, 1982).

Edwin L. Herr is professor and head, Division of Counseling and Educational Psychology, Pennsylvania State University. He received his B.S. degree in business education from Shippensburg State College (1955) and his M.A. degree in psychology and his Ed.D. in counseling and student personnel administration from Teachers College, Columbia University (1959 and 1963, respectively).

A former business teacher, school counselor, and director of guidance, Herr previously served as assistant and associate professor of counselor education at the State University of New York at Buffalo and as the founding director of the Bureau of Guidance Services and the Bureau of Pupil Personnel Services, Pennsylvania Department of Education. He has been involved as a visiting professor or researcher in several European universities and in Japan. In 1976, he served as visiting fellow, National Institute for Careers Education and Counseling, Cambridge, England. In 1979 he served as research fellow, Japan Society for the Promotion of Science at Sophia University, Tokyo.

Herr is immediate past president of the American Association for Counseling and Development, past president of the National Vocational Guidance Association, and past president of the Association for Counselor Education and Supervision. He is the author of over 200 articles and some twenty books. His most recent books include *Career Guidance and Counseling Through the Life Span: Systematic Approaches* (1984); *Counseling Youth for Employability* (1983); *Foundations for Policy in Guidance and Counseling* (1981); *Guidance and Counseling in the Schools: Perspectives on the Past, Present, and Future* (1974). He served as editor of *Vocational Guidance and Human Development*, the second NVGA Decennial Volume (1974).

David A. Jepsen is professor of counselor education in the College of Education, University of Iowa, where he has been teaching, conducting research, and serving as consultant to schools and colleges since 1970. He received the B.S. degree (1960) in education from the University of Northern Iowa and the M.S. (1963) and Ph.D. (1970) degrees in counseling and guidance from the University of Wisconsin-Madison. He was a school counselor for five years and has provided career guidance programming and consultation for such diverse groups as gifted and mentally disabled high school students, undecided college students, and mid-career changers.

Jepsen's primary academic and research interests are in career development and career guidance. His scholarly contributions consist of more than thirty articles and book chapters, many of which seek to synthesize ideas about decision making, human development, and psychological measurement as they relate to understanding people's work lives.

Jepsen is currently serving as editor of the *Vocational Guidance Quarterly,* the official publication of the National Vocational Guidance Association.

Cynthia S. Johnson is cochair of the doctoral program in College Student Personnel, University of Maryland, where she is an assistant professor. Prior to joining the faculty at the University of Maryland, she served as director of Career Planning and Placement at the University of California, Irvine. She received her B.A. degree (1954) in counseling and guidance from California State University at Irvine and her Ph.D. degree in administration and higher education from Michigan State University (1983).

Johnson has been involved in a national grant called Project LEARN, funded by the W. K. Kellogg Foundation. As director of counselor training for that project, she has assisted career counselors in working with computer-assisted guidance. In addition, she has edited several publications, including *Microcomputers and the School Counselor* (1983), *Enhancing Student Development with Computers* (1984), and a special issue of *Personnel and Guidance Journal: Computers and Counseling* (February 1985).

Richard T. Kinnier is an assistant professor in the Department of Counselor Education at Arizona State University. He received the B.A. degree in psychology from Boston College (1971), the M.A. degree in counseling from Teachers College, Columbia University (1973), and the Ph.D. degree in counseling psychology from Stanford University (1982).

Kinnier's major research interests are in the areas of intrapersonal values conflicts and decision making. He is the author of the Values Conflict Resolution Assessment, an instrument designed to assess the extent to which individuals are resolved about and committed to their values conflict choices.

Richard L. Knowdell is manager of employee development for Racal-Vadic, a telecommunications company, and president of Career Research and Testing, a human resource consulting firm. Both organizations are headquartered in California's Silicon Valley. From 1975 to 1980, Knowdell served as chief counselor for the University of California's Lawrence Livermore National Laboratory. He earned his B.A. degree (1969) in behavioral science and his M.S. degree (1971) in counseling psychology from San Jose State University.

Knowdell has written several articles on career development and outplacement counseling in business and industry, his major area of professional interest. He is a founding director of the national Career Planning and Adult Development Network, is currently serving as president of the California Career Guidance Association, and teaches graduate classes at John F. Kennedy and San Jose State Universities.

John D. Krumboltz is professor of education and psychology at Stanford University, having previously taught at the University of Minnesota and Michigan State University. He received his B.A. degree in psychology from Coe College (1950), his M.A. degree in guidance from Teachers College, Columbia University (1951), and his Ph.D. degree in educational psychology from the University of Minnesota (1955).

Krumboltz has received the Outstanding Research Award

of the American Personnel and Guidance Association three times. He has served as president of the Division of Counseling Psychology of the American Psychological Association, as vice-president of the American Educational Research Association, and as a member of the editorial boards of three professional journals. He has written or edited eight books, including *Counseling Methods* (with C. E. Thoresen, 1976), and has published more than one hundred articles in academic and professional journals.

Linda S. Lotto is assistant director for planning at the National Center for Research in Vocational Education, Ohio State University. She was awarded the B.A. degree in art history from Smith College (1969), the M.Ed. degree from Tufts University (1971), and the Ph.D. degree in education from Indiana University (1979).

Prior to joining the National Center, Lotto codirected a study of exceptional urban elementary schools for Phi Delta Kappa. She has published articles on effective schools, school improvement, organizational evaluation, and vocational education. Her research interests center on organizational processes, the administration of educational organizations, and effective policy development.

Carl McDaniels is professor and program area leader in the Counselor Education Program at Virginia Polytechnic Institute and State University in Blacksburg. He is also director of the Virginia Career Information Delivery System–Virginia VIEW and codirector of the Employee Career Development Program at Virginia Tech. Prior to 1969, he taught at George Washington University and earlier served six years as director of professional services at the American Personnel and Guidance Association in Washington, D.C. He has been a high school teacher and counselor and an elementary school supervisor in a U.S. Naval Prison. He received his A.B. degree in psychology at Bridgewater College (1951) and his M.Ed. and Ed.D. degrees in counseling at the University of Virginia (1957 and 1964, respectively).

McDaniels' writing and research interests have focused

mainly on various aspects of career development through the life span, with articles appearing in the *Vocational Guidance Quarterly, Personnel and Guidance Journal, Journal of College Placement, Occupational Outlook Quarterly, The School Guidance Worker, Counselor Education and Supervision,* and *American Vocational Journal.* His books include *Finding Your First Job* (2nd ed., 1981), *Unlock Your Child's Potential* (with D. Hummel, 1982), and *Leisure: Integrating a Neglected Component in Life Planning* (1983).

McDaniels is a licensed Professional Counselor in Virginia and a Nationally Certified Counselor. He has been president of the National Vocational Guidance Association, National Capitol Personnel and Guidance Association, Virginia Vocational Guidance Association, and the North Atlantic Association of Counselor Education and Supervision.

Johnnie H. Miles is associate professor of counselor education at Virginia Polytechnic Institute and State University in Blacksburg. Prior to 1974, she served as a counselor at Indiana University, taught at the junior high school level in the Columbus, Missouri, and Washington Township, Indiana, schools; and worked as a staff intern in human relations for the National Student YWCA and as director of the YMCA-YWCA at Tuskegee Institute. She earned a B.A. degree in biology (1964) from Rust College, an M.S. degree in guidance and counseling (1968) from Tuskegee Institute, and an Ed.D. degree in counselor education (1974) from Auburn University.

Miles has a strong interest in the career development of women and minorities, which occupies a dominant theme in her research, writing, and professional activities. She has written several articles and coauthored others, including "Women and Peers as Counselors" (with H. M. Getz, 1978) and "Black Students' Perception of Counseling Appropriateness" (with J. Walter, 1982). She was coeditor and contributor to *School Guidance Services: A Career Development Approach* (with T. H. Hohenshil, 1976; rev., 1979).

Miles has served in numerous leadership roles, including president of the New River Personnel and Guidance Association, Virginia Association for Nonwhite Concerns, Virginia Personnel and Guidance Association (name changed to Virginia Counselors Association), and chair of the National Vocational Guidance Association's Commission on Career Development of Young Adults. She is also actively involved with state and local government and business and industry in developing materials and programs for the career development of women and minorities in organizational settings.

Juliet V. Miller is associate director of the National Center for Research in Vocational Education at Ohio State University. She also serves as director of the ERIC Clearinghouse on Adult, Career, and Vocational Education. She was earlier involved in counselor education and research related to career development at the University of Michigan and served as consultant in career education and guidance to secondary schools, universities, and employment and training programs. She earned her B.A. degree in English and her M.A. (1964) and Ph.D. (1970) degrees in guidance and counseling, all from the University of Michigan.

Miller has served as president of the National Vocational Guidance Association and currently serves on several editorial boards, including the *Journal of Career Development* and *Journal of Vocational Education Research*. She has written several books, monographs, and articles on career development and guidance, including *A Handbook of Career Guidance Methods* (with R. Campbell, G. R. Walz, and S. F. Kriger, 1973) and *Career Guidance Practices for Disadvantaged Youth* (1974). She is currently preparing a monograph titled *The Family-Career Connection: Improving Career Development Programs.*

Anna Miller-Tiedeman is president, LIFECAREER Foundation, and tutor/adviser, International College, where she provides holistic alternatives for students interested in professional work with the LIFECAREER. She holds the Ph.D. degree.

Miller-Tiedeman's career started unfolding in 1970 at the Appalachia Educational Laboratory, where she began her study and development of career decision making. She continued such work as counselor in a middle school in California and a high school in Illinois. In this latter work she earned the 1981 Outstanding Research Award of the American Association of Counseling and Development for demonstrating gains in ego development from empowerment of career decision making in adolescents.

Miller-Tiedeman has published extensively. She presently leads the shift of the career paradigm from external to internal/external grounds, from particularism to holism, and from work to life. She has two books on these topics in press—*Career Development: Journey into Personal Power* (with D. V. Tiedeman) and *How to NOT Make It—and Succeed: The Truth about LIFECAREER* (with L. Wilson).

Daniel Sinick is professor emeritus of George Washington University, Washington, D.C., where he directed a graduate program in rehabilitation counseling from 1967 to 1980. Prior to that, he played the same role at San Francisco State University and now is consultant to the Western Gerontological Society in San Francisco. He received a B.A. degree in English and education at City University of New York (1936) and an M.A. degree in the same majors at State University of New York, Albany (1937); he received a Ph.D. degree in counseling psychology at New York University (1955). He also studied psychology at the University of New Hampshire, Harvard University, and Columbia University (1944-1946). From 1949 to 1957 he was a counseling psychologist with the Veterans Administration.

Former president of the National Vocational Guidance Association and editor of the *Vocational Guidance Quarterly,* Sinick has also been president of the American Board on Counseling Services, the San Francisco Psychological Association, and other professional organizations. A fellow of the American Psychological Association, he has been a consultant to that organization and to many others. In 1968 he did a major study of retirement planning programs for the U.S. Civil Service Commission. He has been heavily involved in the field of gerontology, constantly blending it with his central interest in vocational guidance. He was the first chairperson of what is now the Committee on Aging and Adult Development of the American Association for Counseling and Development. He has authored over a hundred articles in professional journals and eight books, including *Joys of Counseling* (1979).

Herbert E. Striner is University Professor and a member of the faculty of the College of Business Administration at the American University, Washington, D.C. He is an economist, with A.B. and M.A. degrees in economics from Rutgers University (1947 and 1948, respectively) and a Ph.D. degree from Syracuse University (1951), where he was a Maxwell Fellow in Economics.

During his career, Striner has been at Johns Hopkins University, the Brookings Institution, the Stanford Research Institute, and the W. E. Upjohn Institute for Employment Research. In government he has worked at the National Science Foundation and the U.S. Department of the Interior. He also has served in an advisory capacity to Presidents Kennedy and Johnson on manpower problems.

Striner has published over seventy articles and four books, the latest being *Regaining the Lead: Policies for Economic Growth* (1984), which focuses on a rethinking of U.S. economic policy as it relates to productivity and economic growth. Since 1962, he has specialized in manpower and productivity problems and has served as a consultant on productivity to such corporations as IBM, PPG Industries (formerly Pittsburgh Plate Glass), and Saks Fifth Avenue, as well as with the Australian, Canadian, and Italian governments.

Prior to his resuming a teaching career in 1981, Striner was dean of the College of Business at the American University. He is listed in *Who's Who in America* and *Who's Who in the World.*

Stephen A. Stumpf is associate professor of management and organizational behavior and director of the Management Simulation Projects Group at the Graduate School of Business Administration, New York University. He received a B.S. degree in chemical engineering from Rensselaer Polytechnic Institute

(1971) and an M.B.A. degree from the University of Roches-
ter (1972). After three years of work as an engineer and manager for the Air Force Aero Propulsion Laboratory, he returned
to academe to earn a Ph.D. degree in management/organization-
al behavior and industrial/organizational psychology from New
York University (1978).

Stumpf has written over fifty articles that have appeared
in such journals as *Academy of Management Review, Journal of
Vocational Behavior, Research in Higher Education, Educational and Psychological Measurement,* and *Academy of Management Journal,* among others. His dissertation won two awards,
including the 1979 S. Rains Wallace Award from the American
Psychological Association. He is coeditor of *Management Education* (1982), coauthor of *Managing Careers* (1982), author of
Choosing a Career in Business (1984), and coauthor of *Financial
Services Industry: A Strategic Decision-Making Simulation*
(1984). His research and teaching interests include career development, judgmental decision making, executive education, and
human resource management. He has received many research
and curricular development grants, including support from the
National Science Foundation, the U.S. Department of Labor,
the Spencer Foundation, and New York University.

L. Sunny Sundal-Hansen is a professor in the Counseling
and Student Personnel Psychology Program, Department of Educational Psychology, University of Minnesota. Prior to joining the
counselor education faculty, she was a counselor, English and
journalism teacher, and director of counseling at University
High School and an English teacher at the University of Chicago
Laboratory School and St. Louis Park (Minnesota) High School
where she began her teaching career. She considers her husband,
Tor K. Hansen, and her two children, Tor, 14, and Sonja, 16,
part of her career.

Sundal-Hansen earned her B.S., M.A., and Ph.D. degrees
at the University of Minnesota, the latter in counseling and
guidance in 1962. She has written several articles and monographs primarily on her major specialty, career development,
and edited a book of readings on *Career Development and*

Counseling of Women. Her international interests are reflected in her study as a Fulbright scholar in Norway (1959-60) and in several follow-up studies since then. Her most recent research and writing are on sex-role issues and stereotyping, including a UNESCO invited monograph on *Eliminating Sex Stereotyping in Schools* (1984). Her major efforts since 1976 have been concentrated on BORN FREE, a federally funded national program to reduce career-related stereotyping and expand career options for both women and men.

A frequent lecturer, both nationally and internationally, Sundal-Hansen has been recognized by state and national associations. She was named a fellow of the American Psychological Association in 1978, received the Research Award of the Minnesota Vocational Guidance Association, and Certificates of Recognition from both the Association for Counselor Education and Supervision and the National Vocational Guidance Association. She has been elected president of NVGA for 1985-86. She received the Minneapolis YWCA Award for Outstanding Achievement in Education in 1984.

Donald E. Super, after attaining emeritus status at Teachers College, Columbia University, where he was director of the Division of Psychology and Education, chairman of the Department of Psychology, and director of the Career Pattern Study, has occupied two later positions in the field of career development and counseling. He was for more than three years honorary director and senior research fellow at the National Institute for Careers Education and Counselling and fellow of Wolfson College, Cambridge. He has since then been a research professor at the University of Florida during the academic year and has taught each summer at Virginia Polytechnic Institute and State University. He lives in Savannah, Georgia.

Super, a Southerner by background, spent his early years in Hawaii and went to grade school in New Jersey and to secondary school in France. He received the B.A. and M.A. degrees at Oxford (1932 and 1936), the Ph.D. degree at Columbia (1940), and an honorary D.Sc. degree from the University of Lisbon. His multinational background has led him to work in many countries and to publish in both English and French. His publications include an early monograph on the relations between work and leisure, textbooks on vocational testing and on the psychology of careers, a French treatise on the psychology of interests, and books on career maturity: All these are listed, along with his numerous journal articles and a biographical sketch, in the write-ups of persons receiving Distinguished Scientific Contributions Awards in the March 1984 issue of the *American Psychologist.*

Kenneth R. Thomas is professor and chair of the Department of Studies in Behavioral Disabilities at the University of Wisconsin-Madison. He earned his B.S. degree in psychology (1964), his M.Ed. degree in counselor education (1965), and his D.Ed. degree in counselor education (1969), all at Pennsylvania State University. From 1965 to 1967, he worked as a rehabilitation counselor in the Vocational Evaluation Unit at the Pennsylvania Rehabilitation Center in Johnstown and was an assistant professor at Pennsylvania State University during the 1969–70 academic year. Since 1970, he has been at the University of Wisconsin-Madison, where he has held a variety of professorial and administrative positions.

Thomas has served on the editorial boards of the *Rehabilitation Counseling Bulletin* and the *Journal of Rehabilitation,* is a fellow of the American Psychological Association (Division 22), and is the immediate past president of the American Rehabilitation Counseling Association. His research has focused on the affective meaning systems of rehabilitation clients, students, and professional personnel. He is the author or coauthor of over fifty refereed journal articles and book chapters. He received special recognition for his research in 1976 and 1984 from the Research Awards Committee of the American Rehabilitation Counseling Association.

David V. Tiedeman is professor of higher and postsecondary education and president, National Institute for the Advancement of Career, University of Southern California. He holds the Ed.D. degree.

Tiedeman has gone through the professorial ranks of the Graduate School of Education, Harvard University, where he also served as codirector of the Center for Research in Careers. At Northern Illinois University, he has been professor of leadership and educational policy studies, director of the ERIC Clearinghouse in Career Education, and university coordinator of Vocational, Technical, and Career Education. His research with R. P. O'Hara has been recognized by the Research Award of the American Personnel and Guidance Association, and he has earned the Eminent Career Award of the National Vocational Guidance Association.

Tiedeman has published over a hundred reports, articles, and chapters in books. His primary work is published under the series title *Career Development*; subtitles in this series presently include *Choice and Adjustment* (with R. P. O'Hara, 1963), *Exploration and Commitment* (with G. A. Dudley, 1977), *Designing Our Career Machines* (1979), *Designing Self* (with J. H. Peatling, 1977), and *Journey into Personal Power* (with A. Miller-Tiedeman, in press).

Garry R. Walz is professor of higher and adult education and director of the Educational Resources Information Center, Counseling and Personnel Services (ERIC/CAPS) Clearinghouse at the University of Michigan. He received his B.A. (1949) and his M.A. (1950) degrees in psychology and his Ph.D. degree (1958) in counseling psychology, all from the University of Minnesota. Having previously served as chairperson of the Department of Guidance and Counseling at the University of Michigan, he is currently in the Department of Higher and Adult Education and a member of its executive committee. He has held several national professional offices, among which were president of the Association for Counselor Education and Supervision in 1967 and president of the American Personnel and Guidance Association in 1971. In 1984 he was recipient of the Gilbert and Kathleen Wrenn Award for a Humanitarian and Caring Person.

Walz has designed and directed ten federally funded programs, including National Defense Education Act institutes for counselor preparation. He has been author or coauthor of numerous publications, including *A Strategy for Guidance,* a three-part series on counseling adults in transition; several monographs on change agentry; and numerous journal articles. He also was the coeditor of a nine-volume series on issues in guidance published by Human Sciences Press and has served since 1967 as editor-in-chief of the ERIC/CAPS publication program. He is coauthor of a training program for career development specialists, the Life Career Development System. Recently he has been appointed a member of the editorial board of the *Journal of Career Development.*

C. Gilbert Wrenn, since 1972 professor emeritus of counseling psychology, served on the graduate faculty of Arizona State University from 1964 to 1972. This was preceded by twenty-eight years at the University of Minnesota (1936–1964) and six years at Stanford University (where he received his Ph.D. degree in 1932). He has served as summer professor or visiting lecturer at twenty-two other universities in the United States and four other countries.

Receiving an honorary Litt.D. degree from Willamette University in 1952 and the APGA Nancy Wimmer Award in 1965, Wrenn has during the past ten years been honored with more than ten awards from national and state professional associations. In addition, a special award was established in 1976—the American Personnel and Guidance Association annual Gilbert and Kathleen Wrenn Award for a Humanitarian and Caring Person. Wrenn has published extensively since 1928, with a total of over 400 articles, books, chapters of books, and monographs. Between 1953 and 1964 he served as the founding editor of the *Journal of Counseling Psychology* and between 1961 and 1974 as consulting editor for forty-two personnel and counseling professional titles published by Houghton Mifflin. Wrenn has served as consultant for many national organizations, as trustee of Macalester College, and on the board of directors of Search Institute and of Concerned Friends, Inc. During the past four years, Wrenn was consulting editor for four professional books.

Designing
Careers

❦ ❦ ❦ ❦ ❦ ❦ ❦ ❦

Counseling
to Enhance Education,
Work, and Leisure

C. Gilbert Wrenn

Introduction:
Evolution of Career
Development, 1913-1983

Norman Gysbers, the general editor of this third decennial volume of the National Vocational Guidance Association's (NVGA) series of books, invited me to contribute an introductory chapter to *Designing Careers*. The book is about what is happening now in career development and the work world and what is projected for the future. But back of this decade lies seventy years of NVGA's activity. Before introducing the contents of the book, I would like to place the book in perspective by presenting a sampling of the conditions of American society and of vocational guidance in 1913 and the next decade or two after that.

The thirty-year-old reader of this book will have been personally aware of professional matters for only a part of this past decade. Such a reader would have only heard or read about anything earlier. For readers in the forty-to-fifty age group, the years before 1963 or 1953 would be vague. So perhaps it is not presumptuous for one born in 1902 to recall his impressions of these earlier decades in the life of NVGA.

The World of 1913

My personal impressions of the world of 1913 are very limited, not only because I was just eleven years old but because

1

I was living in a rural area in Florida (as a fairly recent emigré from Ohio) with limited educational and national knowledge facilities. There were, I am sure, many thousands of other rural youth whose homes had only a fireplace for heating, a wood stove for cooking, an open well for water, no transportation except horse and buggy, no nearby library, no radio, no TV, and of course no electricity. Yet youth did not lack in enthusiasm and aspirations, and when they went to a "city," gas lights, streetcars, and Model T Fords gave them a feeling that the future might be wonderful!

Many readers of this book and members of NVGA take for granted experiences and conditions of the present that were unknown to the 1913 founders of an organization to help youth. Our familiar forms of personal security were all unknown: Social Security came into being in 1935; Medicare not until 1965; until Social Security made possible the Federal-State Unemployment Compensation Acts of 1936, only Wisconsin had a public law of this nature, and that not until 1932. Familiar forms of transportation were also lacking or in short supply, the first transcontinental air service beginning in 1930. In 1910 only 181,000 automobiles, trucks, and buses were produced, compared with 1978, when there were 9,176,000 cars produced, with 113,696,000 autos registered and a total motor vehicle registration of 143,750,000. The first "regular TV broadcasts" began in Great Britain in 1937, not until 1939 in the United States. (The first limited color TV service in the States was by CBS in 1951, but the demands of the Korean War delayed progress, and a full-service program—NBC's—did not appear until 1953.)

The reader may not find it easy to realize that the increased mobility of past decades brought about by automobile and air transportation and the more immediate awareness of social changes and of the oneness of the world brought about by radio and TV opened up kinds of vocational planning that were unheard of during the first two decades of our association's history.

In a curious sort of way, the 1930s—the years of the Great Depression with its peak unemployment more than twice that of our peak year 1982, its staggering bank failures, the presence on the streets of once-proud men and women openly begging, the increase in both prostitution and birthrate—were a good decade for vocational guidance! Many more youth and adults were attending school because of the job shortage and so became accessible to vocational planning help; more tests became available and were more widely used; better vocational information became available with the establishment of the United States Employment Service in 1933, which led to the first publication of the *Dictionary of Occupational Titles* in 1939 (followed in 1949 by the first issue of the equally invaluable *Occupational Outlook Handbook*), and the establishment in 1938 of the Occupational Information and Guidance Service in the United States Office of Education. Perhaps an intangible benefit of those traumatic years was that both youth and adults learned more about the critical importance of *work,* not only through the paucity of jobs but through "working to survive," so to speak, in WPA and NYA (Works Progress Administration and National Youth Administration).

In 1913 this country had not yet experienced four major wars—World Wars I and II, the Korean War, and Vietnam—each with its shattering of the values related to national purpose and the integrity of human life, breakup of family and industrial patterns, postwar surges in education and vocational fields, the expanding vocational environments to include the world, together with political, industrial, and technological changes too numerous to mention. The world of work for women in 1913 was a narrow one. The Eighteenth and Nineteenth Amendments to the United States Constitution, each to have profound effects on national, family, and personal lives, were still a dream in 1913. It is difficult now to recall with any sense of realism both the Prohibition decade and the first decade of women's very tentative acceptance of the responsibilities of their right to vote. Both seem unreal. Can the women readers of this book, who are now fighting for equal rights in the legal and economic dimensions of their lives, visualize what it was like to be denied the right to vote—or the feeling of triumph when that victory was won in 1920? For a good many years after 1920, it was not clear that the long struggle had been justified. The majority of women were *not* voting, nor were they engaging in any of the other struggles for equality that so characterize contemporary women. ERA would have frightened some of the women more than the men—as it still does to a disappointing degree.

Comparatively few women were working outside the home in 1913. The United States Census for 1910 reported 20 percent of "females 10 years of age and older engaged in gainful occupations." The occupational fields where females made up more than 80 percent of the workers are of interest (the percentages are approximated from charts of the *Statistical Abstract of the United States,* 1914): launderers and laundresses (98 percent), milliners and millinery dealers (96 percent), trained nurses (94 percent), housekeepers and stewards (92 percent), telephone operators (92 percent), midwives and untrained nurses (88 percent), boardinghouse keepers (85 percent), servants (83 percent), teachers (83 percent), charwomen and cleaners (83 percent), stenographers and "typewriters" (82 percent). On the other end of the line, the physician and surgeon category reported only 6 or 7 percent females; bankers, brokers, moneylenders only 2 or 3 percent.

The overall picture was quite different for one subgroup —55 percent of black females "10 years of age and older" were reported to be in the labor force. (Owing to their highly restricted educational and employment opportunities, the great preponderance of the black female workers in 1910 was to be found in unskilled jobs.) This was a higher proportion by far than among either native or foreign-born white females.

Nor would it be easy to imagine a period without liquor flowing freely and legally. The 1920s were the years of bootleg whisky (which caused many deaths), bootleggers, speakeasies, rumrunners—and a mounting toll of crime and violence. There was reason for the repeal of the Eighteenth Amendment, but the cure may now be seen as worse than the ailment. The toll of at least 8 million alcoholics, the tragedy of which swells to 25 million or more when families are considered, is a very high price to pay for "freedom." Our high schools and colleges might be different places without the appallingly high percentage of students who drink regularly or to excess. "It was not so" in 1913, but NVGA faced equally serious social conditions.

The National Vocational Guidance Association grew out of a society that was cruel to the worker. In 1913 child labor laws existed in what I would guess to be a minority of the states (even with the able assistance of James Cox of Northern Arizona University I was unable to determine the exact number). In this connection it seems significant that, as earlier listed, the 1910 labor force ("gainful occupations") began at age 10—the age of a child. The *Statistical Atlas* listed the 1910 percentage of children "in gainful occupations" for ages 10-13 and ages 14-15. The top ten states, all in the South, for ages 10-13, reported employment ranging from 58 percent to 28 percent for boys, from 39 percent to 6 percent for girls. For the 14-15-year-olds, these same states, with one exception, ranged from 78 percent to 54 percent for boys and from 52 percent to 28 percent for girls (percentages were approximate). These figures suggest that in 1910 there was a great deal of what we would call "child labor." For both children and women, sweatshop conditions often prevailed in factory and field work. Women domestics had their lives controlled by "the lady of the house," and they were paid per month less than what now might be paid per day. Working conditions for men were little better as the Wages and Hours Act was not passed until 1938, and little attention was given to worker health and safety conditions.

It is not surprising, then, to recall that it was a Boston *social worker*, concerned with the working conditions and haphazard employment of urban youth, who first wrote about what might be done in "vocational guidance" (Parsons, 1909). The motivations of those who launched NVGA in 1913 must have been stirred by the Parsons book (in circulation for the preceding four years) and the conditions that motivated its author. The available resources were pitifully small from our point of view. There were no appropriate psychological tests, of course, since the Stanford-Binet first appeared in 1916 and the Otis Group Intelligence Test in 1918. Tests useful in appraising personality traits, so significant in vocational counseling appeared much later—the Strong Interest Blank, for example, in

1927. During my early years in counseling, the 1920s, a rash of "aptitude tests" appeared, but most of them had a very heavy g-factor weighting and were general intelligence tests under the label of aptitude. Universities were early interested in the use of general intelligence (or academic aptitude) tests for selection purposes. Stanford University began using the Thorndike Intelligence Test (group, paper and pencil) in 1924, but Stanford had established a Vocational Guidance Committee about 1915 (Harvard, as I recall, established such a committee a little earlier), and it was "ready" for the testing movement. The Stanford University Committee (E. K. Strong, Jr., chairman) appointed me in 1929 to be its first executive secretary. My first project was not psychological test applications, as might have been expected, but the use of vocational information. I set about selecting vocational books and pamphlets, annotating them, and placing them on a special and easily available shelf in the library. The expectation was that students would eagerly avail themselves of the opportunity to read these materials. They did not! We know better now.

Vocational information was an early interest of NVGA because that was the only *available* resource for guidance. But reliable and useful vocational information, as we understand it, was not available for a couple of decades. As mentioned earlier, one of the counselor's chief reference works in vocational counseling, the famous *DOT* (*Dictionary of Occupational Titles*), was first published in 1939. Other significant publications of the United States Employment Service (established 1933) were still more years ahead of the early days of NVGA. The Bureau of Labor Statistics had been publishing labor information since 1886, but the publications of its early decades were segmented and not too helpful. As earlier mentioned, the first issue of the *Occupational Outlook Handbook* appeared in 1949.

The association established the *Vocational Guidance Magazine* in 1924 (preceded by the *NVGA Bulletin,* 1921-1924), and that was the only vehicle of professional communication for some years. My first published article, "Organizing a Guidance Program in a Small School," appeared in that journal in October 1928. How proud I was of that article, and how pitiful it looks now! The first book to provide an integrated picture of "guidance" in these early days was *Educational and Vocational Guidance,* by William Martin Proctor, published in 1926. This gentleman and gentle man was the reason I went to Stanford University in 1928 for graduate work, and as a student of his, I coauthored the *Workbook in Vocations* with him and Benefield in 1931. (Both books were Houghton Mifflin publications.)

Publications on student personnel work in colleges and universities also began appearing in the 1920s. The first survey of student personnel work in universities was published in 1926 by the American Council on Education. This was followed in 1929 by Esther Lloyd-Jones' description of the student personnel program at Northwestern University.

Several more explicit descriptions of developmental stages or waves of emphasis over the past fifty years are given in two publications (Wrenn, 1983, 1984).

The World of 1983 and Beyond

The twenty-three chapters of this book reflect in various specific ways the conditions of our society and of our professional field in the present decade. There are some general trends and conditions in our society that appear to me to have vital significance for the career development field. I am, therefore, introducing the chapters with a brief preface of personal convictions.

Current Trends. In the 1980s we appear to be responding to these professional, social, and philosophical trends:

1. Vocations and jobs are appraised in terms of emotional satisfaction, value factors, and job environments as well as intelligence, experience, and skills.

2. There is both promise and threat in the rapid expansion of computer technology and robotics; for example, the assembly of an IBM $8,000 PC computer is so completely automated that it requires only ten minutes of a worker's time. One recent projection in the popular press stated that by 1990 there would be 100,000 robots in use and 20 million computers.

3. Women have achieved a degree of power socially, politically, and vocationally that necessitates that men reconsider their part in the functioning of society, particularly their changing position in the labor force and in the family. Note two recent books: Goldberg (1983) and Gerzon (1982).

4. An increasing life expectancy has made retirement and the needs and capacities of older people a solid concern of both students and practitioners in career development. The development over the past ten years of the International Association of Universities of the Third Age and the International Association for Senior Citizens' Colleges highlights constructive concern in other parts of the world.

5. A changing public and student attitude toward schools and colleges is resulting in a compromise between schools' providing students of all ages with learning experiences that *they* want and protecting both society and the students with an adequate level of reading and mathematical literacy.

6. The use of imagery and imagination is an important concern for those who deal with client thinking about vocational futures.

7. Birthrate is an important concern for counselors, teachers, and others whose work is with people because birthrate determines the number of potential clients for a given number of years ahead; for example, the United States Department of Labor projects an increase of 231,000 elementary school teachers and 125,000 childcare workers during the period 1980 to 1990. (See *U.S. News and World Report,* February 7, 1983, for projections in fifty occupational fields.) This projection, for example, may be invalid if the birthrate continues to decline—there were sixteen births per thousand population in 1980, markedly down from the peak year 1957 and still falling.

8. Vocational counselors must balance the realism of the still-prevalent employer attitudes toward the differences in outward appearance of ethnic, age, and sexual minorities against the great need of the client to maintain self-respect and to take risks in vocational planning.

9. Such books as *The Aquarian Conspiracy* by Marilyn Ferguson, *Megatrends* by John Naisbitt, *The Turning Point* by

Fritjof Capra, *Encounters with the Future* by Marvin Cetron and Thomas O'Toole, and *The Evolutionary Journey* by Barbara Hubbard describe and demonstrate a worldwide network of positive thinking about the future of our civilization and our world. At least these writers have convinced me that career development people need to guard against the domination of their thinking and client contacts by short-run pessimism. There are some frightening trends and conditions facing our society and the world. These press on us now. There is also much evidence that the projections of long-term trends (within the lifetime of younger clients) are upward and positive for greater humaneness and justice among the peoples of the world, an acceptance of an integrated body, mind, and spirit in the oneness of a person, and acceptance of the reality of the mystical and transcendental as well as the logical and empirical. My glass of the future is half full and slowly filling. I see no logic or meaning in a concept of a half-empty glass or in a negative interpretation of the future of our species. (This conviction is a personal sharing, not a teaching or a dogma. The older I become, the less dogma I seem to have!)

This Book. Twenty-nine authors from eighteen universities and three government and independent agencies, located in fifteen states from New York to California and Texas to Minnesota, have contributed to this book. Only six of the twenty-nine authors contributed to the 1974 volume—Henry Borow, John Crites, Edwin Herr, Donald Super, David Tiedeman, and Anna Miller-Tiedeman. The writing backgrounds of the authors of this book assure a product that is both contemporary and seasoned. Editor Norman C. Gysbers, a past president of both the American Association for Counseling and Development (formerly the American Personnel and Guidance Association) and the National Vocational Guidance Association and currently chairperson of the board of trustees of the American Association for Counseling and Development Foundation, is a productive and highly respected author in his own right.

I found the book easy reading and written with great clarity. The contents were stimulating and provoked me to considerations that were new to me. All chapters showed the results of what I consider careful scholarship. Two issues of the contemporary scene are hinted at or treated explicitly in many of the chapters: inflation and unemployment. This could be both a strength and a weakness of the book, for both conditions are cyclical in nature. The 1974 volume, written presumably in 1973 before the impact of the 1974 inflationary rise, gave little attention to these topics. Its 1300-item index has one item under *inflation* and fourteen under *unemployment*. Most of the latter refer to unemployment in the world rather than in the United States. All the references to these two topics are by three authors of the twenty-three in the book—Borow, Herr, and Wolfbein.

Following are my capsule reviews of the chapters. Each is just long enough to give the reader a feeling for each chapter.

Part One
The World of Work Today:
Personal, Social, and Economic Perspectives

Chapter One: "Perspectives on the Meaning and Value of Work"—Donald E. Super. The author, a national and international figure in the field, past president of NVGA, the American Association for Counseling and Development (AACD), and the International Association for Educational and Vocational Guidance (IAEVG), opens the chapter by commenting on our current tendency to use the term *quality of life* rather than *work motivation* and to use *life satisfactions* rather than *job satisfaction*. The implications are far-reaching. From the international Work Importance Study that he has been directing, he contrasts the different values accorded to work in different countries and cultures—for example, risk taking is more valued in the United States than in Yugoslavia; economic rewards are a material value in the United States, whereas in Japan they have a psychological prestige value. The concept that "the place of work in life changes greatly with age" is carefully developed, as is the relation of "affective work commitment" to vocational maturity. In the last third of the chapter, the author dips generously into changing career roles and their determinants. This is a most im-

portant section for me, for our professional future lies in understanding technological and other societal changes in this and
other countries as they inevitably affect both career counselor
and career client. It is something of a shock to realize that our
work environment is the world.

   *Chapter Two: "Changing Structure of Work: Occupation-
al Trends and Implications"—Harold Goldstein.* This is a very
helpful chapter, both for practicing counselors and for researchers or writers in the field. The author gives specific and accurate
answers to scores of significant questions on kinds and numbers
of occupations and trends in many fields, often from 1900 on
to 1982, with trends projected into the future. The second half
of the chapter is devoted to an equally careful analysis of how
individuals respond not only to the changes in occupation and
education but to changes in one's total life span and attitudes.
The chapter is loaded with facts, but the writing style is clear
and the sentences are attractive. The treatment of women and
ethnic minorities is both specific and sympathetic.

   *Chapter Three: "Links Among Training, Employability,
and Employment"—Edwin L. Herr.* The author of this chapter—
editor of the 1974 NVGA decennial volume, past president of
AACD, a productive and competent writer—lives up to his reputation in this chapter. The four components of employability
and the thwarting conditions in youths' and adults' adjustment
to work will be found very helpful for practicing counselors.
The comprehensive treatment of training considerations will be
equally helpful to counselor educators. The beginning and closing sections of the chapter evidence long-range thinking and
educational statesmanship of a high order.

   *Chapter Four: "Partnership Between Education and
Work"—Linda S. Lotto.* This chapter provides a much-needed
analysis of the Job Training and Partnership Act (P.L. 97-300).
Although individual benefits are viewed as having primary significance, the author sees benefits to schools, employers, and
society. Having declared these benefits, she looks at the outcomes of previous experiences with such partnerships and is not
greatly encouraged. After analyzing kinds of partnerships and
providing nine case illustrations, the author offers a section en-

titled "Assessing Partnerships: The Tie That Doesn't Necessarily Bind." I like her realistic skepticism, for she goes on to provide *answers,* ways of making the partnership work. The writer's issues and answers are constructive and helpful. She knows her field.

Part Two
Knowledge Base of Career Development

Chapter Five: "Relationship Between Career Development Theory and Practice"—David A. Jepsen. The first section of this chapter provides a clear discussion, very interesting to me, of the theory/practice conflict or confusion. In my own teaching over the years, I often served as a step-down transformer in presenting personality or career theory to practicing counselors, translating theory words into practitioner-behavior words. Yet a counselor explicitly or implicitly relates practice to theory, his own or another's! In the next section, career theories are briefly but appropriately discussed under headings of structural, developmental, and self-concept considerations. The last section deals with the various ways in which career behavior is considered. Careful attention is given to the affect side—the worker's feelings toward the job, the job's contribution to worker satisfaction, and thoughts about self in work roles and various types of overt behavior in seeking information.

The author's summary suggests the value of the proposed informal theory approach for the practitioner/counselor but also poses some issues that must be faced by formal theory builders. The solution, of course, lies in a more effective dialogue between theorist and practitioner.

Chapter Six: "Occupational Socialization: Acquiring a Sense of Work"—Henry Borow. This is a well-written, mature chapter, providing an understanding that is basic to every other chapter in the book—namely, the development of a person's attitude toward the place of occupation in his or her life. Work models and occupational attitudes are important factors in the socialization of a person; Borow devotes over half of the chapter to "work as social bonding." The child is early influenced by the occupations and attitudes of *both* parents (68 percent of school-age children and youth have working mothers) and by the strictly academic expectations of most schools. Peer culture and possible work experience are also factors, but most important are the media—TV, movies, and print. These most often focus on occupational status and neglect work requirements.

Later sections are titled "Growing Up: Acquiring Self-Managed Behaviors," "Learning an Occupational Role," and "The School-to-Work Passage: Discontinuities."

The chapter demonstrates careful scholarship, clear writing, a sense of movement in occupational understanding from childhood to adulthood, and a strong conviction of the importance of the topic. It is, in fact, a chapter, particularly the first and second sections, that should be read and reread by every career development student and practitioner.

Chapter Seven: "Adult Career Development: Individual and Organizational Factors"—Stephen A. Stumpf. This chapter will introduce the reader to two distinct dimensions of life. One is the world of the individual in a business organization and how he or she can contribute to personal career development rather than feeling manipulated by the organization. The other is the world of the organization and the ways it is now contributing or can contribute to the growth of the individual employee. The counselor will find in this chapter six factors in career development for which the individual is responsible and eleven ways in which business organizations are helping. Many studies of particular programs are provided (many references are listed, with six annotated references for suggested reading). The outlook for career development in business organizations is presented as optimistic.

Chapter Eight: "Interrelationship of Gender and Career" —L. Sunny Sundal-Hansen. This is a strong and scholarly chapter, written clearly and with professional competence. The topic is obviously a major factor in any dimension of career development, and the hope is expressed (with great professional courtesy) that it will be considered in every chapter of this volume. The reader might find it interesting to make this the first or second chapter read and then to see how this challenge is met in each of the other chapters. I found the chapter stimulating reading, almost fascinating. (I made several pages of notes, which I cannot use here!)

The writer is committed, knowledgeable, and fair in her analysis of the adjustment problems of both men and women. Many facts and studies are presented, with clarity and conviction. I think the reader is certain to develop great respect for the author, both as a professional and as a writer.

Chapter Nine: "Instruments for Assessing Career Development"—John O. Crites. This is a professionally organized chapter on measurement in a particular area. Major attention is given to two well-known career development inventories, the author's Career Maturity Inventory and the Career Development Inventory by Thompson and others. Both have their roots in Super's (1957) Career Pattern Study. These two instruments are carefully examined, using commonly accepted criteria of evaluation. In a very professional manner, the author discusses the limitations of these and earlier inventories and suggests the work yet to be done. Three other inventories are briefly described.

The concluding section, on future trends, is rich with a discussion of trends and projected developments and contains a sentence that has significant meaning for both practitioner and measurement specialist: "Normative data, rather than predictive validity, thus become more relevant to . . . comprehensive career counseling, since they deal primarily with *how* clients make choices and secondarily with *what* choices they make." The reference list provides an accounting of the author's extensive work in this field over the past two decades and more.

Chapter Ten: "Job Satisfaction: Worker Aspirations, Attitudes, and Behavior"—René V. Dawis. The author has performed a distinct service for the reader by selecting a relatively small number of significant references and research studies from what is apparently a very voluminous literature (he cites one study reporting that by the early 1970s there were over 3,000 publications on job satisfaction).

I find it impossible to do justice in this brief statement to the many facets of job satisfaction understanding presented in this chapter. The author writes clearly and is obviously well informed on both the general literature and the research in the field. It is apparent that his own research in the field extends over many years. The chapter is at times exciting. The final section, on the implications of all this for the career development practitioner, is helpful, as is a list of annotated "Suggested Readings."

Part Three
Facilitating Career Development:
Practices and Programs

Chapter Eleven: "Procedures for Successful Career Counseling"—Richard T. Kinnier, John D. Krumboltz. The chapter opens with an analysis of the confusion caused by an overabundance of theories and printed material. The authors want to help the counseling practitioner have a framework within which he or she can select from the abundance and yet retain a pragmatic and eclectic stance. The framework evolves under polysyllabic headings, but these are quickly interpreted in simple terms, and the text is clear, specific, and helpful. The authors, as experienced counselors in their own right, focus on elements of the client/ counselor relationship and on client learning, with many suggestions and case illustrations. Tables 1 and 2 illustrate the clarity of the specific helps suggested in this case for values clarification and decision making. The chapter is readable, and the authors show a real concern for the nitty-gritty of career counseling. The literature is not neglected, but it does not clog up the text. One section in particular is highly useful to the counselor who is really concerned about the client—"Getting the Job."

The future is seen as hopeful for the development of *self-help* measurements and procedures. The last sentence reads: "Ultimately, individuals will be best served if they are taught and encouraged to be the experts in their own career development."

Chapter Twelve: "Systematic Career Guidance Programs"—Garry R. Walz, Libby Benjamin. For some readers such delivery systems will not be as well known as other phases of a career development program. It is, therefore, helpful to have these authors early on define such a system and carefully describe the development of several kinds of delivery systems. The bulk of the chapter is devoted to what such systems contribute to a program and what is lost without a delivery system. The senior author, a past president of AACD, should know, for he has for more than a decade directed one such delivery system on a national scale, and both authors have written extensively on the research in the field. Their description of six "future images" of guidance systems is good reading. The chapter is innovative and stimulating.

   Chapter Thirteen: "The Computer as a Tool in Career Guidance Programs"—JoAnn Harris-Bowlsbey. The author of this chapter has been deeply engrossed in the computer-guidance field for at least two decades and is eminently qualified to enlighten the reader on the total scope of the field—which is just what she does. A clear distinction is maintained throughout between information systems and guidance (student assist) systems. Some readers will enjoy most her clear picture of the development of the different systems in the 1960s and 1970s and what is happening to them now—the current status of computers, with the new instruments such as the videodisk. Others will read most carefully such practical matters as cost, benefits to students (seven are described), benefits to counselors (four are given), and how many schools use the systems. These and other "practical" suggestions have grown out of the long-term experience of a competent professional. There is one striking quotation with which I heartily agree: "The impact of the microcomputer combined with robotics will be *as great as or greater* than the impact of the industrial revolution."

   Chapter Fourteen: "Serving the Career Guidance Needs of the Economically Disadvantaged"—Johnnie H. Miles. Note that this chapter is one of two chapters on disadvantaged people—one on the poor and one on the physically and mentally handicapped. The poor, whose numbers are variously estimated at between 26 and 34.4 million, or one eighth of the United States population, are composed of diverse ethnic, sex, and age subgroups, including the working poor and the nonworking poor. After sensitizing the reader to the kinds of people involved and the situations in which they live and work, the author outlines the specific career guidance needs of the poor. The balance of the chapter (two thirds of it) is focused on strategies and techniques for helping the economically disadvantaged. Seven strategies are given for helping individuals and five for changing the system or the environment. I cannot overemphasize that this chapter is written to help the counselor and that it does so in a meaningful manner. Few can read this chapter without reflecting "I believe I *could* help more than I am doing—and I will."

Chapter Fifteen: "Providing Career Counseling for Individuals with Handicapping Conditions"—Kenneth R. Thomas, Norman L. Berven. Perhaps 20 percent of the adult population is handicapped, and they represent a wide diversity of people with a wide diversity of disabilities—Thomas and Berven name sixteen of the most prevalent. The authors next examine various work theories as they apply to the handicapped and various career counseling delivery systems such as educational institutions and rehabilitation facilities. The second half of the chapter is devoted to the *practice* of career counseling with the handicapped. This is well organized, following each step through to work adjustment. The authors are optimistic about the future in this field in terms of both public support and technological developments. The chapter has a fifty-one-item reference list and four annotated "Suggested Readings."

Chapter Sixteen: "Career Development Programs and Practices in the Schools"—Juliet V. Miller. As I read this comprehensive and well-organized chapter, I was impressed with the distance we have come from the early days of "guidance in the schools." Such pioneers of the 1910–1920 period as Bloomfield and Davis had almost no resources to meet vocational and other counseling needs of the youth of that period. They would have been overwhelmed with the riches of today! This chapter is comprehensive and clearly written; it could be the *précis* of a strong text in the field. Many individual programs and developments are presented with succinctness and clarity under three heads. The wealth of specific material discouraged any attempt of mine to comment on content. The contemporary nature of this chapter is obvious. Of the numerous references and suggested readings, most were published in 1978 or later. The last fourth of the chapter is devoted to a creative and encouraging "look to the future."

   Chapter Seventeen: "Career Development and Placement in Services in Postsecondary Institutions"—Cynthia S. Johnson, Howard E. Figler. Following a succinct statement on historical background and a review of the state of the art, the authors creatively move into issues confronting career centers. Five opposing views are treated in a straightforward, no-holds-barred fashion. Some exciting reading! I liked particularly the advocation of risk taking in vocational choice in contrast to counseling toward "safe" but perhaps boring occupational niches. The need for negotiation between what a student wants and what the employer wants, the oft-mistaken expectations of higher education with respect to vocational choice, and the equally frequent erroneous career expectations of the client are given equally lively attention. A section on new resources and solutions (cassettes and computers) is contemporary and very helpful. Five major future directions are presented, with much attention to expanded services. The chapter concludes with a presentation of alternative models at seventeen institutions. The writing is clear and uncomplicated. The authors come across as experienced and competent professionals who have a comprehensive understanding of movements in the entire field at the college and university level.

   Chapter Eighteen: "Career Planning and Development Programs in the Workplace"—Richard L. Knowdell. This chapter differs from Chapter Seven in that it is written by an author who has held numerous organizational positions but who is now "outside looking in" at organizational patterns for career development. One function of this chapter is to inform the vocational counselor of the reasons that career development is now a concern of business. Various ways of contributing to the career development of an employee are given, together with who is responsible and which kinds of employees need help. One model career planning program is described in detail. The author describes a new occupation in business, that of the human resource development specialist. All this and much more, clearly and briefly written. This is one of the more specifically helpful chapters of the book.

Part Four
Responding to Emerging Views
of Work and Leisure

Chapter Nineteen: "Changes in Work and Society, 1984-2004: Impact on Education, Training, and Career Counseling"—Herbert E. Striner. The author is thoughtful and low-key about the kinds of changes to be expected and the probable rate of change, but even so the effect is startling. His projections prepare us intellectually for shock, but few of us are prepared emotionally for the new realities of the next twenty years.

The author believes that both industry and government are forced to accept change (to prevent loss of business or loss of elections) but that education, the most important factor in preparing us for change, is not. School systems are not keeping up with present technological or industrial changes, nor are schools preparing us for a drastically different future. He believes that the fault lies in the lack of adequate management principles in education. It is a specifically critical chapter. Be prepared to have your hackles rise!

Chapter Twenty: "Problems of Work and Retirement for an Aging Population"—Daniel Sinick. This excellent chapter opens with a clear picture of an aging population, but the main emphasis is on facts about contemporary retirement patterns in our society and their implications for counselors. The timing of retirement is an important concern; there is a careful discussion of eleven reasons for "early retirement" and eleven reasons for retirement "on time" (traditionally age sixty-five) or later. This is a valuable section of the chapter. Likewise helpful is the last half of the chapter, devoted to a presentation of what society as a whole is doing or can do about retirement and the needs of retirees, what prospective retirees can do, and what the counselor's commitments to the older person are. It is a helpful chapter with both scope and depth.

Chapter Twenty-One: "Work and Leisure in the Career Span"—Carl McDaniels. This chapter is comprehensive, clearly written, and creative. It will command the full respect of the reader, for the author is obviously a competent scholar in this field. Authentic definitions of both *work* and *leisure* are followed by a comprehensive analysis of work and leisure in our society. The review of a rich literature (sixty references and six annotated readings are listed) is stimulating reading (not always true of a review!). The last third of the chapter is devoted to a creative analysis of leisure potentials at six stages in the life span and to a helpful description of possible institutional responses to the "changing role of leisure." A satisfying chapter, written by a past president of NVGA.

Chapter Twenty-Two: "To Be in Work: On Furthering the Development of Careers and Career Development Specialists"—Anna Miller-Tiedeman and David V. Tiedeman. The text of this chapter is as intriguing as its title. The Tiedemans have been proposing for some time the concept that "career is life," a concept that leads to the conclusion that vocational choice should be guided by what one wants to *be* rather than what one plans to *do.* The fact that the job picture changes rapidly, almost from year to year, emphasizes the shakiness of choices based on what one does. A "soft" vocational choice is therefore necessary, one that is admittedly tentative and subject to change. Such choices need not be haphazard but may be related to some substantial principles that appear to govern the universe. (This concept is mindboggling—but read the chapter!) The balance of the chapter is devoted to the expansion of eight ways in which soft career specialists develop and the resulting changes in professional life. Tentative choice is not a new concept, but the authors now give it structure and substance. It is difficult to dispute, and the outcome is a new way of thinking. Some "hard" choices seem unavoidable, but not to be open to change means slow death as the changing present flows by and the laggard is left in a stagnant, slowly circling eddy on the side of the stream.

This is one of the most creative and mind-stretching chapters of the book.

Chapter Twenty-Three: "Major Trends in Career Development Theory and Practice"—Norman C. Gysbers. This chapter by the editor is much more than a wrap-up, summary chapter—it is a major contribution in its own right. The author skillfully brings into sharp focus "four predominant trends in the evolution of career development theory and practice" from among the many trends presented by the authors of the preceding twenty-two chapters. They are (1) the evolving meanings of career and career development, (2) the changing environments and structures in which people live and work, (3) the increasing numbers and diversity of career development programs, tools, and techniques, and (4) the greater number and variety of people and settings being served. Gysbers cites each chapter for its contribution to at least one of these trends, thus providing a very helpful highlighting of what the book is all about. He then enters into a condensed and very contemporary discussion of the meaning of each trend. (Thirteen of the twenty-two references cited are within the period 1980–1983.) Many sentences within these few pages supply a key to an integrated understanding of an entire section of the book.

The chapter concludes with the development of two major perceptions: (1) As concepts of career and career development become more encompassing of the totality of life, people in a greater age range are served, there is a greater diversity of programs to serve them, and career counseling is found in a broad new array of settings, all of which have been influenced by the marked economic, social, and living changes of the past decade. The changes are interdependent and, in a sense, had to develop in this manner. (2) The future will see further emphasis on the developmental focus in career guidance, a movement from the early "vocational guidance" focus and the personal adjustment emphasis of the 1920s, 1930s, and 1940s to the present and future focus on career *development* over a life span.

The chapter is a creative and stimulating ending to this chronicle of the marked changes of the past decade. One is encouraged, even excited, and is reminded that one must be open to still further change! Few of us would want to hazard more than a wild guess at the content of the 1994 NVGA volume. The next decade could be the equivalent of half a century.

Epilogue

This book suggests major changes in societal functioning, in job outlook, in counselor function. There is a tendency to say that all this is exaggerated—"It can't happen here"—or to feel panic-stricken because one believes that it can.

> Some seventy-five years ago, the inhabitants of a remote village saw Halley's comet, a frightening sphere of white light in the heavens, coming closer each night. They became panic-stricken. "It could be the end of the world for all of us!" The pastor noticed their panic, but in looking at the sky he saw something else. So he called the villagers together and said, "I see what you all see, a bright moving star coming closer to us, but I also see all the other stars in the heavens just where they have been night after night. There are thousands of them, and they are not getting closer. They are almost stationary. So place your mind on all the familiar fixed stars, and you won't be so frightened by the bright one."

We also have some "fixed" stars. (1) One distinguishing continuing characteristic of our humanness is our adaptability; when faced with change, we handle it—that is how we have survived. (2) You and I know certain truths to be "self-evident," certain principles of justice and humaneness that will outlast the race. (3) We know certain people whose integrity is deathless, whom we would trust to the end. (4) Most of all, we sense our own potential of strength whose limits have never been tested. With these "fixed stars" in our lives, we can meet dramatic, traumatic change and not panic. The changes suggested in this book are a part of our present world. Past, present, and future are blended into one running stream of time, the true reality. In that stream the rushing waters of the future can be heard, and they become part of the present. When we make these sounds a reality of the present, we contribute to our survival.

References

Gerzon, M. *A Choice of Heroes: The Changing Faces of America's Manhood.* Boston: Houghton Mifflin, 1982.

Goldberg, H. *The New Male-Female Relationship.* New York: William Morrow, 1983.

Parsons, F. *Choosing a Vocation.* Boston: Houghton Mifflin, 1909.

Super, D. E., and others. *Vocational Development: A Framework for Research.* New York: Bureau of Publications, Teachers College Press, 1957.

Wrenn, C. G. "Developments in Vocational Counseling: One Counseling Psychologist's Point of View." *International Journal for the Advancement of Counselling,* 1983, *6,* 255–270.

Wrenn, C. G. "Personal Reflections on My Experiences in Counseling Psychology and in Life." In J. Whiteley and others (Eds.), *The Coming Decade in Counseling Psychology.* Irvine, Calif.: The Counseling Psychologist, 1984.

Part One

The World of Work Today: Personal, Social, and Economic Perspectives

Career behavior and development do not unfold separately and independently from the world of work and the personal, social, and economic environments and structures within it. The relationship is reciprocal and interactive. As a result, professionals need a thorough understanding of the work world so that they are able (1) to appreciate its impact on the dynamics of career behavior and development and (2) to empower individuals with whom they work to become competent, achieving persons by effectively managing their talents in the work environment.

Part One provides professionals with a comprehensive and detailed analysis and discussion of the world of work today and tomorrow. Personal, social, and economic environments and structures are analyzed and discussed, as is the impact that they may have on career behavior and development. The result is a clearer picture for professionals of the work world and its effects on the human career.

Donald E. Super begins the analysis and discussion in Chapter One by examining the changing meaning and value of work through the ages. He traces how understandings of work and the meanings attached to it have changed as cultures have changed. He describes and presents some findings of a major cross-cultural research project, the Work Importance Study, that is under way to assess the values people hold about work. Super also considers how work today is viewed from, and in relationship to, the broader perspectives of life roles and the quality of life. This broader view, he points out, signals the beginning of the movement toward "true career counseling."

In Chapter Two, Harold Goldstein describes the changing nature of work and the industrial and occupational structures that shape work. He also discusses the openness of the occupational structure for women and minorities. He examines how individuals move through these structures as they are building their careers and details the role of education and formal training, as well as the ways firms hire workers. Finally, Goldstein summarizes patterns of worker mobility among employers and occupations.

Edwin L. Herr, in Chapter Three, presents a comprehensive discussion of the connections among training, employability, and employment. He describes major elements of youth and adult employability and some possible counseling, educational, and economic responses to develop it. Employment and unemployment are defined, and solutions to unemployment are considered. Finally, Herr makes distinctions between general and specific employability and draws implications for policies governing counseling and training.

Part One closes with a challenging discussion by Linda S. Lotto in Chapter Four concerning the importance of the partnership between education and business and industry. Examples of effective partnerships are provided, as are criteria for assessing the effectiveness of partnerships. Cautions and suggestions for carrying out such partnerships also are provided.

1

Donald E. Super

Perspectives on the Meaning and Value of Work

Philosophers and social scientists have for some two centuries written and spoken about the meanings of work, about job satisfaction, and about the Protestant work ethic. Psychologists interested in the daily actions and attitudes of normally functioning people have often pointed out that a major theater of normal human behavior is the workplace. Sociologists have relied heavily on occupations as the demonstrably best single index of a person's social origins, education, domestic status, community activities, leisure use, and social status. It is to their occupations that most men, and today most women, devote some eight hours a day, five days a week, for some forty years. They may love their work, they may hate it, or they may more neutrally view it as merely a way of earning a living, of making friends, of passing the time. Many people pursuing the higher-level, more self-expressive occupations work as many as ten or twelve hours a day, five or six days a week, forty-eight or fifty weeks per year, for fifty years—and then, in retirement, continue their oc-

A briefer version of this chapter was used as the keynote address at the Eleventh World Congress of Educational and Vocational Guidance in Florence, Italy, September 19, 1983.

cupational activities in a diminished, more selective way. Many
in lower-level, society-maintaining jobs work as few hours per
day, as few days per week, as few weeks per year, for as few
years as their unions can negotiate for them or as they feel they
can manage—and, in their retirement, drop completely that
which they did to earn a living.

Students of work whose names are familiar to counselors
and who have provided them with insights into this major aspect and determinant of the human condition are Theodore
Caplow, John Crites, Eli Ginzberg, Edward Gross, Robert Havighurst, John Holland, Everett Hughes, Donald Paterson, Kenneth
Roberts, Ann Roe, William Sewell, Morris Viteles, and W. Lloyd
Warner. Roe's (1956) book *The Psychology of Occupations* is a
still valid but already little-read classic that has had no more up-
to-date replacement; my own treatise (Super, 1957) brought together what was then known about careers as lifelong sequences
of study, work, and related roles and helped to put to use in
guidance and counseling what others had found in their research. More recent books such as Osipow's (1983) text have
done a great deal to familiarize counselors with contemporary
approaches to career development, and Kanungo's (1982) *Work
Alienation* has brought some of the motivational aspects of work
into clearer perspective, clarifying both the positive and the
negative importance of work in the lives of men and women in
the world of today. Fifty years ago Hoppock (1935) surveyed
the research and conducted two landmark studies that showed
how important work was in making life satisfying during a
period of deep economic depression; only a decade ago, in a
period of general prosperity, Terkel (1972) interviewed people
in a haphazard but dramatically effective way and portrayed
work as dull and frustrating for large numbers of people. The
outcomes of these two studies cannot be compared, for their
samples and their methods were completely different, but they
do point up the need for careful sampling and for carefully devised methods of collecting and analyzing data on this central
life concern of most men and women. Kanungo's work helps to
point the way, as does the Work Importance Study (Super,
1982).

A Changed Perspective

The approach of recent years has shifted from a focus on work alone as *the* central life concern to an interest in the quality of life, life in which work is *one* central concern in a constellation of roles such as homemaking, citizenship, and leisure that interact to make for life satisfaction. The terms *work motivation* and *job satisfaction* are now perhaps not displaced by, but certainly incorporated into, the terms *quality of life* and *life satisfactions*. This focus on the several life roles, including work and occupation, is so widespread that one finds treatises on the subject in virtually all major languages, in countries of all political orientations, in all disciplines dealing with human behavior and the human condition, and in many popular magazines and newspapers.

This is not meant to imply that social scientists are not interested in work as a subject of theory and research and as an object of action. It is meant to underline the fact that much of the interest and attention formerly paid to work and occupation, with perhaps tangential attention to other life roles, is now directed to the quality of life in general, at school, in the home, at work, in the community, and in the larger world of politics and economics, as the work of Campbell, Converse, and Rodgers (1976) illustrates.

It is not meant to imply, either, that psychologists and sociologists such as those named in the introductory paragraphs of this chapter have been interested only in work and occupation: Some have written also on leisure and on other aspects of the quality of life. My own first book was on leisure, on hobbies in relation to work and to job and life satisfaction (Super, 1940), but so slight was interest in such questions then that the research and theorizing reported therein had no impact on the field. Most of what had been written on leisure was neglected by psychologists, sociologists, and counselors until only a few years ago. Now, however, a whole new field of specialization has been opened up, with its own journals, its own professional associations, and its contributing specialists on theory, research, and practice. Among them are to be found names such as those of

James Chamberlain in Ireland and Lawrence Loesch and Carl McDaniels in the United States, both active in the National Vocational Guidance Association as well as in leisure organizations. They are specialists actively doing research and developing principles and practices for leisure guidance and counseling (Chamberlain, 1983; Loesch and Wheeler, 1982; McDaniels, 1977). Other roles have long had their own specialized attention, roles such as those played in the home and family and in the community. But now, instead of being separate domains in which theorists, researchers, and practitioners function with little or no attention to what is going on in the other relevant domains, they are being brought together in this relatively recent focus on the quality of life, as in Campbell, Converse, and Rodgers (1976) and in the Work Importance Study (Super, 1980, 1982).

The Meanings of Work

Work has meant many things over the ages and, during any one age, to different people. Thus the ancient Greeks, living in a society in which slaves did the menial work and the heavy labor while others pursued either work or leisure activities of their own choice, viewed work as drudgery, for slaves only. Work has been viewed as punishment for our sins, as in much of the Old Testament, the heritage left by Adam and Eve expelled from the Garden of Eden. Medieval monastic orders viewed it sometimes as pure service to God and sometimes as a means of avoiding temptation and sin. During the Protestant Reformation something of the same point of view was elaborated on and stressed; combined with the expansion of trade accompanying improvements in navigation and the opening up of the East and of the New World, this view gave rise to what Weber called the Protestant work ethic. The name was a misnomer, as the Protestant colonies in North America had their share of "no 'count whites," and Catholics from the south of Italy moved to the USA and to manufacturing northern Italy motivated to work hard once they saw opportunities to earn and to save. But this fact seems not to have bothered Weber and his disciples—it was, in any case, a work ethic in which work and virtue were linked, and it tended to produce prosperity. In more recent decades social scientists have been inclined to view work as being engaged in for a variety of reasons combined in various degrees: for survival, for the economic means of living according to one's desires, for social status, for the establishment of a network of friends both at work and (through work) in one's leisure time, and as a means of self-fulfillment. And, as we have seen, most recently writers like Terkel (1972) and Warnath (1975) have played up the frequency with which men and women find work dull and deadening, claiming that work, once viewed as a means of self-expression, has, with mechanization and automation and now especially with computerization, become merely society-maintaining. This distinction, first so neatly made by Havighurst (1953) but noted by many observers of modern society as in Charlie Chaplin's *Modern Times* years before, has been helpful to many researchers, writers, and counselors in considering the meanings of work and the reasons for these meanings.

The distinction, however, antedates the industrial revolution, in which mechanization displaced the drafts. Jean Jacques Rousseau wrote, before the industrial revolution affected countries outside the British Isles, that man, born free, was everywhere in chains. Much handwork—whether in the textile industry as pursued in the domestic system by women and children working at home on contract with manufacturers and wholesalers, in the making of clothing as by the merchant tailors in their shops of cutters, fitters, and sewers, or in the mining and metal industries with their miners, foundrymen, and smiths—was drudgery. Men, women, and children worked as long as sixteen hours a day, for six days a week, in poor lighting, bad air, and cramped space. *Society-maintaining work* is a twentieth-century term, but that kind of work itself is age-old, and so is drudgery.

After the industrial revolution had taken place in Western Europe and North America, Karl Marx wrote that work should be self-fulfilling but had been perverted by the industrial system. His knowledge of economic history therefore seems to have been as limited or as biased as that of many contemporary

writers on work and occupations: Neither drudgery nor alienation from work is new. The economic history of the eighteenth,
nineteenth, and early twentieth centuries describes vividly the
women and children dragging sledges loaded with coal, crawling
on hands and knees through tunnels too small for them to stand
up. The legal slaves of Southern plantations worked and lived
under no worse conditions than did the women and girls in the
textile mills of New England or the factory workers described
by Émile Zola in France and the poor who peopled the works
of Charles Dickens.

The exploitation of labor that Marx lamented, the long
hours and poor working conditions that Dickens and Zola portrayed, were real, but they were not novel: Merely their form
was rather new. What is new today is a more general awareness
of the lack of challenge in much work, of the lack of opportunity to express oneself in work that is regulated and paced by
machines. New too, in the writings of the leisure theorists and
counselors, of the role theorists, of the family theorists and
counselors, of the women's liberationists, and of career development theorists and counselors who have come to understand the
full meaning of the term *career,* is a broader focus that takes
into account the constellation of roles that constitute a career,
viewing study, work, home and family, community service, and
leisure activities as interacting and interdependent.

It was with the objective of putting these roles in proper
perspective that, at the World Seminar on Educational and Vocational Guidance in Lisbon in 1975, I proposed the concept of
life careers as a constellation of roles together with their graphic
representation in a "Life-Career Rainbow" (Super, 1976). In
this rainbow each of the major roles of child, student, worker,
spouse, homemaker, parent, citizen, leisurite, and eventually
pensioner is portrayed as one arc in the rainbow, with its representative color (childhood, for example, is green for growth).
Each role is shaded or colored to show both the amount of time
devoted to the role (life space) and the affect invested in it
(commitment). The shading of the arcs thus makes clear the impact that one role has on another; for example, in portraying
one person's career, the time (space) given to the role of worker
decreases when a new role is added on, that of spouse, and de-

creases again with the addition of homemaker and parent roles. But with the home well established and the children grown up, the time given to the worker role increases again, as may the affect invested in it (depth of shading or color).

Along with this concept of the multirole career went the recognition that these roles are played in a variety of theaters, such as the home, the school, the workplace, and the community. But although each role has its special, if not peculiar, theater, some are played in more than one theater. Thus a working person may take work home in the evening or over the weekend, and similarly a student studies at home as well as at school or at a university (Super, 1976, 1980).

The Career Rainbow brings out, also, the simultaneity and the sequences of the major roles. Thus a person is a child for as long as his or her parents live: The role expectations and requirements change, but just as the young child is expected to obey parents and the adolescent son or daughter is expected to exercise an appropriate degree of independence though still dependent financially and in other ways on the parents, so the grownup is expected to help aging parents cope with lessening energy, endurance, and often finances. While still a child, one adds the role of pupil or student. At some point leisure becomes a real concept, with freedom from domestic demands and from school schedules and homework, and the role of leisurite is added. Similarly, the work role may be taken on while the person is still in school, modifying school schedules and commitments. At the time of marriage, researchers have observed "role diffusion," the fact that newlyweds take on new roles as they build a home and make a place for themselves in the community. At the peak of a life career, in the prime of life, a given person may play as many as seven, eight, or nine roles simultaneously if one thinks in terms of a day or a week rather than in terms of minutes or hours. And just as roles are added, often in sequence as work takes the place of study, so they are dropped with the growing up of children who detach themselves from their parents, with the death of parents who had been dependent financially or psychologically, and with retirement from a job.

Failure to take this multiplicity and interaction of life-career roles into account has been, and to a degree still is, one of the most serious shortcomings of educational and vocational guidance. It is this that has kept those endeavors from becoming career guidance, even with the widespread adoption of that newer term. Recognition of the true nature of a career has begun to transform educational and vocational guidance and counseling and to make career guidance and counseling a reality. With this recognition, and with the development of suitable methods and materials, counseling's concern for human development can manifest itself in career counseling that takes into account the changing life-career roles of developing people, can help them prepare better for their diverse roles and for their role changes, and can thus help them find more nearly complete self-realization as they go through life. A new type of guidance textbook has begun to facilitate such changes in guidance and counseling (for example, Herr and Cramer, 1984).

Values in Work and in Other Roles

In a major, concerted effort to develop a better knowledge base for developmental career guidance, a group of psychologists in a dozen countries ranging from Poland to Portugal in Europe, including both Canada and the United States in North America, joined by India in Asia and Australia in Oceania, and with Zimbabwe and South Africa represented by university researchers with similar interest, have been collaborating in the Work Importance Study (WIS). This study is based on the Career Rainbow concept. It began with each national team doing a review of its national literature on the structure of values, their taxonomy and measurement, and the roles in which youths and adults seek to attain them (Super, 1982).

Two major categories of values have emerged in this work, in studies in several of the countries: extrinsic and intrinsic. *Extrinsic values* are the concomitants or outcomes of engaging in an activity, whatever it may be, whatever the role that provides an opportunity to engage in it. Thus economic security, colleagueship or social interaction, and prestige are values that can be found in or result from a variety of activities but are not inherent in the activity itself. *Intrinsic values* are inherent in the activity itself rather than dependent on the conditions in which or people with whom one engages in the activity. Thus creativity and ability utilization are possible in certain kinds of activity but not in others.

Despite awareness of the fact that values can be sought in all of life's roles, European and neo-European traditions have focused the attention of educational and vocational counselors and of counseling psychologists on work and occupation as the prime means of value realization. This is not surprising in societies in which work is so central to people's lives and, as we have seen, determines many of the nonwork aspects of living. The occupational career has been seen as the self-actualizing role. Thus the Work Values Inventory (Super, 1968), devised in the Career Pattern Study at a time when the focus was on occupational careers, focused on work and had the term *work* in its title.

In launching the Work Importance Study ten years after that inventory was published and some twenty-seven years after it was developed, however, the objective was to devise a measure that could be used to assess values sought or found in any major life role. Although the main interest of the multinational team of project directors was in occupations and occupational careers, they recognized the need to view the work role in the context of other major life roles. People were, they knew, capable of seeking and finding values in a number of roles, so that an important value not sought in work might reveal its importance in being sought in homemaking or in community service, in studying or in leisure activities. Thus economic security can be sought in studying as preparation for a stable job, in working at the job, in marrying a breadwinner who has a stable job, in making home a secure refuge for the family wage earners, in community service that gives one a good reputation and thus reinforces other roles, in conceiving and raising children to work in the family enterprise and to support one in old age, or in leisure activities that bring one clients or customers or that lead to the acquisition or creation of valuable objects such as paintings, pottery, musical compositions, and manuscripts. Altruism, an intrinsic value, can find expression in any of the major career roles—for example, in helping fellow students, in caring for a spouse and children, in social work and in teaching but also in sales and in management and in medicine, and in community service. Charity may "begin at home" and is an established field of volunteer service in the community, but it is also an important source of paid employment for social workers and for managers.

The structure of values, how they relate to one another in substance and in importance, has been found in the WIS to be very similar in countries as different as Australia, Yugoslavia, Portugal, and the United States (Ferreira-Marques, 1983; Lokan, 1983; Nevill and Perrotta, 1983; Sverko, 1982). Canada should also probably be included in such a list, judging by related data from that country's project. But the WIS has also found that there are some real differences between and even within countries. Thus risk taking is more highly valued in the United States than in Yugoslavia and more by Anglophonic Canadians than by Francophonic fellow countrymen. Physical prowess, as contrasted with physical activity, appears to be more important to Americans than to Yugoslavs and even to Australians. In the United States, economic gain or rewards can be differentiated from economic security: Some people are willing to work for greater gains at the expense of security of employment than others. But this does not seem to be true in most other countries studied, for there only one economic factor has been identified, in a scale that includes largely security items but also a few rewards items. In another study, Ronen (1979) has shown that although economic rewards are, in most Western countries, a material value, in Japan they are instead a prestige value, a sign of the esteem in which an employer holds the employee in a society where organizational paternalism and loyalty are valued more than self-realization or the display of wealth.

It is thus amply clear that values are polyvalent, for they can find expression in a variety of ways. The list of values seems to be a universal list in industrialized and somewhat industrialized societies (the newly launched work in India and in Zimbabwe should throw light on its validity in developing countries). But the hierarchal order, the relative importance attached to each value, does, as we have seen and as Hofstede (1980) has also shown, differ somewhat in not unexpected ways when societies differ.

The Place of Work in the Life Span

The place of work in the life of a man or woman changes greatly with age. In childhood it is often seen as a symbol of power and of independence: Children often admire the workers who lift heavy garbage cans and drive earth-moving machinery, and their special heroes include pioneers and space explorers. In adolescence being a worker signifies adulthood and thus has some of the same meanings as having (or shaving) a mustache or using lipstick or smoking. This is true even though dating, sports, schoolwork, and the moratorium on work that is imposed by general education in high school and college make earning a living and pursuing an occupation recede into a future that seems remote to most adolescents. It is true even in schools and colleges in which students pursue vocational or professional courses of study, for the present is a period of study and of preparation for a future, and the time perspective of youth is very limited. Interviews with boys in the Career Pattern Study (Super and Overstreet, 1960; Jordaan and Heyde, 1979) at the ages of fourteen, eighteen, and twenty-five showed that during their secondary school years these typical boys knew little about the world of work, their parents' occupations, and even the occupations to which they then aspired; at age twenty-five their knowledge was still very limited, bearing generally only on what they themselves had done or were actually doing. The future is remote and poorly perceived during the years from fourteen to twenty-five, and so is that which is around the corner or over the next hill. It is in the middle and late twenties that work and occupation are brought sharply into focus; it is when young men and women begin to take stock on where the years have led them, and where they would like to be, that the concept of career takes on meaning, that they conceive of a career as the sequence of positions occupied over a span of time and recognize the substantive connection between one job and the next and the one that follows.

During the late twenties and early thirties, often more

acutely in the late thirties and early forties, the relationships between earlier jobs and later, between work and home, work and
leisure, and work and eventual retirement, are seen rather more
clearly. Not infrequently in the current era of mobility and
change this arousal causes a desire to restructure life and its career roles in an attempt better to attain values that themselves
have become clearer or even changed, to realize an emergent
self. These are the much publicized "career crises," which are
often not crises if the emerging self or the emerging economic
and occupational trends are sensed in time, but developmental
tendencies which can be guided and on which changing careers
can be built.

Socioeconomic status acts with age to fix the place of
work in life. Although the relationship is far from perfect, men
and women tend to pursue occupations that were made accessible to them through their parental status and resources. At the
same time, it is true that, having reached a certain point on the
educational ladder thanks to the start the family gave them,
they may go further because of their own achievements in
school, college, or the world of work: In a democracy, young
adults to some degree make their own status. The fact that it is
the higher-level occupations that give their members the most
freedom for self-expression means that these are the men and
women who tend to find the most satisfaction in their work:
The teacher and the manager tend to carry out their work in
their own individual ways, but the carpenter and especially the
assembly-line worker have little choice about what tasks they
perform, when, and how they perform them. It is not surprising
that those who have the readiest access to educational and occupational opportunities and resources, those whose abilities have
been most highly developed and refined by education both formal and informal and whose interests have found most opportunity to expand and express themselves and thus also to develop,
should seek and succeed in finding outlets that satisfy them
more often than do men and women less well situated and less
well equipped to locate and use occupational opportunities
suited to their potential or emerging abilities and interests.

Here some recent findings of the Work Importance Study

(Nevill and Super, 1983; Super and Nevill, 1983) are especially important. Using the Salience Inventory of the Work Importance Study (a refined instrument now being standardized for publication) and the Career Development Inventory (Super and others, 1981), we examined the relationships among socio-economic status, sex, commitment to work, and career or vocational maturity. Career maturity is here defined as attitudinal and cognitive readiness to cope with the developmental tasks of finding, preparing for, getting established in, pursuing, and retiring from an occupation; just which of these depends, of course, on the life stage of the individual. Using good samples of high school boys and girls in urban, suburban, and rural areas and of college students in a state university that draws from similar areas in another part of the country, we found no simple linear relationships between social status and the various dimensions of vocational maturity in youth or young adulthood. Furthermore, there were no important sex differences in vocational maturity. This was true even though females at both educational (age) levels tend, in young adulthood, to score higher on the cognitive scales of vocational maturity, while their scores on the attitude scales are neither more nor less mature than those of males. But the relationships are more complex than these facts suggest, for females who are affectively committed to work and career, as shown by the Salience Inventory, tend to be more advanced in their career development than males. It may be that, surmounting or having surmounted the psychological and social barriers to becoming committed to a career, girls and young women so committed are more mature vocationally than their male counterparts for whom work is more accessible.

Equally interesting is the finding that males and females who are committed to work and career tend also to be those who are committed to home and family activities and the roles with which they are associated. It should be added here that for both males and females work commitment is related to affective (but not to cognitive) career maturity: It is commitment that is important, rather than sex or socioeconomic status.

A major dilemma faced by many men and women, from the late exploratory stage until retirement, arises from the interaction of the major life-career roles. It has often been pointed out that more time devoted to one role is likely to mean less time devoted to another: The additional time must be taken from some other activity. More emotional commitment to one role must, similarly, have some impact on commitment to another role. Thus more time devoted to homemaking by a newly-wed young man or woman may mean less time to devote to parents or to work, and absorption in work when not working may reduce the amount of attention given to the parents or to the home. Thus, also, hobbies and community service tend to suffer when the role of spouse is being considered and when its obligations are assumed, although some such activities may flourish if they fit in with a pattern of courtship or, later, of establishing a place for the home and family in the community in which the newlyweds live. As life becomes more complex in late adolescence and young adulthood, new roles are thus added, role diffusion is common, and it is only in midcareer that many people find it desirable and possible to focus on a more limited number of roles. This is true of both men and women, even though in midlife women may take on a worker role with the lessening of parental responsibilities. They then reduce the maternal role and sometimes the roles, or parts of the roles, of homemakers and even of spouses.

Roles can, it has been shown (Champoux, 1981; Super, 1940), be supplementary, complementary, or conflicting. For example, model engineers (model railroad builders and operators) were found to be either employed graduate engineers with engineering interests according to Strong's Vocational Interest Blank who found in their hobby an opportunity to express their engineering interests more adequately than they did in their more restricted jobs or people working in other fields such as accounting and sales who also had engineering interests but had no outlet for them in their jobs. The first group were, on the whole, better satisfied with their jobs and even with their lives in general than were the latter group, although some in the latter group liked their work and wanted also the complementarity of their avocation. The first group, for whom the avocation appeared to be supplementary, were expressing dominant interest in two roles, the worker and the leisurite roles. The second group, for whom the avocation was complementary, were in some instances expressing a dominant interest in the avocation for which they would have liked to find an outlet in their work, and in others they were expressing some interests in their work and some in their hobby; the former predominated, and one might hypothesize that for them the two roles were conflicting. It would be interesting to know whether those who practiced engineering in both work and play were better engineers for this engineering commitment and whether the nonengineers were less effective in their work because of involvement in an engineering avocation. Here is a fruitful and long-neglected field for further research: The interactions of internal and external pressures have only begun to be studied, and yet they should be rich in implications for education, guidance, counseling, therapy, and continuing education.

Determinants of Changes in Roles
and in Quality of Life

Changes in the roles people play and in the quality of life are, it need hardly be stated, a function of both individuals and of cultures. People change, and so do the societies, the economies, the communities, and the institutions such as companies and families of which they are parts. Just as human beings have life cycles, so do institutions; crises and critical events affect both people and institutions. And not all development, not all change, is a function of crises.

Verbal and quantitative abilities, for example, have been found to stabilize or even decline in adolescents and adults who virtually give up reading and working with paper and pencil but to increase with age into middle adulthood in those who continue to use these abilities in study, in work, or in their leisure. Abilities can therefore continue to develop if used in any role, be it that of homemaker who does family bookkeeping and accounting, home decorating, menu planning with attention to nutrition, and other "domestic science" activities, that of community service volunteer who participates in fund raising, organizing needed committees, and planning needed community resources and services or family welfare assistance, or that of hobbyist engaging in ballet dancing, painting, musical programs, philately, or other such activities that may stretch the mind as well as the body. The needed opportunities must, of course, be present for the abilities to be put to use, but they can also be found or created by those who have the savoir faire and the drive.

An example or two may help. An unemployed printer, in a city where printing was badly depressed, used much of the free time that he could not avoid having to pursue his hobby of model railroading. Challenged by the local club's need to develop a signal system for its train layout, he became the club expert on electrical signal systems, which, according to the mores, had to be miniature versions of real railroad signal systems. Another member, who knew that the municipal subway system was hard put to find experts to employ in the revamping of its signal system, suggested to the printer that he apply for one of the skilled jobs being advertised. He did so and was hired. His work history proves the ability of a mature person both to learn something new and to put his abilities to work in a new situation.

Another case is one of a type that one sees frequently today, as career women seek self-fulfillment in both domestic and occupational careers. In this case the woman had worked for several years in a biological laboratory, changed to part-time after maternity leave, and then, after having a second child, resigned in order to devote the children's preschool years to them, to their development, and to the home. She foresaw, however, that in her late thirties she might well want to resume her professional work, for with the children in school she would, with her husband's continuing participation, be able to handle the domestic work along with a regular job. But scientific developments in her field were proceeding at such a pace that she knew that, in five or ten years, her knowledge and training would be obsolete. For her the solution seems to have lain in continuing to read appropriate books and journals, buying the important items for her own library and annotating them, taking occasional short-term continuing education courses in her specialty, and getting her former employer to call on her occasionally when the pressures of work would make an experienced person who knew the laboratory a welcome part-time, temporary staff member.

Interests, values, and needs change too, as well as abilities. These changes are partly a function of physical changes: Physical activity has less appeal for those in middle and later life, when the organism is no longer growing and developing, than for young people whose bodies need exercise. Sedentary activities have more appeal in middle and later middle age. Once people have established families and have a place in their community and in their field of work, they tend to have less interest in other people. This is shown in lessened efforts to make new friends, lessened joining of organizations, and lessened activity in them unless elevation to positions of leadership leads to an escalation of activity. One later result is that as friends and colleagues retire, move away, or die, people find that their informal social support systems have begun to melt away, at a time in life when they find it difficult to rebuild them by renewed or continuing community activity. Men and women in the sciences frequently find that their investigative needs and interests decline after they have made their mark, big or small, on their field (Lehman, 1953). This is sometimes because of growing administrative demands on their time: People who build better mousetraps soon have so many people beating a path to their door that they find they have no more time for building still better mousetraps! But sometimes this decline in scholarly productivity or in inventiveness is the result of an intellectual isolation from new sources of creative ideas, an isolation that results from being the local authority in one's field, having one's own projects or laboratories with one's own staff and students who all focus on what the master thinks, with a resulting decrease in the input and assimilation of new ideas from other actual or rising authorities. It is generally the graduate students who, working with several masters, achieve the new syntheses that lead to scientific breakthroughs. It is noteworthy that although this tends to be true in the sciences, some scientists continue to be highly productive in both quality and even quantity after most of their peers have begun a slow decline. And in the social sciences, and especially in philosophy, the peaks of productivity tend to come later and to last longer.

The opportunity structure also changes with time. Social legislation creates or removes barriers to education and to occupations, as we have seen during the last three decades in the cases of racial minorities and women in the United States, Canada, and Great Britain, with handicapped persons in the United Kingdom, the United States, and many other countries, and, in reverse, in countries such as Kenya, Nigeria, and South Africa. Changing technologies also affect opportunities for self-realization in work, increasing demands for the highly skilled and for the highly educated in the technologies and in the social sciences for which they create special needs and decreasing opportunities for the less-educated and less-trained blue- and white-collar workers. Business cycles, too, play a part in increasing or in limiting opportunity, especially the longer-term as contrasted with seasonal cycles. Wars have a somewhat similar effect but often a more visible and drastic one: It was thus that women in war-ravaged countries such as France found themselves needed in fields such as medicine and business management and, having replaced their menfolk, stayed there in greater numbers than in countries less affected by the two world wars. Similarly, in the United States, war gave women opportunities in the semiskilled and skilled trades that they had not had before: During World War I they drove ambulances, cut their hair, and smoked cigarettes in public for the first time, and in World War II they built airplanes, put on overalls, and paved the way for women's liberation.

The effects of equal opportunity legislation are now fairly clear, as women move in greater numbers into such occupations as architecture, engineering, management, medicine, the machine trades, and the military, and as men feel freer to become hairdressers, nurses, and schoolteachers. Smoking, coronaries, and ulcers are beginning to be more equally distributed among men and women, as the latter take on the pressures as well as the privileges of the status occupations, and their life

spans may also become more equal. But the effects of technological change are not so clear. In the most advanced countries
they may lead to the creation of a new leisure class, the soon-to-
be-unemployed unskilled, semiskilled, and even skilled workers.
Such workers will be redundant, for much of what they do in
the shops, factories, and offices of today is increasingly being
done more accurately, more rapidly, and more cheaply by computers and by computer-controlled machines and robots. Even at
the higher levels of work there may in due course be fewer opportunities for the able. Difficult medical diagnoses are quickly
made by medical personnel inputting the data from examinations and tests and getting back from the central computer diagnoses that are based on more data than a physician can weigh in
his or her own mind and on more accumulated knowledge than
the best of students can acquire and retain. More complex managerial decisions are made by managers drawing on up-to-date
information that is organized for them by sophisticated computer programs available to them at their own desks. It will be
the very able men and women who can understand the issues,
recognize the needed data, and work with the high-level programmers in making those programs available who will be in
great demand. The new leisure class will not be an aristocracy
of merit or of wealth but one of intellectual mediocrity and of
diminished work motivation arising at least in part from diminished demand for their work.

In the developing countries, the future is not so clear.
Some are importing the older and current technologies of the
advanced countries: One has only to visit their larger cities to
witness the uncontrolled pollution of the air and of the water
that prevails there as it did in the advanced countries a few decades ago. Industrialization has brought, there as in the United
States, Canada, and Western Europe, large numbers of rural
people to the cities in search of elusive higher standards of living. The less advanced countries seem to be repeating the errors
of the more advanced, and if recapitulation theory is more valid
in this case than it has usually proved to be, they may in due
course also move into the high-tech era. But it is too early to tell.

Changing Roles in Changing Societies

No one knows whether the changes of automation and in computerization will be largely beneficial, largely negative, or merely mixed. There are now many apostles of doom who proclaim a future of boring work for most people, a future in which the least complex jobs will be done by machine, in which even the most complex jobs will also be done by machine, and in which men and women will do the work of serving the machines, whether in mechanical, clerical, managerial, or professional roles. Others foresee economies in which only a very few, very able professional and managerial men and women, and a small number of highly skilled technicians, will be gainfully employed. In such a society the large majority of people would constitute the new leisure class, at first labeled "unemployed" by themselves and by the rest of the world but, as the newly emerging economy and society begin to be better understood, renamed "leisured," given leisure by society. No longer needed in employment for production, distribution, or even service, members of a computerized automated society that produces and distributes all that anyone needs, they will be well supported in their leisure by the economy. Their role will be redefined. They will feel that they have as worthy a place as do those who work to maintain the economy, but a different place. Both groups will need help in seeking and finding self-actualization in their roles, the one in leisure only ("leisure" here in the sense of nonemployment, and including community activities, homemaking, and avocations) and the other in both work and leisure. The workers will be honored for their important contributions to the welfare of all; the nonworkers will need help in finding and using opportunities to earn the respect of others and of themselves. To help both types of people do this will no doubt be one of the greatest challenges to education, to counseling, and to the other institutions that constitute society.

We have, clearly, two conflicting visions of what technological change is likely to produce in the occupational structure, employment, and life-styles of the developed countries.

One could conjure up other possible developments, comparable to those of the Dark Ages, when prosperous Rome was overridden by wave after wave of people from less advantaged societies envious of its wealth, although that kind of apocalypse seems less likely than destruction by nuclear warfare. Assuming that nuclear warfare and related catastrophes can be avoided, what are the implications of the gloomy view of technological change, and what are those of the rosier view?

If the gloomy vision of the effects of technological change is valid, then we will need to develop in our schools and universities curricula that will give young people (and adults in continuing education) an understanding of the multiple roles that constitute careers, a perspective on these roles that will help them to see how life values can be attained in various types and combinations of work, study, leisure activities, community service, and homemaking activities.

Outlets for developing abilities and interests and for the attainment of values must be made visible, appreciated, explored, prepared for, and utilized in each of the available major life-career roles. Guidance and counseling must help people to understand how work that is dull, repetitive, and not self-fulfilling for them may appear otherwise to people of differing abilities and may in any case be worthwhile for them as a means of attaining important values in other roles. Work can provide material support for an otherwise rewarding and self-actualizing way of life. At the same time, of course, the possibilities for self-realization in the higher-level and social service occupations must be made clear, for in these occupations the requirements in time, money, energy, personality, and ability are substantial. If the manpower needs of high-technology economies result in a substantial number of unemployed men and women, in a new leisure class, then education, guidance, and counseling will need to find ways of helping these people to find life meaningful and themselves worthy in nonwork—that is, unpaid—roles.

If the rosy vision is valid, the members of the new leisure class will need education for the other roles that will constitute their careers, education that will enable them to develop their abilities and interests and attain their values. They will need to learn to use nonoccupational—that is, homemaking, leisure, and community service—activities for self-actualization, resources that have too often been viewed as of secondary importance. There are, in the home, in the community, and in the wider world, nonoccupational resources which allow for self-expression, which are currently being exploited for that purpose, but which need to be more highly developed and more greatly valued as means of enriching life. If this vision is valid, the new leisure class will need guidance and counseling for life-career development, for the development of career roles that are nonoccupational, roles that are valued for reasons other than for income.

The question will arise and will disturb many people: How are those youths destined for occupational employment to be differentiated from those who are destined for the new leisure class? In posing this question, the word *destined* has been used deliberately, to point out the problem. Who is to decide what is destiny? In a series of case studies of guidance and counseling in developing and developed countries (Super, 1984), as diverse as Benin and Sweden, this issue emerges in the cross-national analysis as the critical question. Some developing countries were trying to impose destiny on rural youths by preparing them, in school and out of school, only for rural life while opening up some of the opportunities of the industrial world only to some of the youths already living in the cities. Other developing countries had tried this and given up or had tried selection procedures based on attempted counseling that they were not yet able to provide. All were foundering in the face of the problem of deciding, or helping to decide, who should be prepared for a given way of life. In the developed countries more resources were being mobilized for educational and vocational guidance, but the declining state of their economies made it difficult to provide guidance that bore fruit in appropriate occupational employment. In view of these facts, the tasks of guidance and counseling in high-technology economies, in leisure economies, must be expected to be most difficult. If democratic methods are to be used, the need for education to cope with such decision making by youths and young adults will be critical.

If either vision is valid, we as guidance and counseling specialists will need to change our titles, or at least their meanings, to reflect broader concerns and broader functions. Our association may need to change its name to reflect these changes in needs and in services. Will we call ourselves "life-role counselors," which may seem rather grandiose, or, perhaps more easily, "career counselors" in the broad meaning of that term? Will the National Vocational Guidance Association, which in the late 1940s fiercely debated proposals to change its name, become the "National Life-Role Association" or, perhaps better, the "National Career Guidance Association"? Only the future will tell which vision is valid, just how our roles will be defined, and just which titles will be most appropriate. But unless we prepare for the future as we now see it emerging, we will not be prepared to meet the challenge and will be as obsolete in the world of working and living as are archers, fletchers, shoemakers, and thatchers!

Summary

In this chapter we have recognized that the values that people seek in work and in other roles have been a subject of concern to thoughtful people for centuries and that recent years have seen a great increase in the objective study of what people of all ages want from life. We have seen, too, that perspectives toward work, homemaking, and leisure roles have changed greatly within the lifetimes of today's older citizens.

Life is now seen as a continuous process, in which roles and values change with age and with experience despite some continuity, and it is seen as a constellation of roles whose configuration also changes over time. Careers are now viewed in time and in space.

There is a concern not just with work motivation and job satisfaction but also with the quality of life in all its complexities. Educational and vocational guidance and counseling have been rather slow in responding to this broader perspective on life roles and on the quality of life, but movement toward a true "career counseling" has begun to take place.

We have seen, too, that the determinants of change are

varied and numerous, both personal and socioeconomic. People change, society changes, roles change; which change first is a subject of useless debate, for the causes are interactive.

Some implications for action are considered, actions that may be called for if a gloomy vision of increasing unemployment proves true and actions that might be needed if a rosy vision of the effects of technological change is warranted. In either case, education, counseling, and social values need to change in order to help students and adults see and appreciate the fact that values can be attained in varying combinations of life-career roles—the roles of homemaker, worker, citizen, and pursuer of leisure interests and activities.

Suggested Readings

Campbell, A., Converse, P. E., and Rodgers, W. L. *The Quality of American Life*. New York: Russell Sage Foundation, 1976.

Examines the varied aspects of adult life in America, the degree and nature of satisfaction with them, and the causes of satisfaction and dissatisfaction. An empirical study of a national sample of adults. Differs from many studies of the quality of life, especially in Eastern and even Western Europe, in that it deals with all aspects of life, not with work alone. Deals with both objective conditions and subjective states.

Hofstede, G. *Culture's Consequences: International Differences in Work-Related Values*. Beverly Hills, Calif.: Sage, 1980.

Identifies four main dimensions of culture by means of theory and statistical data: power distance, uncertainty avoidance, individualism, and masculinity. The data come from surveys made in subsidiaries of a multinational company in forty countries in 1968 and 1972 and are verified by analyses of other comparable studies. Trends over the span of four years are examined, as are regional clusters of cultures.

Kanungo, R. *Work Alienation: An Integrative Approach*. New York: Praeger, 1982.

Critically reviews the literature in some detail and on it

builds a theory of work motivation and alienation. Proposes a theory and instruments for the study of the positive and negative aspects of attitudes toward work.

Super, D. E. "A Life-Span, Life-Space Approach to Career Development." *Journal of Vocational Behavior*, 1980, *16*, 282–298.

    Develops a theoretical view of careers as constellations of several roles played, some sequentially and some simultaneously, in the life space and over the life span. Each stage in the life span is seen as dominated by certain combinations of roles such as those of worker, spouse, parent, and homemaker at the prime of life, each role having its typical developmental tasks at each stage. Implications for guidance and counseling are briefly considered.

Super, D. E. "The Relative Importance of Work: Models and Measures for Meaningful Data." *Counseling Psychologist*, 1982, *10*, 95–103.

    Describes a model and a set of measures developed to facilitate the study of the relative importance of the major life roles, the reasons for their importance, and the determinants of individual differences in role salience. The implications for practice, in both assessment and counseling, are examined in a later article: Super, D. E. "Assessment for Career Guidance: Toward Truly Developmental Counseling," *Personnel and Guidance Journal*, 1983, *61*, 555–562.

References

Campbell, A., Converse, P. E., and Rodgers, W. L. *The Quality of American Life*. New York: Russell Sage Foundation, 1976.

Chamberlain, J. "Adolescent Perceptions of Work and Leisure." *Leisure Studies*, 1983, *2*, 127–138.

Champoux, J. E. "A Sociological Perspective on Work Involvement." *International Review of Applied Psychology*, 1981, *30*, 65–86.

Ferreira-Marques, J. H. "Values and Role Salience in High-

School Students in Portugal and the USA." Paper presented at annual convention of the American Educational Research Association, Montreal, April 11, 1983.

Havighurst, R. J. *Human Development and Education.* New York: Longmans Green, 1953.

Herr, E. L., and Cramer, S. H. *Vocational Guidance and Human Development in the Schools.* Boston: Houghton Mifflin, 1984.

Hofstede, G. *Culture's Consequences: International Differences in Work-Related Values.* Beverly Hills, Calif.: Sage, 1980.

Hoppock, R. *Job Satisfaction.* New York: Harper & Row, 1935.

Jordaan, J. P., and Heyde, M. B. *Vocational Maturity During the High School Years.* New York: Teachers College Press, 1979.

Kanungo, R. *Work Alienation: An Integrative Approach.* New York: Praeger, 1982.

Lehman, H. C. *Age and Achievement.* Princeton, N.J.: Princeton University Press, 1953.

Loesch, L., and Wheeler, P. *Principles of Leisure Counseling.* Minneapolis: Educational Media, 1982.

Lokan, J. J. "The Factor Structure of Life and Work Values of Students in Diverse Cultures." Paper presented at annual convention of the American Educational Research Association, Montreal, April 11, 1983.

McDaniels, C. "Leisure and Career Development at Mid-Life." *Vocational Guidance Quarterly,* 1977, *25,* 356-363.

Nevill, D. D., and Perrotta, J. M. "The Importance of Life-Career Roles: American, Australian, and Portuguese Patterns." Submitted for publication, 1983.

Nevill, D. D., and Super, D. E. "Career Maturity and Commitment to Home and Work in College Students." Submitted for publication, 1983.

Osipow, S. H. *Theories of Career Development.* Englewood Cliffs, N.J.: Prentice-Hall, 1983.

Roe, A. *The Psychology of Occupations.* New York: Wiley, 1956.

Ronen, S. "A Cross-National Study of Employees' Work Goals." *International Review of Applied Psychology,* 1979, *28,* 1-12.

Super, D. E. *Avocational Interest Patterns.* Stanford, Calif.: Stanford University Press, 1940.

Super, D. E. *The Psychology of Careers.* New York: Harper & Row, 1957.

Super, D. E. *The Work Values Inventory.* Boston: Houghton Mifflin, 1968.

Super, D. E. "Vocational Guidance: Emergent Decision Making in a Changing Society." *Bulletin of the International Association for Educational and Vocational Guidance,* 1976, *29,* 16-23.

Super, D. E. "A Life-Span, Life-Space Approach to Career Development." *Journal of Vocational Behavior,* 1980, *16,* 282-298.

Super, D. E. "The Relative Importance of Work: Models and Measures for Meaningful Data." *Counseling Psychologist,* 1982, *10,* 95-103.

Super, D. E. *Guidance and Educational Mobility in Developed and Developing Countries.* Paris: UNESCO, 1984.

Super, D. E., and Nevill, D. D. "Work-Role Salience as a Determinant of Career Maturity in High-School Students." Submitted for publication, 1983.

Super, D. E., and Overstreet, P. L. *The Vocational Maturity of Ninth Grade Boys.* New York: Teachers College Press, 1960.

Super, D. E., and others. *The Career Development Inventory.* Palo Alto, Calif.: Consulting Psychologists Press, 1981.

Sverko, B. "The Factor Structure of Work Values." Paper presented at the International Congress of Applied Psychology, Edinburgh, July 1982.

Terkel, S. *Working.* New York: Random House, 1972.

Warnath, C. F. "Vocational Theories: Directions to Nowhere?" *Personnel and Guidance Journal,* 1975, *53,* 422-429.

2

Harold Goldstein

❧ ❧ ❧ ❧ ❧ ❧ ❧ ❧

Changing Structure of Work: Occupational Trends and Implications

The constant change that people have come to expect in the world in which each individual builds a career is assuming a new and threatening aspect. It seems to many that a revolution in work has begun—that while such mainstays of our economy as steel mills and automobile plants are closing down, the only new jobs developing are in "high-tech" industries for which few workers are trained and that robots threaten to take jobs from human workers.

In this chapter I try to sort out what is happening to work and what it means for the task of planning careers. I will first review trends in the structure of work—the way it is organized, industrially, occupationally, and geographically. I will then examine the ways individuals move through this structure as their careers develop.

The Changing Structure of Work

Industrial Structure. A profound transformation has been taking place in the work Americans do: a change from producing mainly tangible goods to providing services. At the beginning of

54

this century, two thirds of American workers were employed in agriculture, mining, construction, and manufacturing—the goods-producing industries. By 1940 only half the workers were in these industries, and in 1982, as the century approached its end, fewer than one third were engaged in goods production. The other two thirds were employed in servicing industries—transportation, communications, public utilities, wholesale and retail trade, hotels, and such rapidly growing activities as banking, insurance, repair, education, health, recreation, business and professional services, and federal, state, and local government.

This goods-to-services shift has been going on worldwide, each country being at a different stage in the process. It reflects a number of developments. One of these is mechanization and automation of production in the goods industries, which makes possible more production with few additional workers. Another is the change in consumption patterns: As average income rises, families raise their consumption of basic necessities such as food, clothing, and shelter only moderately and use an increasing proportion of their income to buy such services as recreation, education, and health care. A third development is the industrialization of other countries: With machinery that is often more modern than that of established industries in the United States, and with lower-paid labor, other nations can sell goods more cheaply. This competition has affected such diverse goods-producing industries as textiles, apparel, shoes, steel, automobiles, and electronics manufacturing, but it has less effect on service activities, which are not as easy to export.

This rapid growth of services has enabled our economy to expand employment in the face of mechanization and foreign competition. Despite recurrent fears that these would throw Americans out of work, total employment has continued to rise to new high levels over the entire period since World War II, except for temporary setbacks in recessions. In 1960, when the loss of jobs to automation was widely feared, 66 million civilian workers were employed; by 1981 employment had risen to over 100 million. Most of the growth was in service-producing industries, but 3 million of the additional jobs were in goods production. Manufacturing, which pessimists had seen as the most threatened industry, provided 3 million more jobs in 1981, after twenty-one years of automation and rising imports. Employment in the rest of the goods-producing industries was unchanged: Growth in construction and mining employment offset a decline in farm employment.

The severe depression that gripped the country in 1982, with 12 million people unemployed at year end, has inevitably colored thinking about the future. It has lent credibility to fears about the long-term effects of rising import competition, decay of "smokestack" industries, and job-eating robots. How much of this unemployment is temporary, generated by lack of demand in the depression, and how much results from basic changes in economic structure in the United States and the world is difficult to tell. What we learn from the historical record, however, is that we have frequently had similar fears, but the economy has always bounced back.

It will be easier in the future to bounce back enough to reduce unemployment. Most of the joblessness of 1982 resulted not from failure of the economy to generate more jobs each year but from the faster growth of the labor force in recent years. But this growth is going to slow down because of slower growth in the adult population. Growth of the civilian labor force, which showed an annual rate of 2.2 percent from 1965 to 1975 and 2.7 percent from 1975 to 1979, is expected to slow down to about 1.3 percent from 1985 to 1990 and to only 0.8 percent during the following five years (Bureau of Labor Statistics, 1982b, p. 49). This means that, instead of the 2.6 million new jobs needed annually to take care of additional workers in the late 1970s, we will need about 1.5 million in the late 1980s and only 1 million in the early 1990s. Indeed, if we view the labor force as a resource enabling the nation to get its work done and provide a rising standard of living for the population, the slower growth should cause concern instead of cheering us up.

The shift toward services has had both good and bad effects on the lives of workers. It has meant that a smaller share of all workers are in the industries most sensitive to the business cycle, such as manufacturing and construction, and thus it has contributed to job security. However, mechanization has been less common in services (with some notable exceptions such as communications, utilities, banking, and insurance), so that productivity has risen more slowly and wage rates are about one-quarter lower than in goods industries. The decline in older industries such as textiles, shoes, and automobile manufacturing has been accompanied by a shift in their location away from older centers in the Northeast and North Central states. This has been hard on their older workers with ties to their communities, leaving many of them stranded. The most pervasive effect of the shift has been on the kinds of work people do, since different types of occupations are employed in service industries.

Although the goods-to-services shift is likely to continue, some recent developments may slow it up. The 1970s witnessed a backlash to the headstrong exploitation of science and technology. To protect air and water from pollution, toxic waste disposal is requiring more effort, and special effluent-cleaning equipment is being manufactured, installed, and maintained at factories, electric utilities, and sewage treatment plants. To keep topsoil and poisonous chemicals from draining down the rivers, more labor-intensive farming is needed. Exhaustion of easily found and extracted fuels is requiring more labor in exploring, drilling, mining, production of synthetic fuels, and use of renewable energy from the sun, wind, falling water, and growing plants. Indeed, if energy becomes more costly, its substitution for human labor will be slowed. All these developments mean more jobs—especially in goods production. This increase tends to slow the shift to services. The Bureau of Labor Statistics foresees a further shift of only about 2 percentage points by 1990 (1982b, p. 30).

Much of the fear about the continued shift from goods to services results from a cultural lag in attitudes. In eighteenth-century economic writings, all nonfarm work was considered parasitic on farming, the only significant economic activity, since life depended on food. Gradually, values responded to changing economic reality, and today most people admit that manufacturing, mining, and construction provide necessary goods, but many still see services as parasitic on the goods-producing economy. This view underlies a union official's comment about the service industries: "We can't all live by taking in each other's laundry." In fact, two thirds of us do live in this way. Our service workers provide education so that manufacturing can compete in a world of advanced technology. They also provide medical care, recreation, restaurant meals, police protection, banking, and business and repair services. If two thirds today, why not three quarters tomorrow?

Two other aspects of the industrial structure affect workers' careers—the growth of large firms and the decline of opportunities for self-employment.

Even before the wave of conglomerate takeovers in the 1970s, firms were becoming larger. Retail trade, the stronghold of the "Mom and Pop" enterprise, has been overrun with chain stores. Restaurants, hotels, banks, construction—lines of business in which small firms predominated—have seen consolidation into large enterprises. In 1977, 60 percent of all employees in private enterprise were in firms of 100 or more workers, and 42 percent were in firms of 1,000 or more (Bureau of the Census, 1979, Table 2). When government workers are added, more than half of all employees work for large organizations.

Large organizations tend to have layers of supervisors and little personal contact of the workers with top management—a situation that fosters distrust and a feeling of vulnerability among workers, which lead them to turn to unions for protection and to advance their interests. The larger firms, however, do provide more employment security (the highest rates of bankruptcy are in small firms) and, in many industries, higher wages.

Self-employment has traditionally been an option for many individuals. With its risks and special requirements (such as capital and entrepreneurial skills), it also offers advantages: a chance for better-than-average income and the independence and autonomy that many workers value highly.

Opportunities to go into business for oneself have become restricted in recent years. Self-employment has declined as a proportion of all nonfarm employment since World War II —from 12 percent in 1948 to 7 percent in 1979 (Bureau of

Labor Statistics, 1982a, Tables A-16 and A-17). Only in certain industries is self-employment still a major option: One out of three workers in personal services is self-employed; about one out of five in construction, business and repair services, and engineering, architectural, legal, and accounting services; and above-average numbers in medical services and retail trade.

The loss of opportunities for self-employment, like the concentration of jobs in large firms, has made most workers dependent and has reduced their autonomy.

Occupational Structure. Even more significant than the industry in which a person works is the occupation, for this determines the kind of work he or she does, the education and training needed, the earnings received, the work environment, and the quality of life itself. Changes in the occupational structure therefore profoundly affect the nature of work.

As farm occupations declined, they were first replaced as the largest occupational group by blue-collar occupations, but after midcentury white-collar occupations became the largest group. Farm work involved nearly two out of five workers in 1900 but by 1982 had dropped to less than 3 percent of the labor force. Blue-collar occupations accounted for a relatively stable share of all jobs. White-collar occupations, the fastest-growing group, nearly tripled their share of the total. Service occupations have also been growing, a decline in private household service partly offsetting an increase in other service occupations —protective, food service, janitorial, and health service (Table 1).

In these changes in the occupational structure we can see two forces at work: the changing industrial structure, reflecting the shift from farming to nonfarm industries and from goods to services production, and changing technology and ways of doing business in each industry.

Among white-collar workers the most striking growth in employment took place among clerical and professional occupations. Clerical occupations, the smallest group in 1900, with 3 percent of all workers, quadrupled their share of the labor force during the first half of the century and by 1982 were the largest occupational group. This proliferation of clerical workers has raised costs and pressured industry to find ways to reduce what

Table 1. Occupational Distribution of the Work Force,
1900, 1950, and 1982.

Occupational Group	1900	1950	1982
White-collar workers, total	17.6	36.6	51.6
Professional and technical	4.3	8.6	16.1
Managerial	5.8	8.7	10.9
Sales	4.5	7.0	6.4
Clerical	3.0	12.3	18.2
Blue-collar workers, total	35.9	41.1	31.6
Craftsmen, foremen	10.5	14.1	12.5
Operatives	12.9	20.4	14.0
Laborers, nonfarm	12.5	6.6	5.1
Service workers, total	9.0	10.5	14.1
Private household workers	5.4	2.6	1.0
Other service workers	3.6	7.9	13.1
Farmers and farm workers	37.5	11.8	2.7
Total	100.0	100.0	100.0

Sources: 1900 and 1950: Kaplan and Casey (1958, p. 7). Includes economically active civilian population aged 14 and over. 1982: Bureau of Labor Statistics (1983, pp. 151, 158–159). Includes civilian labor force aged 16 and over. Some changes in occupational classifications occurred between 1950 and 1982.

was seen as the "burden of paperwork." A variety of labor-saving office machines have been introduced, including book-keeping, duplicating, and copying machines and later computers. Four out of five clerical workers are women, and the growth of employment opportunities in this field helped to make possible the massive influx of women into the labor force.

The highly educated professional and technical occupations also increased their share of the work force fourfold from 1900 to 1982 and were the second-largest occupational group. Three major developments generated this rapid expansion: the growth of science and technology, of medical services, and of educational services ranging from preschool through the university and adult education. The occupations involved in these areas account for two thirds of all professional and technical employment.

Two other white-collar occupations, managers and sales-persons, have also been growing, though more slowly, the first because of the increasing size of companies, the second because of the growth of employment in retail trade.

Among the blue-collar workers, craft occupations have been fairly stable. Fast growth in the repair and maintenance crafts, as machinery proliferated in factories, offices, hospitals, and homes, was offset by declines in other crafts whose production work was taken over by machines. Semiskilled operatives—the bulk of production workers in factories—grew during the first half of this century and then declined by 14 percent by 1982. The least-skilled group, laborers, dropped steadily over this period.

Looking ahead to 1990, the Bureau of Labor Statistics foresees faster-than-average growth for service, professional, sales, and clerical occupations, slower-than-average growth for operatives, laborers, and managerial workers, and a continued decline in employment in farm work (1982c, Table C-1). The effect of these trends will be to increase the proportion of jobs for which at least a high school education is required and also the proportion of jobs requiring college education.

Underlying these changes in occupational structure has been the relentless search for ways to replace labor—particularly simple, repetitive labor—by the machine. As machines have become more sophisticated, however, some more-skilled occupations have been affected, such as bookkeepers, machinists, and cabinetmakers. At the same time, the occupations needed to build, repair, and operate the machines are also growing—instrument makers, repair and maintenance technicians, computer analysts, and others.

The search is continuing. The buzzwords of the 1980s are *high tech* and *robotics,* just as the buzzword of the 1960s was *automation.* Experienced counselors have learned to discount apocalyptic prophecies of doom. Nevertheless, the computer is the most pervasive technological innovation of our time, since it affects office work, production control, trade, banking and finance, many services, and government. At the same time that this technology creates jobs for more scientific, professional, technical, and craft workers in computer research, design,

manufacture, utilization, and repair, it also reduces the skill requirements for many workers whose tasks—and jobs—are taken
over by the computer; computer programs are developed to enable workers with little specialized training to use them. Computers used for information storage and retrieval displace li-
brarians and file clerks; those used for preparing copy for
printing displace typists and compositors. The workers operating the computers will require less skill than those displaced.

Robots in the production process replace workers who
perform relatively simple and repetitive tasks. Their effect is to
eliminate many such jobs; the new jobs created in designing,
manufacturing, installing, and maintaining the robots are more
skilled than the jobs eliminated—but they have to be far fewer,
or the robots would not be economically feasible.

In summary, computers tend to substitute less-skilled
people for the moderately skilled, while robots eliminate the
least-skilled jobs. At the same time, both create smaller numbers of highly skilled professional, technical, and craft jobs in
their manufacture and maintenance.

Technological changes affect the work content of occupations. For example, some of the craft workers have seen their
skills eroded as engineers and scientists have introduced new
methods (such as instrumentation and computer-controlled production) that have taken over work decisions once made by
skilled craftspersons on the basis of traditional craft lore and
personal experience—the thickness of a beam needed to support
a floor, the point at which molten metal is ready to be poured,
and so on. Such developments are reducing the autonomy of
craft workers.

In the context of this "high-tech" revolution, the future
of the hundreds of thousands of workers in traditional industries like steel and automobile manufacturing who have lost
jobs from foreign competition as well as the depression of
1982–83 is uncertain. Even with full economic recovery, the
markets these industries once had are not likely to be completely
recovered. Some of the workers will therefore never return to
their previous jobs and will have to seek employment in services
or other industries where wage rates are lower and special train-

ing may be required. Some may have to relocate to other cities —an adjustment made more difficult if their spouses have jobs.

Women and Minorities. An important aspect of the occupational structure is the extent to which the various occupations are open to women and minorities. Recent decades have witnessed the beginning of a revolution in the employment patterns of these groups. Dedication to the principle of equality of opportunity—to which lip service had been paid for a century after emancipation of the slaves—began to be serious under pressure of the civil rights movement, the women's movement, and legislation enacted in the 1960s.

Women entered the labor force in vast numbers during and after World War II. The net addition of 31 million women to the civilian labor force between 1950 and 1982 provided 61 percent of the total growth of the labor force in this period; women were 28 percent of the labor force in 1950 and 43 percent in 1982. Although this vast influx was partly a response to increasing opportunities in the fields traditionally employing women, it also reflected women's desire to work. They found their way into many occupations not heretofore hospitable to them.

Women's share of jobs in every major occupational group increased in this single generation. More than half of the white-collar and service workers—the fastest-growing occupations—are women. Their gains have been more modest in the blue-collar and farming occupations: They hold about 18 percent of the jobs in each of these fields. Most significant are their gains in the professional and technical occupations (from 40 percent in 1950 to 45 percent—more than their share in the labor force—in 1982) and in the managerial occupations (in which their share doubled to 28 percent). Women trying to enter craft and operative jobs had more difficulty; nevertheless, their share of craft jobs rose from 3 percent to 7 percent during this period, and their share of operative jobs from 27 to 32 percent. Since they are well positioned in the faster-growing white-collar fields, women are likely to improve their share of the better jobs in the future.

The gains of blacks and other minorities during the post-

war period exceed those during the previous century. This point
is illustrated by a single comparison of their position in the
white-collar jobs. In 1950 minorities amounted to over 10 percent of the civilian labor force, but they had fewer than 3
percent of the white-collar jobs; that is, their share of the prestigious jobs was about one quarter of what it should have been
if we were to assume that, in the absence of discrimination and
educational disadvantages, minorities should be distributed
among the different occupations roughly in proportion to their
share in the labor force. A generation later, in 1982, blacks and
other minorities, who then amounted to nearly 12 percent of
the civilian labor force, held 9 percent of the white-collar jobs;
that is, their share of these jobs had risen from one quarter to
three quarters of their share of the labor force—a very substantial movement toward parity.

This way of measuring progress toward parity is an over-
simplification for two reasons—first, because minorities have
made greater gains in the lower-paid white-collar jobs than in
the higher and, second, because the equal proportionate distribution of all ethnic groups among occupations is not really an
ideal but rather an arbitrary standard for purposes of comparison and does not necessarily reflect the desires or geographical
locations of the various groups. We use this imperfect measuring stick only to summarize the changes that have taken place
and set them in perspective.

Minorities have made the greatest gains in clerical occupations, where their share of the jobs rose from less than 30 percent of their share of the labor force in 1950 to over 100 percent
in 1982. They have done well in the professional and technical
occupations, where their numbers rose from 38 to 83 percent
of their share of the total labor force. Starting at a lower level
in the managerial and sales occupations in 1950—about one
fifth of their share of the labor force—they attained only half
of their share by 1982. They made substantial gains in the craft
occupations, moving from 38 percent of their share in the labor
force in 1950 to 64 percent in 1982. In 1950 minorities' share
of the jobs in operative occupations was just under their share

of the labor force; in 1982 they had moved up to one-third *more* than their share of the labor force in these fields.

In the occupations at the bottom of the skill or earnings ladder (laborer, service and farm occupations), minorities were much overrepresented in 1950, and their concentration in these jobs was reduced substantially by 1982.

Thus both women and minorities improved their occupational positions impressively during the postwar period, but much remains to be achieved, especially in the higher-paid, more skilled jobs (Kaplan and Casey, 1958, pp. 9, 28, 29; Bureau of Labor Statistics, 1983, pp. 140–143, 158ff.).

Where People Work. This century's major shift in where people live and work has been the movement from farm to city. By World War I half the population still lived in rural areas, but by 1970 nearly three quarters lived in more than 7,000 urban areas. Virtually all of the nation's population growth of 72 million from 1940 to 1970 occurred in metropolitan areas. As the cities swelled, the overflow moved out of the central cities and into the suburban rings around them; by 1980 one and one-half times as many people lived in the suburbs as in the central cities.

At first suburbanization meant long commuting to work by mass transit or private car, but then industry itself began to move out of the central cities in search of both cheap land on which to build spread-out single-story factories and better access to transportation. Trade, finance, and services followed. The economic base of many central cities decayed, leaving a rotting core in the heart of many a prosperous metropolitan area.

At the same time, population and jobs shifted out of the older industrial states of the Northeast toward the South and West. Industries concentrated in these areas, such as textiles and apparel, moved to areas where labor was cheaper. The area stretching from Maine to the Mississippi and Ohio rivers lost nearly 17 percent of all nonfarm payroll jobs in the United States during the period 1939 to 1981—a share that was gained by Southern and Western states. Recent declines in steel, automobiles, and other major industries of the Northeast and North Central states will accentuate this trend.

The population shifts were accomplished by uprooting and migration of millions of people. Those living in the old central cities and in the Northeast find themselves trying to build their careers in depressed areas, while in many areas in the South and West workers live in an atmosphere of boom and growth.

We can summarize this account of the changing structure of work by saying that it is clearly a structure in flux. Rapid and revolutionary changes have been taking place in where the jobs are and the kinds of industries and kinds of occupations in which work is organized. The advantages and perils of self-employment have become an option for fewer workers; instead, many find themselves in large firms, with all this implies in loss of firsthand contact with the people who make decisions affecting their lives. At the same time, women and minorities have been battling their way into a somewhat more equitable share of the higher-skilled, higher-paid jobs.

Moving Through the Structure in the Course of a Work Career

I will now look at how individuals move through the structure of jobs, occupations, and industries as they try to build their careers. This account begins with a description of how men and women workers fit work and nonwork activities into their lives. It then discusses the role of education and formal training, both before and during work life. How people move through labor markets is then described in terms of the way firms do their hiring ("internal" and "external" markets), and the existence of a "secondary" labor market in which the disadvantaged are segregated from the mainstream of the labor force is suggested. Finally, patterns of worker mobility among employers and occupations are summarized.

Life Span and Work Life. As background for considering how people develop their work careers, I will first examine the way men and women fit their work careers into their life spans.

The work careers of men are longer than those of women, although differences have narrowed in recent years. In 1977 the average man had a life expectancy at birth of 69 years, of which he could expect to work 38; that is, he worked for 55 percent of his years on earth, using the remaining 45 percent for schooling in youth and retirement in old age. The average woman, in contrast, had a life expectancy at birth of 77 years and worked 27 years, or 35 percent of her life span, using the remaining 65 percent of her years for education, family raising, and retirement. Thus men had 11 more years to devote to their careers than women did (Smith, 1982).

This picture reflects significant changes since the turn of the century. Men added 23 years to their life span as higher incomes and improved health care prolonged life, but they added less than 6 years—only one quarter of the additional life span—to their work life. The rest of the 23-year gain was divided between longer education and longer retirement. Women, however, added 29 years to their life spans and fully 21 years—three quarters of the additional life span—to work.

With this came a remarkable change in the pattern of work in women's lives. Work became not merely a way of marking time for the few years between school and marriage but a lifetime commitment. The peak work activity of women in 1900 was in the years before marriage (when about one third were in the labor force), and their participation dropped sharply after age 25. In 1977 *two thirds* of all women worked during their early twenties, and—instead of the sharp dropoff thereafter—nearly 60 percent were still working from age 25 to age 44; only after age 55 did labor force participation drop below 50 percent. The need to supplement family income was a major factor in getting women to work more. Thus the patterns of life and work for men and women have become more alike, and most women have long work careers, with brief interruptions or none at all.

In all this discussion of work in people's lives, we should not forget that we are talking about paid work outside the home; both men and women—but especially women—do a lot of work in the home in housekeeping and childrearing whether or not they also work outside.

Rising Educational Attainment. At the same time as the

average life span and work life has been prolonged, more of the years of life have been spent in getting an education. This includes both increasing years of schooling in youth and time spent in mostly part-time schooling or other training in the adult years.

The lengthening of school years in youth has been a response to the shift toward white-collar and skilled jobs. It can be seen in the figures on the highest level of school completed by persons aged 25-29—an age at which nearly all people have finished their formal schooling and gone to work. In 1940, 38 percent of the people of this age had completed at least four years of high school; in 1981, 86 percent had completed that much education. Among blacks and other minorities the improvement was even greater—from 12 percent completing at least four years of high school in 1940 to 79 percent in 1981— not far behind the average for all people (National Center for Education Statistics, 1982, p. 16).

The United States has extended college education to a higher proportion of its population than any other country in the world. In 1940, 6 percent of 25–29-year-olds had completed at least four years of college; in 1981, 22 percent. Among minorities this figure was up to 15 percent in 1981. Enrollment of women for degree credit increased from 35 percent of the total for both sexes in the early 1950s to more than half the total by 1980 (National Center for Education Statistics, 1982, p. 95).

Less than ever is life compartmented into periods of education in youth, work in adulthood, and idleness in old age; instead, a significant portion of adults continue to take education and training at various times throughout their lives. In a single year such as 1978, roughly 40 million adults took such education or training—about one out of four persons 17 years of age or older. More than one third of the courses taken were in schools or colleges, one quarter in private community agencies (such as Ys), nearly one fifth in business firms, one eighth in government agencies other than schools, and others in professional organizations and unions or courses given by private tutors. The principal training given by business firms and government agencies was for their own employees. Most of the courses taken were for the purpose of improving work skills or qualifying the individual for employment; a minority were avocational (Adams and others, 1982, chap. 3).

People get all this education largely because they need it in work. The increasing proportion of white-collar and skilled jobs and rapidly changing technology have forced it. Adult education is a way for those who failed to get enough education in youth to catch up—but a striking fact about the people who take adult education is that they are better educated than the average to begin with: Those with more education are more likely to continue taking courses, partly because of the "continuing education" requirements in many professions but also because these individuals have found schooling an effective way to learn. People whose school experience was frustrating left school early and have little wish to go back. Despite concern about productivity in American industry and about the growth of "high-tech" jobs, few blue-collar workers other than craftspeople participate in adult education or training. Serious problems result at a time when blue-collar workers are being displaced.

One inevitable result of the spread of education is that the less educated are at an increasing disadvantage in the labor market. This can be seen in the high unemployment rates and low earnings of those who dropped out before completing high school. It can also be seen in the advantage of college-educated workers in moving up the career ladder. Once a manual or clerical worker could aspire to become a foreman or supervisor and then move up in the management structure. Now firms hire college graduates—engineers, accountants, business administration graduates—for management trainee positions. This practice has built a ceiling over the heads of those without college education. At one time a significant proportion of top managers in industry were men who had worked their way up from the bottom; more recently they are mainly college graduates.

"Internal" and "External" Labor Markets. The ways workers build their careers depend on how the organizations in

which they work go about hiring and promoting. Some firms are characterized by "internal labor markets," in which a worker enters at the bottom and works up. Others depend largely on filling jobs at all levels from outside.

Firms with primarily internal labor markets usually have a number of "ports of entry" for different occupations. For example, manual workers may enter in helper or laborer jobs and advance by training or experience to operative, craft, or first-level supervisory jobs; secretarial and other clerical workers enter with vocational or business school training and can work up to office supervisory positions; engineers, accountants, and other technically trained professionals enter after college in beginning jobs or management trainee positions and have the best chances of advancing to top-management jobs. In such firms it is not easy to enter high-level jobs from outside; training and experience within the firm are the keys to advancement. Internal labor markets are most common in large firms, in which, as we have seen, most workers are employed.

However, many firms hire extensively from external labor markets for all their positions and bring in midlevel and senior employees from outside. Workers committed to particular occupations by extensive education are more likely to go this route.

The distinction is not generally a hard-and-fast one, and firms differ on the extent to which they adhere to one or another model. Traditional practice, collective bargaining agreements providing for seniority in bidding for promotions, and, in general, the style of management of the individual firm determine the use of internal or external labor markets. The steel industry is an example of the internal labor market pattern. Hospitals, which employ many highly qualified professional and technical workers trained in schools rather than on the job, with little chance of promotion from one occupation to another, are typically users of external labor markets.

The "Secondary" Labor Market. In spite of the occupational gains of minority workers, many of them continue to be at the bottom of the ladder in most measures of economic well-being—earnings, unemployment, and irregularity of work. The unemployment rate for black workers has continued to be roughly double that of whites, in good times and in bad.

On examining the workers most affected by unemployment and low wages (whether or not they are members of ethnic minorities), economists have found that to a great extent they are the same individuals year in and year out: people with low educational levels (many of them school dropouts), irregular work records, low levels of skill, many with police or prison records or physical or mental disabilities. It is hard for them to break into better jobs with training and advancement opportunities, security, and good pay.

It appears that there are two labor markets, and these disadvantaged workers are concentrated in a secondary market characterized by temporary or casual jobs, low pay, and lack of training or advancement opportunities—that is, "blind-alley jobs." Once a worker gets into this pattern, it becomes increasingly difficult to break out. The cumulative disadvantages of such workers make their lives contrast sharply with those of people who finish school and—either immediately or after a short period of trying out jobs—get into jobs with advancement and training opportunities. It is as if some people never manage to jump onto the bus.

It was in an attempt to break this pattern that government-sponsored training programs in the 1960s and 1970s favored admittance of "disadvantaged" or long-term unemployed or members of minorities.

Job Tenure and Occupational Mobility. American workers have traditionally been more mobile in shifting among employers and even among occupations than workers in the more stable and older industrial countries. Entrance into occupations is easier because requirements for formal apprenticeship are not enforced, because only a relatively few occupations (generally those involving public health or safety) have licensure requirements, and because educational levels of applicants are generally high.

Movement from job to job is especially frequent among younger workers who try out different kinds of work during their early years in the labor force. We find more stability among workers near the end of their work lives. A recent survey (Horvath, 1982) shows that among men aged 55-64 the median tenure in their present jobs had been 15 years; among women it had been 9 years. About 30 percent of the men had been with their current employers for more than 25 years. Blacks in this age group had about the same average tenure as whites, but Hispanic workers (many of whom are recent immigrants) had little more than half as much tenure as other ethnic groups. Despite the tendency for older workers to have longer job tenure, a basic or underlying rate of job changing seems to occur at every age level: Roughly 9 percent of the employed workers in every age group had started their current jobs within the previous year.

We find a similar pattern in occupational mobility: It is highest among young workers and decreases rapidly after age 30. Another survey (Rytina, 1982) showed an average annual mobility rate of about 10 percent for men, 11.5 percent for women. (Mobility was defined as a change from one specific occupation—of which there are about 400—to another, whether or not the occupations were in the same major occupational group. A mobility rate was calculated by taking those who changed occupations within a year as a percentage of those employed at both the beginning and the end of a year.) The annual mobility rate for both men and women at age 20-24 was 23 percent; by age 45-54 it had dropped to 4 percent for men and 6 percent for women.

As would be expected, mobility rates were lowest for occupations requiring the highest skills—7 to 9 percent for men entering professional, managerial, and craft occupations, 11 to 14 percent for men entering sales, clerical, operative, and service occupations, and as high as 19 percent for those entering laborer occupations. (These differences also partly reflect the age composition of those entering the various occupations.)

Most occupational shifts were voluntary—more than half of them to get better pay or working conditions. Only about 11 percent of the changes were made because the worker lost a job.

Most older workers have been in the same occupations a long time. One third of those 55 years and older had been in the

same occupation for 25 years or more and another third for between 10 and 24 years. White and black workers had about the
same mobility experience, but Hispanics had been in their occupations for fewer years (Rytina, 1982).

Summary and Implications

Counselors need to be aware of the far-reaching changes
going on in the structure of work in the United States and must
alert their clients to the need to keep in touch with the changing labor market.

Technology and changing consumption patterns are combining to transform the economy to one emphasizing employment in services, with goods production requiring fewer workers. This means more job security in the business cycle but also
slower growth in productivity and in real incomes. At the same
time, a high proportion of workers are employed in large firms—
again offering more job security at the expense of depersonali-
zation and bureaucratization of work life. Similarly, opportunities for self-employment are declining, so that workers have
become more dependent on large organizations and have lost
autonomy.

The changing industrial structure, together with technological change within each industry, has required great increases
in employment of white-collar workers (especially clerical and
professional) and of service workers, while blue-collar workers
have maintained a constant proportion of the labor force. This
trend is raising the educational requirements for work. Its effects on average wages could offset the negative effects of the
shift to a service economy.

As demand for white-collar workers grows, women have
been flooding into the labor force and gaining a larger share of
jobs not only in traditional women's fields like clerical and
some professional occupations but also in the harder-to-crack
crafts and managerial occupations. Minorities are gaining entrance into occupations once virtually barred to them and are
raising their share of jobs in the white-collar and craft fields;
they have moved a good deal of the distance toward parity in

occupational opportunity. The gains of women and minorities do not yet represent achievement of parity, but they are evidence that progress toward this goal can be accomplished by working at it.

First moving into cities, jobs have now decentralized to the suburban rings around the decaying core of metropolitan areas. At the same time, jobs are shifting from the Northeast to the South and West, changing the country's political balance and plunging the two out of five Americans still working in the Northeast into an area of depressed opportunity.

In summary, the changes in structure have been rapid and pervasive.

Turning to the dynamics of the individual coping with the changing structure, we can see how the place of work in the life span has altered. As life expectancy increases, men allocate only a small part of their additional years to work, while women have been allocating most of their additional years to work. The work-life patterns for men and women are converging.

Men and women are getting more formal education, both in the years before work and by employee training and adult education in the work years. This is a necessary response to rising educational requirements of jobs. The presence of so many more educated workers means that the others must get more education merely to compete for jobs. Although the bulk of the work force is better educated, a dwindling but still significant minority are school dropouts, placed at a greater disadvantage—many of them functionally illiterate and unable to cope with the task of learning skills. Because most adults with educational deficiencies do not utilize the extensive resources for adult education, schools must do a better job of reducing the number of their pupils who come out with deficiencies.

The ways in which firms hire, train, and promote their workers affect the individual's opportunities. Firms depending mostly on internal labor markets bring employees in with little skill and help them to advance through training and experience. The skill and productivity of their labor force depend on the effectiveness of their training. Those utilizing external labor markets count on being able to hire qualified workers and give workers less opportunity to acquire skills; for developing these skills they depend on the schools.

Workers who, because of lack of education, fall into a secondary labor market are confined to low-paid, short-term dead-end, and other undesirable jobs and find it hard to break out of this pattern. Adult education provides breakout opportunities for some, but for many others the very difficulties that prevented their profiting from schooling early in life keep them from using adult education resources, and the cycle of failure, poverty, and insecurity is prolonged. Again, effective schools would reduce the seriousness of this problem.

In response to the changing job structure, workers are able to change jobs and even occupations fairly freely. Most of this mobility occurs early in a worker's career, however. By middle age both kinds of mobility are greatly reduced. The prevalence of occupational mobility, together with the extensive opportunities for education and training in adult life, means that decisions about careers and training arrived at in youth are not irrevocable. Those who acquire education maintain flexibility. But those who enter the labor force with educational deficiencies find themselves closed out of many avenues and confined to a cycle of irregular, low-paid employment and frequent periods of unemployment.

For the counselor, these facts of work life point to the need to emphasize education and training to their clients—both during the school years and during the work years. Workers have flexibility in adapting to occupations, but those with better training have greater flexibility and more ability to take advantage of opportunities.

Suggested Readings

Bluestone, B., and Harrison, B. *The Deindustrialization of America: Plant Closings, Community Abandonment, and the Dismantling of Basic Industry.* New York: Basic Books, 1982.

Dramatically traces the history of plant closings and their effects; closes with recommendations of social and economic programs to revive industry or mitigate the effects of industrial decline.

Bureau of Labor Statistics, U.S. Department of Labor. *Occupational Projections and Training Data.* Bulletin 2202. Washington, D.C.: U.S. Government Printing Office, 1982.

    A statistical and research supplement to the 1982–83 *Occupational Outlook Handbook.* Summarizes statistics on employment, estimated replacement needs, and training in many occupations and gives projections of employment change up to 1990 for over 600 occupations.

Bureau of Labor Statistics, U.S. Department of Labor. *Economic Projections to 1990.* Bulletin 2121. Washington, D.C.: U.S. Government Printing Office, 1982.

    Describes the projections of population and labor force growth and of the changing patterns of consumption that underlie the bureau's projections of employment by industry and occupation to 1990.

Magaziner, I. C., and Reich, R. B. *Minding America's Business: The Decline and Rise of the American Economy.* New York: Harcourt Brace Jovanovich, 1982.

    Describes the decline in the growth rate of the American economy and our loss of first place in output and income per worker. Discusses the roles of business and government in this decline and concludes by arguing for an "industrial policy" by which government would aid in making business more efficient and competitive in the world.

Stanback, T. M., Jr. *Understanding the Service Economy: Employment, Productivity, Location.* Baltimore: Johns Hopkins University Press, 1979.

    Analyzes the growth of production, employment, and productivity in the service industries and their geographical location.

References

Adams, A. V., and others. *The Neglected Source of Human Wealth: A Study of Formal Education and Training During the Adult Years.* Springfield, Va.: National Technical Information Service, 1982.

Bureau of Labor Statistics, U.S. Department of Labor. *Labor Force Statistics Derived from the Current Population Survey: A Databook.* Vol. 1. Bulletin 2096. Washington, D.C.: U.S. Government Printing Office, 1982a.

Bureau of Labor Statistics, U.S. Department of Labor. *Economic Projections to 1990.* Bulletin 2121. Washington, D.C.: U.S. Government Printing Office, 1982b.

Bureau of Labor Statistics, U.S. Department of Labor. *Occupational Projections and Training Data.* Bulletin 2202. Washington, D.C.: U.S. Government Printing Office, 1982c.

Bureau of Labor Statistics, U.S. Department of Labor. *Employment and Earnings.* Washington, D.C.: U.S. Government Printing Office, January 1983.

Bureau of the Census, U.S. Department of Commerce. *County Business Patterns, 1977: Enterprise Statistics.* Washington, D.C.: U.S. Government Printing Office, 1979.

Horvath, F. W. "Job Tenure of Workers in January 1981." *Monthly Labor Review,* September 1982, pp. 34-36.

Kaplan, D. L., and Casey, M. C. "Occupational Trends in the United States, 1900 to 1950." Working Paper No. 5. Washington, D.C.: Bureau of the Census, 1958.

National Center for Education Statistics, Department of Education. *Digest of Education Statistics.* Washington, D.C.: U.S. Government Printing Office, 1982.

Rytina, N. F. "Occupational Changes and Tenure, 1981." *Monthly Labor Review,* September 1982, pp. 29-33.

Smith, S. J. "New Worklife Estimates Reflect Changing Profile of Labor Force." *Monthly Labor Review,* March 1982, pp. 15-20.

3

Edwin L. Herr

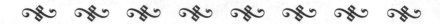

Links Among Training, Employability, and Employment

Employability and the countervailing effects of unemployment on individuals and the larger society have become persistent national issues with important implications for career guidance. This chapter will address the major elements of youth and adult employability and some of the possible counseling, educational, and economic responses to facilitate it. Distinctions are made between general and specific employability and the importance of each in a society undergoing major structural transition in its occupational characteristics. Implications are drawn for policies governing training, counseling and related matters.

Employment: A Structural Transition

For twenty years or more, various observers have characterized the United States as a postindustrial society. Through the years many names have been given to the structural transitions represented by the term *postindustrial*. Toffler (1980), after rejecting many of the recent attempts to name the changes we are experiencing—space age, information age, electronic era, global village, technetronic age, superindustrial age—suggested that the magnitude of upheaval and transformation that will occur is so great that it constitutes a parallel to the two major waves of change that have constituted most of the history of the world: first, the agricultural revolution and, second, the industrial civilization. "The result is the Third Wave of civilization which is among other features highly technological and anti-industrial" (p. 10).

Whether one uses terms like *postindustrial* or *Third Wave,* the effects are the same. The United States has been and is undergoing a major change from reliance on heavy industrial manufacturing of durable goods—for example, steel, furniture, automobiles—to an industrial base that rests on advanced technological innovation applied to the production of goods and a labor force engaged mainly in service occupations concerned with information generation and processing relevant to goods production, transportation, communications, and retailing. The characteristics of these industries are basic to the shape and support of the occupational structure of the United States. At the heart of such transitions are computer technology (Ginzberg, 1982), microprocessors and microcomputers, industrial robots, telecommunications, and electronic data handling (Riche, 1982).

As a result of such mechanization and technological applications, the current labor force is composed of only 3 percent engaged in agriculture, 32 percent in the production of goods (mostly manufacturing), and 65 percent, and increasing, engaged in service occupations (defined in the broadest sense to include all enterprises not engaged in the production of goods—mining, manufacturing, and construction—or agriculture) (Ginzberg, 1982). In comparison, in 1940 approximately 54 percent of the population was engaged in goods production, and at the height of World War II, 70 percent. Perhaps even more dramatic is the statistic that, of all new jobs added to the economy from 1969 to 1976, 90 percent were in services (Ginzberg, 1982).

Employability Defined

Employability, under conditions of either economic change or stability, refers to a composite set of traits and skills that permits the individual to meet the demands of the workplace. Dunn (1974), for example, has defined employability as "the capacity of the individual to function in a particular work situation or occupation." In contrast, "placeability refers to the probability that the individual will obtain work in a particular occupation" (p. 39). Dunn includes under "general employability" factors such as social development, work personality, work methods, work habits, physical tolerance, and basic academic skills. "Specific employability" has to do with the person's ability to perform the work tasks required by a particular job and focuses on technical skills and experience as well as, in the case of handicapped workers, whether the person has physical access to the job site and sufficient mobility to perform the technical aspects of the job within the particular work environment.

In the view of Dunn and others, employability can be broken into its components, which can then be used as bases for assessments of work readiness or as conceptual frames of reference for planning programs of general or specific training. General training is applicable to a variety of work environments and jobs. Specific training deals with performance of skills required in a limited number of jobs (Vandergoot, 1982).

The components of employability are described in a variety of ways and differ with the levels and kinds of work at issue. Both general and specific employability would differ for professional, managerial, skilled, and unskilled jobs. Within each of these categories, specific employability would likely vary for different job families, or occupational clusters.

Regardless of differences in the content of the components of employability, it is possible to speak of them as including such general categories as affective work competencies, industrial discipline, self-management, and occupational or firm-specific task-performance skills. The first three categories are examples of general employability skills; the latter, of specific employability skills.

Affective Work Competencies. Affective work competencies include work attitudes, values, and habits that are manifested in individuals' behaviors in the workplace. The research of Kazanas (1978) has focused on identifying those affective work competencies that are desirable and common across occupations. These are basically the behaviors associated with job adjustment and stability. Kazanas contends that, in an occupational structure that is rapidly changing from a production-oriented to a service-oriented world and one in which machines are performing more of the psychomotor activities once performed by people, workers increasingly face the problem of early obsolescence of specific job skills and knowledge. Therefore, affective work competencies—work values, habits, attitudes—become important to job survival (p. 1). They are the affective mediators that spur people to learn new work tasks, accept work roles, identify with organizational goals. Kazanas identifies sixty-three work competencies that could serve as the basis of general training in vocational education or in other settings. These competencies include such behavior as punctuality, cooperativeness, emotional stability, honesty, dependability, loyalty, and judgment.

Industrial Discipline. The term *industrial discipline,* more common in some European nations (for example, Great Britain) than in the United States, embraces the behavior described by Kazanas as affective work competencies and by Herr (1982) as work context skills. Included might be knowledge and skills associated with effective employer/employee relations, ability to accept supervision, willingness to follow work rules, regularity of attendance, understanding of life in an organization, dependability, teachability, efficiency, pride in work.

Self-Management. Self-management skills are those that relate to career planning and to job search and access. Career planning would include such emphases as decision making, ability to use exploratory resources to reality-test alternative choices, understanding of the constructive use of leisure, personal economics skills, self-knowledge (for example, aptitudes, values, interests), knowledge of career opportunities (for example, occupational alternatives, educational options, the relation between subject matter and content of jobs), and the ability to match personal characteristics to those required in preferred curricula or occupations. Job search and access skills include knowing how to find relevant employers, knowing procedures to use to make contact with employers, being able to manage and respond to the types of conditions and questions likely to occur in interview situations, and having the information and

ability to complete letters of inquiry, résumés, and applications. Career planning tends to include all behavior that has to
do with forging a career, being purposeful, and defining, testing,
and narrowing the field of alternatives from which selection will
be made. Also included are job-search and access skills, the tac-
tics used to convert a preferred choice into a reality.

    With specific reference to job finding, Wegmann (1979),
after an extensive analysis of existing programs of job-search assistance, concluded that "the ability to find a suitable job in a
reasonable period of time demands a series of learnable skills"
(p. 197). Thus, job finding is a learnable skill and one of considerable importance. He cites several surveys indicating that many
applicants for employment do not know how to interview effectively, present themselves physically, or complete appropriate
résumés or job applications. In short, they suffer an absence of
skills as job seekers, and they need counseling in the skills of
finding a job.

    Occupational or Firm-Specific Task Skills. Virtually every
job or occupation has specific technical skills that are required
by it or by the workplace in which the job is done. These skills
are ordinarily the content of specific employability training
either on the job, in an apprenticeship, or in formal education.
In general, the more complex and lengthy the training for the
job, the more likely that the training site will be formal education rather than the work setting itself. Examples of firm-specific training are instruction in how to operate a unique piece of
equipment found only in a particular firm and requiring skills
and knowledge that are present in no other occupation. More
likely to be acquired in a formal education setting are such skills
as typewriting and operation of office machines that are central
to clerical occupations and present in virtually every firm or
enterprise.

The Transition to Work

    The importance of the multiple facets of employability
just described can be seen in studies that describe what happens
in the transition to work and in persistence on the job after

work has been secured. The studies of primary concern here assume that jobs are available and that the loss of a job is not due mainly to economic dislocation. The most employable of people can lose a job if a plant or corporation is closed or moves to a different geographical location. Such situations are not at issue here. Rather, the concern of the next sections is how various components of employability tend to affect the transition and adjustment to work for youths and adults.

Problems and Thwarting Conditions for Youths. In the 1960s a series of studies began that indicated that many young persons experienced difficulties in obtaining and keeping jobs because they lacked skills in job seeking and on-the-job behavior, not because they lacked the technical skills to do the job. For example, Eggeman, Campbell, and Garbin (1969) queried a sample of 763 youth opportunity center counselors in forty-eight of the fifty states about their view of the major problems faced by youth in the transition from school to work. Eighty-six percent of the counselors indicated inadequate training and job skills, lack of information about work and training opportunities, lack of knowledge of the real demands of work and of employer expectations, lack of educational requirements, and lack of prior work experience. Slightly more than 71 percent of the counselors indicated that vocational behavior was a major problem in worker adjustment. This category included poor work habits (for example, absenteeism, tardiness), inability to fill out forms and handle interviews, inability to accept supervision, inability to get along with fellow workers or to cope with real demands of work, and poor attitudes toward work.

Haccoun and Campbell (1972) engaged in an extensive study of the work-entry problems of youth, the outcomes of which Crites (1976) subsequently described as "thwarting conditions" that new workers may experience as they become established in a job. These thwarting conditions were found to be of two classes: (1) those dealing with job performance (for example, responsibility, maturity, attitudes and values, work habits, adjustment to peers and supervisors, communications, taking on new roles, self-image, coping with automation and new technology) and (2) those dealing with job entry, career planning, and management problems (for example, job seeking, interviewing and test taking, geographic mobility, family and personal situational adjustment, job layoffs and rejection, prejudice and discrimination, occupational aspirations and job expectations, career planning and management).

Adams and Mangum (1978), in a major study of youth unemployment, have shown that, beyond a predictable period of trial and experimentation, joblessness among out-of-school teenage youth carries with it a "hangover effect." Such jagged labor market problems among youth do not simply age out but instead are predictive of later labor market problems in early adulthood and beyond, because periods of unemployment represent loss of work experience, information, and skills that may place the person at a competitive disadvantage for available jobs and also have an injurious effect on attitudes toward work.

These studies illustrate that employability for young workers is composed of psychological traits, planning and job-search components, interpersonal skills, and either technical skills or the ability to acquire such skills. These conditions are not all operational for all persons and all work settings. They are sufficiently pervasive, however, to be classified into the various components of employability previously described. In general, adults experience many of the same problems with employability as young workers do, although there are some differences worthy of note.

Problems and Thwarting Conditions for Adults. Just as the youth population is made up of different subgroups that vary in their ability to master the transition from school to work, there are also differences among adult populations in their ability to cope with the demands of the workplace or of work performance. As discussed later in this chapter, estimates are that 20 to 30 percent of the adult population is functionally illiterate: unable to make change, fill out job applications, and deal with other aspects of work-related behavior. Beyond functional illiteracy proper, Northcutt's studies (Knowles, 1977) suggest that only 40 percent of the American adult population is coping adequately with typical life problems (for example, getting work and holding a job, buying things, parenting, managing one's economic life).

The foregoing suggests that some adult populations are in such need of help with basic academic and life-coping skills that these deficiencies limit both their trainability and their likely success in many emerging occupational areas. In other studies of adult adjustment to work, it has been suggested that successful adaptation to work can become a problem if a sequence of adjustments does not unfold effectively. The study by Ashley and others (1980) indicates that these areas of adjustment include performance, responsibility, and organizational, interpersonal, and affective aspects of work.

Compared with youth, the adjustment to work for adults is likely to be multidimensional. Family responsibilities, among other issues, tend to exacerbate the choice of and preparation or retraining for work in ways not experienced by youth. For example, Miller and Oetting (1977) identified some thirty-seven specific barriers to work in eleven categories that were reported by economically and vocationally disadvantaged persons. These barriers included childcare, health, transportation, social and interpersonal conflicts, financial problems, legal problems, emotional/personal problems, drug and alcohol abuse problems, job qualification, discrimination, and language and communication problems.

Employability, Employment, and Unemployment

Employability and Employment. As suggested in the preceding sections, employability and employment are not interchangeable concepts. Employability is the *potential* to perform and to adjust in the workplace. If there are no jobs available in which to act out that potential, the individual remains or becomes unemployed. A person may be able to do a job (be employable) but not be able to obtain a job (be placeable, be employed). Employment, as used in most government statistics, is an estimate that deals only with those who have secured a job and are working. To be more specific, "An employed person is anyone who did any work for pay during the survey week, worked in his own business, profession, or farm, or worked fifteen hours or more as an unpaid worker in a family-run business. That category includes those who were temporarily absent from their jobs because of illness, vacation, bad weather, strike, or personal reasons, regardless of whether they were paid for their time off" (Cerianni, 1982).

Unemployment, as used by the federal government, refers to the condition of those persons 16 years of age and older who had no job during the period of the survey, were able and available for work, and were actively seeking employment. Thus, people who are ill or handicapped and unable to work are not considered unemployed, nor are housewives, retired persons, students, children under sixteen, or anyone who is unable to work, chooses not to work for personal, family, or health reasons, or is not actively seeking a job. The unemployed category also includes persons who have quit their jobs to search for another, new entrants to the labor force who have not worked before, and reentrants who are looking for jobs after a long absence from work (Cerianni, 1982). Discouraged workers, who are not counted in official unemployment statistics, have neither worked nor looked for work during some specified period prior to an enumeration of the work force.

Who Is Employed? To answer the question "Who is employed?" is to experience some constant error because actual employment is always in flux. Nevertheless, employment patterns show intermediate and long-range trends that are instructive. For example, at any given time presently, persons employed in the services sector—hotels and motels; entertainment; personal, medical, and educational services; finance, insurance, and real estate—are far more likely to be employed than those in the goods-producing sector. In the early 1980s, job reductions took place almost entirely in the goods-producing industries, particularly those engaged in and related to marketing higher-priced consumer goods: auto, construction, steel, and related industries (Westcott and Bednarzik, 1981). The decline in employment during 1980 was concentrated in blue-collar occupations; white-collar jobs continued to grow steadily. Between the fourth quarter of 1979 and the third quarter of 1980, jobs in manufacturing declined by 1.1 million and jobs in the construction industry by 300,000. The only services sector industry to experience job loss during the same period was transportation and public utilities industries (70,000 jobs).

Demographic changes in employment follow the job profiles of the industries affected. Adult men made up two thirds of those who lost jobs during 1980. Teenagers accounted for most of the rest of the job losses. Adult women made modest employment gains. Blacks tended to be affected slightly more than whites and to experience longer periods of joblessness. But this statement belies the actuality that black unemployment was more than twice that of whites—in general, 20 percent for black workers and 40 percent or more for black teenagers.

Comparing full-time and part-time workers: The early 1980s saw a marked decline in the number of persons who worked thirty-five hours or more per week and a rise in those who worked part-time as many industries tried to avoid layoffs or job reductions by reducing the length of the work week.

Although much more could be said about who is employed in the labor force, suffice it to say that the incidence of employment/unemployment varies across industries, age and gender groups, and educational levels. In general terms, the shifts reflect the long-term transition in the characteristics of the occupational structure from heavy industrial, manufacturing, blue-collar work to advanced technological, service-producing, white-collar work.

Who Is Unemployed? Unemployment tends to fall most heavily on those persons with little education, few skills, and low incomes (Pierson, 1980). This tends to be true across demographic groups. For example, among men aged 55 to 64 years, the labor force participation rate from 1962 to 1978 fell by over 20 percentage points for those who had not graduated from high school but only 7 points for those with at least one year of college. Among men 45 to 55 years old, the largest decrease in rates was also among the least educated (Rosenfeld and Brown, 1979). Another study of prime-age male workers (Hill and Corcoran, 1979) found that blacks, the poor, the less educated, blue-collar workers, and men under age 45 were more likely than other subgroups to have experienced at least one bout of unemployment between 1967 and 1976. In addition, prime-age black men who headed households were one and one-half times as likely to be unemployed during 1967–1976 as their white counterparts. More than half of all blacks surveyed were unemployed sometime during 1967–1976, compared with about one third of whites. Further, blue-collar workers with lower levels of education were more likely to experience repeated unemployment than white-collar workers or well-educated workers.

Any examination of the unemployment profile must include teenagers and, particularly, black teenagers. Youths between 16 and 24 years of age make up nearly half of all those unemployed (Andrisani, 1977). The unemployment rate of teenagers has typically been two or more times the adult rate, and the unemployment rate of black teenagers has been two or two and one-half times that of white teenagers. Regardless of location, huge gaps in employment status exist between white youths and black youths because of discrimination, inadequate education, changing characteristics of jobs, fluctuations in opportunities in the military forces, and related factors (Iden, 1980).

Three Categories of Responses to Unemployment

It is not unusual for the term *unemployment* to be used as though it had a single meaning. To be more precise, however, there are several types of unemployment (Kroll, 1976), caused by different factors and affecting groups of persons somewhat differently. For example, nonwhites tend to be vulnerable to all types of unemployment—seasonal, frictional, cyclical, and structural—with white youths and women only somewhat less so and adult white males subject largely to cyclical influences only (Pierson, 1980, p. 188). Thus, as economic conditions change and different types of unemployment occur, major changes also occur in the jobless status among various demographic groups. Collectively, these types of unemployment elicit three types of response: counseling, education and training, or economics.

Counseling. In broad terms, counselors of the unemployed need to help them understand and deal with the psychological aspects of unemployment. In particular, counselors must be conscious of the relations between joblessness and mental health. They need to help the unemployed deal with what Lichtman (1978) has observed as an irrational willingness—perhaps even a need—of people to blame themselves for social processes for which they are not responsible. Counselors also need to help the unemployed view themselves as part of a system in which a range of resources are available to them in the event of unemployment or as aids to avoiding unemployment. Counselors also need to recognize that most unemployed persons need more than support. Their problems are likely to be multidimensional and may include such areas as transportation, racial discrimination, lack of basic skills, poor industrial discipline, family discord, and drug or alcohol problems. Where these problems are present, counselors need to coordinate services or experiences likely to be of assistance to the unemployed person in changing the skills or attitudes that led to unemployment while also providing the conditions in which alternative behavior and jobs can be explored.

Education and Training. Education and training in combination with counseling can provide different responses for different types of unemployment. Seasonal unemployment requires that persons entering the work force or changing jobs be informed that it occurs, be assisted in identifying the industries or occupations most likely to be vulnerable, and, if they choose to enter such industries, to be assisted in developing attitudes of flexibility toward the work they do. Cyclical unemployment tends not to be amenable to education and training. Persons actually or potentially affected by cyclical unemployment can be helped to gain some understanding of economic history and of the causes and likely outcomes of a given cycle, along with ways to develop skills or self-employment opportunities that may be less vulnerable to cyclical influences. Although some frictional unemployment is inescapable, its magnitude can be reduced by equipping people with job-search skills, precise knowledge of job opportunities, and other information designed to facilitate the transition and adjustment to work. In response to structural unemployment, education and training can develop initial entry-level skills, job-search strategies, retraining in critical skill shortage areas, and sensitivity to labor market forecasts about changes in the occupational structure and can combine with industry to provide work-study, cooperative education, and apprenticeship programs in areas of emerging need (Herr and Watts, 1981).

Economics. In a sense, neither counseling nor education and training directly controls employment or reduces unemployment. Both represent approaches that are likely to increase people's employability or help them deal with the fact of personal unemployment with lessened stress and psychological trauma. It is, then, economic mechanisms and monetary and fiscal policy, as well as political priorities or values, that have the most direct effect on forms of employment available and, indeed, types of unemployment likely to occur. Such institutions as job development, government-subsidized employment or training schemes, export/import tariffs, protectionism, training/ retraining stipends, tax credits for industry to hire and train unemployed persons, job data banks, transitional services for unemployed workers, and industrial development grants are each economic and, often, political responses appropriate to employment and unemployment.

Since America is now straddling a structural transition to a postindustrial society, it seems mandatory that all three responses cited here and others that might be available must be brought to bear on the dilemmas and needs at hand.

Relation of Training to Employability

In a postindustrial society, knowledge and skills are the basic ingredients of employability. To the degree that training is relevant to the requirements of the occupational structure, it becomes a principal medium of employability among the labor force.

Training takes many forms and is concerned with both general employability and specific employability. Within these two gross classifications, there are many types of content, varying in generalizability across occupations and time. General employability, as suggested previously, tends to be concerned with affective work competencies, industrial discipline, self-management, career planning, and job access. Such content has to do with work attitudes and values, purposefulness, understanding of the organization in which work takes place, ability to take supervision, interpersonal relations and communications with coworkers, decision making and planning about work, as well as job search and access. The attitudes, knowledge, and skills that make up general employability are likely to be durable, resistant to obsolescence, and generalizable.

The importance of general employability skills is illustrated by Osterman's research (1980). Osterman suggests that the key issue in the hiring practices used by firms in the primary labor market, probably the most attractive employment sector because of the opportunities for career ladders, good pay, promotion, security, training, and fringe benefits, is who will become a stable worker. This is another way of saying that what is desired is reliable and mature workers who are able "to learn future jobs, not necessarily the job they are being hired for, since that job is simply the first rung on the bottom of the internal ladder" (p. 26). Such a view also validates the importance of the many aspects of a positive work attitude and of the possession of affective work competencies in general employability skills.

Specific employability is more likely to be technical in content and targeted on particular types of job performance. The types of job performance involved may be industry-specific, occupation-specific, or firm-specific. Because of the effects of mechanization and emerging forms of technology, specific employability skills are likely to become obsolete more rapidly than general employability skills. They are also more likely to be limited to particular occupations or firms. For example, the technical skills required in accounting are likely to have relevance wherever accounting is performed. They are not firm-specific, although there will be variations in the exact procedures used from firm to firm. However, the technical skills of accounting are not the same as those of engineering. Thus, accounting skills are specific employability skills not bound to a particular firm but limited in their generalizability across occupations. The relevant term here is *elasticity*; accounting skills may be relevant to occupations in business and industry other than accounting. Therefore, they have some elasticity: If one cannot find a pure

accounting position, there are other jobs in which such knowledge and skills are useful. However, the elasticity of such skills
does not stretch into health care, the sciences, engineering, the
arts, or other occupations in which the technical content of job
performance is quite different. On balance, general employability skills are much more elastic, applicable, and useful in many
more types of jobs, occupations, or settings than are specific
employability skills.

Because specific employability skills vary widely in their
technical content and academic substance, the ways they are
obtained also vary. The more technical the content of specific
employability skills, the more likely they will be achieved in
formal educational settings. The less technical and more quickly
learned the specific employability skills, the more likely they
will be learned on the job under the tutelage of a master practitioner or supervisor. There are exceptions to these general rules,
and in addition, regardless of the technical content of employability skills, there will likely be some orientation to the expectations and characteristics of the firm in which the skills are to
be employed. Orientation to a firm is in itself a form of specific
employability training.

The Nature of Training. Both general employability and
specific employability training occur in many settings. In some
instances, it is difficult to separate one from the other. Such a
position is inherent in Freedman's (1980) contention that
"training encompasses maturation in general, socialization to
work and the workplace, basic education, and, finally, occupationally related skills. In real life, among real people, these
aspects are interdependent; successful work experience depends
on their coexistence" (p. 1). Freedman contends that, in terms
of the needs for and types of training, "patterns of entry and
skill acquisition are complex, and they vary considerably by
occupation." She divides skill acquisition into two categories:
preemployment training and on-the-job training.

Freedman further contends that over 60 percent of all
jobs do not routinely require preemployment training (Freedman and Dutka, 1980, Table 1). At one end of the scale are jobs
requiring low skills that are learned entirely on the job in less

than three months. This grouping of jobs accounts for about 37 percent of all jobs in the United States. At the higher end of the scale of skills, many better jobs in the insurance industry, for example, are learned on the job by liberal arts graduates who are recruited for such occupations (1980, p. 2). Between such examples are many skilled and semiskilled jobs described as mixed because the nature and extent of preemployment training or on-the-job training tend to be a function of the employer resources and the supply/demand considerations in the local community where such jobs are located. This group includes jobs ranging in complexity from auto mechanic to air controller.

Preemployment training is a function of both public and private educational institutions. Elementary and secondary schools, colleges and universities, area vocational/technical schools, and community colleges are frequently the formal educational settings most visible in preemployment training. However, confining one's thinking to this segment of educational settings significantly underestimates the availability and impact of other preemployment settings. For example, there is a large network of proprietary, trade, business, and related schools that provide specific types of preemployment training. The curricula of these schools vary across the gamut of clerical, cosmetological, computer-programming, aviation, mechanical, and other occupations. Similarly, the armed forces of the United States have an elaborate network of schools that do preemployment training in many clerical, health care, mechanical, and other technical skill areas of importance to maintaining modern military systems. Estimates are that the military probably has the best-organized and the largest system of on-the-job training of any employer. It also has the largest number of vocational and technical training programs maintained by any single establishment anywhere. Such instruction ranges from basic literacy to education at the postdoctoral level (Evans and Herr, 1978, pp. 257–258).

A major category of training that bridges preemployment and on-the-job training is apprenticeship. About 350,000 American workers are engaged in such training currently (Swanson, 1982). Apprenticeship involves formal training programs in which students/workers are provided training agreements that specify the amount of related instruction in a classroom and the amount of learning on the job that will be required to complete the apprenticeship. Apprenticeship training occurs within "apprenticeable" occupations as governed by regulations of the Bureau of Apprenticeship and Training of the Employment and Training Administration, U.S. Department of Labor. As Glover (1981) observes, apprenticeships are regular jobs—not just training positions. Apprentices are involved in regular production work rather than only concentrated training, and they receive progressively increasing wages as their training and skill development advance. Thus, they earn while they learn (p. 100).

Business and industry are also heavily involved in training, sometimes of a preemployment nature, more often on-the-job training. Osterman's conclusion is that, in general, firms heavily engaged in training do not want to train people in skills that are generalizable throughout an industry or occupation—for example, blueprint reading or typewriting. Instead, they try "to shift costs of this training to the school system and to other firms by giving preference to applicants with some previous work experience and by supporting vocational programs in the public schools" (1980, p. 28). What they intend, for the most part, is to provide firm-specific training which does not equip workers with occupational mobility to move to other firms but which does stimulate such mobility within the firm doing the training.

Thurow (1977) observes that, rather than completely trained workers, employers are interested in obtaining employees whose costs of training are low. "Although on-the-job training may be informal, it is still costly in that production slackens while the training occurs" (p. 40). What this view leaves unsaid is that firms vary widely in their ability to provide training for workers. Large firms are more likely to have training departments and to be able to afford the reduction in production during the period that master or veteran workers are training new workers. Many small or geographically isolated firms cannot afford the costs of training. Instead, they must be able to recruit workers whose prior skills or work experience permit them to be trained quickly and whose general employability skills enable them to be stable workers. Thus, for most firms, whether heavily engaged in training or not, industry- or occupation-specific skills that can be taught in a classroom on a preemployment basis are important because they increase the labor pool of employable workers from which large and small firms can choose those to whom they will provide the firm-specific training necessitated by their business or industrial processes. In a sense, preemployment training provides workers with freedom of choice of employment if jobs requiring their skills are available and their technical skills are not obsolete. For firms, such skills typically reduce the length and costs of firm-specific training, whether it is on-the-job or of some other type. Mixing sources and types of training in this fashion spreads the costs of training between the public and the private sectors and may protect workers' freedom of choice if the demand for skills exceeds the supply of such skills but can be a problem for workers whose skills become obsolescent if retraining provisions or opportunities are limited.

If there is an overarching premise associated with job-skill training of either a specific or a general employability focus, it is that such training cannot be seen as isolated from other aspects of a program leading to employability, nor can it be limited to one-shot skill improvement programs. Such training must be seen as part of a developmental process by which participants gain labor market information, an orientation to the behavioral norms and expectations that characterize the workplace, a commitment to future trainability, the work habits by which personal productivity can be maximized, job performance task skills in demand, and the tools of job search and interview by which access to the work force can be enhanced (National Commission for Employment Policy, 1979; Herr, 1981).

Emerging Perspectives on Training, Employability, and Employment. Any informed perspective on the present and future requirements of the American economy must accept the reality that training, employability, and employment are tightly linked. However, the linkages are complex, not simple, in their content and character. Training and employability depend on the availability of an employment environment that provides opportunities for those who are trained in general and in specific employability skills. The employment possibility structure is dynamic as a function of economic policies and events, both domestic and international. Therefore, the linkage of training, employability, and employment is influenced by the provision of information to training settings about areas of emerging demand so that structural mismatches between the employability potential of the labor force and the requirements of the employment structure can be minimized. Such information must also be made available systematically and with sufficient lead time to workers and potential workers so that choice of preparation through training related to occupational availability will be facilitated.

Although such statements are accurate, they are also simplistic. There are structural barriers to meeting such broad general goals which must be recognized and addressed. For one, training in the United States, whether for purposes of general or specific employability skills, has not developed as a system but, rather, as a collection of enterprises in different types of institutions, at different levels, for varying purposes, and having different definitions (Swanson, 1982, p. 40). Such training resembles a patchwork about which available information on access or outcomes is less than is desirable and is not communicated to training settings as comprehensively as would be helpful. Consequently, vocational education and other parts of the training network are frequently criticized for preparing people for jobs that do not exist or with skills so specific that they rapidly become obsolete (Thurow, 1977). In fact, the problem is shared by those who train and those hiring the trainees. Information and cooperation in identifying necessary skills, emerging occupational demands, instructional resources, and school/industry cooperative agreements for joint provision of combinations of formal instruction and on-the-job training each require more systematic attention than is apparent in many parts of the nation.

According to some observers, one of the areas of current deficit in an age of major occupational skill transition is a national training strategy (Choate, 1982). The nation's labor force comprises many subpopulations whose basic academic skills, work habits, and occupation/task-specific skills vary widely in development. These differences are important in providing training for workers displaced or otherwise affected by the onrush of advancing technology, plant closings, and new industrial processes. "Technology and foreign trade are making millions of existing jobs obsolete. The academic and functional skills of most workers are too antiquated for the new replacement jobs that already are emerging" (Choate, 1982, p. 1). However, national training policy covers only a small minority of the existing labor force and, for the most part, not those workers who have had a positive, consistent work life but whose skills are now becoming obsolete. There is no comprehensive policy now in place that assists displaced workers to upgrade their skills or workers still employed to obtain training that will extend their opportunity to take advantage of replacement jobs coming into the occupational structure. When headlines cry out about 12 to 14 million persons, including discouraged workers, being unemployed, many of them because of the structural transition already described, the dimensions of the problem are enormous, costly, and inescapable.

Choate (1982, p. 3) has calculated that the public training programs now available serve less than 8 percent of the population, mostly those who are economically and culturally disadvantaged. Therefore, they essentially ignore the 90 percent of the working population who will need skill retraining and the sharpening of skills if they are to fill the emerging critical technological skills shortages or adapt to the current technological incursions into the fundamental processes of work in this country.

The less-than-comprehensive national training strategies are illustrated by the line of legislation beginning in the early 1960s with the Manpower Development and Training Act (MDTA), the Comprehensive Employment and Training Act (CETA), and, most recently, the Job Training and Partnership Act (JTPA). Although each of these programs has been and will be useful in providing entry-level skill training or income maintenance for some segments of the labor force, primarily those who are economically disadvantaged, the programs have little impact on the training needs of the majority of workers. For example, recent legislation, P.L. 97-300, the Job Training and Partnership Act, cites as eligible those economically disadvantaged youths sixteen to twenty-one and adults twenty-two and older. Ten percent of the funds may be used for participants who are not economically disadvantaged but who have "encountered barriers to employment," including individuals who have limited English-language proficiency, displaced homemakers, school dropouts, teenage parents, handicapped, older workers, veterans, offenders, alcoholics, and addicts. Monies for adult programs may be used for twenty-eight specific activities, including job search, counseling, remedial education, basic skills training, vocational exploration, and customized training. In addition to such services, exemplary programs may be provided to youth, which include education for employment programs, preemployment skills training programs, entry employment experience programs, and school-to-work assistance programs.

The problem that remains as a consequence of the Job Training and Partnership Act and similar legislation has at least two aspects: (1) the complexity, multidimensionality, and often intractability of the employment problems faced by the target groups and (2) the fact that the legislation does not cover the retraining needs of the majority of the labor force, on whose skills and productivity the renewal of the economic progress of the nation rests. In short, it does not deal in sufficient magnitude or comprehensiveness with displaced skilled workers or with workers still employed who need retraining ("Reagan Says Training Must Adapt," 1983).

Issues and Conclusions

As this chapter has illustrated, the United States is in the midst of a comprehensive transition in the types of work likely to be available in the future. Thus, the nature of employability and the content of training must undergo continual change if they are to remain relevant to the emerging occupational structure.

In large measure, employability is learned. The concept can be dismantled into its component parts of general and specific employability and training designed to facilitate the acquisition by youth and adults of the knowledge, attitudes, and skills that make up the various types of employability. In any case, training and employability are linked. Within such a context, several concerns are of interest.

First, although training and employability are clearly linked, the relation between employability and actual employment is more complex. Employment is a function of whether or not jobs are available to make use of the different levels and types of employability that the labor force possesses. If there is a structural mismatch between the skills that the occupational structure requires and those possessed by the labor force, structural, cyclical, and frictional unemployment result. In addition, if the skills required by emerging occupations change more rapidly than the labor force can gain such skills, there are also problems of unemployment and of reduced productivity and economic development.

One of the overriding issues inherent in the first concern is that a sufficiently comprehensive national training policy is not now available to avoid the types of structural mismatches described above. Therefore, the delivery of training that occurs is not well coordinated across public and private sectors, formal education and in-firm settings, preemployment and on-the-job training. These problems are also uneven in their effects across states and localities. A major factor exacerbating these problems is the lack of an information system adequate to the task of informing educators of changing skill and employability requirements and of providing persons choosing work initially or relocating within the work force with sufficiently fine-tuned information about needs and opportunities to permit individual planning to be as effective as it might be. The National Commission for Employment Policy (1981, p. 41) has argued for a labor market and training information system of national scope to aid in diagnosing occupational training problems and assessing programs. Among the factors to be considered in such a system would be projections of job openings, student course performances and enrollments, personnel and equipment commitments, and alternative suppliers of training (p. 46). Such a system would be intended to accurately anticipate structural changes in occupational demand and supply patterns and increase the coordination between institutional suppliers of training and markets for trained or trainable labor (p. 53). If such a system is to be established, planning, shared information, and mutual responsibility among governments, educators, employers, and unions need to reach higher levels of cooperation.

The second concern has to do with the diversity in employability training that is required by the characteristics of the labor force. The labor force, both youth and adult, comprises subpopulations that vary substantially in the development of employability. As described elsewhere in the chapter, a sizable proportion of the adult population is functionally illiterate; other groups have emotional, communication, or interpersonal problems that constrain their employability; still others require retraining in technical skills to replace those work performance skills that are now obsolete. Unless certain groups in the labor force are to be relegated to permanent unemployment and welfare, training for employability must include literacy and numeracy, general employability skills, and occupation-specific technical skills tailored to the requirements of an occupational structure that is itself in flux.

Regardless of which type of employability skill emphasis a particular group of workers needs, it seems clear that the training must be more closely tied to actual job experience in private firms or government agencies than has been the norm to date. A greater emphasis on cooperative education seems warranted. In addition, individuals have to be helped to be job-ready and sufficiently skilled so that their participation in employment is likely to involve permanent jobs and some type of career progression. The latter would imply that a national training policy needs to be coupled with macroeconomic policy designed to expand job creation and to assure continuous attention to worker retraining. Such a perspective seems critical if economic development and worker productivity are to be enhanced. In other words, for the majority of workers who are adequately or functionally literate, who do have general employability skills sufficient to the demands of work adjustment, and who have a positive work history, government policy needs to ensure that work will be available, as will retraining to take advantage of such work. This view recognizes that unemployment is not simply an individual problem. It is, rather, a national problem because each worker is part of a national resource of human capital, which must be invested in, nurtured, and modified in skill potential just as equipment and other capital expenditures are invested in and modified as necessary.

The ramifications of a national training policy such as that described here are enormous. There are needs for general employability skills and literacy to be met throughout the public school system and in other preemployment settings. The debate about whether all students should systematically be provided with initial occupational skills, and career awareness infused throughout their academic experience, needs to be extended. Ways to generate meaningful work experience for students in school need to be expanded. Training for critical skill shortages under the control of educational authorities and in cooperation with that which need such workers must be systematically developed throughout the nation. New efforts in school/industry cooperation and sharing of facilities, personnel, and information need to be developed.

It seems clear that, aside from the programmatic needs of the less job-ready and disadvantaged, the future will require more systematic and comprehensive counseling and approaches to training, employability, and employment for youth and adult workers at all levels of development.

Suggested Readings

Choate, P. *Retooling the American Work Force: Toward a National Training Strategy*. Washington, D.C.: Northeast-Midwest Institute, 1982.

A provocative review of the status of training strategies in the United States and the characteristics of the different subpopulations needing retraining. Recommends policies and strategies pertinent to retraining, counseling, and economic mechanisms.

Osterman, P. *Getting Started: The Youth Labor Market.* Cambridge, Mass.: MIT Press, 1980.

An interesting overview of different perspectives on the transition to work by youth. Discusses initial entry to work, how employers view young workers, and the characteristics of the youth labor market.

Pierson, F. C. *The Minimum Level of Unemployment and Public Policy.* Kalamazoo, Mich.: W. E. Upjohn Institute for Employment Research, 1980.

A comprehensive summary of the causes and forms of unemployment. Discusses historical and potential responses to unemployment and makes recommendations for public policy.

Silberman, H. F. (Ed.). *Education and Work.* Eighty-first yearbook of the National Society for the Study of Education. Chicago: University of Chicago Press, 1982.

An edited compilation of chapters by major authors discussing vocational education in various settings, research in manpower development, career development and vocational guidance, and related topics.

Wegmann, R. G. "Job-Search Assistance: A Review." *Journal of Employment Counseling,* 1979, *16*(4), 197–226.

A comprehensive summary of the characteristics of job finding as a learnable skill; describes major programs across the nation specifically designed to provide assistance in the job search.

References

Adams, A., and Mangum, G. *The Lingering Crisis of Youth Unemployment.* Kalamazoo, Mich.: W. E. Upjohn Institute for Employment Research, 1978.

Andrisani, P. "Internal-External Attitudes, Personal Initiative and the Labor Market Experience of Black and White Men." *Journal of Human Resources,* 1977, *12*, 309–328.

Ashley, W. L., and others. *Adaptation to Work: An Exploration of Processes and Outcomes.* Columbus: National Center for Research in Vocational Education, Ohio State University, 1980.

Cerianni, W. J. "Employment and Unemployment Statistics: How They Are Computed and What They Mean." Pittsburgh, Pa.: Regional Office, U.S. Bureau of Labor Statistics, 1982. Quoted in the Business Report, *Centre Daily Times,* January 30, 1983, p. G-4.

Choate, P. *Retooling the American Work Force: Toward a National Training Strategy.* Washington, D.C.: Northeast-Midwest Institute, 1982.

Crites, J. O. "A Comprehensive Model of Career Development in Early Adulthood." *Journal of Vocational Behavior,* 1976, *9,* 105-118.

Dunn, D. *Placement Services in the Vocational Rehabilitation Program.* Menomonie, Wis.: Research and Training Center, University of Wisconsin-Stout, 1974.

Eggeman, D. F., Campbell, R. F., and Garbin, A. P. *Problems in the Transition from School to Work as Perceived by Youth Opportunity Center Counselors.* Columbus: Center for Vocational and Technical Education, Ohio State University, 1969.

Evans, R. N., and Herr, E. L. *Foundations of Vocational Education.* (2nd ed.) Columbus, Ohio: Merrill, 1978.

Freedman, M. "Training and Motivation." In *A Review of Youth Employment Problems, Programs, and Policies.* Vol. 3. Washington, D.C.: Vice President's Task Force on Youth Employment, 1980.

Freedman, M., and Dutka, A. *Training Information for Policy Guidance.* U.S. Department of Labor, Employment, and Training Administration, R and D Monograph 76. Washington, D.C.: U.S. Government Printing Office, 1980.

Ginzberg, E. "The Mechanization of Work." *Scientific American,* 1982, *247*(3), 67-75.

Glover, R. W. "Apprenticeship Training and Vocational Education as Partners." In K. B. Greenwood (Ed.), *Contemporary Challenges for Vocational Education.* Washington, D.C.: American Vocational Association, 1981.

Haccoun, R. R., and Campbell, R. W. *Work Entry Problems of*

Youth: A Literature Review. Columbus: Center for Vocational and Technical Education, Ohio State University, 1972.

Herr, E. L. "Does Job Training Serve the Needs of People?" In K. B. Greenwood (Ed.), *Contemporary Challenges to Vocational Education.* Washington, D.C.: American Vocational Association, 1981.

Herr, E. L. "Career Development and Vocational Guidance." In H. F. Silberman (Ed.), *Education and Work.* Eighty-first yearbook of the National Society for the Study of Education. Pt. 2. Chicago: University of Chicago Press, 1982.

Herr, E. L., and Watts, A. G. "The Implications of Youth Unemployment for Career Education and for Counseling." *Journal of Career Education,* 1981, *7*(3), 184-202.

Hill, M. S., and Corcoran, M. "Unemployment Among Family Men: A Ten-Year Longitudinal Study." *Monthly Labor Review,* 1979, *102*(11), 19-23.

Iden, G. "The Labor Force Experience of Black Youth: A Review." *Monthly Labor Review,* 1980, *103*(8), 10-16.

Kazanas, H. C. *Affective Work Competencies for Research in Vocational Education.* Columbus: National Center for Research in Vocational Education, Ohio State University, 1978.

Knowles, M. "The Adult Learner Becomes Less Neglected." *Training,* 1977, *14*(9), 16-18.

Kroll, A. M. "Career Education and Impact on Employability and Unemployment: Expectations and Realities." *Vocational Guidance Quarterly,* 1976, *24*(3), 209-218.

Lichtman, R. "Jobs and Mental Health in a Social Context." *Center Magazine,* 1978, *11*(6), 7-17.

Miller, C. D., and Oetting, G. "Barriers to Employment and the Disadvantaged." *Personnel and Guidance Journal,* 1977, *56* (2), 89-93.

National Commission for Employment Policy. *Expanding Employment Policies for Disadvantaged Youth.* Report No. 9. Washington, D.C.: National Commission for Employment Policy, 1979.

National Commission for Employment Policy. *The Federal Role in Vocational Education.* Washington, D.C.: National Commission for Employment Policy, 1981.

Osterman, P. *Getting Started: The Youth Labor Market.* Cambridge, Mass.: MIT Press, 1980.

Pierson, F. C. *The Minimum Level of Unemployment and Public Policy.* Kalamazoo, Mich.: W. E. Upjohn Institute for Employment Research, 1980.

"Reagan Says Training Must Adapt to Changing Job Market." *Education and Work,* January 11, 1983, p. 2.

Riche, R. "Impact of New Electronic Technology." *Monthly Labor Review,* 1982, *105*(3), 37–39.

Rosenfeld, C., and Brown, S. C. "The Labor Force Status of Older Workers." *Monthly Labor Review,* 1979, *102*(11), 12–18.

Swanson, G. "Vocational Education Patterns in the United States." In H. F. Silberman (Ed.), *Education and Work.* Eighty-first yearbook of the National Society for the Study of Education. Pt. 2. Chicago: University of Chicago Press, 1982.

Thurow, L. C. "Technological Unemployment and Occupational Education." In T. Powers (Ed.), *Education for Careers: Policy Issues in a Time of Change.* University Park: Pennsylvania State University Press, 1977.

Toffler, A. *The Third Wave.* New York: Bantam Books, 1980.

Vandergoot, D. "Work Readiness Assessment." *Rehabilitation Counseling Bulletin,* 1982, *26*(2), 84–87.

Wegmann, R. G. "Job-Search Assistance: A Review." *Journal of Employment Counseling,* 1979, *16*(4), 197–226.

Westcott, D. N., and Bednarzik, R. W. "Employment and Unemployment: A Report on 1980." *Monthly Labor Review,* 1981, *104*(2), 4–14.

4   Linda S. Lotto

Partnership
Between Education
and Work

The partnership between education and work is a tenet of faith for most educators concerned with education for work. Expressions of this faith are manifest in legislation, by the private sector, and by the education community. For example, the Vocational Education Act of 1963, as amended in 1976 (P.L. 94-482), requires local advisory councils to be composed "especially of representatives of business, industry, and labor." Sections 121 and 122 of the same law permit the expenditure of federal dollars for work-study and cooperative vocational education programs. The recent Job Training and Partnership Act (P.L. 97-300) is even more explicit about the partnership between education and work. At the local level, training programs will be planned and delivered through Private Industry Councils (PICs), the majority of whose members must be owners of business concerns or other private-sector executives with managerial responsibilities.

Employers, too, are interested in working with educators to improve and extend education and training for work. The availability and quality of such education have become major considerations in relocation decisions. A recent survey by the National Association of Manufacturers (Nunez and Russell,

1982) indicates a clear desire for greater private-sector involvement in planning and even operating vocational education programs.

Across the broader education community there is concern for an education/work partnership. A task force created by
the Education Commission of the States to study the role of
education in economic growth called for an increased partnership between public schools and industry. As reported in the
Chronicle of Higher Education, "The task-force members centered on the notion that the educational system and business
and industry have to get together if the needs of education are
to be met" ("Federal Commitment to Excellence," 1983, p. 10).

Why this pervasive interest in school/work relationships?
Many benefits are thought to accrue from collaboration of
schools with the private sector in educating students for work.
These include benefits to individual students, to organizations
such as schools and firms, and to society as a whole.

Individual Benefits of Partnerships

In preparing for work, students need to develop what
have been called employability skills. These skills encompass
(1) knowledge of the world of work, (2) work values and attitudes, and (3) job-seeking, entry, and maintenance skills. They
build on students' proficiencies in basic literacy skills and prepare them for learning specific occupational skills. The development of all these skills is enhanced through matching skills
taught in the classroom with those used and desired in the
workplace. Through such collaborative activities as supervised
work experience programs, advisory council participation, and
equipment sharing, students learn real-life skills and knowledge
that enhance their employability.

Similarly, real-life experiences can motivate students to
increase performance in nonvocational areas. The challenges of
job tasks may spur students on to higher achievement in reading
or math. The incentive of a paycheck may stimulate appropriate
work values and attitudes and encourage potential dropouts to
complete high school. By increasing motivation through on-the-

job experience, by increasing the precision with which skills taught match skills needed in the workplace, and by providing a relevant and applied setting for learning, the partnership of education and work benefits individual students.

Organizational Benefits of Partnerships

Although benefits to individual students are considered preeminent, the benefits of school/work cooperation to the participating organizations cannot be ignored. Schools in particular have much to benefit. Useem's (1982) "want list" from the public schools in her study is indicative of the kind of benefits schools hope to attain: "Schools' interests ranged beyond traditional kinds of corporate involvement such as plant tours, guest speakers, and participation on vocational advisory boards. Several wanted curriculum advice, especially in computer-related areas, summer or sabbatical jobs for science and math teachers, loaned faculty members from industry, scholarships for math and science teacher trainees, gifts of equipment, work experience placement for students, and broad political support for teachers" (p. 28).

In general, schools hope to secure from the private sector scarce resources that the educational system is unable or unwilling to supply (for example, equipment, teacher training, political support). Other benefits are less concrete and fulfill a general legitimating function for the school (that is, certifying the program or curriculum as "in tune" with the workplace).

Business firms and industries also benefit from these partnerships. Unfortunately, the benefits that accrue to the private sector are all too few, often overlooked, and frequently available from other sources. In the first yearbook of the AVA, only three reasons are listed for industry to become involved with public education: (1) public service, (2) trusteeship or oversight of tax-dollar expenditures, and (3) the need to ensure access to a qualified work force (Burt, 1971, p. 282). Those reasons have been expanded recently as private-sector firms and labor unions increasingly benefit from the customized or contract training services provided them by public education agencies.

Societal Benefits of Partnerships

The benefits to society of education/work partnerships follow from the argument that such partnerships lead to vocational education and training programs relevant to labor force needs. Hence, the products of these preparation programs will readily and easily be absorbed into the labor force as productive citizens. Society benefits in at least two ways from education for work programs tied closely to current labor market needs: (1) decreased unemployment (that is, students are trained for existing jobs, skills, and conditions and hence are readily employable) and (2) increased productivity (that is, relevant training reduces on-the-job training and hence results in more productive workers).

As individuals grow and mature, they must make the often awkward transitions from childhood to adulthood. Part of that passage is the transition from education to work. If that transition is delayed, if education is not appropriate preparation for work, then society as a whole suffers. Gaps must be filled and deficiencies met—and society must provide the resources. The training and education that occur under the various Department of Labor youth programs (for example, Job Corps, various manpower training programs) are examples of social programs enacted to fill the gaps for certain individuals in their transition from education to work.

Additionally, society benefits when education for work and education in work settings enhance the educational achievements of students who might otherwise not succeed. "An educated citizenry" is an old saw but a meaningful one. Secretary of Education T. H. Bell's National Commission on Excellence in Education highlighted the need for increased educational benefits for all members of society: "Our concerns . . . go well beyond matters such as industry and commerce. [They also include] the intellectual, moral, and spiritual strengths of our people which knit together the very fabric of our society. The people of the United States need to know that individuals in our society who do not possess the levels of skill, literacy, and training essential to this new era will be affectively disenfranchised, not simply from the material rewards that accompany competent performance, but also from the chance to participate fully in our national life" (*A Nation at Risk*, 1983, p. 7). When educational agencies collaborate with the private sector to provide cooperative work experience and other learning in work programs, students are provided with real-life incentives for learning, as well as the chance to apply and extend classroom knowledge.

Finally society benefits from private-sector support for its public institutions. Material support in the form of equipment, scholarships, or loaned staff directly reduces the public tax burden. Other forms of support (for example, political, collegial, informational) serve a range of needs that are as critical as direct resource support, or more so. For example, private-sector support of public vocational education can result in increased public resource allocations to vocational education, greater commitment and support from existing constituencies, and a greater sense of community integration and cohesiveness.

A Partnership Sampler

However, despite the widespread rhetorical support for the partnership between education and work, and despite the perceived benefits to be reaped, the school/work partnership ideal has consistently failed to meet the expectations of its supporters. The notion of a vigorous and close interrelationship has just not matured beyond isolated, temporary instances. For example, Useem, in a study of school/industry relations in the high-technology area around Boston, found that "there are a few cases of mutually satisfying cooperative programs between the companies and other sectors of education but, for the most part, school/industry ties are fragmentary, weak, and of short duration" (1982, p. i). Nunez and Russell found that although manufacturers desired a closer relationship with vocational education, the most frequently used form of collaboration—providing work experience for vocational students —was practiced by only 21 percent of the respondents (1982, p. 4).

Although current school/work relationships may not epitomize the closeness and interdependency advocated by some, many partnership activities are now in operation. Instructional programs such as experience-based career education, work experience programs, CETA-like training programs, and planning and advisory groups such as the private industry councils, vocational education advisory committees, and craft committees, as well as numerous occasions of private-sector resource loans and personnel training and upgrading activities are all examples of functional partnerships. A partnership exists; but it seldom fits our image of what a partnership ought to be. It is the intent of this chapter to redress that gap by laying the basis for a more realistic set of expectations, expectations based on current examples of exemplary education/work partnerships and hoped-for benefits.

The range of partnership activities currently under way involving business, industry, labor organizations, and educational agencies is substantial and indicative of the existing capacity for cooperation and collaboration. This section is intended to provide the reader with a sense of those activities, not a survey of them. The sampler is illustrative, not exhaustive, in describing current partnership activities.

Curriculum Planning. One of the oldest and most durable forms of collaborative activity is that in which the educational agency seeks information from business, industry, and labor representatives relevant to curriculum planning. Most often the private-sector representatives are asked to provide (1) labor market information (that is, information about local labor markets and the demand for certain jobs to be filled) and (2) job-task information (that is, information about the tasks required to perform certain jobs). The rationale for this tie is, of course, that educators need to know what jobs and tasks are in demand and how that demand changes over time in order to adequately prepare students for employment.

The preeminent mechanism for obtaining this advice is the traditional advisory committee. Variations exist in the form of craft committees, private industry councils (for the old CETA and the new JTPA training programs), and college and university boards of trustees. These groups are usually permanent structures, and the membership is rotated over time as individuals fulfill their terms of membership. These advisory groups are adjuncts to the educational agency. They are established by the educational agency for its own goals, and the formal purposes describe a one-way flow of information to the school.

The perceived advantages of these types of partnership activities relate to the *currency* of the information obtained and its *relevance* to local labor markets. What is being sought is direct access to the content of jobs and occupations. The current diffusion of advanced technologies into many occupations has increased the press for updated job and job-task information. Vocational education must work with business, industry, and organized labor to keep curricula up to date and relevant to actual jobs and job tasks. The traditional advisory committee may not be a sufficient mechanism for carrying out this partnership function. Additionally, future-oriented research studies may be needed in which trends likely to affect education for work are identified. These, in turn, could be complemented by task analysis or other studies of current performance requirements of jobs.

World-of-Work Knowledge and Experiences. Another popular focus for partnership activities is program enrichment in the sense of providing students with exposure to firsthand knowledge of and experience with the world of work. These activities may be programmatic, as in work experience, cooperative work experience, and clinical or internship programs. Or they may be ad hoc, as in plant tours, classroom speakers, and career nights. Like curricular planning, these types of partnership activities are adjuncts to the educational program and hence are initiated by educators for educators. However, world-of-work activities directly benefit private-sector firms by providing them with (1) access to a pool of trained personnel, (2) a trial employment period after which they may, and frequently do, hire an individual already socialized and trained to their particular firm, and (3) a chance to substantially influence the training of students with regard to vocational skills and work attitudes.

Experiential world-of-work activities are somewhat more complicated to initiate and establish than curriculum planning activities because the costs are greater. Instead of a simple convening, ongoing costs for staff time and salaries are involved. For example, most cooperative work experience programs require a full-time coordinator not only to obtain the "slots" but to actively supervise the students on the job. Private-sector firms must also put up a considerable ante in the form of student wages and decreased productivity among supervisors and others who work with the students on the job on a daily basis. This level of investment requires multiple bureaucratic approvals and elicits more intense scrutiny than lower-cost activities. Ad hoc strategies for providing world-of-work knowledge (for example, speakers or plant tours) are simpler to establish and hence more plentiful. They are also more likely to be initiated informally by teachers, middle managers, and first-line supervisors rather than top management.

It is probably safe to say that, when and where used, world-of-work knowledge and experience activities are generally viewed quite positively. From the educators' point of view, the biggest problem is obtaining enough slots for students. If Nunez and Russell's survey of the National Association of Manufacturers (1982) is any indication, there is a considerable pool of untapped interest out there—roughly twice as many manufacturers reported interest in participating in work experience programs as actually did participate.

But there are drawbacks as well. For example, Steinberg and others (in press) found that part-time work has a small but significant negative impact on grade-point average, particularly for students who work long hours. Whether this finding is sustained for students participating in supervised work experience programs is uncertain. But even these generally popular programs have been faulted for providing primarily youth jobs, little real training, and even less interaction with appropriate adult role models. It seems there is a danger that employers can use these supervised programs as a source of cheap labor without providing much in the way of education and training.

Upgrading Instructional Staff. Education-for-work programs rely on the occupational experience and know-how of their faculty to provide accurate and relevant training. However, full-time teachers often teach about a workplace, an occupation, or a job that existed ten or fifteen years ago and is now radically different—perhaps even nonexistent. The problem of keeping occupational instructors occupationally up to date has been exacerbated by recent technological advances in the workplace. Not only do technological innovations require new job skills (for example, running a word processor instead of a typewriter), create new jobs (for example, robot maintenance and repair), and displace familiar jobs (for example, Linotype operator), but hardware innovations bring implications for the social and organizational systems required to implement them (Tornatsky, Hetzner, and Boylan, 1982). The strategies of bringing industry personnel into the school to teach and taking school faculty members back to the workplace for updating link education and work in an effort to maintain relevant instruction.

The benefits of these activities go beyond simply upgrading instruction. For the private-sector firms involved with personnel "loans" to educational agencies, a major benefit is real control of the curriculum and instruction provided to potential employees. The business or industry supplies only the instructor; actual training is usually done at the school site, with school equipment. Whereas on-the-job training is a business investment in current employees, loaning instructors to teach in occupational education classes can accomplish some on-the-job training objectives with potential employees; that is, the on-the-job training investment may decrease as preemployment training becomes more relevant to company requirements.

For the educational agency (usually a postsecondary-level community college, technical institute, or trade school), the benefits may also exceed curricular relevance. By employing private-sector personnel part-time, the school introduces a measure of flexibility into its instructional staff that traditional staffing patterns would not allow. The biggest hurdle to such flexibility is clearly teacher tenure. Unless a tenured faculty member voluntarily strives to keep up to date in his or her occupational area, few incentives or sanctions are available to the school administrator to stimulate retraining and upgrading. However, part-time faculty members from the private sector are marvelously flexible. They are not eligible for tenure, sometimes not even fringe benefits. And best of all, they are automatically kept up-to-date by their continuing employment in the private sector. However, employing private-sector personnel as part-time teachers maximizes occupational skill proficiencies at the expense of pedagogical skills. These part-time teachers have little knowledge of educational concepts and little commitment to the educational agency at which they are employed. The school administration may find itself in the position of managing an ever-changing pool of transients with little training, interest, or expertise in the core function of the organization—teaching.

Sending regular faculty members back to the private sector for summer or semester internships is another technique for upgrading instructional staff. It is used less frequently than private-sector personnel loans, probably because the initial costs are higher and the ultimate benefits less immediately obvious. Finding internship slots for teachers is analogous to finding work experience slots for students. The business firm is often asked to provide a temporary job for an individual who will require some amount of on-the-job training and then leave. A further complication is that the teacher is asked to take such a position at a salary that is either significantly lower or higher than that paid by the school. In the former case, the teacher will be reluctant to take a cut in wages. In the latter, the teacher will be reluctant to return to the classroom.

The stimulus for arranging these types of partnership activities is usually the school. Once again, this is largely a one-way exchange in which the schools gain relevance, knowledge, training, or even staff from the workplace. The initiating mechanism varies from individual teachers to schools, employers, chambers of commerce (Elliman, 1983), or state education agencies (Thomason, 1983).

Sharing Resources. This type of partnership covers a variety of joint ventures in which the fiscal or material resources of one partner are used for the purposes of the other. This category includes scholarships, equipment loans or gifts, and use of facilities. Useem (1982) cites the following examples in the Boston area:

- Digital Equipment Corporation has donated over $500,000 worth of equipment to the Hubert Humphrey Occupational Resource Center in Boston and has loaned a person to put in substantial amounts of time on curriculum development there (p. 31).
- Wang Labs donated new computer equipment to each of Massachusetts' public institutions of higher education, a gift worth over $3 million (p. 40).
- The Massachusetts Institute of Technology (MIT) has an active Industrial Liaison Program, with over 270 members (generating close to $6 million in revenue annually to MIT), which provides firms with access to MIT's research and staff resources.

Although partnership activities subsumed under this category are often ad hoc, there are some interesting commonalities by educational level. According to Useem (who looked at educational links to high-tech firms in California's Silicon Valley and the Boston Route 128 area), private-sector largesse varies by educational level, the major research universities receiving the most and the public secondary schools receiving very little, if anything. The reason for this almost single-minded focus on higher education is that high-technology firms (and likely others as well) feel they have more to gain from contributing to universities. Not only do they strengthen engineering and other relevant graduate programs, but they stand to benefit from the research carried out at the university.

Sharing resources is a form of partnership in which partners contribute for the benefit of both. By and large these partnerships involve businesses contributing equipment or facilities and schools providing appropriately trained personnel. The problem with these arrangements is that the schools realize immediate benefits, while not only must the private-sector partners wait to realize long-range benefits (in the form of trained personnel), but those benefits are often loosely tied to the shared or donated resources.

Contract Training and Other Joint Ventures. Contract training is a form of partnership in which the educational agency works for the private sector, either a single firm or a group of firms. This category includes in-service training for employees, apprenticeship training for unions, special programs conducted for Private Industry Councils under CETA or JTPA sponsorship, and training as part of state or local economic development efforts. Typical of this category are the following (all from Warmbrod, Persavich, and L'Angelle, 1981).

• *Alabama Technical College's Competency-Based Apprenticeship Training Program.* The college and a local steel corporation are jointly training apprentices in industrial electronics. The program was developed jointly by the college and industry in cooperation with the Bureau of Apprenticeship and Training, U.S. Department of Labor. Coordinators from both education and industry cooperate in identifying instructional content, developing performance-based student activities, and managing and supervising student attendance and progress. Testing, interviewing, and selecting for the program are competitive and follow company, government, and labor union guidelines.

• *Cuyahoga Community College's Machine Tools Training Program for Youth.* This national demonstration project provides twelve weeks of comprehensive training for youths in basic education, personal development, principles of basic machining, and job-search skills. The student is then placed with individual employers for on-the-job training. Program funding, operation, and administration involve major government, school, and industry organizations such as CETA, the Cleveland Machine Trades Association, Cleveland Public Schools, the International Association of Machinists, the United Labor Agency, and Cleveland employers.

• *Miles Community College's Power Plant Technology Program.* At the request of the power company, Miles Community College developed an associate degree program to provide entry-level skills in the field of coal-fired electricity generation. The project is approved by the electrical workers' union and counts toward apprenticeship time.

• *Calhoun Community College's Center for Industrial Development.* A unit of the technical college, the Center for Industrial Development develops customized curricula at the request of business and industry to meet specific technical or managerial training needs. The center was established after extensive discussion with the industrial and business community on ways in which the college could better serve local needs. Specific programs are developed following a request from a business or industry. The center prepares a customized curriculum for the client and submits it for approval. On approval, the center schedules the course and selects and hires the instructors.

• *Ohio State University's Technology Transfer Organization.* The goal of the Ohio Technology Transfer Organization (OTTO) is to establish a network of community and technical colleges working in cooperation with the Ohio State University to provide technical assistance, information, and training to Ohio's small businesses relative to the use of advanced technologies. The project has at its disposal computerized data banks, contacts with the Federal Laboratory Consortium, and technical support for the university and for government agencies such as the Small Business Administration and the National Aeronautics and Space Administration.

What distinguishes this category of partnership activities from the others is (1) the specificity of purpose and (2) the immediate beneficiary. Although the activities just noted are diverse, they are characteristically narrow in focus and explicit about purpose. For example, whereas the local advisory council functions *generally* to provide advice for curriculum planning, contract training and other joint ventures are responses to *specific* training needs of business, industry, and labor unions. And while advisory councils immediately benefit the school, contract training ventures benefit primarily the private sector. Contract training and other joint ventures are not part of the regular educational program of the agencies involved. Instead they are separate and distinct programs, courses, subunits, or activities.

The fact that a community college may run the training program for a local union does not necessarily affect the other occupational courses offered there.

Contract training provides an intense but constrained kind of partnership. The outcomes vary from a single course to an ongoing degree program; the participants may be limited to a single firm and a single college but often include multiple businesses, government agencies, and even other educational agencies. Contract training and other joint ventures are primarily a function of community colleges, technical institutes, and universities. Secondary schools are rarely involved.

Assessing Partnerships: The Tie That Doesn't Necessarily Bind

As is evident from the foregoing examples, the partnership between education and work takes many forms. Therefore, thinking about improving that partnership *in toto* requires recognition that the partnership of rhetoric is not the partnership of practice. Spokespersons advocating closer ties between education and work are in fact describing an aggregate concept manifest in many forms in practice. The partnership to be strived for is not a single ideal but a relationship that varies with the agents and agencies involved and with the relevant issues and is mutually satisfactory.

Our understanding of the education/work partnership— creating, sustaining, or imagining partnerships—can be enriched by examining the experiences of other interagency "partnerships." The school improvement area is particularly useful in this regard because the partnership between knowledge-producing (research) and knowledge-using (practitioner) agencies has a nearly fifteen-year history of program experience (for example, the Research and Development Exchange, the Research and Development Utilization programs), research (for example, Berman and McLaughlin, 1978), and theory-building (for example, Fullan, 1982).

Lessons from the school improvement literature can extend our understanding of school/work partnerships *conceptually*

by comparing analogue conceptualizations of knowledge-pro-
ducing/knowledge-using partnerships with the education and
work arena and *technically* by comparing program experiences
in that area with education/private-sector partnership activities.

   Conceptualizing Partnerships. Early efforts to conceptualize interagency linkages affecting school improvement were
functionally oriented. Once a group of functions believed to be
necessary for school improvement (for example, research, development, dissemination, adoption) was incrementally recognized, the next step was to link those functions sequentially.

> If the functions were necessary and linear
> they could be linked, thereby forming:
> - a system of agencies and agents,
> - with assigned functions and responsibilities . . . ,
> - sharing goals,
> - and directed to productive output which would
>   result in improvement-oriented change in
>   schools [Clark and Guba, 1974, p. 24].

It is not difficult to transpose that picture to the partnership
between education and work. Leaving aside the issue of a system, it is easy to imagine the partnership between education
and work as consisting of—

- Assigned functions and responsibilities (for example, the
  schools do the training in accordance with private-sector
  needs and conditions).
- Shared goals (for example, a productive and skilled work
  force).
- Improvement-oriented outcomes (for example, more efficient training and transition from school to work).

   The problem with this "systems model" for school improvement was that, despite its logical appeal, it was a poor
match for the way things worked in the real world. In comparison, the conventional model of education/work partnerships
may suffer from a similar problem. Most people assume that a
partnership relationship can be characterized similarly to a "sys-

tem"—that is, shared goals, interdependent functions, mutual responsiveness, and common interests in a shared output. "These two almost completely separate organizational systems need to integrate their resources—personnel, facilities, equipment, and materials—in an organized and systematic manner, with knowledgeable leadership, to produce the desired results" (Clark and Rinehart, 1982, p. 2). In practice, however, these ideals are rarely achieved. Instead a sort of centripetal force seems to continually fragment efforts at linkage and collaboration. One explanation for this phenomenon is the varied and variable couplings existing in the organizational contexts of education and work agencies.

Our expectations are for consistently tight couplings. According to Weick (1982), instances of tight coupling share the following: (1) rules, (2) agreement on rules, (3) a system to inspect for compliance, and (4) feedback designed to improve compliance. "In systems that are more loosely coupled, at least one of these four characteristics is missing. Typically the missing component is either consensus on policies and procedures or inspection that occurs frequently enough that significant deviations can be detected" (p. 674). At least one of Weick's four characteristics is missing from many education/work partnerships. Advisory committees make agreements about the procedures and rules for meeting and the topics to be discussed, yet no system works to monitor school compliance with advisory committee advice. Conversely, no system works to provide feedback to advisory committee members about the efficacy of their advice. Advisory committees are partnerships that are loosely coupled.

Partnerships in a loosely coupled world cannot, by definition, meet our expectations for tight coupling. Schools, as Weick (1976), Cohen, March, and Olsen (1972), and others have pointed out, are organizations operating with unclear, ambiguous, and sometimes conflicting goals. The instances in which these organizations will be able to agree to a set of rules and purposes for working with private-sector organizations will tend to be those instances in which the purpose is either very general (for example, advisory councils) or very specific (for example, contract training). In the former instance, disagreements are avoided by setting sufficiently abstract goals that disagreement is difficult. In the latter instance, specific activities are simply enacted by interested and agreeable subsets of individuals.

In the sense of an enduring partnership applicable generally to education and work agencies, shared goals and a reliable division of labor are unlikely. Most private-sector firms are concerned mainly with maintaining a profitable operation. Recruitment, training, and retraining become central occasionally, during periods of expansion, relocation, or shutdown. But in general, training, especially of *potential* employees, is not a central concern for private-sector firms. Schools, in contrast, are concerned primarily with training. Work, student performance on the job, and student placement in jobs are critical only insofar as they affect aspects of the training program—curriculum, recruitment, instruction, equipment. Although it is true that schools tend to provide the instruction while private-sector firms focus on providing (or stimulating) the curriculum, there is considerable latitude in carrying out those roles.

Couplings are not uniformly tight, and hence the uniformity, consistency, and reliability that the term *partnership* connotes are seldom realized in any single activity. The impact of variable coupling on education/work partnerships is to create a range of different partnership activities. No single activity is sufficient to constitute a total partnership, but each is a manifestation of that relationship.

Strategies for Operating Partnerships. Turning from the conceptual to the technical aspects of partnerships, what can be learned about sustaining and creating partnership relationships between education and work organizations from the programmatic experience of school improvement efforts? First, the literature of school improvement suggests that synthetic, or created, relationships are rarely sustained after external funds are withdrawn (Louis and Rosenblum, 1981). When the project funds that supported joint activities dry up, so does the impetus for carrying out the joint activities. Partnerships can be created and sustained as long as policy planners are willing to force-feed them. Clearly a better strategy is to build on and enhance naturally occurring links.

Second, the school improvement literature and the experience of related programs point to interpersonal rather than interagency relationships as key in building partnership activities (Crandall and others, 1982). The interagency partnerships for school improvement originally envisioned by the designers of such programs as the State Capacity Building Project proved to be exceedingly fragile, and, in fact, not the most efficient strategy for linking researchers and practitioners. Instead, the behaviors and attitudes of individuals—principals, teachers, researchers, and linking agents—proved to be critical in stimulating and facilitating school improvement.

In assessing partnerships between school and work agencies, perhaps our expectations have been overly narrow and insufficiently flexible. By looking only for partnerships that are tightly coupled and applicable across a variety of organizational functions, we tend to dismiss those partnerships that are ad hoc, transient, or encapsulated within certain levels or subunits as weak, ineffective, or not enough. Similarly, by holding only a single image of what partnership ought to be, we are blinded to the diversity of partnerships that emerge when we begin to expand our view. By concentrating on interagency relationships manifest by links at the top-management level, we omit many interpersonal links that exist at the individual and subunit levels.

Some Cautionary Notes

So far establishing partnership activities has been treated here as an unequivocally good idea to be cultivated in diverse forms for a variety of purposes. However, from the educator's perspective, the decision to solicit private-sector involvement ought to be made with a clear sense of purpose and an awareness that these kinds of relationships have drawbacks and potentially negative consequences. Consider, for example, the fact that private-sector organizations, like schools, vary in quality, philosophy, and productivity. "Would you be comfortable if you found out that among the companies from which you were seeking advice and counsel, some had routine cost overruns in the millions of dollars on government contracts? . . . It is necessary to examine carefully a company's record, its philosophy, and its management before seeking its involvement" (Pratzner, 1983, p. 2). Moreover, educators seeking internship slots (cooperative work experience) need to have confidence that those slots entail work experiences that are complementary to classroom learning experiences, that appropriate role models and supervision exist, and that organizational management and operations reflect the concepts being taught in the classroom. Similarly, schools seeking equipment loans in order to provide more relevant training may find that donated equipment is provided simply because it is outdated at the workplace.

Beyond simple mismatches of purpose and utility, there are important legal and ethical issues. As public institutions, schools have a clear responsibility to provide equitable opportunities for all students and to strive for the common good. Are those responsibilities abrogated when schools accept corporate funds to meet specific corporate needs? Is there a limit, legal or otherwise, to the school's role in providing firm-specific training?

Yes, if the relationship jeopardizes the school's ability to provide equitable access to quality training programs. Yes, if the selection criteria for the program are especially stringent or if a course is "closed" in any way (for example, open only to employees of a given firm, to individuals who have participated in particular apprenticeship programs, or to members of a certain union). Certain equipment may be available to schools only for the training of employees. Employers in general are unwilling to invest in their competitors' success. Thus, customized or contract training ventures, loans of sophisticated or specialized equipment, and perhaps even access to highly skilled teachers may be contingent on limited access to the training by students.

Another dilemma facing schools wishing to become closely involved with the private sector is the need to maintain an emphasis on *individual educational development* in the face of the private sector's emphasis on corporate, firm, or union success through the *development of a trained labor pool*. Put another way, the school's interest is in placing individuals in jobs or developing employment skills. The firm's interest is in a pool of ready talent that can be drawn on as needed. Additionally, schools are committed to the educational as well as the occupational development of their students. A firm's interest in a potential employee is limited to that individual's performance as an employee. The school must be concerned with a student's total cognitive, social, and personal development.

These issues point up the importance of careful forethought and the development of a clear sense of purpose before jumping on the partnership bandwagon. Partnerships are viable and useful as long as the integrity of each partner remains and there is a common expectation that partnerships will only rarely reflect central organizational interests. The lure of the private sector is a powerful one for many occupational educators but a lure that ought not be taken heedlessly.

Suggestions for Practice

There is, then, no single recipe for education/work partnerships. One element of an effective partnership is simply knowing when to "go it alone." The often-frustrating loose coupling of educational organizations may have the saving grace of effectively preventing the development of overly close ties to other agents and agencies. The following suggestions are directed to educators at *all levels* who need or want to work with the private sector. They are suggestions for occupational strategies to maximize satisfaction and minimize frustration.

1. *Match expected or intended outcomes to the activity.* Not all activities yield the same outcomes. Having a firm representative sit on an advisory council is no guarantee of a subsequent equipment donation. Conversely, merely sitting on a school's advisory council does not guarantee that the curriculum will become specific to a particular employer. Loosely coupled, symbolic activities like advisory councils tend to be good bases for building relationships and generating support and commitment. Tightly coupled, operational activities like contract training provide for short-term, intense relationships.

2. *Remember the quid pro quo.* The basis of all partnerships is that each partner benefits. Industry is under no obligation to subsidize the schools, and the schools have no obligation

to provide firm-specific training. But each partner has legitimate interests that are the basis for the partnership. Those interests must be attended to if the activity is to succeed.

3. *Treat the partnership as generic.* The partnership between education and work is not manifest in the extent of a single school/firm relationship or activity. By focusing on a single relationship or type of activity, one increases the chances for failure and limits the opportunities for working together on a variety of activities.

Summary

The partnership between education and work is both much more and much less than commonly believed. On the one hand, there are a great variety of partnership activities currently in operation, and that number is sure to grow. Both schools and private sectors are benefiting from shared resources, expertise, and capacities. On the other hand, the partnership is clearly not central to either partner, nor ought it to become so. In fact, schools and workplace organizations are very different and reflect different organizational contexts and cultures. The partnership is viable and satisfactory as long as we remember that it is no panacea. The best that can be hoped for or attained is a partnership consisting of many diverse, ad hoc, and short-lived activities, a modicum of symbolic and political support, and a dollop of enduring tension. That is probably a pretty good mixture.

Suggested Readings

1. Developing Partnerships

Elsman, M. *Industry-Education-Labor-Collaboration: An Action Guide for Collaborative Councils.* Washington, D.C.: National Institute for Work and Learning, 1981.

A guide for developing and effectively using local collaborative councils. Material includes purposes, funding, and evaluation as well as sample profiles and a resource guide.

Journal of Career Education, 1983, *9*(4).

A special issue on business/education collaboration designed for educators, business representatives, and other community leaders concerned with the development of comprehensive career education programs.

Topougis, N. J. *Labor and Career Education: Ideas for Action.* Washington, D.C.: Office of Education, U.S. Department of Health, Education and Welfare, 1979.

This handbook provides a sample of specific activities for involving labor in the educational process. The material presented runs the gamut from teacher training to sample lesson plans to an annotated bibliography.

2. *Research and Policy*

Ripley, R. B., and Franklin, G. B. "The Private Sector in Public Employment and Training Programs." *Policy Studies Review,* 1983, *2*(4), 695-714.

In this article Ripley and Franklin provide an overview of public and private employment and training efforts and review private-sector performance. They conclude with suggestions for policy and practice.

Work-Education Councils: The Collaborative Approach. Youth Knowledge Development Report 12.5. Washington, D.C.: Employment and Training Administration, U.S. Department of Labor, 1980.

Work-education councils, conceived by Willard Weitz, were funded in conjunction with the Youth Employment and Demonstration Projects of 1977 as a unique and efficient technique for linking local institutions involved in the broad problems of the transition from education to work. The volume contains the first report of an NIE-funded evaluation and a series of case studies, as well as relevant background papers.

3. Organizational Theory and Analysis

Georgiou, P. "The Goal Paradigm and Notes Toward a Counterparadigm." *Administrative Science Quarterly,* 1973, *18,* 291–
   310.
   Organization theorists have faced many difficulties in
conceptualizing organizational goals and understanding organizational behavior through them. Georgiou suggests that Bar-
nard's incentive-system analysis provides the foundations for a
counterparadigm. Such a perspective can contribute to our
understandings and explanations of education/work partnerships.

Weick, K. E. "Educational Organizations as Loosely Coupled
   Systems." *Administrative Science Quarterly,* 1976, *21,* 1–19.
   Weick proposes that, in contrast to the prevailing image
of organizations coupled through dense, tight linkages, elements
are more often tied together loosely. In this article the concept
of coupling is described and related to organizational behavior.

References

A Nation at Risk: The Imperative for Educational Reform.
   Stock No. 065-000-00177-2. Washington, D.C.: U.S. Govern-
   ment Printing Office, 1983.
Berman, P., and McLaughlin, M. W. *Federal Programs Support-
   ing Educational Change.* Vol. 8: *Implementing and Sustain-
   ing Innovations.* R-1589/8-HEW. Santa Monica, Calif.: Rand
   Corp., 1978.
Burt, S. M. "Involving Industry and Business in Education." In
   G. Law (Ed.), *Contemporary Concepts in Vocational Educa-
   tion.* Washington, D.C.: American Vocational Association,
   1971.
Clark, D. L., and Guba, E. G. *The Configurational Perspective:
   A View of Knowledge Production and Utilization.* Washington, D.C.: Council for Educational Development and Re-
   search, 1974.
Clark, D. M., and Rinehart, R. L. *Structures and Strategies for*

Linking the Higher Education and Employment Communities. Washington, D.C.: American Council on Education, 1982.

Cohen, M. D., March, J. G., and Olsen, J. P. "A Garbage Can Model of Organizational Choice." *Administrative Science Quarterly,* 1972, *17,* 1–25.

Crandall, D. P., and others. "Models of the School Improvement Process: Factors Contributing to Success." Paper presented at annual meeting of the American Educational Research Association, New York City, March 1982.

Elliman, P. J. "Employers Sponsor Technical Scholars." *VocEd,* May 1983, pp. 39–40.

"Federal Commitment to Excellence in Education Urged by Panel." *Chronicle of Higher Education,* May 11, 1983, pp. 5, 10.

Fullan, M. *The Meaning of Educational Change.* New York: Teachers College Press, 1982.

Louis, K. S., and Rosenblum, S. *Linking R&D with Schools: A Program and Its Implications for Dissemination and School Improvement Policy.* Washington, D.C.: National Institute of Education, U.S. Department of Education, 1981.

Nunez, A. R., and Russell, J. F. *As Others See Vocational Education: A Survey of the National Association of Manufacturers.* Research and Development Series, No. 225A. Columbus: National Center for Research in Vocational Education, Ohio State University, 1982.

Pratzner, F. C. "The Business-Industry-Education Bandwagon: A Skeptical View." Unpublished manuscript, National Center for Research in Vocational Education, Ohio State University, 1983.

Steinberg, L. D., and others. "High School Students in the Labor Force: Some Costs and Benefits to Schooling and Learning." *Educational Evaluation and Policy Analysis,* in press.

Thomason, A. J. "Teacher-Interns Update Skills." *VocEd,* May 1983, pp. 43–44.

Tornatsky, L. G., Hetzner, W. A., and Boylan, M. G. "Industrial Innovation Processes: Implications for Public Policy." Paper presented at meeting of the American Association for the Advancement of Science, Washington, D.C., 1982.

Useem, E. *Education and High Technology Industry: The Case
of Silicon Valley.* Boston: Institute for the Interdisciplinary
Study of Education, Northeastern University, 1981.

Useem, E. *Education in a High Technology World: The Case of
Route 128.* Boston: Institute for the Interdisciplinary Study
of Education, Northeastern University, 1982.

Warmbrod, C. P., Persavich, J. J., and L'Angelle, D. *Sharing Resources: Postsecondary Education and Industry Cooperation.*
Research and Development Series, No. 203. Columbus: National Center for Research in Vocational Education, Ohio
State University, 1981.

Weick, K. E. "Educational Organizations as Loosely Coupled
Systems." *Administrative Science Quarterly,* 1976, *21,* 1-19.

Weick, K. E. "Administering Education in Loosely Coupled
Schools." *Phi Delta Kappan,* 1982, *63*(10), 673-676.

Part Two

Knowledge Base
of Career Development

During the past ten years, knowledge about career development has increased dramatically. Increased theory building has expanded and extended the meaning and focus of career development. Expanded research efforts have helped consolidate and unify what is known about career development. To keep abreast of theory and research in this fast-moving discipline, professionals need a state-of-the-art update. This is the purpose of Part Two.

In Chapter Five, David A. Jepsen investigates the relationship between career development theory and practice. He does so in two ways. First, he discusses how theory can be translated into practice by examining formal theories of career development. He gives particular emphasis to barriers that prevent the application of theory to practice. Second, Jepsen reverses the focus and shows how career behavior can be translated into theoretical concepts that, in turn, are useful in career counseling.

Henry Borow, in Chapter Six, provides an in-depth review and analysis of the occupational socialization of young people—how they acquire a sense of work. He begins by considering what he calls "the principal agents" of the work socialization process; namely, family, school, peers, work experience, and the media. Next, he discusses the growing-up process and the development of such career-related behaviors as impulse control, becoming responsibly independent, a sense of destiny control, and achievement motivation. He follows with an explanation of how young people learn occupational roles. Borow concludes the chapter by reviewing some discontinuities in the transition from school to work.

Adult career development from an organizational perspective is the focus of Chapter Seven. Stephen A. Stumpf examines both individual and organizational factors that affect adult career development in business settings. His discussion of such individual factors as personality, interests, social class, and values focuses on how they shape adult career development. His discussion of organizational factors highlights how organizations provide the context, structure, and procedures through which adult career development unfolds. Stumpf also cites specific organizational programs and processes designed to influence adult career development.

The interrelationship between gender and career is the topic of Chapter Eight by L. Sunny Sundal-Hansen. Sundal-Hansen first analyzes the sex-role system that affects career development, then extensively reviews the literature on the career development of women and men. She offers additional insight into the interrelationship of gender and career by comparing the sexual division of labor across cultures. She describes new goals and practices for career guidance and counseling and concludes the chapter by stating, "If career guidance and counseling specialists become conscious of the past sex-role system and its central impact on the career development of women and men and can envision male/female synergy or the sex-role transcendence of the future, then they will commit themselves to developing gender-free career counseling strategies and programs."

A new genre of assessment instruments generally classified as measures of career development or career maturity has been evolving during the past ten years. John O. Crites, in Chapter Nine, examines several of the prominent examples of these instruments using a standard outline. Conclusions about the psychometric adequacy of the instruments are presented, as is commentary about their use in career guidance and counseling.

Chapter Ten by René V. Dawis considers what theory

and research have to say about job satisfaction, worker aspirations, and work attitudes and how these affect, and are affected by, worker behavior. He begins by surveying what the research literature has to say on these topics and follows with a review of theories of job satisfaction. He then describes such correlates of job satisfaction as self-esteem, job involvement, and organizational commitment, as well as positive and negative consequences of job satisfaction. Dawis concludes by drawing some implications that job satisfaction theory and research have for career guidance and counseling.

5

David A. Jepsen

Relationship Between Career Development Theory and Practice

An anecdote is told about a well-known professor who taught a course on career development theory to students preparing to become practicing counselors. The professor, a gifted scholar, had authored several theoretical papers about career development, so the classes were well attended. After the professor delivered each lecture, however, a teaching assistant would meet with the same class in order to clarify the lecture content. The assistant would relay students' questions and comments to the professor. This anecdote illustrates the problems in communication between those who construct career development theory and those who conduct the everyday practice of career guidance. A particular problem, identified by observers of theory and practice (for example, Borow, 1982; Osipow, 1983), is an inadequate translation of theory into the explicit terms useful to practicing counselors.

The purpose of this chapter is to examine the relationship between career development theory and career guidance practice. Application of theory to practice will be treated as a problem in *translation*, as illustrated by the opening anecdote. Two forms of translation will be discussed: (1) theoretical ideas into practical actions and (2) everyday career behavior into theoretical concept systems. The contribution of formal career development theories (such as those summarized by Osipow, 1983) to career guidance practice will be analyzed with particular emphasis on revealing barriers preventing application of theoretical ideas. The discussion of the second translation problem is an attempt to show how career behaviors typically observed in career guidance practice can be translated into theoretical concept systems useful as cognitive tools for counselors.

Before speaking to those problems, I will discuss the major concepts and their particular meanings. I will invoke the convention of using the term *career* to cover human behavior involving work roles and activities. This is not completely satisfying, because *career* often implies roles other than work alone (Super, 1980). The term *career guidance* refers to a broad range of activities purposely undertaken to help people improve the quality of their work life. *Career counseling* is an important subset of these activities, but presumably all activities are organized and planned by practicing counselors.

Translating Theory into Practice

The work of practicing career counselors is, if nothing else, that of real-world problem solving. Counselors are faced with people seeking jobs, searching for a sense of identity and direction, and desiring satisfactions from work and harmony among career roles. In the broadest sense, these people must deal with real-life problems—that is, barriers to personally valued and desired career experiences—and they look to counselors for help. Although counselors perform many tasks, two stand out as generalizable to most career guidance practices (Crites, 1981). The first is *problem identification,* the process of describing and interpreting the clients' problems as the basis for collaborative goal setting. This process is also called "diagnosis" or "needs assessment." The second task is *intervention design,* the process of designing or adapting interventions to reach the clients' goals. This task is sometimes referred to as "treatment selection" or "programming."

These two career guidance tasks, undertaken as planning

for practical action, require deliberate thinking involving ideas about the structure and dynamics of career behavior. Problem identification involves making formal and informal assessments of client status. This requires instrument selection (or development), such as choosing among inventories, questionnaires, or interviewing strategies. The very existence of assessment instruments presupposes some state of theory about the behaviors observed, the logical connections between them, and their sequence (Katz, 1979). In other words, the activity of problem identification is based on explicit or implicit theory about the client's career development.

Intervention design, too, involves planning based on theoretical ideas. For example, Vondracek, Lerner, and Schulenberg (1983) suggested that specific developmental theories are likely to dictate the precise nature of the intervention processes selected, the timing and duration of the intervention, and the evaluation criteria applied to the entire process. Apparently most interventions are designed with explicit or implicit ideas about what conditions influence what behaviors for what kind of people.

Formal career development theory has elicited a variety of reactions from practicing counselors. Two opposite reactions should give a feel for these differences. On the one hand, theory has been embraced by some practitioners who perceive a close tie between a particular theory and their practice. These counselors routinely use the ideas and instruments advocated by a particular theoretical school. They see theory as essential to providing organized and purposeful counseling services. On the other hand, formal theory is eschewed by some practicing counselors; it has no place in their day-to-day activities. They see theory as irrelevant because it does not speak to the essential, idiosyncratic experience of individual clients. Although each of these positions could be elaborated, the point is that both have attractive and unattractive qualities. Hence, it seems likely that many practitioners feel the conflict epitomized by the pull of these two positions.

The work of theorists, in contrast to practitioners, addresses problems involving abstract ideas about real-life phenomena. The theorist's objective is to move beyond observation and description of particulars toward complex explanations such as cause/effect relations. A formal theoretical statement is constructed to clarify and order the theorist's ideas. It usually includes concepts and propositions that are systematized so they can be subjected to certain manipulations such as projections, extensions, and interpretations. The manipulations most important to improving theory are those conducted in behavioral research. Other manipulations occur when practitioners apply theory to organizing and planning their activities. Indeed, Kerlinger (1977) suggested that the most important source of influence on practice is theory.

Theory influences practice at two levels. First, theories or perhaps families of theories help practitioners to distinguish a general perspective, or "world view," about career behavior. Second, specific theoretical statements are invoked by practitioners when setting policy, organizing services, and performing tasks such as problem identification and intervention design.

Perspectives on Career Behavior. Career development theories influence career guidance practice at the broadest level by suggesting general perspectives on career behavior. Theorists are not a monolithic group; they come from various academic backgrounds and construct theories based on substantially different assumptions. One apparent difference is between theories called *structural* and those called *developmental.*

Nearly all career theorists and career guidance practitioners seem to endorse some variation of a developmental perspective on careers. It is nearly a truism to say that "career choice is a developmental process" or "career adjustment is developmental." No one has seriously challenged these points since they were first popularized in the 1950s. The major distinction among career theorists, then, is largely between those who emphasize the structure of personality characteristics (interests, abilities, and other personality traits) resulting from early developmental processes and those who emphasize the processes themselves as they unfold across the life span (for example, conceptualization of self as worker, the capacity to work). Theorists in the latter group focus on the stages and the transitions that describe orderly behavioral changes. Thus, two fundamentally different perspectives, called the *structural* and the *developmental*, can be distinguished.

Theories written from the structural perspective attempt to describe individual differences on selected personality characteristics and relate them to differences among job demands. Among contemporary vocational psychologists, examples include the work of John Holland (Holland, 1973) and the Minnesota theory of work adjustment (Dawis, Lofquist, and Weiss, 1968).

The developmental perspective, in contrast, focuses on intraindividual differences across the life span and how people "grow up into" their work. The dimension along which differences are highlighted is that of time rather than persons. *Development* is generally considered to refer to at least two kinds of qualitative changes: (1) changes in the processes of choosing, entering, and progressing in work roles (for example, Super, 1980) and (2) changes in the ability to cope with the generalized worker role expectations (for example, Neff, 1977).

The developmental perspective includes distinguishable views about behavioral change over time. A particular view of developmental processes, sometimes identified by the metaphor of the growing organism, seems to have guided developmental theory and research in the 1950s and 1960s. This view is generally based on the assumptions that (1) the person is an active agent, (2) development is an internal, self-constructive process, and (3) the succession of changes is discontinuous (Jepsen, 1984). A career theory that presents a contrasting view to these assumptions is the social learning theory of career decision making (Krumboltz, 1979). The attention given by this theory to environmental events and learning histories assumes that changes in career behavior are a function of person/environment interactions. The succession of changes has no apparent upheavals, nor does the behavior change in structure. Thus, within the developmental perspective there exist several distinctly different views about the source and progression of developmental changes.

Evaluation of Current Theories. What is the value of formal career development theory for career guidance policy, organization, and tasks? Specific answers would require careful examination of several theories. Instead we will rely on conclusions from those who have studied theories. For example, Borow (1982) concluded that "the net yield of thirty years of theory making has been somewhat disappointing. Much of the explanation would appear to reside in the flawed quality and dubious relevance of much of theory" (p. 29). Borow identified the problems of existing theories as falling into three categories: problems of scope limitations, methodological problems, and problems of practical applications in counseling. These criticisms are strikingly similar to those offered by Crites (1969) about thirteen years earlier. They seem to summarize frequent criticisms about theory and may reveal barriers to applying formal theory in practice.

Many theories are criticized for *scope limitations* because they are concerned with a relatively narrow range of career behaviors. A given theory may focus on how people choose occupations *or* the kind of occupations they choose or enter *or* the satisfaction they experience on the job. Most theories do not include all three, and consequently they are sometimes called theory fragments or segments (Osipow, 1983; Super, 1980). Another limitation is that the social and economic context of career behavior (for example, job market conditions) is not sufficiently stressed, while psychological aspects of work motivation receive so much attention (Neff, 1977; Vondracek, Lerner, and Schulenberg, 1983; Warnath, 1975). Theories are sometimes viewed as inappropriate for client groups who differ from the majority population on key social or economic variables—for example, racial and ethnic minorities, women, the handicapped, and the poor.

The *methodological problems* criticism refers to problems in the logical methods of theory construction. Most current theories emphasize description rather than prediction (Borow, 1982; Crites, 1969; Osipow, 1983). Few include explicit explanations in the form of cause/effect relationships. Specifically, little attention has been given to predictions about either (1) the complex, multidimensional relations between the developing person and the environmental context or (2) the behavioral antecedents of critical career behaviors such as decisions and satisfactions (Vondracek, Lerner, and Schulenberg, 1983). Since problem identification and intervention design require ideas about the order and sequence of career behaviors, descriptive theories have limited applications.

The third criticism is that both research and practical *applications* are inhibited because the terms used in many theories are not easily converted into concrete, observable behaviors (Osipow, 1983). Furthermore, many theories are not explicit in specifying the connections between antecedent conditions of influence and consequent career behavior response patterns (Borow, 1982). If a theoretical statement contains vague terms and ambiguous relationships, the practitioner is certainly discouraged from making applications.

These three criticisms reveal serious barriers to applying current career development theories to practice. The thesis should not be misunderstood; certainly not *all* theories nor *all* ideas from theories suffer from *all* these problems. There is progress in formal career theorizing; Osipow (1983) viewed current theories as prototypes of the future theories that may eventually serve the same function as theories in the more sophisticated sciences. In the meantime, counselors must *adapt* ideas from current theories to fit their everyday problems. For example, existing segmental theories may be amalgamated into a "local theory"—that is, a theoretical statement that deals explicitly with the critical conditions and problems in the community served. Such adaptations will involve practitioners in a second translation process, that of translating local contextual conditions and clients' career behaviors into theoretical concepts. This requires a different approach to theory by practitioners.

This different approach to the relationship between theory and practice is derived from Kelly's (1955, p. 43) fundamental perspective of the person as a scientist: "The aspirations of the scientist are essentially the aspirations of all men." This approach assumes that practicing counselors function as intuitive scientists in everyday problem solving and, consequently, construct their own *informal* theories as cognitive tools in the solution process. Another way to say this is that when the stakes are high—for example, when considering the importance of clients' welfare—counselors attempt to reason through their response to the situation using essentially the same methods as scientists do.

Counselors' *informal theories* are born out of their personal experiences and their counseling experiences. Williamson (1965, p. 172) observed that "a theory serves as the summing-up of one's life experience to date; it may be a search for an ordering of a myriad of individual counseling cases, as well as originating in the theorist's own personal experiences and observations." Not only do counselors address each individual client as a unique experience, but they also must cope with their aggregate experiences across many clients. Thus, when practitioners are trying to organize and abstract their experiences, their objectives are very similar to those of a scientist.

We are reminded of Lewin's admonition that "there is nothing so practical as a good theory." The point is noteworthy largely because Lewin joins formal theory with practical problem solving in a way that is unfamiliar yet appealing. Whereas common parlance pits theory *against* practice, he upends our expectancies and suggests that, rather than competitors, theory and practice are complementary functions in professional work. Practicing counselors use "theories"—probably not always formal theories but, rather, informal theories—as cognitive tools of the trade.

Translating Career Behaviors into Theoretical Concepts

Practicing counselors who attempt seriously to solve real-world problems function much as intuitive scientists and do invoke theory in their work, albeit at an informal level. The central issue is not *whether* practicing counselors use formal theory or *which* one they will use; rather, it is *what* cognitive tools are useful for their work. Nisbett and Ross (1980) have suggested two general cognitive tools that are used by both the scientist and the layperson: (1) *knowledge structures,* including cognitive schemata such as concepts used to organize and abstract knowledge, and (2) *judgmental heuristics,* the cognitive strategies or rules of thumb used to reduce complex inferential tasks to simple judgmental tasks. Because of space limitations, I will concentrate on knowledge structures—the categories of career behavior and the concepts, or dimensions, underlying the differentiation of categories.

The cognitive aspects of the counselor's everyday problem solving involve constructing *concepts* in order to capture the common qualities experienced by his or her clients as they grow up into changing work roles. Concepts serve the functions of reducing complexity and confusion when organizing observations and of aiding in revealing connections between observed behaviors. They provide the criteria for categorizing observations. A *concept system,* or series of concepts, provides an organized structure for cataloguing categories and suggesting connections. Thus, concepts and concept systems aid counselors in the tasks of problem identification and intervention design.

Practicing counselors frequently criticize the concept systems from formal theory as too abstract, too complex or elaborate, and too peripheral to the events at hand. For example, the concept of vocational maturity offered over twenty years ago has not been utilized to a great extent in writing about career guidance practices. The minimum desirable attributes of concept systems seem to be concreteness, simplicity, and centrality.

Concreteness is the degree of correspondence between a theoretical concept system and the phenomena being observed. Practitioners seek clear, unambiguous links between their ideas and their real-life experiences. Are the concepts clearly associated with the behavior that counselors observe? In formal theory this quality is sometimes called "precision" and is often obtained at the expense of generalizability, the quality of being applicable across several settings or phenomena (Blalock, 1982). This dilemma does not escape the practicing counselor; the more concrete a concept system is, the less generalizable it will be across many clients and settings.

The second desirable characteristic of useful concept systems is *simplicity,* represented by the number of dimensions necessary to define the system. A simple concept system allows counselors to think about and respond to particular individual differences in clients' behaviors. For example, the concept of employment rests on the single dimension of remuneration; to be employed is to do something for pay. The concept of occupation, in contrast, usually requires several dimensions, such as tasks, settings, and responsibilities, in order to give it a full definition. Once again, simplicity is not entirely helpful, because it may isolate the counselor from the more complex concept systems found in formal social science theory. For example, counselors may become unwitting victims of reductionist thinking by reducing all their concepts about client problems to attributes of the person, such as values, abilities, attitudes, and plans, and ignore attributes of social structure such as the job market. On balance, however, practitioners probably seek parsimony in the concepts used to comprehend their counseling experiences.

Finally, concept systems are probably more useful to practitioners if they are *central* to the real-world problems being addressed. Concept systems are considered central when relatively few dimensions are required for the counselors to attribute *meaning* to the phenomena represented. A concept system exhibiting the quality of centrality allows the counselor to comprehend readily *patterns* in his or her experiences with clients. Particular experiences "fit" into the larger concept system; it "clicks," as we often say. As McCabe (1958) suggested twenty-five years ago, the practicality of a theory is a function of the degree to which it has become an integral part of the system by which counselors reorganize past experiences into meaningful relationships and derive meaning from current experience.

A sample of three career concept systems will be considered. Since it seems reasonable to construe career behavior as being expressed through affect, cognition, and overt activity, the three systems will be called (1) the work-affect concept system, (2) the cognitive-activity concept system, and (3) the overt-career-behavior concept system.

Work-Affect Concept System. The work-affect concept system describes the feeling tones associated with concepts of self in work roles—for example, affect toward work activities, work settings, jobs, and occupations. These feeling tones are expressed as emotional responses—both positive and negative—to particular characteristics of work that are experienced either vicariously, as in information about occupations, or directly, as in job situations. When these experiences are repeated, a generalized feeling tone emerges, which may be expressed verbally or nonverbally, consciously or unconsciously. Observers—either the self or a second party—use affect concepts to describe the common qualities of a person's feeling expressions about self in work roles. The concept system described here is limited and omits several attitudes, such as attitudes toward the acts of choosing and preparing for work.

These generalized feeling tones seem to have been distinguished by both theorists and practitioners along two bipolar dimensions, labeled *functional attribution* and *temporal proximity*. The two dimensions allow for the distinction among four major categories of work affect. These categories are familiar in both career development theory and career guidance practice. The functional attribution dimension contrasts the object of affect according to whether it functions as a *means* or an *end*. Affect is expressed toward the efforts and activities themselves (the means) at one pole of the dimension or toward the outcomes and results (the ends obtained from efforts) at the other pole. The temporal proximity dimension contrasts feelings associated with *past* experiences and feelings associated with experiences projected into the *future*.

The first behavioral category includes affect toward efforts and activities (means) previously experienced (past) and is conceptualized as *career interests*, defined as affect toward activities, settings, or roles that may be construed as means toward later or larger purposes. The affect is typically expressed toward experiences instrumental to achieving one's eventual vocational goals. For example, people express positive feelings for activities ("I like to work with my hands") or settings ("I enjoy working outdoors") or roles ("I like what I saw the dentist doing"). This categorical definition of interests is consistent with Osipow's (1979) behavioral analysis of interests as preferences for or rejections of activities, which Osipow contrasted with "abstract affective composites," usually expressed as preferences for occupations.

A second affective category includes the affect associated with means that may occur in the future. These feelings are usually called *career preferences*—that is, feelings about future activities or roles instrumental to achieving goals. The person is expressing affect toward anticipated career experiences, which may be summarized as an occupational field. This fits with Gottfredson's (1981) definition of occupational preferences as "one's likes and dislikes, and they may range from what is desired to what would be least tolerable" (p. 548). Gottfredson equated preferences with judgments of job/self compatibility, a subjective judgment about person/environment congruence (Holland, 1973).

Affect associated with work outcomes and consequences anticipated in the future is often called *work values*. Such values are commonly defined as affect toward anticipated outcomes and results reached through work roles (Katz, 1973; Pryor, 1979). Examples of feelings about outcomes are preferences for feelings labeled as stability/security, income/wealth, adventure/excitement/change/variety, or independence/autonomy. Rokeach (1973) referred to these concepts of feelings as "terminal values," which he distinguished from instrumental values—that is, concepts of feelings about means used to achieve end states, or what I earlier categorized as interests.

Finally, there is affect associated with outcomes or consequences that have resulted from past work roles. We think of this as *job satisfaction*, the affect toward the outcomes resulting from work experiences. Job satisfaction has been given many definitions (see Kalleberg, 1977), but there seems to be general agreement that it is an affective state representing an overall liking or disliking held by a person for a particular job. Translating this category to real-life events presents a serious challenge to practicing counselors and behavioral scientists. Single, direct questions about satisfaction have produced limited and perhaps misleading information; more valid indicators of client satisfaction are obtained from several indirect questions (for example, Kahn, 1972).

The four categories of generalized feeling tones are likely to have different qualities across the life span, thus exhibiting developmental changes. Even career interests, sometimes construed as stable and unchanging, especially when only inventoried interests are considered, are thought by others (for example, Roe and Siegelman, 1964) to undergo important changes. Job satisfaction and work values may be interpreted as changing with accumulated experience, since the available empirical evidence and theoretical statements suggest age-related differences (Jepsen, 1984). Much empirical and theoretical work remains to be done, however, before the nature and timing of these changes are clear.

How do these two dimensions, or concepts, meet the three criteria for usefulness—concreteness, simplicity, and centrality? The contrasting functions of efforts and outcomes and the concept of time seem to correspond to concrete experiences; thus, the work-affect concept system seems to be sufficiently concrete. There are many real-world indicators of the affective categories, as exemplified by the many inventories that focus on expressed interests and values. The experienced counselor may complement the use of inventories with carefully phrased inquiries about client feelings toward particular past activities and roles. However, some interest inventories include items relevant to both the values and the interests categories, making straightforward score interpretations difficult.

The affect system would appear to satisfy the simplicity and centrality criteria, too. The two dimensions cover considerable conceptual territory, although there are clearly other affect categories—for example, attitudes and attributions—that would require other concepts. The two concepts also help to reveal connections between categories of career behavior. For example, the two-dimensional representation of affect alerts the practitioner to the probable and improbable covariations among expressions of affect. As repeated studies have shown, inventoried interests are generally poor predictors of job satisfaction (Gottfredson, 1978). The preceding conceptual analysis suggests that work values are more likely to predict a person's job satisfactions. This relationship has been suggested in several formal theories (for example, Vroom, 1964).

Cognitive-Activity Concept System. Cognitive activity about self in work roles describes the client's thought processes associated with acquiring knowledge about self in work roles. These thought processes are expressed in verbal responses, usually when the person is confronting change in his or her work role—for example, entering jobs, changing jobs, or retiring from work. My discussion will be limited to clients' cognitions about information contained in environmental events rather than information as perceived and transformed by the individual. The latter viewpoint—often called the constructionist perspective—is a part of the recent renaissance in cognitive psychology and has several applications to career development (Stone, 1983).

Another distinction is made between the extent to which the thought content emphasizes qualities of the *self* or qualities of the *work roles.* The latter emphasis suggests an "out there" focus involving thought about the work world, which will be assumed here. The distinction between self-knowledge (knowing who I am) and world-of-work knowledge (knowing about work roles) is common, if simply convenient, in career counseling and career development theory. Nevertheless, it is somewhat artificial for practitioners because clients seldom talk solely about themselves or the work world without some reference to the other topic. The two distinctions represent contrasting world views that counselors may adopt when describing client cognitive activity.

Thought about work roles includes two dimensions. The first, called *perspective,* is the extent to which thought processes are focused on the collective work activity in a social system such as a nation, region, or community, in contrast to the specific work activity of an individual. Thought about the social system has a broad scope and involves learning how the work gets done within a social system—for example, how food reaches our table, how the table is built, how the mail is delivered, how people are healed. Thought about individual positions has a narrower focus on how a single person accomplishes the tasks expected in a job.

The second dimension describes the *complexity* of

thought organization and expression. On the one extreme is the expression of a single piece of information (often in summary form); on the other extreme is the organization of complex information into clients' thought structures. Here the distinction is along a dimension of cognitive complexity from a simple, single piece of information to a complex, organized thought structure.

Four categories of client thought emerge. First, there is the category represented by the intersection of a focus on the individual person at work in the form of a single bit of information. This seems to be represented by *job titles*, convenient abbreviated representations of work roles. Similar labels for this category are Gottfredson's (1981) "occupational images" and Holland's (1973) notion of "occupational stereotypes," impressions of what people in an occupation are like. The job titles known collectively by a person represent his or her subjective opportunity structure. Gottfredson (1981) used the phrase "perceived accessibility of an occupation" to describe the person's estimate of the compatibility of self and job. The single job title most closely associated with one's view of the self is, of course, expressed as the *career choice*.

A second category emerges from attempts to represent the work social system by a single bit of information. The person thinks about the social system in terms of a single dimension. Here we encounter the familiar category of *occupational scales*. Perhaps the most easily recognized scale is social status, which people apply to occupations at a relatively young age. Other one-dimensional scales along which people think about occupations might be sex typing of jobs and common tasks on jobs such as working with people or working with things.

A focus on the social system and complex information structures results in the third category, which we commonly call *occupational knowledge*. Occupational knowledge is construed as a person's factual information about the occupational structure in general. It is the generalized knowledge acquired and stored as one grows older. Like knowledge about comparative religions, the economic structure, and political traditions, it is largely acquired informally. Occupational knowledge resembles

Gottfredson's (1981) "cognitive map of occupations," a generalization about occupations that links the individual occupational images to one another. ACT's World of Work Map (Prediger, 1976) is an elaborate example of knowledge accumulated from research about occupations and serves as an external model for understanding this internal cognitive structure.

The fourth category emerges from a focus on the individual person expressed through complex information systems. We often think of this as *job knowledge*, or the facts known about a particular job or position, usually one for which a person has a strong preference. Here the knowledge is frequently gained through reading information sources, often based on a detailed job analysis (U.S. Department of Labor, 1972), or, more likely, through personal experience in a job.

Comprehending the content of cognitive activity about work roles has been enhanced by a conceptual framework for career awareness (Wise, Charner, and Randour, 1976). These authors suggested that the work content that a person attempts to understand has three dimensions: routines, requisites, and returns. Routines are the required work activities, including content and function. Requisites are factors such as general educational requirements that constrain the eligibility of people to perform a work activity. Returns are the benefits and rewards accrued as a consequence of working. The three dimensions can aid the counselor in understanding occupational knowledge and job knowledge by subdividing the cognitive categories. Indeed, these three career awareness dimensions may emerge as the scales a person uses to structure complex knowledge about work.

The cognitive concept system generally meets the three criteria for usefulness to practitioners. The perspective dimension certainly has concrete referents, and although information structures may be somewhat more difficult to apply to what clients say, frequency of information "bits" is not. Thus, the system would seem to be *concrete*. The two concepts account for most major categories of thought about the work world, thus suggesting that the concept system is relatively *simple* and that it may enhance counselors' differentiations among clients'

thought about the work world. Counselors are better prepared
(1) to give meaning to the progressive *changes* in knowledge,
especially those that accompany increased experience, and (2)
to understand the potential *impact* of such traditional career
guidance tools as occupational information sources. Thus, the
two dimensions seem critical to understanding cognitive behavior and are considered *central.*

    Overt-Career-Behavior Concept System. The third concept
system is defined as patterns of observable action displayed in
response to occupational stimuli (Crites, 1969). Concepts of
overt behavior are not difficult to imagine, probably because of
their public nature. In contrast to the previous two concept systems, overt behavior concepts are represented as three continua
derived from applied behavior analysis: *frequency, duration,*
and *intensity.* The instances of overt career behaviors can be
counted and vary from none or few to many. Career behavior
varies in *duration* from a brief time to a lengthy time and varies
in *intensity* from exerting much effort and energy to exerting
little. For example, the overt career behavior of reading occupational information may involve a few or several instances (frequency) and may take a few minutes or several hours (duration), and the information sources may be searched with a singular purpose or encountered serendipitously (intensity).

    Categories of overt career behavior are differentiated
when the three dimensions are considered simultaneously or in
pairs. Categories emerge when one focuses on the region where
two or more continua intersect. For example, high frequency
and relatively long duration in a work role describe a career behavior pattern that is usually called "job experiences." If the intensity dimension is added as a variable, we are considering *job
involvement,* frequent activity of relatively long duration that
varies in intensity (Weiner and Gechman, 1977).

    Several other categories of overt vocational behavior are
differentiated by the three concepts, and three more will be discussed. *Job tryout experiences* (or reality-testing experiences)
are defined as vocational behaviors occurring with low frequency over a relatively moderate duration and with medium to
high intensity. These patterns of response to occupational stim-

uli do not happen often or for long periods but are marked by considerable expenditure of energy and effort largely directed toward testing hypotheses about the fit of self in the role.

A third overt career behavior is *career role playing.* People occasionally assume work roles under "pretend" conditions for short periods but with relatively low or moderate intensity. The intensity is construed as less than for tryout experiences, since the latter conditions seek to *test* hypotheses about self-in-roles while the former seeks to *develop* hypotheses. This distinction requires adding a cognitive dimension that may be described as *awareness* of the purposes for overt career behavior. Jordaan (1963), for example, has delineated several dimensions of vocational exploratory behavior, which include both cognitive and overt behavior concepts.

A fourth category of overt vocational behavior is the often-used behavioral criterion for career counseling practices, *career information-seeking behavior.* These behaviors vary in frequency and intensity (though probably restricted to the lower ranges) but are usually of short duration. The behavioral activity of *seeking* information should be differentiated from *consuming* information, which is largely a cognitive and affective process. This distinction is consistent with the early definitions of information-seeking behavior as a class of events in which a person attempts to solicit information relevant to his or her future education or occupation (Krumboltz and Schroeder, 1965).

The overt-career-behavior concept system as portrayed in this chapter also seems to meet the criteria for usefulness to practitioners. The concepts of frequency and duration are clearly *concrete* because they can be applied to everyday events through counting or keeping track of time. The correspondence between intensity and concrete events is less clear but may be translated to observable behavior through observing the effort and energy expended. The concept system exhibits only moderate *simplicity.* About the only additional dimension used in applied behavior analysis is topography, the form and shape of overt behavior. The system is nearly exhaustive and may be considered complex. In addition, the dimensions are not clearly orthogonal; that is, frequency may be correlated with intensity as in the act-frequency notion of traits (for example, Buss and Craik, 1981).

The concepts in the system exhibit *centrality* by increasing insights into such behavior as information-seeking and exploratory behavior. For example, the intensity dimension helps to differentiate between high and low personal initiative, as Prediger and Noeth (1979) have, and between purposeful and hypothesis-testing exploratory behavior (Walvoord, cited in Myers, 1978). Furthermore, if a cognitive dimension such as "stated rationale for action" is added, additional insights are available such as exploratory versus terminal job experiences (Phillips, 1982). Thus, the four categories can be applied to adult vocational behavior.

The three concept systems are clearly interrelated. The emergence of career choice in categories of two concept systems, the cognitive (within job title and job knowledge) and the affective (within career preferences), suggests that this simple expression represents both feeling and thought. Perhaps it would be a mistake to overemphasize either facet of this frequently encountered behavior. Likewise, career decision making can be represented as the combination of affective and cognitive behavior involving feelings about future work roles (work values) and thought about self in work roles (job knowledge). The stages in decision making probably describe increasing differentiation of occupational knowledge, career preferences, career interests, work values, and job knowledge. Thus, the dimensions of cognitive and affective behaviors help to clarify such complex notions as developmental stages (Super, 1980) and decision-making stages (Tiedeman and O'Hara, 1963).

Summary and Conclusions

Theoretical ideas serve an indispensable function in career guidance practice, especially in the fundamental tasks of problem identification and intervention design. Formal career development theories provide alternative perspectives for framing practical problems. However, most theories do not offer ideas covering the full scope, sequence, or detail of events typically encountered in career guidance. An alternative form of theory application is the use of informal theory by counselors as a cognitive tool for solving everyday problems. An example of ideas that form an informal theory is the categorization of common career behaviors, including the concepts (or dimensions) describing relationships among categories. The resulting concept systems, though not exhaustive, serve to illustrate the possible application of theory, albeit informal theory, to career guidance practice.

Many challenges remain in applying theory to practice. Challenges to theorists hae been explained elsewhere (Borow, 1982; Osipow, 1983). As a minimum, career development theorists must work toward constructing ideas that (1) cover a broader range of career behaviors, (2) include the social and economic context of careers, and (3) specify the structure and sequence of developmental change. When practitioners are assumed to function as informal theorists (rather than theory consumers only), the challenges to career guidance become more obvious. First, counselors must try to make their knowledge structures more explicit by clarifying the categories they use and specifying the underlying concepts, or dimensions. Second, these categories and dimensions should be examined for their heuristic value. Do they stimulate new and accurate insights during problem identification? Do they suggest more varied and effective interventions? Third, the structures should be tested using empirical methods. Are the categories applied consistently over time? Are the dimensions validated by observations? Both challenges will undoubtedly benefit from continued dialogue between theorists and practitioners.

Suggested Readings

Datan, N., and Ginsberg, L. H. (Eds.). *Life-Span Developmental Psychology: Normative Life Crises.* New York: Academic Press.

The twenty papers in this volume, from the fourth in a

series of conferences on life-span developmental psychology, were planned to create an interface between academic and applied perspectives on the life cycle. Conflicts between theorists and practitioners are explored. The list of contributors contains counseling and developmental psychologists, sociologists, social workers, and gerontologists, illustrating the interdisciplinary emphasis in this new specialty area. Two other volumes with similar format and focus are Turner, R. R., and Reese, H. W. (Eds.), *Life-Span Developmental Psychology: Intervention* (New York: Academic Press, 1980), and Lerner, R. M., and Busch-Rossnagel, N. A. (Eds.), *Individuals as Producers of Their Development: A Life-Span Perspective* (New York: Academic Press, 1981).

Healy, C. C. *Career Development Counseling Through the Life Stages.* Boston: Allyn & Bacon, 1982.

A compendium of replicable career counseling procedures grouped into four of Super's vocational development stages. The author seeks to match counseling procedures with the developmental tasks for each stage, thus demonstrating an application of career development theory to career counseling practice.

Krumboltz, J. D., and Hamel, D. A. (Eds.). *Assessing Career Development.* Palo Alto, Calif.: Mayfield, 1982.

This book comprises fourteen papers on various facets of measuring career education program outcomes. Most papers focus on measurement issues, but the paper by Henry Borow, "Career Development Theory and Instrumental Outcomes of Career Education: A Critique," provides an especially good analysis of current career development theory.

Neff, W. S. *Work and Human Behavior.* (2nd ed.) Chicago: Aldine, 1977.

An excellent and probably underutilized social psychological analysis of human work behavior is presented in a second edition. The cultural and social context for work behavior is analyzed, and a theory of work personality development is proposed with an emphasis on the developing ability to work.

Osipow, S. H. *Theories of Career Development*. (3rd ed.) Englewood Cliffs, N.J.: Prentice-Hall, 1983.

　　The second revision of a volume that attempts to do for
the field of career development what others have done for personality and development—namely, to summarize and compare
important theories. Sociological approaches as well as structural
and developmental theories are included. The introduction and
summary provide especially good evaluations of theory as it relates to career guidance practices.

Williamson, E. G. *Vocational Counseling: Some Historical, Philosophical and Theoretical Perspectives*. New York: McGraw-
Hill, 1965.

　　An acknowledged leader in vocational counseling presents
a personal interpretation of the historical and philosophical
roots of vocational counseling. In the third section, on theorizing and philosophizing about counseling, he argues for a unique
conclusion: "Counseling *as a profession* requires that counselors
learn how to philosophize and theorize about the counseling relationship."

References

Blalock, H. M., Jr. *Conceptualization and Measurement in the
Social Sciences*. Beverly Hills, Calif.: Sage, 1982.

Borow, H. "Career Development Theory and Instrumental Outcomes of Career Guidance: A Critique." In J. D. Krumboltz
and D. A. Hamel (Eds.), *Assessing Career Development*. Palo
Alto, Calif.: Mayfield, 1982.

Buss, D. M., and Craik, K. H. "The Act Frequency Analysis of
Interpersonal Dispositions: Aloofness, Gregariousness, Dominance, and Submissiveness." *Journal of Personality*, 1981,
49, 174-192.

Crites, J. O. *Vocational Psychology*. New York: McGraw-Hill,
1969.

Crites, J. O. *Career Counseling: Models, Methods and Materials*.
New York: McGraw-Hill, 1981.

Dawis, R. V., Lofquist, L. H., and Weiss, D. J. "A Theory of

Work Adjustment: A Revision." *Minnesota Studies in Vocational Rehabilitation*, 1968, *23*.

Gottfredson, G. D. "Why Don't Vocational Interests Predict Job Satisfaction Better than They Do? Unpublished manuscript, Center for Social Organization of Schools, Johns Hopkins University, 1978.

Gottfredson, L. S. "Circumscription and Compromise: A Developmental Theory of Occupational Aspirations." *Journal of Counseling Psychology Monographs*, 1981, *28*, 545–579.

Holland, J. L. *Making Vocational Choices: A Theory of Careers*. Englewood Cliffs, N.J.: Prentice-Hall, 1973.

Jepsen, D. A. "The Developmental Perspective of Vocational Behavior: A Review of Theory and Research." In S. D. Brown and R. W. Lent (Eds.), *Handbook of Counseling Psychology*. New York: Wiley, 1984.

Jordaan, J. R. "Exploratory Behavior: The Formulation of Self and Occupational Concepts." In D. E. Super and others, *Career Development: Self-Concept Theory*. New York: College Entrance Examination Board, 1963.

Kahn, R. L. "The Meaning of Work: Interpretation and Proposals for Measurement." In A. A. Campbell and P. E. Converse (Eds.), *The Human Meaning of Social Change*. New York: Basic Books, 1972.

Kalleberg, A. L. "Work Values and Job Rewards: A Theory of Job Satisfaction." *American Sociological Review*, 1977, *42*, 124–143.

Katz, M. R. "The Name and Nature of Vocational Guidance." In H. Borow (Ed.), *Career Guidance for a New Age*. Boston: Houghton Mifflin, 1973.

Katz, M. R. "Assessment of Career Decision-Making: Process and Outcome." In A. M. Mitchell, G. B. Jones, and J. D. Krumboltz (Eds.), *Social Learning and Career Decision Making*. Cranston, R.I.: Carroll Press, 1979.

Kelly, G. A. *The Psychology of Personal Constructs*. New York: Norton, 1955.

Kerlinger, F. N. "The Influence of Research on Educational Practice." *Educational Researcher*, 1977, *6*, 5–12.

Krumboltz, J. D. "A Social Learning Theory of Career Selection." In A. M. Mitchell, G. B. Jones, and J. D. Krumboltz (Eds.), *Social Learning and Career Decision Making*. Cranston, R.I.: Carroll Press, 1979.

Krumboltz, J. D., and Schroeder, W. W. "Promoting Career Planning Through Reinforcement." *Personnel and Guidance Journal,* 1965, *43,* 19–26.

McCabe, G. E. "When Is a Good Theory Practical?" *Personnel and Guidance Journal,* 1958, *37,* 47–52.

Myers, R. A. "Exploration with the Computer." *Counseling Psychologist,* 1978, *7,* 51–55.

Neff, W. S. *Work and Human Behavior.* (2nd ed.) Chicago: Aldine, 1977.

Nisbett, R., and Ross, L. *Human Inference: Strategies and Shortcomings of Social Judgment.* Englewood Cliffs, N.J.: Prentice-Hall, 1980.

Osipow, S. H. "Career Choices: Learning About Interests and Intervening in Their Development." In A. M. Mitchell, G. B. Jones, and J. D. Krumboltz (Eds.), *Social Learning and Career Decision Making.* Cranston, R.I.: Carroll Press, 1979.

Osipow, S. H. *Theories of Career Development.* (3rd ed.) Englewood Cliffs, N.J.: Prentice-Hall, 1983.

Phillips, S. D. "Career Exploration in Adulthood." *Journal of Vocational Behavior,* 1982, *20,* 129–140.

Prediger, D. J. "A World of Work Map for Career Exploration." *Vocational Guidance Quarterly,* 1976, *24,* 198–208.

Prediger, D. J., and Noeth, R. J. "Effectiveness of a Brief Counseling Intervention in Stimulating Vocational Exploration." *Journal of Vocational Behavior,* 1979, *14,* 352–368.

Pryor, R. "In Search of a Concept: Work Values." *Vocational Guidance Quarterly,* 1979, *27,* 250–258.

Roe, A., and Siegelman, M. *The Origin of Interests.* Washington, D.C.: American Personnel and Guidance Association, 1964.

Rokeach, M. *The Nature of Human Values.* New York: Free Press, 1973.

Stone, G. S. "Cognitive-Behavioral Theory and Its Application to Career Development." In L. W. Harmon (Ed.), *The Individual's Use of Information in Career Development: From Cognitions to Computers.* Columbus: ERIC Clearinghouse on

Adult, Career, and Vocational Education, National Center for Research in Vocational Education, Ohio State University, 1983.

Super, D. E. "A Life-Span, Life-Space Approach to Career Development." *Journal of Vocational Behavior*, 1980, *16*, 282-298.

Tiedeman, D. V., and O'Hara, R. P. *Career Development: Choice and Adjustment.* New York: College Entrance Examination Board, 1963.

U.S. Department of Labor, Manpower Administration. *Handbook for Analyzing Jobs.* Washington, D.C.: U.S. Department of Labor, 1972.

Vondracek, F. W., Lerner, R. L., and Schulenberg, J. E. "The Concept of Development in Vocational Theory and Intervention." *Journal of Vocational Behavior*, 1983, *23*, 179-202.

Vroom, V. H. *Work and Motivation.* New York: Wiley, 1964.

Warnath, C. F. "Vocational Theories: Direction to Nowhere." *Personnel and Guidance Journal*, 1975, *53*, 422-428.

Weiner, Y., and Gechman, A. S. "Commitment: A Behavioral Approach to Job Involvement." *Journal of Vocational Behavior*, 1977, *10*, 47-52.

Williamson, E. G. *Vocational Counseling: Some Historical, Philosophical, and Theoretical Perspectives.* New York: McGraw-Hill, 1965.

Wise, R., Charner, I., and Randour, M. L. *A Conceptual Framework for Career Awareness.* Washington, D.C.: Career Awareness Division, National Institute of Education, 1976.

6

Henry Borow

Occupational Socialization: Acquiring a Sense of Work

More than a few writers have been drawn to the fanciful theme of *Homo sapiens* removed from its ancestral roots and left free to develop in a sequestered, adult-free environment. In *Lord of the Flies,* Golding (1962) paints a disquieting picture of a band of children inescapably bound together by geography, needing to learn how to deal with one another for survival but lacking an adult presence or direct knowledge of how to build a stable social order. Itard's (1932) *Wild Boy of Aveyron* documents the remarkable case of a real child found abandoned, for how long no one could know, in a wooded area near Paris and of the largely futile attempts to humanize this savagelike creature. What impresses the reader of such accounts is that these children are startlingly unlike any we have ever known. However disparate the cultures into which they are born, children universally are tempered in a social crucible, and each exhibits the profound and indelible markings of his or her particular subculture. We refer to this humanizing process as "socialization." Within behavioral science, even the moral sense and its expressive manifestations are assumed to be shaped by the process. McCandless (1967), for example, points to the widely held axiom that conduct derives from social learning, not from assumed innate goodness or evil.

Socialization, then, is the intricate, birth-to-death process by which one acquires one's view of the human world and its institutions, one's beliefs, loyalties, convictions of right and wrong, and habitual response modes. The learning is both formal and informal, deliberate and incidental, conscious and unconscious. When the infant begins to emit consistent overt responses to human stimuli—for example, smiling at the sight of the father's or mother's face—we infer that socialization has begun and will pursue a more or less orderly sequence. Freud's psychosexual theory of personality development (Jones, 1953) and Erikson's (1963) stage sequence of eight psychosocial crises represent specialized conceptual constructions of the socialization process. These explanatory systems, like others, attempt to trace the steps by which the child experiences reality, learns who he or she is (identity formation), comes to apprehend the rules by which the game of life is played, and moves toward responsibly independent and socially productive behavior. One is struck by the discovery that, despite their avowed differences in orientation and methods, several established systems of psychotherapy such as the Adlerian, rational-emotive, and reality therapies link successful life adjustment with appropriate socialization, and each has as the core of its treatment aim the effective resocialization of the troubled client. At stake is the individual's learning of improved self-control, including the adequate management of one's impulses and motives within a human order that establishes institutional expectations and constraints. What this implies with respect to the child's mastery of appropriate task performance and work-relevant behaviors will be considered later in the chapter.

Work as Social Bonding

The character and stability of any society cannot be well understood without knowledge of how that society prepares and deploys its human resources in the production and distribution of goods and services. Work is highly institutionalized and ranks prominently among the institutions to which individuals must accommodate through the socialization process. For the majority of adults, occupation provides a setting in which they are drawn into communion with others and with reality. Both psychological and sociological studies emphasize the pivotal contribution of work to life satisfaction and to self-assessments, favorable and unfavorable, of personal worth. The social meanings and pervasive importance of work have been emphasized by writers from a variety of perspectives (Tilgher, 1931; Roe, 1956; Super, 1957; Gross, 1958; Wrenn, 1964; Neff, 1977).

However cultures may differ from one another, obligatory movement through earlier stages in the life cycle toward socially useful occupational status appears as a recurrent theme. For most contemporary youth the path is not well marked and may be tortuous. Influential writers have analyzed the dilemma of adolescents in the main as one of poor socialization for work life. Erikson (1968), for instance, voices a widely shared interpretation when he concludes, "In general it is the inability to settle on an occupational identity which most disturbs young people" (p. 132).

Making the transition to relatively autonomous adulthood requires that youth confront and resolve a number of sequenced personal choices—for example, the decision to remain in school at the legal school-leaving age or to continue education or enter the labor market on completing high school. It is understandable, then, that these career decisions of middle and late adolescence command our attention. Yet it is increasingly clear that significant work-relevant images and behaviors trace their roots to the individual's earlier history. Long before youth is required by compliance with society's timetables to make educational and occupational decisions, it is possible to observe childhood styles of interaction with the environment, formative self-characterizations, and even nascent conceptions and fantasies of work (Murphy, 1973). In a culture that rewards achieving behavior, mental pictures about one's competence and about self as distant worker-to-be have early beginnings. Such developmental experiences, of course, occurring as they do in a social context, reflect the society's values, customs, and expectations, at least as the child interprets them. We will, accordingly, turn next to an examination of the principal agents of the child's socialization.

The Family Experience. Members of the child's immediate family, generally the nuclear family, make up his or her primary reference group and exert the most pervasive and durable influence on social development. It is in the web of family interactions that the child has his or her earliest learning experiences, observes and imitates the behavior of others, is imprinted by sex typing, acquires elemental rules of conduct, and learns that other people are necessary for the satisfaction of one's wants but that these others also have their needs and rights. It is here, within the intimate family circle, that children begin to gain a sense of their own competence and limitations. Their behavior is shaped by an elaborate but not always consciously applied system of rewards and denials. Since, as McCandless (1967) points out, reinforcers are meted out from a basis of power, the child learns that his or her own responses reap social consequences, good or bad, depending on whether these responses are acceptable or unacceptable.

Luckey (1974) observes that parents make their influence felt on children through their own personalities, their modes of living, and their childrearing techniques. Owing to the shift in family focus in recent years from producer to consumer values, the family functions less visibly as a closely knit economic unit and less often assigns structured work roles to the child. Nevertheless, as we shall see, the time-extended impact of the family experience has a relevance for career that becomes more distinct as the growing child moves beyond the home into the competitive school environment, enters peer-group settings, and, still later, approaches important career choice points. The child who witnesses productive, achieving behavior in the home and whose own developing habits of success have been rewarded will likely be able to transfer such habits to school and occupation (Super, 1957). Family influence on work behavior comes not only indirectly through early habit training and the transmission of attitudes and values; it is, also, more directly evidenced later on when career plans are made. Studies reviewed by Brown (1970), among others, disclose that families, parents in particular, are potent factors in the making of vocational decisions.

Occupational inheritance, a social induction mechanism by which an offspring prepares to enter the occupation of the parent, is now far less common than earlier, but it may still account for significant numbers of young people who enter such fields as medicine, law, small-business operations, and farming. Geography is yet another family-related circumstance in occupational choice. Although the geographical mobility of American youth has increased, many students attend schools and colleges and take part-time employment in the vicinity of their parents' homes, and their job opportunities are defined by the occupational characteristics of the region. Such family-related geographical restrictions on career decisions are especially stringent for severely socioeconomically disadvantaged youth with limited education and marketable skills, who may simply "fall into" whatever low-level jobs exist.

Since about 1965, a significant rise has occurred in the labor force participation rates of married women with children. In 1970, 39 percent of children under age eighteen had working mothers. By 1982, the figure had risen to 55 percent. Somewhat surprisingly, nearly half of the nation's very young children (birth to age five) have working mothers (Bureau of Labor Statistics, 1983). Such demographic shifts mean that larger percentages of young people are growing up in homes with nontraditional divisions of parental roles and functions. Studies reviewed by Portner (1978) make clear that these changes have been accompanied by modifications both in family occupational socialization practices and in their effects. Working mothers with high school diplomas have been shown to maintain firmer control over their children than comparably educated nonworking mothers. This distinction in child management approaches, however, did not hold for college-educated mothers. Several studies have reported that the adolescent children of working mothers of varying educational levels are assigned a greater share of household responsibilities. In comparison with nonworking mothers, those who work are more likely to encourage independent behavior in their children. That the working mother's influence on the child occurs early is supported by the finding that the kindergarten daughters of working women held less traditional sex-role stereotypes than a comparable group with nonworking mothers. College women with working mothers scored higher on measured traits generally identified as masculine characteristics, such as dominance and achievement. They also described their mothers as role models in more positive terms than the college daughters of nonworking women did (Baruch, 1974).

Establishing dependable empirical relationships between family experience and subsequent career-related behavior is not as straightforward a procedure as the foregoing review might appear to suggest. A matrix of interacting causal variables generally exists, and isolating the effects of single determinants of career socialization patterns is a difficult research task at best. Bratcher (1982) maintains that individuals grappling with career decisions are influenced by elements in family relationships that are denied to awareness, and he proposes that the use of family systems theory in career counseling can be helpful with such cases. Finally, it should be noted that many studies of the effects of childhood experience are flawed by the use of retrospective reports and short-term follow-ups. The type of longitudinal research design advocated by Stone and Onqué (1959) and Kahn and Antonucci (1980) has only infrequently been used in studies that may contribute to the understanding of occupational socialization processes. An exception is Moss and Kagan's (1961) use of the Fels Research Institute data in their study of achievement behavior in children.

School as a Socializing Agency. Although the family's role remains primary, urbanization and its consequences have progressively loosened familial controls over members' life space and extended responsibility for inducting the child into society to a number of secondary institutions, chiefly the schools. Dispute has long existed concerning whether the school's influence on its charges should be confined to cultivation of the intellect through formal subject matter instruction, but it is patent that the vast majority of adults, both by explicit commission and by lapsed responsibility, expect the school to guide the social and ethical development of the young.

Entering school for the first time is an event of signal importance, for it exposes children to strange and exciting new vistas that broaden and redefine for them the nature of the social universe. Much of what children now learn about what is expected of them and many of the coping devices for meeting such expectations are acquired through the school experience. Meeting society's impersonal standards, facing competition from others, having one's performance and oneself routinely judged by others—all become part of one's daily encounter with the human world. Later, the student will have to think about his or her competencies and values as he or she arrives at the planning-and-choice checkpoints that are systematically built into the phased educational program.

It is in the school setting that the young child learns that the things adults do for a livelihood are differentially valued. By the time the student has entered junior high school, he or she has assimilated the notion that occupations can be ranked by their social status (Gunn, 1964). The concept of occupational prestige is, of course, woven into society's fabric but is accented by the school's stress on the importance of upward mobility. Despite the presence of programs of vocational training and career education, the typical secondary school judges its success by the proportion of its students who go on to college, ostensibly to prepare for the professions. Whether deliberate or inadvertent, the indoctrination is thorough. The investigation of O'Dowd and Beardslee (1960), among others, strongly supports the conclusion that American college students are greatly influenced in their selection of fields of study by the perceived power of these fields to confer both high social status and a preferred life-style. The social mechanism for raising students' educational and occupational aspiration levels is in keeping with the national ideal of maximizing individual opportunity. However, serious concerns have been raised about the imbalance between the expectations of college graduates and the realities of the marketplace (Freeman, 1976). To adjust labor supply-and-demand ratios, the nation may again do what it has done before —that is, raise educational and other credentialing requirements for entrance into the high-status occupations. By such restrictive means, highly educated job applicants will be allocated in increasing numbers to lower-level jobs. Terms like *underemployment* and *spillover* are now appearing with greater frequency in labor market reports.

The Peer Subculture. The child's peer group operates as another significant socialization agency. In a manner different from but inextricably linked to that of the adult culture, it interprets the social world to the child, introduces him to group rules, tests his resources, and presents him with the consequences of his own behavior. Yet, powerful as the peer cohort is as a humanizing force, its role and function are not well delineated, since the dominant adult society at no point expressly delegates to it a fixed set of responsibilities for guiding the development of its members.

The highly visible and cohesive youth society of the type we have come to know is of comparatively recent origin. Demos and Demos (1973) have persuasively advanced the thesis that the idea of adolescence as a distinct stage of psychological development, significant in itself, was virtually nonexistent until relatively late in the nineteenth century. The Puritan heritage in America carried with it the concept of the child as an immature and imperfect adult. Childhood impulses toward self-assertion and individuality were viewed as unwholesome and as needing to be eradicated on moral grounds through obligatory parental discipline. Even what we think of as the natural paraphernalia of childhood, toys and games, occupied an obscure place in early American family life, an indication that childhood was not a self-justifying stage of human development to be valued in its own right. Corroboration of this view is provided by the primitive artistic portrayals of children in which they appear oddly as homunculi with the bodily proportions of mature adults.

The emergence of a conspicuous youth segment of American society, distinguishable by its particular set of beliefs, practices, and loyalties, may be attributed to the confluence of several late-nineteenth and early-twentieth-century conditions. Urbanization, a steadily rising national standard of living, and, as previously noted, the decline of the family as a strong, functional economic unit diminished the usefulness of children as providers and loosened their moorings to the adult world. Concurrently, middle-class America was witnessing a radical shift in childrearing values, effectively spurred by the child study movement, in which training for psychological independence and competent individuality largely supplanted the earlier emphasis on intensive indoctrination in the rules of etiquette and the virtues of filial obedience. Closely identified with the contributions of G. Stanley Hall, the child study movement laid stress, among its other themes, on the significance of adolescence as a critical stage in human development. Although Hall's critics invoked the phrase "special cult of adolescence" pejoratively to protest what they believed to be his overdrawn "storm and stress" characterization, it is clear that the recognition of adolescence as a special time of life with identifiable problems and cultural markings is closely dated to this period, a time that saw the appearance of early publications on child labor and vocational guidance. A bit later, during the economic depression of the 1930s, the nation's resort to the devices of heightened age, educational, and experience requirements as a means of delaying youth's entrance into full-time employment status placed adolescents in a holding pattern of extended dependency and isolation from the adult world. This condition seems to have further hastened the emergence of a distinct youth culture.

Whatever the social vectors that have coalesced to give the contemporary youth culture its special identity, its wide-ranging effects in modeling, transmitting, and reinforcing the outlooks and tastes of young Americans are undeniable. Powerfully shaped preferences in dress styles, recreational pursuits, and argot all vividly bespeak the presence of peer-group influence. The music recording and marketing industry counts its youth clientele as its primary market, and although the illicit drug traffic may be chiefly adult-initiated and adult-directed, a large and worrisome sector of the drug culture itself is youth-styled.

How child and adolescent peer groups specifically affect

youthful thinking about occupational and life values, however, is a matter about which we still have much less dependable knowledge. The signals and caveats that the young exchange relative to the institution of work appear to be largely covert and arcane, and although numerous surveys of youth work attitudes have been published, systematic investigations of the influence of the youth peer groups themselves on the career-related thinking of their members have not been seriously undertaken by psychologists, sociologists, or counselors. What information exists appears sketchy and anecdotal. The imaginative play and discourse of childhood and preadolescent groups appear to include occasional reference to work, but the contributions of these cohorts to occupational socialization are of an indirect nature, centering on the framing and monitoring of appropriate standards of member conduct, furnishing the individual with feedback on his or her behavior, and providing their own limited theater for the staging of in-group contests of mastery and achievement.

    If one is to judge from the reports of students who appear for counseling, informal discussions among mid and late adolescents and young college adults about plans for occupational life are not uncommon. Such sessions would appear to be marked by a good deal of self-disclosure centering on personal aspirations, vaguely formed plans, and uncertainties about the future. Individual work values are tested in debate, sometimes endorsed by peers, sometimes challenged. There seems little doubt that many youths, facing the imminent prospect of educational and occupational decision making, use the informal peer encounter as a vicarious means of probing the wisdom of tentative aims and of thinking about work meanings. Moreover, the young person's career ambitions may be correlated with the expectations she perceives that her significant others hold for her. Herriott (1961), for example, found that even when adolescents' self-assessments of motivation and competence are held constant, the higher the level of expectation perceived from significant others, the higher the level of their own educational aspirations is likely to be.

    The influence of age and grade mates on one's own out-

look is also to be seen in the shifting group attitudes and senti-
ments that prevail at a particular time. During the 1960s and
early 1970s, a period of much social unrest, the mounting dis-
affection of the young with large-scale institutions such as big
government, corporate industry, and education led many secondary school and college students to profess a rejection of
work in most of its forms on grounds of its alleged degradation
of the human spirit. And yet numerous studies, including the
widely cited Yankelovich surveys and the *Work in America* report, continue to show that youth, over the long stretch, consider career to be an essential way of life (Yankelovich, 1972;
Special Task Force, 1973). With the exception of the greater
emphasis that contemporary youth place on the importance of
interesting work and opportunity for challenge and advancement, their avowed work values remain largely unchanged from
those of their parents' generation. One is reminded here of Erikson's (1962) observation that each succeeding generation, on
the road to maturity, challenges the legitimacy of its predeces-
sor's values but does so in a manner that refurbishes the durable
elements of the past and blends them with the current in a renewal of the species.

    The foregoing discussion has implied that the family, the
school, and the peer group are all limited in their potential as
testing grounds for adequate occupational socialization. In today's world, youth's bridges to career are not easily traversed.
The Vocational Education Act of 1963 and its subsequent
amendments and the career education movement of the 1970s
had a common aim of providing sequential arrangements of
guided functional explorations and skill acquisition experiences
to ease youth's transition to the world of work (Herr, 1972,
1974). Although such model programs provided an urgently
needed corrective to the traditional, narrow-band academic curriculum, social and economic pressures have combined to restrict their scope and impact. A deeply ingrained and tenacious
conviction, historically rooted, that the high school must vin-
dicate itself primarily as a college preparatory institution and as
a vehicle for upward socioeconomic mobility seems repeatedly
to blunt reasoned attempts to improve the school's effectiveness in socializing youth for the workplace.

Work Experience. What of the workplace itself as the milieu for occupational socialization? Few experiences free the adolescent so decisively from the demeaning feeling of dependence on adult beneficence or provide so direct an impetus to independence and sense of personal utility as the fact of being paid for one's competitive worth and economic effort in the impersonal marketplace. Despite the exclusion of large segments of the youth population from full-time gainful employment, the proportions of high school boys and girls engaged in part-time jobs, particularly in the secondary labor market, are probably at their highest point in the last half century. However, we need to know better the impact of this job experience on a person's long-term career history. Does contemporary youth work, for example, in any sense parallel the social induction value of the bygone European guild system for the training of artisans or the more current apprenticeship system? It is a matter of concern among some authorities that as the United States moves toward a postindustrial economy, the proportion of American youth who are prepared for entrance to the labor market through formal apprenticeship stands substantially below that of such countries as Japan, West Germany, and Belgium.

Proposals constantly appear that outline the requisite conditions for arranging the work setting as a social context in which youth can acquire the habits, attitudes, knowledge, and skills conducive to competitive labor market success and long-term career satisfaction. Hamburger (1967), in a position paper prepared for the United States Office of Education, provides a detailed analysis of the potentialities and limitations of school-sponsored work experience in adolescent development, and he points to an impressive array of work-relevant personality variables and behaviors that proponents claim can be nourished through this socialization medium. Among them are responsibility, punctuality, initiative, self-confidence, respect for rules, sense of independence, learning to handle money earned, and learning to work cooperatively with others. Hamburger is duly attentive to the pitfalls associated with much youth work, and he specifies the conditions that must be established if the planned work experience is to be salutary. Programmatic research on the social and personal consequences of the employ-

ment experience of young workers is currently being undertaken by Greenberger and her associates. The findings to date of
this team of researchers present a mixed picture, as will be reported later in the chapter (Greenberger and Steinberg, 1981).

Communication Media. Closely paralleling the institutional influences of family, school, peer group, and workplace
on the child's perceptions of the social world are those exer-
cised by the mass media of communication, both the print
media and the audiovisual media of motion pictures and television. Belief that television may be a shaper of youthful values
and environmental response styles rests on recognition of the
substantial amounts of uncommitted time devoted to watching
TV. American fifth-grade schoolchildren spend 256 minutes per
week on homework, in sharp contrast to 368 minutes per week
for their Japanese counterparts (Garfinkel, 1983). Television
accounts for a good part of this time differential. Although
studies differ somewhat in their findings, there is general agreement that the time given to TV by both elementary and secondary school students in the United States greatly exceeds that devoted to homework assignments.

The lively debates on the effects of TV notwithstanding,
evidence from well-designed studies suggests a strong connection between young viewers' frequent witnessing of television
fiction that makes use of violent themes and their own latent
tendencies to use aggression-oriented approaches to situations.
As for occupational imagery, the television caricaturing of
workers on different rungs of the job status hierarchy conveys
unequivocal messages to youth about the badges of success or
taints of failure that seem invariably to be associated with one's
occupation. Contrast, for example, the stereotyped depictions
of the inept, boorish, and mood-careening bus driver (Jackie
Gleason), in the situation comedy *The Honeymooners* and the
unrelenting machismo of the profane, bigoted shipping department laborer (Carroll O'Connor) in *All in the Family* with the
seemingly omniscient, always self-controlled, and boundlessly
humane physician (Robert Young) in *Marcus Welby, M.D.*

Thus, through family modeling and expectations, school
emphasis on the promised social rewards of academic success,

selective peer pressures, and the persons-at-work vignettes beamed to viewers by TV and other communication media, the maturing child acquires a growing sense, not necessarily consciously reasoned out, of the importance of occupational status to the attainment of social approval and an attractive life-style. As we study these powerful socialization forces, we are able to understand better the previously reported conclusions of Gunn (1964) that youth demonstrate early their ability to rank occupations according to a prestige criterion and of O'Dowd and Beardslee (1960) that college students may be better informed about the status-conferring characteristics of their chosen fields of study than about the specific sets of qualifications and duties they entail. Furthermore, we can begin to understand the widespread tendency among secondary school and college students to exclude entire clusters of occupations from even preliminary exploration in career counseling. This mental screening process, which I have discussed elsewhere under the name "subjective occupational foreclosure," mystifies and frustrates many counselors who routinely encounter it in the career guidance setting (Borow, 1966).

The effects of primary and secondary agencies of socialization on youth's emerging attitudes, aspirations, and attainments are mediated by a pervasive, role-defining socioeconomic class system. The analytical efforts of sociologists such as Warner, Meeker, and Eells (1949), Hollingshead (1949), and Sewell, Haller, and Straus (1957) have produced a set of indicators that render the concept of socioeconomic stratification accessible to measurement. Furthermore, through the use of path analysis and multiple regression analysis, sociological studies have shown that the individual's status origins are to a significant degree predictive of his or her subsequent educational and occupational history (Sewell, Haller, and Portes, 1969). A basic thesis in sociological research, known as the status attainment model, is that socioeconomic status indicators such as parents' educational level, father's occupational status, and source and level of family income are transmitted intergenerationally through a chain of effects and that the predicted outcomes are measurable in terms of the offspring's consequent occupational and income attainments. Reviews of sociological work on the status attainment model have been reported by Featherman (1980) and by Hotchkiss and Borow (1984).

The high degree of generation-to-generation constancy in status attainment, as revealed by sociological studies, serves counselors as a sober reminder that, despite its comparative openness and fluidity, the American social structure still poses formidable barriers to occupational opportunity for those with less favored social-class membership. Sociologists who have worked on the status attainment model do not believe that mobility patterns are unalterably fixed by conditions of socioeconomic origins and, in fact, point out that "external agents might intervene to change educational and occupational attainment levels" (Sewell, Haller, and Portes, 1969, p. 89). Nonetheless, the hope, for example, that narrowing the black/white educational credentials gap would tend to equalize occupational attainment has not been fulfilled. Although the proportion of young blacks earning the high school diploma is approaching that of whites, black high school graduates aged eighteen to twenty-four in 1980 experienced two and one-half times the risk of unemployment of all high school graduates in that age group (Bureau of Labor Statistics, 1980).

Growing Up: Acquiring Self-Managed Behaviors

In contrast to the sociologist's research focus on socioeconomic mobility and on the large-scale institutional forces that direct it, counseling psychologists have looked more closely at the microlevel psychological variables associated with vocational preferences and at both the interpersonal and social influences that facilitate commitment to career planning. Classical vocational guidance was anchored in the psychology of individual differences and chose as its main strategy the assessment of personal characteristics that might be matched to the human trait requirements of various occupations. Stimulated principally by the seminal work of Super (1951, 1953, 1957), investigations of vocational choice behavior began in midcentury to draw increasingly on concepts of human development, and emphasis gradually shifted from the discrete act of choice making to the dynamics of the career maturation process. Super noted the significance of the work in Europe of Lazarsfeld (1931) and Buehler (1933), which set the study of career in a developmental context and which, in Buehler's case, proposed the utility of a psychological life-stage conceptual model.

The introduction of a developmental view of vocational behavior created a hospitable climate for the examination of the cycle of socialization by which the society establishes progressively more complex coping responsibilities for the growing child and guides the child in their mastery. In 1953 Havighurst captured the notion more formally by introducing the developmental task construct, signifying a sequence of time-bound and necessary social learnings corresponding to the successive life stages. Havighurst's view that the key developmental tasks associated with a given life stage absorb substantial amounts of the individual's time, thoughts, and energy provides a rationale for examining the motives, images, and fantasies of children and youth, life stage by life stage, as clues to vocational maturity. Stated differently, the developing cognitive competencies and coping techniques are seen not only as significant indicators of the individual pace of general social maturity but, in a more particular sense as well, as intimations of subsequent career planning and career enactment. These learnings become internalized early, are exhibited as habitual response modes, and become important determinants of how, later on, the adolescent and young adult performs the task-oriented roles of student and worker. Several of these behaviors, discussed briefly here, are closely connected and may, indeed, represent merely different interpretations of the same basic competencies.

Impulse Control. Young infants lack the capacity to tolerate the thwarting of a bodily need. Learning to postpone gratification of a desire until its fulfillment is deemed socially appropriate and, later, learning to curb one's impulse when it intrudes on the rights of others are among the child's most important social lessons. The ability to delay need gratification when circumstances warrant is widely accepted as an index of the child's growth in personal maturity. Studies of parental childrearing patterns show that, ironically, the parent who chooses to avoid frustrating the child by constantly yielding to impulsive demands ends with a child who has neither acceptable internal controls on behavior nor the ability to tolerate frustration. The behavior history of such a child is likely to be marked by procrastination and a disordered arrangement of personal priorities. By contrast, we see another child who is able to delay his playtime activity until he has completed his homework or an assigned household chore. The early and adequate establishment of internal controls on one's behavior prepares the child to confront and master his sequential developmental tasks. The long-range implications for meeting the competitive demand of schooling and for accepting and carrying through a reasoned commitment to planning for career are evident.

Becoming Responsibly Independent. As noted earlier in the chapter, training children in responsible autonomy became a valued childrearing objective in middle-class American society around the turn of the twentieth century, and it remains so. Studies indicate that well-educated parents in particular encourage their young children to explore their environments and to learn about life through the taking of graduated reasonable risks. To deal with tasks of increasing complexity and to make sound personal decisions, the child must learn to draw constantly on her enlarging repertoire of understandings and skills. The resultant expanding capacity for self-reliance and independent judgment will later serve the individual well in interpersonal encounters and in task-centered settings such as the classroom and the workplace.

Destiny Control. Though more tacit than explicitly stated, there is a strong assumption in both childrearing and schooling that the social world in which the child will increasingly participate, despite all its uncertainties and inequities, presents an essentially orderly and rational structure and that, consequently, one's own social actions can have predictable and rational consequences. It is in this belief that the successful child has been trained to understand that he or she has some power to use or to modify the environment toward desired ends and that, with the proper resources and planning, one can make things happen.

The child's intuitive grasp of this concept, which has a profound effect on how that child approaches tasks and problems, is variously termed "internal locus of control," "destiny control," and "sense of personal efficacy." Kahn and Antonucci's (1980) review of the research literature indicates that it is probably through the intimate attachment experiences with the contingently responding mother that the infant develops the primitive perception of personal control that is later generalized to relations with others and interactions with the world. The child who grows up with a sense of destiny control is disposed to engage the environment confidently, to plan courses of action, and to be willing to try to change things. How such personal beliefs may later affect career is pointedly indicated by the statement that "a belief that one's goals are attainable [is] strongly related to a successful transition from school to work" (Employment and Training Administration, 1979, p. 2). In contrast, the infant who has been subjected to prolonged maternal deprivation or the growing child who has experienced bewildering inconsistency in parental reactions—that is, who has learned that his own actions bring irregular and unpredictable social consequences—is likely to exhibit learned helplessness, a social response posture that includes avoiding dealing with the environment out of a feeling that to do so would make no difference. As the latter child grows, his thinking about education and work will be characterized far more by fantasy and fatalism than by informed and realistic planning.

Progressive Mastery. There is a widely observed propensity among healthy infants and young children, loosely analogous to the exploratory drive in laboratory animals, to experience their surroundings actively. These persistent efforts to satisfy an elemental curiosity, to participate in what is going on around one rather than avoid it, and to increase one's manipulation and mastery of the delimited surrounding world are the beginnings of coping behavior. White (1959), who used the terms *competence* and *effectance motivation* to explain how the child learns to deal successfully with his or her environment, has noted that such mastery-building activity is commonly exhibited in children's play. Murphy (1973, p. 172) defines progressive mastery as "a process by which satisfaction is derived from consolidating one's gains and setting for one's self still higher, more complex goals." Implicit in the notion of progressive mastery, then, is a psychological striving to go beyond where one is and to continually extend one's understanding and measure of control. Although it remains for longitudinal research to furnish firmer evidence of the relation between early coping behavior and the progress of career, it seems reasonable to assume the existence of a causal connection between them. Murphy sees an implication for the training and guidance of youth when he proposes that work experiences should be arranged according to degree of complexity and level of integration.

Achievement Motivation. When the child's natural tendencies toward environmental coping and progressive mastery are deliberately encouraged and cultivated as socially valued behavior, that child is likely to acquire a need to achieve at a superior rank. Setting high standards of attainment for oneself and acting commensurately in a manner conducive to meeting these standards is called "achievement motivation." Early training in independence and the social reinforcement of self-initiated problem solving appear to nourish the need to achieve. Children who exhibit strong achievement motivation tend to have parents who (1) set high standards of accomplishment for themselves, (2) specify the behavior that is expected of their children, (3) teach and model the technique for successfully performing that behavior, and (4) reward the behavior when it occurs (Borow, 1968).

An advanced level of achievement motivation is more likely to occur when the child is able to experience a high rate of success in attempts to meet parental expectations and when the mother is the principal agent of social reinforcement. Studies suggest that superior levels of achievement motivation and performance, even among preschool children, are closely and persistently related to school achievement. After comparing children who exhibited independent achievement-oriented behavior with subjects of comparable grade placement who displayed recognition-seeking behavior, Moss and Kagan (1961) concluded cautiously that young children's need to achieve may be a reasonably good precursor of achievement in adolescence and adulthood. Furthermore, students who exhibit achieving behavior are more likely to become adults concerned with their own intellectual competence. Although such findings give no warrant for confident predictions about subsequent work-related planning and attainments, data from the Career Pattern Study for both ninth- and twelfth-grade boys have shown significant correlations between scholastic achievement and level of vocational aspirations, on the one hand, and selected career maturity factors, on the other (Jordaan and Heyde, 1979).

Learning an Occupational Role

Many of the conditions of social and economic change discussed earlier in the chapter have had the net effect of isolating growing children and youths from the intimate presence and realities of a world at work. Because the producing world is less visible to them than to their forebears and because they experience it less directly, the process of learning what it means to be a worker tends to be unsystematic and diffused. Although exceptions to this claim are to be found in the formal curricula of vocational and cooperative education and in special job training projects, such programs reach only a segment of the youth population, often late rather than early, and are too often stigmatized. Such programs probably do not match the thoroughgoing socializing influence of formal work induction practices of past generations, through which close psychological identification with the community of workers was gained and which, especially for young males, afforded the rites of passage into adulthood. Learning the work ethos generally takes place today by less deliberately structured means and embodies a number of psychosocial phenomena, discussed next, that have been closely examined by counseling and career development psychologists.

Reality Testing. The very young child lacks awareness of personal limitations, and the onset of negativistic responses in two- to four-year-olds is thought to be the consequence of an initial cognizance of their own fallibility. Young elementary school pupils, when sharing their fantasies in response to the question "What do you want to be when you grow up?," respond in terms of uncomplicated interest and with little or no recognition of the test of adequacy they will be expected to meet. In contrast to this earlier child self, the adolescent is developing an enlarging critical capacity to gauge his or her assets and limitations. This increased ability for self-evaluation stems both from the individual's maturing intellect and, as mentioned earlier, from the judgments of significant others about one's performance. Accordingly, many of adolescents' social acts are instances of self-exploration by which they test both the appropriateness of their behavior and their competencies. As findings from the Career Pattern Study indicate, the youth's testing the self against social reality sometimes takes the form of exploratory vocational behavior, which provides one basis for the clarification of images of oneself as future worker (Jordaan and Heyde, 1979).

Identity Formation. Intimately bound to ongoing reality testing is the process of identity formation. The maturing youth's attainment of a more realistic self-understanding extends beyond the stocktaking of cognitive and physical abilities to questions of personal values, the kind of person one is, and the types of life experiences likely to enhance that self-image. Erikson (1963) and Tiedeman and O'Hara (1963), among others, have examined identity formation with reference to its meanings for the enactment of successful adult roles, including occupational roles. Current applied systems for assisting counselees with career plans, such as the Work Adjustment Project (Lofquist and Dawis, 1969) and the computerized System for Interactive Guidance and Information (Katz, 1975) rely heavily on the individual's examination and ranking of his or her personal values as means of facilitating work-related self-understanding.

Occupational Role Modeling. The influence of primary and secondary agencies in the child's socialization has been discussed earlier. Some of that influence is seen in the social modeling of occupational behavior, both unintentional and deliberate, by parents, relatives, neighbors, teachers, and older siblings. Work habits, beliefs, and attitudes are exhibited and assimilated.

Because the effects on developing behavior are thought to be both powerful and durable, increasing attention is being given to the development and use of social modeling techniques with children and youth to accelerate career maturity. Krumboltz and Thoresen (1976) illustrate a number of such techniques. One notes, too, the growing use of successful women workers as role models to counteract the effects of occupational sex typing.

How well the foregoing psychosocial processes function in readying youth for satisfying and productive work may be questioned, given the social and economic obstacles to career development discussed in this chapter. Studies have been reported in agreement with the American College Testing (ACT) Program's National Survey of High School Students, disclosing unfocused motives and a serious lack of knowledge about both the occupational world and career-planning methods (Prediger, Roth, and Noeth, 1973). Failure of school youth to initiate occupational exploration and information seeking is also widely found. In the ACT sample, about 40 percent of the eleventh-graders reported never having talked with workers about their jobs or having used the library or school counseling office to consult a job description. The ongoing refinement of career development instrumentation, as reported by Crites in Chapter Nine, makes possible a more systematic and dependable audit of the vocational maturity of youth of varying ages and grade levels and should permit researchers to use scores on such career development questionnaires as indicators of subsequent work adjustment.

The School-to-Work Passage: Discontinuities

Given the growing tendency among American students to combine gainful employment with schooling, considerable interest has been expressed about the impact of this practice on student learning and on socialization for adult responsibilities. Charging that the schools isolate young people from the adult world and shield them from opportunities for self-management, decision making, and learning to work with others, the Panel on

Youth of the President's Science Advisory Committee (1973) advocated workplace experience as an important means of aiding movement toward productive adulthood. However, others have voiced doubts about the value of employment experience for in-school youth. They have argued that, in most instances, neither the schools nor the work-site employers and supervisors provide adequate support and constructive guidance to students in exploiting their outside jobs as a means to effective work socialization. The discussion that follows summarizes selected recent findings on the school-to-work transition.

Impact of Work on Young Workers. A study comparing tenth- and eleventh-graders in first-time jobs and same-grade students without work experience (Steinberg and others, 1979) found that working facilitated modest gains in practical knowledge about the business world, economic concepts, and consumer practices, especially for academically below-average students. However, working had a negative effect on scholastic performance, especially for students who worked longer hours (beyond fifteen or twenty hours weekly). Students who worked were found to have more frequent school absences, to enjoy school less, and to spend less time studying. These evidences of lower involvement with school were thought to explain partially the poorer academic records of working students.

Companion studies by the same University of California at Irvine research team showed that the working high school students spent comparatively less time with their families but not less with peers and that the work obligation did not appear to affect the quality of their family and peer relationships. Although many of the employed students believed that their work served a socially useful purpose, their job experiences, in the main, did not furnish an opportunity for meaningful interaction with adults or for learning social responsibility through interdependence with other workers. These findings have led the research team to question the President's Science Advisory Committee's optimistic assessment of the socialization benefits of the workplace (Greenberger and others, 1980; Greenberger and Steinberg, 1981).

Data from the fifteen-year National Longitudinal Survey

have yielded findings about the relation between the aspirations and work experiences of young workers that have important implications for parents, educators, and counselors. Both white and black youth with higher educational/occupational aspirations made greater gains in subsequent earnings than less ambitious youth. Those with a stronger sense of destiny control, who felt they could influence career outcomes through their own efforts and planning, were shown later to have experienced greater success in the labor market. The published report on this study directs attention to "the potential significance of instilling 'success-prone' attitudes in youth as they proceed from school to their work experiences" (Employment and Training Administration, 1979, p. 111).

Summary

The coming-of-age-as-worker over the individual's life history can best be understood as a social learning process. In myriad ways that we only partially understand, the developing child is imprinted with the beliefs, attitudes, and expectations of the culture. Family, school, and college experiences, among others, continuously shape the child's socialization. The formation of a relatively stable and comfortable self-identity, including an occupational self-identity, requires both a heightened awareness of society's norms and a personal sense of how well and in what ways one can satisfy those norms. A subjective and intimate process of testing oneself through occupational fantasies, aspirations, and plans occurs.

As noted in this chapter, occupational socialization is multidimensional and not always orderly. The inconsistent and conflicting images that the culture presents to the growing child and the sometimes unreasonable demands that it sets may operate as barriers to the acquisition of self-managed behaviors, such as impulse control and achievement motivation. Similarly, the complexity and seeming remoteness of the occupational world may make unduly difficult the important tasks of reality testing and identity formation in the learning of occupational roles. Consequently, the individual's career development may be misdirected and its pace uneven. In its broader sense, the concern of the career counselor is not with the act of decision making alone but with humanizing the occupational socialization experience and facilitating career maturity.

Suggested Readings

Bachman, J. G. *Youth in Transition.* Vol. 2. Ann Arbor: Institute for Social Research, University of Michigan, 1970.

Reports the detailed findings of a large-scale study of family and related background factors in the socialization of teenage youth. Conditions associated with college plans and occupational aspirations are analyzed.

Erikson, E. H. *Identity: Youth and Crisis.* New York: Norton, 1968.

Widely cited neoanalytic classic on the life cycle and its psychosocial stages and the implications for understanding the personal identity dilemmas of youth.

Jordaan, J. P., and Heyde, M. B. *Vocational Maturity During the High School Years.* New York: Teachers College Press, 1979.

Third monograph in the twenty-year Career Pattern Study of the career development of young males. Presents longitudinal data on changes in vocational maturity between the ninth and twelfth grades and identifies early predictors of vocational maturity.

Maizels, J. *Adolescent Needs and the Transition from School to Work.* London: Athlone Press, University of London, 1970.

Report of a British inquiry of problems and changes associated with movement from school to work. Analysis emphasizes school experiences, socioeconomic roles, and work environments as important elements in the transition.

Slocum, W. L. *Occupational Careers.* (2nd ed.) Chicago: Aldine, 1974.

A sociological view of occupational attainment. Includes a treatment of the developmental determinants of career aspirations and decisions.

References

Baruch, G. K. "Maternal Career Orientation as Related to Parental Identification in College Women." *Journal of Vocational Behavior,* 1974, *4,* 173-180.

Borow, H. "Development of Occupational Motives and Roles." In L. W. Hoffman and M. L. Hoffman (Eds.), *Review of Child Development Research.* Vol. 2. New York: Russell Sage Foundation, 1966.

Borow, H. "Effective Task or Work Orientation." In R. Jessor (Ed.), *Perspectives on Human Deprivation: Biological, Psychological, and Sociological.* Bethesda, Md.: National Institute of Child Health and Human Development, 1968.

Bratcher, W. E. "The Influence of the Family on Career Selection: A Family Systems Perspective." *Personnel and Guidance Journal,* 1982, *61,* 87-91.

Brown, D. *Students' Vocational Choices: A Review and Critique.* Boston: Houghton Mifflin, 1970.

Buehler, C. *Der Menschliche Lebenslauf als Psychologisches Problem.* Leipzig: Hirzel, 1933.

Bureau of Labor Statistics, U.S. Department of Labor. *Profile of the Teenage Worker.* Bulletin 2039. Washington, D.C.: U.S. Government Printing Office, 1980.

Bureau of Labor Statistics, U.S. Department of Labor. "Working Mothers." Reported in *USA Today,* July 28, 1983, p. 1.

Demos, J., and Demos, V. "Adolescence in Historical Perspective." In M. Gordon (Ed.), *The American Family in Social-Historical Perspective.* New York: St. Martin's Press, 1973.

Employment and Training Administration, U.S. Department of Labor. *Work Attitudes and Work Experience.* R&D Monograph No. 60. Washington, D.C.: U.S. Government Printing Office, 1979.

Erikson, E. H. "Youth: Fidelity and Diversity." *Daedalus,* 1962, *9,* 5-27.

Erikson, E. H. *Childhood and Society.* (2nd ed.) New York: Norton, 1963.

Erikson, E. H. *Identity: Youth and Crisis.* New York: Norton, 1968.

Featherman, D. L. "Schooling and Occupational Careers: Constancy and Change in Worldly Success." In O. G. Brim and J. Kagan (Eds.), *Constancy and Change in Human Development.* Cambridge, Mass.: Harvard University Press, 1980.

Freeman, R. B. *The Overeducated American.* New York: Academic Press, 1976.

Garfinkel, P. "The Best 'Jewish Mother' in the World." *Psychology Today,* September 1983, pp. 56-60.

Golding, W. G. *Lord of the Flies.* New York: Coward, McCann & Geoghegan, 1962.

Greenberger, E., and Steinberg, L. D. "The Workplace as a Context for the Socialization of Youth." *Journal of Youth and Adolescence,* 1981, *10,* 185-210.

Greenberger, E., and others. "Adolescents Who Work: Effects of Part-Time Employment on Family and Peer Relations." Unpublished paper, Program for Social Ecology, University of California at Irvine, 1980.

Gross, E. *Work and Society.* New York: Crowell, 1958.

Gunn, B. "Children's Conceptions of Occupational Prestige." *Personnel and Guidance Journal,* 1964, *42,* 558-563.

Hamburger, M. "The Significance of Work Experience in Adolescent Development." Position paper prepared for Division of Adult and Vocational Research, U.S. Office of Education, Washington, D.C., January 1967.

Havighurst, R. J. *Human Development and Education.* New York: Longman, 1953.

Herr, E. L. *Review and Synthesis of Foundations for Career Education.* Columbus: National Center for Research in Vocational Education, Ohio State University, 1972.

Herr, E. L. "Manpower Policies, Vocational Guidance, and Career Development." In E. L. Herr (Ed.), *Vocational Guidance and Human Development.* Boston: Houghton Mifflin, 1974.

Herriott, R. E. "Some Social Determinants of Level of Educational Aspiration." Harvard Studies in Career Development, No. 16. Cambridge, Mass.: Graduate School of Education, Harvard University, 1961.

Hollingshead, A. B. *Elmstown's Youth*. New York: Wiley, 1949.

Hotchkiss, L., and Borow, H. "Sociological Perspectives on Career Development." In D. Brown and L. Brooks (Eds.), *Career Choice and Development*. San Francisco: Jossey-Bass, 1984.

Itard, J. M. G. *The Wild Boy of Aveyron*. New York: Appleton-Century-Crofts, 1932.

Jones, E. *The Life and Work of Sigmund Freud*. New York: Basic Books, 1953.

Jordaan, J. P., and Heyde, M. B. *Vocational Maturity During the High School Years*. New York: Teachers College Press, 1979.

Kahn, R. L., and Antonucci, T. C. "Convoys over the Life Course: Attachment, Roles, and Social Support." In P. B. Baltes and O. G. Brim (Eds.), *Life-Span Development and Behavior*. Vol. 3. New York: Academic Press, 1980.

Katz, M. R. (Ed.). *A Computer-Based System of Interactive Guidance and Information*. Princeton, N.J.: Educational Testing Service, 1975.

Krumboltz, J. D., and Hamel, D. A. *Assessing Career Development*. Palo Alto, Calif.: Mayfield, 1982.

Krumboltz, J. D., and Thoresen, C. E. *Counseling Methods*. New York: Holt, Rinehart and Winston, 1976.

Lazarsfeld, P. *Jugend und Beruf*. Jena: C. Fischer, 1931.

Lofquist, L. H., and Dawis, R. V. *Adjustment to Work*. New York: Appleton-Century-Crofts, 1969.

Luckey, E. B. "The Family: Perspective on Its Role in Development and Choice." In E. L. Herr (Ed.), *Vocational Guidance and Human Development*. Boston: Houghton Mifflin, 1974.

McCandless, B. R. *Children: Behavior and Development*. (2nd ed.) New York: Holt, Rinehart and Winston, 1967.

Moss, H. A., and Kagan, J. "Stability of Achievement and Recognition Seeking Behavior from Early Childhood Through Adulthood." *Journal of Abnormal and Social Psychology*, 1961, *63*, 504-513.

Murphy, G. "Work and the Productive Personality." In H. Borow

(Ed.), *Career Guidance for a New Age*. Boston: Houghton Mifflin, 1973.

Neff, W. S. *Work and Human Behavior*. (2nd ed.) Chicago: Aldine, 1977.

O'Dowd, D. D., and Beardslee, D. C. *College Student Images of a Selected Group of Professions and Occupations*. Cooperative Research Project No. 562, U.S. Office of Education. Middletown, Conn.: Wesley, 1960.

Panel on Youth, President's Science Advisory Committee. *Youth: Transitions to Adulthood*. Chicago: University of Chicago Press, 1973.

Portner, J. *Impact of Work on the Family*. Minneapolis: Minnesota Council on Family Relations, 1978.

Prediger, D. J., Roth, J. D., and Noeth, R. J. "Nationwide Study of Student Career Development: Summary of Results." ACT Research Report No. 61. Iowa City, Iowa: American College Testing Program, 1973.

Roe, A. *The Psychology of Occupations*. New York: Wiley, 1956.

Sewell, W. H., Haller, A. O., and Portes, A. "The Educational and Early Occupational Attainment Process." *American Sociological Review*, 1969, *34*, 82–92.

Sewell, W. H., Haller, A. O., and Straus, M. A. "Social Status and Educational and Occupational Aspiration." *American Sociological Review*, 1957, *22*, 67–73.

Special Task Force, U.S. Department of Health, Education and Welfare. *Work in America*. Cambridge, Mass.: MIT Press, 1973.

Steinberg, L. D., and others. "High School Students in the Labor Force: Some Costs and Benefits to School and Learning." Unpublished paper, Program in Social Ecology, University of California at Irvine, 1979.

Stone, A. A., and Onqué, G. C. *Longitudinal Studies of Child Personality*. Cambridge, Mass.: Harvard University Press, 1959.

Super, D. E. "Vocational Adjustment: Implementing a Self-Concept." *Occupations*, 1951, *30*, 88–92.

Super, D. E. "A Theory of Vocational Development." *American Psychologist*, 1953, *8*, 185–190.

Super, D. E. *The Psychology of Careers.* New York: Harper & Row, 1957.

Tiedeman, D. V., and O'Hara, R. P. *Career Development: Choice and Adjustment.* New York: College Entrance Examination Board, 1963.

Tilgher, A. *Work: What It Has Meant to Workers Through the Ages.* London: Harrap, 1931.

Warner, W. L., Meeker, M., and Eells, K. *Social Class in America.* Chicago: Science Research Associates, 1949.

White, R. W. "Motivation Reconsidered: The Concept of Competence." *Psychological Review,* 1959, *66,* 297-333.

Wrenn, C. G. "Human Values and Work in American Life." In H. Borow (Ed.), *Man in a World at Work.* Boston: Houghton Mifflin, 1964.

Yankelovich, D. *The Changing Values on Campus.* New York: Washington Square Press, 1972.

7

Stephen A. Stumpf

❧ ❧ ❧ ❧ ❧ ❧ ❧ ❧

Adult Career Development: Individual and Organizational Factors

Several trends have evolved over the past two decades that define the context of adult career development in business settings. There has been increased acceptance of a life-span perspective of career development (Hall, 1976; Super, 1980); a career involves a person's lifetime. There has been a shift from focusing on career choices to a concern for career transitions that affect individual growth or deterioration (Hall, 1976; Schlossberg, 1981). And there has been growing interest among work organizations in viewing individuals' careers as integral to human resource management systems (Bartol, 1981; Hall and Lerner, 1980; Super and Hall, 1978). This chapter focuses on these trends and examines both individual and organizational factors that affect adult career development in business settings. Future trends are also discussed.

For purposes of this chapter a career is defined as a sequence of work-related positions and activities throughout a person's life. A career encompasses those stages, transitions, and actions that reflect one's needs, motives, and aspirations, as well as societal and organizational needs, expectations, and constraints (Hall, 1976; London and Stumpf, 1982). This definition is more limited than that proposed by Super (1980) in that it excludes nonwork roles. Although nonwork roles such as being a spouse or a parent interact with work roles and affect an individual's choices regarding allocation of time between work and leisure activities, nonwork roles are not considered in this discussion of adult careers in business settings.

The foregoing definition implies that adult career development can be examined from both individual and organizational perspectives—that is, with regard to both individual growth and improved work performance. In addition, the term *career development* is often used in business organizations to refer to the activities that individuals participate in to prepare themselves for various work roles and to refer to the activities that organizations sponsor to affect individual performance.

The two perspectives of adult career development—personal growth and improved work performance—imply some progression or positive change for the individual. Presumably, the individual and the organization are able to detect a change in psychological and/or work-related outcomes. Psychological outcomes include job, career, and life satisfaction; feelings of accomplishment, mastery, and competence; and feelings of self-worth, self-esteem, and success (Hall, 1976; Schein, 1978). Work-related outcomes include work-role changes that involve more interesting or enjoyable work activities, advancement or promotion, and salary increases; and organizational rewards such as power, prestige, and status (Bartol, 1981).

Whether people perceive themselves as developing with respect to their career depends on the nature and magnitude of the changes in psychological and work-related outcomes and the value placed on these outcomes by individuals and their respective organizations. Hence, adult career development, although it has some objective components, is primarily subjective and is a function of what individuals and organizations value and perceive. For example, two individuals with similar work histories and performance records might be offered a job transfer. One individual might perceive the transfer as a positive part of his or her career development as a result of expected changes in job satisfaction, self-esteem, work activities, and status. The second individual might perceive the transfer negatively, given the same general changes. The latter individual may not be inclined to describe the transfer as part of his or her career development. Outside parties, including managers, personnel administrators, and counselors, may also view the transfer as either part or not part of the individual's career development. In any case, they are often confronted with the difficult task of helping the individual adjust to career changes that are perceived to have some negative components. If they try to discuss a negatively perceived change as a developmental experience, they may encounter resistance, resentment, and anger.

These two perspectives of adult career development depart from the more traditional views of general adult development (Levinson and others, 1978; Gould, 1978; Lowenthal and Chiriboga, 1975; Neugarten, 1968). General adult development theory focuses more on the development of *self* in the context of family, work, and community environments. The perspectives in this chapter, however, consider adult career development as a dynamic, interactive process between individuals and organizations. Together these perspectives create the context for individuals and organizations to comanage people's careers for the benefit of both the individual and the organization.

Individual Factors Affecting Adult Career Development

Many individual factors affect adult career development. This chapter discusses six of them: social class; personality, interests, and values; self-knowledge and career plans; career motivation; career stage; and career life cycles.

Social Class. Research on social class as a determinant of career attainment suggests that there is a relationship between parental occupation, education, and wealth and the subsequent occupational status attained by children (for example, Blau and Duncan, 1967). One proposed explanation is that parents and the broader family unit socialize children so that they value, and hence strive for and expect to enter, particular occupations. One primary outcome of socialization is the narrowing of the spectrum of occupations actively considered (Gottfredson, 1981). Therefore, some elements of subsequent adult career development may be partially determined.

Personality, Interests, and Values. Individual differences such as differences in personality, interests, and values are among the most-researched variables in career development. Theory and research support the idea that people tend to develop more productively in work roles and organizational environments that are congruent with their personalities, interests, and values (Holland, 1973; Osipow, 1983; Schein, 1978). To the extent that individuals can achieve a reasonable degree of congruence between their orientation and work-role demands, positive outcomes should result for both them and the organization. Alternatively, developmental demands may become excessive when there is incongruence—whether it is due to a poor choice, lack of opportunities, or work-role changes after initial employment.

Self-Knowledge and Career Plans. During the past decade a rather extensive popular literature has evolved that encourages individuals to conduct self-assessment and to update that assessment every few years (Bolles, 1983; Kotter, Faux, and McArthur, 1978). Self-assessment involves a systematic process of gathering information about oneself and analyzing that information to provide direction for career decisions. Such direction can take the form of specific identity statements that describe aspects of one's identity vis-à-vis one's ego, affiliations, family, and work roles. Self-assessment can also be used to define possible career work roles, to understand personal strengths and weaknesses, to identify training and development needs, and to guide one's career planning. In short, accurate self-assessment provides an information base for meaningful career plans, decisions, and actions.

Career Motivation. The premise that self-assessment and career planning have an impact on adult career development is contingent on individuals' being motivated to conduct self-assessment, to formulate plans, and to implement them. In the absence of career motivation, uncontrollable factors such as age, career stage, external events, socioeconomic status, and individual traits are more likely to explain substantial variation in individuals' careers than controllable factors.

London (in press) describes career motivation as internal to the individual, influenced by the organization in which an individual is involved and the tasks the individual performs in the organization, and reflected in the individual's career decisions and behavior. The individual characteristics that affect career development are categorized into three domains: career identity, career insight, and career resilience. Each domain affects and is affected by situational characteristics and results in decisions and behaviors relevant to that domain.

Career identity is the centrality of one's career to one's self-image. Constructs in the literature such as career salience, job involvement, professional orientation, identification with the organization, primacy of work, need for advancement, and need for recognition are part of career identity. Situational characteristics that affect career motivation via career identity include the objectively determined importance of one's job for the organization, the extent to which a job is challenging, and management's encouragement of professionalism. Also included are management's press for commitment to the organization, the organizationally implied priority of work over nonwork activities, availability of advancement opportunities, and recognition for work performed effectively. Typical career decisions and behaviors that reflect career motivation derived from the career identity domain include identifying with one's career by establishing career plans or giving up other valued outcomes to enhance one's career, demonstrating job involvement, participating in professional activities, exhibiting commitment to the organization, showing devotion to work, striving for advancement, and seeking recognition.

The career insight domain reflects the extent to which one has a realistic perception of one's skills, values, and preferences as well as organizational realities. Career insight variables are goal clarity, goal flexibility, need for change, self-objectivity, and realism of expectations. Situational characteristics that affect career motivation via the career insight domain include structures and policies to facilitate goal setting, organizational flexibility in requirements, and procedures for establishing or changing goals. Also included are opportunities for change, feedback systems (the fairness and accuracy of performance appraisal), and availability of realistic job information (job descriptions and job postings). Career motivation due to career insight can be observed in such decisions and behaviors as establishing specific and moderately difficult career goals, making goal changes that reflect organizational constraints, expressing enthusiasm for new experiences, monitoring one's own performance, and forming expectations that reflect an understanding of the reality of the situation and the organization.

Career resilience is the extent to which one is resistant to career disruptions that could not be easily avoided. Variables such as self-esteem, adaptability, internal locus of control, need for achievement, inner work standards, and need for superior approval are part of this domain. Situational characteristics that affect career motivation via the career resilience domain include positive and constructive feedback to employees, changes in task assignments, job structures, and reporting relationships. Additional situational characteristics are opportunities for individual discretion in determining work methods, opportunity for achievement, incentives for high-quality work, and supervisory consideration and control. Career decisions and behaviors that reflect career motivation derived from the career resilience domain include showing belief in oneself by requesting assignments and sharing ideas, changing work behaviors to meet changing demands, taking control in low-structure situations, working hard to achieve difficult tasks and seeking knowledge of results, taking the time to do the best job possible, and trying to impress one's supervisor.

Career motivation affects the level of career development an individual aspires to achieve. The strength of one's career identity, career insight, and career resilience will partly determine the nature and course of one's development. Situational or organizational factors will often affect the level of motivation exhibited as well as the outcomes of actions taken by goal-directed and motivated individuals.

Career Stage. As suggested earlier, the perspectives of adult career development discussed herein depart from views of general adult development based primarily on career stage and chronological age. However, this departure does not imply that career stage and age have no relevance to adult career development. On the contrary, some individual needs and some organizational factors are likely to change over time in predictable ways. By defining career stages and the major events associated with them, we can identify the different tasks that individuals need to accomplish at different points in their lives and the conflicts they are likely to face during their career development. Career-stage models resemble biological growth-and-decline curves—beginning with an early growth period, then exploration and trial, moving to a period of establishment and advancement, followed by midcareer growth, maintenance or decline, and finally disengagement (Hall, 1976; Schein, 1978; Van Maanen and Schein, 1977).

Van Maanen and Schein (1977) discuss the salient developmental tasks for adult career stages of exploration and trial, establishment and advancement, midcareer, and disengagement. Exploration and trial involve mutual search and exploratory processes between the individual and the organization; each tests and screens the other, makes choices, and experiences a socialization process that is dominated by the organization. The most important developmental tasks of this stage are to evolve an accurate image of the job and the organization; to accept the ambiguities and uncertainties of making career decisions; and to adapt to early job challenges, goals, and feedback.

Establishment and advancement involve establishing one's worth to the organization, taking special assignments and transfers, and becoming visible to those at higher levels. The developmental process involves forming an accurate self-image based on actual work experiences, developing areas of expertise, accepting and managing successes and failures, and establishing supportive relationships with both junior and senior coworkers.

The midcareer stage involves still more growth for some people, leveling off and maintenance of the status quo for others, and even decline for some. Growth often involves promotions, new experiences, greater responsibilities, and higher status. Developmental challenges are to accept success, adjust to new career directions, and work through midlife reevaluations in light of experienced changes. Maintenance—remaining on the same job or experiencing little change in responsibilities or status—requires one to accept what is, feel pride in past accomplishments, value security, become a mentor, develop nonwork interests, and reevaluate what one wants to achieve over the next decade. Decline involves being considered "surplus" or "obsolete" and possibly demoted or reassigned to a lesser work role. Development here requires that one accept shortcomings or failures, begin to consider retirement, emphasize nonwork activities, or withdraw from one work setting to seek another.

The disengagement stage allows one to prepare for retirement, assume an advisory position, and become a mentor to junior coworkers. Development in the disengagement career stage includes becoming concerned with teaching others, making psychological adjustments to retirement, finding new interests and sources of self-improvement, and learning to accept a reduced work role.

Schein (1978) discusses another conceptualization of career stages, general issues to be confronted at each stage, and the accompanying tasks. He defines these stages in terms of the individual's entrance into and exit from work organizations: entry to the world of work (age 16–25), basic training (age 16–25), full membership in early career (age 17–30), full membership in midcareer (age 25+), midcareer crisis (age 35–45), late career in either a leadership or a nonleadership role (age 40+), decline and disengagement (age 40+), and retirement. Because of the substantial overlap in age across these stages, and the likely cycling back to earlier stages as individuals change jobs or career areas, these stages are more like career transitions that often recur than career stages.

Life Cycle. Influences of life cycle on adult career development expand on the career-stage-related factors to include other aspects of the individual's life. Work is viewed as only one of several activities (Gould, 1978; Hall and Hall, 1976; Super, 1980; Vaillant, 1977). For example, being in a dual-career situation, having a large family, or having responsibility for an extended family may consume significant amounts of energy, leaving less energy for work. Demanding hobbies and leisure activities may also vary with one's life stage and compete for one's time. Individuals may therefore be required to develop an effective balance of work and leisure (Near, Rice, and Hunt, 1980; Kabanoff, 1980).

Kabanoff (1980) has identified several general patterns of combining work and leisure, based on five work and leisure attributes: autonomy, variety, skill utilization, pressure, and interaction. The patterns are reflected in individuals who have low (or high) levels of one or more of the five attributes in work and low (or high) levels of one or more of the five attributes in leisure. Different personal and work characteristics such as sex, age, family commitments, and work schedules tend to characterize different work/leisure patterns. Four patterns that evolved from Kabanoff's study suggest that individuals must learn to manage both their work and nonwork activities to achieve life goals. One's self-assessment is likely to identify many family- and leisure-related issues in addition to career-related issues. One's career plans and objectives need to be extended to include the development and balance associated with other life goals.

Organizational Factors Affecting
Adult Career Development

In addition to the many individual factors that affect adult career development, work organizations provide the context, structure, and procedures through which careers evolve, as well as specific programs and processes designed to influence career paths, mobility, and human development. The organizational factors discussed in this chapter are organizational purpose and job opportunities, supervision and performance assessment, career-planning and career development activities, and staffing support systems.

Organizational Purpose and Job Opportunities. A major organizational factor that affects adult career development is the basic purpose of the organization. Developmental opportunities for employees of a university are likely to differ from those of a manufacturing organization, government agency, or research laboratory. Employees of organizations with policies of short-term employment, rapid evaluation and promotion, and specialized career paths are going to experience different developmental opportunities and demands than employees of organizations with policies of secure employment, slow evaluation and promotion, and nonspecialized career paths (Ouchi, 1981). Similarly, an organization with a "high-potential model" of organizational advancement will try to identify exceptional employees early in their careers so that they can receive the developmental experiences necessary to function at higher-level positions and can be promoted earlier (London and Stumpf, 1982). An alternative to the high-potential model can be viewed as an apprenticeship model (Bailyn, 1980). Apprenticeship entails a fairly long period of slow learning and training, resulting in an extended early career period, with incremental challenge through new assignments that are more like transfers than promotions.

The nature and extent of development experienced often relate to individual career mobility. Mobility within and between organizations is affected by the particular skills one possesses relative to those needed, one's marketability, labor market conditions, and barriers to mobility such as giving up retirement benefits, job security, and family-commitment ties (Veiga, 1983). Factors affecting mobility internal to the organization generally relate to past work experiences, duration of current position, availability of career options, and level of exposure. Studies of intraorganizational movement suggest that identifiable patterns of vertical and horizontal movement evolve (Anderson, Milkovich, and Tsui, 1981; Scholl, 1983; Vardi, 1980). Such mobility patterns, or career paths, have generalizable lengths, heights, directions, and overlap. It is therefore possible for individuals and organizations to plan career movement by taking into account these naturally occurring patterns. It is also possible for organizations to design career paths for particular developmental purposes.

Supervision and Performance Assessment. One's supervisor probably has more influence over one's career development than any other single individual. The various roles assigned, the feedback received, the developmental activities made available, and advancement opportunities are generally influenced heavily by one's immediate supervisor (Souerwine, 1981). To the extent that one is responsible for performing a variety of activities that use different skills, is allowed some autonomy in accomplishing the tasks, and acquires useful information on the results of the activities, then adult learning is likely to take place (Hackman and Oldham, 1980).

Information on results relates to both ongoing feedback on the quantity and quality of work performed and formal performance appraisals. Ongoing feedback provides one with the information necessary to alter behaviors to be more effective on particular tasks. Such feedback may be provided by one's supervisor, coworkers, or the task itself. Performance appraisals are generally conducted annually and involve a synthesis of past performance (Storey, 1976; Walker and Gutteridge, 1979). They typically inform the subordinate where he or she stands in the organization, indicate promotion potential, and discuss developmental needs and career opportunities (Latham and Wexley, 1981). If certain skills and abilities necessary to perform effectively need improvement, training and development activities may be made available. These may involve on-the-job training, classroom training, apprenticeship activities, or temporary developmental assignments (Goldstein, 1974). Whatever the form of training, it is likely to require the approval of one's supervisor if it takes place during working hours or is funded by the employer. Hence, a superior/subordinate relationship in which individual and organization career goals are openly shared, discussed, and acted on is central to adult career development in work settings.

In addition to assigning work, providing feedback through performance assessment, and approving or recommending developmental activities, one's supervisor is often a useful role model of effective managerial behavior. One can learn to handle particular situations, problems, and people through observing successful behaviors of others (Bandura, 1971; Weiss, 1977). Hence, learning is often accomplished through modeling.

Career-Planning and Career Development Activities. Organizations' ongoing processes to facilitate adult career development include a wide variety of career-planning and development activities. Following Bowen and Hall (1977), I shall describe four types of career-planning activities: individual activities, counselor/client activities, activities involving one's boss as counselor or coach, and group activities. Potential advantages and disadvantages of each career-planning activity for adult development are discussed, followed by a description of three types of training and development programs (London and Stumpf, 1982, pp. 108–119, 182–183).

Individual activities involve personal planning, perhaps with self-help materials but without the aid of company officials or external counselors. The information used in developing a career plan is generally uncovered through self-assessment and/or available as part of the feedback of either a performance appraisal system or an assessment center. Motivated and persistent people often find this material valuable in setting goals. However, individual career development activities are especially difficult for those who are unmotivated or who require excessive feedback and social support. These people often need additional career-planning assistance before they can establish meaningful plans.

People seeking advice often establish counselor/client relationships through guidance centers, local colleges and universities, community associations, and private counseling organizations (Gutteridge and Otte, 1983; Harrison and Entine, 1976). Counselors help clients explore their needs through interviews and interpretation and feedback of the results of interest and aptitude tests. These procedures tend to be most beneficial when integrated with life and organizational goals. Since people may resist results that disconfirm self-concepts, skillful counseling is necessary for meaningful career management activities.

Counseling assistance in career development offers advantages for information search, employee acceptance, and relevance for subsequent planning. An interview, often conducted by a trained manager or by a human resource professional, is used to determine an individual's strengths and weaknesses along career-relevant dimensions. By focusing on past behavior, the interviewer assists the individual in identifying individual abilities. The rapport between the interviewer and the individual facilitates acceptance of feedback. Such rapport and acceptance of feedback, coupled with the interviewer's knowledge of the organization, help the person develop realistic career plans. The result can be a development program that takes advantage of opportunities, relationships, and activities provided by the work environment, which are also compatible with the individual's personality and nonwork goals.

As previously mentioned, a supervisor can provide counseling or serve as a coach by appraising subordinates' performance, providing feedback, making suggestions for improvement, and providing information on career opportunities. Generally, supervisors are able to observe and to evaluate subordinates' behavior, to know about available career opportunities, and to provide assignments to develop the individual's capabilities. However, some supervisors lack the ability or willingness to appraise and discuss such information with subordinates (Gutteridge and Otte, 1983; Walker and Gutteridge, 1979). Supervisors may not have sufficient influence in the organization to fulfill promises for future developmental assignments. Moreover, subordinates may be defensive when faced with a negative evaluation and/or have difficulty expressing feelings to the supervisor. A management-by-objectives approach that integrates self-assessment, performance evaluation, and goal setting is a widely recommended procedure (Latham and Wexley, 1981). It requires substantial commitment on the part of both the supervisor and the subordinate.

Group activities include assessment centers, business simulations, and life-planning workshops, all of which may be conducted inside or outside the organization to generate relevant career management information. Assessment centers use group discussions and individual decision-making exercises as well as paper-and-pencil tests to generate data about individuals. The results suggest advancement potential and can help identify individuals' strengths and weaknesses for developmental purposes (Boehm and Hoyle, 1977; Freedman, Stumpf, and Platten, 1980).

A program offered in many organizations that was designed by the Center for Creative Leadership for work-related skill assessment allows individuals to manage a simulated organization called "Looking Glass, Inc." (McCall and Lombardo, 1978). Trained staff members observe the Looking Glass participants, evaluate the decisions made (or why they were not made), and provide group and individual feedback on managerial skills. Generally, individuals volunteer for the program to learn more about their skills; no evaluative information is reported to the participant's supervisor or retained within the corporation. Feedback is generally tailored to the areas the participant views as most relevant to current job and career growth.

Life-planning workshops attempt to develop greater self-awareness through interaction with other participants. Groups may discuss cases or simulated problems with which group members are able to identify. Discussion may also deal with participants' problems both in and out of work settings (Kirn and Kirn, 1978). Aspects of group activities that facilitate more effective life planning are the availability of more information and sources of information; shared concerns, which facilitate openness and realistic discussions of career plans; norms for helping others; and the opportunity to develop social skills. In contrast to assessment centers and business simulations, life-planning workshops are generally low-pressure situations oriented toward discovering and revealing one's feelings and goals. Voluntary participation and confidentiality are basic rules for most life-planning activities (Kirn and Kirn, 1978).

Career-planning programs generally integrate several activities. The activities chosen depend on the purpose of the program. Some career-planning programs are intended to have universal applicability; anyone who wishes, regardless of career stage, ability, organizational level, and job function, may take advantage of the program. Other programs are meant for high-potential individuals—those who are identified early in their careers as having good potential for advancement. Still other programs are remedial. These last types of programs are often targeted to the development of particular skills.

Three types of training and development can be distinguished: orientation training, technical skills training, and managerial skills training. Orientation training is used at all levels to

indoctrinate newcomers. New recruits, for example, are frequently given an orientation to the organization, covering its
objectives and offered benefits, as well as formal rules for employees. Orientation sessions may also be held for newly promoted individuals to help them get acquainted with their new
peers, to introduce them to top executives, and to explain required procedures and behaviors.

Technical skills training focuses on introducing employees to new technology, recent advances in the field, or instruction in a new or outside field. The goals are to broaden
perspectives and to guard against professional obsolescence.
Such training may be short-term and offered "in-house" by the
company staff—as would be likely for refresher courses—or it
may be long-term and given "off-site" at a university or a com-
pany-sponsored training institute.

The third type of training focuses on general managerial
skills. This training takes on different forms at different organizational levels. Lower-level managers may be given an opportunity to participate in workshops lasting from several hours
to several days. These workshops may be offered by trainers
employed by the company, consultants, or local university faculty members. Possible topics include time management, budget planning, leadership, decision making, conflict management,
and career planning. Workshops for higher-level managers may
focus on corporate strategy, organization design, productivity,
or economic and political trends and their impact on the organization. The diversity of topics suggests that there are a variety of training methods and types that might be adopted in response to a training needs analysis to facilitate adult career
development (Goldstein, 1974).

Staffing Support Systems. Organizations often establish
formal and informal mechanisms to help them make staffing
decisions such as promotions and transfers. Such staffing support systems provide employees with information and guidance
to use in their adult career development. Formal staffing support systems include (1) promotion and transfer policies to
establish and to clarify the general procedures for making staffing decisions, (2) standard operating procedures to describe spe-

cific procedures on salary and benefit administration, promotion and transfer actions, performance appraisal processes, and career-planning and career development activities, (3) human resource forecasting and planning systems to predict the number and types of people necessary in the future and to formulate action plans for securing the required labor force, (4) succession-planning activities to define the requirements of particular higher-level positions and to determine the availability of candidates and their developmental needs in order to advance into such positions, (5) job-matching systems to align individual abilities and interests with job requirements, and (6) job-posting systems to publicly announce position vacancies in order to encourage employees to apply for openings and to prepare themselves for future openings (London and Stumpf, 1982; Walker and Gutteridge, 1979).

Informal support systems also exist in organizations to facilitate career development (Schein, 1978). Such systems include the social, professional, and patron relationships that provide information, guidance, emotional support, and sponsorship for individuals. The most common form of informal support comes from peers, who often offer friendship and information and act as sounding boards for one's career issues. Role models differ from peer supporters in that a role model may be any work associate—peer, superior, subordinate, or coworker—whose behaviors, personal style, and attitudes are emulated (Shapiro, Haseltine, and Rowe, 1978). Role models can be helpful in guiding one's career development by exemplifying effective work behaviors and attitudes; alternatively, inappropriate behaviors and attitudes can also be identified and avoided.

Peers and role models often influence individual career management, but they have little effect on how the organization manages one's career. In contrast, sponsors and mentors provide informal support through sharing career management information and influencing others in the organizational hierarchy. Sponsors and mentors can be instrumental in facilitating career advancement (Levinson and others, 1978; London and Stumpf, 1982).

Trends in Adult Career Development

In this section I identify several trends in adult career development, based on the view of adult career development as a joint process involving individuals and work organizations. During the latter part of the 1980s and the 1990s, the emphasis is likely to be on defining individual, organizational, and shared responsibility for adult career development; encouraging career exploration and self-assessment; establishing career paths; targeting development to particular individual and organizational needs; matching jobs and people; and integrating career development planning and activities with other human resource functions.

Defining Individual, Organizational, and Shared Responsibilities. Self-assessment and the development of career and life plans will continue to be viewed as the responsibility of the individual. Although organizations frequently provide assistance in these areas through psychological testing, assessment centers, performance feedback, and specialized workshops on career planning, retirement planning, or outplacement, the responsibility for using these opportunities and for forming career and life plans remains with the individual (Walker and Gutteridge, 1979).

The organization's primary responsibility will be to communicate career-related information. This will often take the form of information on Equal Employment Opportunity (EEO) and affirmative action programs and policies; the company's business strategy and economic condition; and personnel function activities, including salary administration, job requirements, training and development options, job vacancies, career paths, and individual feedback on performance and career potential.

Individuals and their organizations will share responsibility for balancing the individual's needs with the organization's goals. Such shared responsibility is apparent when supervisors counsel and coach subordinates for adult career development or when the organization specifies career paths and developmental activities to prepare individuals for target jobs.

Encouraging Career Exploration and Self-Assessment. As

the number and variety of jobs increase in an increasingly complex society, it becomes more important for individuals to explore their environment and themselves to facilitate effective career decisions. Hence there will be more courses and programs that focus on career exploration activities and self-assessment (Hall, 1982). The process of learning about occupations, organizations, and jobs has been found to lead to more realistic expectations about the work roles accepted (Stumpf and Hartman, 1984). In turn, realistic expectations often lead to more realizable career plans, less job dissatisfaction, and fewer intentions to leave an organization or position. Although it is possible that the process of career exploration and self-assessment will cause a current employee to conclude that an alternative organization or position is desired, organizations are beginning to accept this risk. To the extent that positions other than an employee's current one are desired, career plans and developmental activities can be identified and pursued to increase the likelihood of a transfer or promotion into such positions.

Establishing Career Paths. Career planning implies that career paths and the developmental experiences by which one can get from one position to another can be identified. Although there are usually no formal paths between all positions, the most salient paths will frequently be identified on an organizationwide or divisionwide basis.

Development of realistic career paths involves three basic steps: defining work activities, identifying individual requirements, and establishing natural job families (Walker, 1976). The definition of work activities involves job content analyses (Burack and Mathys, 1979), which should integrate what employees say they actually do with what their managers say should be done. Individual requirements in terms of skills and knowledge can then be established on the basis of these identified and acknowledged work activities. These requirements can then be clustered into positions and job families. The existence of formalized career paths communicates to employees specific objectives, identifies the positions of possible role models for them to observe, and suggests a developmental process for target positions.

Targeting Development. As career planning becomes more common, and as organizations continue to spend millions of dollars on training and development, it is increasingly likely that career development programs will link the results of individual assessment and career-planning activities with training experiences. Development, therefore, will go beyond courses and programs to include positions, special projects, short-term assignments, and observing and modeling higher-level personnel. The developmental experiences a person has will be based on targeted development—that is, matching experiences to skills needed for target jobs. Experiences will increasingly be chosen on the basis of the individual's strengths and weaknesses and the type of job the individual hopes to attain. The focus will be on skills that can be developed and on providing experiences that use and enhance current strengths.

Matching Jobs and People. Formal systems to match jobs and people will become common. Computer technology has made complex career management information systems more feasible. Personnel data bases or skills inventory systems have the capacity to retain a complete profile of each employee. The computer profile can be easily revised as employees acquire additional education, gain new skills, and undertake new work experiences. It is also possible to develop computerized records of job descriptions in terms of requirements necessary to perform each job (Colarelli, Stumpf, and Wall, 1982). Computers can then be used to match job vacancies with available high-potential managers. This will be especially useful in large, geographically dispersed organizations, in which it is difficult to provide equal opportunities to all qualified candidates throughout the organization without computerization.

Smaller organizations without the resources or need for sophisticated computerized systems will rely on mechanical means to match individuals and jobs. An index system might consist of a card for each manager and a card for each job. Information about job requirements and individual qualifications expressed in common language will be coded into groups. The groupings show the similarity among different jobs, making it possible to identify paths from one job to another. Individuals who occupy two or three groupings in common with a job vacancy would be selected as candidates to fill the vacancy. The person eventually chosen need not meet all the job requirements, since most companies recognize that some skills can be developed on the job.

Integrating Career Development with Other Human Resource Functions. The importance of relating career development actions to other human resource functions is now being recognized. Organizational career development programs will become closely linked with management training and development to ensure that developmental activities are available and are actually used when needed. In some situations, enactment of the plan will involve new job assignments that are viewed as requisite for subsequent assignments. Staffing decisions that involve transfers or rotational job assignments will begin to take into account the career plans and development needs of employees. To the extent that career plans lead to development, the use of career planning will generate a larger talent pool to consider when making future staffing decisions.

The primary inputs into an organizational career-planning program are individual and organizational needs, goals, and abilities. Data on individuals are generated through assessments of performance and potential, as well as self-assessments of career interests and ambitions. Data on organizational needs and goals may come from job and organizational analyses. Both types of information are necessary to develop realistic career plans. Organizational needs and goals can also be established through human resource planning and then communicated clearly to employees for their use in establishing goals.

Human resource plans will identify future work force needs with respect to specific organizational goals. The organization's forecast of its future staffing requirements will be used to formulate career plans that include expected changes in the organization. This practice should reduce managerial and technical obsolescence, as well as unrealistic and unfulfilled expectations for individual employees.

Summary

Two perspectives of adult career development were proposed—personal growth and improved performance effectiveness. Both perspectives suggest that individuals and organizations should work together to enhance each other. Individual and organizational factors were identified and discussed that affect adult development: on the individual side, social class; personality, interests, and values; self-knowledge and career plans; career motivation; career stage; and life cycle; and, on the organizational side, organizational purpose and job opportunities; supervision and performance assessment; career-planning and career development activities; and staffing support systems. Several trends in adult career development theory and practice also were identified that seem likely to continue through the 1980s and 1990s.

Suggested Readings

Burack, E. H., and Mathys, N. J. *Career Management in Organizations: A Practical Human Resource Planning Approach.* Lake Forest, Ill.: Brace-Park Press, 1979.

A detailed how-to guide on career planning activities in business organizations. Excellent reading for those involved in designing career development programs in business organizations.

Gutteridge, T. G., and Otte, F. L. *Organizational Career Development: State of Practice.* Washington, D.C.: ASTD Press, 1983.

A useful summary and discussion of career development programs used in business organizations. The authors provide some integration of theory with practice to reach a set of conclusions, implications, and recommendations that should be read by anyone who manages a human resource function related to adult career development.

London, M., and Stumpf, S. A. *Managing Careers.* Reading, Mass.: Addison-Wesley, 1982.

   A thorough examination of the empirical and theoretical basis for career management practices in work organizations. The book can help individuals form career plans and assist organizations in designing and implementing successful career management systems. The policies and guidelines discussed are important to human resource program managers and anyone responsible for the careers of others.

Montross, D. H., and Shinkman, C. J. (Eds.). *Career Development in the 1980s: Theory and Practice.* Springfield, Ill.: Thomas, 1981.

   A collection of articles, most written specifically for this book, which review career development theories and outline practices for the 1980s. Career development issues, interventions, and counseling strategies for higher education and work organizations are discussed. Of the twenty-nine chapters, over half are required reading for anyone concerned with adult career development.

Schein, E. H. *Career Dynamics: Matching Individual and Organizational Needs.* Reading, Mass.: Addison-Wesley, 1978.

   This excellent book builds a human resource management model by examining the parallelism between individual and organizational needs throughout the life cycle. An important resource for serious students of career development, career counseling professionals, and managers.

Super, D. E., and Hall, D. T. "Career Development: Exploration and Planning." *Annual Review of Psychology,* 1978, *29,* 333–372.

   A thorough review of the career exploration and planning literature from 1966 to 1975. Half of the review focuses on these topics in educational settings, including instrument development efforts, the nature of exploration, and individual planning efforts. The second half focuses on career planning in work settings. Required reading for all career development research-ers.

References

Anderson, J. C., Milkovich, G. T., and Tsui, A. "Intra-organizational Mobility and Review." *Academy of Management Review,* 1981, *6,* 529-538.

Bailyn, L. "The Slow Burn Way to the Top: Some Thoughts on the Early Years of Organization Careers." In C. B. Derr (Ed.), *Work, Family, and the Career: New Frontiers in Theory and Research.* New York: Praeger, 1980.

Bandura, A. *Psychological Modeling: Conflicting Theories.* Chicago: Lieber-Atherton, 1971.

Bartol, K. M. "Vocational Behavior and Career Development, 1980: A Review." *Journal of Vocational Behavior,* 1981, *19,* 123-162.

Blau, P. M., and Duncan, O. D. *The American Occupational Structure.* New York: Wiley, 1967.

Boehm, V. R., and Hoyle, D. F. "Assessment and Management Development." In J. L. Moses and W. C. Byham (Eds.), *Applying the Assessment Center Method.* Elmsford, N.Y.: Pergamon Press, 1977.

Bolles, R. N. *What Color Is Your Parachute?* Berkeley, Calif.: Ten Speed Press, 1983.

Bowen, D. D., and Hall, D. T. "Career Planning for Employee Development: A Primer for Managers." *California Management Review,* 1977, *20*(2), 23-25.

Burack, E. H., and Mathys, N. J. *Career Management in Organizations: A Practical Human Resource Planning Approach.* Lake Forest, Ill.: Brace-Park Press, 1979.

Colarelli, S. M., Stumpf, S. A., and Wall, S. J. "Cross-Validation of a Short Form of the Position Description Questionnaire." *Educational and Psychological Measurement,* 1982, *42,* 1279-1283.

Freedman, R. D., Stumpf, S. A., and Platten, P. "An Assessment Center for Career Planning and Change." *Journal of Assessment Center Technology,* 1980, *3,* 5-10.

Goldstein, I. L. *Training: Program Development and Evaluation.* Monterey, Calif.: Brooks/Cole, 1974.

Gottfredson, L. S. "Circumscription and Compromise: A Developmental Theory of Occupational Aspirations." *Journal of Counseling Psychology,* 1981, *28,* 545–579.

Gould, R. *Transformations: Growth and Change in Adult Life.* New York: Simon & Schuster, 1978.

Gutteridge, T. G., and Otte, F. L. *Organizational Career Development: State of Practice.* Washington, D.C.: ASTD Press, 1983.

Hackman, J. R., and Oldham, G. R. *Work Design.* Reading, Mass.: Addison-Wesley, 1980.

Hall, D. T. *Careers in Organizations.* Santa Monica, Calif.: Goodyear, 1976.

Hall, D. T., and Hall, F. S. "What's New in Career Management?" *Organizational Dynamics,* 1976, *5*(1), 17–33.

Hall, D. T., and Lerner, P. E. "Career Development in Work Organizations: Research and Practice." *Professional Psychology,* 1980, *11,* 428–435.

Hall, F. S. "Developing and Managing Careers: A Teaching Perspective." In R. D. Freedman, C. Cooper, and S. A. Stumpf (Eds.), *Management Education: Issues in Theory, Research, and Practice.* London: Wiley, 1982.

Harrison, L. R., and Entine, A. D. "Existing Programs and Emerging Strategies." *Counseling Psychologist,* 1976, *6*(1), 45–49.

Holland, J. L. *Making Vocational Choices: A Theory of Careers.* Englewood Cliffs, N.J.: Prentice-Hall, 1973.

Kabanoff, B. "Work and Nonwork: A Review of Models, Methods, and Findings." *Psychological Bulletin,* 1980, *88,* 60–77.

Kirn, A. G., and Kirn, M. O. *Life Work Planning.* (4th ed.) New York: McGraw-Hill, 1978.

Kotter, J. P., Faux, V. A., and McArthur, C. C. *Self-Assessment and Career Development.* Englewood Cliffs, N.J.: Prentice-Hall, 1978.

Latham, G. P., and Wexley, K. N. *Increasing Productivity Through Performance Appraisal.* Reading, Mass.: Addison-Wesley, 1981.

Levinson, D. J., and others. *The Seasons of a Man's Life*. New York: Knopf, 1978.

London, M. "Toward a Theory of Career Motivation." *Academy of Management Review,* in press.

London, M., and Stumpf, S. A. *Managing Careers.* Reading, Mass.: Addison-Wesley, 1982.

Lowenthal, M. F., and Chiriboga, D. "Responses to Stress." In M. F. Lowenthal, M. Thurnher, D. Chiriboga, and Associates, *Four Stages of Life: A Comparative Study of Women and Men Facing Transitions.* San Francisco: Jossey-Bass, 1975.

McCall, M. W., and Lombardo, M. M. "Looking Glass, Inc.: An Organizational Simulation." Technical Report No. 12. Greensboro, N.C.: Center for Creative Leadership, 1978.

Near, J. P., Rice, R. W., and Hunt, R. O. "The Relationship Between Work and Nonwork Domains: A Review of Empirical Research." *Academy of Management Review,* 1980, *5,* 415–429.

Neugarten, B. L. "The Awareness of Middle Age." In B. L. Neugarten (Ed.), *Middle Age and Aging.* Chicago: University of Chicago Press, 1968.

Osipow, S. H. *Theories of Career Development.* (3rd ed.) Englewood Cliffs, N.J.: Prentice-Hall, 1983.

Ouchi, W. G. *Theory Z: How American Business Can Meet the Japanese Challenge.* Reading, Mass.: Addison-Wesley, 1981.

Schein, E. H. *Career Dynamics: Matching Individual and Organizational Needs.* Reading, Mass.: Addison-Wesley, 1978.

Schlossberg, N. K. "A Model for Analyzing Human Adaptation to Transition." *Counseling Psychologist,* 1981, *9,* 2–18.

Scholl, R. W. "Career Lines and Employment Stability." *Academy of Management Journal,* 1983, *26,* 86–103.

Shapiro, E. C., Haseltine, F. P., and Rowe, M. P. "Moving Up: Role Models, Mentors, and the 'Patron System.' " *Sloan Management Review,* 1978, *19*(3), 51–58.

Souerwine, A. H. "The Manager as Career Counselor: Some Issues and Approaches." In D. H. Montross and C. J. Shinkman (Eds.), *Career Development in the 1980s: Theory and Practice.* Springfield, Ill.: Thomas, 1981.

Storey, W. D. *Career Dimensions I, II, III, and IV*. Croton-on-Hudson, N.Y.: General Electric Company, 1976.

Stumpf, S. A., and Hartman, K. "Individual Exploration to Organizational Commitment or Withdrawal." *Academy of Management Journal*, 1984, *27*, 308–329.

Super, D. E. "A Life-Span, Life-Space Approach to Career Development." *Journal of Vocational Behavior*, 1980, *16*, 282–298.

Super, D. E., and Hall, D. T. "Career Development: Exploration and Planning." *Annual Review of Psychology*, 1978, *29*, 333–372.

Vaillant, G. E. *Adaptation to Life*. Boston: Little, Brown, 1977.

Van Maanen, J., and Schein, E. H. "Career Development." In J. R. Hackman and J. L. Suttle (Eds.), *Improving Life at Work: Behavioral Science Approaches to Organizational Change*. Santa Monica, Calif.: Goodyear, 1977.

Vardi, G. "Organizational Career Mobility: An Integrative Model." *Academy of Management Review*, 1980, *5*, 341–355.

Veiga, J. F. "Mobility Influences During Managerial Career Stages." *Academy of Management Journal*, 1983, *26*, 64–85.

Walker, J. W. "Let's Get Realistic About Career Paths." *Human Resources Management*, Fall 1976, pp. 2–7.

Walker, J. W., and Gutteridge, T. G. *Career Planning Practices: An AMA Survey Report*. New York: AMACOM, 1979.

Weiss, H. M. "Subordinate Imitation of Supervisor Behavior: The Role of Modeling in Organizational Socialization." *Organizational Behavior and Human Performance*, 1977, *19*, 89–105.

8

L. Sunny Sundal-Hansen

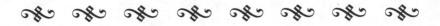

Interrelationship of Gender and Career

To adequately discuss a topic as broad as gender and career in one chapter is truly impossible. Ideally the cultural conditioning and differential socialization of women and men would be integrated into every chapter of this volume, for it pervades every aspect of career development and career guidance. It is a topic that affects all of us at all stages over the life span, from childhood to older adulthood. It also affects our view of the future and men's and women's roles in that future.

It is the purpose of this chapter (1) to provide a systems perspective on the career development of women and men, focusing particularly on the sex-role system that profoundly affects our careers, (2) to examine the impact of growing up female or male on our career development and career decision making, (3) to present data on the sexual division of labor across cultures, (4) to suggest career guidance interventions for changing futures, and (5) to present a career futures scenario as a context for career development and guidance transformations.

A Systems Perspective on Career Development

Essential to a systems perspective on gender and career is the fact that one must examine the social, psychological, political, spiritual, and economic context in which careers of women

216

and men are developed. This examination includes ascertaining the extent to which a culture values individual development or whether societal goals are primary. It also requires awareness of the stage of development of a society on a continuum of rural to industrial to technological. It is also important to know whether the society is democratic or authoritarian, capitalist or socialist or marxist. The degree of literacy and the distribution of women and men in education and work are critical factors, as are the degree of spirituality and the extent to which religion controls or affects other aspects of life, including male/female roles. The stage of development of career guidance and counseling (still often called educational/vocational guidance) in a culture is another part of the system.

Also to be considered are how the society distributes roles in education, work, and family; how independence, dependence, and interdependence are cultivated; and how the policy makers view equality of the sexes. The preparation of girls and boys for their future in the twenty-first century is a major issue. Another is how much counseling relies on classical matching of people and jobs or uses more contemporary developmental methods over the life span. Barriers that may limit career development of either sex need to be examined, as do similarities and differences that may result from the racial, ethnic, socioeconomic, and religious composition of the population. A basic question is how the culture perceives tradition and change and where it lies on the continuum of change in resisting, welcoming, or attempting to manage change.

Definitions. In examining gender and career, it is important to recognize that a sex-role system is at the core of our cultural norms and that it affects both women and men (Chetwynd and Hartnett, 1978). It can best be understood through some definitions, particularly related to sex-role socialization and stereotyping, for these, in turn, lead to the roles that each culture ascribes to women and men.

Stereotyping is the arbitrary assigning of certain habits, abilities, and expectations to people solely on the basis of group membership, regardless of their attributes as individuals. Stereotypes may be based on race, sex, ethnic background, socioeconomic level, age, handicap, sexual preference, or other factors. *Sex-role stereotypes* are beliefs concerning the general appropriateness of various *roles* and *activities* for women and for men. *Sex-trait stereotypes* are those psychological characteristics or behavioral traits that are believed to characterize one sex with much greater or lesser frequency than the other; thus, sex-trait stereotypes undergird both the sex-role stereotypes and sex roles themselves (Williams and Best, 1982). *Sex-difference stereotypes* are perceptions of "typical" characteristics and behaviors of males and females, views of what the sexes "are like" (Kutner and Brogan, 1976). *Sex-role orientation* is the attitudes we have learned through our socialization about masculinity and femininity and masculine and feminine roles. *Gender identity* derives from our basic biological and physiological characteristics and provides a secure sense of one's maleness or femaleness (Bem, 1975). *Sex-role ideology* is a normative view of appropriate behavior of females and males—that is, a view of what males and females "should" do. *Socialization* is the process by which behaviors, roles, attitudes, and beliefs are transmitted to the next generation. The socializing agents (for example, family, schools, churches, TV, peers, work and other organizations) may hold stereotypic beliefs about what are sex-appropriate characteristics. *Career socialization* comprises the lifelong series of differential processes and experiences through which women and men are prepared for the educational, vocational, and life-role options considered appropriate for their sex, race, or class (Hansen, 1979).

The Sex-Role System. At the heart of issues of gender and career is the sex-role system, which is the network of attitudes, feelings, and behaviors that result from the pervasiveness of sex-role stereotyping in the culture. Chetwynd and Hartnett (1978) point out that there are three factors of major importance to the system:

1. The assignment on the basis of sex of one of two different series of personality traits, the masculine and feminine stereotype. The male stereotype is one of dominance, aggressiveness, independence, and problem solving; the female

stereotype is one of dependence, subjectivity, passivity, and subordination.

2. The allocation on the basis of sex of different categories of those activities considered necessary, useful, or appropriate for the sustenance or improvement of living—that is, the division of labor into "men's work" and "women's work."

3. The investing of the male with a higher status or stature than the female; the characteristics and traits associated with men are considered to have more importance and value than those associated with women.

A growing body of literature from psychology, sociology, and cross-cultural research supports the power of stereotypes and the impact of socialization on sex roles. The study by Williams and Best (1982) of children and adults in thirty nations, perhaps the most comprehensive to date, supports the "pan-cultural" similarities in stereotypes. Although the researchers found no cross-cultural tendency to evaluate either of the stereotypes as more favorable than the other (unlike Chetwynd and Hartnett), they found that the male stereotype was more active and stronger than the female stereotype. They pointed out: "Children are socialized toward their adult roles by strengthening agentic needs in boys and communal needs in girls. Concomitant with the development of the different roles, belief systems evolve within the society concerning the psychological characteristics of men and women that serve to rationalize and justify the assignment of the sexes to their different social roles" (p. 241).

Socialization is reinforced by the sex typing of interests, trades, lines of study or majors, and jobs, and it affects what one believes is appropriate to be interested in, to study, to choose, or to do. It is an assumption of this chapter that changes occurring across cultures have made most of our sex-role prescriptions, stereotypes, and gender division of labor dysfunctional and that major changes are needed in the context, content, and concepts of career guidance and counseling to accommodate and manage these changes in ways that will benefit both individuals and society. When sex-role stereotyping is eliminated, people will still be socialized for life career roles, but it is hoped that this socialization will include expanded options for both sexes.

Important to understanding the sex-role system is knowledge of sex differences. In their extensive review of the psychology of sex differences, Maccoby and Jacklin (1974) reviewed all the studies that seemed to provide conclusive findings, those that were inconclusive, and those topics that had not yet been studied. Although their review was criticized by Block (1976), they reported "fairly well established" sex differences in only four areas: (1) Girls have greater verbal ability than boys. At about age eleven, the sexes begin to diverge, with female superiority increasing through high school and possibly beyond. (2) Boys excel in visual-spatial ability. Male superiority on spatial-visual tasks is fairly consistently found in adolescence and adulthood, but not in childhood. (3) Boys excel in mathematical ability. The two sexes are similar in their early acquisition of quantitative concepts during the grade school years, but beginning about age twelve to thirteen, boys' mathematical skills increase faster than girls'. (4) Males are more aggressive. This sex difference is found as early as social play begins, at age two or two and one-half (pp. 351–352).

Maccoby and Jacklin stated that, because of the overlap of ability distribution, no occupation is appropriately reserved for only one sex on the basis of ability patterns. They point out that many popular beliefs about the psychological characteristics of the two sexes have proved to have little or no basis in fact.

A more likely explanation for the perpetuation of "myths" is the fact that stereotypes are such powerful things. An ancient truth is worth restating here: if a generalization about a group of people is believed, whenever a member of that group behaves in the expected way the observer notes it and his belief is confirmed and strengthened; when a member of the group behaves in a way that is not consistent with the observer's expectations, the instance is likely to pass unnoticed, and the observer's generalized belief is protected from disconfirmation. We believe that this well-documented process occurs continually in relation to the expected and perceived behavior of males and females, and results in the perpetuation of myths that would otherwise die out under the impact of negative evidence. However, not all unconfirmed beliefs about the two sexes are of this sort. It is necessary to reconsider the nature of the evidence that permits us to conclude what is myth and what is (at least potentially) reality [p. 355].

Although research has not revealed many well-established, cross-situational sex differences in ability or psychological traits, the widespread stereotypes about sex differences held by both sexes influence judgments of the potentials or quality of work of men and women. The extent to which an individual might pursue a nontraditional occupation or life-style might be influenced by the strength of his or her own stereotypic view of sex differences. The issue seems to be not so much what sex differences exist as what people believe about what sex differences exist (sex-difference stereotypes) and how those beliefs influence attitudes and behavior. Therein lies the power of the sex-role system.

The Impact of Growing Up Female or Male

Career Development of Women. To anyone who has studied the literature on the career development of women, counseling women, achievement motivation of women, women and sex roles, gender and career, occupational/educational distribution, and sex-role socialization, it seems strange that one would have to justify attention to this topic in the 1980s ("Counseling Women," 1973, 1976, 1979). Yet, in spite of recognition of the inattention or minimal treatment given to women's career development for many years, the acknowledgment of barriers to women's careers, and the number of publications attending to women's careers, some textbooks suggest that women's career development has not been studied because it is so complex.

They also propose that societal change is occurring so rapidly that any theoretical proposal or generalization about women's career development is likely to be premature. What is overlooked in such statements is that theoretical propositions about men's career development have been proposed and tested for many years, that men's career development also is increasingly complex, and that men live in the same society in which rapid social change is occurring. Some argue further that what is known indicates that women's career development is not substantially different from that of men, that career counseling is essentially the same for both sexes, and that, therefore, we are creating much ado about nothing—a position challenged by this author and by several professional associations.

One major article that attempts to identify what we know and need to know about a career psychology of women (Fitzgerald and Crites, 1980) offers background in theory, knowledge, attitudes, and techniques for career counseling with women. In spite of these authors' thorough discussion of the limitations of knowledge and practice, of client socialization and counselor bias, their definition of career as "the developmental sequence of full-time gainful employment apart from other life roles" (p. 46) limits the article's usefulness. Using that definition because it can be studied more easily does not seem to provide a satisfactory rationale for this segmented view of women's lives. Worell (1980) observed that a revolution is in process regarding counseling women. If one uses the broad definitions of career as life roles, much of what she says relates to the career development of women. Worell suggested that new theory and research on gender differences and socialization, on the effects of sex-role stereotyping, and on androgyny support new imperatives for revisions in the content and practice of counseling psychology. Among the counseling approaches for new female client groups she identified are (1) career development counseling, (2) life-span development counseling, (3) reentry and adult counseling, (4) family and marital role counseling, and (5) divorce, widowhood, and singleness counseling. Worell also noted the need for new approaches with other client groups such as minority women, lesbians, handicapped women,

female offenders, and corporate women. She identified procedures to use with these new client populations, including guidelines for feminist counseling. She also highlighted the need for
ethical standards in professional practice, particularly the need
to avoid practices of prolonged dependency relationships and of
encouraging women to submit to oppressive and stereotyped
sex-role behaviors within sexual, marital, and work situations.

In examining the literature on career development of
women and men in relation to sex-role stereotyping, Follett,
Watt, and Hansen (1978) noted a striking absence of research
literature on men, in contrast to the abundant literature about
how sex-role stereotypes affect women. Their review of
internal and external barriers to career development included
literature on sex-difference stereotypes, self-concept and self-
esteem, locus of control, motivational variables such as achievement motivation and fear of success, and cognitive variables
such as expectancies and attribution of success. Among the
findings of that review were the following: (1) Sex-role orientation, sex-difference stereotypes, and ego strength all influence
the self-concept, which, in turn, influences educational/voca-
tional aspirations and expectations. (2) Women are more external than internal and tend not to plan or seek information. (3)
There is some evidence that persons who believe they have control over their environment are also likely to be flexible and
innovative in the life roles they choose and in their view of
themselves. (4) Males have higher aspirations and expect more
successful performance, and boys expect to perform better on a
given task. Studies also revealed that women's expectations of
success decline markedly in adolescence, that males tend to
overestimate their performance and females to underestimate
theirs, and that women attribute both success and failure to
internal causes. In examining data on the distribution of women
and men in the labor force, in vocational education, and in
school and college settings, Follett and associates found that the
educational underrepresentation of women in certain subjects
and training programs, not unexpectedly, led to similar occupational underrepresentation.

Although there is a significant gap in theories of women's

career development, a number of researchers have contributed a variety of conceptual frameworks from which to approach the topic. Farmer (1978) developed a conceptual model for explaining the inhibitors of achievement motivation in women, and Harmon (1977) presented a useful analysis of career counseling for women from the perspective of Maslow's hierarchy of needs. Osipow (1975) and his students analyzed factors affecting women's emerging careers, including barriers and family influences. Hansen and Rapoza (1978) assembled and critiqued a series of articles on the career development and counseling of women from a developmental and multiple-role perspective. Hackett and Betz (1981) conceptualized a self-efficacy approach to women's career development based on Bandura's social learning theory. They postulated that, largely as a result of socialization experiences, women lack strong expectations of personal efficacy in relation to many career-related behaviors and therefore fail to fully realize their potentials in career pursuits. The model is useful in integrating existing knowledge, generating research, and guiding interventions.

An important contribution of role theory in career development is Richardson's (1981) model for the intersection of work and family roles. In her analysis, Richardson cited the myth that occupational and family roles are two separate and nonoverlapping worlds. Like Pleck (1977), she demonstrated that there are both tasks and relationships in work and family and how they intersect. Four important assumptions, which affect both men and women, are that (1) major social roles provide the basic structure of the adult life experience, (2) occupational and familial roles (marital and parenting) are the major life roles for adults in our society and set normative expectations, (3) work and intimacy are processes that occur in both occupational and family roles, and (4) gender, race, and class are critical variables that affect the nature and process of role interaction. In discussing the complexity of role interaction, including developmental stage and life-event models, Richardson also analyzed the role conflict and stress involved in combining work and family roles for both women and men, especially in families with young children.

Although the scope of this chapter precludes an exhaustive review of literature on the career development of women, these examples give some indication of the extent to which attention has been given to the topic during the last decade. They also support the need for further study of the vocational behavior and career development of women, who constitute 51 percent of the population.

In summary, the influence of internal and external factors on women's career development has been widely documented in the literature on women, work, and socialization (Follett, Watt, and Hansen, 1978; Safilios-Rothschild, 1980). The lack of career information, adult models, and sense of self-direction; the influence of parents, family, teachers, counselors, and other socializing agents; and sex-role stereotyping and sex typing of occupations have been documented across cultures (BORN FREE, 1978; Secretariat of the Council of Europe, 1982; Williams and Best, 1982; Sundal-Hansen, in press). That the sex-role system has limited women's educational and occupational options, social and intellectual development, and economic status over the life span seems undeniable. The female stereotype, which begins in childhood, is reinforced by the socializing agents, becomes internalized, and continues into middle and older adulthood. The lack of work orientation, lack of planning orientation, lack of role models, lack of self-efficacy, lack of mathematics/science and athletic training, lack of economic independence, and lack of managerial skills, along with the Cinderella syndrome of "Be submissive, dependent, invisible, and passive," have combined into a deficit model that limits women's options, devalues their contributions, and keeps them from developing their human potential in getting the world's work done.

Career Development of Men. It is a fact that men's lives and career development have been studied longer and more intensively than women's. One might read any of the traditional texts on career development, as most of them are written by men and operate from a premise of men and career, often with a separate chapter on women and other "special populations." Most of the recognized theories, except for Roe's, have been developed by men and are about men. The focus here will be on the male sex role, some of the new perspectives on men's career development, and how men are affected by the sex-role system.

As women's lives have been defined by the family and the family life cycle, men's lives have been defined by work, in accordance with the dictum that "vocational success is everything" (Skovholt, 1978, p. 4). The male stereotype includes an expectation that boys will become leaders, be strong and athletic, develop mechanical, analytical, and mathematical abilities, and be competitive, autonomous problem solvers. One of the main messages of this stereotype is that occupational success equals self-worth (Skovholt and Morgan, 1981). One of the differences between the female and male stereotypes is that the male stereotype is more positive, as it is the one that brings the rewards valued in American society—money, status, and power. Several researchers have begun to look at men's lives in some new ways—not just at men and occupational careers but at the balancing of work, relationships, and leisure; the negative consequences of male socialization; male/female employment combinations (for example, dual careers or shared positions); midlife career shifts and preretirement; and sex-role strain. Indeed, rather than addressing men's career development in traditional agentic ways, men themselves are beginning to examine their own lives from a communal perspective, as women have done for a long time (Carlson, 1972).

O'Neill (1981) clearly described the gender-role strain that men have experienced through their early rigid male-role socialization and the consequent difficulty of dealing with the changes in women's roles that became so prominent in the 1970s. He conceptualized six patterns of gender-role conflict that emerge from personal and institutional sexism and sex-role conflict and strain: (1) socialized control, power, and competition issues, (2) restriction of sexual and affectionate behavior, (3) obsession with achievement and success, (4) homophobia, (5) restriction of emotionality, and (6) health problems. He sees all these as emanating from the masculine mystique and value system and fear of femininity.

The male socialization for gender roles has caused considerable emotional pain and violence to men, limiting their emotional development and expression and at times causing physical deterioration. One piece of evidence is that more men commit suicide than women by a ratio of three to one at every age, and of course it is the men who die earlier and have more emphysema and heart attacks. O'Neill makes four recommendations regarding counseling men: (1) Counselors of men must assess the gender-role conflict and strain in men and the degree that gender-role conflicts limit their emotional, interpersonal, and physical lives. (2) Educational and preventive programming is needed to help those experiencing gender-role conflict and strain, including facts about the restrictive effects of being socialized male. (3) Some men will need consciousness-raising experiences to explore their fear of femininity and gender-role conflict patterns. (4) The public needs to understand the oppressive and destructive effects for both women and men. Gender-role conflicts are seen as part of societal discrimination and the maintenance of sexism, which is dangerous and is a form of psychopathology.

Two special journal issues, "Counseling Males" (Sher, 1981) and "Counseling Men" (Skovholt and others, 1978), presented an excellent overview of issues related to men's development in work, family, and parenting and in relation to other men. In "Counseling Adolescent Males" Coleman (1981) offered an insightful picture of male socialization and sexuality. The proliferation of books on the male sex role over the past five years also suggests that men are beginning to discover the disadvantages of rigid male sex-role prescriptions. New options for both women and men are emerging as both sexes begin to understand the negative effects of their socialization and stereotyping on the quality of their lives and to take conscious steps to reevaluate and even transcend their socialization.

Pleck (1981b) presented a new theoretical framework for looking at men's lives. He analyzed male sex-role identity and presented a new paradigm of male sex-role strain, challenging the "myth of masculinity." His cutting-edge book, which reviews research on the male sex role since the 1930s, should be a requirement for counseling theory or career development courses. He also described the work/family system in which men traditionally have carried the provider role and women the nurturer role and how this is changing, women moving more into the work role and men (albeit more slowly) into the family role, necessitating considerable role renegotiation and some stress (1981a). Like Richardson, he used a systems approach, examining the sex-role system in work and family as central to the sex-role changes that contemporary men and women are undergoing. He believes that the emerging role of women in paid work and the consequent overload occurring for employed mothers in two-earner families, combined with the increased supports to families and the enlarged family role for fathers, will transform women's and men's lives and the stucture of society as a whole.

In "The Good Provider Role: Its Rise and Fall," Bernard (1981) pointed out that the male wage-earner or provider role (which eventually became the "*good* provider" role) has been in American society for only 150 years. She cited 1980 as the year of the "fall" because that was the year that (1) the Bureau of the Census stopped using the term *head of household* on census questionnaires and (2) the two-earner family became the majority family pattern in this society. It seems appropriate that the directions in which much of the career development literature is moving—for example, examining the linkage between and changes in work and family (and leisure) roles—are congruent with the changes occurring in society. The sex-trait stereotypes found in Williams and Best's studies (1982)—dominance, autonomy, aggression, exhibition, and achievement for men; abasement, deference, succorance, and nurturance for women—do not seem to fit the changing roles in American society or other societies in change. Freeing women and men from rigid sex-role constraints perpetuated by stereotypes and socialization and implemented in societal institutions, structures, and policies would seem to be a valid goal for career guidance and counseling.

Sexual Division of Labor Across Cultures

Figures on the distribution of women and men in education and work offer additional insight into the impact of gender on career. Elsewhere (Hansen, 1981) I have posited that there are cross-cultural trends in the structure and composition of the labor force, in individual rights and development, in the structure of the family, and in educational goals and programs that indicate that new goals and strategies are needed in career guidance. Reports from the United Nations and the International Labour Office and national documents reflect that individuals within cultures and across cultures are insisting on a greater share in the economic, political, and social opportunities through education and work. The increased participation of women in paid work is an international phenomenon due to a number of factors, including inflation, divorce, widowhood, single parenting, the women's movement, immigration, and women's role in economic development—especially in Third World nations. It is not yet known precisely what the effects of worldwide unemployment are on women's participation in paid work, but unemployment, especially of youth, is an international concern. In the United States, retrenchments and cutbacks in educational and social welfare programs that have acutely affected women and minorities have been of particular concern, especially since 80 percent of those living in poverty in the United States are women and children, many of them minorities.

Occupational Distribution. The increased participation of women in paid work has been acknowledged by many as one of the most dramatic changes of the century. The International Labour Office (1978) reported that women make up more than a third of the world's economically active population, and 46 out of 100 women between fifteen and sixty-four years of age are employed. The percentage of women in the paid labor force varies tremendously from one country to another.

The ways in which women are distributed in work across cultures also gives some indication of their career development. Considerable sex typing of occupations exists across cultures, and although there are variations from one culture to another (for example, dentistry has long been open to women and men in Norway, whereas it has been a male occupation in the United States), there are in most cultures "women's jobs" and "men's jobs" (Holland, 1980). Large percentages of women seem to be concentrated in a few occupations, such as agricultural, clerical, teaching, textiles, and service. It appears that across cultures women fill only a small percentage of managerial, administrative, and executive positions and in most countries are concentrated in a limited number of occupations, mostly at lower levels of pay, skill, and responsibility. There is some variation in the rate of change of occupational distribution from one culture to another, and in some places a few women have entered traditionally male fields such as law, business, medicine, politics, management, ministry, and the trades, but in most cases percentages continue to be small. In Western nations such as the United States, Sweden, and Norway, changes appear to be more rapid and visible; in Japan, slower (Cook and Hayashi, 1980).

In the United States in 1980, women formed 43 percent of the labor force. Of women in the labor force in 1979, nearly 80 percent were in clerical, sales, service, factory, or plant jobs (16 percent professional/technical, 6 percent managerial/administrative, 17 percent service, and 11 percent operatives). Of women heads of household with children under eighteen, 66 percent were in the labor force. Although women, like men, report that they work because of economic need, they earn only 57 percent of what a full-time male worker makes (the wage gap is getting larger, not smaller). The facts of the pay gap are well known, especially that in 1979 women workers who were high school graduates earned less, on the average, than fully employed male workers who had not completed elementary school. Women workers who had graduated from college earned less than men workers with an eighth-grade education. The percentage of women in professional occupations has increased less than 2 percent during the past decade; women constitute 97 percent of all registered nurses, 71 percent of all elementary and secondary school teachers, less than 3 percent of all engineers, and less than 11 percent of all doctors (National Commission on Working Women, 1980).

The problems of minority women are especially acute, with their unemployment rate at 12 percent in 1979 and 30 percent of black women living below the poverty level in 1978. The median annual income of husband/wife families in which both partners were employed in 1979 was $25,290; for black married-couple families, $15,913; and for black families headed by women, $5,888. One has to consider these factors, and particularly the economic disadvantage of minority women, in examining gender and work. It becomes apparent that factors of gender and race interact to keep minority women at the bottom of the socioeconomic ladder. The feminization of poverty has meant that it is women who account for an increasingly large proportion of the economically disadvantaged in the United States, especially displaced homemakers with children (Pearce, 1978).

A number of factors affect women's participation in the labor force. Although work environments change slowly, experiments with new forms of work structures have affected both men and women. For example, in Scandinavia and the United States, developments such as flextime and flexplace are making work more responsive to human needs instead of workers always having to adjust to the needs of the workplace. Flextime, shorter work weeks, and part-time jobs allow people to work hours more compatible with their personal needs and lifestyles. Through shared jobs two persons divide one position—for example, two reporters may alternate work every three weeks or two medical technicians may each work every other week. Companies are beginning to recognize family/work linkages, where child care is provided at the workplace or vouchers are available for workers as part of employee benefits. Maternity, paternity, and personal leaves may be divided between partners to fit family preferences. Multiple benefit packages have been developed, offering employees choices from a variety of rewards. It is now possible to make lateral moves as well as vertical ones. Equal opportunity and affirmative action regulations are opening new options for women and minorities. Quality circles have developed to give employees more input into company decision making, and decentralization of organizations has meant fewer hierarchies and less room at the top. Job-creation efforts have resulted in new entrepreneurial jobs, while other jobs have become obsolete (for example, elevator operators are no longer needed, but emerging high-demand fields are petroleum engineers in Norway, lasar and robotic technicians in the United States and Japan, and geriatric social workers and counselors in several countries). Other major factors that affect women's participation in work are the number and age of children, amount of work experience, and amount of education.

Educational Distribution. Another gender-related factor affecting division of labor is the educational distribution. Although there have been global trends toward women's increased literacy and education, McGrath (1976) called equal education for women "the unfinished assignment." This has been a major concern of the Decade for Women. The movement toward lifelong learning and women's increased involvement in paid work have opened up opportunity for the development of women's potentials around the world. In many nations women are seeking and being accepted into postsecondary and higher education, as mature adult women seeking job skills or personal enrichment, and forming a major part of the new adult education population. They are increasingly entering nontraditional subjects and fields that were formerly male domains and are completing training programs both in the professions and in the trades. Sweden, for example, which is politically committed to equality of the sexes, has developed a system of paying companies for deliberately hiring workers to bring about more equal representation of the sexes.

It is significant that even though several nations have laws regarding equal status for women and men, these do not guarantee equal access to education and to work. In spite of such laws, several nations still reflect traditional patterns of distribution of men and women along sex-stereotyped lines. In Norway, for example, equal numbers of young women and men go on for *gymnasium* education, but most young women still choose the English or language majors and young men the science and mathematics lines. A study by Holland (1980) of gender division of labor in England and Sweden revealed the same stereotypic patterns and division of educational choices by sex. The implications of these patterns for distribution in the labor force and the workplace are obvious and have been analyzed in several countries (Holland, 1980; Secretariat of the Council of Europe, 1982; Vangsnes, 1978). Since educational opportunities often determine occupational opportunities, the subtle effects of the sex-role system on career decision making of young men and women again seem clear. That educational tracking leads to occupational tracking is a fact that militates against women's equal participation in the labor force.

Changing Patterns of Work and Family. Changes in patterns of work and family vary from one culture to another but seem to be most distinct in certain Western cultures such as Sweden and the United States. In the United States there is ample documentation about women's status and employment, and the Bureau of the Census provides regular reports on changing family structures, which are important parts of career data. For example, it is clear that pluralistic family structures are emerging in the United States: The traditional nuclear family (male provider, female nurturer), which constitutes about 20 percent of families; the two-earner, or dual-career, family, which is now over 52 percent of families; the single-parent family, which makes up 20 percent (families headed by women, about 17 percent); and the single person, the communal or extended family, and even the role-reversal family, with smaller percentages. As previously indicated, the intersection of work and family does affect gender roles, division of labor, and relationships in both arenas of life. While many women have sought participation in the work sector, some men have resisted involvement in the family and household-tasks sector, especially if they have traditional sex-role orientations about what women and men should do. Although small changes may be occuring, studies have shown that the amount of men's participation in family work does not increase significantly when a woman enters paid work, with consequent overload problems (Pleck, 1981a). But the increase in two-earner families and other family types, along with the increasing awareness of work/family linkages, appears to be here to stay.

Career Guidance Interventions for Changing Futures

It has been suggested that changing roles of girls and boys, men and women are among the dominant trends across cultures and that these changes are having and will continue to have a powerful influence on work, education, and family. The changes require us to consider an *expanded concept of career* (Hansen, 1977) for both women and men and to develop career guidance goals and methods more congruent with those changes (Hansen, 1981). Besides changes already mentioned in career development of women and men, in work and family patterns, and in educational/occupational distribution, awareness is also needed of the profound transformations occurring in technology and in human perception. The transformational movement, with its advanced views of technological developments and discoveries about creative intelligence and alternative ways of knowing and perceiving, offers new concepts and contexts for career guidance. The imaginative visions of futurist Marilyn Ferguson (1980), physicist Fritjof Capra (1982), astronaut Edgar Mitchell, and futurist Hazel Henderson need to be part of the image of the future presented to youths and adults.

Naisbitt's *Megatrends* (1982), his presentation of ten (and later eleven) trends that will transform American society and reshape our institutions (based on analysis of newspapers across the country in cities of 100,000 or larger), needs to be incorporated into a career guidance curriculum. Cetron and O'Toole's (1982) world forecasts about life and careers for the 1990s and beyond need to be part of basic reading lists of career information and what the future in many arenas of life, including work, may be like. The eleventh megatrend, unfortunately identified by Naisbitt after publication of his book (Zweig, 1983), is of major relevance to issues of gender and career, for this megatrend is "a shift from sex roles to synergy. It reflects a reconciliation between the sexes at a deep level, a greater harmony between qualities we used to consider either masculine or feminine. It could well mean the end of the battle of the sexes. . . . It's a time for rethinking masculine and feminine roles. The new style will be a synthesis of the best qualities and characteristics of each, a reconciliation of what were once thought to be opposite values into a new whole" (Zweig, 1983, p. 138).

Because *imaging* the future has to precede *planning* for the future, the importance of this process of imaging that new synergy of women and men for career development and decision making cannot be stressed enough. In addition, however, because the residues of the old sex-role system are still with us, still so powerful, and still having negative effects, it is necessary to create positive interventions for both youths and adults in curriculum, in counseling, and in programs.

New Goals. Among new goals that seem appropriate for career guidance in light of exponential societal change are the following: (1) the need for career guidance to focus not only on jobs but on life patterns and life roles, including increased preparation for economic independence for women and increased preparation for family roles for men, (2) the need to make students/clients aware of their own career socialization, the ways in which the sex-role system may have limited them but also ways in which they can transcend their socialization and conditioning to more fully develop their potentials, (3) the need to help individuals to *create their own futures* through anticipating future possibilities, identifying societal needs, and creating entrepreneurial activities that help meet those needs—and not just prepare them to fit into a diminishing pool of available occupations, (4) the need to help youths and adults work toward role integration in a society in which work, family, ecological, consumer, and spiritual values may be changing; to help clients see that occupation is only one part of career and to reflect on how work values relate to other life values; to see the interrelatedness of *life roles*—how the various parts fit together—and to negotiate tasks and relationships to improve the quality of life through a more holistic approach to career roles in work, family, education, community, and leisure, and (5) the need to help individuals move beyond the sex-role stereotypes—and other stereotypes of race, class, or handicap—which limit the range of options they are able and willing to consider and choose. Since cultural expectations about what we ought to do and can do affect what we will do, career guidance needs to expand the range of choices that girls and boys, men and women perceive as available to them in their life roles (Hansen, 1981).

Counselors will need to become aware of bias in their own attitudes and behaviors embedded through their own unconscious socialization, as well as in textbooks, tests, and guidance materials, in sex typing of occupations and subjects, in institutional policies, procedures, and structures, and in emerging computer-assisted instruction and guidance as well as other technologies. They will need to increase their efforts to create and implement developmental career guidance programs, reinforce sex-fair career education curriculum (including on-the-job training, computer and other technology experiences, and work experience opportunities for both girls and boys), and reduce the inhibitors of career development in educational structures, policies, and practices. Adults also will need reeducation because of long histories of traditional sex-role socialization, and creative programs of the type emerging in college centers, rehabilitation centers, adult development centers, and community centers will need support.

The hundreds of programs developed and field-tested in the 1970s will need much wider dissemination and implementation. Well over 300 programs were created under the Women's Educational Equity Act and the Vocational Education Amendments, and numerous other programs were developed through the Office of Civil Rights with funding by private agencies, foundations, and corporations (Women's Educational Equity Act Program, 1983). Such programs as BORN FREE, which deliberately seek to reduce stereotyping and expand career options of both women and men, offer useful concepts, models, and processes for trainers, educators, and counselors through focusing on career development, sex-role socialization, and stereotyping, as well as on personal, organizational, and societal change (Hansen and Keierleber, 1978). Hansen and Watt (1979) described a wide range of resources that can be used by counselors and counselor educators interested in concepts and tools for professional renewal in areas of sex equality. The American Institutes for Research (1980) has compiled a selected list of programs that combat stereotypes of sex, race, and handicap in career choice. The extent of use of such programs, resources, and materials will depend in large part on the consciousness of counselors and educators of the pervasiveness and centrality of sex-role issues in career development and their willingness to "own the problem."

Managing and Shaping Change. A growing body of knowledge has emerged in the last five years from many disciplines—physics, psychology, technology, medicine, and religion, to name a few—that describes how the world is changing, a fact few would deny. As pointed out earlier, Naisbitt's *Megatrends* describes the transformation of American culture from an industrialized to an information society, to high tech and high touch, from single options to multiple options, from a national to a global economy. Ferguson (1980) saw a contemporary "paradigm shift," of people "breathing together" to find ways to think about old problems and bring about personal and social transformation—from the inside out. Physicists, astronauts, and futurists offer a new paradigm for perceiving the world, including the world of career, characterized by world views, wholeness, sensitivity, planetary awareness, cooperation, synergy, integration, and connectedness. Interestingly, these are characteristics that in the past have been more associated with women.

That change is occurring more rapidly than people can understand, that there is tension between tradition and change, that there is a "crisis of perception" (Capra, 1982) and a paradigm shift that is already challenging old ways of perceiving, knowing, and inquiring also affect gender and career. The move toward "synergy" that Naisbitt describes is an acknowledgment of role changes described earlier. Old ways of competing and wielding power that cause great stress are giving way to a new kind of cooperation based on individual contribution. "Personal responsibility for excellence—rather than sex-role stereotyping—can be the foundation for this rising mutual respect" (Zweig, 1983, p. 138).

One of the great challenges for career guidance in the future will be to help people cope with and manage the changes in their lives. Many are going to counselors today because they cannot cope with change—divorce, death, job loss, midlife career change, broken relationships, widowhood, separation, immigration. Although there will always be crises and the need for human service providers to help others through crises, attitudes about change may also affect what becomes a crisis. The technological revolution, with its emerging occupations, and the sluggish economy, with its obsolescent occupations, reinforce the need for individuals to be better prepared for change. The need for help in managing a variety of career transitions over the life span has become and will continue to be a major concern of career counseling. The anticipated human effects of technological change, with microcomputers, videodisks, cable TV, telecommunications, space shuttles, and other technological developments potentially dominating people's lives at home, at work, and in leisure provide another area of need for understanding change. Helping people understand and manage life transitions and empowering them to bring about planned changes in their own personal lives and work environments may be one of the major contributions of career guidance, of both women and men.

Knowledge produced during the last thirty years about career development (unfinished and incomplete though it is), organizational psychology and planned change, interpersonal and organizational communications, sex-role socialization and stereotyping, technology and futurism, and changing work and family structures provide a solid base for interventions in developmental career guidance and counseling. A variety of models are needed for creating change and shaping the kind of life and society we want and for helping people redefine goals and objectives as part of a transforming renewal process. Ways to explore a synthesis of technology and psychotechnology, of the rational and intuitive, of the agentic and communal, of mind and body in dealing holistically with career development are needed, to help improve the quality not only of work life but of learning life, family life, and leisure life as well.

Futures Scenario for Designing Careers

Tradition and Change. Several years ago, at an international conference, a man from Nigeria responded to a question about why there were no Third World nations represented in a group discussing sex roles. He said, "It's very simple: In my country there are rules; there are rules for what men do and there are rules for what women do. We follow the rules, so there isn't a problem." Although that is hard to believe even if we acknowledge that there are differences across cultures, for some it is hard to accept that the roles and rules by which men and women learned to behave or to relate to each other are changing (even in national and international conferences).

We live both in a world of tradition and in a world of change. Many of the changes cause tension, fear, and conflict. On the one hand, Margaret Mead said that tradition is what gives structure to our lives, that without it we would face a bleak future. On the other hand, Rollo May spoke positively of creative courage, discovering new patterns and new symbols by which a new society can be built. In the transition between change and tradition, there is fear—about the demise of the family, about who will raise the children, about homosexuality, about unisex, and about change itself. Evidence that many of these fears are unfounded appears in a recent study, *Families at Work* (Harris, 1981). In it the American family was found to be alive and well, with considerable agreement among family traditionalists, feminists, and several other adult groups that women are in the labor force to stay. Although there is concern about pressure on families, citizens have faith in the family's strength and adaptability in a changing world.

Career Futures Scenario. To move from the limiting sex-role system of the past to the synergy of the future, what kinds of changes can career guidance and career development specialists help design? The following "career futures scenario" may help us to know where we as individuals and as a profession are and might be on a continuum of change. If we are successful in empowering people to manage their careers and effect a career development transformation, society might look something like this:

1. Women and men will be able to make choices and decisions more according to their authentic interests, talents, values, and preferences and to explore a wide variety of fields, subjects, and activities not labeled by sex. These changes will allow for development of the multipotentialities that both women and men possess. Children growing up will be exposed to and will be free to explore a wider variety and range of op-

tions in activities, hobbies, interests, roles, and behaviors. They will experience sex-fair childrearing at home and sex-fair education, counseling, and curriculum at school.

2. There will be more equitable distribution of men and women in education and work. Movement will be away from occupational and educational segregation toward more equal distribution of the sexes in all kinds and levels of education and occupation. Business and industry will pay more attention to human needs in the workplace, with flextime and flexplace, parental leave, childcare services available to employees, multiple benefit options, and other kinds of employee assistance programs reflecting a new corporate perspective on, responsibility for, and commitment to the personal and family needs of workers.

3. Women and men will have more solid relationships because they will be able to relate to each other as equals, instead of women being "less than" and men "more than." They will learn to respect each other at home and in the workplace, to resolve conflicts constructively, to negotiate roles and share tasks. They will find creative new patterns for working out work/family relationships in dual careers, in blended families, and in single-parent and other family types.

4. Men and women will have opportunities to decide without guilt whether they want single roles or multiple roles; inside roles or outside roles or both; to engage in role sharing rather than role owning, with women sharing the provider role and men the nurturing role. They will be able to choose sequential roles (fulfilling achievement or nurturing roles in sequence if they prefer) or concurrent roles (carrying multiple roles at one time).

5. Those who have been outside the opportunity structure—particularly youth, racial and ethnic minorities, the poor, the handicapped, and the aging—will have greater opportunity to develop their potential and feel they can have some choices, control, dignity, and self-direction in their lives.

6. Women and men will build better patterns of communication in organizations (including educational institutions such as universities). Instead of women always fitting into male

value systems and structures (competitive and hierarchical), the best female and male characteristics and styles will be adapted into our institutions and organizations, and the contributions of both will be recognized and respected in an evolving equal partnership. This will mean changing role expectations on the job as well as in the family and in the community; it will mean networks and associations that are inclusive rather than exclusive and women assuming a more equal role in professional associations, work organizations, and leisure.

7. Men and women will become much more aware of the power of language, its impact on people's self-concepts, and the negative and positive images it conveys. Since language is one of the most personal means of self-expression both at home and at work, changing it may at first seem difficult. But because people care about the effects of their language on others, they will learn to modify it—to use inclusive language, eliminate demeaning and sexist stories and humor, and include women and their achievements in both written and oral communications, to help them because visible equal partners.

8. Women and men will gradually learn to give up their stereotypes. They will stop labeling people and making assumptions about them because of a single characteristic of sex, race, age, handicap, ethnic group, or sexual preference. They will learn to relate to each other on the basis of their humanness. In short, they will create, adapt, and use programs, materials, and "new rules" that may bring them closer to those values cherished in many Western democracies—equal opportunity, freedom to grow, develop, and choose, and fostering of human intelligence, creativity, and potential.

9. Both women and men will have more opportunities to develop holistically because we will have moved from traditional polarized sex roles through androgyny to sex-role transcendence—"achievement of a dynamic and flexible orientation to life in which assigned gender is irrelevant. Individual behavior and emotional choice is based on the full range of possible human characteristics" (Rebecca, Hefner, and Oleshansky, 1976, p. 147).

10. Men and women in a global, technological, lifelong

learning society will have internalized new ways of knowing, perceiving, and developing creativity and human potentials. They will utilize their new-found knowledge and perceptions to continue to help society change, empowering individuals to bring their best talents to bear on solving complex societal problems—world order, hunger and poverty, ecology, freedom and social justice, interpersonal communication, technological literacy, and human and planetary development. People will have transcended sex roles and moved to synergy, and the old sex-role system will self-destruct.

If career guidance and counseling specialists become conscious of the past sex-role system and its central impact on the career development of women and men and can envision male/female synergy or the sex-role transcendence of the future, then they will commit themselves to developing gender-free career counseling strategies and programs. Such efforts will improve the quality of work life, learning life, and family life into an integrated whole and a better quality of life for all.

Suggested Readings

Bernard, J. *The Female World*. New York: Free Press, 1981.

A prominent sociologist presents a comprehensive picture of the special world of women and analyzes women in a variety of domains from family to social class to politics.

Kahn-Hut, R., Kaplan-Daniels, A., and Colvard, R. *Women and Work: Problems and Perspectives*. New York: Oxford University Press, 1982.

Men and women provide an in-depth examination of various aspects of women's participation in work.

Kanter, R. M. *Men and Women of the Corporation*. New York: Basic Books, 1977.

A well-known consultant to corporations, the author provides a clear picture of the dynamics of male/female interactions in the corporate world. Discusses the psychology of being different in organizations.

McGuigan, D. *Women's Lives: New Theory, Research and Policy.* Ann Arbor: University of Michigan, 1980.

Excellent collection of timely articles on issues in work, education, family, and public policy; special article by Carol Gilligan.

Pleck, J. H. *The Myth of Masculinity.* Cambridge, Mass.: MIT Press, 1981.

An original and insightful analysis of the male sex role, from male identity to a paradigm of male sex-role strain. Challenges many traditional assumptions and biases.

Secretariat of the Council of Europe (Ed.). *Sex Stereotyping in Schools.* The Netherlands: Council of Europe, 1982.

This report of an educational research workshop held in Hønefoss, Norway, provides data from several Western European and North American nations on the pervasiveness of sex stereotyping in elementary and secondary schools.

References

American Institutes for Research. *Programs to Combat Stereotyping in Career Choice.* Palo Alto, Calif.: American Institutes for Research, 1980.

Bem, S. L. "Beyond Androgyny: Some Presumptuous Prescriptions for a Liberated Sexual Identity." Keynote address for APA-NIMH Conference on the Research Needs of Women, Madison, Wis., May 31, 1975.

Bernard, J. "The Good Provider Role: Its Rise and Fall." *American Psychologist,* 1981, *36*(1), 1-12.

Block, J. N. "Debatable Conclusions About Sex Differences." *Contemporary Psychology,* 1976, *21,* 517-522.

BORN FREE. *BORN FREE Training Packets to Reduce Sex-Role Stereotyping in Career Development: Postsecondary/Higher Education, Secondary, and Elementary Levels.* Newton, Mass.: Education Development Center, 1978.

Capra, F. *The Turning Point: Science, Society and the Rising Culture.* New York: Bantam Books, 1982.

Carlson, R. "Understanding Women: Implications for Personality Theory and Research." *Journal of Social Issues,* 1972, *28,* 17-32.

Cetron, M., and O'Toole, T. "Careers with a Future: Where the Jobs Will Be in the 1990's." *The Futurist,* 1982, *16*(3), 11-19.

Chetwynd, J., and Hartnett, D. (Eds.). *The Sex Role System.* London: Routledge & Kegan Paul, 1978.

Coleman, E. "Counseling Adolescent Males." *Personnel and Guidance Journal,* 1981, *60,* 215-218.

Cook, A. H., and Hayashi, H. *Working Women in Japan.* Ithaca, N.Y.: Cornell University Press, 1980.

"Counseling Women." Special issue. *Counseling Psychologist,* 1973, *4*(1).

"Counseling Women II." Special issue. *Counseling Psychologist,* 1976, *6*(2).

"Counseling Women III." Special issue. *Counseling Psychologist,* 1979, *8*(1).

Farmer, H. "Why Women Choose Careers Below Their Potential." In L. S. Hansen and R. Rapoza (Eds.), *Career Development and Counseling of Women.* Springfield, Ill.: Thomas, 1978.

Ferguson, M. *The Aquarian Conspiracy.* Boston: Houghton Mifflin, 1980.

Fitzgerald, L., and Crites, J. "Toward a Career Psychology of Women: What Do We Need to Know?" *Journal of Counseling Psychology,* 1980, *27*(1), 44-62.

Follett, C., Watt, M., and Hansen, L. S. *Selected Review of the Literature on Career Development and Sex-Role Stereotyping in Post-Secondary/Higher Education.* Project BORN FREE. Newton, Mass.: Education Development Center, 1978.

Hackett, G., and Betz, N. E. "A Self-Efficacy Approach to the Career Development of Women." *Journal of Vocational Behavior,* 1981, *18*(3), 326-339.

Hansen, L. S. *An Examination of the Concepts and Definitions of Career Education.* Washington, D.C.: National Advisory Council for Career Education, 1977.

Hansen, L. S. "School Curriculum, Developmental Career Guidance and Changing Roles of Women and Men." Paper presented at International Conference on Guidance Through the Curriculum, Cambridge University, July 3, 1979.

Hansen, L. S. "New Goals and Strategies for Vocational Guidance and Counseling." *International Journal for the Advancement of Counselling,* 1981, *4,* 21-33.

Hansen, L. S., and Keierleber, D. "BORN FREE: A Collaborative Consultation Model for Career Development and Sex-Role Stereotyping." *Personnel and Guidance Journal,* 1978, *56,* 395-399.

Hansen, L. S., and Rapoza, R. *Career Development and Counseling of Women.* Springfield, Ill.: Thomas, 1978.

Hansen, L. S., and Watt, M. A. "Counselor Renewal in Sex Equality." *ACES Journal,* 1979, *19,* 274-287.

Harmon, L. "Career Counseling for Women." In E. Rawlings and D. Carter (Eds.), *Psychotherapy for Women: Treatment Toward Equality.* Springfield, Ill.: Thomas, 1977.

Harris, L. *Families at Work: Strengths and Strains.* Minneapolis: General Mills Corp., 1981.

Holland, J. *Women's Occupational Choice: The Impact of Sexual Divisions in Society.* Reports on Education and Psychology. Stockholm: Stockholm Institute of Education, 1980.

International Labour Office. "Equal Pay for Equal Work." In L. S. Hansen and R. Rapoza (Eds.), *Career Development and Counseling of Women.* Springfield, Ill.: Thomas, 1978.

Kutner, N. G., and Brogan, D. "Sources of Sex Discrimination in Educational Systems: A Conceptual Model." *Psychology of Women Quarterly,* 1976, *1,* 50-69.

Maccoby, E. E., and Jacklin, C. N. *The Psychology of Sex Differences.* Palo Alto, Calif.: Stanford University Press, 1974.

McGrath, P. L. "The Unfinished Assignment: Equal Education for Women." Worldwatch Paper No. 7. Washington, D.C.: Worldwatch Institute, 1976.

Naisbitt, J. *Megatrends: Ten New Directions Transforming Our Lives.* New York: Warner Communications, 1982.

National Commission on Working Women. *An Overview of Women in the Workforce.* Washington, D.C.: Center for Women and Work, 1980.

O'Neill, J. "Male Sex Role Conflicts, Sexism, and Masculinity: Psychological Implications for Men, Women, and the Counseling Psychologist." *Counseling Psychologist,* 1981, *9*(2), 61-80.

Osipow, S. H. *Emerging Woman: Career Analysis and Outlooks.* Columbus, Ohio: Merrill, 1975.

Pearce, D. "The Feminization of Poverty: Women, Work and Welfare." *Urban and Social Change Review,* 1978, *11*(1), 28-36.

Pleck, J. H. "The Work-Family Role System." *Social Problems,* 1977, *25,* 417-427.

Pleck, J. H. "The Work-Family Problem: Overloading the System." In B. L. Forisha and B. H. Goldman (Eds.), *Outsiders on the Inside: Women and Organizations.* Englewood Cliffs, N.J.: Prentice-Hall, 1981a.

Pleck, J. H. *The Myth of Masculinity.* Cambridge, Mass.: MIT Press, 1981b.

Rebecca, M., Hefner, R., and Oleshansky, B. "A Model of Sex-Role Transcendence." *Journal of Social Issues,* 1976, *32*(3), 197-206.

Richardson, M. S. "Occupational and Family Roles: A Neglected Intersection." *Counseling Psychologist,* 1981, *9*(4), 13-23.

Safilios-Rothschild, C. *Sex-Role Socialization.* Washington, D.C.: National Institute of Education, 1980.

Secretariat of the Council of Europe (Ed.). *Sex Stereotyping in Schools.* A report of the Educational Research Workshop held in Hønefoss, Norway, May 1981. The Netherlands: Council of Europe, 1982.

Sher, M. (Ed.). "Counseling Males." *Personnel and Guidance Journal* (special issue), 1981, *60.*

Skovholt, T. "The Impact of Feminism on Men's Lives." *Counseling Psychologist,* 1978, *7*(4), 3-10.

Skovholt, T., and Morgan, J. "Career Development: An Outline of Issues for Men." *Personnel and Guidance Journal,* 1981, *60,* 231-237.

Skovholt, T., and others (Eds.). "Counseling Men." *Counseling Psychologist* (special issue), 1978, *7*(4).

Sundal-Hansen, L. S. *Eliminating Sex Stereotyping in Schools.* Paris: UNESCO, in press.

Vangsnes, K. *Fakta om Likestilling.* Oslo: Likestillingsrådet, 1978.

Williams, J. E., and Best, D. L. *Measuring Sex Stereotypes: A Thirty-Nation Study.* Beverly Hills, Calif.: Sage, 1982.

Women's Educational Equity Act Program. *216 Resources for Educational Equity.* Newton, Mass.: Education Development Center, 1983.

Worell, J. "New Directions in Counseling Women." *Personnel and Guidance Journal,* 1980, *58,* 477-484.

Zweig, C. "The Eleventh Megatrend." *Esquire,* May 1983, p. 138.

9

John O. Crites

❧ ❧ ❧ ❧ ❧ ❧ ❧ ❧

Instruments for Assessing Career Development

Until about 1950, emphasis in vocational counseling was chiefly on the act of career choice making and on the choice itself. How well clients resolved their career problems was typically judged by the specificity and certainty of the clients' choices and the realism of those choices—that is, the correspondence between the clients' personal attributes and the requirements of their preferred occupations. Since midcentury, the focus in vocational counseling theory and research has been increasingly on the developmental and social maturational aspects of career behavior. The newer emphasis has given rise to a genre of assessment instruments generally classified as measures of career development, career maturity, career awareness, and the like. Such instruments enjoy growing recognition and use, and it is with an examination of several of the more prominent examples among them that this chapter deals.

Three common properties mark the instruments to be described here. First, all are operational expressions of the construct of career development, a term connoting "the total constellation of psychological, sociological, educational, physical, economic, and chance factors that combine to shape the career of any given individual over the life span" (Sears, 1982, p. 139). Second, although the concept embraces both career choice content and career choice process, the inventories discussed in this

248

chapter are primarily measures of career choice process. Each assesses "the individual's readiness to choose, knowledge of the choice process, and ability to collect information and weigh its personal value" (Kapes and Mastie, 1982, p. xiii). Finally, all the instruments described are objectively scored, standardized measures of career development, which presumably have certain psychometric properties that can be evaluated by generally accepted criteria (American Psychological Association, 1974).

Each measure of career development is reviewed using a *standard outline* (Anastasi, 1981; Super and Crites, 1962). The outline contains the following categories: content and construction, administration and scoring, standardization and norms, reliability, validity, and use and applicability. The reviews are summative, rather than comprehensive or encyclopedic. (For the latter, see the technical reports on the evaluations of the measures in Buros' *Mental Measurements Yearbook*, 1978, and secondary sources, such as Anastasi, 1981, and Kapes and Mastie, 1982.) General conclusions about the psychometric adequacy of the measures are drawn from the technical data on them, but the emphasis is on their use in individual career counseling, group career guidance, and career development programs.

Measures of career choice process are relatively few. Selected for review in this chapter are two measures, both with roots in Super's Career Pattern Study (Super and others, 1957): the *Career Maturity Inventory* (Crites, 1973, 1978a) and the *Career Development Inventory* (Thompson and others, 1981, 1982). Each is discussed at length according to the following outline:

1. Content and Construction
   a. Items
   b. Response format
2. Administration and Scoring
   a. Administration
      1. Booklets and answer sheets
      2. Procedure (individual/group)
      3. Time
   b. Scoring

        1.   Hand/machine
        2.   Profile
        3.   Printout (interpretive)
3.   Standardization and Norms
    a.   Standardization
        1.   Initial administration
        2.   Applicability
    b.   Norms
        1.   Percentiles
        2.   Standard scores
4.   Reliability
    a.   Interval constancy
    b.   Test-retest
    c.   Equivalence
5.   Validity
    a.   Content
    b.   Criterion-related
    c.   Construct
6.   Use and Applicability

In the interest of completeness and to note new trends in the measurement of career development, three other inventories are surveyed in less detail. They are the *Career Awareness Inventory* (Fadale, 1974, 1979), the *Career Skills Assessment Program* (College Entrance Examination Board, 1978), and the *Career Adjustment and Development Inventory* (Crites, 1975, 1982). A final section of the chapter summarizes some conclusions that can be drawn about the measurement of career development and offers predictions about future directions and trends.

The Career Maturity Inventory

The Career Maturity Inventory (CMI) was the first objectively scored, standardized measure of career development to be published (Crites, 1973). Its antecedents date back to the concept of vocational maturity (Super, 1955) and the research framework of the Career Pattern Study (Super and others,

1957). Its measurement model is a synthesis of the age- and point-scale methodologies used in the Stanford-Binet and Wechsler Adult Intelligence Scale to measure intelligence (Crites, 1961). The basic principle underlying this model is that the items in any measure of a developmental variable must be systematically related to some index of time (chronological age, school grade, job tenure, and so on). Thus, in an instrument designed to assess career maturity (a complex developmental variable), all the items must have demonstrable, empirical relationships to time. Only items that met this criterion were included in the CMI. Moreover, only items that "made sense" theoretically and linguistically were selected for the CMI. Another basic principle followed in its design is that items be both rationally and empirically valid (Crites, 1965). The rational-empirical method of test construction devised for the CMI represents an integration of the two major psychometric methodologies in test psychology, capitalizing on the strengths of each and eliminating the weaknesses of both. The CMI was constructed, then, from a newly formulated measurement model, which not only incorporated the distinction between career choice content and process but built on the combination of the age- and point-scale and rational-empirical methodologies.

Content and Construction. Detailed accounts of how the CMI was developed are available in Crites (1965, 1978a). Presented here briefly are some of the salient features of the CMI's content and construction. Items for both the Attitude Scale and the Competence Test were written from "real life" source materials—for example, client statements in career counseling, career counseling case summaries, and occupational information kits and manuals. The 75-item Attitude Scale assesses "dispositional response tendencies" in career decision making, whereas the Competence Test is more a measure of cognitive skills in career choice. Both parts of the CMI have been studied extensively to determine response bias (acquiescence, social desirability) in the items, and there appears to be no appreciable score variance attributable to this source (Crites, 1971). Moreover, nonsexist terminology and ethnically balanced content have been used in item content and construction.

Administration and Scoring. The CMI is a paper-and-pencil inventory that can be administered either individually or in a group. Testing time for the Attitude Scale is thirty minutes and for the Competence Test approximately one to one and a half hours, but there are no time limits for either part of the CMI, and they can be administered separately. The Career Maturity Profile sheet summarizes scores for the CMI as percentile and standard score "bands." The "Right Response Record" on the extreme right of the profile sheet gives actual responses to CMI items, which are keyed to a self-administered instructional booklet called the *Career Guide* (Crites and Savickas, 1983).

Standardization and Norms. The initial standardization of the CMI was designed to select those items from a pool of over 1,000 that had either linear or monotonic relationships to time across the span from the upper elementary school years to the senior year of high school. Approximately 3,000 students in grades five through twelve were tested in the Cedar Rapids, Iowa, school system during the 1961-62 academic year, and in 1974 nationwide groups of students in grades five through twelve, totaling 8,000-10,000, were tested with the revised edition of the CMI (Crites, 1978a). Separate sex norms are needed, because gender differences have been found, at least on the Attitude Scale Total (Smith and Herr, 1972), and special group differences (ethnic, racial) exist.

Reliability. The stability (reliability) of the CMI presents special problems because, as with any measure of behaviors that change systematically over time (developmental variables), classic test-retest reliability coefficients are inadequate, since they do not estimate (or partial out) that part of the total score variance attributable to maturation. In classical test theory, this variance is considered "error." For the CMI Attitude Scale, for example, the mean test-retest reliability for grades six through twelve, with a year's interval, is .74 (Crites, 1978a, p. 12). But when calculated with Heise's (1969) path analysis technique, which allows for maturational variance, the coefficient increases to .82 (Karren, Crites, and Bobko, 1975). This degree of stability is quite comparable to that of intellective tests (Super and Crites, 1962).

Validity. The "nomonological network" of validity relationships for the CMI is too extensive to review in detail here (Crites, 1974b, 1978a). It encompasses all three kinds of validities, as defined by the APA test standards (American Psychological Association, 1974), including relationships to a variety of stimulus, organismic, and response variables. Perhaps the most meaningful way to summarize these relationships is to review the CMI's *convergent* and *discriminant* validity (Campbell and Fiske, 1959), particularly since some questions about these psychometric properties have been raised (Westbrook and others, 1980). The convergent validity of the CMI has been documented in over 200 studies of the Attitude Scale and the Competence Test. The Attitude Scale correlates in the .30s and .40s with measures of other career decisional variables, such as decisiveness, certainty, realism, satisfaction, and congruence of vocational interests (Crites, 1971, 1974b, 1978a). Furthermore, when the appropriate factor-analytic method—hierarchical (Wherry, in press), *not* principal-axes (as used by Westbrook and others, 1980)—is followed, both the Attitude Scale and the Competence Test "fit" the model of career maturity as hypothesized (Crites, Blaha, and Wallbrown, in press). In other words, their interrelationships "converge" to support their validity as measures of the Career Choice Attitudes and Career Choice Competencies dimensions. Convergent validity for the CMI also accrues from the use of the Attitude Scale and Competence Test as criterion measures or dependent variables in studies of numerous vocational interventions using experimental and control groups. In over 300 investigations, 75 percent have yielded positive results: The vocational interventions produced "gains" in CMI scores as predicted. Thus, stimulus treatments hypothesized to facilitate career maturity, as assessed by the CMI, were highly effective.

The *discriminant* validity of the CMI involves its correlations with intellective tests and indexes—that is, intelligence, reading rate and comprehension, scholastic aptitude, and academic achievement. Westbrook and others (1980, p. 251) contend that, contrary to theoretical expectations derived from the Model of Career Maturity (Crites, 1974a) and the concept of discriminant validity, CMI scales and tests correlate, on the average, less highly with each other than with measures of intellective variables, and they raise the question whether "career maturity" inventories really assess anything different than aptitude and achievement instruments do. At least three comments are apropos of this criticism:

1. Theoretically, it would be inconsistent with the nature of decision making if career maturity measures were *not* related to intellective variables, because career choice is a mental and verbal process that involves comprehension, information, and problem solving—exactly what aptitude and achievement tests assess. There *should* be common variance between the two behavioral domains. Moreover, career maturity indexes that are more cognitively oriented should correlate more highly with intellective measures. And this is exactly the case, as Westbrook and others (1980, pp. 251, 274) have reported: The Competence Test (cognitive) correlates, on the average, significantly higher with intellective variables than the Attitude Scale (conative). In other words, these differential relationships to aptitude/achievement *support* the so-called discriminant validity of the CMI.

2. Empirically, Westbrook and others (1980) fail to recognize that the CMI is related to variables to which aptitude/achievement is unrelated. Reviews of the correlates of the CMI (Crites, 1971, 1974b, 1978a) indicate that it is correlated with a variety of interest and personality variables that are negligibly correlated with intelligence. If the CMI (and other "career maturity" measures) were only indexes of aptitude/achievement, then they should *not* correlate with variables (nonintellective) with which intellective tests are uncorrelated (Super and Crites, 1962; Crites, 1969). It can only be concluded that the CMI assesses *both* intellective *and* nonintellective variance and consequently has "discriminant" validity for behaviors not measured by aptitude/achievement instruments.

3. Conceptually and methodologically, the CMI has been criticized for being too highly related to reading ability tests (Westbrook and others, 1980, pp. 274–275). Several points are pertinent: First, as mentioned previously, the career decisional

process is verbal and would be expected to correlate highly with measures of the ability to read and understand verbal material. Second, reading ability tests are also related substantially to verbal measures of aptitude and achievement, for the same reason. And third, because reading ability is related to both career maturity and intellective variables, it constitutes what Cook and Campbell (1979) call a "third variable," which may explain *why* the CMI is correlated positively with aptitude and achievement measures in Westbrook and others' (1980) study. Although they collected the relevant data, these investigators did not "partial out" reading ability from the relationship between the CMI and intellective measures. If they had, the expectation would be that it would accentuate the "discriminant" validity of the CMI.

Despite criticisms (Westbrook and others, 1980), the CMI has well-established convergent and discriminant validity, documented by over twenty years of empirical research modeled after the American Psychological Association's standards for tests (1974). Detailed information on the validity findings is summarized by Crites (1979).

Uses of the Career Maturity Inventory. The CMI has been used for individual career counseling in many ways. As its construction and development reveal, much of its content came from the comments and concerns expressed by clients in career counseling. These center on the two principal problems encountered by clients in career decision making: indecision and unrealism (Crites, 1981a). The CMI can be used not only for diagnosis of these two general decisional problems but also for finer pinpointing of the factors producing the problems. (See Crites, 1978b, for illustrative case studies, which are too extensive to reproduce here.) Once the client's problems have been assessed with the CMI, a collaborative "feedback" (test interpretation) interview is highly useful in orienting the client to the career choice process, which should generally precede consideration of career choice content. If the latter is introduced prematurely, before problems in career choice process have been solved, the career counseling is likely to be much less effective. Discussion with the client of the CMI results can follow several formats. One is the traditional test interpretation mode of presenting the scores graphically on the Career Maturity Profile sheet and discussing their implications with the client. Another is to interpret "the tests without the tests," what I have called *integrative test interpretation* (Crites, 1981b). In this approach, the counselor interjects the test results verbally, rather than graphically, into the ongoing dialogue with the client, integrating them with the total context of the client's career choice and planning mentation and articulation. Finally, a technique that has been particularly effective with high school students is called "teaching the test" (Crites, 1971; Kapes and Mastie, 1982). The counselor goes over each item in the CMI that the client answered immaturely and explains why a different response is more mature. Crites and Savickas (1983) have prepared a *Counselor's Guide for the Career Maturity Inventory* for this purpose.

In group career guidance, often the problem in interpreting test results—for example, reporting scores on an interest inventory—is that each group member has a different profile. The consequence may be that the counselor ends up doing one-on-one career counseling in a group context (Crites, 1981a). Although this frequently happens with measures of career choice content, it is far less likely with instruments such as the CMI, which assess career choice process, since the components and stages of the decision process are common to all students. The basic principle in interpreting the CMI in group career guidance, therefore, is to focus on *how* career choices are made rather than on *what* career choices to make. All members of the group can participate in a discussion of their scores on the involvement part of the Attitude Scale, for example, and compare their maturity in being engaged in the career choice process with that of others. More important, they can suggest ways in which they can increase their involvement and, with the encouragement of the group, try these out. The group in career guidance with the CMI can become a potent support system for learning *how* to make realistic career choices—a capability that is lifelong across the total span of career development (Super, 1980).

The CMI has been used at both the high school and college levels in comprehensive career development programs (Crites, 1978a, 1981a). The first stage in such programs is "checkpointing the career development" of students, tested in large groups, with the Attitude Scale (Form B-1) total score, which screens those individuals who are less career-mature. Scores from the testing are distributed, and all students below the median are invited to engage in individual career counseling or small-group career guidance, while those above the median can benefit from classroom and/or workshop career development experiences. Savickas and Crites (1983) have prepared and field-tested, for example, a career maturity curriculum for grades nine through twelve, which teachers can present with a minimum of training. In the second stage of the program, additional testing with the Competence Test and scoring of the Attitude Scale (Form B-1) for the "attitude clusters" (Involvement, Independence, and so forth) can provide diagnostic information for planning and implementing either individual career counseling or group career guidance. Programmatic testing with the CMI in stages, then, builds a foundation for differential career development experiences for all students.

   Comment. Although reviews of the CMI by others are available in the *Mental Measurements Yearbook* (Zytowski, 1978) and in Kapes and Mastie (1982), they are based largely on the 1973 edition, which consisted only of the Attitude Scale. In addition, there remain some points at issue that should be addressed (Westbrook and others, 1980). In my judgment, however, there is sufficient positive research evidence on the CMI and enough favorable experience with its use in career development activities, spanning twenty years (1962-1982), to conclude that it can be used with confidence in assessment, diagnosis, intervention, and program evaluation. At the same time, it is clear that additional research is needed. Possible lines of inquiry include validity studies of the assumptions underlying the self-appraisal and goal selection parts of the Competence Test, a Composite Competence Test (short form), stability data on the Competence Test, validity studies of the "attitude clusters" of the Attitude Scale, hierarchical factor analyses of the CMI to test the Model of Career Maturity (currently being conducted by Crites, Blaha, and Wallbrown), and a multitrait-multimethod analysis of the CMI and other measures of career maturity. Research on these problems can advance not only knowledge of the CMI but also our general understanding of the construct of career maturity.

The Career Development Inventory

The background of the Career Development Inventory (CDI) is also that of the Career Pattern Study (Super and others, 1957), in which the concept of vocational (career) maturity was first formulated (Super and Overstreet, 1960). From these theoretical antecedents, Super (1955) developed the Indices of Vocational Maturity (IVM). Early attempts to measure these variables mainly utilized ratings of interview protocols and test scores from trait-and-factor measures. As a "provisional try" at operationally defining the IVM, they were useful, particularly in identifying the *planning* dimension of career development, which is a primary one in Super's theory and research (Super and Overstreet, 1960). The Career Development Inventory (CDI) evolved from this early work and represents a standardized method of assessing the IVM variables. Its preliminary forms were developed as part of the Career Pattern Study but not actually used in it to gather data, the exception being the Adult Form (Zelkowitz, 1974), which has not as yet been published. As the following description of the CDI brings out, most of the available research pertains to the School Form, although there is a College and University Form, which appeared in 1982; consequently, this review deals largely with the School Form.

Content and Construction. The CDI is a rationally derived instrument, the content having been drawn from career development theory and expert judges' knowledge and experience. Items were not empirically selected to be related to a time variable, such as age, but grade differences on scale scores are reported as evidence of construct validity. The two parts of the CDI, each with a separate answer sheet, contain the following scales:

1. *Career Planning* (CP): Of the twenty items in this scale, the first twelve assess "extent of career planning" activity and involvement and the remaining eight "amount of knowl-

edge" that individuals estimate they already have about fields of work they might like to enter after their schooling. The foils are the same for all the stems in each of the subsets of items on planning and knowledge.

2. *Career Exploration* (CE): The first subset of ten items in this twenty-item scale asks the individual to indicate the probability of using several sources of career information. The second subset of ten items elicits the individual's evaluation of how useful that information was. Again, the foils within a subset are repeated.

3. *Decision-Making* (DM): Twenty items compose this scale, the stems of which depict a decisional dilemma with the foils posing alternative courses of action. "The rationale is that students who can solve the career problems in these sketches are more capable of making wise decisions about their own careers" (Thompson and others, 1981, p. 2). The item format of this scale closely resembles several of the subtests (Self-Appraisal, Goal Selection, and Problem-Solving) in the CMI Competence Test. Because of this similarity, as well as substantive overlap, it would be expected that they would intercorrelate empirically in the moderate positive range (.30s–.40s). Common variance would also be predicted, because they involve cognitive functions in arriving at decisional solutions.

4. *World-of-Work Information* (WW): This last scale in Part 1 has ten items on the individual's knowledge of career developmental tasks in the exploratory and early establishment stages and ten items on knowledge of "the occupational structure, of sample occupations ranging from semiskilled to professional and executive, and of techniques for getting and holding a job" (Thompson and others, 1981, p. 2). This scale parallels, but is not identical to, the Occupational Information part of the CMI Competence Test and as such can be considered a cognitive measure of career development.

5. *Knowledge of the Preferred Occupational Group* (PO): This scale is the only one in Part 2 and represents a unique, if not ingenious, attempt to assess how much *accurate* information individuals possess about their preferred occupational group. The latter is elicited from a chart of twenty groups, in-

cluding "write in" options, on the back of the answer sheet. The occupational groups were modified from the Career Planning Questionnaire of the Differential Aptitude Tests, and the questions about them in the booklet cover (1) characteristics of the preferred occupational group, (2) ability requirements, (3) interests, (4) values, and (5) other characteristics. Answers are scored according to objective information or expert judgments.

In addition to these five basic scales, there are three derived or summative scales. One is called Career Development—Attitudes (CDA), which is the sum of the CP and CE scores and which yields a score representing the conative dimension of career maturity. A second is Career Development—Knowledge and Skills (CDK), which is equal to the scores on the DM and WW scales and which defines the cognitive dimension of career maturity. And third, there is the Career Orientation Total (COT), which combines CP, CE, DM, and WW into a composite of "four important aspects of career maturity" but not necessarily a general factor of career maturity, because, as the authors observe (Thompson and others, 1981, p. 3), "it measures only four of the five basic dimensions in Super's (1974) model of vocational maturity." Note also that PO is not included in COT.

Administration and Scoring. The CDI can be administered either on an individual basis or in a group session and takes approximately forty minutes for Part 1 (Career Orientation) and twenty-five minutes for Part 2 (Knowledge of Preferred Occupations). The authors state that Part 1 can be administered in grades eight and above but that the vocabulary of Part 2 (because of the occupational titles) limits its use to grades eleven and twelve. Both parts are applicable to males and females, although there are significant sex differences, particularly during the senior high school years on the cognitive measures.

Standardization and Norms. The School Form of the CDI was standardized on 5,076 students and the College and University Form on 1,826 students. Raw scores have been transformed to both standard scores and percentile ranks. For the School Form, norms were calculated for grades nine through twelve, separately by sex as well as for the total group, and for the College and University Form, norms are given for males and females (no total) by class year. The manual suggests several comparisons that can be made among subgroups and encourages the construction of local norms for the College and University Form, on which there are presently limited data. Special group (ethnic, racial) forms are not reported, but extrapolating from findings with the CMI, there are most likely depressed scores for minorities, although the career developmental gradient still remains (Crites, 1971). Concerning the norms for the CDI, the manual (Thompson and others, 1981, p. 13) states: "The sample is not a representative national sample of ninth- through twelfth-grade (or college) students. The sample does, however, comprise groups that differ in relevant characteristics, for example, urban-suburban-rural, inner city, and regions as well as grade and sex . . . Eastern schools were heavily represented in the standardization group."

Reliability. The only type of reliability estimate reported for the CDI is internal consistency, which, as noted in the discussion of the CMI, actually indicates the homogeneity of a scale, rather than a prediction of how stable the behavior is over repeated testings (Thorndike and Hagen, 1977). Consequently, the Cronbach alpha coefficients given in the manual for the CDI should be interpreted as indexes of scale dimensionality, and they are uniformly high for CDA, CDK, and COT, the composite scales.

The average internal consistencies are also high for CP, CE, and WW, the median coefficients being .89, .78, and .84, respectively. The estimates for DM and PO, however, are .67 and .60. For DM, females had lower average coefficients (.59) than males (.70), and for PO they were lower for grades nine and ten (.55) than for grades eleven and twelve (.66).

Referring to the composite scales, the manual concludes: "These scales clearly have adequate reliabilities for use in individual counseling and in analyses of group differences" (Thompson and others, 1981, p. 14). Yes and no. The absolute magnitude of the alphas is certainly large enough for both individual and group interpretation, but it is the wrong reliability estimate to cite for this purpose. For individual profile interpretation, as well as group difference analyses, it is the stability of the behaviors over time that is at issue, not scale homogeneity. The appropriate reliability estimate for these uses is the stability coefficient (test-retest or equivalence), but none has been reported as yet for the CDI.

Validity. The principal type of validity offered for the CDI in the manual is content validity, based on the many years of theory and research of the Career Pattern Study (Super and others, 1957; Super and Overstreet, 1960). From this work, there has evolved a widely articulated and accepted (with the exception of Westbrook and others, 1980) model of career maturity (Super, 1955, 1974; Crites, 1961, 1973, 1978a), tested extensively by others independently (Gribbons and Lohnes, 1968, 1969, 1982), which provides the conceptual framework for the CDI (as well as for the CMI). Theory, research, informed judgment, and psychometric expertise all contribute to the substantial content validity of the CDI scales.

The construct validity of the CDI derives largely from its factorial structure. Factor analyses by grade (nine through twelve) and sex generally support the CDA and CDK group factors. CP and CD load clearly on CDA, the attitudinal dimension in the model, and DM and WW make up the CDK group factor, which represents the knowledge (competence) dimension. No findings are reported on the COT factor, which appears in the model as a general one, contributed by CDA and CDK.

That curricular differences were found on the CDI, especially on the cognitive scales, among students in academic, general, and vocational/technical curricula is not surprising and is consistent with similar findings on the CMI. In general, the academic (college preparatory) majors score higher on all scales except CP, partly because of their greater academic ability, which enhances their scores on the cognitive scales in particular, and partly because of their deferred entry into the world of work, which depresses their scores (on the average) on CP.

Although it will certainly be forthcoming as the CDI is further researched and results are reported in the literature, no criterion-related validity is mentioned in the manual. Some criterion-related validity may be inferred, however, from the Career Pattern Study findings, and others can be conceived, the CDI being related to other decisional variables (indecision, unrealism, and so forth) and to similar measures, such as the CMI.

Uses of the Career Development Inventory. The CDI *User's Manual* proposes several uses for the CDI (Thompson and others, 1981). Among these are the employment of the instrument for individual diagnosis and prediction in counseling, as a survey tool in planning guidance programs, and as a criterion measure to assess counseling outcomes. Functions in the career counseling process that can be facilitated by use of the CDI, according to the instrument's developers, include selecting a counseling strategy through problem diagnosis, determining the client's readiness for choice making, and focusing on the attitudes, behaviors, and knowledge needed to make good choices. The case studies presented in the *College and University Manual* illustrate how the counselor can perform the foregoing functions with the aid of the CDI. Among the relevant diagnostic concepts discussed in the case studies are "crystallization without exploration" (one-track concentration on a particular career goal), "exploration for specification" (learning how to implement a career choice), and "exploration for scope without depth" (extremely limited career planning and exploration).

Comment. Despite its rich theoretical background from the Career Pattern Study and its psychometric predecessors, the CDI has only made a start on the laborious process of empirical norming and validation. There is no question that it has distinctive prospects as a measure of the career choice process, since it appears to assess attitudes and competencies not defined by the CMI or other instruments of this type. There are bound to be some areas of common variance between the CDI and CMI, if for no other reason than their shared conceptual framework and the variables they are designed to measure. However, it would be erroneous to assume that because some of their scales have similar names, they are measuring the same career choice behaviors. This was a pitfall of numerous studies of the Strong Vocational Interest Inventory and the Kuder Preference Record, which have occupational scales with identical names and yet, because of their significantly different modes of measurement, have little relationship to each other (Super and Crites, 1962). Although comparative studies have not yet been conducted on them, much the same may be concluded about the CDI and the CMI. Different approaches may be necessary to psychometrically assess a particular behavioral domain.

Other Inventories

In addition to the Career Maturity Inventory (CMI) and the Career Development Inventory (CDI), a few other instruments have been developed that should be mentioned. Two of these are still unpublished, Westbrook's Cognitive Vocational Maturity Test (CVMT) and Harren's Assessment of Career Decision-Making (ACDM), and consequently are not generally available for use, except for research purposes. ACT's Assessment of Career Development is more suitable for the survey of guidance services in secondary schools than for individual measurement, although it incorporates parts of the CVMT. Gribbons and Lohnes' (1982) Readiness for Vocational Planning Scales (RVP) are based on semistructured interview data rather than objectively scored inventory responses. There are, however, three other published, objective-type measures of career development available for use in career counseling activities and programs: (1) the Career Awareness Inventory, (2) the Career Skills Assessment Program, and (3) the CAREER Adjustment and Development Inventory. These instruments are briefly described.

Career Awareness Inventory. Developed by Fadale (1974, 1979), this instrument has been published in two forms: Elementary and Advanced. The Elementary version is supposedly applicable to grades three through six and yields seven part scores based on 125 items: Identity, Training, Models, Function, Prestige, Clusters, and Characteristics. The Advanced Form, which was revamped in 1980, is designed for grades seven through twelve. It comprises 133 items divided into the following: Grouping in Occupations, Related Occupations, Work Locations, and Self-Assessment of Career Awareness. Because of the occupational titles in the items, the reading level becomes difficult and particularly poses a problem at the elementary level. Although the inventory was designed to measure "career awareness," a concept often included in career education models, the definition of this construct conceptually or empirically is not explicit. If the Career Awareness Inventory assesses a unified construct, then its parts should intercorrelate in the moderate positive range (.40–.60), but they do not. Rather, they possess considerably less interdependence, a condition that suggests there is more uniqueness than common variance among them. Much further research needs to be completed on the Career Awareness Inventory before even an objective evaluation of its psychometric properties can be made, much less a recommendation of use with students in the elementary and high school grades. Cole's (1982, p. 117) conclusion is that "at this stage, the instrument should definitely be marked 'EXPERIMENTAL.'"

Career Skills Assessment Program. Conceived by the College Entrance Examination Board (1978), this "program" comes from an educational rather than a psychological context because it includes measures as well as instructional booklets. Westbrook and Rogers (1982, p. 127) commented on its construction: "Specification outlines, based on current practices and knowledge in career education, were developed to define the behavior domain. Items were written to match specific instructional objectives. Apparently CSAP is based on actual practices in career education rather than any theory of career development. The instructional objectives are intentionally limited to skills that can be taught in schools and that can be assessed through a multiple-choice item."

In contrast, then, to the CMI and CDI, the CSAP was not theory-derived. Rather, it concentrates on the pragmatic assessment of six content areas: Self-Evaluation and Development, Career Awareness, Career Decision-Making, Employment Seeking, Work Effectiveness, and Personal Economics. No national norms are offered, the recommendation being to derive local norms on the groups tested. Moreover, available data on its psychometric characteristics are practically nonexistent, with the exception of relatively high correlations with verbal ability

(.65-.70). The CSAP obviously needs further study, and there is no basis for recommending its use for other than research purposes at this time.

CAREER Adjustment and Development Inventory. In contrast to the other measures of career development reviewed here, the CAREER Adjustment and Development Inventory (ADI) assesses career adjustment rather than career choice variables. Conceptually, career choice involves selecting between two or more occupations, whereas career adjustment involves getting along and getting ahead in an occupation after it has been selected. A "Model of Career Adjustment" for the establishment stage in early adulthood has been formulated by Crites (1976), and it was from this model that the CAREER ADI was conceptualized and constructed. Work on the model began in 1974-75 as part of a career development program undertaken at Lawrence Livermore Laboratories. Preliminary scales were composed and field-tested to measure the outcomes of the career development interventions. These measures were subsequently refined through a project conducted by the National Center for Research on Vocational Education at Ohio State University, called "A Diagnostic Taxonomy of Adult Career Development Problems" (Campbell and Cellini, 1981), and data were collected for further psychometric research on three representative organizations across the country (commercial, industrial, and research and development). More recently, the CAREER ADI has been administered, on a voluntary basis, in over 100 organizations nationwide to gather still more data for its technical development.

The current edition of the CAREER ADI consists of two parts: (1) ninety objectively scored items on the mastery of six sequential career developmental tasks during the establishment stage and (2) twenty open-ended item stems describing problem situations arising in career adjustment on the job, to which solutions are "written in" (see Crites, 1982, for a copy of the inventory). The scales in Part 1 measure the major career developmental tasks that workers are likely to encounter during the period from occupational entry to midlife (Campbell and Cellini, 1981). In chronological order along the career developmental continuum, they are (1) Organizational Adaptability (Org.), (2) Position Performance (Pos.), (3) Work Habits and Attitudes (Wha.), (4) Co-worker Relations (Cor.), (5) Advancement (Adv.), and (6) Career Choice and Plans (Cho.).

Each scale is composed of fifteen statements of attitudes and behaviors, using the rational-empirical method of test construction originated with the CMI. Items were first written from theoretical constructs drawn from the "Model of Career Adjustment" and are now being standardized empirically against the two principal outcomes of the career adjustment process, success and satisfaction. The "open-ended" stems in Part 2 were composed from a cross-section of "real life" source materials on work-generated problems (supervisor criticism, alcohol abuse, sexual harassment, and so forth). Responses to these stems are being compiled and classified by judges as (1) integrative, (2) adjustive, or (3) nonadjustive career coping mechanisms (Crites, 1976) and will eventually constitute the foils (or options) in multiple-choice questions. In addition, research has been started on Part 3, which will measure the congruence (matching) of the person to position with regard to aptitudes, interests, and values. Thus, the completed CAREER ADI will provide measures of the three central components of the career adjustment process: (1) mastery of career development *tasks*, (2) mechanisms for *coping* with career problems, and (3) extent of *congruence* between the individual and the job.

Future Trends

More than thirty years of research and educational and counseling practice have established career development as a viable construct. Nonetheless, much additional research on its measurement is needed. Additional work on both the CMI and the CDI is required, both to refine their effectiveness as psychometric instruments and to examine their interrelationships. Furthermore, the parameters of the career maturity construct—for example, its multidimensionality—should be more systematically explored. The other inventories reviewed in this chapter, particularly the CAREER ADI as a measure of the career adjustment process, also need to be extensively studied.

Meanwhile, there is sufficient knowledge of the CMI and the CDI to warrant their judicious use as measures of career development and as assessment instruments for vocational interventions and program evaluations. However, precautions are advisable. Underlying the construct of career development is the tacit assumption that career maturity, as measured by the scales of existing career development inventories, is predictive of subsequent choice-making behavior and occupational adjustment. Empirical evidence in support of this critical assumption is accumulating, but longer-range predictive validity studies of career development assessment measures are needed.

The future will likely witness increased use of career development inventories in counseling but with a shift in emphasis. In the past, measures of aptitudes and interests have been used largely to predict educational and vocational behaviors. The focus has been on estimating how well individuals can be expected to achieve academically or occupationally (scholastic and vocational aptitudes) and how long and how well satisfied they would be in different occupations (interests). Unfortunately, the initial promise of these traditional instruments for prediction has been dimmed by their subsequent mediocre validity. As a consequence of their disappointing predictive validity, and with the advent of career development inventories, which focus more on career choice process than on content, there has been a marked shift in the use of tests and inventories from *prediction* to *description* (Zytowski, 1982). Current emphasis is on where individuals stand on the continuum of career development (career maturity) and what problems they are having in making career choices. Normative data, rather than predictive validity, thus become more relevant to the contemporary concerns of comprehensive career counseling, since they deal primarily with *how* clients make choices and secondarily with *what* choices they make. Helping clients learn the "how," based on the descriptive use of career development inventories, will be an important trend in career counseling (Crites, 1981a). At the core of this shift in counseling strategy is the objective of facilitating career maturity—that is, of helping clients plan and manage their career development more independently, competently, and realistically.

Future counseling practice will also place increased emphasis on the delivery of career development assessments to clients. For several years, I have been researching and using the "integrative test interpretation" method, in which test data are introduced into the ongoing dialogue with clients in their career decision making and planning, rather than presenting the results to them in a perfunctory fashion from profiles during a test interpretation interview (Crites, 1981b). Innovative delivery methods will also include increased use of computer-generated hard-copy printouts of profiles and score interpretation forms and integrated reporting services for the career counselor. Examples of the latter are Edit's COPS, CAPES, and COPES, Intran's AIM for the GATB, and ACT's Career Planning Program and Viesa.

The improved application of career development assessment methods foreseen here cannot occur in disjointed and piecemeal fashion. The elements of change must be logically merged with the best of career counseling insights and methods. As conceptual and applied models of career counseling increase in sophistication, the need to adopt the delivery systems approach becomes more apparent. Correspondingly, the need grows to train prospective career counselors in the proper understanding and use of career development assessment methods. The availability of powerful new measurement devices will have no appreciable impact on the quality of career counseling unless practitioners are adequately equipped to use new counseling technologies.

Suggested Readings

Crites, J. O. "Integrative Test Interpretation." In D. H. Montross and C. J. Shinkman (Eds.), *Career Development in the 1980's: Theory and Practice.* Springfield, Ill.: Thomas, 1981. Outlines and offers a rationale for a new approach to test interpretation in career counseling, which integrates the results of assessment with the ongoing dialogue between counselor and client.

Kapes, J. T., and Mastie, M. M. (Eds.). *A Counselor's Guide to Vocational Guidance Instruments.* Washington, D.C.: National Vocational Guidance Association, 1982.
    A compilation of reviews on a wide range of tests and inventories available to career counselors. Reviews have been abstracted and rewritten in a convenient format from the *Eighth Mental Measurements Yearbook.*

Vacc, N. A., and Bardon, J. I. (Eds.). "Assessment and Appraisal: Issues, Practices, and Programs." *Measurement and Evaluation in Guidance,* 1982, *15,* 1-127.
    "State-of-the-art" articles on a variety of topics directly relevant to the work of the career counselor. Particularly noteworthy is the divergence of points of view on the usefulness of testing in counseling.

Walsh, W. B., and Osipow, S. H. (Eds.). *Handbook of Vocational Psychology.* Vols. 1 and 2. Hillsdale, N.J.: Erlbaum, 1983.
    A comprehensive, yet in-depth treatment of the foundations (Vol. 1) and applications (Vol. 2) of vocational psychology. In particular, see Westbrook's chapter "Career Maturity" and Zytowski and Borgen's chapter "Assessment."

References

American Psychological Association. *Standards for Educational and Psychological Tests.* Washington, D.C.: American Psychological Association, 1974.
Anastasi, A. *Psychological Testing.* (5th ed.) New York: Macmillan, 1981.
Buros, O. K. (Ed.). *The Eighth Mental Measurements Yearbook.* Highland Park, N.J.: Gryphon Press, 1978.
Campbell, D. T., and Fiske, D. W. "Convergent and Discrimi-

nant Validation by the Multitrait-Multimethod Matrix." *Psychological Bulletin*, 1959, *56*, 81-105.

Campbell, R. E., and Cellini, J. V. "A Diagnostic Taxonomy of Adult Career Development Programs." *Journal of Vocational Behavior*, 1981, *19*, 175-190.

Cole, N. S. "Review of the Career Awareness Inventory." In J. T. Kapes and M. M. Mastie (Eds.), *A Counselor's Guide to Vocational Guidance Instruments*. Washington, D.C.: National Vocational Guidance Association, 1982.

College Entrance Examination Board. *Career Skills Assessment Program*. New York: College Entrance Examination Board, 1978.

Cook, T. D., and Campbell, D. T. *Quasi-Experimentation*. Chicago: Rand McNally, 1979.

Crites, J. O. "A Model for the Measurement of Vocational Maturity." *Journal of Counseling Psychology*, 1961, *8*, 255-259.

Crites, J. O. "Measurement of Vocational Maturity in Adolescence: I. Attitude Test of the Vocational Development Inventory." *Psychological Monographs*, 1965, *79*(2, Whole No. 595).

Crites, J. O. *Vocational Psychology*. New York: McGraw-Hill, 1969.

Crites, J. O. *The Maturity of Vocational Attitudes in Adolescence*. American Personnel and Guidance Association Inquiry Series, Monograph No. 2. Washington, D.C.: American Personnel and Guidance Association, 1971.

Crites, J. O. *Theory and Research Handbook for the Career Maturity Inventory*. Monterey, Calif.: CTB/McGraw Hill, 1973.

Crites, J. O. "Career Development Processes: A Model of Vocational Maturity." In E. L. Herr (Ed.), *Vocational Guidance and Human Development*. Boston: Houghton Mifflin, 1974a.

Crites, J. O. "The Career Maturity Inventory." In D. E. Super (Ed.), *Measuring Vocational Maturity in Counseling and Evaluation*. Washington, D.C.: National Vocational Guidance Association, 1974b.

Crites, J. O. *The Career Adjustment and Development Inventory*. College Park, Md.: Gumpert, 1975.

Crites, J. O. "A Comprehensive Model of Career Development in Early Adulthood." *Journal of Vocational Behavior,* 1976, *9,* 105–118.

Crites, J. O. *Theory and Research Handbook for the Career Maturity Inventory.* (2nd ed.) Monterey, Calif.: CTB/McGraw-Hill, 1978a.

Crites, J. O. *Manual for the Career Maturity Inventory for Adults.* Monterey, Calif.: CTB/McGraw-Hill, 1978b.

Crites, J. O. "Validation of the Diagnostic Taxonomy of Adult Career Problems: A Pilot Study." In R. E. Campbell and others, *A Diagnostic Taxonomy of Adult Career Problems.* Columbus: National Center for Research in Vocational Education, Ohio State University, 1979.

Crites, J. O. *Career Counseling: Models, Methods, and Materials.* New York: McGraw-Hill, 1981a.

Crites, J. O. "Integrative Test Interpretation." In D. H. Montross and C. J. Shinkman (Eds.), *Career Development in the 1980s: Theory and Practice.* Springfield, Ill.: Thomas, 1981b.

Crites, J. O. "Testing for Career Adjustment and Development." *Training and Development Journal,* February 1982, pp. 20–24.

Crites, J. O., Blaha, J., and Wallbrown, F. H. "The Career Maturity Inventory: Myths and Realities—a Rejoinder to Westbrook, Cutts, Madison, and Arcia (1980)." *Journal of Vocational Behavior,* in press.

Crites, J. O., and Savickas, M. L. *A Counselor's Guide for the Career Maturity Inventory.* Hudson, Ohio: Crites Career Consultants, 1983.

Fadale, L. M. *Career Awareness Inventory.* Bensenville, Ill.: Scholastic Testing Service, 1974; 1979.

Gribbons, W. D., and Lohnes, P. R. *Emerging Careers.* New York: Teachers College Press, 1968.

Gribbons, W. D., and Lohnes, P. R. *Career Development from Age 13 to 25.* Weston, Mass.: Regis College, 1969.

Gribbons, W. D., and Lohnes, P. R. *Careers in Theory and Experience.* Albany: State University of New York Press, 1982.

Heise, D. R. "Separating Reliability and Stability in Test-Retest Correlation." *American Sociological Review,* 1969, *34,* 93–101.

Kapes, J. T., and Mastie, M. M. (Eds.). *A Counselor's Guide to Vocational Guidance Instruments.* Washington, D.C.: National Vocational Guidance Association, 1982.

Karren, R., Crites, J. O., and Bobko, P. "Path Analysis of CMI–Attitude Scale Data in Adolescence." Unpublished manuscript, University of Maryland, 1975.

Savickas, M. L., and Crites, J. O. *A Course for Career Maturity: Grades 9–12.* Hudson, Ohio: Crites Career Consultants, 1983.

Sears, S. "A Definition of Career Guidance Terms: A National Vocational Guidance Association Perspective." *Vocational Guidance Quarterly,* 1982, *31*(2), 137–143.

Smith, E. D., and Herr, E. L. "Sex Differences in the Maturation of Vocational Attitudes Among Adolescents." *Vocational Guidance Quarterly,* 1972, *20*, 177–182.

Super, D. E. "The Dimensions and Measurement of Vocational Maturity." *Teachers College Record,* 1955, *57*, 151–163.

Super, D. E. "Vocational Maturity Theory." In D. E. Super (Ed.), *Measuring Vocational Maturity for Counseling and Evaluation.* Washington, D.C.: National Vocational Guidance Association, 1974.

Super, D. E. "A Life-Span, Life-Space Approach to Career Development." *Journal of Vocational Behavior,* 1980, *16*, 282–298.

Super, D. E., and Crites, J. O. *Appraising Vocational Fitness.* (Rev. ed.) New York: Harper & Row, 1962.

Super, D. E., and Overstreet, P. L. *The Vocational Maturity of Ninth Grade Boys.* New York: Teachers College Bureau of Publications, 1960.

Super, D. E., and others. *Vocational Development: A Framework for Research.* New York: Teachers College Bureau of Publications, 1957.

Thompson, A. S., and others. *Career Development Inventory.* Vol. 1: *User's Manual.* Palo Alto, Calif.: Consulting Psychologists Press, 1981.

Thompson, A. S., and others. *Career Development Inventory: College and University Form, Supplement to User's Manual.* Palo Alto, Calif.: Counseling Psychologists Press, 1982.

Thorndike, R. L., and Hagen, E. *Measurement and Evaluation in Psychology and Education.* (4th ed.) New York: Wilcy, 1977.

Westbrook, B. W., and Rogers, B. H. "Review of the Career Skills Assessment Program." In J. T. Kapes and M. M. Mastie (Eds.), *A Counselor's Guide to Vocational Guidance Instruments*. Washington, D.C.: National Vocational Guidance Association, 1982.

Westbrook, B. W., and others. "The Validity of the Crites Model of Career Maturity." *Journal of Vocational Behavior*, 1980, *16*, 249-281.

Wherry, R. J., Sr. *Contributions to Correlational Analysis*. New York: Academic Press, in press.

Zelkowitz, R. S. "The Construction and Validation of a Measure of Vocational Maturity for Adults." Unpublished doctoral dissertation, Teachers College, Columbia University, 1974.

Zytowski, D. G. "Review of the Career Maturity Inventory by J. O. Crites." In O. K. Buros (Ed.), *The Eighth Mental Measurements Yearbook*. Highland Park, N.J.: Gryphon Press, 1978.

Zytowski, D. G. "Assessment in the Counseling Process for the 1980s." *Measurement and Evaluation in Guidance*, 1982, *15*, 15-21.

10

René V. Dawis

Job Satisfaction:
Worker Aspirations,
Attitudes, and Behavior

In 1973 a Special Task Force to the Secretary of Health, Education and Welfare, reporting on "work in America," documented with statistics and research findings the various dissatisfactions of American workers with the quality of their work lives and the consequences of such dissatisfaction. One of the main problems, the Special Task Force observed, was that "work [had] not changed fast enough to keep up with the rapid and wide-scale changes in worker attitudes, aspirations, and values" (p. xvi).

This chapter examines what research and theory can tell us about job satisfaction, worker aspirations, and work attitudes and how these affect, and are affected by, worker behavior (job performance, turnover, absences, and the like).

The Research Literature

The Study of Worker Behavior. From its very inception (Muensterberg, 1913; Taylor, 1911), the scientific study of worker behavior in the United States was undertaken primarily in the service of the employer. The basic objective of such study was to specify the human requirements of work and the factors

275

that contributed to satisfactory job performance. The well-known Hawthorne experiments (Roethlisberger and Dickson, 1939) began as studies of factors affecting worker productivity. The vocational guidance movement (Paterson, 1938), while seeking to help the individual, focused much of its attention on what was required for the individual to become a satisfactory worker.

The Great Depression brought the first studies of work from the worker's vantage point. The consequences of unemployment for the individual (Bakke, 1934) and its converse, job satisfaction (Hoppock, 1935), were new topics for investigation. This line of research, focusing on the individual's requirements *of* work, was pursued vigorously after the end of World War II. By the early 1970s, Locke (1976) was moved to complain that it was impossible to review the (then) over 3,000 publications on job satisfaction alone. What did this enormous literature show?

Job Satisfaction Research. To begin with, considerable research was devoted to the problem of measuring job satisfaction. Many methods were proposed, but methods based on self-report gained the widest acceptance and use. Hoppock (1935) used such a method in his pioneering study.

In his study, Hoppock found more satisfied workers—over two thirds of those he surveyed—than he had expected to find. In subsequent annual reviews of job satisfaction research from 1935 through 1965, Hoppock and Robinson (reporting in *Occupations* and its successor, the *Personnel and Guidance Journal*) found the percentage of dissatisfied workers to range between 13 and 21 percent, averaging about 15 percent. Nationwide surveys conducted by the National Opinion Research Center, the Survey Research Center, and Gallup since the late 1950s have confirmed that at least 80 percent of respondents say they are satisfied with their jobs. This percentage has not changed much since Hoppock's 1930s study (Chelte, Wright, and Tausky, 1982; Quinn, Staines, and McCullough, 1974; Weaver, 1980).

How, then, do we explain the widespread impression that more and more American workers have become increasingly disaffected with work?

One explanation may lie in the way the survey question is phrased. In the studies just cited, the usual survey question was "All in all, are you satisfied with your job?" When Roper asked his national sample of 5,000 adults, "If you could go back to age eighteen and start life all over again, would you choose a different career or occupation?," over 40 percent said yes. Only 39 percent said they would choose the same career or occupation. This finding has also remained the same over the years (Special Task Force, 1973). In other words, many workers may have adjusted to their current situation but would not hesitate to change for the better.

Another explanation may lie in the difference between overall satisfaction and "facet satisfaction"—that is, satisfaction with particular facets of work, such as pay, supervision, coworkers, working conditions, and type of work. One may be dissatisfied with one or more facets of the job and still be satisfied with the job overall.

Facet satisfaction is different and separable from overall satisfaction. Scales that measure facet satisfaction correlate only moderately with one another and with overall satisfaction (Dawis and others, 1974; Weiss and others, 1967). Weitzel and his colleagues (1973) showed that facet satisfaction could be organized in a hierarchical fashion: a general satisfaction factor; two subgeneral, or second-order, factors (Satisfaction with the Job, Satisfaction with the Organization); and four first-order factors (Personal Progress and Development, Compensation, Superior-Subordinate Interaction, Organizational Context). This structure means that dissatisfaction could appear at the facet level, at the first-order factor level, or even at the subgeneral factor level *without* there being overall dissatisfaction.

Accepting the concepts of facet and overall satisfaction serves only to raise more questions. How is facet satisfaction to be weighted in its contribution to overall satisfaction? Is facet satisfaction compensatory; will satisfaction on one facet make up for dissatisfaction on another? Are there facets that are so important that dissatisfaction on them results inevitably in overall dissatisfaction?

At present, most of the available data to answer these

questions are cross-sectional and therefore amenable only to correlational analysis. The most commonly used multivariate method, multiple correlation, is based on a compensatory model. Furthermore, for multiple correlation, the more predictor variables there are, the less is the differential effect of assigning different predictor weights. For practical purposes, if there are more than five predictors (in this case, facet satisfaction), unit weighting produces much the same results in predicting overall satisfaction as using differential weights (Ewen, 1967). At the moment, then, the questions posed earlier cannot be answered satisfactorily because any "answers" found would only be artifacts of the methodology used.

However, if there is one finding that all observers can agree on, it is the fact of individual differences. People differ in overall satisfaction, in facet satisfaction, and in their weighting of facet satisfaction. How can we account for these individual differences in job satisfaction?

Some Determiners of Job Satisfaction. A reasonable expectation is that if circumstances differ, job satisfaction will differ. The research data (Herzberg and others, 1957; Quinn, Staines, and McCullough, 1974; Weaver, 1980) bear out this expectation: On the average, people in higher-level occupations report higher satisfaction than those in lower-level occupations. People in better-paying jobs are more satisfied than people in lower-paying jobs. People at higher socioeconomic status levels express more job satisfaction than those at lower levels. However, these are *average* findings, and the difference in satisfaction means between extreme groups (say, between the highest- and the lowest-ranked occupations) rarely approaches one standard deviation on the satisfaction scale, while the individual differences *within* any group exceed four standard deviations. Obviously, there are more factors at play.

Several proxies for "internal" factors have been studied—in particular, gender, age, and education. Female and male workers have been thought to differ in their internal factors, and this difference was expected to show up in differing levels of satisfaction. The research findings do not support this expectation (Brief, Rose, and Aldag, 1977; Weaver, 1980). The variable of gender *alone* is apparently a poor surrogate for the internal factors that are presumed to affect job satisfaction.

Research data have consistently supported a positive linear relationship between age and satisfaction. Glenn, Taylor, and Weaver (1977) partialed out the influence of reward variables (income, occupational prestige, authority, autonomy) and education and found a linear age effect for both females and males. Quinn and his colleagues (1974) also observed a striking age/satisfaction relationship.

Studies on the relationship between education and satisfaction (Glenn, Taylor, and Weaver, 1977; Herzberg and others, 1957; Quinn, Staines, and McCullough, 1974; Weaver, 1980) have shown mixed results, more studies showing a negative than a positive relationship. Vollmer and Kinney (1955) showed that the education variable could be confounded with the age variable: Workers with less education who also happened to be older were more satisfied than workers with more education who turned out to be the younger workers. When they held age constant, they found the more educated to be less satisfied than the less educated. One explanation for this negative relationship is that more education can produce higher expectations about the job than are realizable, leading to lower satisfaction. If this conjecture is correct, research should focus not so much on the proxy variables of gender, age, and education as on, rather, the worker's actual expectations, needs, wants, and aspirations about work—in a word, on what workers want from work.

Worker Aspirations. Jurgensen (1978) reported an important study of worker aspirations. In 1945 he began collecting data from job applicants about their preferences (ranking in importance) for the ten job factors listed in Table 1. Over a thirty-year period, some 57,000 applicants for jobs ranging from professional and managerial to laborer and service provided data on their own ranking and, in addition, on how they thought others would rank the factors. Table 1 summarizes the data by gender (a third of the applicants were women) and by five-year groups.

The table shows that, across the years, job applicants agreed about what they wanted most in jobs. Security and type

Table 1. Rank Order[a] of Ten Job Factors over a Thirty-Year Period, by Gender and Time Period.

Job Factor	Own Ranking														Ranking Ascribed to Others 1949–1975	
	1946–1950		1951–1955		1956–1960		1961–1965		1966–1970		1971–1975		1945–1975			
	F	M	F	M	F	M	F	M	F	M	F	M	F	M	F	M
Advancement	3	2	3	2	4.5	3	6	3	6	3	7	3	5.5	2.5	3	3
Benefits	10	9	10	8	10	7	10	7	10	8	10	8	10	8	6	5
Company	5	4	4	4	2	4	2	4	2	5	2	4	2	4	9	7
Coworkers	4	5	5	6	4.5	6	4.5	6	3	6	4	6	4	6	10	10
Hours	9	8	9	9	9	9	9	9	9	9	8	9	9	9	4	6
Pay	8	7	7	5	7	5	7	5	5	4	5	5	7	5	1	1
Security	2	1	2	1	3	1	3	1	7	2	6	2	3	1	5	2
Supervisor	6	6	6	7	6	8	4.5	7	4	7	3	7	5.5	7	8	9
Type of work	1	3	1	3	1	2	1	2	1	1	1	1	1	2.5	2	4
Working conditions	7	10	8	10	8	10	8	10	8	10	9	10	8	10	7	8
	r = .82[b]		r = .88		r = .79		r = .77		r = .58		r = .62		r = .77		r = .85	

[a] Based on median rank for each job factor.

[b] Rank-order correlation between gender groups.

Source: Adapted from Tables 1 and 2 in Jurgensen, C. E., "Job Preferences (What Makes a Job Good or Bad?)," Journal of Applied Psychology, 1978, 63, 267–276.

of work were ranked highest; working conditions, hours, and
benefits were ranked lowest. Men and women were in general
agreement, except for the period 1966–1975. There were age-
group differences for the men but not for the women. With age,
company and benefits became relatively more important for
men. Education-group differences showed similar patterns for
men and women. With higher levels of education, type of work
became more important while security became less important.
Men and women in the same occupation had similar rankings,
except for those in professional and service occupations. Professional women ranked coworkers high, but professional men did
not; the latter ranked security high, while the former did not. In
the service occupations women ranked supervisor and type of
work much higher than men did, while men ranked advancement much higher than women did. These differences in rankings, when the total group is subdivided according to gender,
age, education, and occupation, reflect the existence of individual differences in job-factor importance rankings even if, over
the years, the *average* overall rankings did not change much.

   Job-factor rankings ascribed to others by the job applicants did not correlate highly with their own. Rankings ascribed
to others might be better reflections of one's true rankings,
since own rankings tend to be influenced by social desirability
factors. If this is so, then for both men and women pay emerges
as the top factor on which jobs are evaluated, and coworkers as
the least important.

   Herzberg and others (1957) compiled data on job-factor
importance rankings from sixteen studies covering 16,000 workers and found almost identical results to Jurgensen's. An interesting finding of Herzberg's was that the same job factors were
ranked differently in terms of their importance in contributing
to job satisfaction and to job dissatisfaction. Security, and company and management, were ranked high in contributing to satisfaction but low in contributing to dissatisfaction, whereas
wages and opportunity for advancement were ranked high in
contributing to dissatisfaction but low in contributing to satisfaction.

   Workers, then, differ in what they look for in work. Presumably they differ in what they find in work. How do these antecedent conditions combine to produce job satisfaction?

Theories of Job Satisfaction

Two-Factor Theory. Herzberg's (Herzberg, Mausner, and Snyderman, 1959) was the first of several theories about job satisfaction to attract attention in the 1960s. According to Herzberg's theory, satisfaction and dissatisfaction are separate phenomena and are determined by two different sets of job factors. Achievement, recognition, advancement, responsibility, and work itself—factors associated with the job's content—are responsible for satisfaction and hence are called "satisfiers" or "motivators." Compensation, supervision, coworkers, working conditions, and company policies and practices—factors associated with the job's context—are the determiners of dissatisfaction and are called "dissatisfiers" or "hygienes." The "hygienes" can cause dissatisfaction but not satisfaction; only "motivators" can produce satisfaction.

Herzberg's theory was controversial, but it did generate much research. The results were mixed: Some studies were positive, but more were negative (House and Wigdor, 1967; King, 1970). The idea that "satisfiers" are different from "dissatisfiers" is intriguing but difficult to confirm. We should note that Herzberg's "satisfiers" and "dissatisfiers" refer to *external* rather than internal factors and that Herzberg's theory does not take individual differences into account.

Equity Theory. Equity theory (Adams, 1963; Patchen, 1961) appeared on the heels of Herzberg's theory. Its main idea was that satisfaction depends on one's feeling of fairness or justice—equity—or the lack of it. This feeling results from the comparison of one's situation (outcomes-to-inputs ratio) with that of a reference person. Outcomes are the rewards from, and inputs the investments in, the job. Outcomes differ in importance (valence), and the worker seeks to maximize the *total* valence of the outcomes.

Job dissatisfaction results when inequity is perceived. To reduce feelings of inequity, one may use behavioral means, such as altering inputs or outcomes, or acting on the reference person, or leaving the field; or one may use cognitive means, such as cognitively distorting inputs or outcomes, or choosing a different reference person.

Equity theory has been applied most successfully in the study of pay as a job outcome, but presumably it applies to other outcomes as well. Predictions have been largely supported for the underpayment condition—when one's ratio is less than the reference person's—but not for the overpayment condition (Pritchard, 1969).

Equity theory has identified new determiners of satisfaction to add to Herzberg's job factors—namely, the comparison of what is obtained (own outcomes-to-inputs ratio) with what is desired (reference outcomes-to-inputs ratio). Whereas Herzberg's job factors may be evaluated from an assessment of the environment, equity theory's internal criteria require information about the worker's cognitions.

VIE Theory. Another cognitive theory, one that rivaled Herzberg's in stimulating research, was Vroom's (1964) valence-instrumentality-expectancy (VIE) theory. In Vroom's formulation, the motivation to work is influenced by the level of satisfaction anticipated and the expectation (subjective probability) that working will result in the anticipated satisfaction. In turn, the level of satisfaction anticipated is determined by the instrumentality (effectiveness) of the job in obtaining certain outcomes and the valence (importance) of these outcomes to the worker. Vroom's VIE theory is a more complex way of stating the basic idea in equity theory—namely, that satisfaction results to the degree that one obtains what one desires. (See Mitchell, 1974, for a review.)

Lawler and Porter's Theory. Combining equity and VIE theory, Lawler and Porter (1967) advanced yet another cognitive theory that differed from its predecessors in its reversal of the focus in the attitude/behavior relationship. In equity and VIE theory, the focus is on behavior as resulting from the formation of attitude; in Lawler and Porter's theory, the focus is on attitude as resulting from behavior. For Vroom, anticipated job satisfaction is a determiner of motivation to work, which, in turn, determines work behavior. For Lawler and Porter, job performance is a determiner of job satisfaction (but through an intervening variable—the evaluation of the rewards obtained through job performance when compared with the level of rewards deemed equitable). Vroom's theory is concerned not so much with present job satisfaction as with present job performance. Lawler and Porter's theory is concerned with both. For Lawler and Porter, present job satisfaction is a function of past job performance, while present job performance is a function of effort, moderated by ability and role perception. Effort, in its turn, is a function of the value or importance of the rewards and the expectation that exerting effort will produce the rewards.

At the risk of oversimplifying, the same common elements germane to job satisfaction can be discerned in these theories. First of all, there are the different rewards (or outcomes or job factors) of work. Then, there is the differential importance of these rewards to different individuals. Finally there is the comparison of what is desired (importance of rewards) with what is obtained (actual rewards). The extent to which the two correspond determines the level of job satisfaction for a given individual.

Theory of Work Adjustment. Lofquist and Dawis's (1969) theory incorporates precisely the common elements just identified. In their Theory of Work Adjustment (TWA), job satisfaction is determined by the correspondence of the job's actual rewards ("reinforcers" in TWA) to what is important to the individual ("needs," "values" in TWA). Needs are preferences for particular reinforcers; values are the "importance" dimensions that underlie needs. Needs and values are the individual's requirements of the job, much as the job has skill or ability requirements of the individual. The prediction of job satisfaction is moderated by the "satisfactoriness" of the individual, prediction being more accurate for more satisfactory workers and less accurate for less satisfactory workers. Satisfactoriness is the work environment's evaluation of the worker's job performance, or the satisfaction of the work environment with the individual. It is predicted from the correspondence of the worker's skills or abilities to the skill or ability requirements of the job. In turn, the prediction of satisfactoriness is moderated by the worker's satisfaction, prediction being better for more satisfied workers and poorer for less satisfied workers.

According to TWA, predicting job satisfaction requires identifying the individual's needs and values as well as the environment's effective reinforcers. One way to identify needs and values would be simply to ask the individual, as in self-report measures of needs and values such as the Minnesota Importance Questionnaire (Rounds and others, 1981). Another way would be to infer reinforcer preferences from the person's reinforcement history and experience with reinforcers. Both methods would profit greatly from some system for listing and classifying reinforcers. One such system is shown in Table 2.

Table 2. Classification of Work Reinforcers
Based on the Minnesota Importance Questionnaire.

Type of Reinforcer	Type of Environment	
	Competitive	Noncompetitive
General environmental	*Safety* reinforcers Company policies and practices Supervision—human relations Supervision—technical	*Comfort* reinforcers Activity Independence Variety Compensation Security Working conditions
Social	*Status* reinforcers Advancement Recognition Authority Social status	*Altruism* reinforcers Coworkers Moral values Social service
Self	*Achievement* reinforcers Ability utilization Achievement	*Autonomy* reinforcers Creativity Responsibility

Source: Rounds, J. B., Jr., and others, *Manual for the Minnesota Importance Questionnaire* (Minneapolis: Department of Psychology, University of Minnesota, 1981).

Can job satisfaction be predicted from a knowledge of reinforcer preferences (needs, values)? Research on TWA shows it can be done when such knowledge is combined with information about the reinforcer systems perceived to be present in work environments. This latter information, in the form of incumbent and supervisor ratings, has been published as "Occupational Reinforcer Patterns" (Borgen and others, 1968). A number of studies (Betz, 1971; Lichter, 1980; Rounds, 1981; Rounds and Dawis, 1975; Salazar, 1981; Weiss and others, 1964), both cross-sectional and longitudinal and involving a wide range of occupations, have consistently produced significant correlations in predicting job satisfaction from the correspondence of appropriate Occupational Reinforcer Patterns to workers' patterns of needs. In other words, job satisfaction can be predicted by comparing what is desired (importance of reinforcers to the individual) with what is obtained (reinforcers generally perceived to be present in the particular work environment).

Correlates and Consequences

Some Correlates of Job Satisfaction. From a cognitive standpoint, job satisfaction is a cognition, with affective components, that results from certain perceptions and results in certain future behaviors. As a cognition, it is linked to other cognitions or cognitive constructs, such as self-esteem, job involvement, work alienation, organizational commitment, morale, and life satisfaction. To understand job satisfaction, we must examine its relationship to these other constructs.

Self-esteem, feelings of personal worth and effectiveness, is the product of self-evaluation (Jones, 1973) and can be considered a kind of satisfaction—satisfaction with self. Like job satisfaction, self-esteem may be multifaceted. Korman (1970) identifies three kinds of self-esteem: chronic, task-specific, and socially influenced self-esteem. The complexity of the construct accounts in part for the disconcerting finding that different measures of self-esteem generally do not intercorrelate highly (Crowne, Stephens, and Kelly, 1961).

According to self-consistency theory (Festinger, 1957), self-esteem as a cognition must be consistent with other cognitions, such as job satisfaction. Self-consistency theory would imply that high-self-esteem persons will attribute job satisfaction to internal (self) causes and job dissatisfaction to external causes, while low-self-esteem persons will do the opposite. Further, low-self-esteem persons are expected to be dissatisfied when they succeed and satisfied when they fail. Research findings (Adler, 1980; Dipboye and others, 1978; Greenhaus and Badin, 1974) support the expectations for high-self-esteem persons but not for low-self-esteem persons. Like high-self-esteem persons, low-self-esteem persons tend to attribute job satisfaction and success to internal causes and job dissatisfaction and failure to external causes. These findings are more consistent with a reinforcement view than a self-consistency view (Hill, 1968).

Job involvement (and its opposite, work alienation) has to do with the importance of the job to the worker's self-esteem or self-concept (Rabinowitz and Hall, 1977). The more important successful work performance is to self-esteem, the stronger is the job involvement. The more important work is in defining one's self-concept, the stronger is the job involvement. When the work itself (but not necessarily its compensations and rewards) becomes unimportant to the individual, the individual is alienated from work.

Job involvement can be a determiner of job satisfaction. Correlational data (Rabinowitz and Hall, 1977) support this expectation for intrinsic, but not extrinsic, job satisfaction. However, the correlational data can also support the conclusion that job involvement *results from* intrinsic job satisfaction. Furthermore, job involvement has not been shown to be related to job performance, raising doubts about its relationship to self-esteem. Many of these findings are unfortunately confounded by measurement problems (Lodahl and Kejner, 1965).

Organizational commitment is related to, but is not the same as, job involvement (Mowday, Steers, and Porter, 1979). Organizational commitment is defined by Mowday and colleagues (1979, p. 226) as "the relative strength of an individual's identification with and involvement in a particular organization." In other words, organizational commitment has to do with the importance of the organization to the worker.

Organizational commitment is also different from, but related to, job satisfaction (Mowday, Steers, and Porter, 1979). Satisfaction with the organization could be a cause or an effect of organizational commitment. Both satisfaction and commitment could also be results of the reinforcement provided by the organization. Organizational commitment, therefore, depends on (1) the importance to the worker of membership in a particular organization and (2) the reinforcement value of the organization. When both are high, job satisfaction will be high, at least for those facets of satisfaction involving the organization.

Job satisfaction, job involvement, and organizational commitment are often confused with morale. Current use would favor restricting the term *morale* to denoting a group phenomenon, while *job satisfaction, job involvement,* and *organizational commitment* denote individual phenomena (Blum and Naylor, 1968). Morale depends on (1) the importance to the worker of the work group and belonging in it and (2) the reinforcement value of the work group. Morale is "high" when group members (1) feel they "belong," (2) agree on group goals, (3) make progress toward these goals, and (4) apportion tasks so that each member feels he or she contributes toward achieving group goals (Muchinsky, 1983). Morale has been shown to correlate with job satisfaction (Motowidlo and Borman, 1978).

Finally, there is the relationship of job satisfaction to life satisfaction. The research evidence (Brayfield, Wells, and Strate, 1957; Iris and Barrett, 1972; Orpen, 1978; Schmitt and Mellon, 1980) shows a moderate correlation between the two variables. What is not clear is whether job satisfaction "spills over" to life satisfaction, as Kornhauser (1965) has proposed. The "spillover effect" might occur for the job-involved but not for those who are not job-involved. However, this possibility has not yet been studied.

In summary, the several cognitive correlates of job satisfaction examined here—self-esteem, job involvement, organizational commitment, morale, and life satisfaction—appear to be separate constructs in their own right that differ from, but are related to, job satisfaction. A fuller understanding of job satisfaction can be facilitated by the study of these correlates, explication of the cognitive processes involved, and examination of how these processes, in turn, involve or affect job satisfaction.

Some Consequences of Job Satisfaction. From a behavioral standpoint, job satisfaction is a response (a verbal operant) that has behavioral consequences. On the positive side are tenure, longevity, physical health, mental health, and productivity; on the negative side, turnover, absenteeism, accidents, and mental health problems.

The turnover literature (Mobley and others, 1979; Porter and Steers, 1973) documents a negative relationship between job satisfaction and turnover. Turnover can be predicted from earlier assessments of satisfaction (Anderson, 1969; Hulin, 1966, 1968), and satisfaction is a better predictor than gender, age, education, or number of dependents (Taylor and Weiss, 1972) but not as good as intention to quit (Mobley, Horner, and Hollingsworth, 1978). Dissatisfaction may set off a chain of events that leads to turnover, an event chain that might be called *avoidance* adjustment. Quitting the job is the means by which the individual avoids the aversive condition that is job dissatisfaction. This contrasts with an event chain—initiated by anticipated job satisfaction, such as the attractiveness of an alternative job situation—that might be called *approach* adjustment.

The absenteeism literature (Muchinsky, 1977; Nicholson, Brown, and Chadwick-Jones, 1976) has likewise documented a negative relationship between job satisfaction and absenteeism, despite severe problems in the measurement of absenteeism. Like turnover, absenteeism is a form of avoidance adjustment. Absenteeism is an early-warning indicator of turnover or a substitute for turnover when quitting the job is not possible. In the case of absenteeism, as with turnover, job dissatisfaction functions as a negative reinforcer.

The relationship of job satisfaction to accidents is not as well documented. Negative but low correlations have been reported (Kerr, 1950; Stagner, Flebbe, and Wood, 1952), the usual finding for most accident predictors (Barrett, 1975). Job dissatisfaction might therefore be a factor in increasing the frequency of unsafe behavior, which, in combination with unsafe conditions, makes accidents more likely.

Job dissatisfaction is related to mental health problems:

psychosomatic illnesses, depression, anxiety, worry, tension, and impaired interpersonal relationships (Special Task Force, 1973). Job dissatisfaction is also a risk factor in coronary heart disease. Job dissatisfaction, therefore, can be the occasion for a "spiraling down" of the worker's health, both mental and physical. In the worst case, inability to cope effectively with job dissatisfaction can lead to such dire behavioral consequences as alcoholism, drug abuse, and suicide.

The evidence for the positive behavioral consequences of job satisfaction comes about largely as the converse of evidence for the negative effects of job dissatisfaction. However, there is Palmore's (1969) much-quoted fifteen-year follow-up study showing job satisfaction as the best predictor of longevity, better than physicians' ratings of physical functioning, use of tobacco, or even genetic inheritance.

The evidence is least clear when it comes to the question of job satisfaction as a determiner of productivity or as a contributor to successful job performance. Early human relations theorists (Mayo, 1933/1960) contended that job performance depended on job satisfaction. The Hawthorne experiments (Roethlisberger and Dickson, 1939) and several other studies appeared to support this position. However, other studies showed an absence of relationship or even an occasional inverse relationship (Brayfield and Crockett, 1955). The causal direction of the relationship, when one is observed, also remains unclear (Sheridan and Slocum, 1975). Under certain conditions, performance causes satisfaction (Wanous, 1974), but under other conditions, satisfaction can affect performance (Organ, 1977).

Job Satisfaction and Job Behavior. It is apparent from the preceding section that job satisfaction and job behavior are separate, or separable, domains. The correlation between these domains is minimal at best. Job performance does not have to depend on job satisfaction. Dissatisfied workers have been observed to be high performers as well as low performers; and so have satisfied workers. Nor does job satisfaction have to depend on job performance. High performers have been known to be satisfied as well as dissatisfied; and so have low performers.

The relationship between job satisfaction and job behavior is a special case of the more general relationship between attitudes and behavior. This relationship is low at best and nonsignificant at worst because of the lack in most studies of correspondence between attitude and behavior entities in their target, action, context, and time elements (Ajzen and Fishbein, 1977). When there is high correspondence between at least the target and action elements of attitudes and behavior, strong relationships are observed. When, for example, compensation is contingent on performance, and when monetary reward is important to the worker, satisfaction *can* result from successful job performance (Porter and Lawler, 1968).

It would seem best to think of job satisfaction as an outcome of job behavior. As an outcome, or consequence, of job behavior, job satisfaction can be seen as a *reinforcer* that has consequences for future job performance and other work behavior (absences, turnover). Future satisfactory job performance can be maintained by present job satisfaction. Future absence or turnover behavior can be made more likely by present job dissatisfaction, acting as a negative reinforcer.

Another outcome of job behavior (actual job performance) is employee *satisfactoriness,* the work organization's *satisfaction with the worker.* As an outcome, employee satisfactoriness can function as a reinforcer. It can maintain the work organization's rewarding behavior, which, in turn, can maintain the worker's job behavior (job performance). As a negative reinforcer, employee unsatisfactoriness makes more probable the work organization's behavior to deny wage increases to the worker, to move the worker to a lesser position, or, finally, to terminate the worker.

Implications

What implications does this research literature have for career development practice?

First, we have to conclude that job satisfaction is an important construct to consider in thinking about career development, an important variable to include in the assessment of status and progress in career development, and an important criterion variable to consider in the choice or rechoosing of a career. Along with job satisfaction, we have to consider worker aspirations (needs, values) and worker attitudes, the cognitive correlates of job satisfaction (self-esteem, job involvement, organizational commitment, morale, and life satisfaction). Information on these variables is needed in order to understand job satisfaction—and therefore career development—more fully. Information on worker aspirations and on the reinforcers present in work is especially important for the individual who is choosing a career.

The literature suggests that—just as failure is easier to predict than success—dissatisfaction may be more diagnostic than satisfaction. Dissatisfaction is usually expressed about facets of work that are important. In contrast, expressed satisfaction may be no more than the response felt to be socially desirable or socially required. We may learn more about the individual's career development from knowing what about work is dissatisfying than from knowing what is satisfying.

This is not to say that knowledge about satisfactions from work is not informative. Expressed satisfaction suggests at least a minimal level of adjustment and indicates that the individual will maintain current work behavior. In this regard, facet satisfaction can be more informative than overall satisfaction. Furthermore, knowledge about facet satisfactions is enhanced by knowledge about worker aspirations. Satisfaction in the work facets deemed to be important *is* diagnostic. We also have to find out whether a given individual is "compensatory," willing to trade off satisfaction in some important facets for lack of satisfaction in other important facets, or "noncompensatory" and unwilling to consider any choice that does not meet *all* important aspirations (needs, values).

People differ in what about work is important to them. We cannot—and should not—rely on the demographic characteristics of individuals (gender, age, race, education) as the basis for inferring what is important to them. Within-group differences are so large as to mandate individual assessment.

The hard reality of individual differences has two inescapable implications: (1) general rules, principles, "laws," or conclusions drawn from the research literature will apply only in a probabilistic sense to any individual, and (2) career development counselors and practitioners should be expert in individual assessment.

With respect to the first implication, the busy practitioner does not have the time to translate research findings, typically given as correlations, into probability expectations about the client. As a service to practitioners, expectancy tables should be routinely constructed for those correlational findings that are useful in career development planning or counseling.

With respect to the second implication, assessment is not meant to be limited to psychometric assessment (in my opinion, still the best that is available). The skilled practitioner can use a variety of other assessment means: clinical interviews, records, biographical questionnaires, observations of behavior, and discussions with "significant others." Whatever means are used, the implication remains the same: More expertise in assessment, not less, will be required of the practitioner.

The theoretical literature can be of much practical value in enhancing the career development practitioner's clinical judgment. For example, the distinction between job content and job context factors points up the difference between intrinsic and extrinisic motivation and the need to ascertain both. Feelings of fairness and equity cannot be construed without considering the social comparison process or the social context. Expectations involve not only anticipated rewards but also the anticipation that doing one's job well will lead to the rewards. The perception of the job's "instrumentality" in attaining desired goals should be examined in career planning. Work may be of central importance to many but not all; other motivations have to be considered. The distinctions between job performance (actual job behavior) and *satisfactoriness* (the employer's *evaluation* of job performance) and between the individual's satisfactoriness and satisfaction (the *employee's* evaluation of the work situation) should be useful in understanding the individual's adjustment to work.

The practitioner can "intervene" either through the individual or through the environment. The practitioner can help clients clarify what is important to them—their aspirations, needs, and values—and understand how these shape their satisfactions and dissatisfactions. The practitioner can teach clients how to make reinforcement work for them. Such teaching will be more effective if it takes account of the clients' needs and values—that is, their reinforcer preferences.

This research literature implies that the design and redesign of work must go beyond the present limited focus on tasks and efficiency and should pay much more attention to the effective reinforcers in the work setting, to what is important to the workers. What is important to workers—their aspirations, needs, and values—holds one important key to job satisfaction, just as job satisfaction holds one important key to the fullest realization of human potential in work.

Suggested Readings

Locke, E. A. "The Nature and Causes of Job Satisfaction." In M. D. Dunnette (Ed.), *Handbook of Industrial and Organizational Psychology*. Chicago: Rand McNally, 1976.

A review of the job satisfaction research literature, with special emphasis on the causes and effects of job satisfaction. The major theories and major findings are summarized and discussed in the light of the author's analysis of the job satisfaction concept. Analysis of measurement problems and research strategies leads to recommendations for future research. A good source for the practitioner who wants to know more about the research base of the job satisfaction concept.

Lofquist, L. H., and Dawis, R. V. "Research on Work Adjustment and Satisfaction: Implications for Career Counseling." In S. D. Brown and R. W. Lent (Eds.), *Handbook of Counseling Psychology*. New York: Wiley, in press.

A review of the research literature on work adjustment and work satisfaction, organized around the authors' theory of work adjustment. Implications of this literature are drawn for the career counseling practitioner.

Quinn, R. P., Staines, G. L., and McCullough, M. R. "Job Satisfaction: Is There a Trend?" Manpower Research Monograph
No. 30. Washington, D.C.: U.S. Government Printing Office,
1974.

An examination of national trends in job satisfaction, the
distribution of job satisfaction in the work force, what American workers want from their jobs, the implications of job satis-
faction/dissatisfaction for employees, employers, and society at
large, and approaches to solving problems involving job satisfaction. This research monograph provides the background for the
movement to improve the "quality of work life."

Special Task Force to the Secretary of Health, Education and
Welfare. *Work in America.* Cambridge, Mass.: MIT Press,
1973.

A landmark document that examines the background for
public policy about work. The report goes beyond the need for
increased job opportunity to the need for more satisfying
work. The crucial role of job satisfaction in the work life of the
nation is the basis for many implications, including several
about education in general and career education in particular. A
must for career development practitioners interested in public
policy.

References

Adams, J. S. "Toward an Understanding of Inequity." *Journal
of Abnormal and Social Psychology,* 1963, *67,* 422-436.
Adler, S. "Self Esteem and Causal Attributions for Job Satisfac-
tion and Dissatisfaction." *Journal of Applied Psychology,*
1980, *65,* 327-332.
Ajzen, I., and Fishbein, M. "Attitude-Behavior Relations: A
Theoretical Analysis and Review of Empirical Research."
Psychological Bulletin, 1977, *84,* 888-918.
Anderson, L. M. "Longitudinal Changes in Level of Work Ad-
justment." Unpublished doctoral dissertation, University of
Minnesota, 1969.
Bakke, E. W. *The Unemployed Man.* New York: Dutton, 1934.

Barrett, G. V. "Public Policy and the Prediction of Accident Involvement." In K. N. Wexley and G. A. Yukl (Eds.), *Organizational Behavior and Industrial Psychology.* New York: Oxford University Press, 1975.

Betz, E. L. "Occupational Reinforcer Patterns and Need-Reinforcer Correspondence in the Prediction of Job Satisfaction." Unpublished doctoral dissertation, University of Minnesota, 1971.

Blum, M. L., and Naylor, J. C. *Industrial Psychology: Its Theoretical and Social Foundations.* New York: Harper & Row, 1968.

Borgen, F. H., and others. "The Measurement of Occupational Reinforcer Patterns." *Minnesota Studies in Vocational Rehabilitation,* 1968, No. 25.

Brayfield, A. H., and Crockett, W. H. "Employee Attitudes and Employee Performance." *Psychological Bulletin,* 1955, *52,* 396-424.

Brayfield, A. H., Wells, R. V., and Strate, M. W. "Interrelationships Among Measures of Job Satisfaction and General Satisfaction." *Journal of Applied Psychology,* 1957, *41,* 201-205.

Brief, A. P., Rose, G. L., and Aldag, R. J. "Sex Differences in Preferences for Job Attributes Revisited." *Journal of Applied Psychology,* 1977, *62,* 645-646.

Chelte, A. F., Wright, J., and Tausky, C. "Did Job Satisfaction Really Drop During the 1970's?" *Monthly Labor Review,* 1982, *105*(11), 33-38.

Crowne, D. P., Stephens, M. W., and Kelly, R. "The Validity and Equivalence of Tests of Self-Acceptance." *Journal of Psychology,* 1961, *51,* 101-112.

Dawis, R. V., and others. "Describing Organizations as Reinforcer Systems: A New Use for Job Satisfaction and Employee Attitude Surveys." *Journal of Vocational Behavior,* 1974, *4,* 55-66.

Dipboye, R. L., and others. "Self-Esteem as a Moderator of the Relationship Between Scientific Interests and the Job Satisfaction of Physicists and Engineers." *Journal of Applied Psychology,* 1978, *63,* 289-294.

Ewen, R. B. "Weighting Components of Job Satisfaction." *Journal of Applied Psychology*, 1967, *51*, 68-73.

Festinger, L. *A Theory of Cognitive Dissonance*. New York: Harper & Row, 1957.

Glenn, N. D., Taylor, P. A., and Weaver, C. N. "Age and Job Satisfaction Among Males and Females: A Multivariate, Multisurvey Study." *Journal of Applied Psychology*, 1977, *62*, 189-193.

Greenhaus, J. H., and Badin, I. J. "Self Esteem, Performance and Satisfaction: Some Tests of a Theory." *Journal of Applied Psychology*, 1974, *59*, 722-726.

Herzberg, F., Mausner, B., and Snyderman, B. B. *The Motivation to Work*. New York: Wiley, 1959.

Herzberg, F., and others. *Job Attitudes: Review of Research and Opinion*. Pittsburgh: Psychological Service of Pittsburgh, 1957.

Hill, W. F. "Sources of Evaluative Reinforcement." *Psychological Bulletin*, 1968, *69*, 132-146.

Hoppock, R. *Job Satisfaction*. New York: Harper & Row, 1935.

House, R. J., and Wigdor, L. A. "Herzberg's Dual Factor Theory of Job Satisfaction and Motivation: A Review of the Evidence and a Criticism." *Personnel Psychology*, 1967, *20*, 369-389.

Hulin, C. L. "Job Satisfaction and Turnover in a Female Clerical Population." *Journal of Applied Psychology*, 1966, *50*, 280-285.

Hulin, C. L. "Effects of Changes in Job Satisfaction Levels on Employee Turnover." *Journal of Applied Psychology*, 1968, *52*, 122-126.

Iris, B., and Barrett, G. V. "Some Relations Between Job and Life Satisfaction and Job Importance." *Journal of Applied Psychology*, 1972, *56*, 301-304.

Jones, S. C. "Self- and Interpersonal Evaluations: Esteem Theories Versus Consistency Theories." *Psychological Bulletin*, 1973, *79*, 185-199.

Jurgensen, C. E. "Job Preferences (What Makes a Job Good or Bad?)." *Journal of Applied Psychology*, 1978, *63*, 267-276.

Kerr, W. A. "Accident Proneness of Factory Departments." *Journal of Applied Psychology,* 1950, *34,* 167–170.

King, N. "Clarification and Evaluation of the Two-Factor Theory of Job Satisfaction." *Psychological Bulletin,* 1970, *74,* 18–31.

Korman, A. K. "Toward a Hypothesis of Work Behavior." *Journal of Applied Psychology,* 1970, *54,* 31–41.

Kornhauser, A. *Mental Health of the Industrial Worker.* New York: Wiley, 1965.

Lawler, E. E., and Porter, L. W. "Antecedent Attitudes of Effective Managerial Performance." *Organizational Behavior and Human Performance,* 1967, *2,* 122–142.

Lichter, D. "The Prediction of Job Satisfaction as an Outcome of Career Counseling." Unpublished doctoral dissertation, University of Minnesota, 1980.

Locke, E. A. "The Nature and Causes of Job Satisfaction." In M. D. Dunnette (Ed.), *Handbook of Industrial and Organizational Psychology.* Chicago: Rand McNally, 1976.

Lodahl, T., and Kejner, M. "The Definition and Measurement of Job Involvement." *Journal of Applied Psychology,* 1965, *49,* 24–33.

Lofquist, L. H., and Dawis, R. V. *Adjustment to Work.* New York: Appleton-Century-Crofts, 1969.

Mayo, E. *The Human Problems of an Industrial Civilization.* New York: Viking Press, 1960. (Originally published 1933.)

Mitchell, T. R. "Expectancy Models of Job Satisfaction, Occupational Preference and Effort: A Theoretical, Methodological, and Empirical Appraisal." *Psychological Bulletin,* 1974, *81,* 1053–1077.

Mobley, W. H., Horner, S. O., and Hollingsworth, A. T. "An Evaluation of Precursors of Hospital Employee Turnover." *Journal of Applied Psychology,* 1978, *63,* 408–414.

Mobley, W. H., and others. "Review and Conceptual Analysis of the Employee Turnover Process." *Psychological Bulletin,* 1979, *86,* 493–522.

Motowidlo, S. J., and Borman, W. C. "Relationships Between Military Morale, Motivation, Satisfaction, and Unit Effectiveness." *Journal of Applied Psychology,* 1978, *63,* 47–52.

Mowday, R. T., Steers, R. M., and Porter, L. W. "The Measurement of Organizational Commitment." *Journal of Vocational Behavior,* 1979, *14,* 224–247.

Muchinsky, P. M. "Employee Absenteeism: A Review of the Literature." *Journal of Vocational Behavior,* 1977, *10,* 316–340.

Muchinsky, P. M. *Psychology Applied to Work.* Homewood, Ill.: Dorsey Press, 1983.

Muensterberg, H. *Psychology and Industrial Efficiency.* Boston: Houghton Mifflin, 1913.

Nicholson, H., Brown, C. A., and Chadwick-Jones, J. K. "Absence from Work and Job Satisfaction." *Journal of Applied Psychology,* 1976, *61,* 728–737.

Organ, D. W. "A Reappraisal and Reinterpretation of the Satisfaction-Causes-Performance Hypothesis." *Academy of Management Review,* 1977, *2,* 46–53.

Orpen, C. "Work and Nonwork Satisfaction: A Causal-Correlational Analysis." *Journal of Applied Psychology,* 1978, *63,* 530–532.

Palmore, E. "Predicting Longevity: A Follow-up Controlling for Age." *Gerontologist,* 1969, *9,* 247–250.

Patchen, M. *The Choice of Wage Comparisons.* Englewood Cliffs, N.J.: Prentice-Hall, 1961.

Paterson, D. G. "The Genesis of Modern Guidance." *Educational Record,* January 1938, pp. 36–46.

Porter, L. W., and Lawler, E. E. *Managerial Attitudes and Performance.* Homewood, Ill.: Dorsey Press, 1968.

Porter, L. W., and Steers, R. M. "Organizational, Work, and Personal Factors in Employee Turnover and Absenteeism." *Psychological Bulletin,* 1973, *80,* 151–176.

Pritchard, R. D. "Equity Theory: A Review and Critique." *Organizational Behavior and Human Performance,* 1969, *4,* 176–211.

Quinn, R. P., Staines, G. L., and McCullough, M. R. "Job Satisfaction: Is There a Trend?" *Manpower Research Monograph,* 1974, No. 30.

Rabinowitz, S., and Hall, D. T. "Organizational Research on Job Involvement." *Psychological Bulletin,* 1977, *84,* 265–288.

Roethlisberger, F. J., and Dickson, W. J. *Management and the Worker*. Cambridge, Mass.: Harvard University Press, 1939.

Rounds, J. B., Jr. "The Comparative and Combined Utility of Need and Interest Data in the Prediction of Job Satisfaction." Unpublished doctoral dissertation, University of Minnesota, 1981.

Rounds, J. B., Jr., and Dawis, R. V. "A Comparison of Need-Reinforcer Correspondence Indices as Predictors of Job Satisfaction." *Work Adjustment Project Research Report* (Department of Psychology, University of Minnesota), 1975, No. 48.

Rounds, J. B., Jr., and others. *Manual for the Minnesota Importance Questionnaire*. Minneapolis: Department of Psychology, University of Minnesota, 1981.

Salazar, R. C. "The Prediction of Satisfaction and Satisfactoriness for Counselor Training Graduates." Unpublished doctoral dissertation, University of Minnesota, 1981.

Schmitt, N., and Mellon, P. M. "Life and Job Satisfaction: Is the Job Central?" *Journal of Vocational Behavior*, 1980, *16*, 51-58.

Sheridan, J. E., and Slocum, J. W. "The Direction of the Causal Relationship Between Job Satisfaction and Work Performance." *Organizational Behavior and Human Performance*, 1975, *14*, 159-172.

Special Task Force to the Secretary of Health, Education and Welfare. *Work in America*. Cambridge, Mass.: MIT Press, 1973.

Stagner, R., Flebbe, D. R., and Wood, E. V. "Working on the Railroad: A Study of Job Satisfaction." *Personnel Psychology*, 1952, *5*, 293-306.

Taylor, F. W. *The Principles of Scientific Management*. New York: Harper & Row, 1911.

Taylor, K. E., and Weiss, D. J. "Prediction of Individual Job Termination from Measured Job Satisfaction and Biographical Data." *Journal of Vocational Behavior*, 1972, *2*, 123-132.

Vollmer, H. M., and Kinney, J. A. "Age, Education, and Job Satisfaction." *Personnel*, 1955, *32*, 38-43.

Vroom, V. H. *Work and Motivation.* New York: Wiley, 1964.

Wanous, J. P. "A Causal-Correlational Analysis of the Job Satisfaction and Performance Relationship." *Journal of Applied Psychology,* 1974, *59,* 139–144.

Weaver, D. N. "Job Satisfaction in the United States in the 1970s." *Journal of Applied Psychology,* 1980, *65,* 364–367.

Weiss, D. J., and others. "Construct Validation Studies of the Minnesota Importance Questionnaire." *Minnesota Studies in Vocational Rehabilitation,* 1964, No. 18.

Weiss, D. J., and others. "Manual for the Minnesota Satisfaction Questionnaire." *Minnesota Studies in Vocational Rehabilitation,* 1967, No. 21.

Weitzel, W., and others. "The Impact of the Organization on the Structure of Job Satisfaction: Some Factor Analytic Findings." *Personnel Psychology,* 1973, *26,* 545–557.

Part Three

Facilitating
Career Development:
Practices and Programs

A major goal of Part Three is to acquaint professionals with new developments in career guidance and counseling practices and programs, particularly as they pertain to the career development needs of the economically disadvantaged and individuals with handicapping conditions. An additional purpose is to update professionals about the increasing types, numbers, diversity, and quality of career guidance and counseling programs, tools, and techniques that have emerged during the past ten years. A third goal is to examine changing practices and programs in traditional settings such as schools, colleges, and agencies, as well as to describe new and emerging practices and programs in business and industry.

Richard T. Kinnier and John D. Krumboltz, in Chapter Eleven, acquaint professionals with new developments in career counseling practices by presenting a framework for career counseling and discussing the major tasks involved. The framework that they describe as "elegant in its simplicity" consists of three phases: assessment, intervention, and evaluation. They review in depth the major tasks of career counseling, including cognitive restructuring, clarifying values, self-assessing career-relevant attributes, seeking information, decision making, and getting the job. Looking into the future, they suggest that "Ultimately, individuals will be best served if they are taught and encouraged to be the experts in their own career development."

In Chapter Twelve, Garry R. Walz and Libby Benjamin discuss the increasing attention being given to systematic career guidance programs. They first define what a career guidance system is and then describe its characteristics. Next, they present the current state of the development of career guidance systems, point out limitations of nonsystematic approaches and the advantages of systematic ones, and examine important issues—both current and future—in developing and implementing career guidance programs.

JoAnn Harris-Bowlsbey, in Chapter Thirteen, provides historical perspective and a current status report about the use of the computer in career guidance programming. She describes two types of systems—guidance systems and information systems. She also analyzes the impact of microcomputer technology on career guidance, as well as the use, quality of use, cost, and effectiveness of computer-based systems. The last section of the chapter focuses on future trends. Here Harris-Bowlsbey describes the capability of microcomputers. She also looks at the introduction of the videodisk; some new settings, such as libraries, homes, and workplaces, that will benefit from computer-based career guidance services; new content to be covered; the increased effectiveness of the systems; and how the computer will change the role of counselor.

Johnnie H. Miles, in Chapter Fourteen, begins her discussion of how career guidance can serve the needs of the economically disadvantaged by defining *disadvantaged* as the "economically deprived," the "poor," or "simply those lacking the purchasing power to meet their basic needs." She describes who the disadvantaged are, including in her definition the chronically poor, the unemployed, and the underemployed. Next she discusses why the disadvantaged remain poor, considers issues related to the cycle of poverty, and presents a comprehensive review of career guidance practices that respond to the needs of the disadvantaged. Systematic environmental change strategies are seen as being a key to the success of career guidance for the disadvantaged.

Chapter Fifteen, by Kenneth R. Thomas and Norman L. Berven, focuses on career counseling for individuals with handicapping conditions. The authors open their chapter by reviewing current theories that conceptualize the work adjustment and career development of individuals with handicapping conditions. They describe major career counseling delivery systems, such as educational institutions, public agencies, rehabilitation facilities, and proprietary rehabilitation companies. They discuss assessment and its role in career counseling. Then they examine counseling, vocational training, and job placement as types of intervention strategies and services used to meet the needs of individuals who have handicaps. Legislation and the application of technology to career counseling are among the topics covered.

Career guidance and counseling in the schools is the topic of Chapter Sixteen. Juliet V. Miller outlines the forces for change in the schools during the past decade that have had an impact on career guidance and counseling. She provides a comprehensive overview of program development procedures and innovations and defines three categories of programmatic approaches: systematic planning processes, state models, and collaboration models. Miller looks at trends in curriculum materials, assessment and testing, career information systems, and practices to meet the needs of special populations.

Chapter Seventeen, by Cynthia S. Johnson and Howard E. Figler, focuses on career development programs and services in postsecondary institutions. The authors present a brief historical review of career programs in higher education. They next discuss major themes that have surfaced during the past ten years, among them the developmental needs of clients and the organization and focus of career centers. Negotiation is advocated as a way to bring together the two opposing forces in centers—the forces of brokering and counseling or, as the authors put it, the internal world and the external world. Johnson and Figler also discuss the differing expectations that higher education and students have concerning careers. They emphasize that as long as career centers are required to prove that higher education pays off, centers will not be able to satisfy their clientele no matter what programs are tried. Next, they present some of

the new ideas, tools, and procedures currently available to improve center operations. They conclude with a look at future
trends and a sampling of exemplary state-of-the-art programs
currently being conducted in career centers around the country.

In the final chapter in Part Three, Richard L. Knowdell
is concerned with career development programs in business and
industry. He points out that during the past ten years "career
development has emerged as a distinct component of the human resource development function in business and industry."
He describes how various technological, social, and legislative
phenomena have contributed to the emergence of career development in the workplace. He presents sample career programs
in business and industry and a model career planning program
developed at Lawrence Livermore National Laboratory. He addresses the topic of responsibility for career planning; looks at
who the potential recipients of career planning might be—namely, the potential manager, the stagnated professional, and the
frustrated secretary, to name a few; and discusses the elements
that make up career planning in organizations, including individual counseling, group counseling, workshops, workbooks and
manuals, and career centers. Knowdell closes by examining
some issues that face career development in organizations and
the future of career development in industry.

Richard T. Kinnier
John D. Krumboltz

11

Procedures for Successful Career Counseling

The general goal of career counseling is to help individuals learn how to make a series of career-related choices wisely and confidently. The choices should be based on accurate self-knowledge and careful consideration of a wide variety of alternatives. In retrospect, individuals should feel satisfied about their choices, function successfully in their chosen jobs, and feel prepared to make career changes or adjustments in the future. They should also feel confident and exhibit competence when pursuing new jobs. Any person who can check off these goals as "accomplished" does not need career counseling. A person who seeks career counseling is probably experiencing external or internal blocks to one (or all) of these goals. The purpose of this chapter is to present a practical framework and some procedures by which counselors can help clients remove the blocks and attain the goals.

A Framework for the Essentials of Career Counseling

Horan (1979) concluded that the main phases of counseling could be labeled (1) assessment, (2) intervention, and (3) evaluation. This framework, elegant in its simplicity, also allows

307

great flexibility in process content, goal setting, and recycling back to preceding phases as needed.

Assessment. During the assessment phase, the counseling skills of active listening and empathizing are especially important (see Carkhuff and Berenson, 1976). Before specific plans and goals can be formulated, the counselor should attempt to establish rapport and get to know the client. It is almost universally accepted that the counseling process and outcome will tend to be more favorable when clients believe that the counselor is interested in them and demonstrates an understanding of their needs, concerns, hopes, and dreams. Although the actual modes of listening, exploring, probing, and possibly interpreting will vary as a function of counselor style and theoretical orientation, the open questions are basically the same. All counselors should, in effect, ask their clients:

> Who are you? What is troubling you? Why have you decided to seek counseling now? Tell me more about yourself and what you want. What do you want to gain from counseling?

In the assessment phase, the counselor and client typically reach some kind of agreement about counseling goals and the structure of the sessions. They also need to establish a general plan for pursuing the goals. During this phase the counselor should clarify his or her theoretical orientation, and a "contract" should be verbalized. For example, part of the contract may refer to counselor and client responsibilities in procuring occupational information. It might be generally agreed, for instance, that the counselor will provide referral sources, a reference list of helpful books, names of some employers, and a description of the kind of information available from computer systems. The client may agree to do the "legwork" of writing letters to the sources, reading selected books, visiting employers, and getting the computer printouts. Together, the counselor and client can integrate and discuss the information gathered. Dixon and Claiborn (1981) found that clients are more likely to follow through on their contract commitments if they take an active part in identifying goals and formulating and approving their parts of the contracts as clearly relevant to goal attainment.

The process of exploration and problem identification should include examining the client's beliefs or assumptions about the problem and goals (that is, cognitive restructuring). When both the counselor and the client feel satisfied that personally relevant and realistic goals have been identified, counseling should evolve into the phase of establishing a tentative treatment plan or considering various interventions.

Intervention. The intervention phase essentially consists of all activities that the counselor and client deem potentially facilitative of goal attainment (Horan, 1979). Imagine that a client's problem and goal were identified as "My main concern now is that my job search is not going well. I think a major problem is that I freeze during interviews. I do not like the way I come across and would like to be able to present myself in a more confident and relaxed way." After discussing general types of interventions that exist and considering what might be most helpful for that particular client, the counselor may suggest that the plan include in-session interview role plays and practice. The client may agree to read certain books or to join an assertiveness training workshop.

Evaluation. We have all heard about the numerous interventions used to cure hiccups. Many people swear by a certain "cure"—drinking water, holding one's breath—because after trying various hiccup-cessation treatments they finally found something that worked for them. During their lifelong search for the magic hiccup bullet, they informally and probably unknowingly acted as personal scientists. They experimented with and eliminated various alternative interventions through observing and remembering that the implementation of those interventions culminated only in the continuation of hiccups. Eventually some people find their magic bullets and rely on them until the cure ceases to work. If a previous "surefire" method begins to fail repeatedly, the processes of experimentation and evaluation are usually reactivated. A similar kind of naturalistic experimentation and evaluation often occurs when people try to lose weight, stop smoking, or pursue other problem-solving or self-improvement endeavors on their own.

In one of our career counseling classes, students are asked to describe what they do or what works for them when they experience confusion or conflict about their value priorities. Most of the students have developed personal strategies for values conflict resolution. Strategies like "talking about it with a trusted friend," "going to the mountains for a few days," or "working in the garden" were all adopted as a result of informal trial experimentation and evaluation. The lifelong processes of observing how others resolved their values conflicts, hypothesizing about the most personally appealing or promising strategies, trying some out, and experiencing clarity as a result of implementing certain strategies resulted in the development of highly tailored and effective strategies.

Consider the previous example of the client who lacked interviewing skills and agreed to participate in interview role-playing sessions and join an assertiveness training group. The counselor and client should evaluate how well those interventions worked. Criteria for goal attainment or intervention effectiveness might include the number of job offers received (both before and after treatment), interviewer feedback, and the client's self-ratings of confidence and competence during interviews. If the goals were reached, counseling can be terminated. If not, "recycling" may be initiated. The counselor and client may decide to try new, promising interventions, or they may consider the hypothesis that the "real" problem has not yet been identified (for instance, for as yet unknown reasons the client may not want to get a job at that time or in that particular field). Counseling can always shift back to the assessment phase, where the client and counselor will begin the exploration and problem identification process again.

Major Tasks in Career Counseling

The road to career fulfillment is full of obstacles. The following are among the major ones:

- People acquire inaccurate information or maladaptive beliefs about themselves and the world. They often operate under presuppositions they have never examined.
- People are uncertain about their own priorities. They feel unclear or conflicted about what they really want or value.
- People are unaware of their own abilities and interests and how their skills and preferences are related to the occupational structure in society. They lack a means of obtaining this information.
- Although a wealth of occupational information is available, people find it difficult to ask pertinent questions, to motivate themselves to find answers, to penetrate the overwhelming mass of material, and to distinguish biased information from facts.
- People generally do not have a systematic method for making career-related decisions. They often make decisions haphazardly.
- People find that obtaining a job is a lonely, frustrating task for which they are ill prepared.

For each of these obstacles to career fulfillment, there are tasks that can help to "clear the road." In the following pages, we will present a practical and flexible guide for overcoming many of the obstacles.

Cognitive Restructuring. When couples choose names for their newborn infants, they often disagree on the desirability of a particular name. The husband might say, "A 'Charles' is a stable, happy-go-lucky person whom everybody likes." But the wife might reply, "No, a 'Charles' is a rigid snob." These images associated with various names result from generalizing from extremely limited information or experience. Often people will form strong name associations on the basis of knowing only one "Charles." A similar image-formation phenomenon can occur in all other areas of our lives—including our impressions of occupations.

Any two persons may describe the occupation of accountant similarly, but their personal images of the "typical" accountant probably differ. Their images are based on media stereotypes plus, possibly, a few accountants they each have known or met. Most of the time, we are aware of our minor biases and stereotypes. We correct them to ourselves or cautiously screen them from others. Nevertheless, our numerous personal images and unique perceptions of the world and ourselves do affect what we value and choose. No one possesses "all the facts and just the facts."

The choice of a child's name is a relatively minor decision, but the choice of an occupation has far-reaching consequences. The unexamined presuppositions that we bring to career choice can result in troublesome outcomes (Krumboltz, 1983). Sometimes the biases, misinformation, or distorted beliefs remain unnoticed, are significant, and lead to self-defeating or even disabling experiences. Consider the unnecessary self-limitations produced by beliefs embedded within statements like "I want to be a psychologist, but I won't, because I don't want to learn two foreign languages" and "I want to be a physician, but I won't, because I can't stand the sight of blood." Each statement illustrates conclusions reached from either inaccurate information or irrational thinking: A person can become a psychologist without having to learn two languages, and it is normal to "hate the sight of blood"—yet medical students routinely become desensitized to it.

Lewis and Gilhousen (1981) identified several common anxiety-producing myths associated with career decision making. They include the following: "I must be *certain* before finally deciding on *one* career for the rest of my life"; "My plans for the future should be concise and cannot be changed"; "If I could just do 'X,' I would finally be happy"; "I can do anything if I just work at it"; "My work *is* my life, and my work determines my worth as a person." Those beliefs are not or need not be true. Lewis and Gilhousen suggest that counselors watch for these types of maladaptive beliefs within their clients.

In general, cognitive restructuring involves uncovering or identifying maladaptive thoughts or beliefs that are irrational, exaggerated, or inaccurate and then correcting or modifying them so that they become more adaptive, rational, realistic, or accurate. Of course, a counselor must use discretion. Not every misconception can be confronted—there is not enough time. Only those misconceptions that seem to inhibit clients from achieving their own basic aims should be confronted.

How does one identify these maladaptive beliefs? One way is by simply being vigilant. Counselors should always be on the lookout for evidence of irrational thinking. Sometimes faulty assumptions or irrational conclusions will clearly emerge —for example, "I'll never get a job" or "I suppose if I really wanted an easy job, I could always become a professor." Following such statements, the counselor could invite the client to examine his or her beliefs about the job-search process or about professors.

Maladaptive beliefs are often subtle and hidden. Evidence of their existence will not always be obvious so counselors may have to probe and formulate tentative hypotheses about possible areas of irrationality. A counselor who suspects that such maladaptive beliefs exist can simply present the hypotheses in question form to the client (for example, "From what you have said about working it sounds as if you only respect work that actually produces concrete products. Is that true?").

After beliefs or cognitions have been identified, then what? In general, most cognitive restructuring techniques (see Meichenbaum, 1977) involve confronting, testing, or analyzing the suspected irrational beliefs, faulty thinking styles, inaccurate assumptions, or invalid conclusions. The process may vary depending on a particular counselor's style and client's unique situation. The counselor can didactically present the client with refuting information, as suggested by Ellis (1962), or treat certain assumptions or conclusions as hypotheses to be tested, as prescribed by Beck (1976). For example, a client who is operating under the assumption that professors have an easy life might be encouraged to research the assumption. Such a hypothesis could be tested informally by interviewing several professors about their jobs.

Who is the final judge of whether a belief is "irrational" or "maladaptive"? We would avoid giving labels like these to any belief. Besides, it is naive to believe that the population of counselors is more rational than the population of clients. Yet counselors can serve an important function as impartial providers of information and feedback on issues with which clients are emotionally involved. Furthermore, counselors can serve as sensitive sounding boards and coaches for their clients who are struggling to reinterpret their worlds.

Clients cannot escape the responsibility of being their own final judges. The counselor's major role, therefore, should be to teach clients how to test their own beliefs and become wiser, more rational judges (Mitchell, 1980). The ultimate goal in cognitive restructuring interventions should be to teach clients the art of "autocognitive restructuring." Clients should be trained to recognize, examine, and modify or refute maladaptive cognitions whenever they emerge in the future.

Ironically, the term *cognitive restructuring* sounds Orwellian to some people—conjuring up images of state manipulation and thought control. Actually, the self-enacted version would be treasonous in Orwell's *1984*. In reality, self-directed cognitive restructuring increases self-control by enabling people to be more competent processors of information and accurate interpreters of events.

Clarifying Values. Values are defined as a person's beliefs or standards about preferred modes of conduct and goals worthy of pursuit (see Allport, 1961; Rokeach, 1973). Values serve as guides for how to live today and criteria on which tomorrow's plans and goals are built. Terms like *prestige, power, altruism,* and *adventure* are often considered vocational values— that is, they denote what people want to experience in and gain from their careers.

A teenage boy who can confidently state, "I want a summer job where I can work outdoors, make at least $3,000, and have flexible hours," ostensibly knows what he wants and would not need help in clarifying his values for that particular summer-job decision. In many decision situations, however, it is common to hear people make comments like "I don't know what I want [or believe] anymore" or "I'm not sure how important X [for example, money, fame, security, variety] is to me" or "I feel conflicted—I want X and I want Y, but I don't think it is possible to have [or be] both." Verbalizations like these indicate that the person feels confused, uncertain, or conflicted about value priorities.

The term *values clarification* refers to a particular theory and type of intervention first described by Raths, Harmin, and Simon in 1966. The theory suggests that the process of thinking about and discussing one's opinions on a variety of topics and reviewing one's past behavior and interests can help people become more aware of and clear about what they value in life.

A values clarification intervention basically consists of exercises that stimulate those processes of thinking, discussing, and reviewing. (See Simon, Howe, and Kirschenbaum, 1972, for a sample of exercises.) In essence, the exercises are vehicles for self-examination and practice in decision making. Some exercises invoke hypothetical situations in which choices must be made. Others require participants to identify their interests, typical behavior patterns, or people they admire. A values clarification workshop typically consists of an introductory lecture about the theory and process of valuing and a series of exercises and discussions where participants are continually prompted to reflect on the implications of their responses as they pertain to their own values (Kirschenbaum, 1977).

An explosion in the production of clarification exercises has occurred during the past decade. This is not surprising, given the wide purview of values clarification; it includes almost any strategy that promotes self-examination. It also is not surprising that some confusion and overlap would ensue. Activities that are indistinguishable from values clarification exercises can be found in various manuals under headings like "Life-Planning Exercises" and "Self-Assessment Strategies." Further, there are many other counseling techniques that could be useful for helping people clarify their values but are not clearly part of the values clarification literature—for example, the Gestalt "two-chair" conflict resolution technique.

Consider what this can mean in practice. Imagine that a hypothetical client, Anne, is trying to decide on a major in college. She gets stuck on an important values issue. On the one hand, she sees herself as an altruistic person. Her ideals about helping people and self-sacrifice attract her to the area of social service. On the other hand, she also wants "the finer things in life that money can buy." Her gaze turns toward business.

Given such an "altruism versus income" values conflict, what should she do? If she turns to the manuals or books containing values clarification exercises, she will find hundreds. Which should she use? How will she select? And will she realize that there are other strategies or exercises not labeled "values clarification" that may help her resolve that type of conflict?

For the purpose of helping people like Anne, we surveyed the literature—both in the area of values clarification and in other areas which suggested interventions that seemed relevant to values conflicts. We then attempted to outline the main components (Kinnier, 1982).

For example, many clarification exercises require participants to consider personal values or priorities in light of their mortality. We have all heard of people who became more certain about "the important things in life" after a close brush with death. Allport (1959) labeled the common resulting experience as "decentering." According to him, after such a jolting experience many people are shaken out of their habitual thinking and behavior patterns. Individuals often emerge from the experience with a new and wider perspective on life. Priorities tend to become more clear.

Several values clarification exercises, in effect, attempt to simulate that experience. For example, in the exercise "Life-line," participants imagine that they have terminal illnesses and ask themselves what is ultimately most important to them; in "Epitaph" participants write out their ideal epitaphs; and in "Obituary" they write out how they would like to be remembered after they die. The main component in these exercises appears to be "thinking about personal priorities in light of one's mortality."

Table 1 presents our outline of the main components of clarification strategies, extracted from surveying the literature. We suggest that counselors and clients consider the general strategies, pick those that seem most promising to them, and then construct personalized interventions around the main ideas.

Table 1. Basic Processes Underlying Many Values Clarification
and Related Conflict Resolution Strategies.

1. Identify and analyze the values inside.
    • Identify the specific values related to the issue.
    • Identify alternative positions—either alternatives or the extremes and middle position on the issue.
    • Summarize (describe, list, weigh) possible consequences of living in accordance with each alternative or position.

2. Examine your past experiences, preferences, behaviors, and decisions that are related to the present issue. Look for manifest patterns.

3. Investigate how others view the issue.
    • Talk to others (especially people you respect) about their opinions on the issue.
    • Imagine what those whom you respect would do in a similar situation or conflict.
    • Experimentally "try on" adherence to various positions. Role-play the defense of alternative positions or opinions.

4. Test or confront yourself about tentative choices, positions, or resolutions.
    • Take a (tentative) stand on the issue. Confront yourself (and ask others to challenge you) on your position. Respond to the challenge that your position is unwise or unethical or that you are being hypocritical.
    • Imagine that you are near death. Consider the issue and various alternatives in light of your mortality.

5. Find personal environments that are conducive to thinking clearly about, or temporarily escaping from, the issue (that is, discover your best "incubation" environments)—for example, while fishing, in the mountains, working in the garden, or meditating.

6. Make your "best" tentative resolution, value statement, or policy and live in accordance with it. Revise if (when) necessary and repeat strategies as needed.

Anne, with her conflict between altruism and wealth, might look over the outline and decide that certain strategies do not seem very promising or relevant to her. Presumably she has tried variations of some of these strategies on her own before. (For example, most of us seek out others when we feel confused. Some of us naturally ask ourselves, "What would this or that person do in a similar situation?") In selecting which interventions to try out, Anne can be guided by her previous experience in using variations of these interventions.

Assume that, after considering the list of strategies, Anne selects "role-playing the defense of alternative positions" as promising and worth a try. In the so-called two-chair method, an internally conflicted individual alternately role-plays the expression of both sides of the conflict. According to Greenberg and Dompierre (1981), the process facilitates deeper understanding of the opposing components of the person's conflict and often results in greater integration or resolution.

Anne probably could benefit most from such a strategy if she (and her counselor) tailored that main idea to her particular style and needs. The strategy is most commonly enacted in the counseling session, but she could decide to experiment with it in a variety of environments. For example, she might carry on internal debates during long walks each evening. Instead of the standard two roles, she could set up other creative combinations. She might alternately play the roles of two opposing lawyers arguing each side and then switch to a third role of an impartial judge. The creative variations are limitless.

Another strategy that Anne can consider using is "self-confrontation." The basic idea behind self-confrontation is that, by challenging our beliefs, we can uncover inconsistencies between what we say and what we do (for example, Janis and Mann, 1977; Rokeach, 1979), identify contradictions between self-conceptions and environmental realities (for example, Glasser, 1965), and reduce irrationality (for example, Ellis, 1962). The process may culminate in revised beliefs or in confirmation that our beliefs or decisions are consistent, realistic, and rational.

If Anne confronts her beliefs or behaviors relevant to the conflict, she may be able to uncover and correct certain flaws in her thinking. Her counselor could confront her (or Anne could confront herself) with challenges like "You say you have been a self-sacrificing person, but is that really true?," "Isn't it naive to think you could really be unselfish?," or "You make it sound as if you can only choose to be either completely selfish or completely altruistic. Are those the only two alternatives?"

Of course, the preceding questions are just examples. The exact form of the confrontation should be developed through counselor and client collaboration based on what seems most relevant and pertinent for the client and the particular values issue. The interventions outlined in Table 1 are "skeletal"; the counselor and client are in the best position to mold idiosyncratic flesh to the bones.

Ultimately, the goal of any counseling intervention is to help the client discover strategies that can be successfully reapplied in the future. The client should leave counseling with a personalized intervention outline and be able to state confidently, "When I am unsure of what I want or value, these are the strategies I have found to be most helpful: . . . ."

Our values are never set in concrete. The world changes, we change. Our values are like draft papers. We continually edit and revise them as we live—an addendum one day, a deletion the next. The final versions of our values will be the drafts we were working on when death comes.

Self-Assessing Career-Relevant Attributes. There are basically two broad self-assessment questions that are relevant to career decision making: "What can the person do?" and "What is the person like?" The first question refers to skills or abilities in which the person has already demonstrated competence or aptitude. The second question refers to what is commonly known as personality or psychological characteristics, such as attitudes, interests, and values. When many people, including career counselors, hear terms like *abilities* and *interests,* they automatically think "tests." Yet there are other practical and sometimes more informative and/or quicker methods for finding out what a person can do or is like.

Although testing can yield pertinent and accurate information, much can be learned about what clients can do by simply reviewing what they have done or tried to do in the past. The fact that a teenager once successfully rebuilt a car engine, for example, is a better indicator than any mechanical aptitude test score that she has the ability to be a mechanic. Carefully recalling past performance evaluations and feedback from others is also an important self-assessment strategy. A person who is unsure about his piano-playing ability may learn something about his ability level by trying to recall honestly whether his playing consistently elicited profuse or polite praise. A common memory of many counselors before entering the profession is that many people seemed to seek them out for help or advice on personal problems. This kind of response from others may be indicative of effective listening and helping skills. Obviously, opinions may be inaccurate or a person's memories may be distorted. However, many separate bits of information can converge to form rather accurate profiles of a person's strengths and weaknesses. Thus, the person who received A's in drawing, was praised by several art teachers for her drawings, and won a few prizes in different art competitions can safely conclude that she has a talent for drawing.

A counselor and client can learn much about the client's acquired abilities by asking the right questions, systematically reviewing relevant life events and experiences, and organizing the "data" into compact and comprehensible profiles. The following illustrative open questions are among those that may facilitate the self-assessment process:

> What have you done vocationally and avocationally? What specific skills did these pursuits require? What is your own evaluation of how well you did these things? What other evidence do you have about your skill level—for example, others' evaluations, grades in particular courses, awards, degrees?

We believe that a major role of the counselor in the self-assessment process is to teach the client how to ask relevant probing questions, gather convergent evidence, and summarize the results. Because during counseling the client is, in effect, practicing self-assessment strategies that will be reactivated many times in the future, much of the self-exploration should be done by the client independently between counseling sessions, with the counselor acting as a guide or coach. The client can then bring summaries into counseling sessions, where both the counselor and the client will review the search process and organize and translate the "raw" information into lists of specific skills and proficiency estimates. The discussions should also focus on how those skills could be creatively applied in various occupations.

A similar exploration and organization strategy can be used for creating profiles of interests and other personality variables. The counselor and client can review experiences, activities, and types of people that the client has liked in the past. From prior choices and decisions, deductions about manifest preferences can be drawn. Standard lists of interests or values may be used as prompts for exploration and discussion. Ultimately, a summary list of most-favored preferences can be constructed from the collaborative efforts of the counselor and client inside and outside the counseling sessions.

Sometimes when clients lack experiential knowledge of the extent to which they could do or would enjoy some activity or task, it may be feasible to encourage them to try out a job or activity on a trial basis. For example, a man who is considering a career in sales but does not know how good he would be in saleswork could take a part-time temporary position as a sales clerk. A woman who wants to get an advanced degree but worries that she may not have the ability or perseverance to do graduate work could take one class as a nonmatriculated student and observe her performance and comfort level in the graduate school environment. There is no better way to find out how well a person can do or will like something than by actually doing it. Obviously a person cannot try everything, and many real-life trials would not be feasible or cost-effective. However, the counselor and client should look for, and be open to taking advantage of, these kinds of experiential opportunities.

If, after carefully assessing competencies and preferences in the ways described, the client still lacks specific information or concludes that some information seems inconsistent or conflicting, tests might then be considered. Crites (1981) suggests that tests should be used selectively in response to specific questions that arise in counseling. Test selection and interpretation should be a collaborative task. Crites recommends that results should be discussed "within the client's conceptual and linguistic frame of reference, not psychometric jargon" (p. 80). With the mystique removed and when they are given a major responsibility in deciding what the results mean, clients will be less likely to misinterpret (Stephenson, 1979) and more likely to remember and integrate the information for future decisions (Crites, 1981).

Thus, at a certain point in counseling, the counselor and client may agree that they could benefit from another source of information about the client's interests. It would be the counselor's role to present a descriptive overview of interest inventories and the basics of how to interpret the results of such tests. Selection and interpretation should be collaborative. Since tests are only (rather crude) tools, we think it is preferable to focus only on the results that are most relevant to the client's questions, simplify scores into broad, more easily understood categories, and view the results as working hypotheses—never as definitive answers. On a test like the Strong-Campbell Interest Inventory, for example, the counselor and client may consider the results as new hypotheses to be further explored or tested. The counselor might comment, "One result suggests that you share similar interests with farmers. What does that mean? Why did that particular result emerge? From what you know of yourself, is it accurate? How does it relate to other interests you have? Should we look further into that particular occupation?"

We have tried to outline briefly how the process of self-assessment can be grounded in a counselor and client collaboration of exploration and experimentation. There is no magic test or formula that can summarize once and for all what a person can do and is like. An experimental, tentative, and "hypothesis-testing" approach is therefore most realistic. We emphasized that clients will be best served if they *learn how* to get to know themselves better. They need to learn to ask the right questions and look for information or evidence in a variety of places. Summaries of a person's preferences and ability levels are somewhat like snapshots. They may be fairly accurate reflections of the person, but they are frozen in time. Accurate, up-to-date self-assessment implies constant reassessment.

Seeking Information. People who want to increase their knowledge of occupations have innumerable convenient opportunities to do so. Yet few people take advantage of them. Almost every person we meet can teach us something we do not yet know about at least one occupation. By simply asking individuals we informally encounter in everyday situations—on airplanes, at parties, while standing in line or getting a haircut—to describe their jobs, we can continually add to our reservoir of knowledge. However, the query "What do you do?" is usually a superficial and terminal question. A few more specific inquiries such as "What is a typical day in that type of job like?" or "What is the difference between an agent and a broker?" would both flatter the speaker and educate the questioner.

A lifelong pursuit of information about occupations may arise largely from the individual's interest or curiosity and a creative knack for gaining information from interesting sources. In counseling, both the interest and the skill can be promoted and developed.

Krumboltz and others, during the 1960s, showed that counselors can increase information-seeking behaviors by modeling and by verbally reinforcing clients' statements about their intent to find information (Krumboltz and Schroeder, 1965; Krumboltz and Thoresen, 1964). If clients become aware of the benefits of broadening their knowledge base and receive encouragement from the counselor for their information-seeking efforts, they will tend to continue to seek. The skill of seeking will improve with practice.

Crites (1981) suggests counselor and client collaboration in the information-seeking process. Counselors can share what information they have about certain occupations and can refer clients to the standard sources (for example, the *DOT*, computer information systems, books) for answers to other specific questions. Unfortunately, as Crites (1981) also noted, most counselors regard "the presentation of occupational information to the client as necessary but uninspiring" (p. 81).

Gaining information need not be boring. In his book *Working,* Terkel (1975) showed that researching occupations by interviewing workers can be an inspirational and stimulating experience for the interviewer. An interview need not be a dry question-and-answer exchange about basic duties and qualifications but can reveal a poignant "inside story" of the daily personal struggles that go on beneath the surface.

If counselors can instill this enthusiasm or appreciation for the worker's story into clients as Terkel did for his readers, then these clients may become regular seekers of occupational information. Such seekers should find ample opportunities to expand their knowledge base. While others exchange comments on the weather during airplane flights, parties, and haircuts, these individuals will be learning about occupations.

Together the counselor and client should brainstorm about interesting interview questions and other creative ways to obtain highly relevant information. Certainly the possibility of trial experience on a job should be considered. Part-time volunteer work in a particular work environment may be a worthwhile experience and a source of valuable information.

The two processes of self-assessment and occupational information seeking are complementary. Clients who interview workers, tour job environments, or volunteer in various settings can learn more about occupations and about themselves.

Decision Making. There is a time for broadening options and a time for narrowing them to a choice. According to Borow (1981, p. 144), "Occupational information should be presented in a manner calculated to broaden the range of options and stimulate exploration—not to narrow choice and hasten decisions." Eventually, however, narrowing must occur. Decisions or choices are inescapable: We cannot have it all, do everything, or be in more than one place at a time. Moreover, although there are thousands of occupations, it is unrealistic to hope to find the "perfect" match for a lifetime. When a decision is made, there can be no guarantees about outcomes. Armed only with self-assessment estimates and incomplete information, we confront an unknowable future in a world where perfect matches and decisions do not exist. A client's belief to the contrary may indicate a need for cognitive restructuring.

Prescriptive decision-making models are not formulas or guides for bypassing the complexities or uncertainties of living.

At best, a good model provides a means for organizing information and a method for progressing somewhat systematically from the conceptualization of a problem to a choice.

Although there are numerous model variations in the literature, they appear to be more similar than different. After comparing various models, Jepsen and Dilley (1974, p. 340) concluded that although theoretical assumptions about the decision maker and situation vary, there is significant overlap between the steps in most models: "All see the decision maker as comparing several alternative actions and selecting the one that is 'best'—usually the one with the greatest multiplicative products of values and subjective probabilities summed over all outcomes." In addition to describing the different models as "more complementary than competitive" (p. 346), they noted that "the models are not clearly enough defined nor is there sufficient research evidence to consider discussions about which might be the better explainer or predictor" (p. 346).

Since many models overlap and none has been shown to be superior, it seems reasonable to extract the main components within most of them and create one general framework. Such a framework should be concise enough to serve as a guide yet general enough to be easily adapted to different decision makers and their unique situations. Further, since the conceptual differences between making a decision and solving a problem are viewed by many as minor (see Horan, 1979, p. 175), a *general* framework could incorporate the essential steps in both processes.

A general framework is presented in Table 2, where we have attempted to summarize the main components in most decision-making and problem-solving models. General decision-making stages are listed in the left-hand column. Specific strategies that are common to many models and subsumed under the general stages are presented in the right-hand column. We suggest that counselors and clients adapt the framework to fit their particular styles and needs. They may explore the problem area according to their theoretical orientation, include or skip over parts as needed, and recycle back to preceding steps when appropriate.

The way this framework is applied depends on the type

Table 2. A General Framework for Making a Decision
or Solving a Problem.

General Step	Can Include Any or All of the Following:
1. Define the problem	• Explore and specifically identify a problem area or need for a decision. • Examine beliefs related to the problem. • State goals.
2. Establish a plan	• Outline *how* the problem or decision will be confronted or resolved. • Set a time frame for each phase of the plan and a tentative deadline for solution or decision.
3. Identify alternatives	• Gather information on alternatives, options, choices, or courses of action. • Examine rationales for precluding consideration of potentially desirable alternatives. • List main alternatives or clearly state major options to be considered.
4. Assess self	• Assess relevant skills or personality variables, if appropriate. • Clarify values or list relevant priorities and needs. • Determine importance of pertinent variables.
5. Investigate probable outcomes	• Consider possible consequences, benefits, costs, or risks of each alternative. • Carefully evaluate or weigh each option on predicted positive or negative consequences.
6. Eliminate alternatives systematically	• Compare costs and benefits by constructing a grid containing estimate probabilities that each alternative will yield each weighted value. • Begin crossing off the least desirable options on the basis of summed products for each option.
7. Start action	• Make tentative commitment to try one option. • Make specific plans and then implement the decision or carry out the solution.

Source: Adapted mainly from Krumboltz and Hamel (1977).

of decision or problem confronted and the specific needs and goals of the client. Application variations are almost limitless on many levels.

For example, decisions vary in their degree of importance for the decision maker. Importance obviously should affect length of time and amount of energy given to making the decision. Certainly a major career decision is worth a lot of time and energy. In contrast, a person who is trying to decide whether to take the day or night shift on a job would not need to allocate so much time and energy. Fewer alternatives (day or night shift) and fewer values (for example, "time with my family," "health") would need to be considered.

Theoretically, the number of options or alternatives considered can range from two to infinity. Although it is important not to limit oneself initially to an unnecessarily small list of alternatives, an extremely large list can be unmanageable. A woman who is struggling with the question "Should I have a family or a career?" may benefit from increasing the number of options to be considered. A third class of options that involve balancing both a career and a family should be added to her list before she makes a decision. At the other end of the spectrum, a man who identifies 517 occupations for consideration has constructed an unmanageable list. He should limit the initial list to probably no more than a dozen or so occupations that seem most appealing at first sight. This concept of identifying a manageable list of preliminary alternatives is called "suboptimization." The counselor and client must reach an agreement about an optimal number of alternatives to identify, given their particular goal—enough not to force premature elimination of potentially good choices and few enough to avoid the frustration of becoming overwhelmed.

After identifying the alternatives to be considered and the most relevant and salient values, two questions should be addressed: (1) To what extent will each alternative *probably* fulfill each value? (2) Which alternative seems to be most potentially fulfilling of the combined group of values? The process of answering these questions rarely involves the arrangement of indisputable facts or precise predictions, but, rather, calls for interpretation and probabilistic judgment.

A decision-making grid often serves as an organizational aid for addressing the two questions. Typically, alternatives or options are arranged along the vertical axis, and values are summarized across the horizontal axis. Values can be weighted by assigning numbers in proportion to their importance to the client. If the value of "security" is considered twice as important as either "income" or "variety," for example, then "security" can be given 50 points while each of the others receives 25.

Within the grid, a box is formed for every alternative and value combination, allowing the person to code a response for how likely it is that each alternative will fulfill each value. These responses can take a variety of forms (for example, categories like "yes/no" or "high, medium, low" or numerical scales like "1–10"). As Horan (1979, p. 49) points out, "No one has yet developed an adequate technology for assigning numbers to the objective and subjective values that might accrue from the various alternatives in a decision-making problem."

The choices of how to formulate and respond to the questions are best made by the counselor and client. The way they do that will affect their system of "eliminating alternatives." Typically, for each alternative the weighted values are multiplied by the fulfillment estimates. The products are then summed for each alternative. Alternatives that receive the highest scores are most likely to satisfy the client's values. It makes sense for most people to start eliminating alternatives with the least attractive one (the lowest total score) and then progressively whittle the list down until a few "best" alternatives remain. If necessary, more information can then be collected before the final choice is made.

The last step in decision making or problem solving is to enact the decision or implement the solution. What good is the decision to ask the boss for a raise if the question is never asked? Thus, the decision-making process does not end until a commitment is made and actual follow-through occurs. In the event of continuing hesitation or doubt at this (or any) point in the decision-making process, recycling back to any stage is *always* an option. The decision rests on the collaborative brainstorming and problem-solving efforts of the counselor and client in response to the question "Now what do we do?"

Decision-making models cannot be applied like mathematical formulas. Good career decisions do not neatly pop out at the end of an equation. Decision-making variables are the "stuff of life" and are simply too complex to be accurately reduced to unidimensional scales. When used as a malleable guide, a model can help a person systematically organize and carefully review chunks of especially pertinent information. Though not a panacea for indecision, the model proposed here is at least a rational way to make decisions.

Getting the Job. When the phrase "Do your own thing" was first uttered, it probably seemed clever and creative. Today, it sounds ridiculous. Many job-search tips or strategies, like sayings, songs, and clothes, are also trendy and short-lived. One day they are novel, potent, and popular—the next they are old, worn out, and ridiculed.

The value of certain degrees, work experiences, résumé formats, and interview strategies changes over time. The job seeker and counselor must know or find out what is "in" today within a particular field and desired jobs—for example, what needs exist within the jobs, what impresses interviewers, and what employers want now.

How can the counselor/client team best research these questions? We recommend the following common-sense strategies, which seem fairly resistant to obsolescence:

1. Read the *most current* "how to" job-search books and related literature.
2. Consult with people who are already employed and successful in the job or type of job you want. Ask *them* for advice on how to write your résumé, how to perform in interviews, and where to apply.
3. Treat your résumé like a *draft paper.* Revise it regularly—not only when applying for a job, but several times a year for the rest of your life. Even if you only improve a word here or the way something is formatted there, never stop improving it. Study other peoples' résumés (especially those of individuals who have been successful in getting the types of jobs you want) for ideas on improving your own.
4. *Practice* interviewing within the counseling session and out-

side it (for example, with friends). During the actual job search and in every interview, you are also practicing for future job searches and interviews.

The main themes of these strategies relate to coaching clients to seek advice from the real experts (that is, successful people in the target jobs) and teaching them how to continue to improve their job-seeking skills for the rest of their lives. The concept of "mentoring" seems especially relevant to these themes.

The current literature on mentoring reveals disagreement about the definition of mentoring, the differences among "mentors," "role models," and "sponsors," and how mentoring benefits mentors and their protégés (see Speizer, 1981). While researchers struggle to unravel these issues during the next decade, practitioners can extract some of the main ideas and incorporate them into their practice now.

Basically, a mentor is a knowledgeable and experienced person who helps a less knowledgeable and less experienced person. Typically, a strong emotional bond exists between the mentor and protégé, and both gain something from the relationship (see Levinson and others, 1978). Speizer (1981) noted that many people retrospectively attribute some of their confidence, success, and wise decision making in their careers to the guidance of a mentor.

A client in career counseling may also benefit from mentorlike guidance. In a mentoring role, a counselor can (1) share his or her knowledge of the job market and the job-seeking process, (2) direct the client to helpful sources such as literature, workshops, and employment opportunities, (3) advise the client on how to write a résumé, apply for jobs, perform in interviews, and cope with rejection, (4) provide feedback and coach the client throughout the job search, and (5) support and encourage the client to maintain faith in his or her ability to get a job. Ideally, a client should describe the counselor/client relationship as "My counselor is my ally who truly wants me to succeed. I realize that the ultimate goal of all we do together is to help me become *independently* competent and successful."

Perhaps one of the more important skills a counselor can teach a client in the job-search process is how to seek out other career-related mentors. Most writers in the area of mentoring agree that it is not clear how one goes about finding and establishing mentoring relationships. Yet it seems reasonable to expect that a person who actively seeks information and advice from critical people in the field is more likely to develop mentoring relationships. A counselor can coach the client during a trial-and-error period of seeking mentorlike relationships. The individual who learns how to establish such relationships easily may be at a perpetual advantage for career advancement.

The Future

In spite of the great technological advances we have witnessed during the past decade, we can confidently predict that individuals who are born today will not inherit a quick, simple, and effective method for selecting fulfilling careers. When they ponder what they will do with their lives, they will have to struggle as we did with tentative self-assessment estimates, vast amounts of information, continually changing alternatives, and an unknowable future.

Undoubtedly, during the coming years, self-assessment instruments will become more valid and reliable. In addition, individuals will be able to gain and process more information with greater ease than today. Yet these advances will not "cure" uncertainty or career dissatisfaction. Then, as now, successful career decision making and management will require lifelong self-exploration and ongoing career education and planning.

The recent self-help movement, the personal-computer phenomenon, and shrinking social service budgets may be harbingers of a future in which individuals will be expected and encouraged to be more self-directed in their own career development. We believe that career counselors will more often be called on to educate larger groups of people on the basic components of self-appraisal, information seeking, decision making, values clarification, and job-seeking strategies. Individuals will intermittently call on counselors as consultants or advisers to assist them in tailoring intervention "shells" to their idiosyncratic styles and needs. Ultimately, individuals will be best served if they are taught and encouraged to be the experts in their own career development.

Suggested Readings

Crites, J. O. "Career Counseling: A Comprehensive Approach." In D. H. Montross and C. J. Shinkman (Eds.), *Career Development in the 1980's: Theory and Practice.* Springfield, Ill.: Thomas, 1981.

Crites presents a model of career counseling that integrates diagnostic, process, and outcome components of five theoretical approaches. He shows how such a model could be applied to interviewing, test interpretation, and occupational information seeking in the practice of career counseling.

Crites, J. O. "Integrative Test Interpretation." In D. H. Montross and C. J. Shinkman (Eds.), *Career Development in the 1980's: Theory and Practice.* Springfield, Ill.: Thomas, 1981.

Crites notes disenchantment among many counselors about the usefulness of testing in career counseling. He describes a process of test interpretation in which the client takes an active role in interpreting tests. Specific test results are looked at in response to questions raised during counseling, and the results are discussed in simple, meaningful language rather than psychometric jargon.

Forney, D. S. "The Art and Science of Career Counseling: A Conceptual Framework for Counseling the Individual." In D. H. Montross and C. J. Shinkman (Eds.), *Career Development in the 1980's: Theory and Practice.* Springfield, Ill.: Thomas, 1981.

Forney argues for a more pragmatic, "real world" approach to career counseling. The author provides examples of how counselors can be flexible, practical, and creative in helping clients with their idiosyncratic, immediate, and complex needs.

"Counseling Psychology in the Year 2000 A.D." *Counseling Psychologist,* 1980, *8*(4).

In this issue, nineteen eminent counseling psychologists discuss the future of counseling psychology. Among the recurrent themes, many predict that future counselors will serve more educative/consultative roles for more "self-directed" individuals.

References

Allport, G. W. "Normative Compatibility in the Light of Social Science." In A. H. Maslow (Ed.), *New Knowledge in Human Values.* New York: Harper & Row, 1959.

Allport, G. W. *Pattern and Growth in Personality.* New York: Holt, Rinehart and Winston, 1961.

Beck, A. *Cognitive Therapy and Emotional Disorders.* New York: International Universities Press, 1976.

Borow, H. "Career Guidance Uses of Labor Market Information: Limitations and Potentialities." In D. H. Montross and C. J. Shinkman (Eds.), *Career Development in the 1980's: Theory and Practice.* Springfield, Ill.: Thomas, 1981.

Carkhuff, R. R., and Berenson, B. G. *Beyond Counseling and Therapy.* (2nd ed.) New York: Holt, Rinehart and Winston, 1976.

Crites, J. O. "Career Counseling: A Comprehensive Approach." In D. H. Montross and C. J. Shinkman (Eds.), *Career Development in the 1980's: Theory and Practice.* Springfield, Ill.: Thomas, 1981.

Dixon, D., and Claiborn, C. "Effects of Need and Commitment on Career Exploration Behaviors." *Journal of Counseling Psychology,* 1981, *28,* 411–415.

Ellis, A. *Reason and Emotion in Psychotherapy.* New York: Stuart, 1962.

Glasser, W. *Reality Therapy.* New York: Harper & Row, 1965.

Greenberg, L. S., and Dompierre, L. M. "Specific Effects of Gestalt Two-Chair Dialogue on Intrapsychic Conflict in Counseling." *Journal of Counseling Psychology,* 1981, *28,* 288–294.

Horan, J. J. *Counseling for Effective Decision Making.* North Scituate, Mass.: Duxbury Press, 1979.

Janis, I. L., and Mann, L. *Decision Making: A Psychological Analysis of Conflict, Choice, and Commitment.* New York: Free Press, 1977.

Jepsen, D. A., and Dilley, J. S. "Vocational Decision-Making Models: A Review and Comparative Analysis." *Review of Educational Research,* 1974, *44,* 331–344.

Kinnier, R. T. "Values Conflict Resolution: Development of an Assessment and Comparison of Interventions." Unpublished doctoral dissertation, Stanford University, 1982.

Kirschenbaum, H. *Advanced Value Clarification.* La Jolla, Calif.: University Associates, 1977.

Krumboltz, J. D. *Private Rules and Career Decision Making.* Columbus: National Center for Research in Vocational Education, Ohio State University, 1983.

Krumboltz, J. D., and Hamel, D. A. *Guide to Career Decision-Making Skills.* New York: College Entrance Examination Board, 1977.

Krumboltz, J. D., and Schroeder, W. W. "Promoting Career Planning Through Reinforcement." *Personnel and Guidance Journal,* 1965, *44,* 19–26.

Krumboltz, J. D., and Thoresen, C. E. "The Effect of Behavioral Counseling in Group and Individual Settings on Information-Seeking Behavior." *Journal of Counseling Psychology,* 1964, *11,* 324–333.

Levinson, D. J., and others. *The Seasons of a Man's Life.* New York: Knopf, 1978.

Lewis, R. A., and Gilhousen, M. R. "Myths of Career Development: A Cognitive Approach to Vocational Counseling." *Personnel and Guidance Journal,* 1981, *59,* 296–299.

Meichenbaum, D. *Cognitive-Behavior Modification.* New York: Plenum Press, 1977.

Mitchell, L. J. "The Effects of Training in Cognitive Restructuring and Decision-Making Skills on Career Decision-Making Behavior, Cognition, and Affect." Unpublished doctoral dissertation, Stanford University, 1980.

Raths, L., Harmin, M., and Simon, S. *Values and Teaching*. Columbus, Ohio: Merrill, 1966.

Rokeach, M. *The Nature of Human Values*. New York: Free Press, 1973.

Rokeach, M. *Understanding Human Values: Individual and Societal*. New York: Free Press, 1979.

Simon, S. B., Howe, L. W., and Kirschenbaum, H. *Values Clarification: A Handbook of Practical Strategies for Teachers and Students*. New York: Hart, 1972.

Speizer, J. J. "Role Models, Mentors, and Sponsors: The Elusive Concepts." *Journal of Women in Culture and Society*, 1981, 6, 692–712.

Stephenson, R. R. "Client Interpretation of Tests." In S. G. Weinrach (Ed.), *Career Counseling: Theoretical and Practical Perspectives*. New York: McGraw-Hill, 1979.

Terkel, S. *Working*. New York: Avon Books, 1975.

Garry R. Walz
Libby Benjamin

12

❧ ❧ ❧ ❧ ❧ ❧ ❧ ❧

Systematic
Career Guidance Programs

The developments in today's world that have wrought such change in how we think and how we spend our time have had a profound influence on the guidance profession as well. Stereotypical images of counselors spending most of their work time scheduling students into classes, advising college-bound youth, and engaging in personal therapy just do not fit today's counselors, whose services extend far beyond schools to community and business settings. Heightened demands for equal opportunity and emphasis on new roles for women have had impact on the direction of guidance. Our precarious economy, with concomitant decreases in funds available to support counselors, has made guidance personnel much more sensitive to the need for substantive data that will testify to their worth. Requirements for program accountability, the establishment of career resource centers, increasing use of paraprofessionals and aides, and the introduction of computer-assisted guidance approaches have converged with other forces to change what counselors do and how they do it. The systematic thinking that typifies a technological society has now permeated guidance, and we are at last beginning to "think big," to view guidance from a comprehensive framework as a system that possesses integrated parts and leads to predictable outcomes.

Along with these forces that are pushing guidance toward

change is a major shift in career development theory. Formerly defined narrowly in the vocational realm, career development is now viewed as a lifelong process that encompasses every aspect of an individual's social, emotional, physical, and vocational growth and maturation. Career guidance professionals are consequently broadening their areas of assistance to include occupational and educational awareness and choice, leisure pursuits, self-knowledge, and life skills such as decision making, conflict resolution, and time management. To accomplish such a formidable array of teaching and learning tasks requires that guidance program planners design a developmental program that extends throughout the formal educational experience and continues to assist adults in the process of lifelong learning. Doing so requires a system.

What Is a Career Guidance System?

Webster defines a system (among other descriptions) as "a regularly interacting or interdependent group of items forming a unified whole . . . a group of devices or artificial objects or an organization forming a network especially for . . . serving a common purpose." Current resources that call themselves "systems" are in actuality career guidance approaches designed for a particular grade or age level. Many in truth are organized programs that follow the definition cited above, having interdependent parts and using a variety of strategies to achieve particular outcomes or purposes. Some focus on decision-making skills, some on dissemination of career information, some on career awareness and choice, some on career and midlife change; others focus solely on self-development, self-knowledge, and enhancement of life skills. Valuable as such resources may be, they will have little long-term effect unless they are part of a program of far greater magnitude. Effective delivery of career guidance requires a planned sequence of activities appropriate to varying levels of maturity, each experience building and expanding on what has gone before and supported by core professionals and staff members within the school environment as well as members of the community at large.

A comprehensive, systematic career guidance program does not imply a static, lifeless, totally predictable curriculum. Rather, the very definition of *system*, which presupposes a sequential program developed from a carefully conducted and analyzed needs assessment, demands that within basic parameters the program be fluid, responsive to changing needs, ahead of and ready for emerging needs, and flexible enough to modify particular strategies on the basis of ongoing evaluation of results.

Characteristics of a Systematic Career Guidance Program

To describe what we mean in more detail, then, we believe that a comprehensive career guidance delivery system exhibits some fundamental characteristics. A systematic career guidance program:

1. Is an organized, sequential, comprehensive series of activities and experiences, based on the maturity and readiness of clients. Planning involves articulation between grade levels within the school and between the school and the community. It implies a developmental building on and broadening of what has gone before, with introduction of new concepts and experiences at succeeding stages of maturation and developmental need. Within the school, the program may stand in its own right as a discrete array of services or be integrated into other teaching/ learning experiences.

2. Is based on initial and subsequent needs assessments of clients, program deliverers, and policy makers, analyzed and assigned priorities according to rankings given by those surveyed. The process of determining the greatest needs requires some juggling of priorities to satisfy as much as possible the major needs of all respondents. A side issue here is the compilation and dissemination of the results of the analysis so that all involved in the program are aware of basic program priorities and goals.

3. Is designed to achieve measurable, realistic, and specific objectives, with criteria for successful achievement clearly stated and understood by program deliverers and clients. Essential to successful performance within the program are advance

preparation and information provided to clients concerning what is expected of them and how they will change as a result of going through the program.

4. Has a built-in, ongoing evaluation component that provides continuing feedback to all those involved in the program about the extent to which the broad goals and specific objectives are being achieved, as well as summative evaluation that measures final outcomes in terms of client behaviors and program deliverer satisfaction. The ongoing evaluation is extremely important, as it alerts program planners to the need to alter strategies or modify particular portions of the program to keep it on target with current or changing emphases in the educational and social environment. Important also is a self-monitoring evaluation strategy that allows clients themselves to assess and be cognizant of how they are growing and changing over time.

5. Uses a variety of resources and procedures to achieve stated outcomes, keyed to differing personal learning modes, to the skills of the program deliverers, and to the materials available to implement the program. These approaches may include textual materials, computerized information, audiovisual resources, outside speakers, supervised work experience, and self-awareness activities completed individually or through group process that provide individuals with the excitement of self-discovery and self-insight.

6. Is delivered by personnel highly trained in human relationships; thoroughly knowledgeable about program goals, content, and process; skillful in group work; committed to the importance of career guidance to the lives of youths and adults; flexible about the need to revise or modify strategies in midstream; able to communicate well with people; and sensitive to the needs of those with whom they work.

7. Focuses on both process and product, on deliverers and clients. Desired outcomes will not be achieved unless the delivery process is tuned to client needs and counselor skills. In a truly effective career guidance system, everyone benefits. Counselors hone and enhance their own skills in the process of helping individuals mature and broaden their knowledge; clients

and significant others receive tangible evidence of growth and change; and the program ensures its own expansion and continuance by providing hard data documenting its success.

8. Is designed and planned by a guidance committee composed of representatives from varying publics, including intended program deliverers, experts from other settings, educational and community decision makers, and, in a school setting, parents and the student body. A well-functioning committee is critical to program success, and members should be chosen with care. Inclusion of the principal or other high-ranking educational official gives the school guidance program clout and underscores its importance. Inclusion of individuals from a variety of backgrounds lends depth to the program by bringing to bear a wide range of viewpoints and broadening the program's support base. It also has the serendipitous advantage of uncovering unknown talent among professional and staff personnel that can enhance and enrich the entire career guidance program. The committee's fundamental role is to establish a defensible rationale for the program, assist in making decisions on broad program goals and specific objectives, and help determine the sequence and flow of program content. Implementation of the committee decisions then belongs to program deliverers themselves, who will be more knowledgeable about the kinds of resources, procedures, and strategies that will achieve the agreed-on outcomes.

Current State of Development of Career Guidance Systems

Recommendations for systematic planning of guidance programs did not emerge until the late 1960s. Small wonder, since counselors were almost unheard of before the middle 1950s. The establishment of university graduate training programs and federally funded guidance institutes in the early 1960s substantially increased the number of counselors working in schools, but it must be said that what they did was subject to the interpretation, the orientation, and sometimes the whim of their particular school administrator. The push for accountability in the early 1970s had a salutary effect, as it caused guidance practitioners to scrutinize their role and functioning—to realize that reactive, crisis-centered activities, a primary focus on one-to-one counseling, and involvement in educational duties extraneous to the role for which they had been trained did not contribute to viable documentation of their effectiveness. Increasing demand for supportive research data, plus severe competition for federal and state money and the tightening of funds available to school districts and community service organizations, forced them to adopt new ways of delivering guidance services that would demonstrate positive, recordable outcomes.

Even a cursory examination of the rapidly growing volume of literature on systematic guidance planning reveals how much progress we have made both in our attitudes toward more organized delivery of guidance services and in the production of practical resources for program planners and clients. It is clear that educators today are recognizing the usefulness of a systems approach to guide the design and planning of educational programs. Indeed, the Educational Resources Information Center (ERIC), the largest data base of educational information in the world, swells monthly with documents from local schools and school districts, colleges and universities, community organizations, regions, states, and federally funded institutions describing unique strategies, models, and total guidance delivery systems that are developmentally oriented and meet the needs of individuals for lifelong assistance in career planning and decision making.

Most states now have developed guidelines for comprehensive guidance program planning for K–12 and postsecondary education. The state of California provides a good example. When findings from a statewide study (Guidance and Counseling Task Force, 1975) revealed that over 90 percent of students and adults surveyed were in need of help in planning for the future, the state department of education began assisting schools in creating comprehensive guidance programs that were developmental and consisted of planned sequences of activities based on student needs (Upton, 1982). Georgia, another state that has devoted much effort to organizing guidance services, has a program development guide (Dagley and Hartley, 1976) to help counselors and other school personnel to develop and implement a comprehensive, needs-based career guidance program in their work settings. The *Illinois Career Guidance Handbook* (1971), a compilation of guidelines, activities, and materials dealing with planning, implementation, and evaluation of career guidance programs, also contains an extensive listing of resources within the state that can aid schools in their quest to organize guidance services.

Program models have also been designed by guidance personnel or teams of educators in hundreds of school districts throughout the nation. Many of these are in the ERIC system and can, with appropriate modification for a particular client group, be used in other settings. For example, a special committee that met for two years to formalize guidance services in the public schools of Ann Arbor, Michigan, designed a detailed program for grades 7–12 that is divided into educational guidance, personal/social counseling, and life-career guidance services and is organized around specific tasks and objectives at each grade level. The New York City reference book on guidance in the high school, focusing on the needs of urban students, offers an omnibus counseling model that can be adopted/adapted for use in other guidance programs. See *Resources for Guidance Program Improvement* (Walz, Mamarchev, and Frenza, n.d.), a recent publication of ERIC/CAPS, for detailed information on these and other exemplary guidance programs.

Program designers and deliverers are the target audience for a number of systematic models created to assist them in organizing or reorganizing the delivery of guidance services to a variety of publics. For example, the American Institutes for Research, in Palo Alto, California, worked with a six-state consortium of guidance leaders from state departments of education and major universities. This consortium developed a series of fifty-two competency-based staff training modules, with coordinator's guides, covering a wide array of topics ranging from all aspects of comprehensive program design to specific skill-building activities.

Though still in draft form at this writing, thirty-one modules (*Competency-Based Guidance Program Training Modules,* n.d.) have been created by the National Center for Research in Vocational Education, in consort with other organizations, and are designed to improve the ability of career guidance personnel to meet their clients' developmental needs. The modules train personnel in the five categories of systematic, developmental career guidance program design and delivery: planning, support, implementation, operation, and evaluation. A valuable how-to reference that highlights practical strategies for making the transition from traditional guidance services to effective developmental guidance programs is *Improving Guidance Programs* (Gysbers and Moore, 1981). The authors focus on competencies for participants in the guidance program as well as competency-reporting systems.

In-service leadership training for guidance professionals working in rural or small school districts is the focus of the *Rural America Guidance Series* (1977), a program developed by a consortium of the National Center for Research in Vocational Education at Ohio State University, the Wisconsin Vocational Studies Center at the University of Wisconsin, and the School of Education at Northern Michigan University in Marquette. The sixteen self-contained handbooks in this program, which can be used individually or as parts of broad subsets, contain all the information and materials needed to train guidance personnel in rural and small-school settings to plan, develop, implement, and evaluate comprehensive career guidance programs. The Center for Vocational Education at Ohio State University has also developed a program called the Career Planning Support System, or CPSS (Campbell, 1977), which provides step-by-step procedures for planning new career guidance programs or upgrading and managing ongoing ones, with increased staff/student/community involvement. It contains a coordinator's training guide, a coordinator's handbook, and other reusable resources, including filmstrip/audiocassette tapes and camera-ready masters.

The foregoing are just a few examples of the kinds of resources that have been developed in just the past few years to upgrade the skills of counseling and guidance personnel and prepare them to assume leadership in the movement toward organizing guidance service delivery.

When we shift our attention to materials for program

planners to use in achieving the desired outcomes outlined in their systematic guidance programs, we find literally hundreds of resources available, ranging from games, films, filmstrips, tapes, and single experiences or activities, to kits and units, to broad-based semester or year programs, to sophisticated computerized guidance systems. Readers will already be knowledgeable about many of these detailed programs and strategies, but we stress again the worth of consulting ERIC for resources in areas of particular interest and need. If certain materials are not in the system, users can usually find references in numerous documents that will help them locate the provider of the desired information.

The resources are surely there. Elegant plans exist in abundance. Implementation of systematic guidance delivery is another thing, however, and we must be more cautious in our estimate of how many of these models are actually in place, despite laudable efforts by many professional educators. Among the many reasons for this situation, two of the most important are drastic reductions in material and human resources and strong reluctance to change established routines. Another block to successful implementation is lack of requisite skills among those responsible for delivery, and here we must look to counselor education and training programs. The shift from process to product (that is, from what counselors do to how students are different as a result of what counselors do), the strong emphasis on accountability, and the broadening of the definition of career development to encompass life roles are having profound influences on counselor practice. Few counselors have the competencies needed to perform the full range of activities and services required in designing and implementing a systematic and sequential career guidance program. We must conclude, therefore, that a lamentably large number of forces are operating to inhibit implementation of systematic career guidance services—that in most cases theory is far ahead of practice.

Limitations of a Nonsystematic Approach to Career Guidance

Despite ever-mounting evidence of the need for a more encompassing and systematic approach to career guidance, some guidance personnel have clung to the traditional model of one-to-one counseling. Indeed, many clients will testify to the significant assistance furnished them by a particular counselor in making an important vocational or educational choice. Guidance strategies that worked in yesteryear, however, have not proved to be so successful in today's increasingly complex and unpredictable world. Among the more important limitations of traditional approaches are the following.

Type of Career Guidance Determined by Individual Counselors. The content and focus of the guidance offered a client was determined to a large extent by the interests and skills of a particular counselor. Perhaps this explains why over three fourths of students in numerous state and national surveys reported that they were dissatisfied with the type of guidance they were receiving and that they needed help in planning their future (Harris-Bowlsbey, 1975; Michigan ACT Secondary School Council, 1976; Prediger, Roth, and Noeth, 1973). Counselors apparently were/are "doing their own thing"—that is, providing quasi-personal therapy rather than responding to the broad and frequently expressed student need for assistance in career planning.

Emphasis on Individual Counseling. As individual providers, many counselors virtually excluded other guidance approaches. This narrow focus emphasized dealing with client attitudes and feelings and conversely minimized information giving and skill building as they relate to career development. Further, it greatly restricted the number of individuals served and the amount of time possible to devote to each. Although individual counseling is an extremely important aspect of any career guidance program, it is far from sufficient as a comprehensive way of assisting with career planning and decision making.

Inattention to the Client as a Total Person. Working with individuals according to the counselor's background and orientation provided a fragmented approach to the full range of the person's needs and interests. For example, some counselors emphasized test giving and the use of test results in helping people make decisions; other counselors steered practically all their clients toward further education; still others focused on providing occupational information and discussing training and placement opportunities. The consequence was that a given individual could be very well served in one area but very poorly in another. And even if a student could consult all the counselors in a school setting, the lack of a basic philosophy and rationale for career guidance meant that the assistance provided was still inconsistent in coverage and emphasis.

Difficulty in Assessing Effectiveness and Outcomes of the Career Guidance Program. The great variability in counseling approaches and the lack of a systematic design created several barriers in evaluating the overall effectiveness of the career guidance program. A program that satisfied some people very much and left others disgruntled, depending on the counselor with whom they worked and the conditions under which they sought assistance, made it extremely difficult to determine the impact of the career guidance program on all individuals. The only really meaningful evaluation had to do with how well a particular counselor responded to the needs and interests of a particular person. However, even this form of evaluation was seldom undertaken in practice. Without agreement by the staff on any clear set of goals and objectives or specific criteria by which to assess outcomes, few program planners tried to evaluate what they did or how clients were different; most settled for head counting or anecdotal or testimonial evidence that clients appreciated and benefited from the guidance they were receiving.

A recent study by Campbell and others (1983) supports the need for organized career guidance delivery. The study revealed that clients from a number of settings, including public schools, vocational schools, colleges and universities, and correctional institutions, benefited from career guidance; the evidence suggested that "career guidance interventions achieve their intended objectives *if* guidance personnel ... provide structured guidance interventions in a systematic, developmental sequence" (p. x).

Variation in Counselors' Goals and Methods. Owing to the great variance in counselor goals and methods and the lack of program materials or a systematic design, improvements in career guidance programs occurred primarily through the development of individual counselors' skills rather than program resources. Decisions about the type and content of further training were typically made by counselors themselves, and the result was a perpetuation, even an increase, in the development of separate subspecialties instead of promotion of a consistent and comprehensive methodology for career guidance delivery. Training, ostensibly for the purpose of improving the program, in fact increased the individuality of the interests and skills of different guidance specialists, further intensifying the tendency for the quality and type of career guidance offered to be dependent on the particular counselor to whom clients went for help.

Reactive and Crisis-Centered Orientation. Student self-referral models for counseling led most school guidance programs to be concerned mainly with reacting to crises or problem situations instead of emphasizing student development and building student strengths. If students were achieving reasonably well academically and had clearly identified occupational goals, it was likely that counseling was either cursory or nonexistent. Counselors were often too busy handling the backlog of student crises and major problems to assist relatively trouble-free students in acquiring further self-knowledge and exploring possibilities in developing long- and short-range plans. Consequently, numbers of students were left to their own resources in making important career decisions. Although many students managed this task adequately by themselves, they might have had greater confidence in or improved the quality of their plans and decisions if they had gone through a comprehensive career planning program with the assistance of a qualified counselor.

Advantages of Systematic Career Guidance Delivery

Listed here are some of the more direct advantages of using a systematic approach to the delivery of career guidance. The statements are not definitive. Rather, they are illustrative, and the reader will undoubtedly be able to suggest other possible outcomes. Nor are they mutually exclusive. In actual operation, the systematic use of various human and physical resources to achieve previously identified objectives has a synergistic effect.

Developmental Emphasis. The systematic approach gives

program planners the opportunity to design a proactive delivery system that anticipates needs and problems and develops appropriate responses to them. It emphasizes building on the strengths of individuals to help them acquire the competencies and knowledge they need to prepare for and manage their lives in the present and in the future. The crisis/problem orientation of traditional guidance approaches is discarded in favor of one geared to helping people make decisions based on important personal values and environmental realities. System designers are able to develop and use guidance resources and procedures that address developmental needs across the age range, with the result that at any particular level of maturity the appropriate guidance emphasis is present to assist each individual to move on to more advanced developmental tasks and needs.

Effective Use of Available Resources. Having clearly defined the developmental needs and priorities of clients and the objectives of significant others, program designers can tailor components of the delivery system (counseling, media, information resources, computer-based guidance) to desired outcomes. This tailoring avoids the shortcoming in traditional methods of using or overusing a particular guidance resource, such as counseling, for all guidance objectives and goals whether or not it is the most appropriate one for a particular purpose. Personal counseling is an excellent method of assisting people in self-exploration and examination of attitudes and feelings, but it is an inefficient and costly approach for presenting information. A particular guidance resource should always be selected with the question in mind whether this method is the most effective way to achieve a particular objective.

Amenability to Change and Innovation. In situations in which what guidance is delivered (and how) is a decision of individual counselors, any effort to bring about change is dependent on the extent to which individual counselors are convinced that change is necessary. With clearly stated goals and objectives and specified modes of delivery, it is easier to determine where difficulties exist within the total guidance delivery system and to identify areas needing change and/or improvement. With this comprehensive view of how the guidance program is functioning, it is then possible to provide the training and resources needed by all the staff members to accomplish the new or revised goals and objectives. In the systematic approach, change thus becomes a unified and organized effort wherein the total program staff works together to enhance its services.

Relative Ease of Evaluation. The idiosyncratic nature of traditional guidance delivery precluded any evaluation other than an assessment of the efforts of individual counselors with individual clients. Drawing generalizations about the effectiveness of guidance services was therefore inappropriate and difficult, if not impossible. Rather than an externally imposed condition, evaluation is an internal and necessary component of the systematic approach. Highly specific goals and objectives, including standards for judging behavioral change, become criteria against which to evaluate outcomes for both program and clients. Where there is a discrepancy between proposed and actual outcomes, new methods can be developed and implemented. Thus, at any stage during the program operation, deliverers of the services can provide statistical evidence of how well the program is functioning.

Avoidance of Faddism. Clarity in objectives and modes of delivery also provides insulation against faddism, or opportunistic responses to catchy ideas that have not been completely developed or systematically tested. Guidance has suffered as much from the premature adoption of incompletely developed ideas and approaches as from inability or slowness to change. Implementing a new approach within a systematic design requires an answer to the question whether a particular method will enable service deliverers to achieve their objectives more effectively than with current modes of delivery. Unless convincing evidence is forthcoming, program planners have clear justification for delaying any adoption of a new technique, however attractive it may seem.

Promotion of Community Effort. The assurance provided by the establishment of a program with well-understood goals and a systematic method of delivery fosters a higher degree of participation by significant members of the total community. School personnel, counselors, social workers, and community leaders are stimulated to find ways that they can be involved in helping individuals to plan and manage their careers and future lives. With greater opportunity and desire to participate also comes an enhanced sense of worth, both of the overall program and of the roles of the various participants. People feel good about the services and the ways they have contributed. The program is not the esoteric domain of a few professionals but one that belongs to everyone and for which everyone feels a degree of responsibility.

Zest for Self-Renewal. Typically our learnings are time-bound. They suffice for the moment; but as people and times change, programs may no longer be attuned to individual needs. Because of the developmental perspective, continuous monitoring of outcomes, and openness to change, both the people served by the program and the program deliverers experience an ongoing search for discovery and new learning. Clients, deliverers, and the program itself all benefit. Clients and program staff provide a support for each other's learning and renewing so that synergistically each in turn models and stimulates the other to new goals and new learnings.

Survivability. In our experience, alertness to individual needs and interests and to building relevant responses leads systematic programs to demonstrate remarkable survivability in the face of great challenge and uncertainty. In contrast to traditional programs, staff members are their own best friends rather than their worst enemies. The essence of the systematic approach is not only to be responsive to the existing priorities and needs of the program's many publics but also to be anticipatory of future needs and interests—to be truly proactive. A well-managed systematic program is seldom surprised or unprepared for any assault by critics on its goals or methods.

Launchpad for Learning. The primary objective of career guidance is to assist individuals to acquire the competencies and knowledge they need to fashion life-styles that are appropriate to their needs and interests and to the many roles they will experience in their lifetimes. It is a goal never fulfilled. Rather, the process is one of ongoing exploration, discovery, and acquisition of new skills and knowledge. Individuals who have experienced the breadth and depth of a systematic approach to career guidance truly become "life architects," increasingly competent to cope with change and the realities of living, to image their desired future, and to chart their life's course with greater certainty.

Important Considerations in Program
Development and Implementation

The ultimate effectiveness of systematic career guidance delivery depends largely on how well the program is designed and implemented. Staff members will sometimes devote all their attention to developing an elaborate system and assume that, because of its quality, its effectiveness is a foregone conclusion. Although a good design is a requirement for a good system, high quality in no way ensures adoption or effective delivery. Implementation is a separate strategy in itself and requires the careful attention of the system designers and deliverers if the program is to achieve its stated goals. The authors have developed a systematic change agent strategy for the human services (Benjamin and Walz, 1979a, 1979b, 1979c; Walz and Benjamin, 1977, 1978), and some of its salient features can be extremely helpful in winning support for a more systematic program and delivering more organized services.

As previously discussed, the goals and objectives adopted for the program are not derived from the whims or partialities of the staff but are the result of an ongoing program of needs assessment. Essential to effective implementation is that all who have a stake in the career guidance delivery system have the opportunity for input. This is not a one-time activity but an ongoing process, with regular updating of assessment data to stay on target with the current needs and interests of the participating publics.

Program evaluation frequently leads to voluminous reports that sit on somebody's shelf gathering dust. The guidance staff must be responsible for managing the logistics of compiling the evaluation data. Of utmost importance, however, is that the interpretation of the implications and applications of the data be a consensus of all the participants associated with and served by the career guidance program. Determination of how well a given facet of the program is functioning or of what changes and new emphases should be undertaken needs to be broad-based, involving all parties rather than just a few guidance professionals. This not only ensures that the program is responsive to current and emerging individual needs and interests but also keeps program personnel and significant others aware of the program's progress in achieving stated goals.

Organized delivery of career guidance services will be no more effective than the skills of the persons performing the different activities. The training and retraining of the deliverers is therefore an essential function of effective systems operation. This training has two specific emphases: (1) training in skills needed for the immediate implementation of components of the system and (2) education that prepares program deliverers for performing future roles and activities within the system. Such training and education is closely allied with the information obtained from the ongoing needs assessment and evaluation components of the program. Training is one of the hallmarks of the mature and well-organized program. In contrast to business and industry, which invest heavily in education and training of employees, educators, perhaps especially guidance personnel, assume that people can acquire the knowledge and skills they need through informal personal efforts rather than through a systematic formal program. Such an attitude is anathema to effective career guidance system operation. Few, if any, of the competencies needed to plan and implement a systematic career guidance program are commonly provided in typical graduate training programs. Hence, even recent counselor education graduates need the specific formal training we are describing.

The opportunity to use a wide range of human and material resources and methods is a particularly attractive feature of the systematic approach. If this positive element is to be used to advantage, it requires a commitment of the staff to being "resource-resourceful"—to becoming aware of and seeking out new approaches, techniques, and people that will enhance the pro-

gram. Here ERIC can be most helpful. The ERIC system is re-
plete with resources of personal and program renewal and contains new input each month of resources that have demonstrated their utility in actual field settings. The key to good resource utilization is a judicious mix-and-match approach in
which quality and applicability are the primary determinants
of resource selection.

Future Images of Career Guidance Systems

Career guidance systems are currently in their infancy.
Many states now have systematic career guidance plans and are
strongly encouraging local organizations and school districts to
adopt a systematic approach to career guidance delivery. As we
progress toward the establishment of concrete operational models, several trends are emerging that are likely to be influential
in their development. The following statements suggest some of
the images of what career guidance delivery systems will look
like in the near future and illustrate some of the probable developments and changes.

Service to Individuals over the Life Span. Recognition of
the need to assist people at all ages will lead to establishment of
career guidance systems that offer services to individuals
throughout their lives. Programs may provide particularly strong
interventions and resources at periods of critical life transition—
for example, leaving high school, entering the labor market, and
coping with midlife crises. Beginning in the early years, individuals will be encouraged to think futuristically and to image
probable and preferred outcomes in their life planning. Schools
and colleges will be involved in lifetime maintenance policies.
The already-pervasive adult involvement in lifelong learning and
self-regulated learning experiences will lead increasing numbers
of individuals to use these guidance services throughout their
lives to review and renew life plans and/or deal with critical life
decisions. Much as schools today are involved in developing
individualized learning plans, so, too, schools of the future will
help elementary-age students to create a career development
plan that they will regularly update as they mature. This plan

will be an important item in every individual's personal record, one that the person will use with employers as well as with life-planning consultants in wellness centers.

Community-Based Programs Oriented Toward Service to Family Units and Groups. The desire of individuals for career guidance over the life span will lead to establishment of community-based psychological wellness centers, housed perhaps in intermediate school districts, community colleges, or unneeded school buildings. Although services will continue to be available to individuals, much of the work of community career guidance specialists will be devoted to providing assistance to larger groups such as couples, families, and persons in other kinds of significant relationships. The community guidance program will operate in many ways as a one-stop development center that will offer the information, resources, and counseling desired by individuals and groups of all ages as they experience important life changes.

Efforts to encourage community participation in meeting the needs of all citizen groups are not new; indeed, many communities have been successful in achieving interagency cooperation. But systematic training and program planning are usually lacking. One significant example of effective community involvement in the career guidance process is the community-collaborative guidance team project, coordinated by the National Center for Research in Vocational Education and assisted by the American Institutes for Research and the University of Missouri. The purpose of the project was to train teams of representatives from various community agencies and volunteer groups to design and develop programs that provided assistance to citizens whose career needs were not being met. Evaluative data from the teams in thirty-five communities throughout the country who participated in the project reveal that the concept of community collaboration is promising at this stage in its development and worthy of expansion (*Community Collaboration*, n.d.).

More Intensive and Extensive Use of Technology. To respond to the wide range of needs and interests of clients, career guidance programs will make much greater use of technology than is true today. Computers will be used not only for extensive record keeping but also for helping people with decision making and skill building. Home-based learning systems utilizing television, telephone lines, and microcomputers will flourish, and such a wide variety of programs and resources will be available that there will be a degree of individualization and customization in guidance programs unheard of today. The rising cost of personnel and the demand for accountability in career guidance systems will lead to the replacement by technology of many functions now performed through personal communication between client and counselor. Advising, providing information, and record keeping, and even some of the more esoteric areas such as decision making and life planning, will be either taken over or assisted by technology. This expansion of the use of technology will result in increased centralization and nationalization of certain aspects of career guidance delivery systems. The cost of both the hardware and software associated with different components of career guidance technology will be such that individual guidance units will find it economically undesirable to develop these resources on their own and will instead purchase them from a national source. This will lead to a more uniform methodology and philosophical base than is true today, which, in turn, will provide greater opportunity for research on the effectiveness of career guidance strategies. However, it will also pose major problems concerning who will make the decisions about the values and priorities that pervade the system and its use in a particular setting.

Change in Counselor Role from Individual Service Provider to System Specialist. Counselors of the near-term future will be greater generalists, skilled in areas not now commonly associated with counselor training and function. They will need to be highly knowledgeable about system design and implementation and skillful in the use of a wide array of technological aids. In addition, they will need to be adept at consultation with clients and other educators and peers and able to perform effectively as facilitators of groups of all ages.

Increased Cooperation and Collaboration Among Specialists. Career guidance specialists operating within a systems approach will be more involved in linkages and networking as a means of delivering the most useful services. Natural alliances with teachers, other educational specialists, and experts in the community will be eagerly sought out and established. The question of finding the best resource person with whom to link and collaborate to achieve desired objectives will be ongoing, and working liaisons between and among specialists will be the rule. People of differing degrees of preparation—volunteers, aides, and interns—and of varying subject and professional specialties will join forces. The counselor will serve as a broker of human resources, deciding which individual or which team of individuals can best accomplish particular goals.

This extended cooperation and teaming will both broaden the perspective of career guidance functions and enrich the quality of the experiences that touch those who use the services. The wide range of persons involved and the variance of their perspectives and training will require a high level of leadership and management skills of the counselor/manager. An important shift in thinking will occur wherein counselors will focus on how best to organize available physical and human resources to achieve positive outcomes, rather than on how best to provide personal assistance to clients. The new roles of the counselor/career guidance system manager will be many and varied and will call for persons with broad training, oriented toward designing learning systems that lead to significant personal growth rather than developing esoteric counseling skills.

Tracking Systems That Provide Information on Future Trends. Career guidance systems have many advantages associated with the quality and quantity of resources, but putting them in place within the system requires lead time. Therefore, career guidance systems will possess a tracking component that will identify changes in demographics, local and national legislation, local and national economic conditions, and client expressions of need and interest that have important implications for what the system should provide and how it can best be provided. Information from national data bases, forecasting services, long-range planning and advisory committees, and the creative futuring of the career guidance staff itself will be highly important to program planners in acquiring appropriate physical resources such as hardware and software as well as in staff training and renewal. Decisions and plans will be focused less on today and next week and more on developing scenarios for several years ahead and identifying future levels of new development.

The images presented here of future career guidance systems are neither exhaustive nor definitive; rather, they illustrate some of the significant changes that will probably occur in the thinking behind and the functioning of career guidance systems of tomorrow. They suggest areas of emphasis not present in current career guidance programs and call for shifts in both the thinking and the training of counselors who plan and work in these programs. Taken as a whole, these images of a futuristic career guidance system are full of excitement and adventure. They offer the potential for career guidance that is more enhancing to individuals and more rewarding and satisfying to those responsible for delivering services.

Summary

Effective delivery of career guidance requires a planned sequence of activities, a variety of strategies for achieving identified outcomes, and clearly delineated roles and responsibilities for those who will be involved in providing services—in other words, a system. This chapter outlined the characteristics of a systematic career guidance program, described several state models for organizing guidance services, and suggested resources both for upgrading the skills of professional counselors and for direct use in systematic guidance programs. It was noted, however, that few systems are actually in operation at present, for a number of reasons.

The limitations of traditional methods of providing career guidance were discussed, as were some of the advantages of adopting a planned, systematic approach to service delivery. Several important considerations in the development and implementation of systematic career guidance programs were presented, including the method of implementation, the need for a needs assessment of those who will be involved in the program, the wisdom of including program participants in the interpretation of evaluation data, the type of staff training that is necessary, and the potential benefits of using a wide range of human and material resources.

The chapter concluded with a statement about the trends that may influence career guidance delivery and some images of what career guidance systems may look like in the future. The picture is bright, and the images of futuristic career guidance systems are full of excitement and adventure. They offer the potential for career guidance that is more enhancing to individuals and more rewarding and satisfying to those responsible for delivering services.

Suggested Readings

American Institutes for Research. Fifty-two competency-based staff training modules, plus resource guide. Palo Alto, Calif.: American Institutes for Research, 1978–1979.

Written by a number of authors and produced by a consortium of AIR and six state departments of education and major universities, covering all aspects of career guidance from initial design and development to delivery in a multitude of settings.

Career Planning Support System (CPSS). Columbus: National Center for Research in Vocational Education, Ohio State University, 1977.

A comprehensive guidance program management system offering step-by-step directions through innovative techniques in planning, developing, implementing, and evaluating an upgraded career guidance program that is compatible with student career development needs and resources available in the school and community.

Competency-Based Guidance Program Training Modules. Columbus: National Center for Research in Vocational Education, Ohio State University, n.d.

Thirty-one competency-based, field-tested modules relating to planning, supporting, implementing, operating, and evaluating career guidance programs; include group and individual learning experiences and readings and references to pertinent federal legislation and available resources. In developmental draft form at this date.

Herr, E. L., and Cramer, S. H. *Career Guidance Through the Life Span.* Boston: Little, Brown, 1979.

     Examines research in career development theory and its application to career guidance in schools, communities, and the workplace; identifies planning models and techniques; presents examples of major developmental programs. Revised edition, due in spring 1984, places more emphasis on programs and models in the workplace and business and industry; explores current adult concerns such as dual-career families and working mothers; applies career development theories to special populations; discusses changes in the meaning of work, including job satisfaction and mental health in relation to work or unemployment.

References

American Institutes for Research. Fifty-two competency-based staff training modules, plus resource guide. Palo Alto, Calif.: American Institutes for Research, 1978–1979.

Benjamin, L., and Walz, G. R. *Making Change Happen: A Workshop for Developing Change Agent Skills.* Ann Arbor: ERIC/CAPS, University of Michigan, 1979a. (ED 167 939)

Benjamin, L., and Walz, G. R. *Making Change Happen: Learning a Systematic Model for Change.* Module 51. Palo Alto, Calif.: American Institutes for Research, 1979b. (ED 184 000)

Benjamin, L., and Walz, G. R. *Making Change Happen: Overcoming Barriers to Change.* Module 52. Palo Alto, Calif.: American Institutes for Research, 1979c. (ED 184 001)

Campbell, R. E. *The Career Planning Support System (CPSS).* Columbus: National Center for Research in Vocational Education, Ohio State University, 1977.

Campbell, R. E., and others. *Enhancing Career Development:*

Recommendations for Action. Columbus: National Center for Research in Vocational Education, Ohio State University, 1983.

Community Collaboration for Improving Career Guidance Programs: Preliminary Findings Suggest It Can Work. Columbus: National Center for Research in Vocational Education, Ohio State University, n.d.

Competency-Based Guidance Program Training Modules. Columbus: National Center for Research in Vocational Education, Ohio State University, n.d.

Dagley, J., and Hartley, D. L. *Career Guidance in Georgia: A Program Development Guide.* Atlanta: Georgia State Department of Education, 1976. (ED 160 850)

Guidance and Counseling Task Force. *Pupil Personnel Services in California Schools: Needs, Problems, and a Plan for Solutions.* Sacramento: California State Department of Education, 1975. (ED 120 600)

Gysbers, N. C., and Moore, E. J. *Improving Guidance Programs.* Englewood Cliffs, N.J.: Prentice-Hall, 1981.

Halasz-Salazar, I. *Planning Comprehensive Career Guidance Programs: A Catalog of Alternatives.* Columbus: National Center for Research in Vocational Education, Ohio State University, 1979. (ED 167 797)

Harris-Bowlsbey, J. "Career Guidance Needs of the Nation's Youth and Adults." Report prepared for the National Institute of Education, July 1975.

Illinois Career Guidance Handbook. Springfield, Ill.: State Department of Education, 1971. (ED 205 887)

Michigan ACT Secondary School Council. *A Needs Assessment Report.* Lansing: Michigan ACT Secondary School Council, 1976.

Prediger, D., Roth, J., and Noeth, R. *A Nationwide Study of Student Career Development: Summary of Results.* ACT Research Report No. 61. Iowa City, Iowa: D. Prediger, J. Roth, and R. Noeth, 1973. (ED 083 383)

Rural America Guidance Series. Columbus: National Center for Research in Vocational Education, Ohio State University, 1977.

Upton, A. "The Development of a Comprehensive Guidance and Counseling Plan for the State of California." *Vocational Guidance Quarterly*, 1982, *30*(4), 293-299.

Walz, G. R., and Benjamin, L. *On Becoming a Change Agent.* Ann Arbor: ERIC/CAPS, University of Michigan, 1977. (ED 140 212)

Walz, G. R., and Benjamin, L. "A Change Agent Strategy for Counselors Functioning as Consultants." *Personnel and Guidance Journal*, 1978, *56*(6), 331-334. (CG 016 643)

Walz, G. R., Mamarchev, H., and Frenza, M. *Resources for Guidance Program Improvement.* Ann Arbor: ERIC Counseling and Personnel Services Clearinghouse, University of Michigan, n.d. (CG 016 643)

13

JoAnn Harris-Bowlsbey

The Computer as a Tool in Career Guidance Programs

Somehow 1966 was a magic year for the birth of the use of the computer in support of career guidance. By that year at least nine development teams geographically scattered across the United States were at work. It was an unusually productive and exciting time. An alert profession had been given a new technological tool—dramatically more powerful than any other it had previously used—that needed to be harnessed for the benefit of people trying to make a vocational choice. Several factors made the early days of development exciting. Probably the most important was the attitude of professional sharing that pervaded. The early developers met at least annually over a period of several years, and in those meetings they talked extensively about their work and its problems and potentials. A second very important factor was the pioneer spirit of challenge. Interactive dialogue between a user and a computer had never been written before; large data files had never been searched by a machine; on-line processing had not previously existed; and the problem of interfacing computer text with audio and visual capability was new. No one knew yet whether the computer should speak in the first person ("I will take you to the college search now") or in the generic third person ("The college search can now be

362

selected"). And it was not yet clear whether the computer should serve the counselor or the student primarily, or both. These kinds of challenges not only led to enthusiasm but also fostered the pushing of the then-frontiers of the technology—to make computers control audio and visual devices, although the technology did not exist to do it, and to make the computer unscramble the user's natural language, although that was a tremendous burden on the then-existing memory and storage capacities of the machine.

Another characteristic of the beginning era, one almost now forgotten, was the plentifulness of funding for such research and development. Early developers had budgets ranging from a quarter of a million dollars to three million dollars, and those dollars went a lot further in 1966–1970! Another very pronounced characteristic was the allegiance to a strong theoretical base for the systems under development. Super operationalized his proposed program of career guidance in IBM's Education and Career Exploration System (ECES). Tiedeman operationalized his theory of decision making as he built his decision-making paradigm into the Information System for Vocational Decisions (ISVD). Katz operationalized his theory of decision making as a combination of valuing and probability as he developed the System of Interactive Guidance and Information (SIGI). Others—namely, Roberts, Flanagan, Impelleteri, Silberman, Tondow, and the author—computerized the process that years of counseling experience told them good counselors perform in the registration of students for academic programs and in assistance with educational and vocational choice. The early invitational conferences of the development group provided an unusual blend of the theoretical and the practical, each strength feeding the other.

Historical Perspective

Nine systems were developed during the years from 1960 to 1970 (U.S. Office of Education, 1969), and among these were the predecessors of three systems that are dominant in the 1980s. The IBM Corporation, supported by the work of Donald

Super and his Columbia team, developed ECES I, an elaborate guidance system that included simulated work tasks on film under computer control. Although IBM decided not to market the system, it and its successive versions have been used extensively in the state of Michigan. The Bartlesville Public School System (Oklahoma), under the leadership of Tommy Roberts, developed an elaborate administrative and counselor support system called the Total Guidance and Information Support System (TGISS) for the management of student records. Although this system did not survive, it did test the validity of ways in which the computer could serve as a strong clerical support system to the counselor. Pennsylvania State University, under the guidance of Joseph Impelleteri, developed the Computer-Assisted Career Education System (CACE), and although this system did not survive, it did test two new ideas—the use of slides under computer control to assist a student in selecting a vocational education specialty and the use of the computer for academic advising/course selection. Murray Tondow, of the Palo Alto Unified School District (California), also developed a sophisticated system designed to let the computer do the registration interviews so commonly done by high school counselors. John Flanagan and his team at the American Institutes for Research implemented a system that made use of interest and aptitude test scores to predict satisfaction in potential vocational choices. Although these systems did not live beyond the heyday of early development, they did provide valuable research and experience that were helpful to later developers.

Surviving Systems. Three of the early systems have survived into the 1980s, either in their original form or in a highly altered form. Martin Katz and his colleagues at the Educational Testing Service, funded by the Carnegie Foundation, developed an early version of the System of Interactive Guidance and Information (SIGI), which is still dominant in the field and still actively being developed under Katz's leadership. David Tiedeman and his colleagues at Harvard University, funded by the United States Office of Education, developed the most elaborate of the prototype systems, one that is still ahead of its time conceptually in its guidance theory, its utilization of audiovisual materials, and its ability to use natural language instead of multiple-choice options (Tiedeman and others, 1968). From this very elaborate system, however, some members of the team abstracted a subset of functions that became the early form of the Guidance Information System (GIS), very prominent in the field in the 1980s. The author and her team at Willowbrook High School (Illinois), funded by the Illinois State Board of Vocational Education, developed the Computerized Vocational Information System (CVIS), still used in many schools at this writing, and began the development of a line of products called DISCOVER, now owned and supported by the American College Testing Program (ACT).

The question of survival related to at least three significant variables. First, survival depended on the existence of a key person who could provide continuity to the developmental work and maintain a funding base for its completion. Second, survival depended on finding a way to get the product distributed; of the three surviving systems, two were supported by a not-for-profit organization with significant external funding, and one was supported by a for-profit corporation. Third, survival depended on having a system that was "practical" in that it performed functions that counselors perceived as useful and not too time-consuming in the career guidance of students and also in that it did not require more machine and external-device support than the technology of the time could bear.

Development of Information Systems. This early development demanded attention and required that the guidance and related professions seriously consider the role and the capabilities of the computer. The first government agency to take serious note of these developments was the Department of Labor. In 1968 or so, this agency called early developers and other significant professionals together in a forum to discuss the new technology and its capability to deliver timely occupational information to consumers. Hindsight now tells us that the Department of Labor was attempting to set its own course for the future in regard to the method of delivering localized, timely occupational information on a state-by-state basis. Negating the need for or appropriateness of the delivery of a developmental guidance treatment to users of their later-to-be-national system, the Department of Labor and later the National Occupational Information Coordinating Committee (NOICC) funded the state of Oregon in 1969 to produce a prototype information system, the Career Information System (CIS). This model was disseminated to eight other states in 1975 and to an additional fourteen in 1980 (Dunn, 1982). Out of this strain of development and funding came two information systems—the Oregon Career Information System (CIS) and the Coordinated Occupational Information Network (COIN). The Computerized Heuristic Occupational Information and Career Exploration System (CHOICES) was simultaneously funded by the Canadian Employment and Immigration Agency. In some states the localized version of either a guidance or an information system has been given a new name (such as Illinois' HORIZONS instead of CIS or DISCOVER, California's EUREKA instead of CIS, and Maryland's INFORM instead of COIN), and this fact complicates the practitioner's understanding of the similarities and differences among systems.

Predominant characteristics of the information systems have been their lack of theoretical base, their dedication to well-developed occupational and educational information, and the localization of files for a particular state and even for a number of individual regions within a state. Since the primary purpose of these systems has been to manage and deliver timely, accurate information to individuals who are facing decision points, it has not been necessary for them to subscribe to one elaborate theoretical model; information is a basic necessity in all guidance and decision-making models. These systems leave the self-assessment and didactic functions of guidance to other delivery modes; they confine the use of the computer to searching and retrieval tasks. Localization of occupational and educational files is important, and it has been possible because these systems have been funded and operated by a centralized consortium of agencies.

Current Status of Computer-Based Systems

Types of Systems. The distinction between guidance and information systems still exists. The difference between the two is less sharp than it once was, however; and systems should be viewed in terms of their position on a continuum between guidance emphasis and information emphasis. The prototypal *guidance* system can be defined as one that places emphasis on the assessment of self-variables and the teaching of a decision-making process. In addition to these central foci, the computer is also used to search files, identify options with characteristics desired by the user, and provide detailed information about those options. The prototypal *information* system can be defined as one that places primary emphasis on the searching of .files, usually by variables that are external to the user and inherent in the work tasks.

In contrasting these types of systems, professionals may want to understand the meaning of these definitions in more detail. The guidance systems share at least three characteristics. First, there are on-line assessment instruments that help the user to become aware of relevant self-variables and to organize them in a way that allows a "translation" to occupational choices. One of the major guidance systems, SIGI, places primary emphasis on the awareness and rank ordering of values as a basis for identification of occupations. The other major guidance system, DISCOVER, places emphasis on the assessment of interests, the self-rating of abilities, and the inventorying of values. Each of these, separately and together, is used to identify occupational alternatives. A second common characteristic is the focus on teaching a planful decision-making process that the user may apply to vocational and other choices throughout life. The teaching of the process may be either explicit or implicit. Third, the guidance-emphasis systems also provide searches through files of occupations, but these searches focus on variables about the person rather than variables about the work tasks of the occupation. Searches and files are also provided about financial aid, colleges, graduate schools, technical and specialized schools, and military programs.

Likewise, the information-emphasis systems share some common characteristics. First and foremost, emphasis is placed on file searches and information. There is wide variation across systems in the number and range of files offered, the number and flexibility of the search strategies, and the amount of information provided about occupations or schools. Second, there is very high interest in the development of accurate, timely, and often localized occupational information and the use of the computer as a mode of delivering it to deciders. Third, there is an absence of didactic material (such as instruction about the decision-making process or the organization of the world of work) and of on-line assessment.

In the early 1980s there are four dominant information-emphasis systems—Guidance Information System (GIS), Career Information System (CIS), Computerized Heuristic Occupational Information and Career Exploration System (CHOICES), and Coordinated Occupational Information Network (COIN).

Because the guidance systems perform more functions—that is, the typical search strategies and information files plus additional self-assessment and didactic material—they perform more of the steps that are commonly considered parts of a systematic career guidance process. Although they are not designed to be stand-alone systems and research indicates that they are more effective when used in conjunction with counselor support, they require less counselor support than the information systems. The inclusion of assessment, didactic material, and information files drives these systems beyond the small floppy disks so common in the educational market to larger-size floppy disks or "hard" disks—a fact that may make the guidance system more expensive because of the hardware required to run it.

Microcomputer Technology. The eighties bring the low-cost ($2,000–10,000) microcomputer to the forefront. Many statewide systems are still functioning on mainframes, both minicomputers and maxicomputers. Many large school districts are also operating on mainframes because that is what they already had, and administrators, school boards, and computer screening committees are still trying to enforce centralization of data-processing functions wherever such mainframe machines are already owned by the school district or institution. There is, however, a definite and significant move toward breaking apart the empire of data-processing directors and departments and toward placing many microcomputers in an organization for individuals to use. These may be dedicated to one operation, such as career guidance or information, or they may be dedicated to several at different time periods, including word processing, budget planning, and instruction. New microcomputers with rapidly increasing power and storage capability and decreasing cost become available monthly. It is extremely difficult for developers in the field to keep up with the technology and to maintain myriad versions of software to run on a wide variety of machines in an attempt to meet customer needs. Development is done with full knowledge that the problems of today will be solved by the technology of tomorrow and that there will never be a "finished" product, only one that is in a constant state of improvement and technical evolution.

This decentralization of computer services has both benefits and problems for the developer of computer-based systems and for the counselor. For the developer, decentralization means a whole new arena of marketing. In the past, expensive software could be delivered directly to data-processing personnel who had full knowledge of the technical requirements for implementation and ongoing operation of the software. A short telephone conversation or specification sheet would communicate easily; installation, maintenance, updating, and problem solving could be done with one central agency and directly with expert data-processing personnel.

The new microcomputer technology, with its attendant decentralization of computer services, makes it necessary for developers and marketers to communicate directly with guidance personnel who are not only untrained in technology but, in many cases, wary or fearful of it. Much time and, therefore, money are spent in providing basic computer literacy to the guidance practitioner and in teaching good practices of installation and maintenance of computer software. Yet, in spite of this need to teach first before selling and to do so with many instead of few, software must be kept at an attractive, low price. This is true because of severe budget constraints in the present educational market and because the microcomputer currently serves only one user at a time. This rapid movement toward decentralization of computer resources makes it mandatory that guidance personnel have a strong program of preservice or in-service training to equip them with basic computer literacy to cope with the future.

A second very important trend of the early 1980s is the entry of videodisk technology into the educational and guidance arena. With this technology more than 100,000 frames of visual material can be placed on one disk and randomly accessed by a laser beam under microcomputer control. At this time the technology is expensive and not fully developed. The up-front cost of developing high-quality material for the videodisk is very high, and updating of this material is expensive. Further, some microcomputers can be adapted to control a videodisk and others cannot. There are very few videodisk players in schools and colleges, so that it may be necessary to market a videodisk player in order to sell a disk. Further, at this time there are so few videodisks ready for the educational market that the school, agency, or institution has a difficult time justifying the cost of the player in light of the amount of material that can be used on it. Just as in the microcomputer field, however, the videodisk field is moving technologically forward at a very fast pace—with a concomitant dramatic lowering of prices on players, disks, and mastering. The industry has settled in on one of the two existing technologies, that of the laser beam. Again, it is a difficult period for both developers and consumers. It appears that developers will not be able to recover the high development costs in the near future because of the very limited market and the high cost of updating. And consumers, even if they have the money to purchase players and disks, are confused about which player to buy. Until the industry settles in, equipment could quickly become obsolete. For all these reasons, videodisk development has begun at a very controlled pace.

Use. The use of computer technology for the delivery of guidance and information to students is on a steady increase in the United States. The study done by the Educational Testing Service (Chapman and Katz, 1981) for the National Occupational Information Coordinating Committee (NOICC) indicated that 24 percent of the high schools in the United States have either a guidance or an information system installed to assist with the career guidance program. This percentage is increasing rapidly, owing to the acquisition of microcomputers by schools and universities. In addition to the growth of such systems in schools, there has also been an increase in the number of systems in other locations. Large corporations are leasing or contracting for systems designed to assist their employees with career development within the organization. Libraries and private counseling agencies are offering programs of systematic career guidance utilizing the computer, since that technology is now within cost-feasible reach of such operations. The Army contracted for the development of AREIS, the Army Education Information System, a microcomputer-based system for soldier use.

Quality of Use. In addition to an increasing quantity of computer-based systems in education, there has been a steady increase in quality of the use of systems, although this has not been without its growth pains. In the late sixties, when development of the systems began, there was considerable counselor resistance to the entry of the computer into career guidance. This resistance appeared to be a combination of reticence to allow a cold machine to do those things that empathic, understanding counselors had been doing and some fear of the technology itself and what it might mean to positions and reassignment of work tasks. Over these fifteen years, these fears and the reticence of acceptance have largely disappeared.

One of the most difficult facets of the entry of the computer as a significant tool to assist with career guidance has been learning how to *incorporate* it into a systematic program. In many sites the computer is seen as responsible for career guidance, leaving the counselor free to do other things. This avoidance may result from lack of interest in the career guidance aspect of counselors' work, and indeed, the computer may be welcomed to do that which many counselors find unrewarding or distasteful. It may be due to the lack of comfort that counselors feel with technology. In Holland's terms (Holland, 1973), *S* (Social), the counselor's code, is all the way across the hexagon from *R* (Realistic), the code of a person who feels comfortable with machines. Or, said another way, in Prediger's terms (Prediger, 1981), counselor (working with people) is all the way across the world of work from computer technician (working with things). Or, third, the lack of integration into a systematic program may be due to the counselor's real difficulty, and even aversion for some, with planning and delivering a systematic program, as opposed to responding to the daily pressing need of students in a nonprogrammatic way.

Some progress, though still not enough, has been made in helping counselors learn how to design programs and how to provide them to students through a combination of a variety of modes of delivery, including the computer. There is still intense need for additions and modifications to in-service and preservice counselor education programs that will build competencies for counselors in the areas of general and specific computer literacy, the design of counselor/machine delivery systems, and preferred modes of treatment for different populations. Especially with the advent of the microcomputer, it is essential that counselors acquire sufficient basic computer literacy to understand core, file storage, floppy disks and their varying capacities, hard disks, and basic computer care.

Cost. The cost of the delivery of career guidance and information to students by computer continues to decline as computers and all their related gear provide more capability for fewer dollars. Using the cost figures for one of the more sophisticated microcomputer and software packages, students can be served at a cost of $2–3 per hour, writing off the entire cost of the hardware over a three-year period. Some systems requiring less sophisticated hardware and offering less content can approach the $1–2-per-hour figure. Simultaneously, the mean cost of providing an hour of one-to-one service with a counselor is approximately $15. This is certainly not to say that the computer is providing the same service as the counselor might; however, it is safe to assume that the counselor will not have to spend time doing the kinds of searches, information look-ups, and administration of assessment instruments that computers do.

Selling schools on the cost-effectiveness of computer-based systems, however, is very difficult. None of the professionals who are marketing such systems feels ethically comfortable with trying to sell administrators the notion that if a computer system is added, counselors can be replaced. If, therefore, the product cannot be sold on its replacement value, it must be sold on its enhancement value. In other words, the only ethical way to market a computer-based system is to "tell it like it is." Students will receive more assistance with career planning if a computer system is also there to help, because the counselor's time is insufficient to provide all the needed functions in an individualized manner to students on a one-to-one or even small-group basis.

Selling on the basis of improved service rather than cost replacement is always difficult. Further, although counselors may be highly committed to acquiring and effectively using a computer-based system, they do not have the decision-making authority to appropriate funds of that magnitude. For that reason the first cycle of selling must be done with administrators who control the purse strings. The turnaround time from the beginning of an effort to sell a computer-based system and the date of delivery of the system may well be as long as two years.

Effectiveness. It is not a primary purpose of this chapter to review research studies; rather, the emphasis is on practice and the application of research findings to it. For that reason this section will focus on what the counselor's expectation of computer-based systems should be, based on the findings of the researchers of many different computer-based systems over the past fifteen years. In a sense the counselor might use the lists that follow as a rationale to administration for acquisition of a system and as a set of expected benefits to the career guidance program. First, let us address the benefits that will accrue to students:

1. Students will be highly motivated to engage in career planning and guidance because of the high motivational appeal of the computer and its associated technologies. Several studies have indicated that students prefer to acquire information from the computer over books, files, microfiche, and even people resources.

2. Using the computer-based system for some sustained

period of time will effect a statistically significant increase in certain factors of vocational maturity, such as awareness of need to plan and knowledge and use of appropriate informational resources.

3. Use of a computer-based system will stimulate students to pursue a variety of exploratory activities after leaving the computer terminals. These activities will include using the career library, writing away for more information, talking to counselors, and talking with parents and other significant adults.

4. Use of a computer-based system will cause more traffic to the counselor's office, not less. Students will come to counselors, however, with a much higher level of specificity of questions and will seek assistance well beyond information.

5. Use of the computer, especially a guidance system, will cause the student to say that he or she knows much more about self in the areas the system deals with—that is, values, interests, and/or abilities.

6. Use of the computer-based system will cause students to have a better cognitive understanding of the way the world of work is organized and of occupational duties, training requirements, employment outlook, and so on for the occupations researched at the computer terminal.

7. Use of the computer-based system will cause students to experience a greater degree of specificity of career plans. In other words, students will move in a positive direction on the continuum from "no idea which occupation to consider" to "a very specific occupational choice."

Happily, there will also be benefits for counselors when a computer-based system is added to the career guidance program. Counselors can have the following expectations:

1. Students who use the computer-based system will come to counseling interviews or group sessions much better prepared to deal with the questions at hand. Having already passed the stages of information collection and file searching, they will be ready to ask the counselor for assistance in narrowing choices, making educational plans related to them, or seek-

ing additional input from the counselor. These facts indicate that counselors can have a more productive use of one-to-one or small-group time with students and that the duties performed during that time will be more professional.

2. The computer will provide a wealth of easily accessible and timely information, which the counselor can tap as needed for work with students on a one-to-one or group basis.

3. The counselor's time and effectiveness can be doubled or tripled because part of the work load is being carried by the computer. This means that some students who otherwise would not have received any help at all with career planning will receive at least that which is available by computer. Other students whom the counselor has time to see one-to-one, in small groups, or in career planning classes will make greater progress by far because of the combined treatment than the counselor could have expected to facilitate alone.

4. Career guidance and counseling will take on the level of importance in the student's mind that it richly deserves, because of the student's positive response to the upbeat use of technology. Use of computer-based systems will create an attitudinal awareness of the need to plan on which the counselor can capitalize.

Administrators will also enjoy some benefits from the use of computer technology in the delivery of career guidance services. First, since career planning is of the utmost priority for both parents and students, the administrator will be seen as providing a service to students which is much valued by the taxpaying community and which that community often says is not being adequately provided in other ways. Second, use of the computer for any purpose adds to the general computer literacy of students. Both parents and students know that computer literacy is as basic a skill for the future as are reading, writing, and arithmetic. Obviously, this is a side benefit, but one often mentioned by parents. Third, at the college/university level a strong career guidance and placement program, aided by the computer, will assist with both recruitment and retention in years when attracting a sufficient number of students is critical.

Future Trends

A pioneer like me has been predicting the future of computer-based systems for a long time. Although the trend of my past predictions has been borne out, the rapidity with which I expected computerization of guidance services has not materialized in the past. Now it appears that the conditions are right to accelerate the use of the computer in career guidance and information much faster than at any time during the fifteen years of existence of this field—and this in spite of the budget problems that so many school districts and educational institutions are suffering. What are the conditions that now make predictions about a faster rate of adoptions more believable?

Cost and Capability of Microcomputers. The impact of the microcomputer combined with robotics will be as great as or greater than the impact of the industrial revolution. The cost of hardware continues to decrease while the capabilities of the hardware and its file storage devices continue to increase. Within the first half of this decade all schools will own microcomputers, and within the second half many if not most homes will have a personal computer. The microcomputer will move rapidly from a single-user device with limited storage to a multi-user, multifunction device with ample storage. Computers will suffer obsolescence within a two- to three-year period.

Increased Competition. The much broader availability of microcomputers will cause an increase in the number of profit and not-for-profit organizations that engage in career guidance and information software development. Counselors will have more products from which to choose. Competition among available products will increase, and counselors and other decision makers will need to be even better informed about the products' differences and similarities as a basis for choice. The combination of competition, high cost of marketing, high cost of producing software for an ever-changing technology, and fewer dollars in the educational marketplace will place a severe burden on developers. Some systems will fail because of these conditions. Those with sufficient financial backing will be in a continuous process of new development in order to keep up with the rapidly moving technology and to have a marketing advantage over the competition.

Entry of the Videodisk. Videodisk technology is just beginning to be used in education. Its adoption may be slow-paced because of the high cost of development of material, the high cost of updating, the confusion about which vendors will survive, and the paucity of material available for use on videodisk players. However, because of the major investments risked by videodisk development companies, the technology may survive and continue the current pattern of rapidly decreasing costs. If the technology survives, it is a natural for guidance purposes because of its capability to add audiovisual materials to occupational and college exploration, job-seeking skills acquisition, and assessment.

New Settings. In addition to an increase in the number of microcomputers and software packages available, computer-based career guidance services will appear in a variety of new settings—including libraries, community learning centers, private counseling practices, places of work, and military posts.

For example, as the need to attend to the developmental needs of a growing adult population continues to mount, there will be a definite movement for the provision of services to this large population by for-profit companies and not-for-profit libraries and educational institutions. One of the methods selected by both the for-profit and not-for-profit sectors will be delivery of systematic services by microcomputer, perhaps enhanced by the videodisk. Adult learning centers, which will provide a variety of opportunities for learning as well as for career guidance and development, will become common. Some of these will be found in public libraries, some in university and community college continuing education centers, some in private counseling agencies, and still more in franchised "chains." Adults may engage in learning and career development either by using computer equipment in these locations or by checking out software that can be taken home for use.

The home, therefore, will become another new setting for computer-based career guidance. Such guidance will be available through the purchase, lease, or "checkout" of software for use on a home computer. The entry of the IBM Corporation into the home market will help to effect a change of the home computer emphasis from gaming to learning. Career guidance will also reach the home via the home TV set, which will be linked to a computer network service offering a very large variety of options—from ordering the groceries to midlife career changing.

The workplace will be a third significant new setting. With the release of DISCOVER for Organizations in the early 1980s by the American College Testing Program, the first microcomputer-based product to assist employees with career development became available. As human resource development becomes an even more significant thrust of the eighties, large organizations will provide career development service to their employees in a one-to-one computer interactive mode rather than by hiring career development staff. Company time will be allocated for the use of such systems.

Finally, military posts and recruiting offices will become a fourth significant new setting. During the late 1970s and the early 1980s, the branches of the military spent large sums of money for the development of computerized recruitment systems, officer career development systems, and enlisted personnel planning systems. These systems, now out of field-test mode, will be broadly disseminated and will take on much of the information-giving function that recruiting officers and military counselors had.

Placing systems in these new settings will challenge our professional ethics and roles. What changes will take place in the role of counselors in schools and other settings? Will clients have more help than at present because of the availability of systems in the home, or will they somehow be ill served because of the lack of counselor support systems? Will "stand alone" packages cause concern in counselor camps about loss of positions and job duties, as in the early days of development of computer-based systems?

Content. Accompanying all these changes will be changes —principally expansions—in the capabilities, functions, and content of the systems of the future. There will be a move back toward the theory-based career guidance systems because the technology is there to provide very comprehensive treatment without undue expense. There will be better assessment instruments on-line, some of them in adaptive mode in which one can receive immediate and personalized interpretation and feedback. Administration of a wide variety of assessment instruments by microcomputer, perhaps with videodisk interface, will be common. Those who take tests on paper will commonly receive their scores back on floppy disks for use on the home, school, or community microcomputer.

There will be an increased capability for the interfacing of data files so that they become much more powerful to assist the decider. For example, a good student personnel system will be capable of integrating information from a longitudinal data base of grades and test scores, with new information generated by the student on-line for predicting success in a variety of occupations and educational institutions. States may be able to communicate with one another for the purpose of job placement or to sample the employment outlook for a given occupation in a different geographical location.

Content changes will also include the application of computer technology to new populations and for new purposes. The new populations can be inferred from the new settings that have been mentioned. These populations will be adult learners, employees, homemakers, elementary-school-age children, senior citizens, military personnel, and the handicapped. The last group has been particularly neglected in relation to its career development needs because of the high cost of software development relative to the size of the market population.

But let's daydream some of the new content. As systems move to a more pronounced guidance emphasis, there will be a great expansion of the concepts presented in them. Work will be presented as only one role in a rainbow (Super, 1980) of life roles that make up career. The computer will be used to help individuals to plan for all those life roles and to attain satisfaction through a combination of them. This concept will help with the planning for the increased amount of leisure time that many persons in the society will have.

With the increased capability of the computer and an ac-

companying videodisk, the technology will be able to provide
some of the futuristic ideas developed by Tiedeman and others
(1968) and Super (U.S. Office of Education, 1969) in the very
early stages of development of the field. Tiedeman's proposition
that the computer can be a prosthetic device to teach and support a decision-making process that is later internalized by the
individual can be made to come true. Super and Impelleteri's
(U.S. Office of Education, 1969) dream that the computer can
control audiovisual devices that provide sufficient reality testing of an occupation to forward choice will come true with the
linkage of videodisks to microcomputers. Tiedeman's dream
that the use of a computer can place the locus of control within
the individual will come true as the settings and content change
and as systems are available for use alone in the home and in
adult learning centers.

Improved Effectiveness. All these changes will result in
increased effectiveness of computer-based systems. The combination of more comprehensive content, improved technical delivery, and videodisk enhancement will make the computer an
even more powerful tool for the delivery of career guidance
services than it has been in the past. When such systems are used
in settings where there are counselors, these professionals will
make better use of them because the profession will have given
careful attention to adequate pre- and in-service training. Counselors will be operating from a variety of models of combined
modes of delivery, including the computer plus one-to-one
counseling, the computer plus group or curriculum, and the
computer plus other self-help materials. Considerably more will
be known about learning styles and about the receptivity of different clients to treatment by different modes. Counselors will
be more sophisticated about prescribing a combination of treatment that best fits the learning style of the client. Further,
much more will be known about vocational maturity and about
readiness for career and guidance information. The computer
will be prescribed for students who are at a stage of vocational
maturity to best profit from its use.

Even in settings where the computer provides service
without the counselor, that assistance will be more effective

than it currently is. This will be true because of the expanded assessment content, the alternative routes in the program for individuals of differing levels of vocational maturity, and the audiovisual support of the videodisk. The profession will take an active role in setting ethical guidelines for the development of such systems and in informing users of their opportunities for counselor follow-up and support.

Role Change. How will the computer, then, change the role of the counselor in the future? Clearly, in the future counselors will have to involve themselves less in the provision of career guidance and information. It will be unnecessary for counselors to administer or interpret the typical interest inventories used in career guidance. Ideally, the same will be true of aptitude batteries as more of these are administered in an adaptive mode by computers or more credence is given to the self-rating of abilities or skills by the student. Searching for educational or occupational options in any way other than by computer will become obsolete, as will the provision of information about these in printed form. The computer, combined with the videodisk, will also reduce the need for field trips and other real-life experiences, since the first stages of reality testing can be done through the audiovisual and interactive capabilities of the disk. These facts will leave the counselor with much higher-level tasks with those students who need them—helping students acquire deeper self-understanding as this relates to vocational choice, helping students narrow options by finding bases for comparison and weighting of alternatives, and helping students apply planful decision-making skills. Since the computer alone will adequately meet the needs of a majority of students for career guidance purposes, the counselor should have an increase in time for counseling in a variety of other areas related to personal/social development.

Summary

This chapter has reviewed the use of computers for individual career guidance from the late 1960s to the present. This review covered the characteristics of the early developments, the types of systems that evolved, trends of the present decade, and expected benefits of using computer technology. The chapter ended by delineating expected future trends related to hardware, competition, new technologies, new settings, content of systems, effectiveness, and counselor role change.

Suggested Readings

Johnson, C. (Ed.). *Microcomputers and the School Counselor.* Alexandria, Va.: American School Counselor Association, 1983.

     A collection of eight chapters about the history, selection, management, projected future, and ethical concerns of computer-based career guidance and information systems.

Katz, M. R., and Shatkin, L. *Computer-Assisted Guidance: Concepts and Practices.* Princeton, N.J.: Educational Testing Service, 1980.

     A review of the state of the art of computer-assisted guidance and information systems and their implementation in schools.

Maze, M., and Cummings, R. *How to Select a Computer-Assisted Career Guidance System.* Madison: Wisconsin Vocational Studies Center, University of Wisconsin, 1982.

     A collection of chapters that provide an introduction to the career planning process, to computer-assisted guidance, and to criteria for comparing computer-assisted career guidance systems. In addition, detailed analysis is made of each of four major systems—CIS, GIS, DISCOVER, and SIGI.

Shatkin, L. *Computer-Assisted Guidance: Description of Systems.* Princeton, N.J.: Educational Testing Service, 1980.

     Detailed descriptions of all systems available, including functions, data file, conceptual framework, and hardware compatibility.

Super, D. E. (Ed.). *Computer-Assisted Counseling.* New York: Teachers College, Columbia University, 1970.

A collection of chapters by the early developers of computer-based guidance systems describing their work. Provides a valuable historical perspective.

References

Chapman, W., and Katz, M. *Survey of Career Information Systems in Secondary Schools: Final Report of Study 1.* Princeton, N.J.: Educational Testing Service, 1981.

Dunn, W. *Status of Statewide Career Information Delivery Systems.* Federal Project Report. Washington, D.C.: National Occupational Information Coordinating Committee, 1982.

Holland, J. L. *Making Vocational Choices.* Englewood Cliffs, N.J.: Prentice-Hall, 1973.

Prediger, D. J. "A World-of-Work Map for Career Exploration." *Vocational Guidance Quarterly,* 1981, *30,* 21-36.

Super, D. E. "A Life-Span, Life-Space Approach to Career Development." *Journal of Vocational Behavior,* 1980, *16,* 282-298.

Tiedeman, D. V., and others. *Information System for Vocational Decision Making: Annual Report.* Cambridge, Mass.: Graduate School of Education, Harvard University, 1968.

U.S. Office of Education. *Computer Based Vocational Guidance Systems.* Washington, D.C.: U.S. Department of Health, Education and Welfare, 1969.

14

Johnnie H. Miles

❧ ❧ ❧ ❧ ❧ ❧ ❧ ❧

Serving the Career Guidance Needs of the Economically Disadvantaged

The economically disadvantaged as a group received a great deal of attention in the 1960s and early 1970s. They were the popular focus of formal and informal conversations for professionals and laypersons alike and were included on the agendas for meetings of most major agencies, institutions, and organizations concerned with the well-being of the poor. They were studied and written about and were the direct or indirect beneficiaries of much of the federal legislation generated during that period. The level of attention has declined into the 1980s, resulting in severe cutbacks in appropriations or the elimination of legislation designed to help the poor (Morganthau and others, 1982).

The radical decline of interest does not suggest that the disadvantaged are no longer in need. It does, however, reflect a change in the social, economic, and political climate of our times. The change is evident in the retrenchment behavior of public and private agencies and affects every segment of the population. Already in the least favorable position in our society, the disadvantaged appear to be hurt the most by this trend.

In 1982 alone, billions of dollars were cut from the federal budget for programs that directly benefit the poor. More than $6 billion was cut from the food stamps, Aid to Families with Dependent Children, and jobs programs, and the school lunch program was cut by 30 percent. Eligibility requirements for participation in welfare programs were made more stringent, causing millions of recipients who needed help to lose coverage (Morganthau and others, 1982).

Even though overall assistance to the disadvantaged is declining, they remain a group identified as having tremendous needs and a difficult time adjusting to them (Perfetti and Bingham, 1983; Miller, 1982). Kessler and Cleary (1980), in their research on social class, looked at undesirable life events that required extensive readjustment and found that lower classes experienced more of these events than middle or upper classes. The disadvantaged also appear more vulnerable and reactive to life stressors, particularly to the impacts of health-related events (Thoits, 1982). Thoits also implied that their vulnerability may be due to joint occurrence of many of the stressful events and few available social support resources to cope with these changes. Although it seemed a reasonable conclusion, it was not confirmed by the research.

In the field of guidance, counselors continue to seek out new and creative ways of responding to the disadvantaged. Their efforts are somewhat hindered by the extreme difficulty in defining the population.

Part of the problem stems from the use of the word *disadvantaged,* for it has become a catch-all for a variety of symptoms and syndromes in our society. It is used to describe racial minorities, individuals with cultural differences, the handicapped, women, the unemployed, the educationally deprived, and the socially alienated, to name a few. All too often these groups are seen as one subpopulation, assumed to have the same needs and characteristics and provided service in the same manner. It would be more beneficial to view each group as distinct with unique needs, although there is a core of exigencies common to all.

For the purpose of this chapter, *disadvantaged* will refer

to the "economically deprived" or the "poor," or simply those lacking the purchasing power to meet their basic needs. Included in large numbers are the chronically disadvantaged, who have existed under deprived conditions over a long period of time, and the new disadvantaged, recently thrown into the ranks by loss of job or some other catastrophe.

Lacking financial resources is far from a simple issue, for it creates a complex system of existence for the disadvantaged. Such a condition predisposes members to limited educational and employment opportunities, generates feelings of worthlessness, powerlessness, and despair, and leaves its victims open to discriminatory practices. As a result, the economically disadvantaged are restricted from full participation in the society as they concentrate their efforts on the daily fight for survival.

Who Are the Disadvantaged?

The economically disadvantaged is a population composed of adults and children with heavy representation from racial minority groups. It is a changing population, owing mainly to the shifts in the American economy. As the economy worsens, more individuals and families are drawn into poverty. According to the 1981 *Current Population Reports* (U.S. Department of Labor, 1981), this population contained approximately 26 million people, or roughly 12 percent of the population. A closer examination of those figures reveals some 17 million whites, 8 million blacks, and 13 million female-headed households as poor. Individuals sixty-five and over made up 15 percent of the poor.

The Chronically Poor. A highly visible group of the economically disadvantaged is the chronically poor. They are individuals born into poverty and nurtured in families and environments that regularly experience a lack of resources to meet basic needs. It was this group that became the focal point of efforts during the 1960s and 1970s. In response to their needs for health care, nutrition, education, and work, many programs sponsored by public and private agencies were developed. Fortunately for some, these programs, their own motivation, and the opening up of opportunities permitted them to break the cycle of poverty.

The Unemployed: The New Disadvantaged. Also among the economically disadvantaged are the unemployed, those individuals who do not have jobs but would like them. A recent report from the Bureau of Labor Statistics (May 1983) indicated that 10.1 percent of the population, or 11.2 million people, were unemployed. It was also estimated that another 1.5 million persons were unemployed but not counted in the statistics because they were discouraged and no longer actively looking for work; 2.1 million working part-time who would like full-time work; and another 1 million in government make-work programs (Thurow, 1982). They are called the hidden unemployed.

The unemployed are persons adversely affected by the downturn in the economy. They have lost jobs because of cutbacks in the work force, closing of various businesses and industries, and the changing job market. Technological advances have stimulated rapid changes in the world of work and are altering the types of jobs people do and the ways they do them. Heavy industries, for example, using large numbers of semiskilled and skilled workers, will continue to decline, and high-tech companies from robotics to bioengineering that require highly developed technical skills are expected to grow (Anderson and others, 1981). More industries are looking toward using machines and robots to supply these new skills. Unemployed workers who do not possess the new skills and those who cannot transfer or apply acquired skills in new ways are finding it difficult to reenter the labor force.

Unlike the chronically disadvantaged, the new disadvantaged (former blue-collar and white-collar workers) are having to develop skills in adapting to being unemployed. For the most part, they are highly educated and skilled and highly motivated. They believed in the American dream and worked hard to make it a reality. They bought the homes, cars, and boats and became accustomed to a comfortable way of life. With the closing of factories, cutbacks in other industries, and general recessionary trends, their jobs disappeared and their dreams were shattered.

Feelings of humiliation, uselessness, and loss of status are relatively new to them.

The dynamics of unemployment are widespread, affecting every aspect of the worker's life. Studies of the impact of unemployment on male workers and their families revealed strong feelings about loss of authority as husband and father, loss of self-respect, feelings of hopelessness, anger, and self-blame for unemployment. Also common were marital problems, increases in drinking, and a withdrawal from social contacts outside the family. Children in these families showed sharp behavior changes as well. They concealed the unemployment situation from friends, reduced their involvement in outside activities, expressed embarrassment about their clothing and homes, and expressed negative self-perceptions (Kamarovsky, 1971; Ackerman, 1978).

Unemployment, short- or long-term, is interpreted as restrictive poverty (Jahoda, 1982, p. 21). It negatively affects physical and psychological health and has been positively related to increases in suicides, admissions to mental facilities, and homicides.

The Underemployed: The Invisible Disadvantaged. A less visible group of disadvantaged is the underemployed, those with some measure of employment but below their productive capability. They are the millions of individuals who work part-time or full-time year-round who do not earn wages sufficient to exceed poverty standards. They are called the working poor and are found mainly in low-wage, marginal jobs that require little, if any, job-specific skill, such as farm laborers, unskilled laborers, and operatives. In addition to the working poor, approximately one sixth of the labor force are considered to be near-poor, earning incomes that place them barely above poverty standards. In a struggling economy, they quickly become part of the poverty population.

Although the numbers alone are appalling, they are only mere reflections of the bigger picture. To be disadvantaged implies that individuals or groups are restricted in competing for goals or opportunities valued in the society (comfortable home, education, job, minimum diet). These goals are intricately linked, and blockage in one area inadvertently leads to unequal opportunity in others; for example, lack of an adequate education leads to employment in low-level jobs, which dictates housing patterns in restricted areas and thus limits the quality of education available to children.

Deprivation or a lack of financial resources affects individuals in ways that extend far beyond work and education. The disadvantaged have less access to medical care, legal counsel, recreation, leisure, travel, and cultural activities. The social and cultural exclusions experienced as a result of deprivations make victims of both adults and children, exact a tremendous burden on individuals and families, and therefore make it necessary to consider separately their experiences within the society.

Why Do the Disadvantaged Remain Poor?

In this society a notion of individualism is prevalent that purports that individuals who want to live well can do so on the basis of hard work and merit. If they succeed, it is due to their efforts, and if they fail, they must not have worked hard enough. This view further contends that individuals who are poor and do not succeed are to blame for their circumstance in life. Many American workers subscribe to this basic philosophy. They feel guilty and blame themselves if they are unsuccessful or unemployed. They further feel depressed and humiliated at receiving assistance, and many will wait until it is an absolute necessity before requesting it (McGrath, Manning, and McCormick, 1983).

Although this individualistic view is widely held, there is little evidence to affirm it. As a matter of fact, existing data suggest that the social system under which we live guarantees poverty for millions of Americans. Edmund Gordon (1974, p. 453) put it succinctly as he wrote: "It is difficult to embark upon a serious discussion of low-economic- and social-status persons without realizing that their position in our society's hierarchy is not accidental. These people are held back, in part, because of the nature of the economic and political structure of our society which has maintained segments of its population at differing levels of reward and participation, both as a function of the competitive traditions and as a device for controlling the demands of wage earners."

The poor do not choose to be deprived. They remain poor in large numbers because access to income through work sufficient to raise them out of poverty is beyond their reach owing to high unemployment, low educational attainment, insufficient job skills, racism, discrimination, and lack of political support.

Breaking the Cycle of Poverty

Although there are no definitive solutions to the cyclical problems of poverty, short of altering the overall health of the economy, there is widespread acceptance that education is crucial to the process. Following that line of reasoning, schools generally are identified and heavily relied on to respond to the challenge of helping the disadvantaged, particularly children and youth. It has been presumed that schools, through guidance and instructional personnel, could mobilize resources to help students who are disadvantaged as well as those from more advantaged backgrounds.

There is one note of concern, however. Schools tend to be microcosms of the larger society and inculcate its major values and views. School systems have been found not only to mirror the views of society but to inadvertently contribute to maintaining them. The disadvantaged in some schools continue to battle against lower expectations and lack of encouragement and reinforcement, and they receive a large proportion of the disciplinary decisions in schools (Morgan, 1980). Moreover, they are disproportionately placed in general and vocational curricula, a fact that in itself limits their career options. Through the use of traditional practices (ability grouping, tracking), the educational process assists in reinforcing the socioeconomic structure of the society.

For schools to assist the disadvantaged in breaking the cycle of poverty, they must withdraw from use of some traditional practices and develop facilitative learning climates that respond to individual needs of students rather than dictates of society. Within these types of climates, guidance and other school personnel can develop practices and programs to assure the disadvantaged a basic education, adequate vocational skills for employment, practical knowledge and understanding about the environment and how it works, and a sense of well-being about themselves within that environment.

Career Guidance Practices

Career guidance is an organized, systematic program to help the individual develop self-understanding, understanding of societal roles, and knowledge about the world of work (Srebalus, Marinelli, and Messing, 1982, p. 255). Though sometimes considered identical to career education or career counseling, career guidance is unique. It generally includes a range of structured learning activities that concentrate on decision making and action planning, and it is available to all. Career education is an effort aimed at refocusing education in ways that will help individuals acquire and use the knowledge, skills, and attitudes to make work meaningful (Sears, 1982). In contrast, career counseling is a one-to-one or small-group interaction between client(s) and a counselor with the goal of helping the client(s) integrate and apply an understanding of self and the environment to make the most appropriate career decisions and adjustment (Sears, 1982, p. 139). Career guidance is designed for use whether or not a problem exists, and, like career education and career counseling, has potential for use with the disadvantaged.

Much has been written about the use of career guidance and various career guidance strategies with the disadvantaged. However, little information exists to conclusively channel efforts in program development or the selection of appropriate techniques. In short, there is a lack of research evidence on what works effectively with the disadvantaged that can guide such efforts. Career guidance practices in general are designed and implemented for the purpose of responding to developmental needs and ultimately to the facilitation of individual career development. These practices help individuals acquire and use information, develop decision-making skills, and learn about themselves, others, and the world of work. For such practices to be relevant, responsive, and effective, they need to be contained in and implemented as part of a systematic, comprehensive guidance program.

A comprehensive guidance program includes all the services a client might need in one setting. It might include information services, career counseling, assessment, consultation, placement, and follow-up. To the extent possible it allows the integration of career information into other activities and functions within the agency. Creating such a program requires systematic planning. The first and most important step is to conduct a needs assessment to identify which groups need the program and to determine what their needs are and why. Having access to data on needs helps to ensure that practices will be relevant and to avoid a trial-and-error mode each time a practice is used.

Planning should be an integral component of any program unit regardless of the client group (Herr and Cramer, 1979) but takes on greater importance in work with the disadvantaged. Not only does it permit the development of relevant programs based on clearly specified needs, but it might identify counselors as sensitive to the needs of the disadvantaged and capable of delivering services.

Career Guidance Needs of the Disadvantaged. Career guidance needs are developmentally oriented and emerge out of a natural pattern of maturation. As individuals grow and interact with the environment, their needs unfold, having been influenced by family and cultural background, socioeconomic status, race, sex, and educational achievement.

Several needs have been found to be crucial to career growth: a positive self-concept, awareness and understanding of the world of work (Super, 1957), and decision-making skills (Tiedeman, 1971). Feck (1971), in looking at the needs of urban disadvantaged youth, identified some fifteen basic needs, which included career-related needs. They were (1) security and stability in one's environment, (2) successful educational experience, (3) recognition for achievement, (4) love and respect, (5) legal sources of finance, (6) financial management, (7) proper housing, (8) good health, (9) development of basic communication skills, (10) salable work skills, (11) an appreciation of the meaning and importance of work, (12) successfully employed or adult peer-group models, (13) positive self-concept, (14) job opportunities and qualifications, and (15) socially acceptable attitudes and behaviors.

Recent research indicates that the disadvantaged have those needs but others as well. They need an open system of opportunity (Griffith, 1980), a strong feeling or sense of control (Kelsey, 1983), information on world of work and available resources (Williams and Whitney, 1978), and appropriate education, training, and counseling (Smith, 1980). The new disadvantaged, in addition, appear to need understanding, acceptance, and assistance in realizing that some aspects of their present situations are beyond their control (Shifron, Dye, and Shifron, 1983).

Herr and Cramer (1979) concluded that most people share those same basic needs. However, they indicated that disadvantaged youth are less likely to fulfill those needs, because of environmentally imposed problems. It appears that temporary or prolonged deprivation creates economic, social, and psychological concerns or problems for the disadvantaged that are qualitatively and quantitatively more intense. In essence, the environment intensifies the needs of the disadvantaged. It is therefore crucial for counselors to learn as much as possible about how the lives of the disadvantaged are affected by those forces and to use that knowledge in program development and delivery of services.

The identified needs of the disadvantaged fit well within the broad goals established for a comprehensive career guidance program. According to Sears (1982, p. 139),

> Career guidance includes those activities and programs that assist individuals to assimilate and integrate knowledge, experience, and appreciations related to:
>
> 1. Self-understanding, which includes a person's relationship to his/her own characteristics and perceptions and his/her relationship to others and the environment.

2. Understanding of the work of society and those factors that affect its constant change, including worker attitudes and discipline.
3. Awareness of the part leisure time may play in a person's life.
4. Understanding of the necessity for and the multitude of factors to be considered in career planning.
5. Understanding of the information and skills necessary to achieve self-fulfillment in work and leisure.
6. Learning and applying the career decision-making process.

Well-developed programs that respond to the goals just stated would have direct applicability to the needs of the disadvantaged. Consequently, counselors may balance and integrate services for the disadvantaged within the total guidance framework. As a matter of fact, Miller and Leonard (1974) indicated that most guidance practices are applicable for use in responding to the needs of the disadvantaged. In highlighting twenty-two guidance practices (career days, group procedures, placement, achievement motivation training, decision-making training, work experience programs, and others), they encouraged practitioners to try out and evaluate the practices as the needs of their clientele suggest.

Miller and Leonard (1974) went one step further and suggested that the environment contains many barriers that prohibit positive development for the disadvantaged. They stated, "It may well be that traditional guidance goals and approaches will have little impact on the lives of disadvantaged clients unless the counselor is also willing to exert a strong influence on the environment. The role of the guidance staff when working with the disadvantaged should include special activities designed to modify the environment to make it more supportive of the client" (p. 58).

In analyzing the needs of the disadvantaged, it seems clear that career guidance programs need to focus attention on the disadvantaged as individuals and members of a group and on the environment in which they live. Much of the assistance

previously provided and the career guidance strategies used concentrated on change in behavior of the disadvantaged individual
or group, giving little attention to the environment. This chapter will therefore focus primarily on change in the environment
as a means of helping the disadvantaged.

   System Change Strategies. Considering the differential
impact of the environment on the disadvantaged, it is reasonable to contemplate the environment as a target for potential
change (Miller and Leonard, 1974; Atlas, 1975; McDavis, 1978;
Jones and Stewart, 1980). System change approaches are relatively new in the field of counseling but are rapidly gaining acceptance. These approaches are concerned with creating positive
climates for learning and personal development. Thus, the counselor may occasionally need to intervene in existing systems
(classrooms, families, institutions, and so forth) to help reduce
negative barriers for clients.

   Gunnings and Simpkins (1972) described an approach to
system change counseling called the systemic approach. In this
approach, the authors contend that clients' behavior may be
more a function of their response to the environment than of
intrapsychic concerns or conflict and, in fact, may be symptoms
of a system's problem. The approach suggests that the client
and counselor work together to evaluate the environment to
identify the problem, design the strategy for action, and jointly implement that strategy. The counselor, in many instances,
may need to teach the client the skills needed for managing the
system and also may assist in implementation if the client lacks
the influence, power, or skills to affect the system. Using system change strategies that help remove barriers in the environment may help in reducing the feelings of powerlessness and
hopelessness often held by the disadvantaged and also help in
building trust in the counselor (Miller and Oetting, 1977).

   Gunnings and Simpkins' (1972) position on system
change has been supported by other writers (Pine, 1976; Banks
and Martens, 1973; Warnath, 1973). The views are clear on the
necessity of such approaches, and the authors are equally clear
about the need to have a support system from which to operate.

   Atkinson and others (1977) undertook a study to determine whether constituent groups were supportive of such change activities. They found that students, parents, administrators, teachers, and counselors viewed traditional and activist roles (ombudsman and change agent) as appropriate school counselor functions. Teachers, however, were not as supportive of the ombudsman role as counselors and were in agreement with administrators on the change agent role as a less legitimate function than the more traditional roles. The primary result of the study was that counselors who have interests in being change agents need to develop a support system of constituent groups within the school and to recognize that such support may be more readily available from parents and students than from fellow educators.

To perform effectively as change agents, counselors must first be committed to the role. Second, they will need a full understanding of how the system or institution works and functional skills in at least one planned change strategy. Jones and Stewart (1980) described a systems model for change agents that eliminates the guesswork in institutional change. The model contains ten sequential components, beginning with the counselor as change agent and tracking the process through each dynamic phase from diagnosing the organization to monitoring the change in operation. The procedures are presented in a manner descriptive enough for the novice counselor to implement with additional reading.

Counselors are encouraged to develop change strategy skills, especially if such training was not included in their counselor education programs. Reading, participation in in-service activities, and advanced graduate study are recommended avenues to acquiring the skills. In addition, counselors will need to develop professional reputations that attract clients and engender respect and cooperation from colleagues.

Counselors are also being called on to be change agents for the profession. Wrenn (1983) challenged counselors to be as concerned about the profession as they are about their clients. He enjoined them to be less security-oriented and less conservative and to become more risk-taking and active for the benefit of the profession. He indicated that unless counselors take more risks and get involved in actions that promote the profession, they may be as "vulnerable as their economically and psychologically uneasy clients" (p. 323). As counselors become more involved in actions to change the system for the profession, they will, one hopes, gain knowledge and skills that can be used in helping their clients.

One approach to change the system for the benefit of clients is through the use of support groups. Support groups have received increased attention in recent years and are being used more extensively with varying clienteles—for example, older persons (Waters and Epstein, 1980) and adults who were victims of sexual abuse as children (Courtois and Watts, 1982). Such groups are now recommended for use with the unemployed (Shifron, Dye, and Shifron, 1983). Other examples of support groups are those for single adults, parents without partners, families of the terminally ill, and parents of handicapped children; perhaps the most widely known is Alcoholics Anonymous.

Caplan (1974) stated that the concept of support groups/ systems focuses on helping people mobilize their strengths and resources to manage the strains and challenges in their lives. The concept not only is therapy-oriented but also provides the framework for pulling together people whose presence provides support, confirmation, encouragement, and assistance (Pearson, 1983). The effectiveness of support groups/systems results from sharing common experiences/problems, giving and receiving emotional support, and joining together to explore coping strategies. The presence of support systems contributes to positive mental health (Waters and Goodman, 1981), and the absence of support systems has been found to be associated with increased mortality rates (Berkman and Syme, 1979). Support groups are excellent tools for use with the disadvantaged.

Shifron, Dye, and Shifron (1983) indicated that the use of support groups with the unemployed can be highly effective. Although counselors can do little to create jobs to combat unemployment, "counseling and therapeutic efforts should be aimed toward asisting individuals in developing adaptive strategies . . . to help unemployed persons to maintain their physical and psychological wellness" (p. 528). Intervention with the family is one way to approach counseling the unemployed, since the condition affects the entire family system. The authors suggest that getting the family members involved in support groups could help the unemployed adapt in a constructive manner.

Individuals in transition (new disadvantaged) or those in relatively fixed circumstances (chronically disadvantaged) or children from these families may also benefit from support groups. Often the expected sources of support in families and home communities may not be available. Counselors "may help people identify existing supports and learn how to access additional supports" (Waters and Goodman, 1981, p. 356). In schools or other agencies, counselors may help in establishing support groups based on the needs of students.

Summary

Career guidance programs for the disadvantaged need to focus not only on client change but also on system change, especially since the disadvantaged are more likely than their nondisadvantaged counterparts to encounter barriers to their development within the environment. Coupled with basic career guidance programs, system change strategies can assist in creating environments in which the disadvantaged may grow productively.

Suggested Readings

Atkinson, D., Morten, G., and Sue, D. *Counseling American Minorities.* Dubuque, Iowa: William C. Brown, 1983.
    Provides a thorough description of the four major minority groups in America and presents a minority identity development model that has great utility for helping counselors understand the minority client's attitudes and behaviors.

Herr, E., and Cramer, S. *Career Guidance Through the Life Span: Systematic Approaches.* Boston: Little, Brown, 1979.
    The authors set out a compendium of career guidance

techniques for use at the elementary, junior high, senior high, and higher education levels and devote a chapter to career guidance for adults. The extensive listing includes numerous techniques that would be excellent for use with all clients.

Longstreet, W. *Aspects of Ethnicity.* New York: Teachers College Press, 1978.

    The author has devised a format for ongoing research to increase teachers' awareness and knowledge of the ethnically different. Although the profile was designed for teachers, it has tremendous potential for counselor use.

Sue, D. *Counseling the Culturally Different: Theory and Practice.* New York: Wiley, 1981.

    Presents a conceptual framework both for understanding and for providing services to culturally different clients. Considerable attention is focused on how the culture-bound and class-bound values of traditional theoretical approaches act as barriers to effective cross-cultural counseling. The author explores a relatively new area—the political context and its impact on counseling.

References

Ackerman, R. J. *Children of Alcoholics: A Guide for Educators, Therapists, and Their Parents.* Holmes Beach, Fla.: Learning Publications, 1978.

Anderson, H., and others. "Where the Jobs Are—and Aren't." *Newsweek,* November 23, 1981, pp. 88-90.

Atkinson, D., and others. "The Role of the Counselor as a Social Activist: Who Supports It?" *School Counselor,* 1977, *25* (2), 85-91.

Atlas, J. "Consulting: Affecting Change for Minority Students." *Journal of Non-White Concerns,* 1975, *3*(4), 154-160.

Banks, W., and Martens, K. "Counseling: The Reactionary Profession." *Personnel and Guidance Journal,* 1973, *51,* 457-462.

Berkman, L., and Syme, S. "Social Networks, Host Resistance, and Mortality: A Nine-Year Follow-up Study of Alameda County Residents." *American Journal of Epidemiology,* 1979, *109,* 186-204.

Caplan, G. *Support Systems and Community Mental Health.* New York: Behavioral Publications, 1974.

Courtois, C., and Watts, D. "Counseling Adult Women Who Experienced Incest in Childhood or Adolescence." *Personnel and Guidance Journal,* 1982, *60,* 275-279.

Feck, V. *What Vocational Education Teachers and Counselors Should Know About Urban Disadvantaged Youth.* Center for Vocational Technical Education, Information Series, No. 46. Washington, D.C.: U.S. Government Printing Office, 1971.

Gordon, E. "Vocational Guidance: Disadvantaged and Minority Populations." In E. Herr (Ed.), *Vocational Guidance and Human Development.* Boston: Houghton Mifflin, 1974.

Griffith, A. "Justification for a Black Career Development." *Counselor Education and Supervision,* 1980, *19*(4), 301-310.

Gunnings, T., and Simpkins, G. "A Systematic Approach to Counseling Disadvantaged Youth." *Journal of Non-White Concerns,* 1972, *1,* 4-8.

Herr, E., and Cramer, S. *Career Guidance Through the Life Span: Systematic Approaches.* Boston: Little, Brown, 1979.

Jahoda, M. *Employment and Unemployment.* Cambridge: Cambridge University Press, 1982.

Jones, M. D., and Stewart, N. R. "Helping the Environment Help the Client: A Sequenced Change Process." *Personnel and Guidance Journal,* 1980, *59,* 501-506.

Kamarovsky, M. *The Unemployed Man and His Family.* New York: Octagon Books, 1971.

Kelsey, E. F. "The Relationship of Locus of Control to Career Decision Making Styles of Black Adolescents." Unpublished doctoral dissertation, Virginia Polytechnic Institute and State University, 1983.

Kessler, R. C., and Cleary, P. D. "Social Class and Psychological Distress." *American Sociological Review,* 1980, *45,* 463-478.

McDavis, R. "Counseling Black Clients Effectively: The Eclectic Approach." *Journal of Non-White Concerns,* 1978, 7(1), 41-47.

McGrath, P., Manning, R., and McCormick, J. "Left Out." *News-week,* March 21, 1983, pp. 26-35.

Miller, C. D., and Oetting, E. "Barriers to Employment and the Disadvantaged." *Personnel and Guidance Journal,* 1977, *56* (2), 89-93.

Miller, J. "Lifelong Career Development for Disadvantaged Youth and Adults." *Vocational Guidance Quarterly,* 1982, *30*(4), 359-366.

Miller, J., and Benjamin, L. "New Career Development Strategies: Methods and Resources." *Personnel and Guidance Journal,* 1975, *53*(9), 694-699.

Miller, J., and Leonard, G. *Career Guidance Practices for Disadvantaged Youth.* Washington, D.C.: National Vocational Guidance Association, 1974.

Morgan, H. "How Schools Fail Black Children." *Social Policy,* 1980, *10*(4), 49-54.

Morganthau, T., and others. "Reagan's Polarized America." *Newsweek,* April 5, 1982, pp. 16-19.

Pearson, R. "Support Groups: A Conceptualization." *Personnel and Guidance Journal,* 1983, *61*(6), 361-364.

Perfetti, L., and Bingham, W. "Unemployment and Self-Esteem in Metal Refinery Workers." *Vocational Guidance Quarterly,* 1983, *31*(3), 195-202.

Pine, G. "Troubled Times for School Counseling." *Focus on Guidance,* 1976, *8*(5), 1-16.

Sears, S. "A Definition of Career Guidance Terms: A National Vocational Guidance Association Perspective." *Vocational Guidance Quarterly,* 1982, *31*(2), 137-143.

Shifron, R., Dye, A., and Shifron, G. "Implications for Counseling the Unemployed in a Recessionary Economy." *Personnel and Guidance Journal,* 1983, *61*(9), 527-529.

Smith, E. "Career Development of Minorities in Nontraditional Fields." *Journal of Non-White Concerns,* 1980, *8,* 141-156.

Srebalus, D., Marinelli, R., and Messing, J. *Career Development Concepts and Procedures.* Monterey, Calif.: Brooks/Cole, 1982.

Super, D. *The Psychology of Careers.* New York: Harper & Row, 1957.

Thoits, P. A. "Life Stress, Social Support, and Psychological Vulnerability: Epidemiological Considerations." *Journal of Community Psychology*, 1982, *10*(4), 341–362.

Thurow, L. "The Cost of Unemployment." *Newsweek*, October 4, 1982, p. 70.

Tiedeman, D. "The Agony of Choice: Guidance for Career Decisions." In R. Pucinski and S. Hirsch, *The Courage to Change*. Englewood Cliffs, N.J.: Prentice-Hall, 1971.

U.S. Department of Labor. *Current Population Reports*. Washington, D.C.: U.S. Government Printing Office, 1981.

Warnath, C. "The School Counselor as an Institutional Change Agent." *School Counselor*, 1973, *20*, 202–208.

Waters, E., and Epstein, L. "No Person Is an Island: The Importance of Support Systems in Working with Older People." *Counseling and Values*, 1980, *24*, 184–194.

Waters, E., and Goodman, J. "I Get By with a Little Help from My Friends: The Importance of Support Systems." *Vocational Guidance Quarterly*, 1981, *29*(4), 362–369.

Williams, J., and Whitney, D. "Vocational Interests of Minority Disadvantaged Students: Are They Different?" *National Association of Student Personnel Administrators Journal*, 1978, *15*(4), 20–26.

Wrenn, C. G. "The Fighting, Risk-Taking Counselor." *Personnel and Guidance Journal*, 1983, *61*(6), 323–326.

Kenneth R. Thomas
Norman L. Berven

15

Providing Career Counseling for Individuals with Handicapping Conditions

A mistake frequently made by counselors and laypeople alike is to think of individuals with handicapping conditions as belonging to one largely undifferentiated group variously known as the "handicapped" or the "disabled." In fact, the range and diversity of individuals with handicapping conditions are quite extensive. According to Wright (1980), the total number of persons having one or more disabilities may be as high as 20 percent of the American adult population, the most prevalent disabilities being musculoskeletal conditions (for example, arthritis, spinal cord injury, amputation, and back injuries); cardiovascular disorders; respiratory conditions; psychotic, psychoneurotic, and behavioral disorders (including alcohol and other drug abuse); mental retardation; vision, hearing, and speech impairments; digestive disorders; and neurological conditions (for example, epilepsy, multiple sclerosis, and cerebral palsy). Great diversity exists among individuals affected by these different handicapping conditions. Further, great diversity exists among those affected by the very same condition (see research reviews provided by Shontz, 1971, 1975; Wright, 1983). Referring to people as "the handicapped" or "the mentally retarded" obscures this diversity and contributes to debilitating stereotypes.

A related problem is the tendency to emphasize the differences rather than the similarities between individuals with and without handicapping conditions. Although it is true that the personal, social, and vocational behavior of individuals with a handicap can be severely affected by their disability, it is an unfortunate consequence of society's response to misfortune that these people are often treated as deviants, not only by their families and acquaintances but also by the agencies and professionals they turn to for assistance. Actually, individuals with handicapping conditions are far more similar to than different from other persons seeking career counseling. They may, however, have some unique problems and needs that require specialized services. It is, therefore, incumbent on the counselor who works with them to be cognizant of the special problems that may occur and the special services and techniques available.

The purpose of this chapter is to provide (1) a description of current theories that have been developed to conceptualize the work adjustment and career development of individuals with handicapping conditions, (2) an overview of the major career counseling delivery systems available for such persons, (3) information on the special career counseling techniques used, and (4) an analysis of the effects of technological, professional, and legislative developments on future career counseling practices.

Current Theories

The most extensive effort to conceptualize the vocational behavior of individuals with handicapping conditions was conducted by Lofquist and his associates at the University of Minnesota (although there have been significant other such efforts—for example, Hershenson, 1974; Osipow, 1976). Over a period of several years, under the auspices of the "Minnesota Studies in Vocational Rehabilitation—Work Adjustment Project," Lofquist and others formulated and tested what is commonly called the

Minnesota theory of work adjustment (Lofquist and Dawis, 1969, 1972).

Essentially, the Minnesota theory of work adjustment is based on the trait-factor concept of correspondence between the individual and the work environment. That is, *"correspondence can be described in terms of the individual fulfilling the requirements of the work environment, and the work environment fulfilling the requirements of the individual"* (Dawis, Lofquist, and Weiss, 1968, p. 3). The process by which the individual seeks to achieve and maintain correspondence is called "work adjustment," and the stability of this correspondence is referred to as "tenure in the job." Two other important concepts are "satisfaction" and "satisfactoriness." Satisfaction refers to the extent to which the work environment (reinforcer systems provided) fulfills the requirements of the individual (his or her needs). Satisfactoriness concerns the extent to which the individual (his or her abilities) fulfills the requirements of the work environment (its ability requirements). Taken together, these two concepts indicate the correspondence between the individual and the work environment and can be used to predict job tenure. The Minnesota theory has generally served as a major theoretical basis for assessment and occupational choice in the provision of career counseling services to persons with handicapping conditions.

McMahon's (1979) model of vocational redevelopment also offers potential as a paradigm for understanding the career development and work adjustment of persons with handicapping conditions. This model was specifically developed to explain and predict the vocational redevelopment of midcareer physically disabled persons. Basically, it hypothesizes that work adjustment is the "goodness of fit" between commensurate sets of worker dimensions and job dimensions. The worker dimensions are needs and competencies, and the job dimensions are job reinforcers and job demands. McMahon proposes that, by using these constructs, one can mathematically derive both objective and subjective estimates of worker/job fit, the worker's understanding of the realities of the job, and the worker's level of self-assessment. In addition, he contends that the event of midcareer physical disability is important (in vocational redevelopment) only to the degree that it alters the needs or competencies of the worker or the reinforcers or demands of the job. The worker's degree of worker/job fit before becoming disabled is also considered a primary factor in predicting vocational redevelopment. Despite the lack of empirical support, McMahon's model of vocational redevelopment provides a useful strategy for assessing and ameliorating the career development problems of midcareer physically disabled individuals. In fact, the model also seems applicable to individuals with mental or precareer disabilities.

Although virtually all the major career development and occupational choice theories (discussed elsewhere in this volume) will facilitate understanding the vocational behavior of individuals with handicapping conditions, the major theorists have seldom considered the impact of disability. The one exception is Super (1957, pp. 271–275), who briefly discussed the nature of disability, its effects, and vocational guidance considerations in *The Psychology of Careers*. Generally, however, the generic theories present certain practical and theoretical limitations (Conte, 1983; Schlenoff, 1975) when applied to individuals with a disability or vocational handicap.

Primary Career Counseling Delivery Systems

Professionals from a variety of counseling and human service disciplines may offer career counseling services to individuals with handicapping conditions. However, rehabilitation counseling is the profession most closely identified with the provision of such services. Rehabilitation counselors are trained to understand the medical and psychosocial aspects of various disabilities and their impact on career development and potential. They are also skilled in providing the full range of specialized career counseling services that may be required. About 25,000 rehabilitation counselors are involved in providing career counseling and related services to individuals with handicaps in the United States through an extensive network of interrelated service delivery systems.

The variety of social institutions that offer career counseling to individuals with a handicapping condition is quite extensive. Among those agencies and facilities whose services are specifically designed for handicapped people are the state vocational rehabilitation agencies, Goodwill Industries of America, and the Jewish Vocational Service. In addition, handicapped persons, as members of society at large, have access to traditional career counseling resources such as the public schools and state job-service offices. A recent and potentially significant delivery system is the proprietary rehabilitation company, which is retained mainly by insurance companies to serve worker's compensation cases.

Educational Institutions. The role of educational institutions, especially primary and secondary schools, in providing career counseling and preparation for handicapped individuals is often underestimated. However, the school, much like the family, creates a social climate that not only influences occupational choices and expectancies but also provides critical academic, vocational, and social skills. Moreover, the public school's involvement in providing career counseling services and experiences for handicapped students has expanded in recent years owing to the passage of the 1975 Education for All Handicapped Children Act (P.L. 94-142). This legislation mandates that the states provide education for all handicapped children between the ages of three and twenty-one. It was followed by the passage of P.L. 94-482, the Education Amendments of 1976, which directs that a specified percentage of vocational education monies be set aside for handicapped, disadvantaged, and certain other special-needs populations.

In the case of cognitively and/or behaviorally disabled adolescents, the responsibility for providing career awareness and exploration in the schools often falls almost exclusively on the special education teacher, who includes vocationally relevant content in the curriculum and works cooperatively with local industries and businesses to establish job sites as part of a work experience program. Brolin and Kokaska (1979) recommended that, during high school, occupational guidance and preparation form at least half the curriculum for most handicapped students. However, even current patterns of service recommend closer cooperation among the special education teacher, the vocational education teacher, and the school counselor, plus the addition or easy access of a rehabilitation counselor to the public school's staff.

Vocational/technical schools, colleges, and universities may also play an important role in the career development of handicapped individuals. All three types of institutions have made significant architectural and programmatic changes in recent years to accommodate handicapped students. Some of these changes resulted from the mandates of Section 504 of the Rehabilitation Act of 1973 (P.L. 93-112), which prohibit the exclusion of handicapped individuals from programs and activities at institutions receiving federal monies. Others are the result of Public Law 94-482, which has served as a catalyst for improving vocational education services for both handicapped youth and adults. However, it should be observed that many institutions of higher learning have traditionally worked closely with the state divisions of vocational rehabilitation in providing vocational training (education) and student services for handicapped individuals. Vocational/technical schools and community colleges have been especially attractive training sites for handicapped persons because of their proximity and the variety, types, and levels of program options. Virtually all types of colleges and universities are presently attempting to eliminate barriers and provide services that will facilitate successful program completion by handicapped students.

Public Agencies. The state/federal vocational rehabilitation program, with its large network of state vocational rehabilitation agencies, is clearly the largest career counseling delivery system developed specifically for handicapped people. Created as the result of the 1920 Civilian Rehabilitation Act, the program enables eligible handicapped adults to receive a variety of coordinated services designed to help them become gainfully employed. Initially the program focused only on persons with a physical handicap, but it now provides services to persons with any type of handicap.

The range of services offered by the state agencies is quite broad. For example, funding can be provided for physical restoration, psychological evaluation, vocational evaluation, work adjustment training, vocational training, and job placement. The rehabilitation counselor is the key professional person in this system. The counselor determines eligibility, provides career counseling, develops an individualized written rehabilitation program (IWRP), facilitates job placement, and generally coordinates the client's program from acceptance to closure (after sixty days of successful employment).

Overall, the performance of the state/federal rehabilitation program has been impressive. Literally millions of handicapped persons served through the system have been placed in employment, and cost/benefit ratios reported for the program have generally been favorable (see, for example, Parker and Thomas, 1980). The program is not without its limitations, however. For example, the system itself, especially because of time and funding restrictions, appears to promote adherence to a limited range of counseling approaches, and it tends to lack responsiveness to clients with chronic or erratic physical, developmental, or behavioral problems. For additional information on the history, structure, and operation of the state/federal vocational rehabilitation program, see Wright (1980) and Rubin and Roessler (1983).

Another highly visible government agency that provides career counseling to individuals with handicapping conditions is the Veterans Administration. Evolving in 1933 from the old Veterans Bureau, the Veterans Administration has been authorized over the years to provide a wide range of medical, educational, and vocational benefits and services to disabled veterans through a network of regional offices and hospitals. In addition, it provides support to a variety of private agencies that offer career counseling services to veterans, including those with disabilities.

Rehabilitation Facilities. Although there are others, the primary types of rehabilitation facilities whose programs include career counseling for individuals with handicapping conditions are rehabilitation workshops, comprehensive rehabilitation centers, and psychosocial rehabilitation programs. The Commission on the Accreditation of Rehabilitation Facilities (CARF) sets standards for such facilities in twelve program (service) areas.

The rehabilitation (sheltered and/or transitional) workshop is a type of facility found in several hundred American communities. Some of these facilities are administered under the auspices of Goodwill Industries of America, the National Association of Jewish Vocational Services, the National Easter Seal Society, or other national organizations, but many others have only local administrative structures. Although the range and quality of services offered vary considerably, these facilities typically provide vocational evaluation and counseling, work and personal adjustment training, vocational training, sheltered and transitional employment, job readiness training, and job placement services to both moderately and severely handicapped individuals. Usually, clients participating in the programs are being simultaneously served and funded by state and local government agencies such as the state division of vocational rehabilitation and local developmental disabilities, mental health, and social service agencies. In recent years, the clientele of rehabilitation workshops has consisted mostly of persons with cognitive, emotional, or behavioral (for example, alcoholism) problems; however, persons with physical handicaps are also served.

Because the rehabilitation workshop must play both a production and human service role to survive economically, it offers a unique opportunity to evaluate and train clients under real and simulated working conditions. For example, a client's productivity rates and general work habits can be closely monitored, and the work environment itself can be altered to promote more satisfactory work and personal adjustment. In addition, individuals are able to learn more about their own interests and abilities by participating in the different types of work activities that the workshop provides.

A major limitation of the rehabilitation workshop as a career counseling delivery system is that, in American society, workshops carry a negative social stigma and act to segregate individuals with handicaps from other workers. Moreover, the types of work activities provided in the workshop are often lim-

ited to routine assembly, packaging, and service tasks. As rehabilitation workshops continue to expand their efforts to
establish arrangements with industry that would involve evaluation and training at the industrial site itself, both these limitations may be neutralized somewhat. Currently, however, such
facilities present special problems when working with the
higher-functioning client (Neff, 1977). An excellent source of
information on the history and development of the rehabilitation workshop in American society is Nelson (1971).

The comprehensive rehabilitation center is another type
of rehabilitation facility that offers career counseling services to
individuals with handicapping conditions. A distinctive feature
of the comprehensive rehabilitation center is that it offers a
wide range of medical, psychological, physical, social, educational, and vocational services under one roof. The service delivery system is either multidisciplinary or interdisciplinary and involves such professionals as psychologists, rehabilitation counselors, occupational therapists, psychiatrists, physical therapists,
rehabilitation trade instructors, speech and hearing therapists,
rehabilitation nurses, recreational therapists, orthotists, and
physiatrists.

Depending on the nature and quality of its staff and on
the focus and range of its services, the comprehensive rehabilitation center can provide a truly remarkable milieu in which to
implement career counseling services. Not only can counselors
utilize the diagnostic and treatment services offered by other
professionals, but they can also use "job tryouts" in a wide
range of training areas to complement traditional vocational assessment techniques. In addition, special services and facilities,
such as libraries and computerized information systems, can provide clients with "state-of-the-art" occupational information resources. Although the comprehensive rehabilitation center has
the disadvantage of being located far from the client's home
community and family and tends to promote the selection of
career options that are congruent with the training programs offered at the center itself, it is an excellent delivery system for
clients who require a full range of rehabilitation services as they
prepare for competitive employment.

Another type of rehabilitation facility that can provide

career counseling services is the psychosocial rehabilitation program, often modeled after Fountain House in New York City,
serving individuals with chronic psychotic disorders. These facilities may provide residential (halfway houses, group homes,
supervised apartments, or other specialized living arrangements),
recreational, day treatment, and community support services, as
well as vocational programming. Such programs have made community treatment available for many individuals who are so severely handicapped that, only a few years ago, they would have
been institutionalized indefinitely. Psychosocial rehabilitation
programs may provide any of the wide range of career counseling services found in other types of rehabilitation facilities.

Proprietary Rehabilitation Companies. The most recent
career counseling delivery system that focuses on individuals
with handicapping conditions is the proprietary, or private, rehabilitation company. Although it is not known exactly how
many of these companies exist, a nationwide survey of members
of the National Association of Rehabilitation Professionals in
the Private Sector (NARPPS) indicated that 206 of the 268
individual and institutional NARPPS members represented
5,285 staff members employed in 1,245 offices (Matkin, 1982).
Rehabilitation companies range in size from large, nationwide
corporations such as International Rehabilitation Associates and
Crawford Rehabilitation Services, Inc., to small one- or two-
person operations.

The clients served by proprietary companies are individuals who have incurred an injury or disease that affects ability
to work and is covered by worker's compensation, disability, or
another type of insurance. Services provided are of two types.
One type is a full range of career counseling services to assist the
individual in identifying an appropriate career goal, preparing
for the career, and attaining a suitable adjustment on the job.
The services are generally funded by the insurance company,
which may benefit a great deal financially if the individual can
successfully return to work. In contrast to other service delivery
systems, which seek to *maximize* career potential, proprietary
rehabilitation companies typically seek only to return an injured worker to the *preinjury level* of employment. This philos-

ophy is consistent with the purpose of worker's compensation insurance coverage and results in less frequent use of long-term vocational training and more rapid job placement.

The second major type of service is consultation and expert-witness testimony regarding the impact of disability on career and earning potential, in order to establish equitable financial settlements in worker's compensation or personal injury cases. Similar expert opinions are often required in determining eligibility for Social Security Disability Insurance and Supplemental Security Income benefits. Proprietary rehabilitation companies have been among the fastest-growing career counseling delivery systems, and there is every reason to believe that this growth will continue.

Other Agencies and Programs. A wide variety of other agencies and programs participate in the delivery of career counseling services to individuals with handicapping conditions. Virtually any hospital, institution, or community-based program serving individuals with handicapping conditions may provide career counseling services as a part of its programming. Examples include hospital departments of rehabilitative medicine, cancer centers, psychiatric institutions, independent living centers for individuals with severe physical disabilities, community-based mental health and developmental disabilities programs, and alcohol and other drug abuse programs. An increasing number of programs are including rehabilitation counselors on staff in order to provide career counseling and related services. In general, specialized career counseling systems have grown and become increasingly diverse in recent years, resulting in the availability of services to a much wider range of individuals with handicapping conditions.

The Practice of Career Counseling

Individuals with handicaps may have extensive and complex career counseling needs. Consequently, a diverse array of services, sometimes extending over long periods, may be required to assess needs, establish career goals, and devise career counseling plans.

Assessment. Assessment in the career counseling process has two primary objectives: establishment of a career goal and specification of strategies and services required to achieve the goal. Accordingly, assessment involves developing an information base about the individual, developing an information base about alternative occupations and corresponding work environments, and making predictions about likely functioning in those occupations and environments. Relevant assessment information would include physical capacities, psychological functioning, social skills, appearance, aptitudes, academic and vocational skills, interests, needs, work habits, financial resources, the influences of family and friends, and a wide range of other characteristics that might influence work adjustment.

When career counseling needs are less complex, a sufficient information base can sometimes be developed through interviews, supplemented by limited psychological testing and reports from other agencies and professionals who have worked with the client. For many individuals additional assessment may be required, including more extensive interviewing and evaluations by medical specialists, psychologists, and other professionals. Sometimes an intensive vocational assessment may also be required, which involves full-time assessment activity for a period of days or weeks and includes traditional psychological testing and the observation of work performance in controlled work environments. In general, this sequence of assessment procedures continues until the individual's assets, limitations, and preferences are well enough defined to specify a career goal and the strategies and services required to achieve the goal.

A variety of assessment tools are commonly used in career counseling for individuals with handicaps (Neff, 1977; Vocational Evaluation and Work Adjustment Association, 1975). One general category of tools is *psychometric or psychological tests,* characterized by the typical paper-and-pencil and apparatus tests used with other populations to evaluate intelligence, achievement, aptitudes, dexterity, interests, and personality. Psychometric devices are widely used in assessment of individuals with handicaps; however, the presence of functional limitations associated with handicapping conditions can pose serious problems in adhering to standardized procedures and can also affect the meaning of test scores in other ways (see Berven, 1980). Consequently, other types of assessment tools may also be required, many of them developed within rehabilitation settings because of the limitations of psychometric devices.

The other most commonly used tools make use of different types of work situations, either simulated or real, as assessment tools. One category is *work samples,* which use simulations of *work activities* performed in actual jobs or clusters of jobs. Individuals are observed performing the simulated work activities under standardized conditions, inferences are made about abilities and skills, and potential interests are explored. Work samples are often developed locally, representing occupations that are prevalent in the local labor market. In addition, a number of commercially available systems are widely used, such as the Philadelphia Jewish Employment and Vocational Service (JEVS) Work Sample System, the Singer Vocational Evaluation System, and the Valpar Component Work Sample Series.

Another category of tools is *situational assessment,* which provides simulations of *entire work environments* within rehabilitation facilities. The demands of typical work environments are simulated, and performance can be observed. Generally, production subcontracts are used, often light assembly and packaging, and individuals are paid wages on the basis of their piecerate production. In contrast to work samples, which focus on ability and skill in performing individual job tasks, the focus of situational assessment is on general work behaviors, such as quality and speed of production, attention to task, attendance and punctuality, response to supervision, and coworker relations. Consequently, situational assessment can help determine job readiness or employability in general and can help identify deficiencies in work behaviors that may require intervention.

A final category is *job tryouts,* or on-the-job evaluations, in which the individual is placed in an actual job for a limited time. Job tryouts will usually provide the most definitive information by which to predict work adjustment in a particular occupation, both satisfactoriness and satisfaction.

Intervention and Services. Counseling, vocational training, and job placement are three general categories of intervention strategies and services that are used to meet the career counseling needs of individuals with handicaps. Many of the specific strategies and services are the same as or similar to those used with other clients. However, there are also a number of other strategies that have been developed within rehabilitation programs to meet the special needs of individuals with handicaps.

Counseling strategies provide primary intervention techniques throughout the career counseling process. Since career counseling is conceived of as a process with the joint participation of the counselor and the individual with a handicap, regular face-to-face contact typically occurs. Counseling strategies are used to facilitate decision making about career goals and career counseling plans. Other counseling strategies are directed at problems and barriers to the achievement of career goals. For example, counseling strategies can be used to develop social skills, to deal with a lack of family support, or to build self-confidence. Where services are provided by other agencies or professionals, counseling strategies can be used to help the individual utilize those services effectively. For example, individuals may require assistance in mobilizing themselves to begin a new vocational training program or to follow through with some other aspect of the career counseling plan. Counseling is also important in the continuing assessment of problems and needs that emerge in implementing a plan. For example, during participation in a training program, study skills deficits or interpersonal problems with an instructor may emerge; such problems must be identified and dealt with when they arise.

Individual counseling strategies are frequently used in career counseling for individuals with handicaps. Group counseling strategies have not been as fully utilized, but their use appears to be growing. A number of structured group counseling programs developed for individuals with handicaps have been reported in the literature, including Personal Achievement Skills (Roessler, Milligan, and Ohlson, 1976) and Structured Experiential Training (Lasky, Dell Orto, and Marinelli, 1977). Current practice in both individual and group counseling tends to draw from a number of theoretical approaches, with no single approach predominant.

Vocational training is used to develop the knowledge, skills, and behaviors required to achieve the career goal. The same resources for vocational training that are used by other individuals are often used by persons with handicaps. These resources include colleges and universities, adult education, vocational/technical schools, business and trade schools, and apprenticeship programs. In addition, a number of more specialized training resources are often required.

One specialized type of program is *work adjustment training,* which focuses on the development of general work behaviors and skills, such as hygiene and grooming, attendance and punctuality, interpersonal behavior on the job, quality and quantity of work, or other skills and behaviors required for success in almost any type of employment. In addition, such training can assist individuals in building confidence in their ability to succeed vocationally and in developing concepts of themselves as productive workers.

Work adjustment training typically occurs in a rehabilitation facility where a competitive work environment is simulated. Individuals perform real work, often under industrial subcontracts, and are paid on a piece-rate basis. To the extent that the environment effectively simulates a competitive work environment, individuals can become aware of the social roles and other behaviors expected in such settings. Various aspects of the work environment can be modified to determine effects on behavior, to build tolerance for the demands of competitive employment, and to promote necessary changes in behavior.

Another specialized training strategy is *transitional employment,* pioneered at Fountain House in New York City. It was originally developed for use with persons having chronic psychiatric disorders (Beard, Schmidt, and Smith, 1963) and has since been adapted for persons having other disabilities that pose special work adjustment problems. It involves the use of jobs in the competitive labor market, secured by the agency, which are used as training sites. The jobs are typically unskilled, semiskilled, or lower-level clerical or service positions, for which employers often have difficulty finding and retaining reliable workers. The agency assumes responsibility for the position and ensures that someone will be present at all scheduled times to perform job duties in an acceptable manner. Agency personnel train and supervise the individuals who fill the positions, have back-ups available if someone is unable or fails to attend work, or, if necessary, temporarily fill the position with an agency staff member. Individuals are paid the prevailing entry-level wage for the position.

Transitional employment can be used to develop appropriate work habits and behaviors, as in work adjustment training, and to help people build confidence in themselves as capable workers. For some persons transitional employment is used as an alternative to work adjustment training in a rehabilitation facility. For others it provides an intermediate step between the rehabilitation facility and competitive employment. A rehabilitation agency may have a number of transitional employment sites available in a variety of positions and work settings. Some of the transitional sites will provide placements for several persons in one location; others involve only a single placement in one location. Individuals may use more than one site, progressing from group to individual sites with increasing demands as skills, behaviors, and confidence improve.

On-the-job training is similar to transitional employment in its use of community job sites. However, rather than focusing on general work habits, behaviors, and adjustment, it focuses on the knowledge and skills specific to a particular occupation. For some individuals on-the-job training provides an alternative to business, trade, or vocational/technical schools or other formal training programs. When no formal training program is available, on-the-job training may provide the only choice. A progressive wage scale may be established consistent with increasing productivity over the course of training. Some agencies participate financially in reimbursing the trainer/employer for the costs of training, which may allow for the prevailing wage to be paid to the individual. There may also be an agreement between the employer and agency that the individual will be hired as a regular employee, assuming satisfactory performance at the conclusion of training. Such an arrangement can be particularly beneficial for a person who is capable of learning a particular job but requires a long time to do so, as the sponsoring agency can reimburse the employer for additional costs and limited productivity during the initial period of employment.

Job Placement. Job placement involves acquiring employment consistent with the individual's career goal and achieving a successful adjustment on the job. Job placement involves not only *employability,* the likelihood of achieving a successful adjustment on the job in a particular occupation, but also *placeability,* the likelihood of actually obtaining employment in the occupation (Gellman and others, 1957). Very often the knowledge, skills, and personal characteristics influencing placeability are quite different from those influencing employability. Further, individuals with handicapping conditions may experience some unique placeability problems.

An important consideration in placeability is the attitudes of employers toward individuals with handicaps, which influence their willingness to hire. Research suggests that, overtly, employers tend to express positive attitudes toward people with handicaps; however, the frequency with which they actually hire such people is often much lower than would be predicted on the basis of their expressed attitudes (Schroeder, 1978). Employers, as is true of people in general, will often overestimate the impact of a disability on job performance and underestimate the capabilities of a person who is handicapped.

The most common employer concern is the higher costs assumed to be associated with hiring an individual with a handicap (Corthell and Boone, 1982). These perceived added costs include reduced productivity, increased absenteeism, higher turnover, greater risk of accidents and injury, higher rates for worker's compensation and health insurance coverage, and the need for expensive physical modifications of the work site. However, research has shown that these concerns are usually unfounded and that the hiring of individuals with handicapping conditions may even result in *reduced* personnel costs (for example, see Wolf, 1973-74).

Legislation and tax incentives have been used to encourage the hiring of individuals with handicaps. The Rehabilitation Act of 1973 (P.L. 93-112) requires that affirmative action policies be followed in the hiring of individuals with handicaps by federal agencies, public and private organizations receiving federal financial assistance or grants, and all employers who have contracts with the federal government in excess of $2,500, as well as subcontractors. As an example of tax incentives, the Federal Revenue Act of 1978 created the Targeted Jobs Tax Credit Program, which provides tax credits toward the partial wages of people with disabilities who are hired, as well as other target groups. As another example, the Tax Reform Act of 1976 provided for tax deductions to compensate employers for removing architectural and transportation barriers to employment of individuals with disabilities. Various state and local government units have also implemented affirmative action, civil rights, and tax incentive provisions to promote the employment of people with handicaps. Such legislation and incentives have helped a great deal in expanding employment opportunities for individuals with handicapping conditions.

Characteristics of the individual can also result in barriers to placement. Knowledge and skill in identifying job openings and marketing oneself to employers are important aspects of placeability, as are grooming, appearance, and interpersonal skills. In addition, fear can be a significant barrier to seeking employment, and frustration and discouragement can become barriers to continuing a job hunt in the face of rejection. Financial disincentives are also sometimes associated with employment. The loss of benefits from public assistance, Social Security, worker's compensation, or other types of insurance is sometimes greater than the financial returns from employment, and employment is often perceived as a less secure source of income. Such considerations can be critical to the success of placement efforts and to whether job seeking is even begun.

Two general classes of techniques are used in job placement with individuals with handicapping conditions: (1) instruction in job-seeking skills and the facilitation of independent job seeking by the individual and (2) job development on the part of the career counseling professional in locating job leads and actively marketing the individual to employers. Either class of techniques, or both, may be indicated for a particular client.

There are a number of program models and curricula for *instruction in job-seeking skills,* such as the widely used Minneapolis Rehabilitation Center (1971) job-seeking curriculum. These programs focus on such topics as identifying sources of job leads, making inquiries about job openings, identifying and describing vocational assets, answering difficult questions about disabilities and personal or employment problems, completing job applications, and handling job interviews. Instruction may be provided individually or in groups, extending from one to two days, followed by regular contact to provide ongoing support, structure, and resolution of job-seeking problems. Research has shown that such job-seeking programs can improve rates of job acquisition (for example, see McClure, 1972).

A widely used extension of job-seeking-skills programs is the *job club* (Azrin and Besalel, 1980). The job club provides group instruction in job-seeking skills, along with continuing group sessions and the use of a "buddy system." Job seeking is conceptualized as a full-time activity, and the group meets as often as daily until placements are achieved. The group sessions and buddy system provide structure and supervision of job-seeking activities, mutual support, and the sharing of job leads and other resources, such as transportation. Research has shown that the job-club method may be substantially more effective in serving individuals with disabilities than job-seeking instruction alone (Azrin and Phillip, 1979).

Some individuals have such severe deficits in placeability and/or employability that the prospects of successful placement through independent job seeking are extremely limited. For such persons an active *job development* approach may be indicated. Deficits in placeability may be due to the severity of disability, limitations in work experience, a poor work history, difficulty in assertively responding to employer concerns, or a variety of other factors that might lead a potential employer to conclude that an individual is a poor employment risk. However, the career counseling professional may be able to intervene on behalf of the individual, respond to employer concerns, and achieve a successful placement. Marketing approaches used in business have been applied to job development, including market analyses to identify the needs of consumers (employers) and promoting the product (the person seeking employment) through advertising, sales, and personal follow-up techniques (Corthell and Boone, 1982). One innovative marketing technique in job development is the *employer account system* (Molinaro, 1977). A wide range of services is offered as a package to major employers in the community, the career counseling professional serving as "account manager." One of the services offered is a pool of prescreened candidates for employment, along with follow-up services to assist those hired in making a successful adjustment on the job. Other services may include consultation on worker's compensation, affirmative action compliance, certain tax incentive programs (for example, the Targeted Jobs Tax Credit Program), and information, referral, and counseling of "troubled employees." A successful employer account system results in a mutually beneficial relationship between a rehabilitation agency and an employer, resulting in job opportunities for individuals served by the agency.

It is sometimes necessary to modify or restructure existing jobs in order to accommodate the severe employability deficits that can be associated with disability. *Job modification* involves changes in job tasks, such as raising or lowering equipment or the use of fixtures, jigs, communication aids, or other assistive devices to make job tasks consistent with an individual's physical or mental capacities; it may also involve modifications of the work environment, such as the removal of architectural barriers, so that the individual is able to move about the workplace. *Job restructuring* is the creation of new part-time or full-time positions by rearranging the tasks performed in a group of jobs through combining, eliminating, redistributing, adding, or isolating individual tasks (Mallik, 1979). Although limitations associated with disability might have kept an individual from performing any of the original jobs *in toto,* one or more of the new positions created through job restructuring become consistent with the individual's capacities. Job modification and job restructuring are both based on job analysis and often require the assistance of industrial or rehabilitation engineers; although such procedures are sometimes costly, many applications are inexpensive. Job modification may require nothing more than a resequencing of job tasks or the use of a simple, homemade jig. A common example of job restructuring is job sharing, which might accommodate the needs of a person who does not have the physical endurance to work full-time. A leader in the area of job modification and restructuring is the Job Development Laboratory at George Washington University (Mallik, 1979).

After placement has been achieved, *follow-up* is often required to facilitate adjustment on the job (Dunn, 1979). Beginning a new job can be a stressful experience, requiring adaptation to the job itself, to the social milieu of the workplace, and to problems that occur off the job in fulfilling outside responsibilities and maintaining interpersonal relationships. Continued monitoring of the individual and the work situation is typically required until a satisfactory adjustment has been attained. Intervention may be required with the individual and perhaps with supervisors and coworkers as well. Identification and use of models in the workplace can be helpful in understanding and conforming to the behavioral expectations of the work environment, and the use of a buddy system can promote social integration into the work force. Group counseling can be provided for individuals who have recently begun employment to provide assistance and support. In addition, where serious adjustment problems are anticipated, an agency sometimes provides job coaches to work alongside an individual in order to provide in tensive supervision, structuring, and encouragement.

Employment Options. Whenever possible, employment in the competitive labor market is the goal of career counseling services. Doeringer and Piore (1971) have distinguished two sectors of the competitive labor market: the *primary* labor market, comprising more "desirable" jobs in terms of wages, fringe benefits, opportunities for advancement, security, working conditions, and equitable, nonarbitrary supervision, and the *second-*

ary labor market, comprising jobs that have few "desirable" characteristics but do provide more tolerant work environments in terms of the skills, productivity, work habits, and behaviors required of workers. Some individuals who are unable to meet the employability demands of jobs in the primary labor market can be successfully placed in the secondary labor market.

For persons with such severe deficits in employability that competitive employment is not feasible, other employment options may be rquired (Vash, 1980). One option is *fully integrated employment* but with some significant accommodations, such as waivers of examinations and other employee selection procedures, reduced productivity demands with corresponding reductions in wages, greater flexibility in scheduling of work hours, or continued intervention of a job coach. Another option is *semi-integrated employment,* such as the Business Enterprise Program, established by the Randolph-Sheppard Act of 1936, through which persons who are blind operate vending stands in public buildings. Other examples are work crews of individuals with disabilities, who perform janitorial, groundskeeping, or other types of work, and group placements, in which several individuals perform work in a competitive business or industrial setting that would ordinarily be performed by one or more regular employees. Another commonly used option is *segregated employment,* exemplified by sheltered workshops, where all or most of those employed have disabilities or other special needs and where considerable accommodation is possible. Although most segregated employment settings are sponsored by government or private nonprofit organizations, there are also successful profit-making ventures of this type, including some that are owned and operated by people with disabilities (see Vash, 1980). A final option is *homebound employment,* including telephone solicitation, mail order sales, and the manufacture of clothing, toys, or other goods in the home, which are then sold on consignment in a "homecraft" store. Computer and communication technology are opening a wide range of home-based employment opportunities in the primary competitive labor market, not only for individuals with handicaps but for others as well.

Future Perspectives

Legislative accomplishments during the 1970s have had a dramatic impact on the practice of career counseling for individuals with handicapping conditions. As a result of federal legislation, career counseling services have been offered to a wider range of people with more severe handicaps. Although it is unlikely that the next several years will see legislative developments as revolutionary as the Rehabilitation Act of 1973 or the Education for All Handicapped Children Act of 1975, how these laws and subsequent amendments are interpreted by the courts will continue to have far-reaching implications. The extent to which all handicapped individuals will be fully served will depend on the increased availability of funding to implement these legislative provisions, which will, in turn, depend on the general state of the economy and governmental budgeting priorities. The increasing inclusion of mandatory rehabilitation in the worker's compensation legislation of the individual states has expanded the provision of career counseling services to industrially injured workers. The documentation of positive cost/benefit outcomes of mandatory rehabilitation is expected to result in a continuation of this trend and a continued concurrent growth in the proprietary rehabilitation service system.

Legislative initiatives have also resulted in expanded employment opportunities, both through affirmative action requirements and through financial incentives to employers to hire persons with handicaps. Federal affirmative action provisions have been controversial but have remained in force, and similar provisions have been increasingly enacted at state and local levels. Such initiatives should continue to expand employment opportunities in future years, but negative stereotypes held by employers and society in general will continue to pose significant barriers to the full integration of individuals with handicaps into the work force. Moreover, the success in implementing progressive concepts such as normalization (Flynn and Nitsch, 1980) and mainstreaming (Stephens, Blackhurst, and Magliocca, 1982) will depend on the expansion and improvement of current delivery systems and support networks.

Technological advances also have the potential to dramatically expand career opportunities for individuals with handicaps in future years. The recent development of several technological support systems for visually, orthopedically, and hearing-impaired persons has laid the foundation for the invention of even more portable and effective assistive devices (for example, see Pati, Adkins, and Morrison, 1981; Resnick, 1980; Vanderheiden and Grilley, 1976). Such innovation will allow individuals with handicaps to perform functions that were not previously possible and, consequently, to engage in a wider range of occupational activities. The increasing application of microcomputers to problems associated with disability should have a particularly significant impact in future years, as discussed in recent special issues of two computer journals, *Computer* (Hazan, 1981) and *BYTE* (Dahmke, 1982).

The technology of career counseling practice itself is also likely to improve. Vocational assessment is an area of practice where recent advances have been particularly significant. Of the seventeen commercially available vocational evaluation systems reviewed by Botterbusch (1982), only two were available in 1970. Advances in future years should focus on building documentation of the reliability and validity of these systems for use in career counseling. In addition, the use of actual job sites for vocational evaluation and training purposes should increase. It is also expected that microcomputers will find greater use in career counseling practice. Computer-administered vocational assessment procedures will provide more efficient administration, scoring, and interpretation methods, and increasing use of computerized occupational information systems should make available larger and more up-to-date occupational information banks. Microcomputers will also be increasingly used in vocational and work adjustment training to develop academic and vocational skills (for example, see Crimando and Sawyer, 1983). Such applications should enhance both the effectiveness and the efficiency of career counseling practice for individuals with handicapping conditions. Finally, computer and telecommunication technology will be increasingly applied in the professional education of career counseling professionals, enhancing the development and assessment of professional competence and bringing professional development opportunities to remote sites (Berven and Scofield, 1980; Bruyere, 1982; Bruyere and Vandergoot, 1982; Chan and Questad, 1981). The growth in technology will probably also result in increasing specialization as counselors emphasize particular aspects of career counseling services (for example, assessment or job placement) or concentrate on serving particular client groups, such as emotionally disturbed, mentally retarded, or hearing-impaired persons (Thomas, 1982).

Summary

Although individuals with handicapping conditions share many characteristics with nonhandicapped persons, there may be some differences in their career counseling needs, which require different types of services. A variety of rehabilitation agencies and facilities are available to provide career counseling and job acquisition services to handicapped individuals, the rehabilitation counselor being the primary service provider. Various career assessment, counseling, work adjustment, vocational training, and job placement techniques enable counselors to help handicapped individuals to capitalize on their vocational assets and to lead productive and satisfying work lives. With the advancement of medical, engineering, educational, and counseling technology and the increased social awareness of the special problems and needs that handicapped individuals may have, the prospects for such persons and for society in general should become increasingly brighter.

Suggested Readings

Bolton, B. (Ed.). *Vocational Adjustment of Disabled Persons.* Baltimore: University Park Press, 1982.

The only recent book to focus exclusively on the practice of career counseling for individuals with handicapping conditions. Chapters are included on assessment, career planning, and job placement. Relevant literature is reviewed, and practical strategies and techniques are discussed.

Parker, R. M., and Hansen, C. E. (Eds.). *Rehabilitation Counseling: Foundations—Consumers—Service Delivery*. Boston: Allyn & Bacon, 1980.

This book provides an overview of the field of rehabilitation counseling. It includes eleven chapters, many by well-known contributors, covering such topics as the impact of disability on the individual, the world of work and disabling conditions, and placement and career development in rehabilitation.

Stolov, W. C., and Clowers, M. R. (Eds.). *Handbook of Severe Disability*. Washington, D.C.: Rehabilitation Services Administration, U.S. Department of Education, 1981.

This book discusses the medical, psychosocial, and vocational aspects of a number of specific disabilities. It was intended as a text for course work on medical aspects of disability in graduate rehabilitation counseling curricula and as a reference for practicing rehabilitation counselors. All chapters are written in a standard format, and much valuable information is provided about practical career counseling implications associated with a wide variety of disabilities.

Wright, G. N. *Total Rehabilitation*. Boston: Little, Brown, 1980.

This 830-page text is the most comprehensive and authoritative source available on the history and practice of vocational rehabilitation in the United States. Includes major sections on foundations, resources, assessment, counseling, and placement. Provides up-to-date information on a variety of career counseling techniques and resources for counselors who work with handicapped individuals.

References

Azrin, N. H., and Besalel, V. A. *Job Club Counselor's Manual: A Behavioral Approach to Vocational Counseling*. Baltimore: University Park Press, 1980.

Azrin, N. H., and Phillip, R. A. "The Job Club Method for the Job Handicapped: A Comparative Outcome Study." *Rehabilitation Counseling Bulletin*, 1979, *23*, 144–155.

Beard, J. H., Schmidt, J. R., and Smith, M. M. "The Use of Transitional Employment in the Rehabilitation of the Psychiatric Patient." *Journal of Nervous and Mental Disease,* 1963, *135,* 507-514.

Berven, N. L. "Psychometric Assessment in Rehabilitation." In B. Bolton and D. W. Cook (Eds.), *Rehabilitation Client Assessment.* Baltimore: University Park Press, 1980.

Berven, N. L., and Scofield, M. E. "Evaluation of Clinical Problem-Solving Skills Through Standardized Case-Management Simulations." *Journal of Counseling Psychology,* 1980, *27,* 199-208.

Botterbusch, K. F. *A Comparison of Commercial Vocational Evaluation Systems.* (2nd ed.) Menomonie: Materials Development Center, Stout Vocational Rehabilitation Institute, University of Wisconsin-Stout, 1982.

Brolin, D. E., and Kokaska, C. J. *Career Education for Handicapped Children and Youth.* Columbus, Ohio: Merrill, 1979.

Bruyere, S. M. "The Use of Telecommunications Technology in the Training of Rehabilitation Personnel." *Journal of Rehabilitation,* 1982, *48*(1), 60-64.

Bruyere, S. M., and Vandergoot, D. "Electronic Communication in Rehabilitation: The Future Is Now." *Journal of Rehabilitation,* 1982, *48*(4), 49-53.

Chan, F., and Questad, K. "Microcomputers in Vocational Evaluation: An Application for Staff Training." *Vocational Evaluation and Work Adjustment Bulletin,* 1981, *14,* 153-158.

Conte, L. E. "Vocational Development Theories and the Disabled Person: Oversight or Deliberate Omission?" *Rehabilitation Counseling Bulletin,* 1983, *26,* 316-328.

Corthell, D. W., and Boone, L. *Marketing: An Approach to Placement.* Menomonie: Research and Training Center, Stout Vocational Rehabilitation Institute, University of Wisconsin-Stout, 1982.

Crimando, W., and Sawyer, H. "Microcomputer Applications in Adjustment Services Programming." *Vocational Evaluation and Work Adjustment Bulletin,* 1983, *16,* 7-12, 34.

Dahmke, M. (Ed.). "Computers and the Disabled." *BYTE,* 1982, *7* (Whole No. 9).

Dawis, R. V., Lofquist, L. H., and Weiss, D. J. "A Theory of

Work Adjustment (a Revision)." *Minnesota Studies in Vocational Rehabilitation,* 1968, *23.*

Doeringer, P., and Piore, M. *Internal Labor Markets and Manpower Analysis.* Lexington, Mass.: Heath, 1971.

Dunn, D. J. "What Happens After Placement? Career Enhancement Services in Vocational Rehabilitation." In D. Vandergoot and J. D. Worrall (Eds.), *Placement in Rehabilitation: A Career Development Perspective.* Baltimore: University Park Press, 1979.

Flynn, R. J., and Nitsch, K. E. (Eds.). *Normalization, Social Integration, and Community Services.* Baltimore: University Park Press, 1980.

Gellman, W., and others. *Adjusting People to Work.* Chicago: Jewish Vocational Service, 1957.

Hazan, P. L. (Ed.). "Computing and the Handicapped." *Computer,* 1981, *14* (Whole No. 1).

Hershenson, D. B. "Vocational Guidance and the Handicapped." In E. L. Herr (Ed.), *Vocational Guidance and Human Development.* Boston: Houghton Mifflin, 1974.

Lasky, R. G., Dell Orto, A. E., and Marinelli, R. P. "Structured Experiential Training (SET): A Group Rehabilitation Model." In A. E. Dell Orto and R. G. Lasky (Eds.), *Group Counseling and Physical Disability.* North Scituate, Mass.: Duxbury Press, 1977.

Lofquist, L. H., and Dawis, R. V. *Adjustment to Work: A Psychological View of Man's Problems in a Work-Oriented Society.* New York: Appleton-Century-Crofts, 1969.

Lofquist, L. H., and Dawis, R. V. "Application of the Theory of Work Adjustment to Rehabilitation and Counseling." *Minnesota Studies in Vocational Rehabilitation,* 1972, *30.*

McClure, D. P. "Placement Through Improvement of Client Job-Seeking Skills." *Journal of Applied Rehabilitation Counseling,* 1972, *3,* 188-196.

McMahon, B. T. "A Model of Vocational Redevelopment for the Midcareer Physically Disabled." *Rehabilitation Counseling Bulletin,* 1979, *23,* 35-47.

Mallik, K. "Job Accommodation Through Job Restructuring and Environmental Modification." In D. Vandergoot and

J. D. Worrall (Eds.), *Placement in Rehabilitation: A Career Development Perspective.* Baltimore: University Park Press, 1979.

Matkin, R. E. "Rehabilitation Services Offered in the Private Sector: A Pilot Investigation." *Journal of Rehabilitation,* 1982, *48*(4), 31-33.

Minneapolis Rehabilitation Center. *Job Seeking Skills: Reference Manual.* Minneapolis: Multi Resource Centers, 1971.

Molinaro, D. "A Placement System Develops and Settles: The Michigan Model." *Rehabilitation Counseling Bulletin,* 1977, *21, 121-129.

Neff, W. S. *Work and Human Behavior.* (2nd ed.) New York: Atherton Press, 1977.

Nelson, N. *Workshops for the Handicapped in the United States: An Historical and Developmental Perspective.* Springfield, Ill.: Thomas, 1971.

Osipow, S. H. "Vocational Development Problems of the Handicapped." In H. Rusalem and D. Malikin (Eds.), *Contemporary Vocational Rehabilitation.* New York: New York University Press, 1976.

Parker, R. M., and Thomas, K. R. "Fads, Flaws, Fallacies, and Foolishness in the Evaluation of Rehabilitation Programs." *Journal of Rehabilitation,* 1980, *46*(1), 32-34.

Pati, G. C., Adkins, J. I., and Morrison, G. *Managing and Employing the Handicapped: The Untapped Potential.* Lake Forest, Ill.: Brace-Park Press, 1981.

Resnick, J. B. "Rehabilitation Engineering." In E. L. Pan, T. E. Backer, and C. L. Vash (Eds.), *Annual Review of Rehabilitation.* Vol. 1. New York: Springer, 1980.

Roessler, R., Milligan, T., and Ohlson, A. "Personal Adjustment Training for the Spinal Cord Injured." *Rehabilitation Counseling Bulletin,* 1976, *19,* 544-550.

Rubin, S. E., and Roessler, R. T. *Foundations of the Vocational Rehabilitation Process.* (2nd ed.) Baltimore: University Park Press, 1983.

Schlenoff, D. "A Theory of Career Development for the Quadriplegic." *Journal of Applied Rehabilitation Counseling,* 1975, *6,* 3-11.

Schroeder, J. G. *Attitudes Toward Persons with Disabilities: A Compendium of Related Literature.* Albertson, N.Y.: Human Resources Center, 1978.

Shontz, F. C. "Physical Disability and Personality." In W. S. Neff (Ed.), *Rehabilitation Psychology.* Washington, D.C.: American Psychological Association, 1971.

Shontz, F. C. *The Psychological Aspects of Physical Illness and Disability.* New York: Macmillan, 1975.

Stephens, T. M., Blackhurst, A. G., and Magliocca, L. A. *Teaching Mainstreamed Students.* New York: Wiley, 1982.

Super, D. E. *The Psychology of Careers.* New York: Harper & Row, 1957.

Thomas, K. R. "A Critique of Trends in Rehabilitation Counselor Education Toward Specialization." *Journal of Rehabilitation,* 1982, *48*(1), 49–51.

Vanderheiden, G., and Grilley, K. *Non-vocal Communication Techniques and Aids for the Severely Physically Handicapped.* Baltimore: University Park Press, 1976.

Vash, C. L. "Sheltered Industrial Employment." In E. L. Pan, T. E. Backer, and C. L. Vash (Eds.), *Annual Review of Rehabilitation.* Vol. 1. New York: Springer, 1980.

Vocational Evaluation and Work Adjustment Association. "Vocational Evaluation Project Final Report: The Tools of Vocational Evaluation." *Vocational Evaluation and Work Adjustment Bulletin,* Spring 1975, pp. 49–64.

Wolf, J. "Disability Is no Handicap for DuPont." *Alliance Review,* Winter 1973–74.

Wright, B. A. *Physical Disability—a Psychological Approach.* (2nd ed.) New York: Harper & Row, 1983.

Wright, G. N. *Total Rehabilitation.* Boston: Little, Brown, 1980.

16

Juliet V. Miller

Career Development Programs and Practices in the Schools

Several developments have combined during the past decade to create a redefinition of career development programs in the schools. The first major change was the increased use of the career development knowledge base for the improvement of school-based programs. Drawing on the work of developmental psychology, career development researchers have provided theory and research that more clearly define the nature of the career development and the career decision-making processes. Career development theory and research provided key concepts that formed the basis for career development program goals. These concepts included an emphasis on career development as a lifelong process, a recognition of the influence of self-concept on career development, a description of the career decision-making process, an appreciation of the interrelatedness of all aspects of human development, and a description of career maturity at various developmental stages.

Another important development has occurred in the legislative arena. Federal legislation in the areas of vocational education, career education, and special education has supported the improvement of career development programs (Herr, 1979). Through this federal legislation, guidance has received direct funding that has resulted in the development of more comprehensive programs and in expanded roles for school counselors.

Still another trend that has influenced career development programs is the increased emphasis on equalization of employment and educational opportunity. Herr (1979, p. 16) stated that "school counselors have sometimes been chastised for not taking into account the differences in needs of different student populations." This emphasis on increased equity has resulted in the development of career guidance programs that are responsive to the needs of special groups such as women, minorities, and the handicapped.

Economic issues have also created a force for change. As property tax levels for the support of public education have reached higher levels, the public has demanded increased accountability for all educational programs. Guidance has not been exempt from these pressures. As the accountability model was applied to guidance, the definition of guidance shifted from that of a constellation of ancillary services to that of a systematic comprehensive program. Gysbers and Moore (1981, p. 8) indicated that this movement "served as a stimulus to continue the task of defining guidance developmentally in measurable individual outcome terms—as a program in its own right rather than as services ancillary to other programs."

A final influence on school-based career development programs was the application of technology to guidance. Although research and development on the use of computers in guidance was conducted as early as the 1960s, recent developments such as the improvement of computer technology and federal efforts including the National Occupational Information Coordinating Committee (NOICC) have increased the development and use of computer-based career information systems. This increase has stimulated an examination of human/machine interaction in the delivery of guidance services—a trend that will continue into the future.

These forces for change during the past decade resulted in the development of new career development programs and practices in the schools. This chapter provides an overview both of comprehensive program development procedures and of innovations in specific areas of career guidance practice. Broad programmatic approaches are described under three categories: systematic procedures that direct local school guidance staff members through the program improvement process, state models for career guidance, and models for using collaboration to enhance school-based career guidance programs. Trends in particular career guidance practices are organized around four practice areas—career development curriculum materials, new developments in assessment and testing, the increased use of career information systems, and career guidance practices to meet the needs of special populations. The final section of this chapter suggests probable future trends in school-based career guidance programs.

Comprehensive Career Development Programs

The several forces for change in career guidance that have occurred during the past decade have resulted in a broader definition of career guidance as a systematic, coordinated program of activities to enhance the career development of all students throughout the K–12 school experience. This broadening reflects a shift from the view of guidance as a support service to guidance as a program that is accountable for specific educational outcomes. Systematic programs are a response to criticisms that guidance lacks clear, assessable outcomes that contribute to broad educational goals (Herr, 1979). Major efforts have occurred at the national, state, and local levels to specify program goals and objectives and to describe systematic planning procedures for developing comprehensive career guidance programs. Campbell and others (1983) described the important outcome areas that have been used in research and evaluation studies of career development programs, including improved school involvement and performance, personal and interpersonal work skills, preparation for careers, career-planning skills, and career awareness and exploration skills.

A variety of models and materials have been developed to support the improvement of career guidance through the use of systematic program development and improvement procedures.

These resources can assist local school district guidance staff members as they design career guidance programs to meet the particular needs of their student population. Through efforts at both the national and state levels, major advances have been made in defining career guidance goals, identifying guidance program resources, and evaluating career guidance outcomes. I shall review these efforts by examining national efforts, state career guidance models, and approaches that support collaboration between the school and the community.

National Efforts. Several projects at the national level have developed systematic career guidance program planning materials that local schools can use to strengthen their guidance programs. These comprehensive planning systems are designed to help local guidance personnel develop career guidance programs based on needs assessment, goals and objectives, sequenced activities, systematic management procedures, and ongoing evaluation (Gysbers, 1978). They are designed to provide both pre- and in-service training to guidance personnel to help them develop the skills needed for systematic program planning. Most of these systems include support materials such as lists of suggested goals, needs assessment instruments, planning forms, and descriptions of guidance strategies.

One example is the Career Planning Support System, developed by the National Center for Research in Vocational Education at Ohio State University and approved by the U.S. Department of Education's Joint Dissemination Review Panel, which endorses and recommends programs for national dissemination. This system includes procedural guides, audiovisual materials, survey instruments, and staff training materials to help local personnel use a step-by-step process to assess, plan, develop, implement, and evaluate their guidance program. The six steps supported by the system are orientation, assessing needs and resources, specifying goals and student behavioral objectives, generating alternative methods, designing program evaluation, and implementing the program (Shaltry and Kester, 1977).

Another system is the Comprehensive Career Guidance System, developed by the American Institutes for Research. The twelve modules in the initial set are organized under the broad categories of orientation, structuring, implementation, and cost-impact decision making (Dayton, 1976). Later, through the Consortium on Competency-Based Staff Development project, the American Institutes for Research, in cooperation with six states, formed a consortium to expand these counselor training materials to include other important areas related to comprehensive career guidance programs.

In their book *Improving Guidance Programs,* Gysbers and Moore (1981) provided a comprehensive approach that grew out of their earlier work through a U.S. Office of Education grant to assist all states in developing and implementing comprehensive career guidance programs. The steps in this model are getting organized, assessing your current program, selecting and using a developmental career guidance model, how to get there from where you are, and conducting evaluation.

These comprehensive models for career guidance program improvement have been applied in local school districts throughout the country. It is important to note that use of these models requires administrative support, guidance staff commitment, financial and time resources, and continuing application. Districts that have invested in these efforts have been successful in developing more comprehensive programs, in coordinating resources within the guidance program, and in improving administrative support for the career guidance program.

State Models for Career Guidance. States also have focused on the development of comprehensive career guidance models. As local school districts have experienced pressures for change, they have turned to state departments of education for leadership. Responding to these requests for help, state departments have developed models and materials to assist local districts in strengthening their career guidance programs. State departments have collaborated with local districts by seeking their involvement in developing comprehensive career guidance models and by providing in-service training to guidance staffs as they support the application of these models.

Upton (1982) described efforts in California to develop guidelines for comprehensive guidance programs. The resulting model states that a comprehensive guidance program should "assist students in their personal, social, educational, and career development; recognize that individuals need a personalized developmental approach to learning experiences; assist students in the development of specific proficiencies; develop a learning environment that is primarily preventive; orient its services and curriculum toward the future; provide for human equity; utilize all available resources in school and community; and utilize a systematic approach to planning, implementation, and evaluation" (p. 296). These California guidelines also propose criteria that can be used to identify successful programs. Through application of this model, the California Department of Education has stimulated the improvement of local guidance programs.

Through its Comprehensive Career Guidance Project, the Georgia Department of Education developed a model and transportable packages to support the improvement of career guidance that are designed to support the achievement of desired student outcomes. These materials are designed to assist counselors and other school personnel in their effort to design programs to meet the life career development needs of students in grades kindergarten through twelve. The basic guidance model encompasses three life domains—career planning, interpersonal competence, and work and life skills (Dagley and Hartley, 1976). A variety of materials were generated through this project, including competency rating scales to assess student needs, career guidance activity guides for various grade levels, and staff development training manuals.

The Programmatic Approach to Guidance Excellence (PAGE) includes in-service and preservice training materials for planning comprehensive career guidance programs. The system, developed at Eastern Illinois University and the University of Illinois, focuses on three important areas of the total guidance program—program planning, curriculum-based guidance, and job placement (Peterson and others, 1977). This system has been used extensively to support career guidance program development, as reported by Treichel (1979), who presents six case studies that illustrate applications of the PAGE system for career guidance program improvement in local districts in Illinois.

Collaborative Models. Two major emphases, career education and community collaboration, have stimulated the expansion of comprehensive career development programs. Career education, a major educational movement during the past decade, was defined by Hoyt (1977, p. 5) as "an effort aimed at refocusing American education and the actions of the broader community in ways that will help individuals acquire and utilize the knowledge, skills, and attitudes necessary for each to make work a meaningful, productive, and satisfying part of his or her way of living." Although the concept of career education was initiated at the national level, states were encouraged to develop career education models. As these models were developed, it became clear that career development is a major component of career education and that career guidance is a major vehicle for delivering the goals of career education. Career education is a broader concept than career guidance, encompassing not only career development but also career preparation and focusing not only on guidance but also on instruction both in the classroom and in the community.

Through a contract with the Office of Career Education, U.S. Department of Education, the American Personnel and Guidance Association conducted a project to clarify the role of the school counselor in career education. This report (Burtnett, 1980) suggests that career education challenges counselors to collaborate with other school staff members. A model is presented that clarifies the role of counselors in planning, implementing, and evaluating career education. Within this framework, counselors can function at five levels: expert knowledge, leadership, management, direct services, and indirect services. This model suggests that career education encourages counselors to consider broad areas of collaboration rather than focusing solely on guidance program goals and activities.

The community collaboration model, developed at the National Center for Research in Vocational Education under the sponsorship of the Office of Vocational and Adult Education, U.S. Department of Education, provides another example of collaboration. "Community collaboration for improving career guidance is an attempt to obtain cooperation from local agencies, organizations, and knowledgeable individuals to provide assistance to citizens whose career needs are not being addressed" (Jones and others, 1981, p. 3). The goal of community collaboration is to use a team of representatives of several community agencies to design collaborative career guidance programs. It expands the role of career guidance programs in the schools to include collaborative activities to meet the career development needs of identified groups within the community. It combines the resources of several community agencies, which share the goal of supporting career development, to provide services to various groups, such as employees in business and industry, unemployed individuals, out-of-school youth, and in-school youth. This collaborative model has several advantages, including the sharing of expertise and resources, improved communication and articulation among institutions, and services that are more responsive to individual needs.

Trends in Career Guidance Practices

As definitions of career guidance have become more comprehensive to include expanded career development goals, to stress the diverse needs of all students, and to focus on extending career guidance to all grade levels, a corresponding increase in the variety of career guidance strategies has occurred. Analysis of these emerging career guidance strategies indicates that current developments in this area have focused on the need to use the total personnel resources of the school and community in career guidance programs, the need to apply new technologies to the delivery of career guidance programs, and the need to design new career guidance activities for special student populations. The following description of these new guidance strategies is organized around the areas of guidance curriculum, assessment and testing, career information systems, and guidance practices for particular populations.

Career Development Curriculum. Comprehensive planning procedures have been used to develop guidance goals and objectives that provide a basis for developing career development curriculum materials designed for use with individuals, small groups, or classroom-size groups. The focus of these materials is on specific skills and knowledge within the broad career development areas of self-awareness, career awareness, career decision making, and career implementation. During the last decade, many curriculum materials have been developed. Burtnett (1980) and Campbell, Rodebaugh, and Shaltry (1978) provided descriptions of career development curriculum materials. In addition, many of these materials are available through the Educational Resources Information Clearinghouse (ERIC) system.

The Career Decision Making program (CDM), developed by the Appalachia Educational Laboratory through a project directed by David Winefordner (Appalachia Educational Laboratory, 1978), consists of approximately fifty individual products that can be used as a semester course, a six- to-eight-week exploratory course, or independent units for secondary school students. The CDM program has two components: (1) the Exploring Career Decision-Making (ECDM) curriculum materials and (2) the Career Information System (CIS), a comprehensive organization and management system for career information resources. The fifteen ECDM curriculum units are designed to help students develop career planning and decision-making skills. Each unit is self-contained and employs a variety of materials and techniques such as filmstrips, worksheets, and hands-on activities.

Using comprehensive planning procedures to assess student needs, the guidance staff in Mesa, Arizona (McKinnon and Jones, 1975), developed a comprehensive career development curriculum. The curriculum is based on five career development areas—solving problems, understanding self and others, understanding the world, obtaining skills and experience, and achieving identity. Twenty-four units were developed, five at the elementary level, nine at the junior high level, and ten at the senior high level, representing a total of 250 hours of instruction time. The curriculum units follow a standard format, with a learner's guide and a teacher/counselor booklet. This comprehensive curriculum has been implemented districtwide.

Tennyson and others (1980) described a comprehensive framework for career development education that has been used in Minnesota. They indicate that career development education is "a systematic approach to career development, incorporating appropriate career education interventions in the classroom and curriculum. Career development education becomes a vehicle for unifying curriculum around student needs" (p. 3). Their guide provides a conceptual basis for developing programs, a curriculum management process, a taxonomy of career development instructional objectives for grades kindergarten through twelve, and a description of strategies and resources for program development.

Assessment and Testing. Assessment and testing have long been an integral part of the career guidance process. During the past decade, several developments have occurred that have strengthened and expanded this component of career guidance by measuring a greater variety of career-related personal attributes, by improving test interpretation reports, and by addressing issues of bias in testing and assessment. A special issue of the journal *Measurement and Evaluation in Guidance* (Jepsen, 1982), an article by Miller (1982b), and the recently published book *A Counselor's Guide to Vocational Guidance Instruments* (Kapes and Mastie, 1982) provide comprehensive information on these developments.

To respond to the increased emphasis on accountability, many states have adopted statewide assessment programs to measure achievement on specific objectives related to all subject areas, including career development. In addition, the National Assessment of Educational Progress (1977) has developed objectives and conducted an assessment in the career and occupational development area. These assessment programs, like career maturity inventories, provide information about the current status of students on important career development objectives that can be used for planning and evaluating career development programs.

In the past, a series of specific tests including aptitude, achievement, and interest measures have been administered to provide information for use in career planning. It has been difficult to relate results from various instruments and to relate test results to occupational options. Multidimensional instruments are now available that integrate several types of measures into one instrument, provide reports that organize test results for use in career planning, and list appropriate career opportunities for further exploration. The Career Planning Program (American College Testing Program, 1976), the Differential Aptitude Test Career Planning Profile (Super and Bowlsbey, 1972), the Planning Career Goals (American Institutes for Research, 1977), and the Kuder Career Development Inventory (Kuder and Diamond, 1975) are examples. These inventories provide comprehensive information that supports both career exploration and career decision making.

A final assessment emphasis has been the development of guidelines and instruments to ensure unbiased testing for special populations. The National Institute of Education developed guidelines to evaluate sex bias in career interest inventories (Diamond, 1975; Tittle and Zytowski, 1978) that recommend criteria for evaluating the instrument, technical information, and interpretive materials. A number of instruments have been developed to respond to the needs of racial, ethnic, and handicapped groups, including nonreading assessment procedures, alternative forms of existing instruments with simplified reading levels, and non-English versions of existing instruments. The Nonreading Aptitude Test Battery (U.S. Employment Service, 1981), the Self-Directed Search—Form E (Holland, 1977), and the California Occupational Preference Survey: Spanish Version (Knapp and Knapp, 1974) are examples.

Career Information Systems. Current, comprehensive, and accurate career information is needed to support the career-planning process. Career guidance programs always have provided career information but have been confronted with the need to find effective methods of collecting, organizing, evaluating, updating, and disseminating this information. In addition to the need to provide information about occupational and educational opportunities, career guidance needs to help individuals relate career information and personal characteristics to support the career exploration and career decision-making processes. Two new guidance strategies, computer-based career information systems and career resource centers, have improved the use of career information in career planning.

Since computer-based career information systems are

treated extensively in another chapter of this volume, individual systems are not reviewed here. It is important to note, however, that career guidance personnel need to integrate the selection and use of these systems into the total guidance program planning process. Specifically, the guidance staff needs to develop skills in evaluating systems, giving feedback to system developers to improve systems, designing comprehensive guidance programs that use these systems in combination with other guidance practices to meet identified student needs, and monitoring the use of computer systems to ensure their appropriate use by students and staff.

As computer-based systems, career information media materials, and written career information resources have proliferated, career resource centers have been developed to support the acquisition, organization, dissemination, and use of these resources. Career resource centers provide physical facilities for the storage and use of career information, are staffed by professionals and paraprofessionals who can provide assistance in the use of career information, and assist students, teachers, counselors and the community in the use of career information for career planning and curriculum development. Several writers (Axelrod and others, 1977; Moore, 1981; Wood, 1976a, 1976b) have developed guides that describe the steps required to develop and operate career resource centers, including design of physical facilities, staff selection and training, materials evaluation and acquisition, specific services, and methods for evaluating the effectiveness of the career resource center.

Career Guidance for Special Populations. A major trend in career guidance programs in the schools has been the focus on developing career guidance practices and materials that support equitable career planning for all individuals. This includes programming to reduce sex-role stereotyping in career planning and to meet the unique career development needs of such groups as the handicapped, the gifted and talented, the bilingual, and Native Americans. Since other chapters in this book provide a detailed review of career guidance for particular groups, this section will describe sample career guidance practices for special populations in the elementary and secondary schools.

A number of programs have been developed to reduce sex-role stereotyping in career planning and decision making. *Born Free* (Hansen, 1977) is a comprehensive program to reduce career-related sex-role stereotyping in educational institutions from elementary through postsecondary and to expand career options through increasing instructors' and parents' awareness of their own socialized attitudes and behaviors. Another program, *Freestyle* (Science Research Associates, 1978), is a television series that was shown on public television and a career awareness curriculum to link the series to classroom activities. The program, funded by the National Institute for Education, is designed to encourage nine- to twelve-year-olds to freely explore their interests, develop their skills, and choose their career paths.

Career guidance programs have also been developed for the handicapped. Counselors have become increasingly involved in developing individualized educational plans for the handicapped, and guidance programs have tailored career guidance practices to the needs of the handicapped. Dahl (1982) provided a framework for analyzing the possible barriers to employment for the handicapped—unrealistic attitudes and options, inadequate skill development, barriers in the physical environment, and communication problems. Several writers (Johnson and others, 1980; Neeley and Kosier, 1977) described programs designed for particular handicapped groups, and Hohenshil and Maddy-Bernstein (1980) identified guidance resources for the handicapped.

Gifted and talented students have also received attention as career guidance programs have been coordinated with emerging programs in gifted education. Miller (1981) and Kerr (1981) have reviewed the needs of gifted and talented students and described career guidance models for this group. Typical needs of the gifted and talented are choosing from many career options, identifying career options that allow them to express multiple talents, resolving conflicts between personal goals and societal expectations, maintaining career aspirations, and resolving conflicts between work and home roles. Kerr (1981) describes individual career guidance practices and overviews career guidance programs developed for the gifted and talented.

Recent interest in bilingual education has stimulated the development of bilingual career information resources for Spanish-speaking and bilingual students. *Trabajamos! (We Work!)* (Education Development Center, 1980) is a three-week course designed to help portray non-sex-stereotyped, nontraditional occupational roles for elementary school Hispanic girls. Rios (1976) reports on the development of twelve bilingual career education curriculum units to provide career information for Spanish-speaking migrant students at the elementary level. Castro (1981) has developed a *Resource Guide for Career Counseling Spanish-Speaking and Chicano Students*. This guide provides general information that counselors need to understand about this group and suggests career guidance practices that are appropriate for Spanish-speaking students.

Several career guidance resources have been developed for Native American students. The Far West Laboratory for Educational Research and Development (Banathy and Studebaker, 1977) developed a twelve-unit instructional program, Native American Career Education (NACE), to introduce junior high school students to career planning. Hollow and Heuving (1979) developed Indians in Careers, which presents interviews with ten Native Americans who have maintained their Indian identity while contributing to the world of work—thus providing models to other Native American youth. Graves (1980) developed a workbook to help Native Americans with career planning, and the Colorado River Indian Tribes (1976) developed a career guidance program for Indian youth that is designed to increase their awareness of occupational opportunities through a variety of career exploration activities.

A Look to the Future

This chapter has summarized developments in career guidance programs in the schools during the past decade. These have been stimulated by several forces for change, such as new understandings of the career development process, legislative mandates, an increased emphasis on equity of educational and employment opportunities, a demand for educational accountability, and applications of new technological developments to guidance. A major consequence of these forces for change has been the emergence of comprehensive career guidance programs that are designed to provide career development assistance to all students throughout the school experience. Examples of these comprehensive programs are found in models for comprehensive career guidance programs developed at the national and state levels. Career guidance practices have also been expanded and improved, with major innovations evident in the areas of career guidance curriculum, assessment and testing, career information delivery, and guidance practices for special populations. As a concluding statement, it is appropriate to look to the future of career guidance programs in the schools. Several writers (Hays, 1982; Herr, 1982; Miller, 1982b; Walz and Leu, 1979) have discussed future trends that will influence career guidance and probable responses to these trends.

Future Trends. Future trends in American society, the world of work, and education will reshape career guidance goals and delivery systems in the future. In the broad social context, this society will continue to seek responses that enable us to remain economically competitive with other nations while also expanding the equality of educational and occupational opportunity for all citizens. Most experts agree that the shift from an industrial to an information society has occurred, but the implications of the shift are not completely clear at either the national policy-making or the personal career and educational decision-making level.

The movement into the information society is changing the occupational structure and creating new human/technology mixes in the workplace. The demands of particular jobs are changing as technology is used to support many job functions. The influence of this change is mixed—some jobs becoming more routine and less skilled, other jobs becoming more highly skilled. The distribution of jobs is shifting away from manufacturing-related toward service and information-related jobs. The basic resource in the information society is information or knowledge that results in new technological developments. There is a growing recognition that educated human resources are crucial to future progress. New solutions are being sought to persistent problems in productivity. The quality-of-work-life movement seems to be gaining wider adoption as a viable approach to increasing productivity. This means that more employees are involved in management functions such as job redesign and problem solving. Employers are valuing a new set of skills in their employees, including problem solving, group leadership, and creative skills. The demographics of the work force will continue to change. Women will continue to choose to enter the labor force in greater numbers. The changing occupational structure will force a redistribution of the existing labor force, resulting in unemployment, career change, and underemployment for many adults. As the population ages, the needs of older workers will demand greater attention.

Education is also changing. The demand for excellence in education is increasing as policy makers recognize the important link between the quality of education and the achievement of other national goals. Recent criticisms of education focus on the need for educational reforms that will result in better-prepared citizens. The National Commission on Excellence in Education (1983) has made recommendations encouraging a more clearly prescribed curriculum in the areas of English, mathematics, science, social studies, and computer technology; higher performance standards and expectations; a longer school day and year to provide more time for education; reforms to increase the excellence of teaching; and strategies for providing leadership and fiscal support. This report is stimulating discussions at the state and local levels that undoubtedly will result in educational reforms.

Another major trend is the application of technology to education. For the first time, a number of communications technologies, including television, telephone, and computer, have been linked together and are available at a cost affordable by many individual citizens. A main characteristic of the information age is the ready availability of information and knowledge to all world citizens. Whereas particular institutions, particularly the school, were previously the major access points for knowledge, learning, and information, this is no longer true. In the future, education will occur in settings other than the school. As these technologies become cost-effective, many groups, including commercial institutions, will become more interested in developing and providing educational services. School personnel need to recognize this trend, to determine new ways to apply technology within the school setting, and to establish channels for influencing and collaborating with non-school-based education.

New Directions for Career Guidance. The future trends will influence career guidance in several ways. Career guidance personnel need to reexamine and redesign both the goals and delivery systems of career guidance in light of these trends. A reexamination of the goals and purposes of career guidance highlights several new areas of emphasis. There is a need to upgrade career information resources to reflect the major changes occurring in the occupational opportunity structure—shifts in occupational distribution, influences of technology on particular occupational areas, and new employment patterns for certain groups, such as women. Career guidance needs to incorporate new goals aimed at helping students develop skills that are particularly important as the quality-of-work-life measures are adopted. The image of the "ideal worker" is changing to include emphasis on such skills as problem solving, group membership, leadership, and creative skills. Career guidance needs to help students strengthen these skills. It is also important for career guidance programs to stress skills required for successful career change that results from changes in occupational demand as well as from personal growth. This includes helping students understand how basic skills are transferable to different occupational areas and helping them learn how to create job opportunities. Life-planning goals in nonoccupational areas such as family and leisure will become increasingly important as employment patterns become more complex and fluid. Individuals will experience more frequent job changes, there will be a greater need to coordinate the career plans of family members, and more children will be raised in families where all adults are working outside the home.

The current emphasis on excellence in education will

have implications for career guidance goals. Educational institutions will probably become more prescriptive in curriculum selection and will set higher standards for performance. This will be true in both secondary and postsecondary institutions. Students need assistance in developing individual educational and career plans in light of these changes. Career guidance needs to maintain students' right to informed freedom of choice by helping them understand standards and requirements, by facilitating the achievement of their full potential, and by ensuring equity of opportunity for all students. The historical mission of guidance in supporting the balance between individual and societal needs will continue to be important.

The delivery systems used in career guidance programs will also be modified. If new proposals related to curriculum and amount of time spent in school are adopted, the organization of career guidance programs will need to be examined in such areas as scheduling of guidance activities and use of classroom guidance activities. Guidance personnel need to be involved in educational reform activities to ensure the continuing role of career guidance in helping students develop individual educational and occupational goals. Another trend related to educational excellence may be the increased use of performance testing to verify student achievement. Guidance personnel have expertise and experience in the area of assessment and testing. It will be important for them to be involved to help guarantee appropriate administration, interpretation, and use of these testing procedures.

The use of technology is another trend that will influence the delivery of career guidance programs. As in other occupational areas, technology will be used to perform an increasing number of counselor functions, will alter the existing role of the counselor, and will move career guidance services out of the school into other settings, such as community organizations and the home. Already career information and testing activities are being performed by the computer. In the future, computer applications will focus on higher-level operations such as test interpretation, interviewing, and teaching career-planning skills. Computer-based career guidance services are available currently in libraries, churches, and community organizations. In the future, they will also move into the home. The expansion of technological applications in career guidance and the use of these technologies to provide career guidance services in new settings will require counselors to redefine their current role and to coordinate service with other institutions.

School-based career guidance personnel increasingly will collaborate with career guidance efforts in other settings to meet the needs of nonschool clientele. Perhaps a future chapter on this topic will be titled "The Role of the School in Life Career Development," rather than "Career Development Programs and Practices in the Schools." Whereas to date most programs have been targeted toward individual institutions, future programs will be designed for many groups and delivered through collaborative activities involving many institutions. School guidance personnel will be involved in designing and delivering comprehensive programs not only for students who attend their schools but also for out-of-school youths and adults.

Finally, it is important to comment on career guidance personnel in the future. There is increasing national concern about the excellence of teachers. There is also a need to reexamine the excellence of counselors. As technology and increased use of collaboration influence the role of the school counselor, there is a need to revise statements of counselor role to reflect new competencies that are important, such as consultation and coordination activities with parents, teachers, software developers, and nonschool institutions. Additionally, competencies that have previously been important (for example, acquisition and filing of occupational information, test administration) may become less important. Once this revised counselor role has been developed, there will be a need to examine its implications for counselor selection, training, and staffing patterns. Such an analysis may result in revised selection criteria for students in counselor education programs, new patterns of differential staffing, new programs for upgrading counselor skills in the in-service settings, and new career ladders to encourage effective counselors to stay within the profession of school counseling.

Suggested Readings

Campbell, R. E., Rodebaugh, H. D., and Shaltry, P. E. *Building Comprehensive Career Guidance Programs for Secondary Schools.* Columbus: National Center for Research in Vocational Education, Ohio State University, 1978. (ED 186 714)

    A handbook of programs, practices, and models of career guidance for secondary schools, intended to provide information about systematic program development models and career guidance techniques to help local guidance departments improve their programs. Includes extensive reference to examples of various guidance practices.

Gysbers, N. C., and Moore, E. J. *Improving Guidance Programs.* Englewood Cliffs, N.J.: Prentice-Hall, 1981.

    Contains comprehensive information needed to design developmental career guidance programs. Provides a comprehensive review of information, suggests specific steps to be followed, and includes extensive references to other works that will be helpful in career guidance program development.

Hays, D. G. "Future Shock and the Counselor." In E. L. Herr and N. M. Pinson (Eds.), *Foundations for Policy in Guidance and Counseling.* Falls Church, Va.: American Personnel and Guidance Association, 1982.

    This chapter resulted from a National Institute of Education contract to study policy issues related to guidance and counseling. Hays reviews future trends related to human issues such as society and education. He then draws implications from these trends for the role of the counselor and the nature of guidance and counseling.

Herr, E. L. *Guidance and Counseling in the Schools: The Past, Present and Future.* Falls Church, Va.: American Personnel and Guidance Association, 1979.

    A report of a project sponsored by the U.S. Office of Education to describe the current status of guidance and to suggest directions for guidance in the 1980s. Includes sections on historical perspectives, current practice, emerging directions, professional preparation, and unresolved problems. Appendixes contain statements on the role and preparation of counselors.

Kapes, J. T., and Mastie, M. M. (eds.). *A Counselors' Guide to Vocational Guidance Instruments.* Falls Church, Va.: National Vocational Guidance Association, 1982.

This handbook provides reviews and descriptions of assessment instruments that can yield useful information for career planning and career guidance program development. Forty instruments are reviewed in the categories of multiple aptitude batteries, interest inventories, work values measures, career maturity instruments, card sorts, and instruments for special populations; over seventy other instruments are described.

National Commission on Excellence in Education. *A Nation at Risk: The Imperative for Educational Reform.* Washington, D.C.: U.S. Department of Education, 1983.

The major report of the National Commission on Excellence in Education, formed by the U.S. Department of Education to study the current status of secondary education and to suggest educational reforms to improve the quality of education. Provides national direction for secondary education that will influence local and state educational agencies.

References

American College Testing Program. *Career Planning Program.* Iowa City: American College Testing Program, 1976.

American Institutes for Research. *Planning Career Goals.* Monterey, Calif.: CTB/McGraw-Hill, 1977.

Appalachia Educational Laboratory. *Career Decision-Making Program: Final Report.* Charleston, W. Va.: Appalachia Educational Laboratory, 1978. (ED 164 915)

Axelrod, V., and others. *Career Resource Centers.* Sault Ste. Marie, Mich.: Eastern Upper Peninsula Intermediate School District, 1977.

Banathy, B. H., and Studebaker, D. P. *Native American Career*

Education: A Curriculum Guide. San Francisco: Far West Laboratory for Educational Research and Development, 1977. (ED 147 595)

Burtnett, F. E. (Ed.). *The School Counselor's Involvement in Career Education.* Falls Church, Va.: American Personnel and Guidance Association, 1980.

Campbell, R. E., Rodebaugh, H. D., and Shaltry, P. E. *Building Comprehensive Career Guidance Programs for Secondary Schools.* Columbus: National Center for Research in Vocational Education, Ohio State University, 1978. (ED 186 714)

Campbell, R. E., and others. *Enhancing Career Development: Recommendations for Action.* Columbus: National Center for Research in Vocational Education, Ohio State University, 1983.

Castro, R. *Resource Guide for Career Counseling Spanish-Speaking and Chicano Students.* San Jose, Calif.: San Jose City College, 1981. (ED 205 695)

Colorado River Indian Tribes. *Career Guidance for Indian Youths.* Parker, Ariz.: Colorado River Indian Tribes, 1976. (ED 132 366)

Dagley, J., and Hartley, D. L. *Career Guidance in Georgia: A Program Development Guide.* Atlanta: Georgia State Department of Education, 1976. (ED 160 850)

Dahl, P. R. "Maximizing Vocational Opportunities for Handicapped Clients." *Vocational Guidance Quarterly,* 1982, *31,* 43–52.

Dayton, C. *A Validated Program Development Model and Staff Development Prototype for Comprehensive Career Guidance, Counseling, Placement and Follow-up.* Palo Alto, Calif.: American Institutes for Research, 1976.

Diamond, E. (Ed.). *Issues of Sex Bias and Sex Fairness in Career Interest Measurement.* Washington, D.C.: National Institute of Education, 1975.

Education Development Center. *Trabajamos! (We Work!)* Newton, Mass.: Education Development Center, 1980. (ED 200 352)

Graves, M. A. *Here I Am—Where Do I Want to Go? A Career Interest Survey for Native Americans.* Seattle: United Indians of All Tribes Foundation, 1980. (ED 192 989)

Gysbers, N. C. "Comprehensive Career Guidance Programs." In R. E. Campbell, H. D. Rodebaugh, and P. E. Shaltry (Eds.), *Building Comprehensive Career Guidance Programs for Secondary Schools.* Columbus: National Center for Research in Vocational Education, Ohio State University, 1978.

Gysbers, N. C., and Moore, E. J. *Improving Guidance Programs.* Englewood Cliffs, N.J.: Prentice-Hall, 1981.

Hansen, L. S. "Born Free: An Applied Developmental Intervention to Reduce Career-Related Sex-Role Stereotyping in Elementary, Secondary, and Higher Education Settings." Paper presented at annual convention of the American Psychological Association, San Francisco, August 26–29, 1977. (ED 150 495)

Hays, D. G. "Future Shock and the Counselor." In E. L. Herr and N. M. Pinson (Eds.), *Foundations for Policy in Guidance and Counseling.* Falls Church, Va.: American Personnel and Guidance Association, 1982.

Herr, E. L. *Guidance and Counseling in the Schools: The Past, Present and Future.* Falls Church, Va.: American Personnel and Guidance Association, 1979.

Herr, E. L. "Comprehensive Career Guidance: A Look to the Future." *Vocational Guidance Quarterly,* 1982, *30,* 367–376.

Hohenshil, T. H., and Maddy-Bernstein, C. *Resource Guide: Vocational Counseling for the Handicapped.* Blacksburg: Virginia Polytechnic Institute and State University, 1980. (ED 186 789)

Holland, J. L. *Self-Directed Search—Form E.* Palo Alto, Calif.: Consulting Psychologists Press, 1977.

Hollow, E., and Heuving, J. *Indians in Careers.* Seattle: United Indians of All Tribes Foundation, 1979. (ED 184 779)

Hoyt, K. B. *A Primer for Career Education.* Washington, D.C.: Office of Career Education, U.S. Office of Education, 1977.

Jepsen, D. A. (Ed.). "Symposium: Testing for Career Counseling, Guidance, and Education." *Measurement and Evaluation in Guidance,* 1982, *15,* 141–163.

Johnson, N., and others. "A Career Awareness Program for Educable Mentally Retarded Students." *Vocational Guidance Quarterly,* 1980, *28,* 328–334.

Jones, G. B., and others. *Community Collaboration for Improv-*

ing Career Guidance Programs. Columbus: National Center for Research in Vocational Education, Ohio State University, 1981.

Kapes, J. T., and Mastie, M. M. (Eds.). *A Counselors' Guide to Vocational Guidance Instruments.* Falls Church, Va.: National Vocational Guidance Association, 1982.

Kerr, B. A. *Career Education for Gifted and Talented.* Information Series No. 230. Columbus: National Center for Research in Vocational Education, Ohio State University, 1981. (ED 205 778)

Knapp, R. R., and Knapp, L. *California Occupational Preference Survey: Spanish Version.* San Diego, Calif.: EDITS, 1974.

Kuder, F., and Diamond, E. *Kuder Career Development Inventory.* Chicago: Science Research Associates, 1975.

McKinnon, B. E., and Jones, G. B. "Field Testing a Comprehensive Career Guidance Program, K-12." *Personnel and Guidance Journal,* 1975, *53,* 663-667.

Miller, J. V. (Ed.). "Special Issue on Career Education for the Gifted and Talented." *Journal of Career Education,* 1981, 7 (4).

Miller, J. V. "The Future of Career Guidance." Paper presented at convention of the Minnesota Vocational Guidance Association, Minneapolis, November 2, 1982a.

Miller, J. V. "1970s Trends in Assessment for Career Counseling, Guidance and Education." *Measurement and Evaluation in Guidance,* 1982b, *15,* 142-146.

Moore, E. J. *Establishing a Career Center in the Secondary Schools.* Columbia: College of Education, University of Missouri, 1981. (ED 203 197)

National Assessment of Educational Progress. *Objectives for Career and Occupational Development: Second Assessment.* Denver, Colo.: Education Commission of the States, 1977.

National Commission on Excellence in Education. *A Nation at Risk: The Imperative for Educational Reform.* Washington, D.C.: U.S. Department of Education, 1983.

Neeley, M. A., and Kosier, M. W. "Physically Impaired Students and the Vocational Exploration Group." *Vocational Guidance Quarterly,* 1977, *26,* 37-44.

Peterson, M. P., and others. *Programmatic Approach to Guidance Excellence (PAGE 2).* Charleston: Eastern Illinois University, 1977.

Rios, E. T. *Development of Career Awareness Materials for Spanish-Speaking Migrant Children: Grades K-6.* San Jose, Calif.: Educational Factors, 1976. (ED 132 312)

Science Research Associates. *Freestyle Guide.* Chicago: Science Research Associates, 1978. (ED 170 543)

Shaltry, P., and Kester, R. J. *Coordinator's Training Guide: Career Planning Support System.* Columbus: National Center for Research in Vocational Education, Ohio State University, 1977.

Super, D. E., and Bowlsbey, J. H. *DAT Career Planning Profile.* New York: Psychological Corporation, 1972.

Tennyson, W. W., and others. *Career Development Education: A Program Approach for Teachers and Counselors.* Falls Church, Va.: National Vocational Guidance Association, 1980.

Tittle, C. K., and Zytowski, D. B. (Eds.). *Sex-Fair Interest Measurement: Research and Implications.* Washington, D.C.: National Institute for Education, 1978.

Treichel, J. *Optimizing Planning Techniques for Career Guidance: Six Case Studies.* Urbana: Department of Vocational and Technical Education, University of Illinois, 1979. (ED 189 422)

Upton, A. L. "The Development of a Comprehensive Guidance and Counseling Plan for the State of California." *Vocational Guidance Quarterly,* 1982, *30,* 293-299.

U.S. Employment Service. *Nonreading Aptitude Test Battery.* Washington, D.C.: U.S. Government Printing Office, 1981.

Walz, G. R., and Leu, J. *Futuristic Images of Guidance and Student Services.* Ann Arbor: ERIC Clearinghouse on Counselor and Personnel Services, School of Education, University of Michigan, 1979.

Wood, R. A. *Establishing a Career Resource Center.* Palo Alto, Calif.: American Institutes for Research, 1976a. (ED 140 198)

Wood, R. A. *Establishing a Career Resource Center: Coordinator's Guide.* Palo Alto, Calif.: American Institutes for Research, 1976b. (ED 140 197)

Cynthia A. Johnson
Howard E. Figler

17

Career Development and Placement Services in Postsecondary Institutions

During the past ten years, significant changes have occurred in the way postsecondary institutions are organizing, administering, and delivering career development and placement services. This chapter examines these changes and discusses current practices in the implementation of today's comprehensive career development program.

Historical Review

Over the past six decades, career development theory has moved from Parsons (1909) to Perry (1970). Parsons' early contributions to the career field have been expanded and replaced by new research and theory. Perry's developmental approach, translated by Knefelkamp and Slepitza (1976) to the career field, shifts the decision-making focus from the counselor to an "internal locus of control" of the individual student.

Concurrently, resources in higher education have diminished because of decreasing enrollments, double-digit inflation, and taxpayers' revolts. In addition, new tools in theory and technology have been made available to the career development professional. An increasing number of career centers have become theory-based and begun to use video technology and computer-assisted guidance and information systems.

These shifts in focus and practice have continued and accelerated from 1975 to the present. The result is more centralized career centers that emphasize career development and placement, rather than the traditional placement function.

The State of the Art

Several major themes have surfaced during the past ten years. Career centers now emphasize that a career is an ongoing process and therefore view their mission as an educational one, rather than one in which providing outcomes (counting the people placed in first jobs, for example) is the measure of success. This focus on development reflects the unpredictable nature of a person's career. Career centers wish to teach students methods of self-assessment and self-marketing.

There is also a greater emphasis on delivery of career services through many modes of service, rather than simply relying on students' referring themselves for individual contacts in the career center. This "outreach" orientation (Drum and Figler, 1976) acknowledges that many students can be reached if the center initiates contact with them. Often the focus is on groups of students that may be reluctant to seek help (for example, minority students, off-campus students). Many of these programs take place outside the center.

Developmental Needs of Clients. In the past, a career center adviser may have felt that a student with certain abilities or academic background "should" enter certain fields, but today there is greater appreciation for individual differences and the unique nature of an individual's development. The decline of the one-career phenomenon and reduced loyalty to the organization one joins have made counselors cautious in predicting or influencing the course of an individual's career.

There is now more emphasis on psychological satisfaction as well as utilitarian goals. Career seekers today are as likely to emphasize personal relationships (at work), creativity desired,

and integration of work with one's life-style as to focus on economic needs. People are thus choosing careers in the hope of
finding not only economic security but self-expression and a
commitment to something beyond their own personal gains.
Such emphases have led career centers to view both paid and
nonpaid work as contributors to career satisfaction.

Career Center Organizations. The merging of the placement perspective with "do it yourself" services has created a
two-headed nature in many career centers that can be confusing to the student. Nonetheless, the dual emphasis will continue. Placement methods have been updated to reflect current
technology. Many offices use computers to organize their recruitment programs and job referral systems. Many have also
developed contact networks among alumni and other professionals in the community. Students are benefiting from these
services, but they also recognize that other job and career opportunities exist beyond the recruitment programs, placement
files, and alumni networks. The alert students take advantage of
both—they use contacts from the placement part of the career
center and learn methods for developing their own contacts as
well.

Many career planning and placement centers increased
their staffs between 1975 and 1981. "Over 40 percent of the
total group surveyed indicated they added to their staffs, while
only 7.2 percent reported cutbacks," according to Weber (1982,
p. 6). They have more professionals, especially counselors, available to talk with students and provide programs for them. Peer
counselors have been made available at some colleges and universities in order to extend the center's services to larger numbers of students. Although it is unlikely that career planning
and placement staffs will increase in coming years, most colleges
and universities will maintain their centers because institutions
increasingly recognize the role of a career center in "selling" the
institution to prospective students.

Issues Confronting Career Centers

Current practices reflect the influence of Richard Bolles
(1983) on the career-planning profession. The impact of *What*

Color Is Your Parachute? and related books during the past ten years has encouraged career counselors and their clients to believe that self-identification of goals and self-management of the career search would yield positive results. Although the importance and validity of "self-empowerment" (Bolles, 1983) continue to be affirmed, career counselors are learning the limits of teaching these approaches and the importance of synthesizing self-help methods with methods of helping students to become connected with present and future labor markets.

Much of the tension in career development today results from the clash of opposing views—the counseling approach (shift the responsibility for decision making and development of career alternatives to the client) and the broker approach, which seeks to arrange opportunities for the individual. Although many acknowledge that self-help, as aided by counseling, can promote higher accomplishments, many complain that it is unrealistic. Some are encouraged by the counselor's support; others feel the counselor is "copping out" of responsibility. Their resentment springs from the legitimate frustrations of trying to find employment with limited resources.

The debate between counseling and "placement" rages on, but it masks several more specific conflicts. First, a synthesis is needed between the labor market approach to career decisions and individual-centered career development. Currently these factions are at war. Each believes that the other is quite unhelpful and even harmful to the student. Because any career is the result of a negotiation with life and its work opportunities—more specifically, a dialogue between the individual's needs and an organization's requirements—the career center must accurately mirror this dialogue. Instead of fighting about which is the better of the two, the career center must learn to embrace both, so that the student can know "where the jobs are" and how best to compete for them. Apparently, in their haste to make the client self-initiating and all-powerful, career centers have overlooked the finite time and space in which a client operates. No one expects or wants the career center to regress to the old information-giving days, but balance is needed between internal processing and external data, between "I can do anything" and "Here is what is available." Our task is to offer a combination of services that balance economic anxiety and appropriate idealism.

Second, much career counseling assumes that there is no distance or isolation problem for clients seeking their career. Yet even commuting to school is difficult enough, let alone finding the time to get downtown or out of town for a career-related conversation. Centers now assume that students can appear in person to gather information. By sending students out to find information on their own, counselors may frustrate clients rather than encourage them.

Third, the issue of vocational training is unresolved. College graduates do not know how much of it is required for entry-level jobs or where they would get it. Career centers can provide some guidelines for making decisions about job training and information about where training is available.

Fourth, there is little acknowledgment that career decisions are made in conjunction with other people. Most of our counseling and other methods assume individual autonomy. No principles of compromise with others, family priorities (either family of origin or acquired family), or negotiation with significant others are proposed. Each career decision is made as part of a social system, and our methods should incorporate this view. By implying that autonomy is the "right" way to make a decision, career centers may unwittingly make people uncomfortable about considering the views of others.

Fifth, no psychology of risking is applied to the career decision-making process. Although it is perhaps not stated, low risk or near certainty of outcomes is assumed to be desirable. "Pick the career that is the 'best bet,' " we hear. However, given that many highly secure careers are considered boring, risk represents an adventure and an opportunity for achievement. The career center can advocate the virtues of risking and can help people to learn their personal risk styles, understand probabilities, and make choices.

Need for Negotiation. The concept that will bring counseling together with brokering, the internal together with the external world, is negotiation. All career development is negotiation between what students want and what the employer or market wants from them. In their haste to praise and embolden the individual decision maker, career centers have lost sight of this ongoing and productive tension between buyer and seller. The market often tends to have its way with people, because it offers dollars for the job it wants done. However, individuals can modify the employer's priorities, and adapt them to themselves, by being creative, insistent, and patient. They thus engage in the art of compromise, between "what you want done" and "my way of doing it." Therefore, a career center's task is to acknowledge the competing forces and equip the client to handle both sides.

When helping the client to negotiate the best deal possible, the career center must proceed to the next level of career counseling, which is often alien ground—helping clients to see how they might express important values in their work, even when these values may conflict with economic realities. Reconciling love of work with probability of success is a crucial issue for anyone choosing a career. Economic factors are weighed very differently by different individuals, even though everyone is confronted with the same economic conditions. Writers who write and dancers who dance for the sheer love of it are the far and inspiring edge of this idea. Career counselors can help their clients to envision their own versions of success, rather than accepting norms thrust on them. Advancement, status, security, and material gain are one-dimensional versions of success, yet they are unconsciously reinforced by counselors. A well-placed question or two ("How would *you* define success for yourself?") may unlock the person's desire to be more creative about shaping his or her goals, as expressions of his or her values.

Thus, the earlier view that one must reconcile oneself to the prevailing job market and the more recent view that one extracts the maximum from supposedly flexible jobs can be synthesized. Career counselors step down from the ideal pedestal of career fantasies, yet they do not descend into making clients supplicants to an unyielding labor market. The negotiation process is continual. The individual learns to play the system for all its worth, enjoy its rewards, accept its requirements.

The career center thus helps the individual to manage not

one but two balancing acts, that between the self and the marketplace and that between paid and unpaid work. Idealism gives way to the synthesis of realism, but enterprising clients can still bargain and barter for every last ounce of satisfaction they can get.

As counselors work to achieve the blending between self-directed careers and providing the information that students need to manage their plans, they should keep in mind two powerful undercurrents that feed the five problems described earlier, assured that they will not be solved easily.

Expectations of Higher Education with Respect to Careers. Although it is seldom fully and overtly stated in a college catalogue, the belief is widespread that college courses are vocational, that they can be marketed in areas of employment. "What is your major?" is tantamount to asking "Where do you hope to work? " in the minds of many students, if not in the minds of faculty members, parents, and administrators of the college as well.

Although it is quite difficult to correlate college programs with job marketability, the belief dies hard. Colleges promote the vocational attitude by elevating programs that are vocationally successful. In general, college has always been touted as the pathway to economic heaven. Although the economic benefits are probably demonstrable over the long run, the typical students' requirements are more severe. They want results *now*—in the first job. They believe their academic programs should reveal obvious pathways to the labor market.

As long as career centers are saddled with the necessity of "proving" that higher education pays off, they will be quite unable to satisfy their clientele, no matter how diverse and sophisticated their programs. The specter of "What do I do with my major?" (whether I like my major or not) hangs heavily over the career center and clouds its efforts to expand the student's array of career alternatives.

Expectations of One's Career. A job was once viewed primarily as a way to earn a living. The transition to the word *career* signals a shift to work as a way of life. Just as a marital partner is now expected to be far more than an economic and parental partner, so individuals expect their career to provide excitement, status, social relationships, new forms of learning, new challenges—all this *and* economic security. Few careers can shoulder that burden well. The notion that one can "have it all" in paid employment places great pressure on the individual and a corresponding burden on the career counselor. "Having it all" often means reaching the highest position in an organization *and* making enough money to satisfy all material needs (plus a few fantasies) *and* enjoying your work as fully as you would like *and* getting time off from work whenever you want it. A few people may fulfill most of these needs in their careers, but a much larger number will get less than they had hoped for.

The economic structure simply cannot support these psychological expectations. For every climber who "gets it all," fifty bruised and battered egos lie in his or her wake. Grandiose expectations or obsessive career dreams can distort the career counseling process and obliterate the joy of attainable gains.

The Role of Education

The decline of liberal education in the eyes of career-oriented students is not isolated from the problems already mentioned. Both education and careers are viewed in a utilitarian way. "What can each do for me, in tangible terms?" As economic anxieties deepen, the student looks for more immediate benefits from education—access to the first job, entry to graduate and professional schools, and indexes of economic gain that will accrue from the degree.

It is the liberal educator's view that if one learns for the long haul, sees "the big picture," and cultivates problem-solving ability, the career will develop on its own. In a climate that emphasizes short-term profits, however, that view is often overlooked.

Some would pit technology against liberal education in this battle for the future direction of career centers, but that would be a false and unproductive contest. Technology is here to stay. The problem is that technological students do not prepare themselves "liberally" and liberal arts students do not prepare themselves "technologically." This artificial separation of the two cultures of higher education (and thus of the career world) creates a deeper problem for career centers than any temporary turn in the economy. Neither the technology majors nor the business majors can take fullest advantage of their potential in the job markets, because their higher education has not taught them to value interconnectedness of knowledge and *all* problem-solving skills (technological and others), which they will need. The idea of having a "major" in the first place encourages the false impression that we are all specialists. In reality, the higher you advance in any employment capacity, the more "general" your responsibilities become.

New Resources and Solutions

Now career centers in postsecondary settings are facing problems never envisioned by pioneers in the field of vocational guidance and career education. A broader and more comprehensive scope of service is being demanded by a larger constituency of students, faculty members, and alumni as well as business and industry.

There are, however, new solutions. For example, career professionals have new tools of both theory and technology to assist them.

Theoretical Foundations. There are many categories of career theories in the literature. Crites (1969) reviewed the major theories and organized them into five categories: trait-and-factor, client-centered, psychodynamic, developmental, and behavioral.

The developmental work of Super (1975), that of Knefelkamp and Slepitza (1976) and their adaptation of the Perry scheme, and Krumboltz and Baker's (1973) early and more recent work on behavioral and social learning theory are a few examples of new theoretical tools available to the practitioner. However, as stated by Super (Montross and Shinkman, 1981, p. ix), "Theorists tend to be the despair of practitioners, because they know what to do but usually stop short of spelling out programs and procedures, and practitioners tend to be the despair of theorists because they do things with too little knowledge of what to do or how to do it." Although handy "how to do it" career workshops still abound with questionable conceptual frameworks and outcomes, there are now more comprehensive career centers based on theoretical foundations. Translation models such as Knefelkamp and Cornfeld's (1976) work with Holland typologies are available to translate theory into practice.

A theoretical knowledge base also exists for the developmental style and stages of the new adult learners who are coming to the career center in increasing numbers. Aslanian and Brickell (1978) reported that over 40 million adults are in some stage of career transition. Many of the structurally unemployed persons and career changers are returning to the college campus. Chickering (1980) stated that we now have the research and theory to understand the individual needs of these adults.

Technology. Career centers are increasingly turning to technology to extend their resources and individualize the career-planning and placement process. Whereas the late 1960s and 1970s were a period of new developments, experimentation, and increasing technological innovation, the 1980s should be an exciting period of technological refinement and expanded application (Johnson and Riesenberg, 1979). Examples of the use of technology include—

- Increased use of video equipment to assist in relieving counselors of repetitive tasks, improving interview skills, and delivering high-quality information.
- Twenty-four-hour phone lines to serve off-campus, alumni job seekers.
- Audiotapes that provide academic information and enable students to hear a career presentation they could not attend.

The availability of the low-cost microcomputer and an increased supply of software are enabling more career centers to use this new technology.

Using the New Tools. In addition to the new theory and technology available to the practitioner, the body of knowledge about how best to use these tools is expanding as the profession increases its empirical research and publishes the results. Graduate training programs for future professionals are increasing in number and will assist career development and placement centers in moving toward a new level of professionalism.

Some career centers are finding creative solutions to the problem of the increased span of population to be served by developing new delivery systems that include group work in the form of classes and workshops and utilization of technology to free staff persons.

Theory and technology combine to meet the career guidance needs of the adult learner in a project called LEARN. Now in its second phase, this project will include a computer-assisted software system for the adult in career transition. Videotapes have already been developed to support this project (Johnson, in press).

Computer software, some of it already available, will enable adults in transition to review their life roles on the basis of Super's theory, to ascertain what skills or learning has occurred in those life roles, to learn how to develop a portfolio to receive academic credit for prior learning, to go through one of two interactive adult career guidance and information modules, and to enter an educational brokering module should they seek further education or certification. Martin Katz of the Educational Testing Service (ETS) will use his value theory for one adult guidance system, and JoAnn Harris-Bowlsbey and Donald Super, in cooperation with the American College Testing Program, will develop the second guidance component. Arthur Chickering and his colleagues at Memphis State will add a computer program that will enable adults to assess their learning styles and their stage of ego development. The W. K. Kellogg Foundation has funded the Council for the Advancement of Experiential Learning and ETS with over $5 million to develop these and other systems.

Future Directions

The philosophy of career centers during the past ten years, "We can teach you to find your ideal careers, and you can learn to do this for yourself," was quite sound and educationally correct in concept but has proved difficult to translate into effective services for college students. The philosophy assumed (1) a robust labor market that would accept the aspirations of most college graduates and find places for them that would fit their needs, (2) a college student who would have the personal maturity and skills to implement such a strategy on his or her own once taught what to do, and (3) a college or university that would approve and tolerate this pure educational approach without being concerned about immediate results—that is, the performance of graduates in entry-level labor markets.

None of these assumptions proved especially true. The number of college graduates, plus the large numbers of returning students, has surpassed the number of readily available jobs at levels the graduates would view as suiting their abilities and education. Most recent graduates have had difficulties putting into practice a do-it-myself strategy without other kinds of assistance from the college's career office. Finally, many colleges have found it necessary to pay much closer attention to the "placement" results of their graduates, for purposes of attracting more students, maintaining effective relationships with alumni, and convincing funding sources that their academic pro grams are justified.

All these factors are expected to continue; therefore, the career center can no longer assume that a self-directed strategy, properly taught on a one-to-one or group basis, is sufficient to satisfy its clientele. The foregoing realities have laid the ground work for the following future directions.

Demand for Services. The career center is no longer the relatively minor part of a counseling or student services program that it once was. Demand for career help is increasing as colleges attract large numbers of students whose career prospects are uncertain. In addition, there is an increasing desire to find a direct relationship between one's academic program and career opportunities. Career services are often perceived by the student as having a greater "payoff" than other student services. In some cases, their effect may be crucial to the future of the college or university, particularly at colleges where a large number of students have come to college for vocational preparation. Such students are probably in the majority among college students today.

Relationship of the Career Center to the Institution. The career center's new synthesis of self-direction with labor market realities will lead to more partnerships between centers and business and industry. In an effort to bridge the gap between students' aspirations and economic realities, centers will arrange new "experience" programs and will serve as clearinghouses for all such programs that are available to students through academic courses or noncredit arrangements. Centers will encourage more students to use such programs and will invite more businesses—large and small—to participate. Similar programs will be developed with nonprofit organizations.

Professionals in Career Centers. Career centers will continue to attract people with professional backgrounds in counseling, psychology, and related fields. However, it will be increasingly necessary that centers attract people having business experience, personnel training backgrounds ("human resource development"), experience with a variety of labor markets, and understanding of how professional networks develop and are used by entry-level individuals. In some cases, these latter skills and experiences may outweigh the counseling credentials. It is likely that counselors will often be teamed with people having the kinds of backgrounds just mentioned.

Expanded Services. Many of the new and expanded services will respond to what Krannich (1983, p. 9) called the need for recareering skills, "the process of repeatedly acquiring marketable skills and changing careers in response to the turbulent job market of the high-tech society." Krannich therefore emphasized that the former ideal of "career *planning*" is inappropriate and must be modified with three new emphases: (1) acquiring new marketable skills through retraining on a regular basis, (2) changing careers several times during a lifetime, and (3) using more effective communications networks for finding employment.

Career centers will adopt these emphases by showing their students how to combine the merits of a general education with ways of acquiring work-specific skills. Some work-specific skills can be acquired in academic programs; others will have to wait until the person graduates or be obtained concurrently with college studies. The concept of recareering emphasizes that college graduates are not likely to obtain their ideal career on graduation and that instead they will have to piece together several jobs into the pursuit of a goal; their success will depend on the ability to negotiate with a turbulent set of labor markets.

The following expansions of services will be seen in the immediate future and, in fact, are presently practiced by some college and university career centers. They represent an effort to find the balance between the self-initiated, self-directed pursuit of an ideal career and the realities of a labor market that changes unpredictably, requires people to retrain frequently, and often makes it difficult for them to discover and pursue opportunities on their own.

1. *Work experience.* Career centers will find many new ways and enlarge old ones for enabling students to obtain "work experience" during college. The center will enable students to learn the career development process as they acquire this experience, but the emphasis will be on arranging situations that will make this experience readily available.

2. *Contact networks.* Career centers will create ways for students and graduates to make far greater use of initial contacts that will help them in job searches. They will initiate or enlarge existing networks of alumni or professionals in the community so that students can explore career alternatives and contact people who can provide advice or "leads" for prospecting in the labor markets.

3. *Training resources.* Given the rapid pace of technological change, students need to be well informed about work-specific skills needed in entry-level jobs and where they can acquire these particular skills. Career centers will help students by learning what skills are currently in demand, identifying sources of training, and helping students decide how they would like to acquire these skills without undermining their general education.

4. *Labor market specialist.* The purpose of labor market specialists will be to help students expand their awareness of ca-

reer possibilities. Though recognizing that it is impossible to "know" a labor market that is inherently chaotic and continually changing, career centers will endeavor to provide students with enough information that they will know the kinds of entry-level jobs typically available to college graduates, how these opportunities relate to academic preparation, the weight given to general education in the typical equations, and trends toward self-employment versus working in organizations. These staff members will also be aware of trends toward or away from small-business opportunities and relative demand in various sectors of the entire labor market. Computer systems will aid the staff in this regard, as will cooperation with other career centers.

5. *Communication skills.* The generic skills of writing and speaking will continue to be emphasized in career centers, in the form of preparation of job-related written materials and interview skills. Poor communication skills are so often the downfall of job candidates, despite their academic preparation or work-specific skills, that centers must concentrate their attention here if their graduates are to reap the rewards they expect as a result of their education.

6. *Job search.* Career centers will continue to emphasize the mechanics and positive attitudes of the job search, because they are directly related to the student's immediate desire to make a successful transition from school to the "adult" status of being employed. Centers will expand their emphasis on *directness* in the application process, because of its efficiency. Students will be exhorted to identify whom they want to work for (through a combination of self-assessment, work experience, research, and labor market data) and contact these people as directly as possible, by telephone, by in-person methods, or perhaps by some form of video network.

Greater attention will be given to earlier stages of the job search—getting organized and making initial contacts—than on the latter stages closer to hiring decisions, because career centers have access to students largely during the early stages.

Delivery of Services. Members of the career center staff will do less one-to-one counseling and group work than they previously have done, and more administration of programs and indirect services, because of the new multiservice orientation of the center, where many students will seek work experiences, labor market data, training oportunities, or other services rather than counseling or workshops. Career centers will emphasize educating students by having them learn career development through experience. Many counselors believe that the principles of self-directed pursuit of career goals become evident when making choices of work experiences and adjusting to one's mistakes.

Career services will continue to be centralized in the career centers themselves, perhaps even more than before, rather than being distributed to academic departments or elsewhere. The new emphasis on specific information and networks, and the continuing emphasis on individual counseling, necessitate that all services be offered by the professional staff members who can provide them most effectively.

Alternative Models of Success

Today's students (and people in general) view their careers differently in several ways, and these have been aptly reported by certain authors. Hall (1976) emphasized the decline of loyalty toward organizations, the increase in loyalty toward oneself, and the nurturance of individual goals. Ferguson (1980) called attention to greater autonomy and self-reliance, rather than dependence on government or other external agencies for help (informal networks among people have aided this trend); increase of the win/win orientation, in which people cooperate to make everyone's job positive rather than compete for the few desirable jobs; humankind as a partner with nature rather than its foe; and individuals' interest in serving both themselves and their community rather than having to choose between the two. Finally, Slater (1983) proposed that money may not be the prevailing theme of all job and career seekers. He indicated that models of success are developing in which money is secondary or even totally absent as a factor of importance.

These themes would seem to belie the emphasis on labor market data and competition noted in this chapter. However, their sum effect will be to increase the number of options available, so that students can incorporate as much or as little competition into their career choices as they prefer.

The authors mentioned previously describe varying views of the meaning of work in one's life. As students become acquainted with these ideas, they will learn that success can be defined in many ways. With the help of career center programs, students will learn that choosing one's own version of success is part of the career choice process. Individuals will vary widely in how much they embrace competition, material gain, creativity, autonomy, self-employment versus being employed by others, self-gain versus other-directedness, free time, economic self-sufficiency, and other dimensions of career choice. As the synthesis between self-direction and labor market realities is shown by career center programs, students will discover how many degrees of freedom they have in defining their own models of success. The most effective centers will enable students to have as much freedom as possible to pursue the "success" they want, by teaching them to reconcile personal priorities with needs for economic resources.

Exemplary State-of-the-Art Programs

Peer Counseling—University of Maryland Career Development Center. Undergraduate students are paid to perform many functions traditionally done by professional counseling staff members, including giving advice about career-planning strategies, critiquing résumés, and referral to resources. Peer counselors also screen clients to determine whether they need career counseling with a professional staff member. Ten peer counselors represent a wide variety of undergraduate degree programs.

Cornell University. Forty peer volunteers work three to four hours per week to perform many prejob activities with clients, such as mock interviews, review of résumés, and distribution of self-help materials. The program, managed by a student coordinator, serves as a publicity vehicle for other services of the career center.

Dickinson College. In a residential setting, "career assistants" conduct most of their counseling activities in residence halls and other locations away from the career center. Paid undergraduates are trained to assist students with their career directions, job-search strategies, and general career indecision. They also conduct workshops and act as liaisons with academic departments. Career assistants represent a variety of undergraduate liberal arts majors.

Outreach—University of North Carolina at Greensboro. A question-and-answer column in the student newspaper provides the principles of career development for students and informs students about all services and programs of the career center. The center uses this column to confront issues important to students and conflicts regarding their career plans.

University of Texas at Austin. The career center distributes a book to all liberal arts students detailing careers of recent liberal arts graduates from the University of Texas. Representative graduates are profiled, and graduates from all academic departments provide quotations about "how liberal education affected my career." The center maintains and updates this data base and disseminates information about career experiences and profiles of liberal arts graduates to all departments.

Ohio State University. Undecided students identify themselves during orientation and are assigned to specially trained academic/career advisers at that time. All students who declare themselves undecided are required to enroll in a credit course that introduces career development concepts, decision-making strategies, and principles of academic and career planning. Undecidedness is viewed as a constructive part of human development.

University of Maryland Career Development Center. A career supplement is produced in the daily newspaper four times each year and is distributed to 50,000 students. Funded by employer advertisements, the supplement contains essays about job-search strategies, explanations of labor market trends, summaries of career-planning and placement services in the center, examples of experiential learning such as internships, and other self-help articles. All material is written and edited by the staff of the career center.

University Center at Binghamton, SUNY. "Quick reference guides" contain much of the career center's self-help information. They are standardized and coordinated in a single format with a highly visible logo, so that the center publicizes itself through dissemination of these materials. Over thirty such guides cover topics related to the tasks of career development. Through the guides, complex tasks are broken down into smaller, more manageable units. The guides are cross-referenced and also refer to materials available in the center's Career Resource Area. These guides are distributed at workshops, campus events, and student affairs programs and are also available as individual handouts on a display rack in the center.

Use of Computers—Michigan State University. Computers are used to handle students' requests for competitive recruitment schedules in a fair and efficient manner. Students rank the recruiters with whom they wish to interview; requests are matched to requested degree, date of graduation, and student priority. The system enables the placement center to track no-shows, as well as analyze recruiter trends and salary survey information.

Use of Computers—University of Missouri-Columbia. Computers are being used extensively by the staff for a variety of functions. SIGI (System of Interactive Guidance and Information) is used by close to 1,000 students a year to help them clarify their work values and examine appropriate careers. EUREKA's Micro-SKILLS is also used extensively in the adult evening career services as a tool for helping adults examine which skills they have and how these might transfer to various careers. The center is also conducting evaluations and research on other career guidance software programs and sees itself as an active field test site.

In addition to career guidance and information software, the center uses computers in the following ways: (1) to produce *The HUNTER,* the center's biweekly, nationwide job listing, (2) to store, sort, and retrieve information on alumni career advisers, (3) to list, store, and provide accountability for the job-locator program, (4) to provide an annotated bibliography of all career center resources, which can be retrieved by key words, (5) as a tool in staff training (the center has computerized the twenty most frequently asked questions and where to locate answers, and (6) for all correspondence, mailing labels, scheduling of meetings, and so forth.

In serving the 25,000 annual career center users, computers help increase staff time and efficiency.

Faculty Involvement—Alma College. Alma College provides a model of how faculty members are integrated into the career development program. They are introduced to a series of five career modules that correspond to students' needs at each year of their education, and they serve as career-planning advisers in conjunction with their academic advising. Computer-assisted guidance and the career resource center are used by students and faculty members as sources of information.

Alumni—Ohio State University. In the Partners in Education program, 900 alumni from the Columbus area volunteer to meet with students. University College staff members conduct seminars for alumni regarding how to work with students who contact them. Students are provided a list of available alumni through their academic advisers, placement offices, career libraries, and freshman orientation and career courses; they attend orientation sessions and workshops before seeing the alumni.

Alumni—University of Missouri-Columbia. ASK (Alumni Sharing Knowledge) has students spending time with an alumnus at his or her place of employment for career exploration purposes. Alumni profiles are computerized, so that students can select alumni on the basis of a variety of specific variables (for example, career field, geographical locations, college major, sex). Alumni are also pulled from this pool for summer jobs or internship possibilities, for panels, or to help students relocate in an unfamiliar part of the country.

Experiential Learning—University of California, Berkeley. SCOPE (Survey of Career Options and Professions through Exploration) is a program that sponsors a broad range of experiential learning opportunities in various off-campus settings. For students developing their own internships, learning objectives are drafted. In all types of internships sponsored by SCOPE, the role and meaning of field learning are highlighted in relation to comprehensive career planning. Through the "Evaluating Your

Internship" workshop, students returning from work assignments discover skills and knowledge acquired as well as attitudes and values affected. A notation is made on the academic transcript for those who complete the SCOPE program.

Career Resource Center—Florida State University. The Curricular-Career Information Service (CCIS) is a multimedia self-service career resource center established in 1972. It has books, pamphlets, audio- and videotapes, slides, filmstrips, computers, and trained career guidance technicians to help learners choose a major or career. Special equipment and materials are available for handicapped students. Assistance is provided for questions about occupations, job outlook, vocational schools, graduate programs, job-hunting techniques, résumé writing, interviewing, and many other career-related topics. CCIS holds weekly workshops and clinics. A course in career planning is incorporated into CCIS and offered for one, two, or three credit hours. This course, offered each fall and spring semester, is open to all students. In addition to services, CCIS provides training for ten to twenty interns annually. It also provides a setting for numerous grant-supported research and development projects.

Cornell University. The center offers a comprehensive collection of printed resource materials, organized according to domains of the world of work. Substantial research of existing printed materials culminates in the publication of *Where to Start,* an annotated bibliography of career resources that is considered a standard among career-planning and placement offices.

Extern Program—Swarthmore College. One-week work experiences are arranged between undergraduate students and alumni during vacation periods. The career center engages students in choosing externship sites according to personal interests and values, rather than liberal arts major field of study. Students are required to develop goals and structure for the experience in cooperation with their externship supervisor.

Summary

This chapter has reviewed some of the changes that have occurred in career development. We identify current issues in the field, including the tension between advocates of the counselor and broker approaches to career decision making. We suggest that an appropriate role for career center professionals would be to help the student negotiate between the need to make the client self-initiating and happy in a career and the reality of the job market.

The new tools of theory and technology are discussed, as are future trends. A more complete treatment of the use of computers is found elsewhere in this book.

Finally, we identify a number of exemplary programs in which concrete examples of future trends are cited.

Suggested Readings

Burck, H. D., and Reardon, R. C. (Eds.). *Career Development Interventions.* Springfield, Ill.: Thomas, 1984.

Examines numerous counseling strategies for assisting clients with their career development, including information, self-assessment, tests, contractual arrangements, group processes, and computer technology. The authors also offer chapters on programmatic strategies that bring indirect service to clients: community resources, career planning through instruction, and career resource centers. Programmatic and counseling strategies are then applied to special client categories, such as women, disabled persons, and ethnic minorities. Programs in organizations, ethical issues, and accountability concerns are also incorporated into this comprehensive text.

Montross, D. H., and Shinkman, C. J. *Career Development in the 1980s: Theory and Practice.* Springfield, Ill.: Thomas, 1981.

A book of contributions from leading theorists and practitioners in the career development field. Offers major theories of career development and the perspectives of program leaders in higher education and organizations. Reveals both similarities and differences between colleges and organizations with regard to career counseling, supportive resources, and the organization of career services. Special topics include liberal arts students, minority students, off-campus learning, computerized career guidance, placement, systems approaches in organizations, job

analysis, assessment centers, career management, women in organizations, and midcareer development.

Powell, C. R., and Kirts, D. K. *Career Services Today: A Dynamic College Profession.* Bethlehem, Pa.: College Placement
Council, 1980.
    Describes the full range of services that exist in career
planning and placement offices of colleges and universities.
Gives attention to career counseling, job-search programs, career
resources, campus interviews, and employer relations. Treats career services as part of an institutional system, in which leaders
of career offices must be effective managers. Traces the development of the career-planning profession to its respected status
today.

References

Aslanian, C., and Brickell, H. *Adults in Transition.* New York:
College Entrance Examination Board, 1978.

Bolles, R. N. *What Color Is Your Parachute? A Practical Manual
for Job-Hunters and Career Changers.* Berkeley, Calif.: Ten
Speed Press, 1983.

Chickering, A. W., and Associates. *The Modern American College: Responding to the New Realities of Diverse Students
and a Changing Society.* San Francisco: Jossey-Bass, 1980.

Crites, J. O. *Vocational Psychology.* New York: McGraw-Hill,
1969.

Drum, D., and Figler, H. E. *Outreach in Counseling.* Cranston,
R.I.: Carroll Press, 1976.

Ferguson, M. *Aquarian Conspiracy: Personal and Social Transformation in the 1980s.* Los Angeles: Tarcher, 1980.

Hall, D. T. *Careers in Organizations.* Glenview, Ill.: Scott, Fores-
man, 1976.

Johnson, C. S. "Adults and Technology." *NASPA Journal,* in
press.

Johnson, C. S., and Riesenberg, B. "Technology and Student
Services Personnel: Current Use and Future Application." In
F. R. Brodzinski (Ed.), *New Directions for Student Services:*

Utilizing Futures Research, no. 6. San Francisco: Jossey-Bass, 1979.

Knefelkamp, L. L., and Cornfeld, J. L. "The Holland Typologies: Aid to Understanding the Counselor and Designing the Counseling Environment." Unpublished paper, University of Maryland, 1976.

Knefelkamp, L. L., and Slepitza, L. A. "Cognitive-Developmental Model of Career Development—an Adaption of the Perry Scheme." *Counseling Psychologist,* 1976, *6,* 53-58.

Krannich, R. L. *Re-careering in Turbulent Times.* Manassas, Va.: Impact Publications, 1983.

Krumboltz, J. D., and Baker, R. K. "Behavioral Counseling for Vocational Decisions." In H. Borow (Ed.), *Career Guidance for a New Age.* Boston: Houghton Mifflin, 1973.

Montross, D. H., and Shinkman, C. J. *Career Development in the 1980s: Theory and Practice.* Springfield, Ill.: Thomas, 1981.

Parsons, F. *Choosing a Vocation.* New York: Houghton Mifflin, 1909.

Perry, W., Jr. *Intellectual and Ethical Development in the College Years.* New York: Holt, Rinehart and Winston, 1970.

Slater, P. *Wealth Addition.* New York: Dutton, 1983.

Super, D. E. "Vocational Guidance: Exploration and Emergent Decision Making in a Changing Society." *Bulletin of International Education and Vocational Guidance Association,* 1975, *29,* 16-23.

Weber, D. M. *Status of Career Planning and Placement.* Bethlehem, Pa.: College Placement Council Foundation, 1982.

18

Richard L. Knowdell

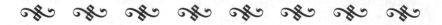

Career Planning and Development Programs in the Workplace

During the last decade, career development has emerged as a distinct component of the human resource development function in business and industry. Many programs have focused on meeting the requirements of the organization, and others have stressed the attainment of personal goals. Some have attempted to meet the needs of both the individual and the organization. This chapter will address the emergence of these programs and describe a variety of career assessment, planning, and guidance programs and techniques in the workplace.

Why Career Development in the Workplace?

When many of our business leaders left school in the 1950s, the common goal and ambition they shared was to secure a job or trade and remain in that vocation until retirement. Career guidance then was quite simple—just identify the job, land it, and work happily ever after. Now, after thirty-odd years in the workplace and a variety of job changes and career shifts, it is quite clear to many that career guidance is not a simple and one-time activity: It is a critical, lifelong activity. As the need to attend to career guidance and career decision making has moved from the traditional school-age bracket to span the whole adult life cycle, so has the setting for career guidance expanded from the campus to include the work site. This past decade has seen a phenomenal growth in number and scope of career guidance and development programs in business and industry (Knowdell, 1981, 1982; Leibowitz, 1980; Trammell, 1980; Lopez, Ruckmore, and Kesselman, 1980). A variety of technological, social, and legislative phenomena have had an impact on occupations and the world of work. Following are brief descriptions of these phenomena and some ideas on how they contributed to the current emergence of career planning and development programs in business and industry.

Equal Employment Opportunity and Affirmative Action. The federal equal employment legislation of the 1960s and 1970s has contributed to the need for career guidance in the workplace. Many organizations with disproportionately few minority and female employees have hired skilled guidance counselors to recruit minority workers and orient them to the workplace. Even companies with large minority work forces have found that women and minorities were underrepresented in all but entry-level and clerical occupations. Many managers were given the additional title of "affirmative action coordinator" and charged with "counseling" women and minorities about the promotional opportunities within the organization and guiding them through the educational and political steps that can lead to higher-level assignments. Some organizations have instituted career development workshops specifically for the advancement of minority employees.

Succession Planning and Manpower Forecasting. The need to project the future requirements and openings for key personnel, as well as the tracking of these "fast track" employees, has long been a concern of top management (Burack and Mathys, 1979; Moore, 1979). Although a few organizations have reserved counseling for succession planning for the favored "fast track" few, more and more companies are viewing the need for guiding and tracking employees as applying to all employees in the organization. In some, the use of tuition reimbursement programs to prepare the employee for a new job within the organization is tied to a documented consultation with the career adviser or counselor.

Management Selection and Development. The slotting of the wrong person into a management position can prove disastrous for both company and individual. In many industries and professions—for instance, medical care and engineering—most managers are selected and/or promoted strictly on their "technical expertise," with very little knowledge of how well they are able to manage. Few of those selected have received any formal management training in college. If the new manager does not possess the skills and aptitudes to manage, the failure can cost the company thousands of dollars to select and train a replacement. The personal cost can be worse. The "failure" at the management job can deflate the worker's self-esteem and stigmatize the person with peers, superiors, and family. Fortunately, most large organizations have coupled in-house management development programs with competent career counseling that is designed to assist potential managers in deciding whether or not to move into management. Much of this counseling is provided by management development specialists or trainers with advanced training or degrees in counseling.

Technological Change. Probably the most visible reason for the emergence of career counseling in the workplace is the magnitude and rapidity of technological change. Over half the occupations that Americans will fill in the year 2000 (just sixteen years from now) have not yet been designed. The thousands of people who received keypunch training in the early 1970s have found that technology has now skipped that process altogether. Secretaries, drafters, cashiers, and even career counselors are now required to work with computer terminals as a routine aspect of their jobs. Guidance counselors are increasingly being called on to assist employees in adjusting to changes on the job as well as to prepare them for the inevitable changes that each of us is facing. For each new high-technology profession that emerges, scores of routine service occupations are required for support. Thus, not only will the technological revolution generate many high-tech jobs, but it will also confound an individual's range of choices by creating a vast array of nontechnical service occupations (Heffernan, 1981).

Social Change. Throughout most of history there has been strong social pressure prescribing particular jobs according to gender, social class, or ethnic background. During the 1950s and 1960s, guidance counselors were reminded of these restricted job options by the different occupational scales on the Strong Vocational Interest Blank for males and females, as well as the accompanying blue and pink test booklets. As recently as ten years ago, the Help Wanted sections of major newspapers were segregated by "male" and "female" jobs. The 1980s are seeing the range of career choices for each individual as ever broadening. The military has abolished separate women's services and is increasing its numbers of women on shipboard and piloting military planes. Legislation now makes it illegal to restrict job assignments or promotions because of gender. As the range of options for each worker broadens, the need for career guidance assistance in choosing and navigating the appropriate path becomes more pronounced. One result of this change in the social fabric has been the emergence of industrial career development programs designed to assist both individuals and organizations in dealing with rapid change.

Career-Planning Programs

Career-planning programs are almost as varied as the organizational cultures in which they occur.

National Semiconductor, a large high-technology manufacturer in California, has a career development program that has been in place for six years. Initially involving individual career counseling with a professional counselor, this program has shifted to a high reliance on managers to conduct counseling. Employees are referred to local colleges for testing and share the results with the manager before the counseling session.

Apple Computer has a formal program that includes open-enrollment career-planning classes led by a professionally trained counselor. The counselor uses a variety of standardized tests and calls on a company staffing specialist to provide up-to-date information on company jobs. (This is necessary because the company is growing too rapidly to commit job descriptions and job paths to writing.)

Both Anheuser-Busch and Union Carbide's Nuclear Division restrict their career development programs to salaried or exempt employees. The Anheuser-Busch program is individualized for each division and may include job posting, performance appraisal, individual counseling, workshops, career development networks, and executive development programs.

The Union Carbide program, though patterned after the Livermore program described in the next section, differs in that it requires 20 percent participation on the employee's own time and uses technical employees and managers as subject matter advisers in lieu of a "professional" counseling staff.

Bache Halsey Stuart Shields has a career development program specifically for exempt females in the personnel and training division. This is a very informal program that revolves around breakfast meetings and strives to enhance personal and professional growth.

A Model Career-Planning Program

As interest in career planning in business and industry intensifies and becomes more widespread, it seems appropriate to present a model program. The career-planning program at Lawrence Livermore National Laboratory is presented, not because it is a typical program (it is not), but because it contains most of the elements of successful programs and has gained a reputation as a model for other, more recent programs. Established in early 1975, the career development program was designed to serve employees in all occupations and at all levels in the laboratory's 7,000-plus work force. With a primary focus on career/life planning (rather than career pathing), the program's major objective is to assist employees in taking control of and managing their own careers. The three major components of the program are a career information center, individual career counseling, and career assessment workshops.

The career information center contains numerous volumes of occupational information, college catalogues, and communication and personal growth books, and for some time it included a computerized occupational information retrieval terminal. The center is open to any employee during normal work hours and over the noon hour.

Individual counseling is also available to the employees. Areas addressed by the counselors in addition to career development are educational planning, personal and family crisis, financial planning, preretirement planning, and vocational rehabilitation. Counseling is provided by full-time counselors, as well as an adjunct cadre of physicists, engineers, chemists, or administrators who spend 10–15 percent of their time providing career counseling to other employees.

The most visible component of the career development program is a series of seminars conducted six or seven times each year. Open to employees in all occupations and at all levels, these seminars are conducted during work hours and involve forty hours of participant time over seven weeks. The seminars are highly experiential and are limited to eighteen employees per session. Following is an outline of the career-planning seminar series:

> *Week 1—Orientation to career planning.* This half-day session includes an overview of career planning, participation in sample exercises, and a discussion of the level of participant commitment required.
>
> *Week 2—Assessment workshop.* Two days of intensive assessment activities involve the identification of values, personality style, communication mode, and vocational interests and include training in decision making and strategy planning.
>
> *Week 3—Individual interview.* A structured one-hour interview focuses on specific behaviors involved in past achievements and is recorded on videotape for use in the following week's activities.
>
> *Week 4—Motivated skills workshop.* Three miniseminars totaling about ten hours allow the participants, working in small groups, to clearly identify each individual's motivated skills and most effective work style. This technique, the Livermore Achievement Motivation Process (LAMP), uses group consensus and focuses on individual strengths.

Week 5—Individual counseling session. During this one-hour session, each participant meets with a counselor, reviews reasons for attending the workshop series, and discusses the development of an individualized career strategy plan.

Week 6—Career strategy assignment. During this period each participant gathers information on options and develops a career strategy plan.

Week 7—Career strategy seminar. During this final session, each participant presents the "what, how, when, and where" of his or her career strategy plan and receives feedback and support from the other seventeen seminar participants.

Employee interest in the Livermore program was high during the initial years, and demand for both counseling and workshops has constantly grown over the years. The vast majority of questionnaires sent to both participants and supervisors twelve months after workshop attendance continue to yield reports of increased career growth and improved morale.

Responsibility for Career Planning

As career planning in organizations becomes a frequent topic of discussion, a complex and controversial issue soon develops: Whose responsibility is career development? As with many other issues, the answer often lies in the eye of the beholder. Responsibility and function can vary greatly, depending on the perspective of the individual examining the issue. It may be helpful to view the issue of responsibility from four perspectives: those of the organization or top management, the supervisor, the trainer or counselor, and the individual worker (Griffith, 1980; Gutteridge, 1980; Kaye, 1981; Leach, 1981; Mamarchev, 1982; Morgan, 1980; Schein, 1978; Walz, 1982; Zemke, 1980).

The Top-Management Perspective. Top management often views career development as a process or program that can ensure efficient succession planning and realistic manpower planning. To the top manager, who really takes the organization's perspective, a good career-planning program should identify those individuals who will be able to fill key slots in the organization during the coming years. In addition, career development is seen as an efficient process for identifying the training and development needs of the candidates for these future positions. For some organizations, career-planning programs are also seen as methods for facilitating the departure of individual employees whose long-term potential does not lie within the organization. Given this perspective, for a career-planning program in an organization to be successful, top management must (1) view the program as contributing to the ultimate financial profitability of the organization and (2) visibly support the program with adequate budget and personnel allocations.

Role and Perspective of the Supervisor. The supervisor has traditionally viewed career development as a help and a hindrance. On the positive side, career development is seen as an aid in motivating and directing employees in their daily tasks. On the negative side, career development is viewed as just one more time-consuming supervisory task dictated by management whim. The 1980s have seen the first-line supervisor's role in career development move into prominence. The supervisor is in an ideal position to assess, counsel, and coach the employee for optimal career development. Many large organizations are instituting programs to provide career counseling skills to supervisors in order to enable them to effectively guide the careers of their subordinates. But learning counseling skills is not enough. To really ensure an effective program, the supervisor must actively take on the responsibility of acting as a career coach and must accept this role as a legitimate supervisory function. Ideally, the supervisor should view career development techniques as tools to enhance and simplify the supervisory role (Pinto, 1980; Kaye, 1980).

Role and Perspective of the Employee. Historically most employees have viewed career development as a means of identifying and navigating career paths within the organization. To these employees, career development was synonymous with upward mobility. Consequently, employees have taken a relatively passive role in organizational career development. A frequent pattern has involved looking to the organization "to develop my career." Now both the perspectives and roles of employees are changing. Many of the most successful career development programs of the 1970s and early 1980s have stressed the importance of each individual employee's assuming responsibility for his or her own career development. In these programs employees are required to gather information on career paths, initiate planning sessions with supervisors, and develop written career strategy plans.

Role of the Career Counselor. The past decade has seen the emergence of a new occupation, that of the human resource development (HRD) specialist (Connelly, 1979; Hutcheson and Chalofsky, 1981; Lipsett, 1980; Peck, 1979). Often these practitioners are industrial trainers or personnel generalists going under a new name. Some are recent graduates with human resource development specializations in graduate schools of business and organizational behavior. A few are professional counselors who have made successful transitions from the public sector. Whatever their origin, these new professionals must assume a major role for ensuring the success of the organization's career development program. In many cases, they act as career counselors, conducting assessments and providing occupational information. Many conduct training classes to equip supervisors with career coaching skills. Others consult with top management to ensure organizational support for career development. Some have taken on the unfamiliar tasks of marketing and promoting career development within the organization. Others are conducting outplacement and preretirement counseling for obsolete employees. The latter half of the 1980s will see many traditional counselor education programs move toward equipping their graduates with the skills to function as human resource development specialists.

Recipients of Career Planning in Industry

To understand industrial career-planning programs, it is useful to examine some of the typical employees who need and use the services of these programs.

The Potential Manager. Today's organizations, especially those in the high-technology area, are staffed with numerous professionals who are confronting the choice of becoming managers or remaining in their professional or technical tracks. These men and women are the products of technical education programs that did not include skill-building courses in management skills. They are questioning whether they possess management skills or whether they would find the role of manager satisfying. These questions, as well as where to acquire management skills, can be effectively addressed by an organizational career-planning program.

The Stagnated Professional. Many mature organizations, those with a work force whose average age is around forty-five, have middle-aged employees who were once highly productive and creative but have now stagnated and are performing at a marginal level. These employees may be experiencing feelings of isolation, are unsure how their careers are going, and may be questioning how their personal value systems mesh with the values of the organization. These individuals have lost touch with their motivated skills, the sources of their past creativity. A career development program can reconnect these stagnated professionals with their skills and talents. This reawakening of motivated skills can either make the employee a valued contributor to the organization again or serve as a motivator to move on to another organization. In either case, the results are positive for both the organization and the individual.

The Frustrated Secretary. Many secretaries and other clerical workers, though quite competent and productive in their jobs, feel blocked from moving into professional positions. This blockage stems from a number of sources: institutionalized sexism; little knowledge of the paths to upward mobility within the organization; and, in some cases, the absence of any real "bridge jobs" that span the gap from clerical to professional ranks. Many of the career development programs of the early 1970s were designed specifically for this group, and most subsequent organizational programs have included it as a target population.

The Entry-Level Employee. One of the largest segments in a typical organization is made up of assemblers, laborers, or service workers who have recently entered the work force. Having resolved the initial task of obtaining employment, these workers, poised on the first steps of career ladders, are in need of information. They are asking such questions as "Is this the right ladder or path for me? What skills must I possess to move up the ladder? Where and how can I acquire these skills? Will the organization provide me with tuition assistance or time off from the job to pursue this training?" These questions and others can be effectively addressed by an organizational career development program.

The High-Tech Specialist. The computer revolution has seen the rise of a highly visible employee: the computer scientist or engineer who can help our high-technology organizations stay competitive in the rapidly changing hardware and software products market. Prime targets of technical recruiters, or "headhunters," these professionals frequently move from one employer to the next by responding to monetary enticements. Many of these professionals are now questioning the wisdom of this rapid jobhopping and are considering the dangers of overspecialization and the advantages of charting a path within one organization. An effective career-planning program can assist these much-sought-after workers in focusing on their own needs and charting meaningful career strategy plans.

The Employee Approaching Retirement. As the mean age of the work force increases, larger proportions of workers are approaching retirement age, many with feelings of uncertainty and fear. Although many organizations offer information on benefits, insurance, and tax issues, few have historically dealt with the psychological effects of retirement. During the last few years, several organizational career development programs have expanded to include preretirement counseling. This counseling, often available to spouses as well, has focused on identifying appropriate retirement activities and exploring sources of identity and opportunities for accomplishment in retirement.

The Industrially Injured Worker. Until recently, many industrially injured workers, no longer able to perform the occupation for which they were hired, were relegated to insurance pension checks and the resulting feelings of uselessness. As more and more organizations have become "self-insured"—that is, have discontinued paying worker's compensation insurance premiums—they have taken on the role of providing vocational rehabilitation counseling. The result has been the identification of rewarding alternative careers for injured workers and a swift return to productive employment. In some organizations, rehabilitation counseling is seen as just one of the roles of the career counselor or human resource development specialist.

The Surplus Worker. Historically, when business changes generated workers without sufficient work, organizations chose one of two paths: abrupt dismissal or absorption of the surplus workers into different jobs within the organization. Both these paths can be detrimental to the workers. The trauma and rejection of being fired are readily apparent. The stagnation associated with working in an alien job is less apparent but often more devastating in long-term effect. The last few years have seen the rise of outplacement counseling as a method for helping surplus workers. Like more traditional career counseling, outplacement involves the identification of strengths and the development of a career strategy plan, but in this case the goal is outside the organization. In some organizations, outplacement is a duty of the career counselor.

Elements of Career Planning in Organizations

Individual Counseling. Individual employee counseling is probably the most widespread form of career counseling provided in the workplace. For the professional counselor with a traditional Rogerian orientation, the industrial counseling model might seem alien. In industry, it is not the nondirective, client-centered model that is preferred but, rather, an active form of problem solving that is directive, intense, and often brief. Typical areas of focus in individual employee counseling include—

- Academic and educational planning
- Financial planning
- Stress management
- Career decision making

- Personal growth
- Job transitions
- Personal crisis
- Substance abuse problems
- Vocational rehabilitation
- Preretirement planning

In many organizations most of the employee career counseling is the responsibility of the manager; in others the responsibility lies with the employee relations manager; still others utilize professionally trained counselors hired specifically for their counseling skills; in a few organizations the counseling tasks are referred to outside consultants, often based at a local university.

Group Counseling Workshops. The most popular format for the delivery of career-planning and development services in the workplace is probably the workshop or seminar (Schalders, 1980). Usually led by a professional counselor or a training specialist, these workshops range from information-giving lectures to structured assessment techniques to "touchy-feely" experiential exercises. The nature of the workshop often depends on the training of the leader as well as on the culture of the organization. Some organizations opt for after-hours workshops, either during the lunch hour or for two hours after work. A more popular practice is to offer workshops on company time. Typical formats call for half- or full-day modules. Some organizations prefer homogeneous groups (all secretaries or all managers, for example); others believe that heterogeneous grouping enhances communication and learning. Attendance at some career-planning workshops is mandatory, but the most successful programs are voluntary. A typical workshop will have fifteen to twenty-five participants and one or two leaders. Following is an outline of a typical career-planning workshop for employees at a medium-sized company:

Module One: Who Am I? Part I

- Introduction to Career Planning
- Interest Assessment
- Career Values Clarification

Module Two: Who Am I? Part II

- Personal and Management Styles
- Identifying Motivated Skills

Module Three: What Options Do I Have?

- Career Paths in and out of Organizations
- Lateral Career Change Possibilities
- Education and Training Requirements

Module Four: Career Goal Setting/Implementation

- What Is the Best-Fitting Career Goal?
- Why Is It the Most Appropriate Goal?
- How and When Will the Goal be Pursued?

Each module can be conducted in a three- to four-hour session (one module each week for four weeks) or in a two-day intensive workshop.

Workbooks and Manuals. Although many career development workshops include the use of looseleaf manuals to organize information gathered during the learning process, a number of early programs relied on a stand-alone workbook for career planning. These self-paced manuals generally focused on self-assessment and contained space for focusing on a career goal and outlining a career strategy plan. A major problem with the workbook approach involves the extremely high proportion of employees who started but failed to complete the workbook. Most organizations have found that the personal interaction from individual counseling or group workshops is necessary for effective career planning, and the number of workbook programs has decreased since the 1970s.

Career Centers. Most organizations that have developed career-planning programs have also established career centers. These centers contain both company-specific information and general information about occupations as well as college catalogues and personal growth publications. Some centers are staffed by career information specialists or interns from local university counselor education programs. Interesting career cen-

ter components include videotapes of selected jobs and computerized occupational information systems. Organizations have
found that career centers serve to increase the visibility of the
career planning program (Moir, 1981).

    Assessment Instruments. Career-planning programs in or-
ganizations use some of the same instruments that are used by
counselors in educational institutions. Following are some typical instruments in use today:

Interest Assessment

- Strong-Campbell Interest Inventory
- Career Assessment Inventory
- Holland's Self-Directed Search

Values Assessment

- Career Values Card Sort
- Super's Work Values Inventory

Personal Style/Management Style

- Myers-Briggs Type Indicator
- Performax Personal Profile System
- LIFO
- I Speak Your Language
- BEST Behavior Profile
- FIRO-B

Transferable Skills Identification

- The Quick Job-Hunting Map (Bolles)
- System for Identifying Motivated Skills (Haldane)
- Motivated Skills Card Sort (Knowdell)
- Livermore Achievement Motivation Process (LAMP)

    By far the most popular and acceptable assessment instru-
ments are personality style (the more acceptable term in industry is *management style*) devices that are quick-scoring and describe behavior in terms of a simple four-part model. The least
popular are clinical assessment tools that appear too "psychological."

Staffing Patterns

There are several routes to the role of career counselor in an industrial setting. Some organizations prefer to hire professional career counselors, trained at the master's level. Many institutions tend to assign career development duties to personnel generalists with degrees in business administration, hoping that they will learn career development techniques from books or short courses. Others rely on management training staff members to develop career workshops for employees. A few organizations supplement core staffs of professional counselors with "adjunct counselors and trainers"—that is, full-time technical and management employees who also hold advanced degrees in psychology. Occasionally, an organization will contract with a university or consulting group to staff its career development program. The fastest-growing staffing practice involves having the professional counselors and trainers train managers and supervisors to carry out routine career counseling and coaching duties with their subordinates. A common point of entry to an organization for professional counselors is through an internship sponsored by a local university.

Evaluation

For a career development program to survive, it must be viewed by the organization as effective. Although a few organizations use pre- and posttests, the most common means of evaluation is the questionnaire. Workshop participants can be polled at the conclusion of the workshop and again nine or twelve months later. Supervisors can also be queried about the effect of the program on their subordinates' behavior. A few organizations have developed quantitative procedures for measuring changes in the cost of recruiting, training, and retaining employees.

Some Issues Facing Career Development in Organizations

Career Pathing Versus Career/Life Planning. Many of the earlier career development programs tended to fall into extremes—that is, some were highly restricted and focused solely on the individual's current job, while others dealt not only with an individual's career but with his or her personal life as well. The appropriateness of either of these extremes will continue to be dictated by the philosophy of the particular organization. A more common trend in the 1980s is to view career development as the process for meeting the developmental needs of the individual while addressing the profitability of the organization. This trend has resulted in a wide variety of programs focusing on a full range of orientations, such as premanagement training, assertiveness training, preretirement planning, stress management, goal setting, and career strategy planning.

Information Versus Experiential Activities. In general, the more conservative organizations prefer programs that are primarily informational in content. These programs focus on communicating information about career paths and describing particular jobs within the organization. More innovative organizations prefer programs with a heavy dose of experiential exercises, such as team building, values clarification, management style assessment, and effective communication. A growing trend in the 1980s is the combining of experiential exercises, assessment instruments, and factual information.

Confidentiality of Information. The confidentiality of client information will probably continue to be an issue that is voiced when discussing career-planning programs. Many managers have expressed the fear that career counselors will withhold valuable information that comes to light in counseling sessions and can be useful to the organization in forecasting future personnel needs. Employees, however, have expressed fears that career counselors might reveal information given in confidence that could eventually be used against them by management. In practice, most successful programs have been able to maintain client confidentiality while gaining the trust and respect of management. This has been accomplished by assertive behavior by counselors in dealing with their supervisors and by continually discussing ethical issues in counselor meetings. Nevertheless, the subject of confidentiality should remain an appropriate topic for counselor and management discussions in the years to come.

Therapy, Testing, and Other Taboos. Although most counselors will agree that all career counseling can be "therapeutic," many organizations will shy away from counseling that is perceived as therapy. Therefore, it is often important that the counseling office look very much like a "business office" and that the counselor look and act like a businessperson.

Another taboo in many organizations involves standardized testing. These organizations, in an overreaction to the criticism of selection tests by equal opportunity employment officials, have often forbidden the use of any tests for any purposes. As we move through the 1980s, this tendency is starting to shift, and organizations are now evaluating the appropriateness of tests according to individual circumstances.

Another critical aspect of an industrial career counseling program is the terminology associated with career activities. Although there is wide variation from one organization to the next, certain words are more acceptable in the workplace than others:

Less Acceptable in Organizations	*More Acceptable in Organizations*
Personality style	Management style
Life planning	Career management
Life values	Career values
Needs	Requirements
Outcome	Result
Facilitate	Teach

Thus, to be acceptable in an organizational setting, the nature of a particular practice may not be as critical as the label by which it is known.

The Future of Career Development in Industry

It seems clear, as we look to the future, that the unhalting acceleration in technology will require employees to maintain and increase their technological literacy just to perform their current jobs. In addition, the exploding numbers of different jobs that result from this new technology will increase the frequency and complexity of career decision making with which workers will be confronted. This phenomenon alone indicates the importance of career counseling in the work site. In addition, the coming years will require increased attention to assist the potential managers in making appropriate decisions and successfully moving into management ranks. As the work force ages, preretirement counseling will continue to grow in importance. As workers become obsolete, outplacement counseling will become more commonplace. Some of the 1970s' "faddish" innovations such as job sharing and flextime should take root as economically advantageous practices. Organizations will begin to rely more on career development to enhance the promotion of managers from within as well as decreasing turnover as employees focus on developing career paths within the company. Indeed, as we move from the 1980s into the 1990s, career planning should become entrenched as a critical element in industrial human resource development programs.

Suggested Readings

Burack, E., and Mathys, N. *Career Management in Organizations: A Practical Human Resource Planning Approach.* Lake Forest, Ill.: Brace-Park Press, 1980.

    This comprehensive volume presents career planning in an organizational frame of reference and contains numerous descriptions of practical programs and techniques currently being used in organizations.

Gutteridge, T. G., and Otte, F. L. *Organizational Career Development: State of the Practice.* Washington, D.C.: ASTD Press, 1983.

    Presents the results of an extensive study of career-planning practice in thirty-nine U.S. organizations. The various elements of organizational programs are described and discussed.

Hagberg, J., and Hirsch, S. "Burning Issues in Career Development." *Career Planning and Adult Development Journal,* 1983, *1*(1), 18-24.

This journal article describes the issues from the points of view of the various players in career development—that is, the manager, the organization, the HRD specialist, and the individual—and points out the appropriate roles and responsibilities of each.

Imel, S., Knowdell, R. L., and Lancaster, A. S. *Career Development in the Workplace: A Guide for Program Development.* Columbus, Ohio: ERIC Clearinghouse on Adult, Career, and Vocational Education, 1982.

This guide is designed to assist the practitioner in implementing a career-planning program in an industrial setting. Included are charts, forms, and questions that must be addressed during the development of successful programs.

Kaye, B. *Up Is Not the Only Way: A Guide for Career Development Practitioners.* Englewood Cliffs, N.J.: Prentice-Hall, 1982.

This book for career development practitioners points out the numerous alternatives to upward mobility in organizations and outlines strategies for career movement.

Knowdell, R. L., and others. *Outplacement Counseling.* Ann Arbor, Mich.: ERIC Counseling and Personnel Services Clearinghouse, 1983.

This monograph traces outplacement from its emergence in executive terminations to its spreading use with employees at all levels in both public and private organizations. The use of outplacement as a career development tool for stagnated professionals is explored.

References

Burack, E., and Mathys, N. *Human Resource Planning: A Pragmatic Approach to Manpower Staffing and Development.* Lake Forest, Ill.: Brace-Park Press, 1979.

Connelly, S. L. "Career Development: Are We Asking the Right Questions?" *Training and Development Journal,* 1979, *33* (3), 8-11.

Griffith, A. R. "Career Development: What Organizations Are Doing About It." *Personnel,* 1980, *57*(2), 63-69.

Gutteridge, T. G. *Career Planning and Development: Perspectives of the Individual and the Organization.* Madison, Wis.: ASTD Press, 1980.

Heffernan, J. M. *Educational and Career Service for Adults.* Lexington, Mass.: Lexington Books, 1981.

Hutcheson, P. G., and Chalofsky, N. "Careers in Human Resource Development." *Training and Development Journal,* 1981, *35*(7), 12-15.

Kaye, B. L. "How You Can Help Employees Formulate Their Career Goals." *Personnel Journal,* 1980, *59*(5), 368-372.

Kaye, B. L. "Career Development: The Integrating Force." *Training and Development Journal,* 1981, *35*(5), 36-40.

Knowdell, R. L. "Career Planning in Industry: A Model Program That Works." *Career Planning and Adult Development Newsletter,* 1981, *3*(4), 1-2.

Knowdell, R. L. "Comprehensive Career Guidance Programs in the Workplace." *Vocational Guidance Quarterly,* 1982, *30*(4), 323-326.

Leach, J. J. "The Career Planning Process." *Personnel Journal,* 1981, *60*(4), 283-287.

Leibowitz, Z. "Career Development at All Levels at Goddard Space Flight Center." *Career Planning and Adult Development Newsletter,* 1980, *2*(8), 1-2.

Lipsett, L. "A Career Counselor in Industry." *Vocational Guidance Quarterly,* 1980, *28*(3), 269-272.

Lopez, F., Ruckmore, B. W., and Kesselman, G. A. "The Development of an Integrated Career Planning Program at Guld Power Company." *Personnel Administrator,* 1980, *25*(10), 21-23, 26-29, 75-76.

Mamarchev, H. L. *Career Management and Career Pathing in Organizations.* Ann Arbor: ERIC Counseling and Personnel Services Clearinghouse, University of Michigan, 1982.

Moir, E. "Career Resource Centers in Business and Industry." *Training and Development Journal,* 1981, *35*(2), 54-57.

Moore, L. L. "From Manpower Planning to Human Resources Through Career Development." *Personnel,* 1979, *56,* 9-16.

Morgan, M. A. *Managing Career Development.* New York: Van Nostrand Reinhold, 1980.

Peck, T. P. *Employee Counseling in Industry and Government.* Detroit: Gale Research, 1979.

Pinto, P. R. "Career Development Trends for the 80s—Better Managers, Higher Productivity." *Training,* 1980, *17*(40), 31-33.

Schalders, W. N. "Developing an In-House Career Planning Workshop." *Personnel Administrator,* 1980, *25*(10), 45-46.

Schein, E. *Career Dynamics: Matching Individual and Organizational Needs.* Reading, Mass.: Addison-Wesley, 1978.

Trammell, C. "Career Planning in Union Carbide's Nuclear Division." *Career Planning and Adult Development Newsletter,* 1980, *2*(12), 1-2.

Walz, G. R. (Ed.). *Career Development in Organizations.* Ann Arbor: ERIC Counseling and Personnel Services Clearinghouse, University of Michigan, 1982.

Zemke, R. "Take the Time to Chart Your Career in HRD." *Training,* 1980, *17*(4), 27-30.

Part Four

Responding
to Emerging Views
of Work and Leisure

Designing Careers provides professionals with the best in contemporary thought about education, work, and leisure and the impact of these components on the human career. But it is more than a state-of-the-art presentation. *Designing Careers* is forward-looking; it examines and discusses future trends and issues. While the authors of chapters in the preceding parts all had something to say about the future, the authors of chapters in Part Four focus specifically on the future and what it may hold for the theory and practice of career development.

Chapter Nineteen by Herbert E. Striner begins by looking at events that may take place in our society during the next twenty years and that may cause us "to change the ways we educate, train, and counsel our work force." Demographic factors, economic factors, rate of change, and the role of the public sector are discussed, as are some of the effects of change on workers and the workplace. Based on this discussion, Striner focuses on how we can deal with the problems of change. He looks at the need for changes in institutional relationships and investment in human capital. He ends by describing some of the tasks that will have to be faced if we are to meet the challenges of the future, among them needed changes in education, educational leadership, and the way education relates to business, industry, and labor.

Major issues during the next decade and beyond for our country are problems of work and retirement for our aging population. Daniel Sinick, in Chapter Twenty first describes the graying population, considers what is meant by retirement, and talks about the dynamics of retirement timing—why people retire when they do. Next, he turns to societal concerns about our graying population, older people's decreased participation in the labor force, and retirement practices, putting forth possible solutions to these concerns. He evaluates how emerging career design concepts can be useful and effective in working with older people on the challenges of work and retirement. In his final section, Sinick describes the commitments professionals in counseling will need to make to respond to these challenges.

Another major issue both for this and subsequent decades is leisure. Chapter Twenty-One, by Carl McDaniels, is based on the premise "that work and leisure are part of one's career and that both merit attention by career guidance/counseling professionals." McDaniels begins by defining work, leisure, career, and career development. He establishes a framework for the interrelationship of work and leisure—what he calls "the work/leisure connection." He addresses some unresolved questions concerning leisure, such as the following: Do we live in a work or leisure society? Is leisure a dirty word? Can leisure satisfaction replace job satisfaction? Which way leisure counseling? Then McDaniels presents a life-span approach to work and leisure, using six life stages to examine leisure identities, interactions, and roles. In the concluding section, he discusses some needed institutional responses to the changing role of leisure/work in America.

In Chapter Twenty-Two, Anna Miller-Tiedeman and David V. Tiedeman challenge the field in general and career development specialists specifically to think, feel, and act in new ways. "In thinking of life-as-career developing, we would like career development specialists to help clients discipline themselves to live the wholeness of life in their careers. . . ." The authors emphasize the point that career development should be described in terms of what a person wants to *be* rather than what a person plans to *do*. They discuss the extrapolation and transformation scenarios of career development as ways of perceiving the work world and conclude that a transformation perspective is required to live in the world of today and tomorrow. They describe how this shift in thinking (from extrapolation to transformation) is similar to the shift of thinking that has occurred in our understanding of the physical world. They point out the necessity of "soft" career choices; choices that are open to change rather than "hard" specialization characterized by the belief that there is one job for life. The chapter concludes with eight life-in-career processing skills that career development specialists must know so that they, in turn, can help their clients master them and with the challenge for career development specialists to be true to their own "soft specializing careers."

Part Four is wrapped up by Norman C. Gysbers in Chapter Twenty-Three. Gysbers brings into focus four major trends in the evolution of career development theory and practice from among the many trends identified by the authors of *Designing Careers*. These four trends are the changing and broadening meanings of career and career development; the changing nature and structure of the environments in which the human career interacts; the increasing number, diversity, and quality of career development programs, tools, and techniques; and the increasing number of people being served by career development programs and services. Gysbers weighs the collective impact of these trends on the theory and practice of career development in the future.

19

Herbert E. Striner

❧ ❧ ❧ ❧ ❧ ❧ ❧ ❧

Changes in Work and Society, 1984-2004: Impact on Education, Training, and Career Counseling

This chapter does not predict the specific work that people will be performing twenty years from 1984. To do so would be fool-hardy in the extreme. Major innovations in technology, changes in social values, or shifts in resource use or availability, among other factors, could cause economic changes altering the world of work. This chapter is about the changes which we can see or sense will take place during the next twenty or so years and which will affect our economy, causing us to change the ways we educate, train, and counsel our work force.

Some changes are easier to perceive than others. For example, changes in age composition of the population, male/female ratios, and educational characteristics are far more pre-dictable than changes in other factors affecting the economy. Changes in technology, foreign competition, and consumer pat-terns will result in very different skill needs. In addition, the tempo of change has changed. Change occurs more rapidly, giv-ing us and our institutions less time for dealing with new needs.

509

Hence, what this chapter seeks to deal with is not only the nature of projected changes that will confront us but also the changes we must be ready to make in our institutions, relationships, and even values if we are to cope with a highly dynamic future. And a major conclusion of this chapter is that unless we, as a nation, are willing to make necessary changes in our educational institutions, adequately financed, this nation will not be able to sustain its historical level of economic growth and improvement in its standard of living.

Patterns of Change

Demographic Factors. Given the demographic changes now evident, we do know that between 1984 and 2004 three major changes in the age distribution of our population will occur, for three major groups and at three different times.

Between 1984 and 1990, the 22-44-year-old population will increase more rapidly than any other group. It will plateau in 1990 for five years and then drop sharply in 1995 until well after 2004. A second major population shift will take place in 1990, when the 45-64-year-old group will launch an increase of major proportions lasting until the year 2015. As the third major shift, beginning in 1995, the 15-24-year-old cohort will grow sharply until the year 2007. These three changes will, we can say with a fair degree of certainty, call for an expansion of secondary and postsecondary educational facilities beginning around 1995 (for the 15-24-year-old cohort), an increase in health services and different living arrangements (for the 45-64 cohort) beginning around 1990, and a tapering off in 1990 of the major types of family expenditures usually related to family formation activities normally associated with the 22-44-year-old group.

Economic Factors. Beyond the fairly predictable population shifts and resulting impacts on services and products that one can logically associate with them, we can also superimpose patterns that have become evident for *all* age groups. Although manufacturing has gradually accounted for less and less of our work force, while the services have grown to assume close to 70 percent of the resources of the working population, the terms *manufacturing* and *services* have themselves begun to lose meaning. By 2004 the definitions of these two apparently opposite terms will have little relation to the definitions of 1984. The auto worker on an assembly line in 1980 was still doing many of the same jobs performed by an earlier counterpart. By 1990 the widespread use of robots for welding, painting, shaping, and moving will have changed the role of the assembly-line worker to that of a programmer or maintenance-service worker. Though employed in the manufacturing part of the automotive industry, the "production" worker will produce services, not cars. The same will be true in many of the so-called manufacturing industries, such as steel, tires, and chemicals. And this shift in job content has been occurring at far faster rates than previously experienced.

Rate of Change. There are several reasons for the rapidity of this change. The first is the nature of new knowledge itself. Knowledge is the only almost uncontrollably, exponentially increasing phenomenon. New knowledge is the basis for opening up horizons for innovation in many areas simultaneously. Serendipity and human imagination guarantee uses of new knowledge beyond the original purpose. Synthetic fibers, envisioned originally for textiles, became the basis for thousands of other products. Mendel's inquiry into the genetic properties of plants in the late 1800s had, in less than 100 years, produced a potential new industry—the production of new species of beings, or exact copies of desirable plants or animals. This is no mere progression of knowledge in a linear manner. It is an explosion that in a matter of one or two lifetimes will change not just industries but whole concepts of what is real and not merely fantasy. The "fantasy" in 1960 of walking on the moon became a reality on July 20, 1969.

A second factor that "forces" the pace of change and affects the world of work is the presence in such countries as Japan, West Germany, and France of coalitions of institutions that leapfrog the usual market-oriented, profit-motivated factors for affecting change with speedier mechanisms.

Japan is perhaps the best example of this new approach to

"forcing" the future, which, in turn, affects rates of industrial change in other countries, including the United States. Japan has, with almost no natural resource found within its own boundaries, seized the automotive, steel, optics, electrical appliance, camera, watch, and television industrial leadership from the United States, Germany, and Switzerland. Contrary to what we would like to believe, this is no product of an "unfair" coalition of government and industry, a few years ago described as "Japan Incorporated." All major nations have what can be described as arrangements to protect or subsidize domestic industries. The only real difference is how intelligently it is done and how pervasive it is in the normal scheme of things. As in the United States, neither Japanese industry nor the government of Japan is controlled by the other. The big difference between government/industry relations in these two countries is that in the United States, government and industry view each other as adversaries, while in Japan they view each other as key actors on the economic scene that must work well together in order to achieve national economic and social goals. And above all, people are viewed as the key resource for economic growth. As a result, the risk of new ventures, expanding overseas markets, planning by government and industry to achieve scientific and industrial breakthroughs, and maintaining a highly educated and skilled population are jointly shared responsibilities in Japan. This team produces changes far more rapidly than is possible when government and industry are adversaries. But in a competitive world, with expanding international competition, when an advance occurs in one country, the other nation's industries must follow suit as quickly as possible or lose the race for markets. The net result is that a quickening pace of industrial change, in products, processes, and markets, means that, during the next twenty years, skills and projections for what new skills will be needed will be highly transitory.

Some Effects of Change

The implications of these changes for education, industrial production, and shifts in our economic structure are basic. They are also fundamental for the role of government in our society. The Japanese model is not unique. In other major industrial nations, since World War II, new partnerships between industry and government have emerged in order to produce, compete, and share the rewards of capitalism more effectively than has been the case in the United States. France and West Germany are two examples. I believe that, within the next decade, a similar change in this fundamental relationship will take place in the United States. It must, if we are to deal with the fundamental flaws that have affected our economy since the early 1970s.

Since the early 1970s, the United States has performed poorly compared with every other major industrial nation, with the exception of Great Britain, with regard to rates of unemployment, productivity gain, and economic growth. For example, between 1974 and 1981, the unemployment rate in the United States was well above that of Japan and West Germany and usually above that of France as well. The rate of annual gain in productivity in the United States has remained well below that of these three major industrial competitors during the same time period. Between 1977 and 1982, the U.S. rate was around zero. The basic problem has to do with the relationship between the private and public sectors of our society. The countries that have done best have viewed government as a necessary source of investment in human resources in order to maintain a vigorous economy. Key to the maintenance of a vigorous economy is a labor force that has an educational level and the skills required to serve the institutions and industries in that society and economy. So we return to the question of what our world of work will look like during the next two decades.

Since 1974 the sharpest rate of increase in employment has been in the services sector. Manufacturing employment in 1981 was well below the figure for 1972. Wholesale and retail employment was in 1982 well above the 1972 level but had plateaued since 1979. Services is the obvious growth area. But services includes the so-called high-tech areas as well as non-high-tech areas.

What are the service jobs in the former? Obviously, we would include computer scientists, engineers, laboratory biologists, and computer programmers. But we would also include a spectrum of jobs ranging through such diverse categories as secretaries, security guards, office machine maintenance and computer maintenance workers, and elevator repair personnel. *High-tech* is an umbrella term that must be broken down into far more meaningful categories if it is to be of any analytical use to us. Every high-tech worker, in the stereotypical sense, has a complementary high-tech partner who looks very much like what we have always called a "service" or "blue-collar" worker. In some of the high-tech industries, the employees who do rather mundane work probably outnumber the professional personnel. One of the largest of all such industries is health care. The miracles of plastic heart transplants, CAT scanners, exotic lab tests all exist in hospitals where over 90 percent of the employees are nonsupervisory, with relatively low salaries. Neither the bedpan nor the ambulance driver has been, or is about to be, replaced.

Although some of these jobs will be relatively unchanged, most will change. Too many of the support personnel in medical institutions will be increasingly trained in higher skills merely because they are a part of a more and more complex system. The logic will soon be inescapable, for economic reasons, that an ambulance driver who only drives is a wasteful luxury. He or she will become part of a rescue team, trained in a variety of skills. This transition has already begun to take place in many medical centers. But the untrained, low-literacy-level, low-paid hospital worker will also have to be replaced by a higher-skilled individual. As medical and health practices become more complex, a truly unskilled, semiliterate attendant becomes a menace —a bull in a medical china shop. There are far fewer simple tasks for even an attendant to do. Technical, written instructions are more present than ever, not only in hospitals but in almost every sphere of activity. The implications for training and education are immense.

When we leave the high-tech industries and look at what one might term normal business services, once again we are confronted by service workers—the maintenance workers (for offices and buildings), secretaries, protection services, copy center operators, equipment mechanics, motor pool operators, and so on. Equally important, of course, in the categories of manufacturing, wholesale, and retail industries, these same types of service workers are found, not only in abundant numbers, but often in the majority. Just as in the case of support workers in high-tech industries, it would be a mistake to be unaware of the increasing complexity of the work that will be done by these people and of the increase in education, training, and retraining that must be envisioned for such jobs.

General Motors and IBM have far more people maintaining, guarding, repairing, typing, filing, and marketing than manufacturing cars, computers, or typewriters. Manufacturing jobs not only account for a minority of all U.S. workers, these jobs also account for a minority of the jobs in manufacturing industries.

The Public Sector

Beyond the industries we generally think of as fundamental to our economy, the role of government—federal, state, and local—as an employer has become increasingly significant in this economy. Government is both a direct and an indirect employer. The first, direct impact grows out of those who are employed by government agencies in order to carry out the many functions that have come to be expected of our governments. The second, indirect impact grows out of the operations carried out by the private sector at the behest and funding of government.

To begin with, government as a direct employer is of considerable significance. In 1981, federal, state, and local government employees accounted for 18 percent of our nation's total labor force. Interestingly, the federal portion accounted for about 18 percent of all government employees. Political rhetoric notwithstanding, it is most unlikely that any of our governmental sectors will recede in employment significance during the next twenty years.

But beyond these types of service and professional jobs, government will also be a source of demand for a large number of jobs that we seem to be ignoring, both for the present and for the future. This is the present and continuing need for skilled workers who are not a part of the services, professional, high-tech, or communications "revolution"—welders, sheet-metal workers, carpenters, mechanics, machinists, and others in the construction and related industries. Beginning in 1982, there was a rapidly emerging recognition that the public "plant and equipment" of our nation had been allowed to decay at a rate nothing short of a crisis. The interstate highway system, 20 percent of our bridges, a large part of our municipal water systems, a significant proportion of our dams, and other public facilities such as jails, courts, and street systems were all in need of repair, replacement, or expansion. Upwards of $90 billion per year between 1983 and 1993 is seen as a necessary rate of expenditure, above and beyond what has been planned for, in order to deal with such needs. This is equivalent to about 2 million jobs in the directly related and support industries, most of which are "blue-collar"—not high-tech—workers.

What we are confronted with is a nation that has failed to maintain its public plant and is now about to be forced to play "catch-up." But, as the largest industrial nation, with the largest share of its population living in or around metropolitan areas, the United States will find that the need to maintain *and* expand the public plant capable of sustaining such intense concentrations of population will continue to call for people doing jobs that, for the most part, cannot be done by machines, at least in the near future. As machinery has been substituted for labor (as has occurred in road building), the experience has been a decrease in the use of manual workers but an increase in the demand for skilled operators and maintenance personnel.

Counseling, Training, and Skill-Needs Information

Given all the foregoing predictions, how do we counsel and train people for the next twenty years? In one sense we can, and in another sense we cannot. Let us look at this question from the time perspective as well as the skill, or education, perspective.

If, as we seem to believe, skill needs shift fairly often, and many skills obsolesce quickly, we must be less specific for the year 1995 than 1987. Most of the large computer companies can tell us in 1985 what they guess their demand for employees, by type, will be in 1987, and this guess will be much closer to reality than a 1985 estimate of such a need in 1995. But even the 1985 guess of job-skill needs in 1987 will have to be updated by some means if we are to do a decent job of counseling and planning for training. Most major industrial nations, such as West Germany, France, Belgium, and Sweden have a far better mechanism for obtaining information from companies on their current skill needs and short-term projected needs than exists in the United States.

In most of these countries, most companies *must* report job vacancies. Hence, counseling and training can be far more effectively tailored to the real-world situation. In the United States, the individual state employment services do not have such information. They have only reports on vacancies that employers are willing to list with them. In many instances, the employment service listings are so inadequate that to take them seriously as an index of training need would be to mislead those involved in training or placement. It is to the benefit of both industry and training programs to obtain real job- and skill-needs information, and the longer we do without such a system, the longer will our efforts to match training to demand be frustrated.

But even if we have such information, we are confronted by a second problem, the ability of counselors and trainers to utilize the information and translate it into an operationally significant placement and training effort. Such a training effort includes the problem of realistic curriculum development. There is only one way to deal with both these problems: We must develop a serious, close working relationship among the counselors, trainers (or educators), and industry people.

Only by bringing together those who are on the supply side (counselors, trainers, and educators) with those on the demand side (industry users) can we be certain that the job-needs data are translated into meaningful programs. Without this relationship, all must remain as it is, far from rational and mostly ineffectual.

The Skills Problem—What Is It?

Thus far, I have been concerned with the time perspective of the question about future job needs and how our institutions can deal with them. In dealing with future job needs, I have also touched on content, but in a superficial way. The major question on content has two aspects, market skills and supportive skills. Market skills are those about which employers talk when they describe the nature of the job to be done. But underlying any set of market skills are the supportive skills. It is in this latter category that the United States is in most jeopardy and in most need of change. From custodial work to computer maintenance, from sales clerk to marketing manager, from gas station attendant to electronics technician, the ability to read, write, and do basic computations is now a must. Reading charts properly to determine which oil filter is used in a particular car make and model is as necessary as reading a price and stock number on an item purchased in a department store. These are very basic jobs, not at the high end of the skill ladder. But 20-30 percent of persons over sixteen years of age in the United States do not read at the level necessary to perform such work. Using statistics from a 1979 Ford Foundation report, William McGowan (1982, p. A27) wrote that about 25 million Americans cannot read at all and 35 million more are functionally illiterate. (This same figure of 60 million appeared in a *New York Times* article on September 16, 1982, p. B6.)

The problem of defining illiteracy is a difficult one. There are two studies that have been looked to as helpful, carefully researched efforts to determine the level of adult illiteracy in the United States. The first, supported by the Division of Adult Education, U.S. Office of Education (University of Texas at Austin, 1975), showed that between 14 and 24 percent of the U.S. adult population lacked the reading skills to function effectively in our society. The second study, supported by the Ford Foundation (Hunter and Harman, 1979), estimated that about 60 million adults in the United States lacked sufficient reading comprehension skills to function effectively.

As McGowan (1982) comments, recent cuts in federal aid

to help deal with this problem only continue a several decades' record of earlier federal inactivity. "Right-to-read programs" instituted in both Democratic and Republican administrations have received little real funding commitment. In a world based more and more on communications, the unemployability and low-productivity implications of illiteracy are of major proportions.

This nation is now confronted by a catastrophe that no major institution seems to be taking seriously. The results of an inadequate level of investment or effectiveness of program in the areas of literacy and science education do not fall solely on the less fortunate members of our society. If during the next decade we do not take adequate steps to reduce the magnitude of this basic-skill problem, we will have consigned a significant portion of our population to the scrap heap of unemployability, thus guaranteeing continued high levels of unemployment, welfare outlays, smoldering hatred, class conflicts, and the natural increase in antisocial behavior—all of which translates into a social environment in which few civilized individuals wish to exist.

Currently, growing awareness of the mediocrity of our nation's primary and secondary education has begun to result in a new dedication to fundamental changes in curriculum and a willingness to accept higher budgets for school systems. At present no major nation in the world faces the industrial future with a labor force and educational system so inadequate for the tasks ahead as we do in the United States.

Dealing with Our Problems

If we are to deal with the problems raised thus far in this chapter, several things must occur. All will be difficult to achieve, mainly because they involve changing perceptions, institutions, motivations, and values.

Institutional Relationships. To begin with, we must come to understand that ours is a society based on conflict and adversarial relations. Although this may seem natural to us, it is quite unnatural in nations that have been besting us in education, economic growth, and economic productivity. In West Germany and Japan, as examples, government and industry see each other as "social partners" for achieving the social and economic objectives that the nation sets as a priority. In West Germany, by law, every company with 2,000 or more employees must have 50 percent of its board of directors selected by the workers. I am not necessarily recommending that we do the same; I am, however, citing this practice as evidence of a very different perspective and set of values in a *capitalist* country. We must begin to understand that management, labor, and government must evolve new ways of operating together in a more harmonious manner to achieve the goals of our society.

Investment in Human Capital. We must also realize that the key to our future is the acceptance of the necessity to invest heavily and continuously in our human resources. This is as necessary as investment in equipment and capital, a need now universally accepted. And we must invest much more at both the early levels of education and later ones. With respect to the former, 95 percent of Japanese children graduate from high school, compared with 74 percent in the United States. Japanese schools are in session five and one-half days per week, about ten months of the year. The result is that a graduate of a Japanese high school has the equivalent of about four more full years of schooling than a U.S. high school graduate. And the quality is far superior. While 20–30 percent of all U.S. adults lack sufficient reading and communication skills to cope with everyday life, fewer than 1 percent of Japanese adults are in this category. And their language is infinitely more complicated to master than ours. "The great accomplishment of Japanese primary and secondary education lies not in its creation of a brilliant elite . . . but in its generation of such a high *average* level of capability. The profoundly impressive fact is that it is shaping a whole population, workers as well as managers, to a standard inconceivable in the United States, where we are still trying to implement high school graduate competency tests that measure only minimal reading and computing skills" (Rohlen, cited in Office of Economic Research, 1982, p. 11).

At the other end of the education or skill ladder, since

1969 every adult in West Germany has been entitled to up to two years of retraining, with all costs paid by the government, with a stipend inversely related to the last level of income. Thus, an individual, employed or unemployed, who wishes to retrain for a higher skill and currently makes the equivalent of $8,000 per year, can pursue a free retraining program full-time and receive 95 percent of his or her salary. This program has provided continual availability of an up-to-date, high-skill labor force for industry as well as a mechanism for social and skill mobility. This German program is based on the United States' World War II G.I. Bill program! It involves no bureaucratic overhead, no community organization, no endless number of local or federal officials. Neither did our World War II G.I. Bill. We have managed to forget our own experience, while the West Germans built on it. The French copied the West German program in 1972.

The success of such institutions as street academies, job corps centers, and what are usually called alternative educational systems serves to highlight the shortcomings of our traditional institutions. Why can we often provide the means of motivating students in so-called second-chance institutions when they have been cast aside by traditional educators as not capable of being motivated? Large numbers of our young people who have been either pushed out or pushed through our public institutions, as either dropouts or graduates, have few basic or vocational skills. High school graduates who cannot read at the fifth-grade level tell us less about the youths than about the systems and its teachers and administrators. These "products" will, during the next two decades, also be part of our society and economy. How we choose to deal with them, the system, and the unmotivated educators who helped produce them should be an issue of honest discussion and debate. A part of the answer to a more effective educational training system will be the increasing use of new technologies for teaching.

We are now no longer experimenting with how to use computer-assisted techniques for teaching. We know it can be done. But a major question is whether educators will permit it. Personal insecurity, concern over having to be retrained, and

just plain ignorance will all tend to pose obstacles to the introduction of new techniques and technologies into education.
This issue must be joined by the educators, administrators, public officials, and consumers, both individual and corporate.
Much strife will probably be involved. But if the education
establishment itself does not take the lead, others will. And if
industry is forced to begin to provide literacy training so that it
can provide skill training, a mighty force will have been set in
motion for questioning the continued support of a public
school system that "isn't doing its job!" Productivity in education is a key barometer for continued existence, as it was for
the continued leadership of such major industries as steel and
autos in the United States, cameras in Germany, and watches in
Switzerland. Not only does nature abhor a vacuum, but after a
while people do not like paying taxes for something they are
not getting. By 1994, and certainly by 2004, education in the
United States, kindergarten through Ph.D., will look very different, either of its own volition or of someone else's.

The future society, the work in it, and our means of preparing for it will all be related to a world of the mind, not of
the back or the muscles. Obviously, education and training will
be a driving force. But education and training will also be a
driven force. All the social institutions that affect output, industry, government, and labor will depend on a form of education
throughout the life of an individual for the efficiency of the
economy. But education, as an institution, will be held to a
much tighter responsibility for producing the type of individual
the society will depend on. That our educational institutions as
they are presently constructed and as they presently function
can meet these needs is, I believe, doubtful.

The Tasks Ahead. The major elements of our economy
and society are industry, government, and labor. All who are in
the work force find themselves in one of these categories. Industry cannot for long ignore changes in the marketplace; to do so
invites loss of markets. The indicator of failure to adapt is a
cruel one, loss of business. Government too must respond to the
changes in its various constituencies. Not doing so can lead to
election losses. Finally, labor, whether organized or unorganized,

has quick indications from management regarding its claims for higher wages or different conditions of work. For all these groups there are mechanisms, however imperfect, that in fairly short order apprise them of the fact that they must change.

As educators, counselors, or educational administrators, we have far fewer mechanisms for forcing us to adjust when we are not functioning or producing adequately. We are protected to a greater degree than many others in the society. There is a mystique about the classroom. Tenure is not only a device for protecting us as "seekers after the truth"; it has also been developed as an ironclad insurance policy against almost any inquiry, justified or not, into what we are doing and for what we should be held accountable.

A major problem in changing the educational institution is that it is difficult to change it from the outside. The tradition of academic freedom, the aura of professionalism, and the complexity of the subject fields themselves make change difficult unless it is generated within the institution itself. But given a continuing resistance to change within, change will eventually be forced on the institution, possibly in destructive ways, should it not serve the legitimate needs for which the educational institution exists.

There is need for educational leaders to do several things. First, there must be a frank evaluation of how adequate our educational techniques and institutions are for meeting the needs of our society. Can we really provide what is needed in order to educate, train, and retrain those needed for the world of the next decade or two? If we find we cannot answer this question positively, then we must determine what part of the problem is internal and what part is beyond our ability to control. Certainly the training of primary school teachers to use new computer-assisted technologies in classroom activities, for example, is both an internal problem and an external one. But if we have resistant teachers, unwilling to change teaching techniques and use the new software and hardware available, we can hardly make a legitimate case for lamenting an inadequate line item in a school budget for such materials. The educational establishment must first get its own house in order. If educators were to list the sorts of problems that usually come to mind when we suggest that we "get our own house in order," the following would be on most such lists:

1. Educators must stop blaming unrealistic curriculum on the unwillingness of others, whoever they may be, to work with the school system when educators themselves have made a major effort to protect the school system from outside influences.

2. We must now develop new alliances and relationships in order to better educate children and adults for the very complicated emerging society. Administrator/teacher teams should take the first steps to build such new relationships into an ongoing school program.

3. University and secondary school instructors rarely meet to discuss problems that can be dealt with only if they do meet and talk together. The same is true for primary and secondary school instructors. The same is true of vocational programs, which very rarely bring the business "consumer" into the school to help develop a realistic program.

Even though most of us admit to the legitimacy of such a list, and many readers could add other items, we will not be able to deal effectively with them until we accept a fact of life in education for which there is an industrial analogue. These sorts of problems are management problems! Until educational administrators cease to view themselves as administrators and begin to view themselves as managers, the educational institution will not be able to function effectively. An administrator's self-image is one of following regulations, enforcing guidelines. A manager is trained to take the leadership in using resources more effectively, designing and redesigning organizational structures so they serve changing needs, and, most significant, working with the front-line workers in whatever ways are necessary to achieve maximum productivity. There is a world of difference between an administrator and a manager, including how they are trained. Our schools of education have to start changing curricula so that we can manage, not just administer.

A trained manager does not, like most school administrators, present a budget as a means of just achieving a narrow goal, such as "meeting grade norms." A manager would present an educational budget supported by the needs of the educational institution as well as those of the most significant consumers or users. Management means strategies for achieving objectives, not merely appearing for hearings.

Just think of the managerial effectiveness of having a joint vocational-school/business-leader team appearing at budget hearings! Such an alliance not only improves the curriculum, it also puts clout into a budget presentation. Indeed, with corporate executives often complaining about problems of functional illiteracy, why haven't reading and special education teachers, along with major industrial leaders, formed a national alliance to support their efforts to develop better-staffed and better-funded reading programs? Good managers naturally use such relationships to achieve goals. Most administrators do not—it is not in their "job description."

A good manager is sensitive to the use of leverage, alliances, and even crisis situations in order to bring about change. Most often what we perceive as problems are not the real problems—management, or its absence, is. We too often grumble about "too many meetings." This is not really the problem. The problem is that poor administrators often use meetings as a device for putting off a decision or shifting responsibility. They are lacking in managerial training or leadership or both. The good manager views a meeting as part of a spectrum of actions in order to move toward achieving a goal, including rethinking job descriptions, organizational structure, and the criteria for judging effectiveness and results. And key to this effort is a very different perception of the relationship between the different members of the organization. Management and unions, teachers and administrators (managers) have to relate differently to each other. The model exists now in industry. Schools of education, boards of education, teachers, and current administrators need to begin to look at them. A response that "they do not apply" is as meaningless as General Motors' response that the Japanese management style would not work with U.S. workers; witness Honda's auto plant in Ohio or Nissan's truck plant in Tennessee. Educators will ignore organizational models that are in different types of endeavors but could be equally effective in education only at their own peril.

A lack of good management also impinges on the sorts of factors that we often see as being external, or not really within our control. In reality, we have suffered from too many administrators who are either so supine or so inadequately trained in management that they have not been able—or willing—to place blame properly for poor educational programs. For example, inadequate surveys by state employment services make it impossible to establish proper vocational education programs. Obsolescent equipment, including computers, given for tax benefits hardly produces the sorts of skills employers often call for. Budgets that cut foreign language programs lead to graduates whom major multinational corporations view as inadequately trained in foreign languages to compete with foreign competitors. Supine educators will have to take different positions than hitherto in educating the community to how these external forces affect the ability of the educational establishment to produce what is expected.

Our schools of education need management courses that equip our teachers and counselors to pursue strategies that focus on relationships, sources of leverage, analytical techniques, marketing strategies, and other abilities vital to their functioning as educators in a world competing for scarce resources. In my experience, educators who look to leaders in business, labor, and government as potential partners in the effort to create a more productive educational institution are usually surprised. They are surprised by the willingness of such people to share in this venture; they are surprised that so many educators have not previously made such an effort; and they are surprised by how many good ideas they have been able to get from these "nonprofessionals." But then, too few educators are aware of how much education goes on in industry, most of which would be highly impressive to any first-rate educator.

Much of what I have said applies to businesspeople as well. Since they suffer when the schools produce "inadequate products," there is no excuse for them not to seize the initiative. They would do this if they were receiving faulty parts from a supplier! People in industry must begin, also, to forge new, more effective partnerships with those who are entrusted with supplying them with their major resource—skilled personnel.

Most of those who read this chapter will have been concerned about, involved in, or confronted by some of the items I have discussed. Although, I hope, some of my insights will be new and will be seen as valuable, in most cases we have already been aware of the important problems. To deal with them, though, we really do have to be prepared to know what we believe should be done, be willing to take positive steps personally to achieve what we believe in, and, finally, even be willing to change ourselves, if the situation requires it. If, as we face the next twenty years, we believe they will call for different types of jobs, skills, and training, we should internalize the following:

> You can't be what you want to be
> By being what you are.
> Change is required!

A Final Word

When one writes about the future, there is usually an unconscious mental tug-of-war within one's mind. On the one hand, the effort is made to predict, or guess about, what can happen, realistically speaking. By that I mean being willing to assume certain major changes but not Buck Rogers flights of fancy into the future. On the other hand, ultraradical events do happen, leaving prudent predictors looking conservative and leaving willy-nilly, fanciful predictors looking like invincible sages.

Thus far, I must confess to having peered into the future with considerable caution. But there are some changes that could unhinge assumptions and institutions should they happen by the year 2004. Permit me to illustrate with a few examples.

Although we educators often tip our hats to the observation that school and education are not necessarily the same,

what we do in practice belies what we say. Institutional creden-
tialization is, by and large, our method of measuring education.
But now we are surrounded by computers, terminals, and games
that can bring the best of educators and learning experiences
into the home or workplace, over and over again. Would I rather
learn appreciation of music from a boring, second-rate instructor who is paralyzingly "live" in a class or from videotapes in
my home, featuring Leonard Bernstein and Leontyne Price and
even bringing back the recorded insights of a Toscanini or Robe-
son? No contest. The technology and low costs of satellite, on-
command education, retrieved at will and repeated as often as
necessary, promise to make continuing education a reality long
before the educational institutions are comfortably geared up
to dispense it in the form of credit-hour modules. Credentiali-
zation can more easily be managed by qualifying examinations
than many of us would like to think.

But striking at an even more basic concept of education
is to question the assumption of a given learning potential for
each individual. Are these natural abilities given, once and for
all? Research in recent years leads us to believe not. The brain
is increasingly being perceived as capable of different levels of
potential, depending on many types of external or internal af-
fectors. Chemical, electrical, and genetic manipulation are seen
as capable of unlocking new capacities. The learning capacity
may be subject to change both before and after birth. Bio-
genetic engineering could by 2004 change the learning abilities
of children.

Away from the world of the mind, by 2004 the just barely emerging revolution in energy could be a reality. Energy is
the basis for economic growth. Massive irrigation, cheap fer-
tilizers, high-grade metals, fast transportation, the ability to
communicate by other than personal face-to-face means—none
of these would exist without the availability of energy derived
from wood, coal, oil, gas, water power, or scarce nuclear materials. All forms of energy sources are costly, relatively speaking,
some more so than others. And for the ones that are often low-
cost, such as coal, attendant problems of pollution impose costs
on the atmosphere, which, in turn, affect health. But on the

horizon is a form of energy that would be available from water, literally. Using hydrogen as it exists in the water molecule as the source of nuclear power could assure us of both plentitude and safety, to a degree not now possible. This could revolutionize our civilization and what we choose to do with and in it as nothing else since we harnessed steam and created the first industrial revolution. Cheap and safe energy could bring water to the deserts, nourish populations with new crop areas, create new mass transportation networks, lower the cost of raw materials, create the basis for industries and skills not yet envisioned— and, obviously, throw all our current predictions right out the window.

That these *sorts* of events will happen, though perhaps not these particular ones (although I would not bet against it), is not only possible but probable. The history of our civilization is that exactly these sorts of events have happened time and time again. And, with each one, the sophisticated pundits have pronounced that the last of the miracles has taken place.

By 2004 one or more "major breakthroughs" will once again have occurred. The world will be different from what we have envisioned, with one exception. Only one result has always been the same after each major change in our civilization: The possessor of information, the person who could communicate, as contrasted with the person who had to seek information or obtain help in order to communicate, has increasingly been the elite. Every activity that advances civilization places a higher premium on the ability to adapt, which, in turn, depends on learning. Whatever the future, it will call for the utmost imagination and effectiveness in the use of our human talents to educate and train.

Suggested Readings

Freedman, D. H. *Employment Outlook and Insights.* Geneva: International Labour Office, 1979.

A collection of papers, by an international group of economists, that analyzes the emerging skill needs of the economies of Western Europe, the United States, and Japan against current and projected work populations there. Old approaches concerning manpower policies are found seriously wanting in most countries. The 1973 recession provided a stark example of how poorly prepared industrial countries are for dealing with economic emergencies affecting work and employment. Different approaches are suggested for moving in new directions in order to achieve a healthier balance between needs of the economy and needs of the labor force. This is a valuable work for understanding the larger world picture as it affects the United States.

Palmer, J. L., and Sawhill, I. V. *The Reagan Experiment*. Washington, D.C.: Urban Institute Press, 1982.

A collection of papers examining the effects on the U.S. economy of the early years of the Reagan administration. Studies by highly competent researchers clearly show the key role of government in such areas as employment training, education, income security, health, housing, and transportation. It is clear that a society based only or largely on responses to market phenomena is not what most Americans envision concerning a decent standard of living or way of life.

Simon, J. L. *The Ultimate Resource*. Princeton, N.J.: Princeton University Press, 1981.

An excellent study of the resources problem confronting nations as they seek to develop their economies. In sharp contrast to similar studies, it concludes that the ultimate critical resource is people. It is this resource, through its imagination, invention, and innovation, that truly is the controlling factor affecting every other so-called natural resource.

Striner, H. E. *Continuing Education as a National Capital Investment*. Kalamazoo, Mich.: W. E. Upjohn Institute for Employment Research, 1971.

Examines the role of retraining as a factor in industrial growth and productivity. Makes comparisons among the United States, West Germany, France, and Denmark, emphasizing the effects of a right to retraining as a key factor affecting employment, employability, and economic growth. Concludes that unless the United States undertakes such a national program, the problem of structural unemployment will continue to grow, unrelieved by periods of expanding economic output. Productivity growth, it is concluded, will also have to decrease.

References

Hunter, C. S., and Harman, D. *Adult Illiteracy in the United States.* New York: McGraw-Hill, 1979.

McGowan, W. "Iliterasee att Wurk." *New York Times,* August 19, 1982, p. A27.

Office of Economic Research, New York Stock Exchange. *People and Productivity: A Challenge to Corporate America.* New York: New York Stock Exchange, 1982.

University of Texas at Austin. *Adult Functional Competency: A Report to the Office of Education Dissemination Review Panel.* Austin: University of Texas, 1975.

20

Daniel Sinick

Problems of Work and Retirement for an Aging Population

Older people represent an increasing proportion of the population but a decreasing segment of the labor force, with variations according to sex, ethnicity, and occupation. Labor force participation is particularly affected by the timing of retirement, which is influenced by numerous factors leading individuals to favor early retirement, "on-time" retirement, or later retirement. Retirement poses problems both for society and for individuals; it also offers opportunities for proper societal solutions and for informed decision making by individuals.

This opening paragraph is a compressed preview of this chapter's contents. Work, aging, and retirement are interactive variables giving rise to national concern, increased understanding, and coming to grips with the challenge. Although aging is the central, pervasive variable, attention is focused on work—its satisfactions and discontents—and "life after work" (Osgood, 1982).

Only recently has retirement emerged as a social institution affecting large numbers of people. Three requirements had to be met: sufficient numbers of people reaching retirement age, an economy that could supply support for retired persons, and systematic support in some form of social insurance. An undergirding social philosophy, also required, erected a landmark structure of "old age insurance" in Germany in 1891. Not so well known is the fact that seventy was then adopted as the compensable retirement age; in 1916 it was lowered to sixty-five. Other nations, it should be noted, have systems based on earlier ages.

The Graying Population

Increasing Proportion of Older People. Declining birthrates, declining death rates, and lengthening life spans have combined to increase the proportion of older people. Birthrates have declined from 32.3 per thousand in 1900 to 23.7 in 1960 and 16.2 in 1980, death rates from 17.2 in 1900 to 9.5 in 1960 and 8.9 in 1980. Life expectancies at birth have risen from 46.3 years for males and 48.3 for females in 1900 to 66.6 for males and 73.1 for females in 1960 to 69.8 for males and 77.7 for females in 1980.

The net effect has been that the proportion of people 65 years of age or older has increased from 4 percent of the total population in 1900 to 9 percent in 1960 and 11 percent in 1980, with 18 percent projected for 2030. These percentages assume dramatic significance when translated into numbers and then into individual human beings reaching the retirement stage or waiting in the wings. Stage fright is not surprising in this situation.

Lessening Labor Force Participation. Decreasing proportions of people 65 years of age or older have been either working or looking for work. The decrease has been much greater for men than for women. The percentage of men 65+ in the labor force has gone down from 63.4 in 1900 to 33.1 in 1960 to 19.1 in 1980, with 14.3 percent projected for 1995. Participation of women 65+ went up from 8.3 percent in 1900 to 10.8 percent in 1960 but has since gone down to 8.1 percent in 1980, with 6.8 percent projected for 1995.

Also pertinent to retirement are labor force participation figures for people approaching age 65. For 1900 available percentages are for ages 45 to 64: for men 90.3 percent, for women 13.6 percent. For the closer age range of 55 to 64, percentages for men have declined from 86.8 percent in 1960 to 72.3 percent in 1980, with 66.5 percent projected for 1995. For women 55-64 the picture is different: from 37.2 percent in 1960 to 41.5 percent in 1980, with 42.3 percent projected for 1995.

   Sex, Race, and Occupational Differences. Male/female differences in longevity and labor force participation are indications of the diversity of the graying population. Black, white, and other skin colors, as well as "collar colors," may in some respects represent a wholesome heterogeneity. In other respects, however, ethnic and occupational differences, together with sex differences, hardly justify the levity of "Long may they live!"

   Nonwhites in general have a shorter life span, a smaller proportion 65+, a higher rate of 65+ labor force participation, lower-level jobs, and lower incomes. Nonwhites are disproportionately laborers, operatives, and service workers, while women have more than a fair share of clerical, sales, and service jobs. Although some of these jobs carry the spurious dignity of "white-collar work," the pay tends to be lower than that of other workers, whether white-collar professionals, blue-collar skilled workers, or "sports collar" technicians.

   Sex, race, and occupation thus have implications for the next section, on the timing of retirement. People with lower pay and less adequate retirement income may of necessity retire later, unless compelled to retire earlier because of poor health or physical disabilities. Job dissatisfaction spurs earlier retirement at any occupational level, but lower-level workers— white or nonwhite, male or female—have less autonomy within their jobs and less control over their retirement.

Dynamics of Retirement Timing

   It is time to consider what is meant by *retirement* and why workers retire at the usual age, earlier, or later. Variously defined, retirement is generally associated with cessation of work—whether a job, an occupation, or a career. That traditional interpretation is grossly inadequate for reasons related to reality and practicality and to the guidance profession. The reality is that many so-called retirees do not retreat into thumb twiddling but advance into further use of their hands or heads. They can profit from guidance expertise throughout the life span.

Retirement timing is basically related to legislation designating the customary retirement age and associated monetary benefits. Social Security's age sixty-five, adopted in 1935, was raised in 1978 to age seventy for most employment settings; for most federal government employees the 1978 legislation eliminated any mandatory retirement age. In 1961 employees aged sixty-two became eligible for reduced Social Security benefits. Despite these legislated variations, sixty-five seems to continue operationally as the usual, or "on time," retirement age.

Retirement before age sixty-five ("early retirement") has been a significant trend since 1961; since 1978 a concomitant trend has been retirement past age sixty-five. Earlier and later retirement possibilities have thus increased the options for those able to make retirement decisions. Although reasons for retiring are numerous, some major ones affecting retirement timing are presented here. Because many workers are forced to retire for such reasons as layoffs or poor health while others eagerly enter the retirement realm, to be borne in mind is the influence of the voluntary/involuntary dimension, which cuts across the two broad categories of early retirement and on-time or later retirement.

Early Retirement. This now-familiar phenomenon, a distinct departure from the conditioned response of retirement at age sixty-five, has been facilitated by a number of general factors. One is the availability of Social Security benefits from age sixty-two on, plus cost-of-living increases legislated in 1974. Another is an apparent weakening of the work ethic, an opposing view being that not working may be equally ethical. A further factor stems from the lengthened life span and parallels the increase in divorces rather late in life: When a particular marriage or employment lasts a long time, some individuals tire and retire.

Individuals is a key word, however, in retirement. General factors are accompanied by specific factors affecting retirement timing. For any individual, general and specific factors may be in conflict. Not all the specific factors listed necessarily apply to any individual, and those that do may include conflicting ones.

- Adequate retirement income. A primary requirement for early retirement is sufficient income, usually from multiple sources. Social Security benefits, which cover about 90 percent of workers, must ordinarily be supplemented by income from other pension plans, from savings, or from other sources. Major public pension plans cover military employees and civilian employees at various levels of government, government being the largest employer in the United States. Private pension plans cover about half of the workers in the private sector. Some employers offer financial incentives for early retirement.

- Poor health, disablement, or excessive physical/environmental demands. Poor health is the predominant reason offered for early withdrawal from the work force, as indicated by a number of studies. Kingson (1982, p. 117) suggested, however, that " 'poor health' is considered an acceptable reason for leaving work. Consequently, there is an incentive to mask other reasons for leaving work by claiming health problems" (p. 117). In the retirement literature, health itself often masks the incurrence of disabilities. Disabilities are incurred on the job as a result of carelessness as well as excessive work demands, or off the job. "Poor health," physical disablement, or work demands may call for a baleful eye of the beholder (or emotional disablement) to constitute a reason for early retirement.

- Dissatisfaction with work or job. Early retirement is spurred by dissatisfaction with one's work, unless the beholder is especially beholden to the particular job. Aspects that satisfy or dissatisfy may reside in the characteristics of the work performed (such as creativity and variety or their absence) or in the job setting (such as coworkers and company policies). This distinction can provide practical decision-making assistance to the graying population beset by the prevalence of blue-collar blues and white-collar woes. Analyzing apparent dissatisfaction can clarify the Hamlet-like decision of "to retire or not to retire?"

- Desire for a new career. This inclination may transcend

the notions of work demands and job satisfaction, its source sometimes being internal and long-standing. It is often an impulse not reflecting impulsiveness but a postponed correction of a previous occupational path. Mistakes made in initial career choices are later recognized as remediable. Remediation is facilitated by the increased acceptance of second and third careers. Instead of an old impulse newly revived, the desire for a career change may come from a person's developmental change, the next factor presented.

• Changed values, needs, or interests. Early retirement—whether toward a new career or toward other uses of oneself—may spring not out of the past but from the unfolding features of the inner person. Personal development combines stability and flexibility, the latter allowing for modifications, for example, of one's hierarchy of needs (too often regarded as fixed for life). Thomas (1978), who saw value changes as significant motivators, found in a study "a subtle shift in emphasis from dominant cultural values, such as success and prestige, to more self-determined values, such as being with family, community service, or more time for leisure" (p. 18).

• Desired or required presence at home. The family and community loom larger later in life to many whose waking hours were mainly spent as working hours. Either success achieved or frustration suffered may finally bounce people from the workplace back to the famly—or as much of it as is intact by that time. In some settings the concept of family extends to the community, whether for socialization or service. Family situations sometimes necessitate a person's early retirement to assist with domestic matters such as health problems.

• Desire for leisure. Surcease from toil is a prime motive for early retirement. Simply not working, or, simplistically, "not doing anything," seems attractive after a lifetime of little leisure. (Basques must work hard, to exclaim in their proverb: "How good it is not to do anything, and then rest afterwards.") The avoidance motivation of some is matched, however, by the approach motivation of others, who look to leisure for avocational activities to which they can now devote some of retirement's free time.

• Dismissal because of incompetence or lack of work.

538   Part Four: Emerging Views of Work and Leisure

This obviously involuntary reason for early retirement is related to the traditional rationale for retirement in general: to get rid of "deadwood," especially when layoffs are seen as necessary. Despite the experience and maturity enhancing the competence of many older workers, they are often the first to go. Seniority, an inherent safeguard ("First hired, last fired"), has a whiplash effect when years of employment are combined with age to justify early exiting.

• Pressures from employer or coworkers. In instances when dismissal from employment cannot readily be legitimized, older workers are otherwise importuned into early retirement. Employers reassign workers to unfavorable tasks or locations. Employers and competing coworkers drop hints that older persons "lose their marbles" and ought to make way for younger workers. The Louis Harris survey conducted for the National Council on the Aging (NCOA) (1981) found that younger persons themselves disapprove of the notion that older workers should retire to make room for them.

• Availability of part-time or self-employment. The same NCOA study reported that three fourths of the workers surveyed would prefer some kind of part-time paid work after retiring. For many workers, presumably, the sooner part-time paid work becomes available, the earlier the retirement—other factors not interfering. Availability has increased in recent years because part-time flexibility also serves the convenience of employers. Self-employment carries a built-in attraction to workers who would prefer to "be their own boss," but its desirability is impaired by the failure rate of self-run businesses.

• Positive anticipations of retirement. This catch-all category may include some or all of the ten factors presented, plus any others affecting early retirement. The sum total of factors entering into an individual's early retirement is seldom the result of an additive process, conscious or unconscious. It is more likely to represent a Gestalt of pleasant expectations, a generalized feeling that retirement will be "good"—or at least better than a continuation of one's employment. A single factor may disproportionately affect voluntary as well as involuntary retirement, but the global feeling probably also comes into play.

"On Time" or Later Retirement. As noted previously, the tradition of retirement at age sixty-five has caused that age to persist as normal, or "on time," retirement. Also noted have been trends diverging in both directions from that traditional age. The trend since 1961 toward retiring before age sixty-five has been discussed in the immediately preceding section, on early retirement. The trend since 1978 toward retiring later than age sixty-five is combined in this section with "on time" retirement, in view of the commonality of the retirement-timing factors. Still to be borne in mind is the voluntary or involuntary nature of different factors. As with early retirement, eleven factors are again presented.

• Retirement income accrual necessary. Many desirous of retiring early cannot do so for lack of adequate retirement income. Whereas such adequacy ordinarily depends on having more than one income source, roughly two thirds of persons sixty-five or older have only one source, Social Security. The inroads of inflation over the lengthened life span, moreover, can sorely attenuate otherwise adequate income. By postponing retirement, therefore, workers hope at least to build up their retirement benefits (based on age plus years of employment) and perhaps accumulate savings.

• Peak earnings hard to part with. Increased retirement benefits and accrued personal savings are likely during the years of employment just prior to retirement because most employees reach their highest level of earnings at that time. The generally long climb up the pay scales to their peak earnings—probably with many a bleak plateau on the steep way up—can easily render many workers who are eligible for retirement reluctant to give up "the fruits of their hard labor."

• Favorable ratio between health and physical/environmental demands. How employees regard themselves and their situation has much to do with their retirement timing. Their positive perception of the ratio between health and demands, for example, could make them stay on while others retire early. Even severe disabilities are perceived differently and lead to different decisions. Disparities between subjective perceptions and objective realities are sometimes so wide as to suggest emotional disturbance, a disability properly falling under the term *emotional health* rather than the misused *mental health.*

• Satisfaction with work or job. Misused or confused terms abound in this vital area of one's satisfaction as a basis for continued employment. A distinction is useful between the work one does and the particular job in which one does it; either may serve as a basis for "employment satisfaction" or "job satisfaction," the accepted term. Less distinctive variables, however, are "job satisfiers" and "job dissatisfiers," as well as "intrinsic" and "extrinsic" rewards. Experts differ on the intrinsic/extrinsic nature of such variables as variety and recognition. Most workers nevertheless recognize the value of psychic income.

• Retention desired by employer. Complementing satisfaction of the employee as a basis for continued employment is employer satisfaction *with* the employee, commonly called "satisfactoriness." Satisfactory older employees are often retained despite their usually higher pay because of higher competence, group morale, the cost of new hires, or other considerations. Retention of older workers could grow into a significant trend if their assets are increasingly recognized and qualified younger applicants become scarcer as the labor force shrinks.

• Loosened family ties. The extended family reached out to the workplace to maintain its embrace and bring the worker back home, whether at the end of the workday or at the end of the work life. The rise of the nuclear family, the geographical dispersion of family members, the breakup of families through divorce and otherwise may make workers approaching retirement feel they "can't go home again." If early retirement beckoned, it may then be cast aside in favor of continued employment, especially if credence is given the "one big happy family" concept of many employers.

• Unavailability of other employment. Sometimes early retirement from one's present employment is desired, but opportunities for employment elsewhere are lacking. Job switching is often precluded by a restricted labor market. Or, despite the present employer's desire to retain the employee, the reasons for retention are not necessarily a basis for hiring. If the employee has in mind more than switching jobs—namely, seeking employment in a new occupation—that aim might be nullified by lack of transferable skills or of other pertinent worker characteristics.

• Delayed retirement credit utilized. The 1977 Amendments to the Social Security Act legislated a delayed retirement credit of 3 percent for each year that workers postpone the acceptance of benefits beyond the sixty-fifth birthday. These increments are effective through age seventy-one. Designed to counteract the trend toward early retirement, this measure is one of the emerging incentives for employees to continue to work.

• Unpreparedness for use of free time. Unknown numbers of employees postpone retirement because they feel unprepared to put all that free time to fruitful use. Society has truly failed to provide individuals with self-actualizing alternatives for use of time. Eligible retirees hear retired friends tell how they "kill time," perhaps forever fishing or golfing, or participating in childish community programs. It has been said that people would like to be immortal but don't know what to do on a rainy Sunday afternoon.

• Inertia. This refers to a common human characteristic as well as "the property of matter by which it remains in a state of rest or, if it is in motion, continues moving in a straight line, unless acted upon by an external force." Inertia lets valid opportunities for early retirement pass by, makes the motion of employment little different from a state of rest, and keeps employees in ruts that turn into graves. The stagnation or linearity of employees, old or young, needs to be acted upon by an external force called career counseling.

• Negative anticipations of retirement. In addition to specific negative factors already mentioned, a nebulous dread of retirement hangs like a pall over many people. In view of society's work ethic, loss of status is anticipated, of a sense of usefulness, even of one's identity. In view of society's youth orientation, retirement is taken to betoken old age. It is a short step from there to regarding retirement as a harbinger of death. Carried away emotionally, people facing retirement sometimes engage in self-pity and anticipatory grief.

Societal Concerns and Solutions

Societal concerns have arisen from the increased proportion of older people in the population, their decreased participation in the labor force, and the divergent trends toward earlier and later retirement. The discussion of retirement timing indicated some pertinent concerns and tentative solutions. For presentation here, five broad concerns have been selected, together with "solutions" adopted or proposed or projected. Valid aims and valiant efforts, it is hoped, will yield results of value both to society and to individuals.

Financing Support for Retired Persons. This concern has generated emotional and political reactions that confuse issues and impair solutions. A "hot potato" at the time of this writing, its treatment here can only summarize some of the issues and solutions, readers further interested being referred to longer discussions (Borgatta and Loeb, 1981; Hendricks and Storey, 1982; Congressional Budget Office, 1982).

The broad Social Security system and other public retirement systems are accompanied by many sporadic, unsystematic private pension plans. The helter-skelter welter of coverage and benefits results in comfortable retirement for some and poverty for others. Inequities exist under all plans, for individuals and various segments of the population. Young and old are put asunder by distorted, divisive interpretations of population trends, as though an inverted pyramid top-heavy with retired persons were weighing down current workers.

That issue pertains mainly to Social Security, to which both employers and employees contribute. Question 1: Is the population pyramid inverted even by the projected 18 percent in 2030 of people sixty-five and over? Question 2: Is the weight of financial support borne by current workers or by prior contributions of retired workers? Controversy rages around other questions: whether the Social Security system is actuarially sound, whether the eligibility age for benefits should be raised, whether benefits should be equalized for married and unmarried couples, whether cost-of-living increases should continue, and whether the amount retirees may earn with no benefit reduction (the "earnings test") should be eliminated. All issues and proposed solutions are tainted by biases based on carrot-or-stick motivators to influence retirement timing, budget balancing versus human beings, and rugged individualism versus government responsibility.

Although most private pension plans require no employee contributions, most workers covered by such plans end up with no retirement benefits. They may leave or be laid off before "vesting," before the minimum number of years usually required. "Some workers are victimized by such sinister practices as being fired just before they are eligible to receive benefits or through hanky-panky played with pension funds in mergers, as well as by mismanagement, bankruptcies, and the like" (Special Task Force, 1973, p. 72). Retirement benefit credits are not transferable from one pension plan to another. Among solutions that have been suggested are "instant vesting" on induction into employment, transferability or portability of pensions from one employer to another, stringent monitoring of pension fund management, individualizing of pension accounts along the lines of Keogh plans and Individual Retirement Accounts, overall coordination of the plethora of private pension plans, and synchronization of public and private retirement arrangements.

Utilizing Older Persons as Capable Older Workers. Partly to reduce the proportion of retired persons and partly to put their potentials to continued use for their and society's benefit, three major approaches have been emphasized and variably implemented.

The first two operate in combination: increasing the recognition of older workers' capabilities and decreasing discriminatory employment practices. Older workers' capabilities have been demonstrated in numerous studies comparing older and younger workers (Meier and Kerr, 1976). In job performance—clearly the most realistic criterion—older workers fare favorably in terms of productivity, accuracy, attendance, injuries, morale, turnover, and supervisors' ratings. Foner and Schwab (1981) cogently counteracted sterile stereotypes of older workers' reduced productivity, slower reactions, diminished strength, declining intelligence, and senile symptoms. Half-truths at best, negative stereotypes can worsen older workers' self-images and become self-fulfilling prophecies.

Even more must employers be disabused of negative notions that lead to discrimination against older workers. As "attitudes cannot be taught but must be caught," the best source of enlightened views is employers who have had eye-opening experience with older workers. Although attitudes cannot be legislated either, it was doubtless in the hope that behavior can be that the Age Discrimination in Employment Act (ADEA) was adopted in 1967 and amended in 1978. Covering persons aged forty to seventy, the law prohibits discrimination because of age in such matters as hiring, compensation, and retention. Two drawbacks are that ADEA does not apply to the large number of small employers and that "the more subtle forms of age discrimination in employment often remain difficult to document and prevent" (Kingson, 1982, p. 112).

Utilization of older workers has been facilitated by an increased variety of alternative work patterns (McConnell, 1980). In addition to part-time employment, which has been augmented by job sharing and work sharing and by tax incentives, work patterns include otherwise flexible scheduling, shorter work weeks, and shorter work years, with overtime discouraged and sabbaticals encouraged. Jobs have been redesigned to reduce physical demands and enhance psychological rewards; a useful matching instrument is GULHEMP (Koyl, 1970), a functional profile of General physique, Upper extremities, Lower extremities, Hearing, Eyesight, Mentality, and Personality. Older workers are reassigned or at least rotated. Retraining is provided. Among related practices in some European countries (Morrison, 1982, p. 277) are mobility allowances, employer subsidies, older worker quota systems, and specialized employment services. Some employers in this country supplement external public and private employment services with an "outplacement" service to terminated employees to help them find other suitable jobs.

Facilitating Education and Training of Older Persons. The two key terms in this heading point up the dual facilitating purpose. Training has an occupational orientation—toward making a living—and education, broadly interpreted, is oriented toward living. Professional occupations pride themselves, however, on how education constitutes their training. Just as working and living are interactive, training and education are complementary.

Education—whether to deepen knowledge, enrich skills, or widen occupational and leisure horizons—now presents increased options for older persons. Adult education programs and community colleges are widely available. Four-year colleges are more accessible with acceptance of high school equivalency diplomas and credit for life experience. Elderhostel is a special program providing college experiences. Some employers provide paid or unpaid educational leave; tuition assistance or voucher plans are available at some educational institutions.

Training and retraining of older workers are mainly to upgrade their knowledge and skills. Despite the obvious process of obsolescence, lamented Atchley (1980, p. 16), "there is no mechanism for periodically updating knowledge systematically." Initial training of employees is assumed by about 50 percent of employers as an essential responsibility, the other half expecting new employees to be fully trained. Retraining of older workers, if assumed by a high proportion of employers, would help the utilization of large numbers of older workers.

To facilitate the education or training of older persons, special considerations and procedures need to be taken into account. Approaches successful with young learners may not work with oldsters. Yet in the United States little is heard of andragogy, the needed counterpart to pedagogy. Although both terms are etymologically sexist, *pedagogy* referring to boys as learners and *andragogy* to men, the latter is addressed to older persons.

Older persons learn best when they feel a need to learn, when they can tackle in an informal atmosphere realistic problems that draw on their experience. As techniques found useful with older persons, Botwinick (1978, pp. 305–307) suggested slowing the pace, avoiding anxiety arousal, organizing tasks into larger and more meaningful units, and combining visual and auditory modalities. A relevant technique endorsed by industrial gerontologists is the "discovery method" (Belbin, 1970), which minimizes verbal instruction or physical demonstration and allows learners to discover the how and why of increasingly difficult tasks.

Making Retirement a Period of Transition. If retirement is to carry promise instead of threat, it needs to be based as much as possible, first of all, on personal preferences regarding retirement timing. Timely preparation for retirement is a second prerequisite for satisfaction with life after retirement. As a process rather than a point in time, finally, retirement is most efficacious when made a gradual transition.

Employees' personal preferences concerning when they ought to retire, to be valid bases for rational decision making, need to be relatively free of emotion, "intuitive" hunches, and external influences. Preferences are not to be whims born of impulse. They can be logically formulated (rather than merely "felt") after due consideration of the many retirement-timing factors previously delineated.

Logical formulations leading to rational decisions about retirement timing and related matters can profit from preretirement planning programs. Such programs, under various names, are increasingly offered by public and private employers, trade unions, and more or less commercial entrepreneurs. Program content goes beyond the traditional focus on finances to include individual or group discussion of health, housing, consumerism, legal affairs, use of time, and other matters of adjustment and readjustment. These programs are proliferating so rapidly that pertinent periodicals may be the best source of recent information (for example, *Aging and Work, Generations,* and *The Gerontologist*), as about other topics in this chapter. Olson (1981) reviewed literature on retirement preparation programs, Migliaccio and Cairo (1981) presented an annotated bibliography, and the entire Summer 1982 *Generations* was devoted to "The Older Worker: Employment and Retirement."

Retirement as a transition has come to be recognized as an opportunity for "rehearsal" of retirement roles. Rehearsal can lessen the stage fright associated with negative anticipations of retirement. It is the customary abruptness of retirement that makes it a traumatic experience for many employees. Self-employed people, with greater control over the situation, more often practice transitional retirement, by means of part-time employment. Other workers use that method, too, but may have available any of the alternative work patterns previously presented that lend themselves to a transition. That the notion of transition has caught on is evidenced by the multiplicity of pertinent terms one encounters in addition to *transitional: flexible, gradual, partial, phased, tapered, temporary,* and *trial* retirement. Transitional retirement, it should be noted, may also afford an opportunity for accrual of added retirement income.

Helping to Fulfill the Promise of Retirement. Whether having positive anticipations of retirement and looking forward to it or having negative anticipations and dreading it, most retirees find actual retirement to pose less threat than promise and pleasure. Most express satisfaction in their retired status, even though some studies show loss of social status, diminished income, or deteriorated health. The proof of the pudding is not in objective statistics but in subjective reactions (Foner and Schwab, 1981, p. 104). Nonetheless, toward fulfillment of retirement's promise two approaches seem appropriate. One is to extend the helping-people-help-themselves philosophy of preretirement programs to the provision of postretirement programs. The other is to expand retirees' options for fruitful use of their free time.

"Postretirement programs are still in the pioneering stage," McClelland (1982, p. 55) pointed out, "but a growing number of corporations are starting them." Companies see benefits to themselves as well as to retirees. Positive attitudes toward the company thus engendered in retirees may be spread to neighbors and the community at large. Feedback can be obtained regarding the effectiveness of preretirement programs. Retirees can be kept available as resource persons for preretirement programs or in-service training. They can also be called on for part-time or peak-period work. Retirees benefit from continuing company contact in additional ways. They may be able to continue or renew personal contact with other retirees or current employees. As postretirement programs develop, retirees may receive support and assistance in various areas of adjustment.

A significant area of adjustment involves the free time that retirement makes available. Although in a materialistic society "time is money," anything free is of questionable value. Disposable income is greatly appreciated, while disposable, or discretionary, time is depreciated, in part because retirees often lack income but have lots of time. "What to do with free time" is a major problem, moreover, to retirees; that problem was ranked third, behind health and finances, by members of the American Association of Retired Persons.

Several things can be done to help retirees know what to do with free time. Transitional retirement, if it provides extended vacation time and liberal leaves of absence, grants opportunities for exploring and selecting options for use of time. Preretirement and postretirement programs can be of assistance in retirees' consideration and experiencing of broadened options. Retirees are helped to recognize that free time can be used for continued work in some form (part-time, temporary, volunteer), as well as for leisure activities. For selection and pursuit of active or passive avocations, retirees can be helped to develop "leisure competency" (Tedrick, 1982).

Career Design Concepts and Counseling Commitments

In concluding this chapter, it seems well to be guided by the volume's title, *Designing Careers: Counseling to Enhance Education, Work, and Leisure*. Some facts having been presented about the graying population, numerous details on the dynamics of retirement timing, and relevant concerns and "solutions" of society, implications are needed for career development and counseling. If quality is to be attained by aging individuals in their work, in their retirement, and in life generally, where do career design and counseling come in?

These career guidance concerns are not prominent in the

retirement literature. Much of the literature emphasizes not only economics but macroeconomics rather than individual-oriented microeconomics. "Human capital" is mentioned as often as human beings. Economists, however, can also be humanists. Morrison (1982, p. 283), for example, in deploring the increased pension costs of the early retirement trend, declared that that trend "may also be dysfunctional because it limits the human potential of millions of persons."

To maximize individuals' self-actualization over the lengthened life span, optimally designed life/work careers can benefit from career development theories and counseling concepts. Pertinent adult development theories have been presented in various books (for example, Herr and Cramer, 1979) and articles (Tolbert, 1980; Wortley and Amatea, 1982). The limited space here permits the presentation of selected concepts largely reinforcing those inherent in the earlier material. The chapter closes with guidance and counseling commitments to the aging population—which includes everybody from the cradle to the grave.

Career Design Concepts. Only in recent years has adequate attention begun to be given to the aging process and retirement, mainly because life has lengthened and more people reach retirement ages. Textbooks on human development and developmental psychology now go beyond adolescence into adult development and aging. The full continuum of life is now treated, with the help of such terms as *life span, life cycle,* and *life course.* A primary concept for career design, then, is that planning can occur throughout life.

Planning can first be emphasized separately as a central guidance concept. With respect to retirement, planning and preparation have been found in a number of studies to yield greater satisfaction with life after retirement. Preretirement planning programs can contribute to such satisfaction by providing what sociologists call anticipatory socialization, or preparation for a change in role or status. The dynamic dilemmas of retirement timing and related societal concerns indicate, however, that tentative planning—even for retirement—should start early in life. Atchley (1980, p. 188), an authority on retirement, pointed out that "many gerontologists are pessimistic about the possibility of completely resocializing older people to lead a 'new life' " and suggested that planning "must begin early."

That planning can occur throughout life has increasingly been recognized. Adopting an internal locus of control, individuals can exercise a maximum of freedom of choice in regard to an initial occupation and perhaps subsequent ones. Career choosers often become career changers. Instead of restricting themselves to a linear life in a single career, people can anticipate discontinuities and avoid crises or convert them into opportunities. Viewing careers both subjectively and objectively, people can combine emotion and reason in reaching sound decisions based on consideration of relevant factors. "What factors," asked Kingson (1982, p. 123), "operate throughout the life cycle to cause some people to face favorable and others unfavorable retirement circumstances?"

Among the factors to be considered, in addition to external realities, are values, needs, and interests. Although individuals—and counselors—usually pay careful attention to changes in the labor market, for example, they are less likely to credit inner changes. Yet developing individuals are composites of consistency and change. New motivations must be taken into account, as well as new "measurements," if tests and inventories are adequate to keep up with subtle changes in individuals. People's own perceptions are highly pertinent. The "career clock" suggested by Kimmel (1974, p. 253) is a different kind of measure: individuals' subjective sense of being "on time" or "behind time" in their career development. The relevance of this concept to retirement timing is especially clear, but the concept is equally applicable to other periods in people's lives.

Assessment or appraisal of older persons may require a reorientation among guidance personnel accustomed to dealing with younger persons. Tests and inventories constructed for young students may lack construct or other validity for older workers, for whom even face validity is generally an important motivator. Artificial instruments seemingly unrelated to real life do not always evoke performance or results of evaluative value.

Norms for youngsters may simply be inappropriate for older persons. Minimal use of standardized tests therefore suggests itself, with greater reliance placed on such indices as work history and life history, interests and activities outside work, and demonstrated functional abilities. Interviews can elicit most of this information and can surpass interest inventories, for example, in tapping duration, intensity, and underlying values. Longitudinal information is, in general, more useful with older persons than cross-sectional test data.

Long-range life planning, to be most effective, must attempt to integrate work, education, family, and leisure. Such integration in the retirement years is, in turn, most effective if achieved—or even sought—in one's earlier years. These four aspects of life need not proceed single file in a fixed sequence but, rather, march together all through life, one or another moving ahead as the four undulate forward. Perhaps family leads first, education then edging into the lead, then work, and finally leisure. Having education leave the procession completely at some point is far less integrative than having it drop back ("drop out"?) for a while but ever marching forward. Both education and work may continue into retirement, whether toward paid employment or just enjoyment. Family is indeed familiar as a favorable walking companion throughout life, as is leisure.

Leisure is of particular importance in the later years because of the free time released by retirement and the added duration of such time caused by lengthened life. Leisure often lends itself to integration with family, education, and work. Although work may cease after retirement, leisure activities may conform to either of two pertinent theories: that these activities "spill over" from work in the form of similar or related activities or that leisure activities serve to compensate for psychological satisfactions unfulfilled by work. The vast variety of leisure activities, their probable relationship to work, and their likely significance in the lives of individuals combine to suggest that career counselors need also to be leisure counselors. "Leisure Counseling" constituted a special issue (vol. 9, no. 3, 1981) of *The Counseling Psychologist*.

Counseling Commitments. Expertise in leisure counseling is only one of a number of areas to which career counselors who deal with older persons need to be committed. Other areas, preceding and following retirement, are delineated in this chapter, such as the dynamics of retirement timing. As adult development occurs, many individuals can benefit from counseling related to inner and outer changes. One-time counseling for all time is desirable, to avoid lifetime client dependence on counseling assistance, but that sound precept should not preclude continued service to those who need it.

"What about gerontological counselors?," some might ask. "Shouldn't they be the ones to do career counseling with older persons?" It is indeed professionally imperative that guidance counselors not compete, but rather collaborate, with gerontological counselors. Such collaboration parallels that of rehabilitation counselors with social workers. The latter are typically well trained in various aspects of social work but lack the special expertise of *vocational* rehabilitation counselors. Gerontological counselors are similarly broadly trained but lack the special expertise of *career* counselors, who are backed by over seventy years of vocational guidance. As recently as 1980 did a leading university program in gerontology announce the launching of a specialization in occupational gerontology (Andrus Gerontology Center, 1980).

The focus of this master's program is on a locus for career counselor commitment—actual workplaces where employees age toward and after retirement. The program, at the Leonard Davis School of Gerontology, University of Southern California, covers "assessment of older employee performance, the retraining of middle-aged and older workers, the design of retirement counseling, and the sensitizing of supervisory staff to the outcomes of the aging process. Persons completing this education should be prepared to participate in the formulation of employer policies which deal with age discrimination legislation limiting mandatory retirement, job change in later life, the problem of obsolescence, and the outcomes of trends in early or deferred retirement" (Andrus Gerontology Center, 1980, p. 43).

If guidance knowledge and skills can be added to gerontology programs, gerontological knowledge and skills can be
added to guidance programs. The aim is optimal combined service to older persons in their places of employment. School settings, employment services, and other guidance loci external to
workplaces have long been recognized as insufficient by the National Vocational Guidance Association (NVGA), whose Committee on Career Guidance in Business and Industry has striven
to bridge a broad gap. Another parallel with rehabilitation counseling is the lamentable lack in business and industry and other
employment settings of qualified professionals in Personnel and
related departments. That the need is there is evidenced by a recommendation of a conference sponsored by the Work in America
Institute (1981, p. 3): "Organizations should provide for career
counseling for all employees throughout their careers."

Other NVGA committees illustrate the literal commitment of this organization to life career counseling, such as the
Committee on Career Change and Retirement Planning and the
Committee on Leisure and Career Development. Pertinent articles appear frequently in the *Vocational Guidance Quarterly*.
Aging-oriented efforts have also been made by the American
Association for Counseling and Development (AACD) and its
other divisions, some of which have produced relevant special
issues of their journals. AACD has a Committee on Adult Development and Aging, and several divisions have similar committees.
AACD's *Personnel and Guidance Journal* pioneered a special issue in November 1976 on "Counseling over the Life Span." More
recently AACD has published counselor training materials resulting from projects sponsored by the federal Administration on
Aging.

Career counselors who wish to be committed to the field
of aging can gain encouragement from several quarters. The
field is relatively new, its rapidly increasing sophistication indicated by the titles of the AACD training materials: *Counseling
the Aged* (Ganikos) in 1979 and *Counseling Older Persons*
(Myers, Finnerty-Fried, and Graves) in 1981. Numerous resources are available toward attaining needed professional development in counseling older persons (Sinick, 1979). Related dis-

ciplines constantly contribute to the widening and deepening pool of knowledge. The National Rehabilitation Association's *Journal of Rehabilitation* had a special issue in 1981 (October/November/December) on "Rehabilitation of Older Persons." The American Psychological Association's *Counseling Psychologist* has had special issues on counseling adults, and its Division on Adult Development and Aging is growing in numbers and expertise. That is true of other organizations in the intensely interdisciplinary field of aging, among them the Gerontological Society of America, the Western Gerontological Society ("with a national voice in aging"), and the National Council on the Aging.

Suggested Readings

Foner, A., and Schwab, K. *Aging and Retirement*. Monterey, Calif.: Brooks/Cole, 1981.

    The sociologist authors bring both perspective and practicality to retirement policies and problems. They dwell on "the dynamic interplay between the individual and the society." A glossary, review questions, and ample references qualify this book as a text.

McCluskey, N. G., and Borgatta, E. F. (Eds.). *Aging and Retirement: Prospects, Planning, and Policy*. Beverly Hills, Calif.: Sage, 1981.

    A relevant array of fourteen chapters addressing components of the aging/retirement complex. Adding up to more than the sum of its parts, this compact book by cogent authors, including the editors, is indeed a thoughtful, sage publication.

Morrison, M. H. (Ed.). *Economics of Aging: The Future of Retirement*. New York: Van Nostrand Reinhold, 1982.

    The editor and eleven others, from a variety of vantage points, examine economic and related trends, work-life patterns, and retirement flexibility, with a look at experience in other countries. Attention is given to policies and practices in both the public and private sectors.

Osgood, N. J. (Ed.). *Life After Work: Retirement, Leisure, Recreation, and the Elderly*. New York: Praeger, 1982.

Comprehensive coverage of the titular topics by sixteen scholarly authors, mainly sociologists. The life-cycle approach highlights differential experiences related to sex, ethnicity, and occupation. Extensive reviews of literature and abundant bibliographical references.

O'Toole, J., Scheiber, J. L., and Wood, L. C. (Eds.). *Working: Changes and Choices*. New York: Human Sciences Press, 1981.

A rich multidisciplinary mix of sixty-three articles by many well-known authors. Alternative work patterns and other concerns of older workers are covered against a broad background of work meanings, attitudes, and public policies. Numerous leads to additional literature.

References

Andrus Gerontology Center. *Work, Aging and Retirement: Changing Concepts in Our Society*. Los Angeles: Andrus Gerontology Center, 1980.

Atchley, R. C. *The Social Forces in Later Life: An Introduction to Social Gerontology*. (3rd ed.) Belmont, Calif.: Wadsworth, 1980.

Belbin, R. M. "The Discovery Method in Training Older Workers." In H. L. Sheppard (Ed.), *Toward an Industrial Gerontology*. Cambridge, Mass.: Schenkman, 1970.

Borgatta, E. F., and Loeb, M. B. "Toward a Policy for Retired Persons: Reflections on Welfare and Taxation." In N. G. McCluskey and E. F. Borgatta (Eds.), *Aging and Retirement: Prospects, Planning, and Policy*. Beverly Hills: Sage, 1981.

Botwinick, J. *Aging and Behavior: A Comprehensive Integration of Research Findings*. (2nd ed.) New York: Springer, 1978.

Congressional Budget Office. *Work and Retirement: Options for Continued Employment of Older Workers*. Washington, D.C.: U.S. Government Printing Office, 1982.

Foner, A., and Schwab, K. *Aging and Retirement*. Monterey, Calif.: Brooks/Cole, 1981.

Ganikos, M. L. (Ed.). *Counseling the Aged: A Training Syllabus for Educators.* Washington, D.C.: American Personnel and Guidance Association, 1979.

Hendricks, G., and Storey, J. R. "Economics of Retirement." In M. H. Morrison (Ed.), *Economics of Aging: The Future of Retirement.* New York: Van Nostrand Reinhold, 1982.

Herr, E. L., and Cramer, S. H. *Career Guidance Through the Life Span: Systematic Approaches.* Boston: Little, Brown, 1979.

Kimmel, D. C. *Adulthood and Aging: An Interdisciplinary, Developmental View.* New York: Wiley, 1974.

Kingson, E. R. "Current Retirement Trends." In M. H. Morrison (Ed.), *Economics of Aging: The Future of Retirement.* New York: Van Nostrand Reinhold, 1982.

Koyl, L. F. "A Technique for Measuring Functional Criteria in Placement and Retirement Practices." In H. L. Sheppard (Ed.), *Toward an Industrial Gerontology.* Cambridge, Mass.: Schenkman, 1970.

McClelland, M. A. "Post-Retirement Programs: A Growing Trend." *Generations,* 1982, *6*(4), 55, 75.

McConnell, S. R. "Alternative Work Patterns for an Aging Work Force." In P. K. Ragan (Ed.), *Work and Retirement: Policy Issues.* Los Angeles: Andrus Gerontology Center, 1980.

Meier, E. L., and Kerr, E. A. "Capabilities of Middle-Aged and Older Workers: A Survey of the Literature." *Industrial Gerontology,* 1976, *3*(3), 147-156.

Migliaccio, J. N., and Cairo, P. C. "Preparation for Retirement: A Selective Bibliography, 1974-1980." *Aging and Work,* 1981, *4*(1), 31-41.

Morrison, M. H. "Conclusion: The Future of Retirement." In M. H. Morrison (Ed.), *Economics of Aging: The Future of Retirement.* New York: Van Nostrand Reinhold, 1982.

Myers, J. E., Finnerty-Fried, P., and Graves, C. H. (Eds.). *Counseling Older Persons.* Washington, D.C.: American Personnel and Guidance Association, 1981.

National Council on the Aging. *Aging in the Eighties: America in Transition.* Washington, D.C.: National Council on the Aging, 1981.

Olson, S. K. "Current Status of Corporate Retirement Preparation Programs." *Aging and Work,* 1981, *4*(3), 175-187.

Osgood, N. J. (Ed.). *Life After Work: Retirement, Leisure, Recreation, and the Elderly.* New York: Praeger, 1982.

Sinick, D. "Professional Development in Counseling Older Persons." *Counselor Education and Supervision,* 1979, *19*(1), 4-12.

Special Task Force to the Secretary of Health, Education and Welfare. *Work in America.* Cambridge, Mass.: MIT Press, 1973.

Tedrick, T. "Leisure Competency: A Goal for Aging Americans in the 1980s." In N. J. Osgood (Ed.), *Life After Work: Retirement, Leisure, Recreation, and the Elderly.* New York: Praeger, 1982.

Thomas, L. E. "Values, Mid-Life Reversal, and Career Counseling." *Counseling and Values,* 1978, *23,* 17-24.

Tolbert, E. L. "Career Development Theories: What Help for Older Persons?" *Journal of Employment Counseling,* 1980, *17*(1), 17-27.

Work in America Institute. *The Future of Older Workers in America: Report of a Symposium.* Scarsdale, N.Y.: Work in America Institute, 1981.

Wortley, D. B., and Amatea, E. S. "Mapping Adult Life Changes: A Conceptual Framework for Organizing Adult Development Theory." *Personnel and Guidance Journal,* 1982, *60*(8), 476-482.

21   Carl McDaniels

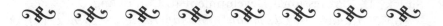

Work and Leisure
in the Career Span

For the first time in the sequence of National Vocational Guidance Association (NVGA) decennial volumes (Borow, 1964; Herr, 1974), the topic of leisure has been elevated to the status of a chapter. There are evident and obvious changes in the United States and other Western industrial nations suggesting that the topic of leisure deserves attention in a book of this importance. Some of these changes are—

- Shorter workdays and workweeks
- Longer and more frequent vacations
- Earlier and financially better retirement
- Greater availability and acceptability of leisure options
- Higher levels of interest by many in leisure
- More unemployment and underemployment

The thesis of this chapter is that work and leisure are part of one's career and that both merit attention by career guidance/counseling professionals. There are signs of taking leisure seriously—for example, the creation of NVGA's Commission on Leisure and Career Development; an increasing number of articles on leisure over the last decade in the *Vocational Guidance Quarterly, Personnel and Guidance Journal, The School Counselor,* and other professional counseling periodicals; some new books focusing on leisure counseling; and occasional convention programs. The larger body of knowledge in the area, though, is still coming from the traditional recreation field, which, in many universities or community agencies, has been renamed leisure studies or services. Publications such as *Leisure Sciences, The Journal of Leisure Research,* or the "Leisure Today" section of the *Journal of Health, Physical Education and Recreation* report regularly on the topic. International reputations have been established for many writers in the leisure field. American examples are de Grazia (1962), Kelly (1982a), Kaplan (1975), Neulinger (1981), and Murphy (1981). European examples are Parker (1971), Roberts (1981), Dumazedier (1967), Veblen (1899/1935), Anderson (1974), and Pieper (1964). A good background in the leisure literature could be developed by studying the writings of these authors. Another ten or so professionals in counseling, cited at the end of this chapter, are also building a foundation for a more compatible relationship between work and leisure.

This chapter (1) presents some working definitions of important terms, (2) establishes a framework for the interrelationship of work and leisure, (3) states some unresolved issues, (4) briefly describes a life-span approach to work and leisure, and (5) suggests some needed institutional responses to the changing role and concept of leisure.

Definition of Terms

Both *work* and *leisure* are terms that have a great deal of personal meaning for people. Academic definitions can be stated here, but the average person already holds a rather firm idea of both, which will not be altered by such definitions. To many, work is what you get paid for, and leisure is what you do not get paid for—as simple as that! Several years ago a group of elementary school youngsters defined leisure as—

> Free time or play time,
> When there ain't nothing to do,
> When school is out,

When studying is done,
When I get to do what I want to do, and
When the family does things together.

Adults might define *leisure* in similar terms, including elements such as time, free choice, and family activity. There is no one accepted or established theoretical or common definition of *leisure*.

For purposes of this chapter, definitions of *work, leisure, career,* and *career development* are taken from a recent report by Sears (1982), which was reviewed by a panel of career guidance experts, the NVGA Board of Directors, and *Vocational Guidance Quarterly* editorial reviewers. The definitions are:

- *Work*—a conscious effort, other than having as its primary purposes either coping or relaxation, aimed at producing benefits for oneself and/or for oneself and others.
- *Leisure*—relatively self-determined activities and experiences that are available due to having discretionary income, time, and social behavior; the activity may be physical, intellectual, volunteer, creative, or some combination of all four.
- *Career*—the totality of work and leisure one does in a lifetime.
- *Career development*—the total constellation of psychological, sociological, educational, physical, economic, and chance factors that combine to shape the career of any given individual over the life span.

Sears developed these definitions except for the crucial addition of the word *leisure* in the definition of *career*. This addition is absolutely imperative if adequate attention is to be given to the concept of leisure. Expressed as a formula, career equals work plus leisure (C = W + L), a formulation I first suggested nearly twenty years ago (McDaniels, 1965). The linking together of work and leisure to form the basis for a career over one's life span combines all three terms in a holistic framework. Through this linkage, leisure can be placed in the proper perspective as an important component of a career. Counselors and teachers can recognize the importance of leisure in elementary school, middle/junior high school, and senior high school. Counselors and other adult service providers can assist a person in dealing with both work and leisure in one relationship—a career.

The Work/Leisure Connection

Work. The past, present, and future of work have been adequately discussed in this and the two preceding NVGA decennial volumes. For the 1980s and beyond, as NVGA begins its seventh decade of services to its members and the public, this book presents a variety of scenarios for the future.

Several writers are significant because of their views of the future of work. Chief among these are Sar Levitan and Clifford Johnson in their book *Second Thoughts on Work* (1982a) and Levitan with William Johnson in *Work Is Here to Stay, Alas* (1973). These authors suggested, as the titles imply, that we are not rapidly headed for a world without work. They viewed young people as being willing to work and as having work available to them. In a *Monthly Labor Review* article (1982b), Levitan and Clifford Johnson speculated that the pace of robotics will be more evolutionary than revolutionary because of (1) the costs involved, (2) the questionableness of the need to further automate some processes, (3) the need to maintain a humanizing factor in delivering goods and services, and (4) the natural slowness to adapt to such changes after an initial surge. They predicted that women and blacks will continue to join and stay in the labor force in record numbers. They saw an increasing number of men over fifty-five years of age retiring. These men have already established identity and self-esteem through thirty years or more of employment and are now ready for full-time leisure. The reason for retirement is more a despair over work than an anticipation of the joys of leisure.

Freeman (1979) speculated that the major challenge in the future will be to keep an increasingly well-educated labor force satisfied with "desirable jobs." Ginzberg (1979) discussed the same problem. He stated that bad jobs (those with low pay, unattractive fringe benefits, little job security, and unfavorable opportunity for advancement) are being created more rapidly than good jobs (those with high wages, attractive fringe benefits, job security, and favorable opportunity for advancement). Ginzberg noted that women, blacks, handicapped, and young people occupy many of these "bad jobs" and expected that they are likely to stay in these until there are enough "good jobs."

James O'Toole (1981) wrote that management must perceive employees differently during the next decade. There will be a need for flexible policies that respect different worker motivations and values as these change over the worker's lifetime. O'Toole called for very sensitive management in order to increase worker satisfaction and hence productivity. Employer openness is likewise reflected in Rosow's essay (1980). Rosow predicted greater employee satisfaction and company productivity resulting from a wide variety of alternative work patterns designed to improve the work environment. Some examples are flextime, shared time, part-time, four-day weeks, and worker participation in decision making. Nollen (1982) addressed a similar theme. He stated that over 12 percent of the labor force was already on a flextime program, with growing acceptance by both employees and employers because flextime is not a costly change to either. A flextime schedule generally showed higher productivity, better job satisfaction, and increased leisure for workers.

Many of the current and predicted changes in the workplace are coming about because of changes in the workers. Two leading exponents of the new worker are Daniel Yankelovich and Bernard Lefkowitz (1982a), who described a basic change in the ethos and philosophy of the American worker. As a result of the social movements of the 1960s and 1970s, a new breed of worker emerged who plays by new rules. Yankelovich labeled these workers "nontraditionalists." They are under thirty-five years of age and make up about 44 percent of the labor force—a growing minority. Other workers, labeled "traditionalists," are over thirty-five years of age and constitute a shrinking majority of 56 percent. The nontraditionalists may enjoy their work, but they are more interested in leisure as a major source of life satisfaction. Yankelovich and Lefkowitz (1982b) see the next decade as a time of attempting to balance the rising expectations of the nontraditional employee against the economic, social, and political realities of the workplace.

Stern and Best (1977) called for increased options for employees who want more than the usual cycle of education-work-retirement (leisure). They reported that many (not all) workers want more leisure and in more useful time periods—not just an hour a day here and there, but extended vacation periods for renewal and self-fulfillment. For many workers, this leisure is more important than additional income and a shorter workday/week. Best, in his significant book *The Future of Work* (1973), speculated that as more employees move toward basic security and affluence, there is a widespread tendency to give up additional material goods in favor of nonmaterial goals, resulting in a more comfortable balance and integration of work and leisure. He believed employees will attempt to break down the compartmentalization of their lives, building toward a better, truer quality of life, self-actualized through *both* work and leisure.

Schumacher (1977), the British economist, wrote about "good" work in jobs that are meaningful and in smaller employment settings. He advocated developing more "cottage industries" in which an individual or a small group of people produce goods and services needed by the population for a decent existence. Similarly, Fain (1980) reported a steady increase in self-employment in America. During the 1970s, the number of self-employed grew by 1.1 to 1.3 million. Fain estimated that 1.5 million people were partly self-employed while holding down another job. Fain reported an increase in self-employment, especially in the sixteen to forty-four age category, with a median income of $20,000.

Will job dissatisfaction drive people to seek life satisfaction through leisure? A case can be made for both sides of this question. A number of studies show job satisfaction holding steady, but a growing number show a steady decline. Chelte, Wright, and Tausky (1982) conducted a review of all major studies on work dissatisfaction undertaken in the last twenty years. The authors concluded that there has been *no* significant decline in overall worker job dissatisfaction during the period 1959–1979. They reported that all the major survey researchers found a generally stable pattern over this period, acknowledging some exceptions to the long-term trend. Their results were confirmed by a recent study of 7,000 American and Japanese workers by Kalleberg and others at Indiana University (1983). Kalleberg reported 81 percent of the American workers satisfied, compared with 53 percent of the Japanese. American workers were reported as more willing to work harder than Japanese workers (68 versus 44 percent) and twice as willing to accept the goals and values of the employers. The authors admitted that they were "surprised" that American workers were so much better satisfied with their work and willing to work even harder. These and other results suggest that there may not be gross job dissatisfaction; however, some 20–30 percent of the American labor force may seek satisfaction through alternatives such as leisure. In a labor force of 110 million, a formidable number of workers may turn to leisure for fulfillment and satisfaction.

The foregoing selected probes into the future of work can be summarized as follows:

1. More changes can be expected in both workers and the workplace during the next decade.
2. More and more people are seeking a balance of work and leisure in their careers.
3. More varied patterns of work will permit larger amounts of leisure.
4. More people are seeking life satisfaction through self-employment.
5. Many employees want extended periods of leisure, often at the cost of pay increases.

Leisure. There are many reports on the status of work; there are far fewer reports on leisure. Few national, comprehensive reports on leisure are noted in the professional journals.

Probably the best continuing coverage of the expansion of leisure activities over the past decade has been in *U.S. News & World Report*. The staff of this weekly newsmagazine has done a real service in bringing together bits and pieces of information on leisure and blending them into a total picture. The most recent update appeared in the August 10, 1981, issue ("Our Endless Pursuit of Happiness," 1981). This report estimated that Americans would spend *$244 billion* on leisure in 1981, a 321 percent increase in sixteen years. Leisure expenditures were $77 billion more than on defense, and leisure spending accounts for one of every eight consumer dollars. Foreign visitors spent another $12 billion on leisure in this country in 1980. Estimates included expenditures of $2.2 billion on camping, hunting, and fishing. *U.S. News* reported that an estimated 55 million people exercise regularly, almost twice the number twenty years ago. The number of best-selling workout books is noteworthy.

Tables 1, 2, and 3 indicate the large numbers of Americans participating in leisure activities. Earlier articles in *U.S. News & World Report* have stressed the steady increase in dollars spent on leisure and the number of participants and spectators. The scope of these reports does not cover the magnitude of volunteer or education/self-improvement activities also considered leisure activities.

Table 1. Spectators.

Event	Numbers (in millions)
Automobile racing	51.0
Thoroughbred racing	50.1
Major-league baseball	43.7
College football	35.5
College basketball	30.7
Harness racing	27.4
Greyhound racing	20.8
NFL football	13.4
Minor-league baseball	12.6
NHL hockey	11.5
Soccer	11.4
NBA basketball	10.7

Table 2. Participants.

Activity	Numbers (in millions)
Swimming	105.4
Bicycling	69.8
Camping	60.3
Fishing	59.3
Bowling	43.3
Boating	37.9
Jogging/running	35.7
Tennis	32.3
Pool/billiards	31.9
Softball	28.5
Table tennis	26.9
Roller skating	25.4

Table 3. Spenders.

Items	Costs (in millions)
TVs, radios, records, musical instruments	$21,612
Wheel goods, durable toys, sports equipment, boats, pleasure aircraft	$15,446
Nondurable toys, sports supplies	$14,017
Magazines, newspapers, sheet music	$ 8,881
Books, maps	$ 6,962
Admissions to amusements, theater, opera	$ 6,424
Golf, bowling, sightseeing, other fees	$ 6,150
Flowers, seeds, potted plants	$ 4,500
Radio, television repair	$ 3,658
Clubs, fraternal organizations	$ 2,295
Parimutuel net receipts	$ 1,898
Other	$14,581

Sources: Basic data from A. C. Nielsen Company, U.S. Department of Commerce, Daily Racing Form.

Tables 1, 2, and 3 are reprinted from *U.S. News & World Report*, August 10, 1981, pp. 62, 63. Copyright, 1981, U.S. News & World Report, Inc.

Two recent studies by the New York–based Research and Forecasts group provide further insight into the scale of leisure in America. The first, *Where Does the Time Go? The United Media Enterprises Report on Leisure in America* (Research and Forecasts, 1982), is probably the most comprehensive study on leisure. Over 1,000 people were interviewed in a carefully drawn nationwide sample. Some of the highlights of this report are the following:

- Reading a newspaper and watching television head the list of leisure activities Americans choose to participate in every day.
- Children in families in which both parents are employed outside the home get more daily attention than children in traditional families in which only the father is employed.
- Fathers in dual-career families spend much more of their leisure time in childrearing activities than fathers in traditional families.
- Television is not a disruptive force in American families; it actually may help bind families together.
- Although watching television takes up more of our free time than any other leisure pursuit, six out of ten Americans say they do not pay close attention to television programs and often do other things while the TV is on.
- Parents who watch a lot of television daily are as likely as parents who watch little television to participate in activities with their children, interact with their spouse, and participate in community affairs.
- Half of all couples in the United States watch television together every day or almost every day. An additional 35 percent watch together at least once a week.
- The top objective of Americans during their leisure hours is to spend time with their families. Eight out of ten Americans (79 percent) report that spending time with their families is the most important use of their leisure time, followed by seeking companionship (68 percent), relaxing (67 percent), learning new things (60 percent), thinking and reflecting (57 percent), and keeping informed about local, national, and international events (52 percent).
- Nearly half of all Americans (46 percent) say they participate in community volunteer activities. Dual-career parents and the parents of older children are the most active volunteers.
- Americans with few responsibilities to other family members

have the greatest amount of leisure time. On a weekly basis, senior citizens have the greatest amount of leisure time (forty-three hours), followed by teenagers (forty-one hours), single adults (thirty-eight hours), childless couples (thirty-seven hours), parents with adult children (thirty-one hours), single parents (twenty-five hours), parents in traditional families where only the father is employed (twenty-four hours), and, finally, dual-career parents (twenty-three hours).

- Single parents, surprisingly, say they have more free time than other parents with young children in America.

The second Research and Forecasts study, *The Miller Lite Report on American Attitudes Toward Sports* (1983), reported the result of a random sample through 1,139 national telephone calls. The main finding was that *96.3 percent* of the sample related to sports in an active or passive way at least once a month. Of those in the sample, 42 percent participated in some form of sport activity daily, swimming being the most popular. Other activities included jogging or running, tennis, bicycling, and bowling. Daily calisthenics showed a substantial number of regular adherents. People gave the following reasons for participation: to improve health, enjoyment, release of tension, and improved mental attitude. Finally, three out of four American parents reported that they sometimes or frequently engaged in some kind of athletic activity with their children, and 81 percent reported that they frequently watched their children compete.

The results of these three major series of findings may be viewed in a number of ways. In light of the previous findings on work and its future, the results on both leisure and work take on a somewhat different cast. The problem is, for the most part, that the findings are viewed separately—not as part of a holistic approach to people. The findings are not interpreted in terms of careers, which, by definition, relate work and leisure. A brief summary of the findings about leisure is difficult, but the following are inescapable:

1. Leisure is a major American enterprise, growing rapidly every year in magnitude and importance.

2. The family is a major focus of leisure activities.
3. Television viewing, as well as spectator and participant sports, takes up a great deal of Americans' time.
4. The American public is seriously involved in volunteer activities.
5. American workers view leisure as a necessity, not a luxury. They want more of it.

Viewed collectively, these summary findings on the work/leisure connection suggest some major changes over the next decade for both aspects of one's career. Leisure time and activities have been growing at a fast pace. Work and workers are probably in the most fluid state they have been in during the past forty to fifty years. Changes now under way in work and leisure will have significant impact on both work and leisure. A growing segment of the population is seeking increased satisfaction from life. These people are seeking satisfaction in work if they can find it there; if not, through leisure; or, under the best of conditions, through both. In some cases, they may look for ways to turn their leisure into work in a smaller, more satisfying self-employment setting. Individuals entering the labor force, employees looking for new direction in their lives, and preretirees are seeking a balance between work and leisure in their careers. Until now, career counseling has not been of much assistance because leisure has not been related to work. New programs providing career development assistance are needed that combine leisure and work.

Some Unresolved Issues

If all the present and future trends continue, a number of unresolved issues will remain. Presently, the shifts in the marketplace and the workplace are evolving into significant societal trends. National policy directives and solid research and development activity are not addressing the changes. Few universities have ongoing research programs investigating work or leisure. Occasionally an association such as the Association for Higher Education or NVGA will publish a book, but such groups do not promote sustained research and development activities. The

Work in America Institute, the W. E. Upjohn Institute for Employment Research, and the National Center for Research in Vocational Education at Ohio State University are notable exceptions and have an ongoing interest in work.

Only a few centers for the study of leisure exist. The best known of these is the Leisure Behavior Research Laboratory at the University of Illinois, Champaign-Urbana, which is producing highly significant studies by both faculty members and graduate students. The groups that study work seem to show little interest in leisure, and the leisure centers show no visible interest in work. Therefore, unresolved issues in the work/leisure connection go mainly unattended in a never-never land of potentially overlapping interests. It may be that vocational guidance professionals who have no proprietary interest in either topic can best resolve the issues noted in the following paragraphs.

Do We Live in a Work or a Leisure Society? A host of studies have appeared in the *Monthly Labor Review* attempting to answer this question. Moore and Hedges (1971) traced the history of the work/leisure trends over the past century, finding a reduction in the workweek from the middle 1800s until the 1940s. Since then the workweek has remained at around thirty-five to thirty-nine hours. The downward trend clearly seems to have leveled off. Hedges and Taylor (1980) reported a number of workers still working over forty hours. They also reported an increasing effort among employees to obtain more and longer periods of paid leave rather than reduction of the workday/week. They found that 5 percent of all collective bargaining agreements in recent years included provisions for extended paid leaves—sabbaticals. Hedges (1980) found a slight increase in the percentage of workers who were employed on a five-day, forty-hour schedule. She did not report significant gains in the four-day, forty-hour option except in very special situations where energy conservation was a concern or difficult transportation problems existed. No current or immediate future trend suggests that the United States is becoming a nonworking society. Increases are occurring in holidays, paid vacations, and retirement benefits and in money to spend on leisure, but clearly there is no move toward a leisure society.

Is Leisure *a Dirty Word?* Put another way, leisure gets no respect! Some people in the career education movement much prefer the term *nonwork* or *unpaid work.* Yet, clearly, most people explore vocational interests through leisure activities. The vocational education literature is void of any mention of the term *leisure.* Nevertheless, millions of people each year use skills learned in vocational education classes for such leisure pursuits as cooking, photography, home repair, animal raising, sewing, flower gardening, furniture refinishing, and on and on—the list is almost endless.

The conventional wisdom is that leisure is not supposed to lead to any other activity. Leisure is thought of in an abstract way, as an end in itself. It is not a matter of serious concern or study at the university or the elementary/secondary school level. To be sure, a number of colleges and universities have renamed their recreation programs "leisure studies," but their interest is in mostly traditional recreational activities, with very limited interest in the intellectual, creative, or volunteer aspects of leisure. A few sociologists, such as John Kelly at the University of Illinois, psychologists, such as John Neulinger at New York University, and economists, such as John Owen at Wayne State University, have evidenced solid and sustained interest in leisure.

The connotation of words is important. For example, persons interested in vocational development seem to be taken more seriously if the interest is labeled "career development." *Leisure* may simply mean play, free time, laziness, idleness and not be recognized as a $244 billion-a-year multiphased industry affecting the life of every man, woman, and child. *Leisure* may be an abused and misunderstood term. Maybe we do need another word that can command some respect.

Do Schools Prepare Students for Leisure? Remember the Seven Cardinal Principles of Education—1918? Remember principle number six—"worthy use of leisure time"? This principle was reaffirmed by a 1946 National Education Association study as an important school objective. There is not a great deal of evidence that this objective has been met very well. The notable exceptions are art, music, dance, drama, physical activities (for all students), crafts, and so forth, which are respected for contributing to student development. A balanced leisure program is often the first thing to be affected by budget cuts in school divisions across the country. At best, a mediocre job was being done in the preparation of youth for "worthy use of leisure time"; now the nation's schools seem headed for a period of time targeted for something even less.

Clearer standards must be set for the inclusion of leisure counseling in career guidance. As it has turned out, over sixty years of a vague cardinal principle has accomplished little. Goals and objectives need to be established and monitored. Mundy and Odum reported goals for leisure education in their book *Leisure Education: Theory and Practice* (1979). The National Recreation and Park Association also conducted an active program, Leisure Education Advancement Project (LEAP), which attempted to implement a good plan of well-developed goals and objectives.

Again, intervention by career guidance professionals may be necessary to implement leisure education in the schools. Mundy and Odum suggest an alliance with career education to make both programs stronger. In order to combine leisure education with career education, the broader definition of career (career equals work plus leisure) must be accepted.

Can Leisure Satisfaction Replace Job Satisfaction? If the high level of job satisfaction reported by Kalleberg and others (1983), 80 percent, holds true on a national scale, an overwhelming percentage of workers are happy with their jobs. From another standpoint, 20 percent of workers are dissatisfied; therefore, of 100 million people, approximately *20 million workers* are unhappy with their jobs—a large enough number to merit considerable attention in attempting to find suitable life/ leisure satisfaction. Further, with an unemployment rate near 10 percent, another 10 million do not have any job with which to be satisfied or dissatisfied. So a combination of unemployed and unhappy workers may reach 30–35 million. Could more adequate leisure programs help to make their lot more attractive? Could, as Schumacher and others suggest, some of those with a high level of leisure skills put these satisfying activities to work in self-employment or small-business settings? In effect, by putting their leisure to work, Americans might become employed and satisfied.

Although no documented body of knowledge exists on the impact of leisure on career satisfaction, there are some indicators that leisure can be highly satisfying. Both studies by Research and Forecasts (1982, 1983) suggested a high degree of leisure satisfaction. Kelly (1982a) advocated leisure as the central source of intrinsic satisfaction, as opposed to the extrinsic satisfaction from a product or service rendered. He thought leisure was a key to life satisfaction and a place to grow and expand in both intimacy and identity. Further, Kelly reported that one's leisure identity grows and expands throughout the life span to accommodate changing family, social, and economic situations. Yankelovich and Lefkowitz (1982b), writing in a special issue of the *National Forum* on leisure in America, reported that surveys over the past quarter century showed a strong trend toward seeking life satisfaction in activities that do not depend heavily on acquisition of goods and services. They agree with Kelly that, for a growing number of Americans, satisfactions will emerge through self-fulfillment, self-actualization, and self-expression—mainly in leisure activities.

Another dimension of the satisfaction issue is addressed by Lefkowitz in *Breaktime* (1979). Lefkowitz defined *breaktime* as life without work. He followed 100 people who were out of work for various reasons and found that many of them were reasonably satisfied with their "breaktime." Lefkowitz described people as being in search of "ease"—that is, relief from daily pressures. They were seeking personal well-being, differentiation, and additional support for family and friends. For the most part, they found what they wanted while on their breaktime and at ease. They stayed out of work for two years or more before 60 percent of them returned to some type of regular employment. Forty percent or so continued to live off the underground economy and still had not returned to work when Lefkowitz's study was complete.

In short, some people can be quite satisfied with leisure even on a full-time basis. This finding was supported by studies conducted by Tinsley and associates at Southern Illinois University. Tinsley and Teaff (1983) described a group of 1,649 persons, fifty-five to seventy-five years of age, highly satisfied with the psychological benefits of their leisure. Some of the satisfactions mentioned were companionship, compensation security, service, and intellectual esthetics. The issue is still unresolved, but there are strong indications that leisure satisfaction could replace or complement job satisfaction for some people.

Which Way Leisure Counseling? Until a few years ago, most of the writing in the field of leisure counseling was by people in the field of recreation/leisure services. They seemed to know the leisure area quite well but had limited credentials in counseling. Interest in leisure by recreation professionals seems to be less evident at the present. No clear indication exists of the direction of future interest in the area.

An emerging specialty, leisure counseling, seems to be of some interest for a few counselors and psychologists. The following have written on leisure counseling: Edwards (1980), Edwards and Bloland (1980), Loesch (1980), Loesch and Wheeler (1982), Overs, Taylor, and Adkins (1977), and Tinsley and Tinsley (1982). The Fall 1981 issue of *The Counseling Psychologist* was devoted entirely to the topic of leisure counseling. Many of the recent developments in the new field of leisure counseling were summarized by Peevy (1981), who defined leisure counseling over the life cycle as "that approach through which a person professionally prepared in leisure aspects of counseling attempts to help a counselee to accomplish the developmental tasks of each life stage through the selection and use of appropriate leisure activities" (p. 134).

At the present, it is difficult to see exactly which way leisure counseling will go—to recreation or counseling professionals. Bloland and Edwards (1981) speculated that leisure counseling will be a short-lived specialty and will be taken into and considered part of the larger arena of career counseling. If the formula advanced earlier in this chapter, C = W + L, is expanded to career counseling = leisure counseling + work counseling, or CC = LC + WC, the direction will be clear. Some counselees may seek help in either the leisure or the work area or both. A skilled career counselor of the future should be able to provide assistance in both areas separately or in a combined holistic approach. Unless the leaders in the field of career counseling are more open to leisure counseling than in the past, the specialty may have no place to go except to leisure/recreation professionals or may be left to float free without strong professional roots.

A Life-Span Approach to Work and Leisure

This section will focus on the interaction between work and leisure at various periods throughout the life span. Career development is assumed to be a part of the larger concept of human development. The well-known work of Erikson, Havighurst, Levinson, and other human developmentalists undergirds the ideas expressed here. McDaniels (1973, 1976, 1977) has provided a basis for the role of leisure in career development. A more detailed study of a life-span approach to work and leisure can be found in *Leisure: Integrating a Neglected Component in Life Planning* (McDaniels, 1982). A summary of that material follows.

Readers should note the important ideas of Rapaport and Rapaport (1975) in *Leisure and the Family Life Cycle*, which substantiate the significant influence of the family in the origin, development, and nurture of leisure interests, experiences, and activities. Sociologist John Kelly of the University of Illinois has conducted extensive research on the influence of the family on leisure in the United States. For a detailed discussion of his concept of leisure and the "life course" (his term for life span) see *Leisure* (1982a) or *Leisure Identities and Interactions* (1983). Kelly emphasized a three-stage, life-course approach to leisure: preparation, establishment, and culmination. He described each major stage by distinct leisure identities, interactions, and roles.

This section emphasizes six stages that could easily be combined into Kelly's three periods or could form four or five epochs. Stages are not defined by hard and fast age barriers. They serve as guidelines for organization and agency planners as well as broad frames of references for individuals. They are flexible time frames. Some individuals go back and pick up activities from earlier stages. Others, for unexpected reasons, move forward to earlier retirement.

Childhood: Birth to Twelve Years—the Awareness Stage. The stage of childhood is divided into preschool and elementary school years because during the first five years the home is the major influence in children's development, but during the next seven years the school also becomes a factor. Childhood is an important stage because it provides opportunities for becoming aware of available leisure activities and experiences for testing these activities.

The preschool years are important building blocks in the establishment of leisure awareness. During this stage, children can begin to learn about the wide range of leisure activities, as well as their likes and dislikes—what is fun and what is not. They also have an opportunity to observe adult values of the significant people in their lives in relation to work and leisure roles.

The elementary school years, roughly ages five through twelve, are a time of expansive opportunities for leisure awareness. Basic human physical, psychological, intellectual, and social dimensions and capabilities grow at a rapid pace during this period, and new activities can be introduced. Usually, eye/hand coordination improves; manual dexterity and small and large muscles come under control. Children of elementary school age need to develop an awareness of a wide range of leisure-related activities, events, and experiences. They need the encouragement and the freedom to try out as many things as possible. They need to understand that not being good at everything is normal. They can learn about their different abilities and interests through leisure. By encouraging the development of leisure awareness, counselors can help children recognize their multiple dimensions, including their intellectual, physical, creative, social, artistic, and mechanical characteristics and interests.

If all these dimensions are valued equally, then every child should enjoy some important, genuine success with leisure activities. The continued development of the leisure self-concept is important. Ample opportunities to test and refine likes and dislikes contribute to a better self-understanding.

Adolescence: Twelve to Eighteen Years—the Exploration Stage. Adolescence is the time when most individuals are in a period of rapid change physically, socially, economically, intellectually, and emotionally. All these aspects of the person play a role in the development and expansion of the leisure activities in which people may engage later in life. Adolescence is a time for exploring leisure.

The school should provide leisure exploration through classroom activities and through extracurricular activities. Opportunities exist for exploration in obvious subjects such as home economics and industrial arts. Music classes are another obvious place to explore work/leisure potential. In English classes exploration through writing activities can result in far-reaching leisure or work possibilities. Through extracurricular activities such as intramural and interscholastic athletics (for males *and* females) as well as lifetime activities such as bowling, skiing, jogging, swimming, and hiking, both sexes can explore leisure interests. Equally important are competitive and non-competitive activities in drama, public speaking, and art, through which students can move from exploration to preparation, if the skill and interest are present. Finally, all sorts of games such as chess, backgammon, and bridge can be explored to test interests and skills.

The family continues to be the single most significant influence on the leisure exploration of the adolescent. In cooperation with school and nonschool agencies, the family can provide an extremely wide array of useful, exploratory leisure and work experiences. In large population centers, nonschool agencies such as YMCA or YWCA, Scouts, Youth Clubs, and 4-H are providing exploration activities not provided by the schools.

The educational system is structured so that students are expected to make both educational and vocational decisions during adolescence. At this time, teachers and counselors should be helping students examine the relationship between leisure and work. Students can learn to relate leisure interests to an occupation. They can also relate an occupation to their preferred leisure activities. However, before making a choice, students must be aware of available options. Students must obtain information about the world of work and the world of leisure. Adolescence must be a time for exploring *both*.

Young Adulthood: Eighteen to Twenty-Four Years—the Preparation Stage. As young adults, age eighteen to twenty-four, individuals reach the crest of physical, intellectual, and social development. They have more freedom than in earlier years in making decisions about how to spend their time. Young adults probably have fewer financial responsibilities and less commitment to or investment in jobs than they will later, so they have greater freedom to participate in leisure activities. Furthermore, education is a personal choice (a leisure pursuit) for the first time; it is now an option, not a requirement. Adult education, higher education, vocational education, correspondence study, and the military are just some of the educational options open to young adults. The preparation stage is also a time for risk taking and exploration, a time for trying new things and testing new possibilities. Leisure activities can be a part of this exploration process. In the transition from school and parental influence to a life-style of personal choice, young adults can prepare for a lifetime of leisure activities. Young adults seeking employment may use the available time to prepare for productive work or to engage in leisure activities or some combination of both.

In most communities, the number of young adults continuing their education and the number working are about equal. For those in postsecondary education, the leisure options are quite different than for those working full-time; however, interesting leisure opportunities exist in both educational and work settings.

For young college students, occupational choices can emerge from leisure interests in areas such as student union/ government, musical, art, or drama organizations, social groups, and intercollegiate athletics. Popular leisure programs have been reported by the Leisure Exploration Services (LES) at Southern Illinois University, the Leisure Resource Room at Texas Woman's University, and the Leisure Fair at the University of Oregon.

Young workers should continue leisure activities started in childhood or adolescence. This is a time of preparation for lifetime and life-style leisure activities, building on new interests or expanding on older ones and available because of newly acquired money, time, or social approval. Moreover, young workers who are dissatisfied with their occupations can seek life satisfaction or develop new work skills through leisure.

Adulthood: Twenty-Four to Forty Years—the Implementation Stage. In the next life stage, adulthood, most people are working full- or part-time. Their jobs may be instrumental in determining leisure pursuits and the time available for leisure. Job expectations can influence leisure; for example, an executive may carry on business while playing golf, or coworkers may expect an individual to bowl or play softball on a company team. The types of company benefits or opportunities provided for leisure are also important. Chosen leisure activities may depend on whether the individual works alone or in a group. Paid vacations may be a source of expanded leisure activities. Adults have the freedom to choose among leisure activities from archeological digs to singles camps to family vacations to camping to tours to fishing. The choice of leisure activities is an individual decision.

A new potential for leisure comes to married adults through their families. Families can make leisure planning a part of their regular activities. Family-oriented leisure pursuits can also become a source of additional income—for example, growing an expanded garden, planting a tree farm, or forming a family musical group. Parents who remain at home caring for children may find useful opportunities for leisure activities through volunteering. Volunteer activities may help a person keep job skills current. During this period some adults quickly become disenchanted on the job, feeling that their work is dull, boring, or generally unfulfilling. For these adults, leisure may replace work as a major source of life satisfaction and may be valued more highly than work. In adulthood, leisure may begin to bring a new meaning to life. For fortunate adults, work and leisure complement each other, yielding equal satisfaction. For those not happy on the job, leisure may provide the principal meaning to life.

Midlife: Forty to Sixty Years—the Involvement and Reassessment Stage. At midlife most people are at the peak of development in many continuing leisure interests. Whatever a person likes to do, the person probably does with some degree of expertise, and at this stage an adult may become a consultant to family and friends.

During the midlife stage, a number of experiences may affect an individual's leisure. For example, during midlife a person may experience job dissatisfaction, perceiving that a career plateau has been reached and further promotions or occupation-related changes are unlikely. People can use leisure activities to provide alternative life satisfaction. At this time, individuals may have more time for leisure activities because children are leaving the home, parents have died, or job responsibilities are lessening. More money may be available for leisure pursuits if the individual has reached the peak of earning power at the same time that family financial responsibilities have decreased. For the out-of-work individual, leisure may be the major or only source of life satisfaction.

Midlife is also the time when people begin to prepare both psychologically and financially for retirement. Development of leisure interests that can be continued during retirement will provide continuity from a full-time work life to a full-time leisure life. Midlife is also a time to build possible part-time income-producing skills related to leisure interests.

Retirement: Sixty Years Plus—the Reawareness and Reexploration Stage. The retirement stage involves total identification with and fulfillment of the desire for leisure. Full-time work is or soon will be only a memory. Time is now available—vast amounts of time! For some people, there is too much time. During retirement, leisure activities can now provide alternative uses of time. Although there is an increase in discretionary time, income may decrease. The retired person's leisure activities may change because of reduced income; an individual may no longer be able to afford the things previously enjoyed. The availability of community resources can also affect the leisure activities of retired persons. Some communities have very few leisure activities for retired people. Others, especially retirement communities, provide a great many leisure activities and opportunities for the development and pursuit of leisure interests. Work-related volunteer groups such as civic clubs, unions, or professional associations may provide a new source of leisure satisfaction for retirees.

The best preparation for retirement is a carefully planned change over a period of years, eliminating the dramatic shock of full-time work one day to full-time leisure the next. If work has given the person satisfaction, then planned leisure could provide the same satisfaction. The transition from full-time employment to retirement can be made more easily by individuals who have developed leisure interests throughout their lives.

Institutional Responses Needed
to the Changing Role of Leisure

This final section focuses briefly on some needed institutional responses to the changing role of leisure/work in America. These responses are necessary if there is to be a smooth transition through the various leisure life stages. So far, most agency or institutional programs have been passive, nonassertive programs. If the scenarios developed in this chapter are anywhere near the target, our major institutions and agencies will need to develop more active, assertive, positive programs. Some suggestions for action are spelled out here.

Parents and the Home. For most people the core of leisure exists in the home. For children it is the central place to learn both work and leisure values. Kelly (1982a, 1982b) as well as Rapaport and Rapaport (1975) supply ample evidence of the importance of the family and the need for early support for leisure awareness and exploration. The Research and Forecasts (1982) study further confirmed that most leisure activity is centered in the home. How can parents promote leisure? First of all, parents can serve as role models for their children with respect to leisure attitudes and activities. If the parents have an active leisure life emphasizing variety and intensity, they will serve as positive models. If parents present a passive leisure life, they will serve as negative models. For example, if a family volunteers at a local senior citizens' center three days a week, the children will benefit from illustration of one of the rewards of leisure altruism. At least the children will be aware of one leisure option involving significant members of the family, and at best, the children will be a part of the volunteering as well.

Second, parents can take full advantage of community opportunities involving families in the physical, creative, or intellectual aspects of leisure. For example, families can take in local arts and crafts shows, community children's theater, story hours at the local library, family fun runs. Parents can talk about *their* childhood leisure activities with the adults in their family. For a more detailed account of the role of the family in leisure activities, see Hummel and McDaniels (1982).

Schools and Youth Groups. Under the best conditions, the schools would adopt an active leisure education program as advocated by Mundy and Odum (1979). Other options are adoption by schools of the Leisure Education Advancement Project (LEAP), available from the National Recreation and Park Association and described by Lancaster and Odum (1976) and adoption of the "Life. Be in It" program, also sponsored by the National Recreation and Park Association (1981). Further, adaptations by schools of career education programs to include leisure as well as work would complement the work of a leisure education thrust. These programs would be effective only if the definition of career as C = W + L were used. Unification of leisure and career education would best serve the interests of the young people.

Other school exploratory experiences could be adapted at little or no cost. For example, some very successful "leisure fairs" have already been held in elementary and middle/junior high schools. At these fairs young people can get a firsthand look at crafts *and* meet craftspeople. Students can watch some leisure models in action. Another variation of the leisure fair is to bring craftspeople into the school for a day to paint, knit, weave, and so on. Another way to introduce intellectual leisure activities is through a wide variety of games. These can be simple board games, card games, or more complicated computer games using skills from different school subjects. The objective is to allow students to explore games as a source of fun and learning.

Many young people belong to youth groups that serve a significant leisure function. In addition to their present activities, youth groups can teach youth to transfer leisure skills to occupational settings. For example, in the many 4-H programs involving animals, related jobs could be demonstrated. Scouting outdoor experiences could relate to the employment opportunities in forestry, wildlife management, and farming, as well as various aspects of agribusiness. Music, art, and drama clubs can accomplish the same objective by bringing in former club members who work in set or costume design, music arranging, or art store retailing.

Emphasizing Leisure in the Workplace. Enlightened places of employment have sponsored progressive programs of industrial recreation for many years. Recently employer leisure programs have experienced a resurgence of activity. For example, Sentry Insurance provides a comprehensive recreation facility including a gym, outdoor play areas, and jogging areas, and employees are urged to use this facility at appropriate times. This is one dimension of a concern for employee leisure in the workplace. Increasingly, employers are adding employee assistance, human resource development, or even employee career development programs. In most instances, these programs emphasize only the work aspect of the employee's life. A notable exception is the Employee Career Development Program at Virginia Tech. This program, now in its fifth year of operation, has a backlog of staff members waiting to enter the six-week career development workshops. One of the premises of this program is the concept of $C = W + L$, and the participant's leisure and work roles are emphasized along with his or her roles as a student and family member.

Many of the staff members who attend these workshops or take advantage of individual counseling express great satisfaction at having the opportunity to systematically examine both their leisure and work roles, relating the two. Often workshop participants are satisfied with their jobs but feel they need changes in their life because of aging, shifting finances, family responsibilities, or work load. They are often assisted in becoming aware of leisure options, exploring these options, and planning future activities. Still others are genuinely unhappy with their jobs but feel they are place-bound. Often a change in their leisure is about all that can be accomplished to provide life satisfaction. Most often the leisure option is not one they have actively pursued previously. There has been a high degree of satisfaction with the work/leisure emphasis presented in this program. For more details, see McDaniels and Hesser (1982, 1983).

Community Agencies Assisting Adults. One of the major ways that community agencies can contribute to people's leisure options is to provide extensive adult/vocational education opportunities. Too often these opportunities for adults are available only on a limited basis—odd hours, odd locations, odd costs, and so on. Adults can expand their own enjoyment directly and increase self-satisfaction or, if they can develop sufficient skill, can use their leisure-learned activity to earn additional income on a part-time or full-time basis. Further, an expanding option for older adults is the Elderhostel program now available throughout the United States and overseas. Many of these program offerings are purely for pleasure, but some may be a vestibule to skill development and an eventual income source. Such a course might be in calligraphy or nature crafting, for example.

Community agencies can also assist in leisure development by providing ample opportunities for volunteering. This leisure activity can be a source of self-esteem and self-confidence for the volunteer. In addition, volunteers can test the particular places of employment and the employers. The employers also get to take a good look at the volunteers—are they on time, diligent, and conscientious? If the volunteers and the employer develop a mutual friendship, then a part-time or full-time position may be in the offing if agreeable to both.

Organized clubs can be sources of excellent leisure satisfaction. Clubs offer opportunities for joining together with others who share similar interests, such as Sweet Adelines or barbershop quartets, iris clubs, chess clubs, or racquetball clubs. In addition to the pure joy of close harmony with others, there are always opportunities to write articles about different experiences, to teach others how to achieve certain skill levels, or to open up a small neighborhood garden shop to sell exotic plants and shrubs.

Summary

This chapter has focused on the similarities and differences between work and leisure. The role and definition of each were examined separately against a backdrop of our changing social and economic conditions, then as a part of the formulation Career = Work + Leisure ($C = W + L$). The role of leisure in career development over the life span as viewed in five age-related epochs was then examined. The chapter closed with a description of how various agencies and institutions can help to facilitate the optimum role for leisure in career development.

Suggested Readings

Edwards, P. B. *Leisure Counseling Techniques.* (3rd ed.) Los Angeles: Constructive Leisure, 1980.

Edwards has operated Constructive Leisure in Los Angeles, California, for a number of years. This manual spells out her theory and practice of leisure counseling. She is a frequent contributor to the literature in the leisure field. A pair of articles by Edwards and Bloland noted in the bibliography are particularly insightful.

Kelly, J. R. *Leisure.* Englewood Cliffs, N.J.: Prentice-Hall, 1982.

This is probably the one book to read if you are going to read only one in the area of leisure. It is a comprehensive coverage of all major topics. Kelly is a sociologist in the Leisure Behavior Research Lab at the University of Illinois, Champaign-Urbana. His 1983 book *Leisure Identities and Interactions* is making a significant contribution to the literature. He has the freshest thinking in the field right now.

Lefkowitz, B. *Breaktime.* New York: Hawthorn Books, 1979.

This is not the usual research report. The author, a journalist, reported case studies on 100 people who dropped out of the labor market on breaktime. The book is a very readable and fascinating report of their plight. Lefkowitz is now associated with Daniel Yankelovich and frequently coauthors with him.

Levitan, S. A., and Johnson, C. M. *Second Thoughts on Work.* Kalamazoo, Mich.: W. E. Upjohn Institute for Employment Research, 1982.

   This is a revision of Levitan and W. B. Johnson's *Work is Here to Stay, Alas* (1973). It takes a broad view of the evolution of work in America. Even though it makes heavy use of statistics to prove certain points, it has plenty of charts, graphs, and illustrations to make the reading interesting. The best book of its kind.

Parker, S. *The Future of Work and Leisure.* New York: Praeger, 1971.

   A Britisher who does a good job of tackling the tough assignment of trying to look at both work and leisure. Many of his forecasts have proved correct, so others look even better now. A revision of this book is supposedly in the works. A must.

Roberts, K. *Leisure.* (2nd ed.) New York: Longman, 1981.

   This short (140 pages) paperback book by another Britisher is tops. It is brief and to the point and reflects a good knowledge of the literature not only in this country but in Europe as well. A sociologist like Kelly, Roberts has keen insights into the leisure/work relationship.

References

Anderson, N. *Man's Work and Leisure.* Leiden, Netherlands: Brill, 1974.
Best, F. "Introduction." In F. Best (Ed.), *The Future of Work.* Englewood Cliffs, N.J.: Prentice-Hall, 1973.
Bloland, P. A., and Edwards, P. "Work and Leisure: A Counseling Synthesis." *Vocational Guidance Quarterly,* 1981, *30*(2), 101–108.

Borow, H. (Ed.). *Man in a World at Work*. Boston: Houghton Mifflin, 1964.

Chelte, A. F., Wright, J., and Tausky, C. "Did Job Satisfaction Really Drop During the 1970's?" *Monthly Labor Review,* 1982, *105*(11), 33–38.

de Grazia, S. *Of Time, Work, and Leisure*. New York: Twentieth Century Fund, 1962.

Dumazedier, J. *Toward a Society of Leisure*. New York: Free Press, 1967.

Edwards, P. B. *Leisure Counseling Techniques*. (3rd ed.) Los Angeles: Constructive Leisure, 1980.

Edwards, P. B., and Bloland, P. A. "Leisure Counseling and Consultation." *Personnel and Guidance Journal,* 1980, *58* (6), 435–440.

Fain, T. S. "Self Employed Americans: Their Number Has Increased Between 1972–79." *Monthly Labor Review,* 1980, *103*(11), 3–8.

Freeman, R. B. "The Work Force of the Future: An Overview." In C. Kerr and J. W. Rosow (Eds.), *Work in America—the Decade Ahead*. New York: Van Nostrand Reinhold, 1979.

Ginzberg, E. *Good Jobs, Bad Jobs, No Jobs*. Cambridge, Mass.: Harvard University Press, 1979.

Hedges, J. "The Workweek in 1979: Fewer but Longer Workdays." *Monthly Labor Review,* 1980, *103*(8), 31–33.

Hedges, J., and Taylor, D. "Recent Trends in Worktime: Hours Edge Downward." *Monthly Labor Review,* 1980, *103*(3), 3–11.

Herr, E. L. (Ed.). *Vocational Guidance and Human Development*. Boston: Houghton Mifflin, 1974.

Hummel, D., and McDaniels, C. *Unlock Your Child's Potential*. Washington, D.C.: Acropolis Books, 1982.

Kalleberg, A. L., and others. *Indianapolis/Tokyo Work Commitment Study: Preliminary Results*. Bloomington: Institute for Social Research, University of Indiana, 1983.

Kaplan, M. *Leisure Theory and Practice*. New York: Wiley, 1975.

Kelly, J. R. *Leisure*. Englewood Cliffs, N.J.: Prentice-Hall, 1982a.

Kelly, J. R. "The Centrality of Leisure." *National Forum*, 1982b, *62*, 19-21.

Kelly, J. R. *Leisure Identities and Interactions*. Winchester, Mass.: Allen & Unwin, 1983.

Lancaster, R., and Odum, L. "Leisure Education Advancement Project." *Journal of Physical Education and Recreation*, 1976, *47*, 43-44.

Lefkowitz, B. *Breaktime*. New York: Hawthorn Books, 1979.

Levitan, S. A., and Johnson, C. M. *Second Thoughts on Work*. Kalamazoo, Mich.: W. E. Upjohn Institute for Employment Research, 1982a.

Levitan, S. A., and Johnson, C. M. "The Future of Work: Does It Belong to Us or to the Robots?" *Monthly Labor Review*, 1982b, *105*(9), 10-14.

Levitan, S. A., and Johnson, W. B. *Work Is Here to Stay, Alas*. Salt Lake City, Utah: Olympus, 1973.

Loesch, L. *Leisure Counseling*. Ann Arbor: ERIC/CAPS Clearinghouse, University of Michigan, 1980.

Loesch, L., and Wheeler, P. *Principles of Leisure Counseling*. Minneapolis: Educational Media, 1982.

McDaniels, C. "Vocation: A Religious Search for Meaning." *Vocational Guidance Quarterly*, 1965, *14*(1), 31-35.

McDaniels, C. "The Role of Leisure in Career Development." In International Association for Educational and Vocational Guidance, *Fifth World Congress, ACTES Proceedings*. Quebec: International Association for Educational and Vocational Guidance, 1973.

McDaniels, C. (Ed.). *Leisure and Career Development at Mid Life*. Blacksburg: Virginia Polytechnic Institute and State University, 1976. (ED 155 577)

McDaniels, C. "Leisure and Career Development at Mid-Life: A Rationale." *Vocational Guidance Quarterly*, 1977, *25*(4), 356-363.

McDaniels, C. *Leisure: Integrating a Neglected Component in Life Planning*. Columbus: ERIC Clearinghouse on Adult, Career, and Vocational Education, National Center for Research in Vocational Education, Ohio State University, 1982.

McDaniels, C., and Hesser, A. "Career Services for Adult Workers at Virginia Tech." *Career Planning and Adult Development Newsletter,* 1982, *4*(11), 1–2.

McDaniels, C., and Hesser, A. "Outplacement: An Occasion for Faculty Career Development." In *Outplacement Counseling.* Ann Arbor, Mich.: ERIC/CAPS Clearinghouse, 1983.

Moore, G., and Hedges, J. "Trends in Labor and Leisure." *Monthly Labor Review,* 1971, *94*(2), 3–11.

Mundy, J., and Odum, L. *Leisure Education: Theory and Practice.* New York: Wiley, 1979.

Murphy, J. *Concepts of Leisure.* (2nd ed.) Englewood Cliffs, N.J.: Prentice-Hall, 1981.

National Recreation and Park Association. "Life. Be in It." Alexandria, Va.: National Recreation and Park Association, 1981.

Neulinger, J. *Introduction to Leisure.* Boston: Allyn & Bacon, 1981.

Nollen, S. D. *New Work Schedules in Practice.* New York: Van Nostrand, 1982.

O'Toole, J. *Making America Work.* New York: Continuum, 1981.

"Our Endless Pursuit of Happiness." *U.S. News & World Report,* August 10, 1981, pp. 58–67.

Overs, R., Taylor, S., and Adkins, C. *Avocational Counseling Manual.* Washington, D.C.: Hawkins, 1977.

Parker, S. *The Future of Work and Leisure.* New York: Praeger, 1971.

Peevy, E. "Leisure Counseling: A Life Cycle Approach." Unpublished doctoral dissertation, Virginia Polytechnic Institute and State University, 1981.

Pieper, J. *Leisure: The Basis of Culture.* New York: Pantheon, 1964.

Rapaport, R., and Rapaport, R. N. *Leisure and the Family Life Cycle.* Boston: Routledge & Kegan Paul, 1975.

Research and Forecasts, Inc. *Where Does the Time Go? The United Media Enterprises Report on Leisure in America.* New York: United Media Enterprises, 1982.

Research and Forecasts, Inc. *The Miller Lite Report on American Attitudes Toward Sports.* Milwaukee, Wis.: Miller Brewing Company, 1983.

Roberts, K. *Leisure.* (2nd ed.) New York: Longman, 1981.

Rosow, J. W. "Personnel Policies for the 1980's." In C. S. Sheppard and D. C. Carroll (Eds.), *Working in the 21st Century.* New York: Wiley, 1980.

Schumacher, E. F. "Good Work." In D. W. Vermilye (Ed.), *Relating Work and Education: Current Issues in Higher Education 1977.* San Francisco: Jossey-Bass, 1977.

Sears, S. "A Definition of Career Guidance Terms: A National Vocational Guidance Association Perspective." *Vocational Guidance Quarterly,* 1982, *31*(2), 137–143.

Stern, B., and Best, F. "Cyclic Life Patterns." In D. W. Vermilye (Ed.), *Relating Work and Education: Current Issues in Higher Education 1977.* San Francisco: Jossey-Bass, 1977.

Tinsley, H. E. A., and Teaff, J. D. *The Psychological Benefits of Leisure Activities for the Elderly: A Manual and Final Report of an Investigation Funded by the AARP Andrus Foundation.* Carbondale: Southern Illinois University, 1983.

Tinsley, H. E. A., and Tinsley, D. J. "A Holistic Model of Leisure Counseling." *Journal of Leisure Research,* 1982, *14* (2), 100–116.

Veblen, T. *The Theory of the Leisure Class.* New York: Viking Press, 1935. (Originally published 1899.)

Yankelovich, D., and Lefkowitz, B. "Work and American Expectations." *National Forum,* 1982a, *62*(2), 3–5.

Yankelovich, D., and Lefkowitz, B. "American Ambivalence and the Psychology of Growth." *National Forum,* 1982b, *62*(3), 12–15.

22   Anna Miller-Tiedeman
David V. Tiedeman

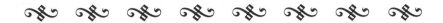

To Be in Work: On Furthering the Development of Careers and Career Development Specialists

To Be in One's Doing

"Remember for any given job, most people don't want it, most don't have the talent for it, and even fewer are willing to make an effort to obtain it. The secret to forecasting your personal work future, then, consists not so much in analyzing the opportunities in the general environment, but in deciding what you want to be when you grow up" (O'Toole, 1982, p. 4).

Notice that O'Toole does not say "deciding what you want to do" when you grow up; he says "deciding what you want to be" when you grow up. When *career* is simply taken as "one's course through life," as we herein define it, the difference between "doing" and "being" in work is simply the difference between helping a client follow what she or he feels is right at the moment or confusing the client's direction by what the counselor thinks the client should or ought to do, such as pay-

591

ing attention to the work/career hot spots. Hot spots do not bring joy in work unless you feel they are truly for you.

When you use your activity, whether paid or unpaid, to further complete yourself, you are coming from what you want to "be," not "do," in your life. "Doing" follows; it does not lead.

Some may ask, "But who can afford to do that?" We reply, "Who can afford not to?" Those who follow who they want to "be" (whether working for someone else or working for oneself) usually find themselves feeling positive and ready to take the next step because they are following what they want, not what someone else suggests they need or should be doing. Many who follow the latter prescription are now unemployed and do not know what to do next. They are waiting for something to "open up" or someone to tell them again what they "should" or "ought to" do. Christopher Malicki, twenty-nine, was one of those persons. According to the *Los Angeles Times* (May 30, 1983), Malicki did what displaced workers are supposed to do when their blue-collar jobs disappear. He spent nine months intensively training to be a robot technician, an obvious career of the future. But five months after graduation, only six of the twenty-six class members had found jobs; Chris remained unemployed.

By contrast, those who define their work situation by who they want to be are usually employed in some way (perhaps in a home-based business or perhaps by someone else). Because they are following who they want to be, they relate more effectively to what they are going after.

"To sell your time for money is always a bad bargain, because it's wasting one of your most precious assets, and you won't be issued any more of it," the author of *Room at the Top,* John Braine (1970, p. 76), once observed. And it is doubly a bad bargain to sell your time for money in something that does not further who you want to be, because when the job is finished, you not only do not have a job, you do not have direction, because you let it come from someone else. Do not underestimate the power in feeling confident that you can continue to pursue in many ways what you love and care about. When a door closes, a window opens. All of us have had that experience at one time or another; we just forget it from time to time.

In thinking of life-as-career developing, we would like career development specialists to help clients discipline themselves to live the wholeness of life in their careers; to help clients create themselves again this moment, and again in a later moment, and again in a still later moment—continuously! In so doing, career development specialists and their clients must work from the *personal theory* of their clients, not from the so-called *scientific theories* on which career development specialists now work, which are really reductionistic, not processional (see Wilber, 1983).

Not to Be, Just to Do, or to Be?

Such is life's perpetual question in the human career. Shakespeare snared human attention for several centuries with a simpler question: "To be, or not to be?" Today's futurists expand Shakespeare's simpler question and reverse its order for their purposes. That is, futurists today speculate on three major human states for tomorrow: doomsday (not to be), extrapolation (to be by just doing again what has been done), and transformation (to be by knowingly acting on personal knowledge).

The doomsday (not to be) scenario and the extrapolation (to be by just doing again scenario) are commonplace in career psychology. However, the transformation (to be by knowingly acting on personal knowledge) scenario is neither commonplace nor now trusted in career psychology. Instead, the transformation scenario is ordinarily just erroneously equated with some of the excessive practices in the "hippieism" of the 1960s. However, "hippieism" is a far cry from working to be more comprehensive by direct connection with your own intelligence, which is the essence in transformational thought. This purpose should be the major purpose in educated living in all at all times, as Krishnamurti (1974) argues.

Futurists used the doomsday, extrapolation, and transformation scenarios to organize a portentous meeting in 1980—namely, the First Global Conference on the Future (Feather,

1980). Quite significantly, futurists there also deliberately excluded doomsday scenarios from the conference agenda. They
did so not to stick their heads in the sand, as ostriches do when
they experience danger from which they cannot flee, but to
make a conference statement to the world that all in attendance
considered continuation of human consciousness too important
a universe matter to waste time debating how humans will disappear in universe. We too dedicate ourselves to this principle in
this chapter: For us the human career is also too precious in
universe evolution to let it disappear thoughtlessly.

　　Having eliminated the doomsday scenario, we discuss just
the extrapolation and transformation scenarios in terms of career, starting with extrapolation. The extrapolation scenario is
the way present career development specialists have been trained
to conceive the future: by looking backward. The Bureau of
Labor Statistics offers classic and widely used examples of the
extrapolation scenario in its work force predictions. These predictions generally underlie a lot of the now-popular writing
about what work is going to be in the short-range future. For
instance, Ehrbar (1983), in an article in *Fortune* magazine,
used extrapolation data provided by the Bureau of Labor Statistics to claim that the greatest number of jobs in the years ahead
will open for secretaries, nurse's aides, janitors, sales clerks,
cashiers, and other such clerical and service employees. The article also suggested that data-processing mechanics, computer systems analysts, and computer operators, along with occupational
therapists and the like, will be in much demand.

　　The extrapolationists suggest what occupational trends
look like based on past data. In numbers, Ehrbar's article suggested: health care, 17.5 million new jobs; secretaries, 700,000
more will be needed in the coming decade; and telecommunications is expected to add 125,000 jobs this decade. Real estate,
economics, and waste management will also have additional
jobs. But the Labor Department predicts that, in 1990, 117 million people will be in the work force or trying to be. This will
by then be a far inadequate proportion of our population who
are in need of incomes, if dynamics in the income distribution
system remain as they are today (see Fuller, 1983).

While looking at the foregoing information, consider that even though the telecommunications industry may be adding 125,000 jobs in the next decade, that industry has already eliminated 100,000 jobs by introducing the computer into its operations (O'Toole, 1983). And although the Bureau of Labor Statistics suggests that 700,000 secretaries will be needed in the future, Marvin Cetron (1983, p. 16) discusses the present use of the "word lexicon." According to Cetron, some 6,000 word lexicons are already in use; "after a person dictates into the machine, a word lexicon types up to 97 percent of what was said." In addition, it can translate the material into nine languages, including Hebrew and Japanese. These machines, Cetron suggests, "will eliminate 50 percent of all clerical and stenographic jobs."

In addition to the word lexicon in use now, the introduction of the microcomputer into the office has reduced the need for secretarial work as we once knew it. Where each executive used to have a secretary, many of them now have microcomputers and share clerical employees. So the computer and the word lexicon have changed and will continue to change the workplace dramatically, particularly the communications workplace.

Delaware's Governor Pierre S. du Pont IV, who recently chaired an ad hoc National Committee on Displaced Workers, suggests that the "effect of new technology on employment will be dizzyingly swift. It is entirely possible that the changes recorded in the last eighty-nine years will be matched and surpassed by the changes in the final twenty years of this century" (Ehrbar, 1983, p. 107).

Now, if you subscribe to fairy tales and Mother Goose, you may want to follow the extrapolationists, as some think extrapolationists "know." But it is our opinion that the transformation scenario is the one that will carry you through the merry-go-round of technology, and through being and living transformation (coming from what you think and who you want to be), you will be able to catch two brass rings: "income" and "satisfaction."

Our reading in futures literature suggests that, except for

very immediate tomorrows and for very broad and not too useful job categories, no one really knows what is coming up in the way of work careers, not even the Bureau of Labor Statistics. Futurist James O'Toole (1982) plainly states such a conclusion this way: "We simply don't know what specific knowledge people will need after their school years, because what people need to know is changing moment by moment." He goes on to suggest that "the best education for the future will be one that develops the general ability to think clearly and use information well" (p. 5). Furthermore, Larry Schrank of Honeywell Corporation suggests that, in the changing nature of work, people "will need to seek out new training opportunities a number of times during their career" (Borders, 1982, p. 72). Toffler (1981) additionally states that employers in the 1990s will need men and women who accept responsibility, who understand how their work dovetails with that of others, who can handle even larger tasks, and who adapt swiftly to changed circumstances.

Finally, Borders (1982, p. 77) encapsulates as follows the consequences of what uncertainty about the future portends for today's living: "It's very likely that no one today knows what the most exciting, powerful, and important new careers (jobs) will be because they have not yet been developed. . . . Therefore . . . the best way to predict the future is to create it." Toffler (1981, p. 166) supports this notion, saying, "Instead of merely receiving our mental model of reality, we are now compelled to invent it and continually reinvent it." That is the transformation scenario.

Whether you choose the extrapolation or the transformation scenario as your fundamental perception of tomorrow's work, you will be forced to become more comprehensive. Practically, you will become more comprehensive because you will need to keep yourself employed and this is your best avenue to that goal. Personally, you will need to become more comprehensive to save yourself from boredom. We seldom think of boredom, because such thought is too scary. We might then "have to" do something about it. But we must today know when we are bored or go bananas tomorrow. Intelligence just

keeps telling many of us that there is more to life than we
presently let ourselves know and do in work.

What implications does all such advice to become more
comprehensive and to act more generally—advice that liberal
educators have continually offered career counselors—hold for
tomorrow's career development specialists? We see two major
implications.

First, career development specialists usually help people
define work/career possibilities. But, extrapolative methods notwithstanding, no one knows what work/career possibilities are
going to be tomorrow. Therefore, if tomorrow's career development specialists are to help consciousness advance further into
life-as-career, former methods of "testing and telling," pointing
out trends, helping individuals get what someone else created in
career development assistance, will, at last and for certain, have
to be integrated into a view that shows individuals how to create what they themselves want, not just "get" what others
offer. Individuals of such understanding fully realize that they
predict their future by what they choose. This is now an accepted principle in the quantum mechanics view of universe:
Universe is as we think it is, as we choose it to be.

Second, tomorrow's career development specialists will
discover a parallel between how the universe works and how life
works as they switch their attention from work to life as implied at the beginning of our chapter. When one thinks of life
as-career, important principles from life at the microscopic
level in the physical realm can be applied to life at the macroscopic level in society. These principles are helpful in personally guiding yourself to get from A to Z in your career, either as
just a citizen or as a citizen who also hopes to make a living as a
career development specialist.

In order for tomorrow's career development specialist to
shift from only helping tomorrow's citizens fit into yesterday's
work (extrapolation) to helping them repeatedly create their
own emerging life niches (transformation), three important
understandings are essential:

1. As noted more fully later, the view of the physical world

shifted (transformed) in the 1920s from its old mechanistic and reductionistic, Newtonian/Cartesian form to the more expansive and comprehensive new quantum model, and a similar transformational shift has not yet found its way into career theory.

2. Life-is-career, and since without life, career does not exist, we need a transformation dynamic life/career theory that is consistent with the new quantum theory.

3. Individuals need to be encouraged to develop a variety of soft specializations.

Hard specialization limits choice. Hard specialization occurs when citizens believe that one particular job or occupational focus will carry them throughout life. Life does not work that way. Life continues to dance, working and winding its way into broader and more varied development.

We are reminded of an engineer whose friend bet him he could not pass the entrance examination for dental school. He did and entered dental school and is now a dentist. Life dances in interesting ways. When life purpose and development are pressed back by thought into specialized corners (hard specialization), the need to become more comprehensive has to go somewhere. And that somewhere is usually the body. We therefore believe that hospitals are the best career redirection centers we have in the society. In hospitals patients find reasons to change their life course: "I can't do that anymore, my doctor advises against it." Or "I can't do that anymore for physical reasons." And many more such "reasons."

Hard specialization sentences each of us to incompleteness for however long we remain blindly specialized. But it is easy to "soften" hard specialization when one follows feeling and thought. We know a psychologist who recently started doing some TV work relating her psychology background to health concerns. She now has a regular three-minute segment on a local news station. What once was a hard specialization has become a soft specialization and includes using what she knows more broadly (more comprehensively).

The life force in universe, echoing down its continuing

15-billion-year-old movement into ever more generality, favors soft specialization, as we move up in our consciousness, or in our human intelligence, if you prefer. From time to time this life force gives us manageable movements while still keeping us from being more general unless we deliberately choose to freely follow throughout our lives that inevitable movement in human intelligence into ever further comprehensiveness. Failure to move into more comprehensiveness as life forces kick us into doing from time to time causes us stress because we then specialize too long and too other-directedly, two things at marked variance with intelligence in universe. This condition has two important consequences for those who aspire to soft career development specialization.

First, soft career development specialists are in both a strategic and vulnerable position with regard to this quaking life force, which is always active in the human career. Since life is always at work in the human career, soft career development specialists will never themselves want for work when they focus on life as career developing in clients rather than on the jobs then considered available or likely to become available.

Second, unless the career development specialist knows life-as-career, it will be difficult for him or her to counsel another from that assumption. Let's admit we all guide others in accordance with our own career theory.

Emerging career development specialists therefore need to soft-specialize so as to alleviate stress both in citizens whom they help toward some eminent specializations for them and in themselves. How? By simply mastering the new science. That is our next point.

Life/Career and the Play of Dynamic Universe

Life in Career. What does the seemingly strange combination of career and modern physics, a quantum mechanics of holism instead of a Newtonian/Cartesian mechanics of reductionism, have in common with the more modern career development specialization that we recommend? It is simple. Both modern physics and modern career development specialization work with life, but at different levels of abstraction. And since people have life, the principles about how life works in the universe are important to how process works in individual careers, at the very least.

Life is as much a process phenomenon as is any other physical phenomenon in the universe; so is career, because life-is-career. The logic is simple:

1. Life works the way the universe works.
2. Without life, career does not exist. Therefore,
3. Life is the essence of career developing, and one basically understands how life works in career by understanding, not just parroting, how the universe itself works.

Although this fact is logically simple, we in the Western world have somehow managed to make it outrageously complex because in Western physics of the past 400 years (Capra, 1975) we have continually reduced irreducible life to seeming elements. We have thereby built our career development systems on the former Newtonian/Cartesian ("Newcar") model: The sum of the parts equals the whole. In this Newcar model, the universe is like a machine. This model has today been superseded by the quantum model of physics: The whole is more than the sum of its parts. The universe in the quantum model is therefore more like thought—it is all connected.

Career development in today's popular culture mostly takes place within the Newcar assumptions about universe, which viewed the career as external to and separate from the person. However, quantum physics suggests that everything is connected, we get what we look for, and universe is in us, not out there. Therefore, life-is-career, life is in citizens, it is the mainframe of their life direction, and down deep they know it. Thus, in order to help citizens format their careers, career development specialists first need to reformat their own former assumptions if they are to be of optimum help to citizens (students and adults) by providing what students and adults need when they are ready. Universe works in rhythms; citizens do too; so do their careers.

Quantum Physics Principles at Play in Life Career. In stating our simple principle that career is merely life action in the universe, we feel as Buckminster Fuller must have felt when told by a businessman: "Bucky, I'm very fond of you so I am sorry to have to tell you that you will never be a success. You go around explaining in simple terms that which people have not been comprehending when the first law of success is 'Never make things simple when you can make them complicated' " (Fuller, 1983, p. 18). However, some readers may suggest that we are using complicated concepts when we postulate that physics exists in life, which in turn exists in career. After all, how many people understand physics? To say nothing of grounding career in physics through life as well! Nevertheless, we find that those marvelously rich concepts in the new physics are extremely helpful to us in talking about life in career. We also think they will hold similar richness for you if you open your mind to them.

What, then, does modern physics say to tomorrow's soft career development specialists that will be useful in helping individuals in their soft career developments? Modern physics has principles that will change the way you think, the assumptions on which you operate, the way you deal with your career, and the way you deal with your clients. That seems a tall order, but here is how it works. (See also Miller-Tiedeman and Wilson, 1984, which further explains the herein-suggested parallelism of the new physics and career, using cases and examples.)

1. *The Heisenberg uncertainty principle.* The uncertainty principle notes that when you focus on one aspect of something, you miss another aspect of it (Capra, 1982). For instance, when clients talk about one work possibility, they rule out others. In other words, communication exacts the price of particularization. This price appears everywhere in career development specialization because specialization is largely conceptual, never only experiential. Specialization thereby "hardens" rather than "softens" because it is then based in incompleteness of knowing. In other words, when clients consider how they feel about something, they miss how they think about it. When counselors talk about what someone wants to *do* in a work career, they

miss what their clients want to *be*. When counselors talk with clients about collecting information, they miss the information clients were born with and all they have collected in their living to date. When two people talk, one frequently makes a point while the other is busy silently countering it with another point the first person missed.

Counselors have intimate familiarity with this uncertainty principle in their work almost without realizing it. After all, the uncertainty principle in career conversations defines the very essence of counseling work. If clients were certain, they would not need counselors. Since counselors help clients see what they mean, not just what they say, counselors continually deal with the more complex spectrum of meaning, not just with the utter certainty of only one particular.

2. *Bohr's complementarity principle*. The complementarity principle suggests that there are two complementary but necessary descriptions of universe: a wave description and a particle description. As dictated by the uncertainty principle, both descriptions are accurate so far as each goes, both are limited, and both are needed for a more complete picture.

In counseling work the complementarity principle manifests in the reliance of counseling on multiple descriptions of persons: interests, personality, needs, ability, and the like. Since each of these parts is accurate only in its limited context, all personal descriptions are needed in their complementariness for the client and the counselor to understand the client as a whole.

Contrary to the presently extant striving for understanding in Western culture, then, independence does not exist in universe. Instead interrelationship, interconnection, and interpenetration exist. Everything is of a whole; everything is connected; life works in career in relationships, not in separations.

3. *The whole is more than the sum of its parts*. Technologically, humans initially experienced this ephemeralization principle (that is, getting more for all with less expenditure of energy per unit produced) on a massive "realistic" scale in the 1860s when one of the world navies began using three-metal alloys in gun construction. At that time naval engineers bet a country's control of the seas on the then-observable fact that

the tensile strengths of alloys are greater than the tensile strengths of their pure metal parts. The world then had a "real" illustration of the invisible ephemeralization working in combinations of things. A sea-controlling navy at last bet its supremacy on what it could not "see"—the ephemeralization arising in energy unions of the "seen" (three metals) and the "unseen," the value invisibly added to the sum of strengths of individual metals when combined in their alloyed state.

Surprisingly, in career psychology we presently "bury" the ephemeralization value arising from the wholeness of individual action in the "errors" of our external models of individual differences on which we presently "guide" the careers of those we help. For instance, in "predicting" for another, we use the person's supposedly "objective" parts (the known to us) but not the person's subjective (the known to the other). But the whole being proves more than the sum of the "objective" parts under personal observation and action in career—that is, when the person wholeheartedly implicates herself or himself in the solutions of personal career unfoldments. Extrapolative "prediction" in career psychology thereafter always proves less consequential for individual action than does personal transformative understanding of career, because extrapolative "prediction" bears error that personal transformative understanding has accommodated.

4. *The principle of dissipative structures.* Going beyond the new physics, Prigogine (1980) introduced the principle of dissipative structures. The theory of dissipative structures explains order arising out of seeming chaos. Energy is ordinarily used and consumed smoothly in physical structures. But energy flow within a structure causes perturbations from time to time. Perturbations may be small or large. Small perturbations are merely dampened down in the system and do not cause a structural change. This is how self-organizing systems both let life exist in them and maintain their continuity. Human being and environment are continually shaken up in these small ways without reorganizing themselves. This is what life does in universe—continually regenerates. For instance, Capra (1982, pp. 271–272) reports such frequent, small, and non-system-reorgan-

izing perturbations in body physiology as follows: "The pan-
creas replaces most of its cells every twenty-four hours, the
stomach lining every three days, our white blood cells every ten
days, and 98 percent of the protein in the brain is turned over
in less than one month. All these processes are regulated in such
a way that the overall pattern of the organism is preserved."

When perturbations in a structure's energy system become large, they overwhelm the structure's normal self-sustain-
ing reactions and cause a structural change in the energy system.
Dossey (1982, p. 84) characterizes such large perturbations
underlying structural change in physiological systems this way:
"Increasing complexity generates a need for increasing energy
consumption from the environment, which in turn gives rise to
increasing fragility. . . . If the internal perturbation is great
enough, the system may undergo a sudden reorganization, a
kind of shuffling. And 'escape to a higher order' organizing in a
more complex way." (Such "escape to a higher order" is comprehensiveness.)

Principles of dissipative structure under conditions of
large perturbation abound, quite obviously, on the level of social relationships as well. In divorce, for instance, the adults and
the children experience shaken, rearranged lives. In addition,
during 1982–1983 over 12 million unemployed people in the
United States had their lives seriously shaken and rearranged by
the loss of their jobs. Furthermore, over 13 million teenaged
women have had their lives shaken and rearranged by pregnancy
in the past several years. Finally, 57,000 people in New York
City are now out of work, many of them roaming the streets
and sleeping in cardboard boxes. All these people experience
major perturbations in their lives, perturbations that change
their life systems. Furthermore, it is probably safe to assume
that these people have had very little schooling about how to
think movement and change—in short, to think life as career.

What, then, do we conclude from these four major principles of the new science? Simply this: Magnificent and powerful
insights into the social level of ordinary human experience in career arise from applying the major principles presently known
to be at play in the microscopic physical world. In fact, we have

personally made several principles from the microscopic world the wellspring of our thought, which gives life the principal focus in our new career physics as the basis for our view of the emerging soft career development specialist.

Emerging Soft Career Development Specialization in Life/Career

Remember, our major principles are, first, that as long as you have life, you have career. When you die, your career dies with you. That is the way life and death are; you have no choice in either matter. When you die, the job you worked at or had is still there for somebody else to do, but your ephemeral career is gone. Therefore, it is important to commit to life in your ephemeral work, not to your job. When you commit to life during ephemeralization in career, you realize that both paid and unpaid work are part of your life, and you do both at different times for different reasons. Furthermore, a comprehensive theory of the human career must, for us, embrace the idea that the reality of the microscopic physical world has applications to the more macroscopic level of ordinary human experience in career. After all, the human career and universe physics are part of each other. Since we can take neither from us, we had best work with both in us. We can thus have the power of the hard-come-by universe principles enunciated in the previous section.

Since any form of hard specialization limits the general principle that all in universe is in continuous motion, as modern physics holds, we suggest escape from such a trap for life career by pursuing soft career development specializations from time to time in our individual careers with a sense of uncertainty that keeps our own careers somewhat open and therefore always transformable (soft). During the past seventy years of its growth, the theory of career in psychology has mostly been limited to the incisive details of just action (extrapolation scenarios) and to just action in only hard occupational specialization at that. The theory of career has therefore not simultaneously been open to considering the parallel between universe principles and career as life, as we do herein (transformation scenarios).

The result is a present hard specialization theory of career, which is—

1. Of the Newcar genre (the parts equal the whole), not the quantum mechanics genre (the parts are more than the whole).
2. Of acts (doing), not of life (being).
3. Of occupation (just doing), not of career (being while doing).
4. Of history (done), not of a living sense of the future in the present (being human).

Since individuals still have to specialize (but softly, we suggest) in order to maintain their sanity and to gain accomplishment even as individuals are continuously subjects of the utter openness of their intelligence, tomorrow's soft career development specialists should help all citizens softly specialize on the better and more open system bases, which are—

1. Of a quantum mechanics theory of universe, not a Newcar theory.
2. Of life (being), not acts (doing).
3. Of career (being while doing), not of occupation (just doing).
4. Of living a sense of future in the present (being human), not living blind reverence for history (done).

In order to achieve this recommended shift in career view from hard to soft, a work specialty must be kept as a living phenomenon in individuals, not permitted to deteriorate into just mechanistics, so that we, as tomorrow's soft career development specialists, can reverse our present reductionism in Western culture (extrapolationism) with hard specialization and instead empower individuals to live career holistically (transformation) with soft specialization. But to do this, the soft career development specialist has to stop telling other people "how to do it"; she or he must assume that if those being helped know "why" they want to do something, they can invent the "how."

Someone else's "how" is not going to do a person much good and will not be nearly as interesting to this person. For instance, Tim Gallway, in *The Game of Inner Tennis* (1982), suggests that telling someone "how" inhibits optimum performance. So the following discussion does not tell you how; it merely helps you form the why.

Emerging soft career development specialists must, in our book, therefore help all citizens continually develop their intelligences. Each of us uses his or her intelligence all the time. However, like Pooh Bear, we ordinarily use our intelligence by just circling the trees of our experiences again and again without catching on to the fact that we are our own intelligence doing so. When we, like Pooh Bear, have an experience of stepping into our own tracks in intelligence as we circle, and recognize that we have ourselves been making all those tracks we formerly considered made by widgets and the like, we have moved up a level in our intelligence. The level to which we have then moved in our intelligence is that of being able both to have an experience and to think about that experience virtually simultaneously. We become more comprehensive in our action at that moment.

We have experiences of things while thinking about them quite often. However, we seldom think of that experience as being comprehensive. When you now do so because we suggest that you do, you will then introduce still a third level into your consciousness: (1) you will have an experience (2) of which you are conscious and (3) in which you become aware of unfolding comprehensiveness itself in your thought system.

There are eight of these third-level, comprehensiveness-mastery skills for personally knowing your life comprehensively in your career. These knowing-how-you-know skills are not sold by any publisher. Instead, these skills are in each person, in a unique constellation. And soft career development specialists must therefore essentially know these skills in themselves if they, in turn, are to help students and adults master these skills in themselves. We therefore offer several prompts for doing so.

The principles of knowing life-as-career depend first on your knowing both life and career experientially. Live discerningly! We gave you opportunities for such an experience in earlier sections. We are not writing of the "ordinary"; we are writing of the "unusual." Surprisingly, the "unusual" is easier to know than the "ordinary" just as soon as you realize that the "unusual" is trustfully personal.

The comprehensive principles of life-in-career depend next on recognizing experientially the three levels of self-consciousness in yourself: (1) self-reference, (2) self-comprehension, and (3) consciousness of the personal comprehension process. This last level is available to all but mostly unused by all.

If you keep this three-level framework in mind, you will find yourself quickly able to help another into consciousness of life-in-career. However, there are eight life-in-career processing skills we also use, along with their appropriate recognition and change cues, when we work with someone in her or his mastery of consciousness in the comprehension process. These life-in-career processing skills and their appropriate recognition and change cues are the following:

1. *Partialize*—that is, know chosen specialties to be just parts of life-as-career developing, not its whole.

Watch your language. How you say something determines what you mean. Asking a client, "Have you decided on a career?," suggests to a client that a career is something you decide on, not something you have. "Where do you want the work part of your work career to go?" suggests that a career development specialist conceives the career as Webster first defined it, "a course or path through life," and knows there is a work part. If the career development specialist does not see career on a broader band, then it is not likely she or he will be able to help clients see career differently either. To see that the work career is only a part of the career, emerging soft career development specialists will themselves have to think more generally.

2. *Temporize*—that is, know each part of work career as potent in a short and finite time interval, not forever.

Learning to learn is an important career development skill in temporizing. Learning to learn helps clients deal with the temporariness of the partial work opportunities and the other facets of their careers. A good check to determine whether one knows temporariness emotionally is how quickly one accommodates, without frustration, but with expectation of change. If you do not accommodate, you are ordinarily mad, angry, upset instead.

3. *Sequentialize*—that is, know that certain combinations of parts in an individual's career are of greater potential for particular purposes than other combinations.

Encourage clients to experiment with combining internal information in different ways, risking outcomes. That way clients can gain the experience that comes with risking and learning, risking and learning, again and again—in sequences of events. Career development specialists need to build clients' confidence for risking sequential solutions and stop trying to save the client time by acting as if the client's future were known to the specialist link by link. Instead, "it all depends" on connections in the client's consciousness. Therefore, encourage clients to keep the fabric of their experience together in sequence by honoring their good as well as their not-so-good decisions about life events. (See Fuller, 1982, for several "fairy tale" illustrations of this point.) Right and left decisions provide balance in life, just as tacking into the wind does in sailing. If you were sailing and wanted to reach a destination, you would tack to starboard and port (go left and right) until you came to your destination. In sailing, there is no such thing as a good tack and a bad tack if you are not racing. The same is true of sequences of appropriate life decisions in career.

4. *Intuit*—that is, know perception and conception of wholes not dictated by parts.

Get students and clients to know themselves capable of receiving information on many frequency bands besides the verbal band. We all receive all information in universe; we do not all read or acknowledge all the information all the time. And yet some of us acknowledge and act on the information without explicitly realizing it. Therefore, clients need work with the invisible career skills: confidence, courage, faith, and intuition, to name a few.

5. *Intelligentize*—that is, experientially ground intuitions in incisive detail sufficient to command personal faith in chosen action based on a personal theory (sense of a whole) rather than on utterly complete understanding or dogma.

Toffler (1981) suggests that we no longer receive long

strings of information organized into wholes for us. Instead, we receive bits and pieces and have to make the wholes ourselves. This is what many people today find confusing. They are accustomed to other people making their meaning and wholes. Therefore, citizens who want their careers to advance by soft specialization will have to learn how to make individual meaning rather than just to accept societal meaning. The invisible career skills will be needed again for this purpose: Organization, or meaning making, is different for each individual. And what makes sense to us may not make any sense to you. Clients need help in trusting what they know about their own meaning-making machine, their intelligence.

6. *Invest intelligent intuitions with utter faith*—that is, when intuition comes, act in now experience without fully knowing the consequences.

Stop perpetuating the myth that we have to understand ourselves fully before we can act. That myth stands in the way of intelligence. We all know who we are, we know our experience, we all intuit. We do need to periodically organize the "who" we consider ourselves to be. Our "whos" change from moment to moment. That makes organizing and reorganizing a full-time job if we let it become so. The invisible skills of faith and courage are therefore important here. We could all relax by treating career as just the path we leave behind us as our ever more comprehensive and always active intelligence tells us what we need to do. That is what is happening to you right now as you read this.

7. *Review*—that is, from time to time, (a) reconsider what was made to happen, (b) reconsider thoughts and feelings about it, and (c) continually open consciousness to energies in universe that enliven thought and power in a more holistic (theoretical) fashion.

There is power in thought. It is another invisible career skill—one that we do not use often. Clients need to be encouraged to periodically take time out for themselves to reassess and decide whether life is going the way they want it to go. Help clients understand that "life feels a lot lighter when we are aware that it is a grand experiment; for the universe is a laboratory where there are no mistakes—only different outcomes" (Berkus, 1982).

8. *Comprehensivize*—that is, know self as a whole spirit in the universe and career in full harmony with one's senses of that spirit in their now moments of its comprehension—that is, recognize that comprehensiveness arises (a) from knowledge within yourself to the effect that there is more than you are presently considering and (b) from accepting yourself as source of this moreness.

When a client discusses doing something that seems out of line for that client, encourage her to go ahead. When we reach out, it very often looks crazy to someone else. For instance, personal experience finds us reaching outside the present area of career development for larger principles to guide our work in career developing. In doing so, we are able to become more comprehensive about former career development. For us, it meant reading outside the then-prescribed field. For others, reaching out may mean attending a conference on how to make widgets in the Appalachian mountains. But whatever a person's reach, encourage it. People grow broader and deeper in very interesting ways. For instance, there are teachers who are seriously trying to leave teaching. They are bored and feel unchallenged, among other reasons. They know they are not growing, and some of them are deciding to venture forth and do something different (become more comprehensive). Similarly, we meet engineers who are studying law, a lawyer who becomes chairman of the board in a large bank. All are becoming more comprehensive in the human career. What is a challenge to one person is a boring experience to another. Like an ever-revolving door, the dance of life encourages us to learn one thing, then add to that, or do something completely different. For instance, a dermatologist friend quit a very lucrative practice at fifty-nine in order to study child psychiatry. She finished when she was sixty-five. She was becoming more comprehensive at a time in her life when many would have been hanging up their occupational spikes. But she knew what many are today coming to know, that life keeps growing. It is only when you try to stop life from growing that it withers and dies.

Living the New Career Physics Professionally

We noted earlier that the shift in career paradigm from doing to being additionally burdens emerging soft career development specialists. The additional burden that the "being" career paradigm places on emerging soft career development specialists is that of being alive in their own careers in order, in turn, to model and to help students and clients to be alive in their careers. This requirement demands not only that emerging soft career development specialists be transformed in more comprehensive consciousness but also that they not be overly concerned with professional requirements that are themselves antithetical precepts to life-in-career. In the previous section we indicated how career development specialists will need to live and to work in their general practices. Here we attend directly to the political process in which life in career finds adequate nurturance.

Given the foregoing eight comprehensiveness conditions necessary for any citizen to keep her or his several lifetime specializations in career soft rather than letting them deteriorate into hard specializations, what are the conditions we should ourselves entertain if we, tomorrow's soft career development specialists, are to professionalize our "help" in empowering such feelings, thoughts, and action? We presume it self-evident by now that if tomorrow's soft career development specialists elect to help individuals softly live several specializations through their careers without letting any one specialty hardly determine those careers for the individuals, they must first and foremost live that ethic themselves. If soft career development specialists do not see the parallels between universe principles and career, then they cannot guide on them; if they do not see life as fully interconnected, then they are not going to guide someone on that principle either. Therefore, tomorrow's soft career development specialists must see life as holistic and make it so in their professional relationships if they are to guide from that assumption.

What does this general principle mean for the work of the modern soft career development specialist?

First, keep freedom more fully available in individuals' lives at all times. Growth or self-transcendence happens in openness, not in social controlledness (Krishnamurti, 1974; Fuller, 1983). Advocate growth (soft specialization), not just maintenance (hard specialization) in career, which our present society both defines and considers "enough."

Second, champion human development throughout the lifetime, not just in schooltime. To do this, you must bring the attention of individuals, through their schools and through society in general (wherever you elect to work), on "communication of that which is central to the transformation of the human mind and the creation of a new culture. Such a fundamental transformation takes place when the child, while being trained in various skills and disciplines, is also given the capacity to be awake to the processes of his thinking, feeling, and action. This alertness makes him self-critical and observant, and this establishes an integrity of perception, discrimination, and action, crucial to the maturing with him of a right relationship to man, to nature, and to the tools man creates" (Krishnamurti, 1974, pp. 7–8). Krishnamurti's simple principle holds for all persons alike—female and male, young and old—despite his old-time use of "sexist" language and his intended pronouncement concerning just children.

Third, read outside the present career development field and integrate the academic disciplines you are required to and/or elect to study.

Fourth, empower thinking in decision and choice throughout life—not just thinking in decisions among externally arranged and permitted choices, but also thinking in decisions among internally perceived, conceived, elected, and pursued choices as well.

Fifth, if you elect to work solely with the work careers of others, let those whom you "help" know that *vocation, occupation, job,* and *position,* as commonly used, are concepts of mere social convenience (hard specialization), not of "reality" (soft specialization). As is now known and acted on in the new science, "reality" is what we attribute to the universe seemingly outside our skins, not to what any human actually knows universe to be. This principle holds for external facts/data on position, job, occupation, and vocation as presently used in the psychology of career. But remember that the career is both an internal and an external matter. Ignore one or the other part of career at the expense of only limited empowerment of the fuller power in universe, which is freely available to us whenever we dare use it in the more comprehensive forms it prefers.

Sixth, and finally:

- Do not attempt to monopolize your professional help. To monopolize your professional help in Western social forms is to make it hard specialization, to kill the life in your own career, and to deny life in the careers of all.
- Do not specialize in one thing overly long in your life. Life diversifies; let your career follow suit (soft specialization).
- Do not rely overly long on what another seemingly knows about you. You will never glimpse truth very fully in the concepts of another. Truth largely rests only in your serious interpretations of your own feelings, thoughts, and action.
- Do not let any one of what we call the "scholastic disciplines" monopolize that which you practice. To practice professionally is to act in the fuller knowing of your own intentionality and motivations, not to rely on the seemingly more complete explorations and subsequent action prescriptions of another about your professional practice (hard specialization). Live and die by your own mistakes, not someone else's! Softly specialize.
- Do not spend your professional career politicizing your profession (hard specialization). Let temporality, not authority, except for the authority of truth, live in your profession. Let your decisions and the decisions of those you help have social power in their actions of the moment. Associate with professionals of similar mind and action, but do not let your associations determine you (soft specialization).
- Do not attempt to change society concerning your profession (hard specialization). Individuals must transform themselves to gain, first, intuitive and, later, developed comprehension of transformation in their own career systems (soft specialization).

To the extent that society becomes internalized in citizens, and only to that extent, will individuals themselves change their society. Hence, empower individuals with transformative capacity and you will have changed your society enough. Let those who themselves act transformatively in their society change their society further for themselves and for all they include in their society.

"Anything Written Here May Be Wrong"

What, then, of a little concluding heart-to-heart advice just to aspiring soft career development specialists who practice in a society with that holistic understanding of life-as-career we present herein? In his fascinating novel *Illusions,* in which a pilot is in quest of the *Messiah's Handbook,* Richard Bach (1977) closes his writing of the then presumably found *Messiah's Handbook* with the admonition "Anything written here may be wrong." We similarly close our pretension to this *Messiah's Career Handbook* for you, tomorrow's soft career development specialists: "Anything written here may be wrong." If you live the modern world view in assisting citizens into temporary career specializations, you will come (1) to know this uncertainty principle at an intense feeling level in you, (2) to know some of the potential difference between seeming truth and personally confirmed observations, and (3) to bear the effective tension between the two in your work. Help all citizens do the same and you will have further empowered the career of each—occupational information, *Dictionaries of Occupational Titles,* professional studies, professional supervision, professional programs, program accreditations, facility inspections, degrees, and counselor, psychologist, or physician licensing all notwithstanding. Forget such hard specializing.

To thine own soft specializing career be true, O tomorrow's soft career development specialists! That is our primary and only dictum both in making life your own career and in helping others do so as well. The human career will live forever in pursuit of this softly specializing dictum.

Live the Messiah of your career, and career joyfully, knowing the truth of e. e. cummings' advice (quoted in Fuller,

1981, p. xii): "To be-nobody-but-yourself—in a world which is doing its best, night and day, to make you everybody else— means to fight the hardest battle which any human being can fight—and never stop fighting."

Suggested Readings

Miller-Tiedeman, A., and Wilson, L. *How to NOT Make It— and Succeed: The Truth About Your LIFECAREER.* Los Angeles: LIFECAREER Press, 1984.

    A popular account of the operation of new science principles in the life of career. Cases and other examples are included.

    The two books by Fritjof Capra listed in the References, Fuller's 1981 book, and Krishnamurti's, Prigogine's, and Wilber's books also listed there rather fully underpin the new science and its accommodation in the perennial philosophy that form this chapter. They provide a set in which process, system, and consciousness are given incisive detail in comprehensive contexts.

References

Bach, R. *Illusions: The Adventures of a Reluctant Messiah.* New York: Dell/Eleanor Friede, 1977.

Berkus, R. *Life Is a Gift.* Encino, Calif.: Red Rose Press, 1982.

Borders, J. "Careers of the Future." *Black Collegian,* Aug.-Sept. 1982, pp. 69-80.

Braine, J. "Starting Afresh: A Discovery of Vocation." *Quest,* 1970, pp. 70-76.

Capra, F. *The Tao of Physics: An Exploration of the Parallels Between Modern Physics and Eastern Mysticism.* New York: Bantam Books, 1975.

Capra, F. *The Turning Point: Science, Society, and the Rising Culture.* New York: Simon & Schuster, 1982.

Cetron, M. J. "Getting Ready for the Jobs of the Future." *Futurist,* 1983, *17*(3), 15-23.

Dossey, L. *Space, Time and Medicine.* Boulder, Colo.: Shambhala, 1982.

Ehrbar, A. F. "Grasping the New Unemployment." *Fortune,* May 16, 1983, pp. 106-112.

Feather, F. (Ed.). *Through the 80's: Thinking Globally, Acting Locally.* Washington, D.C.: World Future Society, 1980.

Fuller, R. B. *Critical Path.* New York: St. Martin's Press, 1981.

Fuller, R. B. *Tetrascroll: Goldilocks and the Three Bears.* New York: St. Martin's Press, 1982.

Fuller, R. B. *Grunch of Giants.* New York: St. Martin's Press, 1983.

Gallway, T. *The Game of Inner Tennis.* New York: Bantam Books, 1982.

Krishnamurti, J. *Krishnamurti on Education.* New York: Harper & Row, 1974.

Miller-Tiedeman, A., and Wilson, L. *How to NOT Make It—and Succeed: The Truth About Your LIFECAREER.* Los Angeles: LIFECAREER Press, 1984.

O'Toole, J. "Second Industrial Revolution Calls for Generalists." *Transcript,* 1982, *2*(11), 2-5.

O'Toole, J. "Getting Ready for the Next Industrial Revolution." *Phi Kappa Phi Journal,* 1983, *63*(1), 16-19.

Prigogine, I. *From Being to Becoming: Time and Complexity in the Physical Sciences.* San Francisco: W. H. Freeman, 1980.

Toffler, A. *The Third Wave.* New York: Bantam Books, 1981.

Wilber, K. *Eye to Eye: The Quest for the New Paradigm.* Garden City, N.Y.: Doubleday Anchor, 1983.

23

Norman C. Gysbers

Major Trends
in Career Development
Theory and Practice

As we approach the close of the twentieth century, the world in which we live and work continues to change and become more complex. Vast and far-reaching changes are occurring in the nature and structure of the social and economic systems in which people live and the industrial and occupational structures where they work. Individuals' values and beliefs about themselves and their society are changing, as are the ways they look at and understand their own growth and development—their career development. More and more people are looking for meaning in their lives, particularly as they think about the work they do, their situation as family members and as individuals, their involvement in their community, their role in education and training, and their involvement in leisure activities.

This book, through its twenty-two chapters, provides, in part, a chronology of these changes as they affect the career development of individuals, but it is much more than a chronology of people, places, and events in the evolution of career development theory and practice. This book helps us to understand these changes, and hence career development theory and practice, in the context of the times in which we live and work from sociological, psychological, and economic perspectives. This book

618

is a source of ideas, techniques, and resources to help us work more effectively with individuals and their career development needs, concerns, and plans.

Rather than summarize what has been discussed in previous chapters, the intent of this chapter is to bring into sharp focus four predominant trends in the evolution of career development theory and practice from among the many trends identified by the authors of the chapters in this book that may have substantial impact on the future of career development theory and practice. What are these predominant trends? They are as follows:

1. The meanings given to career and career development continue to evolve from simply new words for *vocation* (occupation) and *vocational development* (occupational development) to words that describe the human career in terms of life roles, life settings, and life events that develop over the life span. Super in Chapter One, Jepsen in Chapter Five, McDaniels in Chapter Twenty-One, and Miller-Tiedeman and Tiedeman in Chapter Twenty-Two described and commented on this evolution of meanings.

2. Substantial changes have taken place and will continue to occur in the economic, occupational, industrial, and social environments and structures in which the human career develops and interacts and in which career guidance and counseling takes place. Goldstein (Chapter Two), Herr (Chapter Three), Borow (Chapter Six), Dawis (Chapter Ten), and Striner (Chapter Nineteen) provided in-depth analyses of these changes from a variety of perspectives.

3. The number, diversity, and quality of career development programs, tools, and techniques continue to increase almost in geometric progression. Crites (Chapter Nine), Kinnier and Krumboltz (Chapter Eleven), Walz and Benjamin (Chapter Twelve), Harris-Bowlsbey (Chapter Thirteen), and Miller (Chapter Sixteen) discussed these developments in detail.

4. The populations served by career development programming and the settings where career development programs and services take place have increased greatly and will continue to do so. Lotto in Chapter Four, Stumpf in Chapter Seven,

Sundal-Hansen in Chapter Eight, Miles in Chapter Fourteen, Thomas and Berven in Chapter Fifteen, Miller in Chapter Sixteen, Johnson and Figler in Chapter Seventeen, Knowdell in Chapter Eighteen, and Sinick in Chapter Twenty documented and described this major trend in the field.

To carry out the intent of this chapter, the first section traces and summarizes each of these four trends. The last section of the chapter brings these trends together and looks briefly at the future of career development.

Evolving Meanings of Career and Career Development

Modern theories of career development began appearing in the literature during the 1950s. At that time the occupational choice focus of the first forty years of career development was beginning to give way to a broader, more comprehensive view of individuals and their occupational development over the life span. Occupational choice was beginning to be seen as a developmental process. It was during this time that the term *vocational development* became popular as a way of describing the broadening view of occupational choice.

In the 1960s, knowledge about occupational choice as a developmental process increased dramatically. At the same time, the terms *career* and *career development* became popular, so that today many people prefer them to *vocation* and *vocational development*. During this period, a common definition referred to *career development* as "the total constellation of psychological, sociological, educational, physical, economic, and chance factors that combine to shape the career of any given individual" (National Vocational Guidance Association, 1973, p. 8).

This expanded view of career and career development was more useful than the earlier view of career development as occupational choice because it broke the time barrier previously restricting the vision of career development to a cross-sectional view of an individual's life. As Super and Bohn (1970, p. 15) pointed out, "It is well . . . to keep clear the distinction between occupation (what one does) and career (the course pursued over a period of time)." It also was more useful because it enabled career development to become the basis for organizing and interpreting the impact that the role of work has on individuals over their lifetimes.

In the 1970s, the definitions of *career* and *career development* used by some writers became broader and more encompassing. Jones and others (1972) defined *career* as encompassing a variety of possible patterns of personal choice related to an individual's total life-style, including occupation, education, personal and social behavior, learning how to learn, social responsibility, and leisure time activities. Gysbers and Moore (1975, 1981) proposed the concept of life career development in an effort to expand and extend career development from an occupational perspective to a life perspective in which occupation (and work) has place and meaning. They defined *life career development* as self-development over the life span through the integration of the roles, settings, and events of a person's life. The word *life* in *life career development* means that the focus is on the total person—the human career. The word *career* identifies and relates the roles in which individuals are involved (worker, learner, family, citizen), the settings where individuals find themselves (home, school, community, workplace), and the events that occur over their lifetimes (entry job, marriage, divorce, retirement). Finally, the word *development* is used to indicate that individuals are always in the process of becoming. When used in sequence, the words *life—career—development* bring these separate meanings together, but at the same time a greater meaning emerges. *Life career development* describes people, unique people with their own life-styles.

Similarly, Super (1975, 1981) proposed a definition of *career* as involving the interaction of various life roles over the life span. He called it the "life career rainbow." "Super emphasizes that people, as they mature, normally play a variety of roles in many different theaters. . . . For Super, the term *career* refers to the combination and sequence of all the roles you may play during your lifetime and the pattern in which they fit together at any point in time" (Harris-Bowlsbey, Spivack, and Lisansky, 1982).

Wolfe and Kolb (1980, pp. 1–2) summed up the life view

of career development when they defined *career development* as involving one's whole life: "Career development involves one's whole life, not just occupation. As such, it concerns the whole person, needs and wants, capacities and potentials, excitements and anxieties, insights and blind spots, warts and all. More than that, it concerns him/her in the ever-changing contexts of his/her life. The environmental pressures and constraints, the bonds that tie him/her to significant others, responsibilities to children and aging parents, the total structure of one's circumstances are also factors that must be understood and reckoned with. In these terms, career development and personal development converge. Self and circumstances—evolving, changing, unfolding in mutual interaction—constitute the focus and the drama of career development."

Changing Environments and Structures

The nature, shape, and substance of career development and the practices of career guidance and counseling are not separate and independent from the economic, occupational, industrial, and social environments and structures in which they take place. Our understanding of career development and how we practice is closely related to what happens in these environments and the changes in them that have occurred and will occur in the future. Not only are the changes within environments important, but so are the interactive effects that occur across environments as a result of change.

What are some of these changes? Since 1900 our country has undergone substantial changes in its economic, occupational, industrial, and social environments and structures. Occupational and industrial specialization has increased dramatically and apparently will continue to do so. Social structures and social values have changed and will continue to change, becoming more complex and diverse. New and emerging social and political groups are challenging established groups, demanding equality. People are on the move from rural to urban areas and back again and from one region of the country to another in search of psychological, social, and economic security.

Today, changes such as these and others that have been well documented by authors of previous chapters continue at a rapid pace. Here are just a few specifics to sum up what has been stated before:

1. We have moved from a goods-producing economic base to a service/information economy. This does not mean that goods-producing industries are no longer important or that people will no longer find employment in them. What it does mean is that more and more workers will be employed in service/information industries. "Two years ago the number one occupation in the United States, which had long been laborer, became clerk. The number of workers in agriculture fell to a low of 3.5 percent. Information/knowledge occupations, including all persons who process and disseminate information, increased from 17 percent in 1950 to 60 percent today" (National Association of Manufacturers, 1982, p. 2).

2. We are continuing to experience rapid acceleration in the use of high technology and automation in the workplace through the continued introduction of new and more highly sophisticated automated techniques, machinery, and computers of all types and sizes.

3. We live in a world economy closely linked by fiscal policies, energy resources, multinational corporations, competition for raw materials, and the sales of goods and services.

4. We continue to experience population shifts that find people moving from the North and Northeast to the South and Southeast.

5. We continue to see changing demographic patterns in our labor force. "After more than two decades of growth, the United States population in the 16-24 age range peaked at 36 million in 1980. The Department of Labor predicts a 10 percent decrease in this age group by 1985 and another 7 percent drop, to 30 million, by 1990. As the number of younger workers declines, there will be a demographic 'bulge' in the prime-age (24-44) work force—from 39 million in 1975 to an estimated 60.5 million in 1990. Many experts also believe there will be a shift away from early retirement" (National Association of Manufacturers, 1982, p. 2).

What about tomorrow? What will likely happen in the future? Experts who study change tell us that the pace of change in the future will be even more rapid. Governor Pierre S. du Pont IV, who chaired a recent ad hoc National Committee on Displaced Workers, concluded that "it is entirely possible that the changes recorded in the last eighty years will be matched and surpassed by the changes in the final twenty years of this century" (Ehrbar, 1983, p. 107).

One note of caution is needed, however, as projections are made about what the future will look like. In the same issue of *Fortune* magazine that carried Ehrbar's article, the following statement also appeared: "The far-off will not be that far-out." Although changes will occur, and with increasing rapidity, the familiar lines of our economic, occupational, industrial, and social environments and structures as we know them today, in all probability, will still be visible.

Increasing Numbers, Diversity, and Quality of Programs, Tools, and Techniques

A number of chapter authors have documented very well the rapid expansion in and the almost bewildering diversity of programs, tools, and techniques available today to use in assisting individuals with their career development. It is projected by these same authors that this expansion will continue into the foreseeable future. Further, it is clear from previous chapters that these programs, tools, and techniques are better organized, are more frequently theory-based, and are used more systematically than ever before. It also is projected that these emphases will continue into the foreseeable future.

Let us look more specifically at what is involved in this major trend. The theory and research base of counseling psychology has been expanded and extended substantially during the past twenty years but particularly during the past ten. Growth in the theory and research base for career psychology has been equally dramatic during this same period. One result has been an interesting convergence of ideas from counseling and career psychology concerning human growth and development and the interventions to facilitate it. This convergence of ideas has stimulated a new array of career guidance and counseling programs, tools, and techniques. These new programs, tools, and techniques are emerging from this convergence through the application in career counseling of concepts from marriage and family counseling (Zingaro, 1983) and cognitive-behavioral psychology (Keller, Biggs, and Gysbers, 1982). We are also seeing it through the application of contemporary thinking about personal styles (Pinkney, 1983), learning styles (Wolfe and Kolb, 1980), and hemispheric functioning to career guidance and counseling.

A recent publication by the National Vocational Guidance Association also documents this trend from another perspective—*A Counselor's Guide to Vocational Guidance Instruments*, edited by Kapes and Mastie (1982). In it are reviews of career guidance and counseling instruments. A number of them have been around for a long time. However, there are some that have been developed more recently, and they represent new directions for the field. There are new instruments in the traditional category of interest inventories, but the new directions for the field are in the categories of work values, career development/maturity, and card sorts.

There also are encouraging signs that career and labor market information, important tools in career guidance and counseling, are continuing to improve. Not only have the nature and content of career and labor market information been improving, but so have the relations among the producers and users of such information (Drier and Pfister, 1980). A major step was taken in 1976 to facilitate this trend—the establishment of the National Occupational Information Coordinating Committee (NOICC) and the corresponding State Occupational Information Coordinating Committees (SOICCs) by the Vocational Education Amendments of 1976. Their charge was to improve communication and coordination between the federal and state agencies that produce career and labor market information and the agencies and individuals that use it. NOICC and the SOICCs are also charged with developing and implementing an occupational information system to meet the common occupational information needs of vocational education and employment and training programs at the national, state, and local levels. Finally, NOICC and SOICCs are mandated to give special attention to the labor market information needs of youth, including such activities as encouraging and assisting in the development of local job outlook data and counseling programs for youth in correctional institutions and out of high school.

Recently, NOICC joined forces with other government agencies including the Department of Labor and the Department of Defense to upgrade counselors' knowledge of career and labor market information. The effort is called the Improve Career Decision Making project. It is designed to help counselors in training and on the job to become knowledgeable about career and labor market information concepts and sources and become skillful in their use.

In addition, there are encouraging signs that delivery systems for career and labor market information using state-of-the-art technology are being put in place with increasing frequency across the country. In 1979 NOICC assumed responsibility for assisting states in developing and implementing career information delivery systems. Commercial vendors, publishers, and others also have become very active in making such systems available for use in a broad array of settings with an equally broad array of people.

Finally, it is clear that career guidance and counseling programs, tools, and techniques are more frequently theory-based. Matthews (1975) pointed out several years ago that there were some missing links between materials and people and that one of them was the lack of an organizing philosophy. "In essence," she stated, "we are now confronted with random materials in search of a philosophy" (p. 652). According to a number of authors of previous chapters, this point has been recognized, and now theorists, researchers, and practitioners are devoting more time and energy to organizing and using career guidance and counseling programs, tools, and techniques in comprehensive, systematic ways that are theory-based.

Expanding Populations and Settings

At the turn of the century, career guidance and counseling (then called "vocational guidance") was designed to help young people in the transition from school to work to make occupational choices in line with their understandings about themselves and the work world through a process called "true reasoning" (Parsons, 1909). Today, young people are still the recipients of career guidance and counseling, and they will be in the future. Additional populations to be served by career guidance and counseling have been added over the years and have included such groups as individuals with handicapping conditions, college students, the disadvantaged, and the unemployed. As the world in which we live and work continues to become more complex, the needs of people in these populations for career guidance and counseling will increase, not decrease.

As new concepts about career and career development began to appear and evolve, it became obvious that people of all ages and circumstances had career development needs and concerns and that they and society could and would benefit from comprehensive career development programs and services. Two such concepts, in particular, have had an impact. First was the shift from a point-in-time focus to a life-span focus for career development. And second was the personalization of the concept of career (the human career), relating it to life roles, settings, and events. By introducing these two concepts, the door was opened for career guidance and counseling personnel to provide programs to a wide range of people of all ages in diverse settings.

These newer concepts of career and career development emerged as a result of and in response to the continuing changes that are taking place in our social, industrial, economic, and occupational environments and structures. Because of these changes, adults and adult career development became a focal point for an increasing number of career development theorists and practitioners in the 1970s (Campbell and Cellini, 1981). This focus persisted into the 1980s and, in all probability, will continue to do so into the foreseeable future. As a result, institutions and agencies that traditionally served adults have added career development components. And new agencies and organizations were established to provide adults with career development programs and services where none had existed before.

Career development programs and services in business and industry also became a focal point in the 1970s and 1980s. This trend, too, will continue and probably be intensified into the foreseeable future. More businesses and industries, as well as many other organizations, are realizing the benefits of career development programs and services for their employees. And if employees benefit, then the organizations benefit also.

The Future

The four predominant trends discussed in this chapter—the evolving meanings of *career* and *career development,* the changing environments and structures in which people live and work, the increasing numbers, diversity, and quality of career development programs, tools, and techniques, and the greater number and variety of people and settings being served—are not separate and discrete. They are closely linked and related. This brief look at the future therefore examines the collective impact these trends may have on the theory and practice of career development.

The behavior of individuals is, in part, determined by their thought processes. The language people use represents their underlying conceptual schemata, and, in turn, their conceptual schemata determines their behavior (Gerber, 1983). As definitions of *career* and *career development* have evolved, becoming broader and more encompassing, particularly during the past ten years, there has been a corresponding broadening and expansion of programs and services to people of all ages and circumstances. What was once thought of as mainly for young people is now for everybody. What was once thought of as a program in schools is now taking place in a whole new array of settings, including public and private agencies, institutions, and business and industry.

Although it is clear that broad definitions of *career* and

career development open up more possibilities and opportunities for programs and services for individuals and groups than narrow definitions, it is equally clear that other variables are involved. The changing economic, occupational, industrial, and social environments and structures in which people live and work have created conditions and needs not previously present that require more attention by individuals to their career development. In addition, a more complete understanding of human growth and development from counseling and career psychology and the corresponding improvement of intervention strategies and resources have helped in the expansion and extension of career development programs and services for more people in more settings than ever before.

As these trends converge, they have begun to shape a new focus for career development programs and services for the future. What will that focus be? Will future programs and services be remedial, emphasize crises, and deal with immediate concerns and issues in people's lives? Will they be developmental and emphasize growth experiences and longer-range planning activities? Or will they do both? The sense of the trends discussed in this chapter and in the literature in general clearly indicates that career development programs and services of the future will respond to people's developmental, longer-term career needs as well as to their more immediate career crisis needs.

Traditionally, career development programs and services focused on immediate problems and concerns. Personal crises, lack of information, a particular occupational choice, and ineffective relationships with spouses, children, fellow employees, or supervisors are examples of the immediate problems and concerns of people to which counselors are asked to respond. This focus for career development programs and services will continue, and new and more effective ways of helping people with their problems and concerns will continue to emerge. However, to help people meet the challenges they may face in the future, this focus for programs and services is not sufficient. What is needed is a developmental focus.

The developmental focus for career development programs and services is not new. It has been part of the professional literature for a number of years. Gordon (1974), for example, pointed out that traditional practices had tended to overemphasize selection and placement instead of nurturing interests and aptitudes. Tennyson (1970, p. 262) made the same point when he stated that "guidance personnel have been inclined to capitalize upon aptitudes already developed rather than cultivating new talents" in their clients. What is new is the sense of urgency about the importance of helping people toward the goal of becoming competent, achieving individuals— of helping people focus on their competencies (skills) rather than only on their deficits as they are involved in their career development over the life span.

What began at the turn of the century under the term *vocational guidance,* with a selection and placement focus, and then shifted in the 1920s and 1930s to a focus on personal adjustment, has now assumed a developmental focus. Selection, placement, and adjustment remain but are encompassed in the concept of career development over the life span. Societal conditions interacting with our more complete knowledge of human growth and development in career terms, as well as with the broader array of tools and techniques, have brought us to the realization that career development is a life-span phenomenon and that all individuals can benefit from career development programs and services whatever their ages or circumstances.

References

Campbell, R. E., and Cellini, J. V. "A Diagnostic Taxonomy of Adult Career Problems." *Journal of Vocational Behavior,* 1981, *19,* 175-190.

Drier, H. N., and Pfister, L. A. (Eds.). *Career and Labor Market Information: Key to Improved Individual Decision Making.* Columbus: National Center for Research in Vocational Education, Ohio State University, 1980.

Ehrbar, A. F. "Grasping the New Unemployment." *Fortune,* May 16, 1983, pp. 106-112.

Gerber, A., Jr. "Finding the Car in Career." *Journal of Career Education,* 1983, *9,* 181-183.

Gordon, E. W. "Vocational Guidance: Disadvantaged and Minority Populations." In E. L. Herr (Ed.), *Vocational Guidance and Human Development.* Boston: Houghton Mifflin, 1974.

Gysbers, N. C., and Moore, E. J. "Beyond Career Development —Life Career Development." *Personnel and Guidance Journal,* 1975, *53,* 647-652.

Gysbers, N. C., and Moore, E. J. *Improving Guidance Programs.* Englewood Cliffs, N.J.: Prentice-Hall, 1981.

Harris-Bowlsbey, J., Spivack, J. D., and Lisansky, R. S. *Take Hold of Your Future.* Iowa City, Iowa: American College Testing Program, 1982.

Jones, G. B., and others. *Planning, Developing and Field Testing Career Guidance Programs: A Manual and Report.* Palo Alto, Calif.: American Institutes for Research, 1972.

Kapes, J. T., and Mastie, M. M. (Eds.). *A Counselor's Guide to Vocational Guidance Instruments.* Washington, D.C.: National Vocational Guidance Association, 1982.

Keller, K. E., Biggs, D. A., and Gysbers, N. C. "Career Counseling from a Cognitive Perspective." *Personnel and Guidance Journal,* 1982, *60,* 367-371.

Matthews, E. "Comment." *Personnel and Guidance Journal,* 1975, *53,* 652.

National Association of Manufacturers. "Perspective on National Issues: America's Human Resources Keys to Productivity." (Pamphlet.) Washington, D.C.: National Association of Manufacturers, 1982.

National Vocational Guidance Association. *Position Paper on Career Development.* Washington, D.C.: National Vocational Guidance Association, 1973.

Parsons, F. *Choosing a Vocation.* New York: Houghton Mifflin, 1909.

Pinkney, J. W. "The Myers-Briggs Type Indicator as an Alternative in Career Counseling." *Personnel and Guidance Journal,* 1983, *62,* 173-177.

Super, D. E. "Vocational Guidance: Emergent Decision-Making in a Changing Society." *Bulletin—International Association of Educational and Vocational Guidance,* 1975, *29,* 16-23.

Super, D. E. "The Relative Importance of Work." *Bulletin—*

International Association of Educational and Vocational Guidance, 1981, *37,* 26–36.

Super, D. E., and Bohn, M. J., Jr. *Occupational Psychology.* Belmont, Calif.: Wadsworth, 1970.

Tennyson, W. "Comment." *Vocational Guidance Quarterly,* 1970, *18,* 261–263.

Wolfe, D. M., and Kolb, D. A. "Career Development, Personal Growth, and Experimental Learning." In J. W. Springer (Ed.), *Issues in Career and Human Resource Development.* Madison, Wis.: American Society for Training and Development, 1980.

Zingaro, J. C. "A Family Systems Approach for the Career Counselor." *Personnel and Guidance Journal,* 1983, *62,* 24–27.

Name Index

Subject Index

Abilities, changes in, 41-43

Absenteeism, and job satisfaction, 289

Accidents, and job satisfaction, 289

Achievement motivation, for self-management, 178-179

Administration on Aging, 553

Adolescence, leisure in, 577-578

Adult career development: analysis of, 190-215; background on, 190-192; and career paths, 207; exploration and self-assessment for, 206-207; and human resources, 209; individual factors in, 192-198; jobs matched to people for, 208-209; organizational factors in, 198-205; readings for, 210-212; responsibility for, 206; reviewed, 13; summary on, 210; targeting, 208; trends in, 190, 206-209

Adults: computer systems for, 377; education for, 68-69; leisure for, 579; and transition to work, 84-85

Affect, in work-affect theory, 144-147

Affective work competencies, and employability, 80-81

Affirmative action: and handicapped persons, 425; and workplace programs, 483

Age, and meaning of work, 37-38

Age Discrimination in Employment Act (ADEA) of 1967, 544

Aid to Families with Dependent Children, 385

Alabama Technical College, apprenticeship program at, 117

Alma College, faculty involvement at, 477

Alumni, and career centers, 477

American Association for Counseling and Development (AACD), 9, 10

American Association for Counseling and Development Foundation, 9

American Association for Higher Education, 569

American Association of Retired Persons, 548

American College Testing (ACT) Program, 150, 181, 264, 269, 443, 453; and computer systems, 365, 378, 468

American Council on Education, 7

American Institutes for Research

644

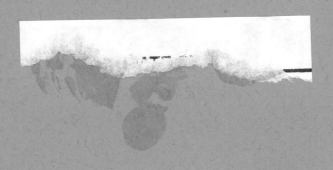